Queens of Sicily

By the Same Author

Margaret, Queen of Sicily

Sicilian Queenship

Kingdom of Sicily 1130-1266

Women of Sicily

The Peoples of Sicily

The Ferraris Chronicle

Sicilian Studies

Sicilian Court Culture 1061-1266

Sicilian Food and Wine

Sicily: The Time Traveler's Guide

Norman-Arab-Byzantine
Palermo, Monreale and Cefalù

SICILIAN MEDIEVAL STUDIES

Queens of Sicily
1061-1266

The Queens Consort, Regent and Regnant
of the
Norman-Swabian Era
of the
Kingdom of Sicily

Jacqueline Alio

Copyright © 2018 Calogera Jacqueline Alio. All rights reserved.

Published by Trinacria Editions, New York.

This book may not be reproduced by any means whatsoever, in whole or in part, including illustrations, photographs and maps, in any form beyond the fair-use copying permitted by the United States Copyright Law and the Berne Convention, except by reviewers for the public press (magazines, newspapers and their websites), without written permission from the copyright holder.

The right of Calogera Jacqueline Alio to be identified as the author of this work has been asserted by her in accordance with the Copyright, Design and Patents Act, 1988 (UK).

Legal Deposit: Library of Congress, British Library (and Bodleian Libraries, Cambridge University Library, Trinity College Library, National Libraries of Scotland and Wales) under ALDL registration 1.3616605, Italian National Libraries (Rome, Florence).

The title of this book was assigned a Library of Congress Control Number on 28 September 2017. On the same effective date, copyright of this work was pre-registered with the United States Copyright Office under number PRE000009910 in the class "Literary Work in Book Form" with the title *Queens of Sicily 1061-1266: The Queens Consort, Regent and Regnant of the Norman-Swabian Era of the Kingdom of Sicily*. Identifying information was registered by the British Library through Bibliographic Data Services on 29 September 2017. Some material contained herein previously appeared in *Margaret, Queen of Sicily* © 2017 Calogera Jacqueline Alio, and is used by permission.

Except where otherwise indicated, all translations contained herein are by Calogera Jacqueline Alio. Illustrations, photographs, maps, image editing and cover design by Louis Mendola with a copyright license to the author. Additional credits in acknowledgments. The text of this monograph was double-blind peer-reviewed.

ORCID identifier, Calogera Jacqueline Alio: 0000-0003-1134-1217

Printed on acid-free paper.

ISBN 9781943639144 (softcover)
ISBN 9781943639205 (hardcover)
ISBN 9781943639151 (ebook)

Library of Congress Control Number 2017956440

A CIP catalogue record for this book is available from the British Library.

PROLOGUE

"All my possessions for a moment of time."

— Queen Elizabeth I

From the battlements atop a square tower, Bishop Richard Palmer surveyed the Bay of Naples, where twenty royal galleys were anchored, their grayish sails barely visible against the cloudy winter sky of late afternoon. Then he fixed his gaze on his counterpart, addressing the shorter man sternly in Norman French.

"It seems obvious enough that the poor girl is seasick, or worse, and you want to continue by sea? And I am to accept *your* unsolicited advice? Were Joanna not to arrive safe and sound in Palermo, I should advise my lord, the King of Sicily, that this debacle was a disgrace of *your* making. Be assured that the immunity clerics enjoy in our beloved England doesn't exist in *this* realm. And that William can be just as vindictive as Henry. Bishop or not, you'd pay for your stupidity with your life, at the edge of a Saracen's scimitar, I promise you!"

"Well, I, uh, suppose that I'm — without words."

"I know. The decision has been made. We'll spend Christmas here and then continue by land to Salerno and Calabria. Assuming that Princess Joanna is well enough to travel. Whatever she was in England, the girl is already a queen to the Sicilians. Now get the hell out of my sight!"

As the shaken man descended the steps, a young lady-in-waiting ascended them. The two met along the way but did not exchange words with each other, only emotionless glances.

"Your Grace," the woman greeted Bishop Palmer, bowing her head very slightly.

"My Lady, your problem, *our* problem, has been solved."

"I overheard you. Would you really punish a prelate that way?"

"Not I. You think a Muslim considers it sinful to kill an infidel, even a bishop?"

"Good God!" gasped the woman.

"Maiden, you will find that this kingdom is very different from the one you know, God save them both. I'm still not fully accustomed to this place, and I left England before you were born. How is Princess Joanna?"

"Better, I think. The nausea has passed. She's resting."

"If the weather permits, I would like to set out for Salerno the day after the Epiphany. Maybe even sooner." As the prelate spoke, the lady-in-waiting stared at the surrounding mountains, which formed a crescent around the city.

"It's colder than I expected. I see snow on the mountains. Does it ever snow down here near the coast?"

"More often than you might imagine, but nothing like Winchester."

"But I see palm trees."

"And I have seen them covered with snow."

"There's a volcano," she blurted out, pointing to Mount Vesuvius, "with fumes coming out of it! What if it erupts?"

"Pay it no heed. There's an even higher one in Sicily. You'll

PROLOGUE

be able to see it from the monastery at Bagnara, our last stop in Calabria." With this, the bishop smiled to himself at the woman's astonishment.

"How long to Palermo?" she asked.

"I've done it by land in a fortnight. We'll take at least four weeks. I've already sent word to King William about our delay. Most of the galleys will go ahead of us with their cargo and anybody who is not needed here. They'll sail tomorrow morning. Take a few knights with you and go down to the harbor, to my flagship, to remove from it whatever supplies, clothes and other effects you and the other ladies need. The queen's trunks are already being brought to her."

"Is there anything else?"

"Please assure your lady that the accommodations in Palermo will be much better than what we have here. There, until the wedding, she'll be lodged in a palace called the *Zisa* amidst lakes and lemon trees in the *Genoard*, the royal park."

"It sounds delightful," she said as she smiled up at him.

"It is what the Arabs of the city call 'Paradise on Earth.'"

"Arabs!"

"You best become accustomed to their presence, young lady, for they are the most loyal of subjects. They make up the royal bodyguard and they are the kingdom's finest archers. The king's harem is guarded by Arab eunuchs."

"A harem!" she screeched, crossing herself.

"Woman, did you believe all the world to be just like the only piece of it you have ever known?"

CHRONICON
ROMUALDI II.
ARCHIEPISCOPI SALERNITANI.
In Christi nomine incipit Chronica.

DE ÆTATIBUS.

Rima mundi ætas est ab Adam usque ad diluvium, côtinens annos, juxta Hebraicam veritatem mille sexcentos quinquaginta sex, juxta septuaginta verò Interpretes duo millia ducentos quadraginta duos ; generationes verò juxta utramque editionem numero decem, quæ universali est deleta diluvio , sicut primam cujusque hominis oblivio demergere consuevit ætatem . Fuerunt Noë filii tres , ex quibus ita. sunt ortæ gentes . De Japhet quindecim . De Cham triginta . De Sem XXVII. Sem annos duos post diluvium genuit Salem : à quo Samaritæ & Indi . Sale genuit Heber : à quo Hebræi . Heber genuit Falech , cujus tempore turris ædificatur , & linguarum divisio fit . In solo Heber prisca remansit lingua, quia in ea conspiratione non fuit . Turris verò duo millia CLXXIV. dicitur passuum . Hanc Nembroth gigas construxit . Hac ætate Scitharum regnum oritur , ubi primus regnavit Ihannus . Tunc & regnum Ægyptiorum ubi primus regnavit Thoës. Dehinc regnum Assiriorum , ubi primus regnavit Belus , quem dicunt Saturnum quidam : deinde Ninus, qui condidit

Ninivem . Hoc tempore Abraham nascitur : & post mortem Nini à Semiramide Regina reædificata est Babylonia, ubi regnavit annos quadraginta .

Secunda ætas à Noë usque ad Abraham generationes juxta Hebraicam veritatem complexa decem , annos autem ducentos nonaginta duos ; porrò juxta septuaginta Interpretes anni MLXXII. Generationes verò XI. hæc verò quasi pueritia fuit generationis populi Dei, & ideo in lingua inventa est Hebræa, à pueritia namque homo incipit noscere loqui, quæ idcirco appellata est , quòd fari non potest . Ab Adam itaque usque ad Abraham juxta Hebraicam veritatem computantur anni mille nongenti quadraginta octo, secundùm septuaginta Interpretes fiunt anni tria millia trecenti quatuordecim .

Tertia ab Abraham usque ad David generationes juxta utramque auctoritatem XIV. annos verò, secundùm Hebræorum auctoritatem nongentos quadraginta duos complectens; juxta septuaginta verò Interpretes anni tria millia CXXXVII. hæc velut quædam adolescentia fuit populi Dei, à qua ætate incipit homo posse generare , propterea Matthæus Evangelista generationum ab Abraham sumpsit exordium , qui etiam pater multarum gentium constitutus est , quando mutatum nomen accepit . Ab Adam verò juxta Hebræorum auctoritatem usque ad David fiunt anni duo millia octingenti nonaginta , secundùm septuaginta Interpretes tria millia CV. Cur autem annorum hæc diversitas sit, in sequentibus ostendetur .

Quarta à David usque ad transmigrationem

Ba-

The 1725 edition of the chronicle of Romuald of Salerno

PREFACE

"One life is all we have and we live it as we believe in living it."

— Joan of Arc

They are the semi-forgotten women of history. Some of them are little more than names mentioned in passing in medieval chronicles or charters. Only a few stand out, and only because they were called upon to step into roles more important, more visible, than what was otherwise envisaged for them. In an age when the typical woman could aspire to nothing more grandiose than a convent or a kitchen, queens were very special indeed, destined to confront challenges beyond field and forge. Queens consort, regnant and regent were a breed apart.

To ignore queenhood is to overlook an important part of the history of womanhood.

Queenship always engendered a certain mystique, a quasi-mysticism, and Walter Bagehot famously observed that, "we must not let in daylight upon magic." Yet the reality of queenly life could be very different from popular perceptions. In the following pages, we shall see how dangerous, indeed fatal, it could be to stand so closely to the seat of power, or even to wield that power.

In widowhood, three of these women actually ruled Sicily as regents: Adelaide del Vasto, Margaret of Navarre, Constance of Hauteville.

We shall seek to discover something of their personalities. Conventional wisdom suggests that women are more inclined than men to use force of argument instead of the argument of force. Was that the case of Sicily's queens? Sometimes, perhaps, but history tells us that Margaret of Navarre, probably the most powerful of the women profiled here, and one of the most fondly remembered, was willing to imprison criminals and adversaries without batting an eye, even when their guilt was questionable. Indeed, there is credible evidence to suggest that she acted to target a few of her husband's opponents for assassination following a baronial revolt. When Joanna of England learned that her brother, Richard Lionheart, had been killed by an arrow, she had the archer who loosed it tortured to death. Here we find the queen not as shrinking violet but she-wolf.

Sicily's first queen, Elvira, achieved her reginal status with the coronation of her husband, Roger II, as the first Sicilian king in 1130. Amongst the women whose stories are told here are the three who were wed to Roger I, the father of Roger II. This is why we look to 1061, the signal year the Hauteville brothers of Normandy came to Sicily and the year Roger I married Judith of Evreux, as the beginning of our journey, even though Judith was never a queen.

That path shall take us through Sicily's Norman period, and thence through the Swabian era of the Hohenstaufens, from the Battle of Messina in 1061 to the Battle of Benevento in 1266, key events in the rise and fall of these dynasties. The polyglot *Regnum Siciliae,* the Kingdom of Sicily founded by Roger II, encompassed not only the island from which it took its name but most of the Italian peninsula south of Rome, along with

Malta and, at times, a chunk of Africa. It was one of Europe's most prosperous realms, and an experiment in multiculturalism.

Queens were all but ignored by Thomas Fazello, author of the first general history of Sicily, a lengthy, post-incunable tome published between 1558 and 1560, where Margaret, as regent for William II, is conceded just a few sparse lines. She is one of only four Sicilian queens before 1266 whose stories have been the subject of detailed biographies worthy of their dignity, the others being Joanna and Isabella "Plantagenet" of England (in 1850) and Helena Angelina of Epirus (in 1791). It is this book's objective to fill a void by bringing to light the others, whose stories have been largely neglected. Along the way, we shall explore some of the intricacies and nuances of queenship into the middle years of the thirteenth century, particularly in the Kingdom of Sicily.

The legacy of these eighteen women is inextricable from the cultural heritage of southern Italy.

None of these women chose to be queen, and in youth few foresaw being crowned, but each rose to face the challenges of complexity, even adversity, that the duties of queenship entailed.

Here we shall celebrate the distinctly feminine virtue of perseverance.

Seven centuries was a long time to wait.

Acknowledgments

Writing history is a sacred trust.

The author wishes to thank the cooperative staffs of the Vatican Apostolic Library, the British Library and other libraries and archives where charters, letters and chronicles mentioned in this volume are kept, including repositories at Palermo, Naples, Munich, Pamplona, Zaragoza, Toledo, Barcelona and Kew, which permitted her consultation of these precious documents, of which rather few are available on the internet.

Thanks to the Archdiocese of Palermo for permission to photograph the crown of Constance of Aragon shown on this book's cover, and to the Metropolitan Museum of Art for permission to publish the photograph of the pendant of Queen Margaret through the OASC program. The latter is far superior to the photographs taken by the author at The Cloisters, in Manhattan, a few years ago.

Special thanks to the colleague who generously provided the transcript of his unpublished interview with the late Princess Urraca de Bourbon of the Two Sicilies in Palermo in 1994.

Sincerest gratitude is expressed to the two colleagues who reviewed the manuscript of this monograph prior to publication. Heartfelt thanks to the author's fans, thousands of readers who constitute a "tribe" that enthusiastically welcomes publication of each of her books. Such a following is a rare phenomenon in the world of academic publishing, where a printing of more than a thousand copies of a work like this one is the exception rather than the rule.

Many thanks to the publisher for making this volume available in paperback at a price affordable to students and underfunded libraries in a market where academic monographs of this length typically sell for two or three times the price of this one and include but a tiny fraction of the number of figures, maps and tables seen in the following pages.

The author alone is responsible for the positions, conclusions, and any errors, present in the pages that follow.

— C. Jacqueline Alio

Pietratagliata, Palermo, November 2018

CONTENTS

Prologue	v
Preface	ix
Introduction	1
Maps	51
1. Backstory	67
2. Judith of Evreux	83
3. Eremburga of Mortain	101
4. Adelaide del Vasto	107
5. Elvira of Castile	127
6. Sibylla of Burgundy	147
7. Beatrice of Rethel	155
8. Margaret of Navarre	163
9. Joanna of England	313
10. Sibylla of Acerra	357
11. Irene Angelina of Constantinople	371
12. Constance of Sicily	381
13. Constance of Aragon	409
14. Yolande of Jerusalem	425
... of England	435
...cia	453

17. Elisabeth of Bavaria	461
18. Beatrice of Savoy	469
19. Helena Angelina of Epirus	475
Epilogue	485
Genealogical Tables	487
Timeline	495
Appendix 1: Assizes of Ariano	509
Appendix 2: Margaret's Pendant	533
Appendix 3: Joanna's Betrothal	537
Appendix 4: Constance's Crown	545
Appendix 5: The Contrasto	549
Appendix 6: Coronation Rite	567
Appendix 7: The Last Queen	575
Notes	595
Sources and Bibliography	669
Index	705

INTRODUCTION

"Whatever women do they must do twice as well as men to be thought half as good."

— Charlotte Whitton

For too long have the voices of medieval women gone unheard or unheeded. The women whose stories are told in this book deserve to be remembered as something more than footnotes to history. How we remember them is nearly as important as why we remember them. This is a plea not for idolatry but for accuracy.

This work is about the women who stood at the apex of society in the Kingdom of Sicily, and in a few cases actually governed it. It is obvious enough that any study of this era must also consider the history of the society itself, and that includes its kings.

However, this is not an exhaustive history of the Kingdom of Sicily, its kings and institutions, about which many volumes have been written. At best, we can consider these when it is necessary or appropriate. Our focus shall be the queens and the world they knew. True, this era is framed by the battles of Messina (1061) and Benevento (1266), but a book such as this one is not the venue for detailed accounts of such events.

We shall venture into largely uncharted territory, for only a few of our countesses or queens have ever been the subject of a biography.

What is presented in these seven hundred pages is not intended to be explicitly analytical, anthropological, revisionist or even monarchist. It is, first and foremost, factual, historical and biographical. So much the better if a certain queen's story makes for an interesting narrative.

"Narrative is the lifeblood of history," declared Barbara Tuchman. "To offer a mass of undigested facts, of names not identified and places not located, is of no use to the reader and is simple laziness on the part of the author, or pedantry to show how much he has read. To discard the unnecessary requires courage and also extra work."[1]

Whilst a historical work may have "entertainment value," most of us read history out of curiosity, to learn something from it. Ideally, it should be interesting, even enlightening, and perhaps inspiring, avoiding the semantic and the pedantic. Some works are purely pedagogical.

Medieval biography should be treated as a subfield of medieval history. Many scholarly histories published nowadays include commentary regarding historiography, such as earlier scholars' observations about, for example, the life of Eleanor of Aquitaine. Since very little has ever been published about most of the women whose stories appear here, the author has elected, for the most part, to place such commentary and references in the endnotes rather than the main narrative text, where tangential or parenthetical remarks about sources or prior research might prove distracting to the reader more immediately interested in reginal biography than scholarship and methodology. Such an approach differs somewhat from that of the typical dissertation-cum-monograph because this work is intended for consultation by thousands of scholars, reginaphiles and Siculophiles rather than perusal by a doctoral committee of three or four professors followed by a few dozen more who may read it over the next decade.

In keeping with that *modus operandi,* these prefatory pages, rather than those in the numbered chapters, consider a few concepts germane to this work, either as integral components of medieval Sicilian history or our means of studying it. The commonality of these otherwise disparate topics is their relevance to the status and place, and even the historiography and sociology, of medieval Sicilian reginal biography.

The Journey

Historical biography, by its nature, breathes life into what otherwise would be a scattering of cold facts and details about the personal experience of somebody who is not here to tell her own story. In this noble endeavor the remote past, most often, is less cooperative than the recent past, rendering the biographical treatment of Queen Cleopatra more intrinsically challenging than one about Queen Victoria. Sometimes, of course, it is the very abundance of information that complicates the task of writing a biography, just as sorting through an entire deck of cards to find the queen of diamonds is harder than selecting a random card from a stack of five or six.

In a perfect world, a biography would be more than the sum of the parts of a woman's life. It would express something of her personality. Unfortunately, that is not always possible.

Despite the challenges inherent in unearthing the story of a medieval queen, this author's experience does not support the theory, espoused by twentieth-century historians such as Kenneth Bruce McFarlane, that a meaningful biography of a medieval figure is impossible to write. Nowadays medieval studies are increasingly multidisciplinary, involving such traditional fields as art and literature but also newer ones like forensic genetic (DNA) analysis, historical climatology and phylogeography, to mention just three.

Much is unsaid or understated. Sometimes, however, the existing record vouchsafes us a touch of emotion, telling us that Isabella of England, whilst riding in a cortege along a winding street to meet her future husband, pulled back the hood of her cloak to reveal her stunning beauty to a cheering crowd of onlookers clamoring to see her face, or that Margaret of Navarre shed a tear of disappointment when unjustifiably reproved by a nasty kinsman.

One may take solace in the fact that these biographies of women were written by a woman, but all of our principal contemporaneous sources are the work of men, many of them monks. To this implicitly patriarchal fraternity, the young aristocratic woman was an ethereal creature, a swan among crows, unless she was called upon to govern a kingdom. Thenceforth, depending on the sycophancy of the chronicler or annalist, she might be subjected to the same harsh criticism as a king, almost as if she assumed male gender by stepping into a role usually filled by a man.

Yet there was still a "double standard," articulating one norm for men and another for women. Rumor mongers dared to "slut shame" Queen Margaret for an imagined sexual liaison simply because she smiled at a certain man, who was her cousin. No contemporary Sicilian chronicler criticized Sicily's kings in this manner, despite the numerous bastards spawned by them.

It falls to the biographer to separate likely fact from likely fiction surrounding the life of her subject. Even the simplest facts and their implications might be viewed differently by two or three biographers writing about the same historical figure. In interpreting essential facts, the biographer should consider such factors as historical context with an eye to making presentation of her subject's experience clear, understandable, readable. But nothing must ever be embellished to the point that it becomes historical fiction. Jumping to conclusions means jumping into an abyss.

One such abyss is a queen's "private life," the modern phrase often being a euphemism for references to sexual activity or sometimes even gender identity.[2] Like any other aspect of the subject's life, this must be based on fact and context rather than speculation. It is not always easy to glean personal details from what were essentially public sources.[3]

A veil of mystery shrouds much about life in the Middle Ages. For better or worse, perceptions of some important queens have been shaped in the public mind by erroneous "facts" or even fictional accounts. If just a few of the women whose stories are told in these pages have fallen victim to this phenomenon it is only because so little has been written about most of them at length, in detail, or in English.

A woman writing about another woman may bring a sympathetic, sisterly perspective to her telling of the story. That being the case, objectivity must not be subverted by passion, for biography's noblest purpose is the expression of truth.

The modern study of queenship inevitably dovetails with the most essential tenets of what we now call *feminism,* an ideal of equality between men and women, and it is inextricably linked to our efforts to evince the unencumbered female spirit. Feminism should not be defined by woman's oppression but by her triumphs. It should not be equivocal or ambivalent. The fact that a book about queens is read by far more women than men tells us that we still have far to travel in achieving a more balanced equilibrium between sisters and brothers, wives and husbands, queens and kings.

We shall know our queens by mononyms: Elvira, Margaret, Joanna.

Was Sicilian queenship a movement or just a moment?

It was, at the very least, a lingering moment, but if we think of a woman's leadership style as an art, even as an embodiment of self, it transcends facile definition. It is unique to each woman who assumes it, whether she is Margaret of Navarre or Margaret Thatcher. It is cause for contemplation, if not celebration.

Sicily, of course, had many queens after the Hauteville and Hohenstaufen reigns, but only a few of them lived on the island and fewer still actually governed the kingdom as regents.

Points of View

Objectivity is an elusive holy grail of historiography.

There is no sole "arbiter" of history. History is not religion. Like science, it has experts but no "authorities."

Historicity is sometimes difficult to establish. In historiography, the aphorism, favored by the astrophysicist Carl Sagan, that "absence of evidence is not evidence of absence" is occasionally appropriate where prosopography or context strongly support a thesis under discussion but for which a *res ipsa loquitur* evidentiary model is lacking. This is relevant where, for example, a particular charter or letter refers to an earlier one that has not been preserved for posterity; we may reasonably presume the first letter's existence.

In general, the author has sought to avoid overzealous speculation of the kind one sometimes encounters in academic papers (in social science), where a theory may be built upon a supposition in turn based on a speculative presupposition, leaving us with a fragile house of cards lacking a supporting foundation. An academic paper may wander into a subtle existentialism when a scholar feels compelled to find a neoteric angle in a historical subject; consequently, some topics have been studied to death yet much that is written about them lacks perspicuity. Moreover, medieval Sicily has become a rather popular academic theme, yielding a plethora of dissertations, ranging from the recondite to the pedestrian, during the present century. This could lead one to conclude that past scholarship has been surpassed by recent papers; it has not, for most of the work of long-deceased scholars like the distinguished Evelyn Jamison (1877-1972) has withstood the test of time. The same could be said of the work of scholars like her student, Marjorie Chibnall (1915-2012).

Unlike Jamison, who had to travel to Italian archives and libraries to consult certain sources, many scholars working outside southern Italy today have not spent sufficient time in the regions that comprised the Kingdom of Sicily to write about it very adroitly; this is clear from a review of their work, which may lack a clear sense of the most rudimentary ethnography. For example, although the language of the Sicilian School of poetry that enjoyed the patronage of Frederick II has changed over time (and has local dialects), listening to its modern form, which is still spoken by some Sicilians, affords the researcher insight into the nuances of this tongue.

Beyond the investigation of ethnography, on-site investigation offers advantages in many aspects of research, such as gauging the distance, and hence travel time, between the locations mentioned in chronicles and letters. It also facilitates the accurate identification of certain places, which sometimes proves elusive even in the efforts of seasoned scholars. A sense of space is also important, providing us with (for example) an idea of the vertical distance traversed by the arrow that killed a son of Queen Margaret during a revolt outside Palermo's royal palace or the area covered by Monreale's mosaics. For the historian, the altitude and terrain of the mountains crowned by the castles of Taormina and Troina is something that should be seen firsthand. (Although it could be argued that no medieval European society was truly isolated, one may well justify a highly localized emphasis if a study's focus were, for example, the women of a specific city; of course, most of our queens traveled around the kingdom and their lives were influenced by events that occurred far beyond its borders.)

In other words, experiencing the places known to her subject(s) is one of many things that inform a biographer's knowledge and point of view. Biography must be more than a chimeric concept. There cannot be a foreground without a background.

Biography is not physics. It offers us few unifying theories beyond the essential realities of birth, conflict, struggle and death. If the queens of Sicily were united by a single ideology or "world view," it was simply raw grit and daily survival. The Sicilian court was unique but it was never Camelot.

We need not be obsessed with "established" or "conventional" views of a series of women about whom, with two or three exceptions, too little has been published to form the basis for rigid opinions. In that regard, more has been written about the kings than the queens, with much of the traditional criticism of the Hauteville and Hohenstaufen monarchs emanating from a certain city on the Tiber.

Papal interference in Sicilian affairs, though by no means unknown during the Norman era, intensified under Swabian rule after 1198 with the looming possibility that Frederick II, the young King of Sicily likely to become Holy Roman Emperor, might end up ruling most of the Italian peninsula, effectively surrounding the territory controlled directly by pontiffs for centuries. By 1220 Frederick's Sicilian and Imperial dominions did indeed encircle the Papal State. Yet beyond its immediate political considerations, papal policy influenced longstanding attitudes in what is now Italy. Some of those attitudes survived into the twentieth century.

The Battle of Benevento of 1266 was a turning point, its outcome merely confirmed by the ultimate demise of Hohenstaufen power at the Battle of Tagliacozzo two years later.

INTRODUCTION

These losses left the defeated Hohenstaufens and their Ghibelline supporters disparaged by the Angevins and Guelphs. In succeeding generations, the popular work of Dante, himself a Guelph, and contemporaries like Boccaccio ensured that this egregiously slanted point of view became ingrained in Italian culture, indeed shaping much of its ethos.

Nobody could prophesy this in the thirteenth century. It is one of the reasons, but (as we shall see) not the only one, for the absence of substantial biographies of the queens of Sicily's Norman-Swabian era.

Reginal Culture in the Kingdom of Sicily

Despite some striking similarities between one kingdom and another, and extensive contact between certain courts, European queenship was inseparable from local culture, social norms and law. Joanna of England may have encouraged the veneration of Thomas Becket in Sicily, but Monreale, the Sicilian cathedral where the saint's earliest public image was rendered in mosaic as an icon, is unlike anything she could have known in England or Normandy. Whatever could be said of Joanna's father, Henry II, his court did not have a harem guarded by eunuchs. Clearly, certain things were different in the Kingdom of Sicily, which seems to have been far wealthier than any realm from whence her foreign queens came.

Even if it is not our chief focus, a consideration of queenly life as it existed elsewhere is at least tangentially relevant to our studies because most of our queens' marriages were "exogamous." With few exceptions, these women hailed from lands far beyond the Italian peninsula. Among our queens, the most obvious example of a life spent in several countries is Constance of Aragon; though born in Portugal she was raised in Spain, and she wed the King of Hungary before marrying Frederick. She knew life at three courts.

As we shall see, the Italian realms known to our countesses and queens underwent much change between 1061 and 1266. What began as a patchwork of duchies and counties became a multicultural kingdom in 1130, yet by the end of Norman-Swabian rule in 1266 it was well on its way to becoming a monocultural European state with its own language. The Arabs, Byzantines and Jews contributed greatly to this, but the Sicilian, Apulian and Neapolitan cultures that we have inherited, clearly manifested in the southern Italian kingdoms that existed into the nineteenth century, were born of Norman and Swabian rule.

Apart from art, architecture, chattels and charters, a few subtle traces of the Norman presence remain, some more evident than others, in the people themselves. There are the genetic haplogroups, of course, along with obvious physical traits like red hair and rosacea. The Sicilian language has a few words from Norman French, along with others from Greek, Arabic and German.

The Norman-Swabian era coincided with what we now call the "age of chivalry," itself part of what has been termed a "twelfth-century renaissance." Sicily's queens witnessed this European movement firsthand. As a patron of the island's greatest monastery, with its striking Norman, Fatimid, Comnenian and Provençal influences, Queen Margaret actively, purposefully fostered it. Her daughter-in-law, Joanna of England, learned about chivalric culture at her mother's court in Poitiers.

True, her sexuality, and especially the ability to produce heirs, ensured a noblewoman's place in society, but it was her inner strength that sustained her. Courtly chivalry was expressed in Sicily in the *Contrasto* of Cielo of Alcamo, a poem he may have intended as something of a parody of what already existed elsewhere. Cielo's contemporary, Giacomo of Lentini, in daily life a royal notary, is credited with inventing the sonnet.

INTRODUCTION

Literary chivalry was much romanticized, reflecting, among other things, a conventional, masculine, cisgendered view that gave rise to the enduring, if often deceptive, image of the damsel as a submissive, albeit beguiling, object of desire endowed with great beauty and charm but little intellect of her own. Like so many other clichés of the Middle Ages, this one is largely divorced from reality. Even for the woman who became a queen, life was often precarious and difficult. The role of Constance of Aragon, who oversaw matters in Sicily during her husband's absence, was not very different from that of a baroness managing a feudal estate whilst her spouse was away fighting.

Chivalry's jousts, tournaments and pageantry glamorized the cult of the mounted warrior, but unlike knights, nobles and kings, men charged with the dirty business of sustaining the tenuous *status quo,* troubadours and minstrels sold dreams. They were entertainers, expressing lofty ideals in a cruel, unforgiving, imperfect world. Romantic love itself was little more than a myth where it presupposed that courtship culminated in a wedding; marriages within every social class were arranged by parental consent, or in any case could not be contracted without it. The eloquent knight courting a lady was as rare as the marriage arranged on the basis of love rather than expedience.

When they weren't kow-towing to the king or coercing serfs, knights were killing, raping and pillaging. Morality was the purview of churchmen, who were known to engage in some occasional mischief of their own.

Until around 1200, the vernacular language of the Sicilian court was Norman French, even though some courtiers spoke Arabic or Greek as their mother tongue. German made inroads during the brief Sicilian reign of Henry VI, father of Frederick II. By the second or third decade of Frederick's reign, the earliest form of the Sicilian language was in common use in everyday speech. This was the tongue of poets like Cielo of Alcamo and Giacomo of Lentini, and Frederick himself composed a few poems in Middle Sicilian.

Cielo's *Contrasto* (translated in Appendix 5) is the lengthiest surviving poem written in Sicilian. The oldest extant copy of it, like much early poetry of the Sicilian School that flourished at Frederick's court, bears the linguistic influence of later copyists, hence its similarity to Tuscan. For Middle Sicilian in its purest form we must look to a later work.

Written around 1290, the account of the War of the Vespers of 1282 from the point of view of John of Procida, onetime chancellor of King Manfred and a planner of the revolt, is the oldest surviving narrative work written in an Italian language, yet it appeared in English only during the twenty-first century; few scholars outside Italy have ever heard of it.

The memoir of John of Procida, *Lu Rebellamentu di Sichilia contra Re Carlu,* brings us such words as these, addressed to Peter III of Aragon and referring to Constance Hohenstaufen ("your consort, our sovereign lady"), Manfred's daughter:

"Ricomandamunj a la vostra signuria et a la signura vostra muglerj, la quali è la nostra donna a ccui nuj divimu purtari liancza, mandamuvj prigandu chi vui ni digiatj liberari e trayri et livari di li manu di nostri et di li vostri nimichi, sì comu liberau Moises lu populu di li mani di Faraguni, actali chi nuj poczamu tiniri li vostri figloli per signurj et divinjari di li perfidi lupi malvasi devoraturj."

Which is to say:

"We wish to submit our fealty to your authority and that of your consort, our sovereign lady, to whom we dutifully convey our homage, praying that you may deign to free us of our enemies just as Moses delivered his people from the hands of the Pharaoh, so that we may ensure our children's future, secure from the deceitful, devouring wolves."[4]

INTRODUCTION

Not everything of length written in Middle Sicilian deals with conflict, and here a good example is the *Contrasto,* mentioned earlier. The focus of most poetry of the Sicilian School was love. Dante recognized the significance of the Middle Sicilian language expressed in Cielo's poem, though he discerned in it no particular beauty:

Et dicimus quod, si vulgare sicilianum accipere volumus secundum quod prodit a terrigenis mediocribus, ex ore quorum iudicium eliciendum videtur, prelationis honore minime dignum est, quia non sine quodam tempore profertur, ut puta ibi: *Tragemi de'ste focora, se t'este a boluntate.*[5]

After 1282, the island of Sicily was separated from the peninsula politically, if occasionally united with it through dynastic marriages, and its society was essentially monocultural. By 1300, Italy's last Muslim communities, at places like Lucera in Apulia, were little more than a memory. In truth, this latinization was a gradual but real process of acculturation that had begun the moment the Normans conquered Palermo, but the "Latin" culture one identifies with southern Italy today is rooted in the society that existed by the dawn of the fourteenth century, when the Aragonese ruled Sicily and the Angevins ruled the southern part of the peninsula. Nevertheless, the society that emerged in southern Italy was more portmanteau than palimpsest, for it reflected the influence of the cultures present here during Norman and Swabian rule.

One of the things that distinguished the Hauteville and Hohenstaufen reigns was the population itself. There was diversity in faith, language and thought. Science and philosophy thrived. Sicily's queens were familiar with this world; those who governed as regents actively promoted it.

It is this eclectic mix that characterized, and perhaps even defined, the Sicilian environment during the Norman and

Swabian eras. Such diversitude is generally appreciated more in our time than it was in times past; Salvadore Morso and Michele Amari, whose earliest treatises appeared in the first half of the nineteenth century, were Sicily's first modern Arabists of note.

In these pages, we are concerned with the Kingdom of Sicily in its European and Mediterranean contexts. If any of the queens whose stories are told here referred to "Italy" it was in purely geographical terms. Often, the so-called "Lombards" were simply peninsular Italians of the landed nobility, despite the gentilic originally being intended to identify those descended from the Longobards who established Italy's first medieval monarchies.

Sources and Scholarship

As we shall see, the study of Sicilian medieval queenship straddles several fields and disciplines. Unfortunately, a good deal of what little, until the present century, has been published about Sicily's first few queens is simply incorrect.

A review of the existing research (secondary literature) is important in this kind of work. However, this book is not an appropriate forum in which to rebut other scholars' flawed research findings or the increasingly hypothetical, whimsical theories advanced in the papers presented at academic conferences and in specialized journals. Some studies blatantly violate the heuristic principle of *lex parsimoniae* advocated by William of Ockham that the simplest explanation of an event about which little is known is usually the most likely one.

For various reasons, many papers and monographs published today, even when peer-reviewed, focus on what is sometimes called "microhistory," resulting in the verbose study of a single charter, icon, object, chattel, church or localized event. In this volume such topics are presented in the appendices and notes.

It is not this monograph's purpose to focus on etiology or prolix analyses for their own sake.

The reasoning behind this is simple. Some weeds blossom into wildflowers, but others remain mere weeds, serving no greater purpose than to occupy space in an otherwise virtuous flower bed. The author has sought to bring you an orderly garden, not an untamed jungle. Let us leave the weeds to thrive someplace else.

At all events, the author's research was based overwhelmingly, nay almost entirely, on contemporary "primary" sources (chronicles, charters, letters, architecture) rather than secondary literature. This is amply set forth in the bibliography, notes and appendices.

The chronicle of Hugh Falcandus was published in the sixteenth century, that of Romuald of Salerno in the eighteenth. A few sources sometimes cited by historians, such as the chronicle attributed to "Matthew Spinelli of Giovinazzo" and the Arabic letters "discovered" by the abbot Giuseppe Vella, are forgeries; this problem also plagues the diplomatic record, where we occasionally find apocryphal or unauthorized charters.

Few chronicles written in the Kingdom of Sicily were published in English translation until the twenty-first century. Much of what is affirmed in chronicles is attested in charters as to persons, places and dates, if not other details, thus bringing us a certain concordance. Like the synoptic gospels, different chronicles sometimes offer us slightly varying accounts of the same events; this is the case of the descriptions of the deeds of Richard I of England and Philip II of France at Messina in 1190, when Queen Joanna was released from captivity.

The author's archival research was augmented by visits to the places where some of our queens were raised, such as certain localities in England, France and Spain, as well as Italy.

Only a few original manuscript sources were available for digital download; two rare examples are the invaluable *Historia*

Bizantina (or "Synopsis of Histories") of John Skylitzes, copied in Greek in Palermo during the middle of the twelfth century and kept in the Biblioteca Nacional de España in Madrid, and the *Liber ad Honorem Augusti* of Peter of Eboli, written in Latin verse at the royal court and retained at the Burgerbibliothek in Berne. These codices are unique, each existing in its entirety in only one precious copy.

The general scarcity of detailed information about medieval queens can be attributed to the rather obvious nature of the available sources. Unless a queen ruled in her own right, became a regent, or somehow played a prominent role in a historical event, there was little need to mention her in a chronicle or charter. Under most circumstances, the birth of a king's daughter was less likely to be recorded than the birth of the same king's son, who inherited a place of precedence in the line of succession under the principles of Salic Law. In most cases, royal daughters (princesses) are not mentioned explicitly, by name, until their betrothals, which made these women "newsworthy" in the eyes of the men writing about them.

In rarer cases, a few of a queen's letters survive. Enough of the correspondence of Eleanor of Aquitaine (1122-1204) is conserved to offer us a clear impression of her opinions, and Anna Comnena (1083-1153) wrote a history expressing, amongst many other things, her thoughts about the Normans who reached the Byzantine Empire, not that queens were the only women writing anything during the twelfth century.[6]

Greater information is available when a woman like Adelaide, Margaret or Constance was a regent. These women also issued charters (decrees), of which some survive, and a photographic sampling appears in this volume. Several fine compilations of reginal charters and decrees have been published. Noteworthy among these is Theo Kölzer's *Urkunden und Kanzlei der Kaiserin Konstanze, Königin von Sizilien 1195-1198* in the fine *Monumenta Germaniae Historica* series.

INTRODUCTION

Most of the extant charters issued by Sicily's regents fall into either of two broad categories. Some deal with the rights of monasteries while others concern such matters as feudal rights (manors, privileges, serfs). Charters are informative, but only to a certain degree, for they do not typically concern sweeping issues or major events. The chronicles provide us with far more information, even in those cases, such as that of Hugh Falcandus, where the chronology of events is occasionally inexact.

Veracity is the most important element in this kind of research. Being our chief sources, chronicles, letters and charters should, in a perfect world, corroborate presumed facts. In some cases a fact or conclusion is attested by more than one source. Where slightly contradictory accounts exist regarding such details as dates, these are rarely matters of great import. Of far greater concern are those particulars that involve events, especially where there is little or no corroboration.

Certain sources have become known to us rather recently. A series of letters between Frederick II and his heir, Conrad, was rediscovered in a library during the present century and published in 2017. The Assizes of Ariano (1140) and the *Ferraris Chronicle* (1228) were found during the nineteenth century. Yet historians already suspected that such manuscripts likely existed; the onetime existence of the letters was surmised from other sources, the Assizes were sometimes alluded to over the centuries as "Roger's laws," and part of the *Ferraris Chronicle* was extracted from a lost (complete) version of the chronicle of Falco of Benevento, of which contemporaneous copies survive.

So solid is the framework of sources supporting our knowledge of Sicilian history into the thirteenth century that no hypothetical discovery of long-lost documentation is likely to alter it significantly. That having been said, it would be encouraging to find information about the regents Adelaide and Constance beyond what we already have.

We know the most about Margaret, hence the exceptional breadth and depth of the chapter dedicated to her. The comparatively extensive information known about Margaret lends to her story a quasi-literary "narrative arc" that makes it especially interesting.

In such exhaustive detail is Margaret's regency chronicled that for this reason alone her story overshadows all the others. It may be stated, *arguendo,* that much more is known about Margaret than any other European queen regent of her century, making the fact that her first biography was written only a few years ago all the more astounding.

In recent years, much has been written about Leonor (Eleanor) of England, Joanna's sister, who wed Alfonso VIII of Castile, and while little of that work seems to shed new light on her life, it is far more voluminous than what has been published about Joanna.

The significance of much that is presented in this volume transcends Sicilian history. The documents relative to Joanna's betrothal are a rare treasure, and an object lesson in how reginal marriages, dowries and dowers were conceived and formulated during the twelfth century.

Another interesting case is Joanna's niece, Isabella of England, about whom we know something beyond the typical facts thanks to certain records kept about her as a maiden during the reign of her brother, Henry III. Here is the perfect example of the attestation of statements by chroniclers like Roger of Wendover in such resources as the Close Rolls and Patent Rolls preserved in Britain.

Much is made of the biased tone of chroniclers like Hugh Falcandus and perhaps Matthew Paris, yet it is remarkable that they are so accurate so much of the time. This reflects more than serendipity in the case of Falcandus, who was actually present at the royal court in Palermo.

The dates of death of some queens were drawn from

necrologies compiled at monasteries or elsewhere. It should be noted, however, that certain medieval sources, such as annals, occasionally recorded incorrect dates.

An obvious — if isolated — case of a solution to the problem posed by missing documentary records is the epitaph over Margaret's tomb in Monreale, which offers us a fine example of the importance of researching *in situ* instead of relying exclusively on works consulted in a library or on the internet. As stated earlier, visiting the places known in youth to the women destined to become Sicily's queens has taken the author across western Europe. As queens, most of these women resided principally in Palermo, the kingdom's capital. Anybody seeking to gain more than a superficial knowledge of them owes it to herself to discover this fascinating city. Palermo boasts more surviving churches, chapels and castles from the twelfth century than any other city in Europe; for information on these the reader is commended to the author's concise guide *Norman-Arab-Byzantine Palermo, Monreale and Cefalù*.

For an informed comparison, the more curious reader (or serious scholar) is also advised to visit certain regions of northern and southern Spain, specifically Navarre, Aragon, Catalonia and Andalusia, whose multicultural medieval history is rather similar to what one finds in Sicily. With good reason, medieval writers sometimes compared Norman-Arab Bal'harm (Palermo) to the cities of Andalusia; Malaga has a similar geographic situation along rivers running through a valley encircled by mountains near a coast, while Granada, Cordoba and even Seville had a rather similar layout and architecture. Some of the gardens and pools at the Alhambra (Granada) and the Alcazar (Seville) evoke something of the atmosphere of those that once existed in Palermo, especially in the parks surrounding the Zisa and Cuba palaces (see note 248). Except for a particularly arid part of Andalusia's Almería province near Tabernas, the topography and agriculture of these Spanish regions is strikingly similar to what one finds in southern Italy.

Compared to her more refined sister cities in Spain, modern Palermo, the city as we see it today, is a diamond in the rough, crude and unpolished. The Sicilian capital is noisy and chaotic, but unlike her Iberian siblings she still has her tenth-century souk, now an unkempt street market called *Ballarò*.

Although we must work with whatever information, however limited or limiting, is available to us (hence the brevity of some biographies that appear in these pages), a woman's life is worth more than a few words on a piece of parchment. The diplomatic record may be sufficient in the writing of a prosaic academic paper or even in formulating a dissertation suitable for eventual incarnation as a monograph, yet an accurate, insightful biography necessitates work far beyond the consultation and study, however diligent, of chronicles and chartularies. This is even truer when writing a collection of biographies.

With one or two exceptions, most obviously Elisabeth of Bavaria, all of these women shared the experience of living in southern Italy, and some died here.

Visiting the places in countries, besides Italy, where Sicily's countesses and queens lived in girlhood was highly informative to the writing of this book, but even more useful is a familiarity with the most important localities of the *Regnum Siciliae* known to these women as adults. Naturally, this includes Palermo, as we have seen, but also Salerno, Bari, Messina, Catania and Naples as well as Potenza, Brindisi, Acerra, Andria and San Marco d'Alunzio, amongst many others. A knowledge of the kingdom's hinterland — its castles, abbeys, towns, mountains, forests, fields and agriculture — is also highly advantageous: Cava, Caccamo, Cosenza, Gerace, Lecce, Lucera, Stilo, Sicignano, Melfi, Maniace, Mussomeli and countless others.

It is a very honest, pragmatic, human approach to biography to learn as much as possible about how the subject lived, what she saw, what she ate, the people and places she knew. Even costume, regalia, iconography, mosaicry, numismatics and heraldry are relevant. This is nothing less than the context that transforms a name on the page into a person about whom we want to learn more.

The physical appearance of some queens is known to us, if only in a very general way, from how they are depicted in contemporary illuminations or otherwise described; Joanna "Plantagenet" of England had blonde hair and Constance Hauteville had reddish hair. The entombed remains of some queens shed light on their physical nature. Constance of Aragon seems to have been reasonably slender; the same can be said of Margaret of Navarre if the image of her engraved on a pendant is accurate, most of what was left of her body being destroyed in a fire, along with the porphyry tomb that preserved her until a fateful bolt of lightning struck Monreale's splendid church in 1811.[7]

Original sources are everything. Inclusion in this volume of both surviving codices of the Assizes of Ariano, already published in one of the author's previous books, may seem like an exercise in redundancy, but this legal code is a common thread running through the Hauteville reigns and into those of the Hohenstaufens, and it was deemed inappropriate (even presumptuous) to refer the reader to *Margaret, Queen of Sicily* simply to consult these texts, which are difficult to find elsewhere. If the Kingdom of Sicily boasted anything like a formative constitution, it was the Assizes of Ariano.

Among the secondary literature of greatest value were studies on very specialized topics, such as a particular chronicle or the monastery endowed by Queen Margaret at Maniace. A rare treasure is the detailed biographical study of Helena Angelina of Epirus published at Naples in 1791. In Italy, biographies of *any* women other than saints were all but unknown until the twentieth century.

The research strategies and methods that resulted in this volume are conventional and transparent enough. This work reflects no "agenda" or "mission" apart from the author's intent to present accurate history in a rigorous manner.

Queenship and Identity

Beyond its historical lessons, important as they are, how relevant is medieval queenhood?

In a society dominated by men, women were long viewed not only as the weaker sex but the less intelligent, less motivated one. In view of serious research, those perceptions have gradually fallen by the wayside.[8]

Much of it has to do with personhood and what is now called "female agency," the natural right of a woman to entertain her own views and to shape her own destiny. This empowerment is feminism in its purist form.

Medieval women's roles were highly defined by female bodies, and there weren't many choices. Depending on the social *stratum* into which she was born, a woman might be valued chiefly for bearing children, working on a farm, performing household chores, or having sex. What was normal was not usually regarded as particularly humiliating, for societal norms were (and still are) overwhelming. Rare was the woman who felt free enough to bridle at the duties imposed upon her, or the way she was exploited.

In passing, we may note that such conditions were not much different in the Muslim world than in Christian dominions.

The fact that a woman encumbered by such conditions, indeed defined by them, might be a great thinker had little to do with it. In short, it was a man's world, and few women escaped its rigid limitations. In this patriarchy, the woman who achieved her intrinsic social or intellectual potential was the uncommon exception, and typically she was an aristocrat or a nun (or both).

Yet Sicily seems to have been slightly more enlightened than other realms where fundamental women's rights were concerned. Under Arab influence, there was somewhat higher literacy among girls than what one encountered in northern Europe, and by around 1140 the Normans had codified a law making rape a serious crime, though principally for assaults on nuns. Despite the enduring historical image of chivalrous knights, sexual predation was fairly frequent in every social class.

How does a woman separate her true self from the conditions thrust upon her? Even a queen, a woman of society's most privileged caste, might be forced to compromise.

Queens, being one of the very few classes of medieval women afforded the opportunity to reach their intellectual and social potential as thinkers and doers, offer us a great deal to study.

Significantly, queenship was the only role of the medieval European woman defined chiefly by its public function.

Only one of the queens in our elite sorority was born in Sicily. Most often, the princess who married a foreign king left her natal family and homeland, never to see them again. Crowned in a far country, she embraced its people, culture and traditions as her own.

The medieval concept of monarchy was inextricably linked to a rudimentary precursor of what today would be called national identity, even ethnicity. This involves, among other things, a distinct culture and language associated with a certain place, and here an example similar to Sicily is Catalonia; during the fourteenth century both were part of the "Crown of Aragon," and the modern Sicilian language bears distinct traces of Catalan. Today both regions, though belonging to larger nations, enjoy a fair degree of political autonomy, a fact that recognizes their medieval heritage.[9] Normally subdued, the Sicilians' sense of independence rises from the ashes every now and then, if discreetly.[10]

In medieval monarchies, queens and kings were the symbolic embodiment of nationhood, a status nurtured in Sicily by the Normans and then the Swabians.

In a perfect world, it would be gratifying to learn something about the wives of Sicily's emirs, especially the consorts of the local Kalbids. Alas, we know very little about them.

As an emirate, Sicily was part of the Fatimid Empire. As a kingdom, it was a sovereign country. The emirate knew prosperity, the kingdom knew greatness. That greatness owed more than a little to a few stout-hearted queens.

The fact remains that we can learn and know only so much about them, much less their emotions and motivations.

Were any of these women even more than an archetypal she-wolf, perhaps attaining the character of a natural leader, an "alpha" female? Clearly, the regents rose to face adversity, and Joanna showed great strength following her husband's death. Only Constance, the daughter of Roger II, was a true heiress, and her self-confidence is obvious enough from her actions. The personality of her namesake and successor, Constance of Aragon, also seems to have been a strong one, certainly by the time she wed Frederick II.

Here one is reminded of the overzealous, misdirected attempt by Ernst Kantorowicz to paint Frederick as a "modern" monarch, an idea that later had to be debunked by more judicious scholars.

Though surely exceptional in some ways, most of our queens were nothing more or less than women of their time. Looking back across the dense mists of centuries, many aspects of day-to-day life were very different from what we experience today. Even prosperous Sicily was essentially an agrarian society. Although the Arabs and Templars devised an early form of the check, coins were the chief currency, with barter the preferred method of exchange for many everyday transactions. Life spans were generally shorter. Disease was rife and efficacious treatments rare. Girls could be married at the age of fourteen and were expected to bear children by twenty. Childbirth was often fatal to the mother, even (as we shall see) when she was a queen. Infant mortality rates were high, with superstition governing what usually passed for the practice of medicine. Children born outside marriage were stigmatized and persons having physical impairments were mocked. The class into which a woman was born marked her for life, with a clear social line drawn between noble damsels and common wenches. (For the reader less than conversant with the realities of European medieval life, the author suggests Morris Bishop's book, *The Middle Ages,* as a suitable primer.)

Objectives

This work is not a general disquisition on queenship or the role of women in medieval society, important as both topics are, although it provides source material for scholars writing about these subjects. Nor is it intended as a detailed study of peripheral topics such as the endowment of a specific monastery by a Sicilian queen or the political reasons, real or imaginary, behind this or that royal marriage, subjects more suited to a concise paper, article or chapter than a tiresome treatise or a whole book. The marriage of Isabella of England to Frederick II was certainly part of a strategy by both her brother and her husband to curtail the ambitions of the King of France, and this was widely known at the time, but few of us are inclined to dedicate an entire dissertation or monograph to such a subject.

While the nature of queenship, with special reference to the queens of Sicily in the context of Norman and Swabian tradition, is considered from time to time, this volume is essentially a biographical reference work. Though queenship, feminism and gender identity are certainly, immediately pertinent to our study, and must not be overlooked, they are not, as an object of exhaustive analysis, the central focus of this work.

More generally, the study of queenship as a social or anthropological phenomenon sometimes sits uneasily with traditional biography, adding to it an unnecessary layer of conjecture or hypothesis.

Geographically, the essential orientation is southern Italy. By necessity, much is presented about this region and the characteristics that distinguish it from others, both socially and geographically. Because such context is important, the Kingdom of Sicily might be considered a silent, omnipresent "character" or a unifying, underlying theme in the story of these queens.

Whereas the author's *Margaret, Queen of Sicily* was presented in a narrative style more akin to storytelling, a format likely to garner criticism in academic circles, this book, by comparison, makes for slightly less engaging, if no less interesting, reading. Like *Margaret,* however, it presents reginal biographical information never before published, not even in Italian.

It is our intent to focus on queens without being myopic or misandric. By necessity, many facts about their husbands' reigns are considered, but an effort has been made to avoid such details overshadowing the stories of the queens themselves. Here one obvious example amongst many is the complex relationship of Sicily's kings with the popes, a subject about which volumes have been written, works to which the reader is referred for further elucidation. The alternative to this, and something that the author has eschewed, would have been lengthy forays into complex topics which, though peripherally relevant, could prove distracting in a biography. Entire treatises have been dedicated to the implications and effects of the apostolic legateship granted to the rulers of Sicily; for our purposes a succinct explanation suffices.

INTRODUCTION

Biography presents certain challenges not always encountered in other forms of history writing. It is human nature for different people to perceive dissimilar qualities in the same person, most often (in daily life) based on that person's relationship to them as parent, spouse, child, sibling, friend, mentor or colleague. Naturally, it is possible for biographers to diverge in their views of the same historical figure. Indeed, it could be argued that this is sometimes preferable so that one biographer's account is not "flat," and identical to another's, and therefore lacking in individuality. The major biographies of Frederick II written during the twentieth century (Kantorowicz, Van Cleve, Abulafia) by historians born and educated in different countries (Germany, the United States, Great Britain) clearly reflect differences in thesis, emphasis and tone. Language sometimes accounts for part of this, especially where a translator seeks to capture not only the literal meaning but the actual, intended sense or tenor of an author's words. The biographer's personal background and world view also come into play, informed by the era in which she lives. Her knowledge of the subject's social and physical environment is required if some sense of reality and empathy is to be conveyed, lending accuracy and verisimilitude to the writing. The present work could not have been undertaken competently without a knowledge of, for example, particular faiths, languages, customs and places.

These challenges are not indifferent, and each biographer confronts them in her own way. In writing the following eighteen biographies, which vary greatly in length and detail, the author has sought to avoid excessive psychological or anthropological speculation about why a woman did (or did not do) something, seeking instead to concentrate on the known facts, context and circumstances without arbitrarily ascribing a modern personality or mentality to somebody living in a multiethnic, medieval Mediterranean monarchy.

Feminism and Multiculturalism

The most obviously feminist element in our study is, quite simply, the empowerment of a few women in an age of entrenched patriarchy. In that respect, Sicily's queens were hardly unique for women of their special rank and status, as there are many contemporaneous examples of strong regents and consorts in the Norman, Iberian, German and Byzantine spheres, all of which touched Sicily. Studies published during the last few decades have revealed such realities, even if this is the first one to do it for Sicilian queens collectively.

Sicily's queens regent navigated this environment with the help of *familiares* (trusted counsellors), prelates and indeed an array of advisors and various experts.[11]

Until now, what was missing, in view of the dearth of serious reginal studies (explained later), was solid support for the thesis that, based on her actions and importance, one Sicilian queen may have stood above the others. Modern scholars are sometimes reluctant to declare a single figure of a certain era to stand out from her peers, but in certain cases the evidence speaks for itself.

After years of study, it is the author's contention that in the Norman-Swabian Kingdom of Sicily the evidence constrains us to recognize Margaret of Navarre as the realm's most distinguished queen, with Constance Hauteville, who was likely her protégée, as a close second.

Be it agreed that a paradigm of feminism is intrinsic to a proper study of Sicilian queens, multiculturalism (or diversity) is equally relevant in any study involving medieval Sicily.

Norman-Fatimid-Byzantine-Swabian Sicily was nothing if not a multicultural society, albeit more so at its apogee than during its senescence. The author co-wrote a book introducing it, *The Peoples of Sicily: A Multicultural Legacy*. Among the many facts presented in that volume intended for a general readership, mention is made of the Arabs' introduction of Hindu-Arabic numerals and paper, the former from India and the latter from China, probably via the Silk Road. Both developments, incidentally, facilitated education at a rate greater in Sicily and Spain than in most other parts of Europe.

The Sicilians themselves were diverse in faith, customs, language, law and even cuisine. Medieval Sicily was influenced by Africa and Asia as well as Europe.

Woe betide the queen who failed to grasp the complexities of this polyglot milieu.

In no other part of Europe, not even in the Iberian lands, do we see such a rich tapestry woven of such varied threads existing in the same society. We must look to contemporary Jerusalem (until 1187) to find something recognizably similar to Palermo's twelfth-century multicultural mosaic; the stout Romanesque architecture of the Holy Sepulchre Church, a vestige of that era, vaguely resembles the syncretic Norman-Arab ecclesial style seen in Sicily.

As we have said, the greater number of women in Norman-Swabian Sicily were afforded more rights and opportunities than the majority of their sisters elsewhere in Europe because Muslim society fostered a higher rate of literacy among girls, while the legal codes (of 1140 and 1231) addressed the rights of women in some measure.

The lessons of Sicily's multicultural experiment transcend Eurocentrism, touching a place in the human spirit where what unites us is far greater than whatever might divide us. One need not be a European Christian, or even a woman, to appreciate the stories of Sicily's queens.

Gender identity, or our view of it, has become ever more complex, at some times recognizing equality but at others celebrating the differences between the sexes. This is reflected in language. In English, a tongue generally lacking gendered nouns, "neutral" words such as *actor,* following the format of *doctor,* are making *actress, adulteress* and *directress* obsolete, even in British usage. These words, of course, are rooted in Latin, whose structure is retained in *dominatrix* and *testatrix*. Words like *emperor* and *empress* have not vanished, and in Italian we still find *dottoressa, studentessa* and *senatrice*. King and queen, *re* and *regina, könig* and *königin* remain unchanged.

Beyond gender, medieval society has left its mark on language in such words as *peasant, bastard, jester* and *rogue*. That the literal meanings of these terms are so often overlooked in our times can make it difficult for the modern reader to appreciate some of the situations and facts presented in a work such as this one.

But feminism and equality have always been about much more than language.

Certain medieval queens, particularly the regents, exemplified a kind of protofeminism. Some degree of intersectionality, the multifaceted identity of a queen as woman, wife, mother, leader and symbol, was inherent in her status, and in these pages an effort has been made to present Sicily's countesses and queens with an eye to describing these various roles. There may have been other facets; Margaret, for example, was the *de facto* protector of the kingdom's religious minorities, the Muslims and Jews. More than a reflection of one or another form of feminist theory, these biographies, considered collectively, are a simple expression of women's history. Little of this is truly "revisionist," for one cannot revise histories that, for the most part, had not yet been written in much detail. At all events, it is always important to view each woman in the context of her era, not ours.

It is equally important to recognize what each woman actually did. Following the death of Roger I, his widow, Adelaide, continued his policies. As regent, Margaret, who had to govern a much larger territory than Adelaide, clearly supported some policies at variance to those of her husband, William I. The regency of Constance Hauteville was too brief to offer us much insight into her divergence from the policies of her husband, Henry VI, with whom she seems to have differed occasionally. Each regent was assisted by competent, if sometimes controversial, courtiers.

We know more about irrepressible Joanna's life after the death of her first husband, William II, than during his reign, but she was never a regent. Joanna's niece, Isabella, also seems to have had a rather independent spirit, and we know something of her life in England before marrying Frederick II. In the veins of both ladies coursed the blood of Eleanor of Aquitaine who, as it happened, visited Sicily twice.

Movements

Reginal biography is hardly new, but today it is much more than it ever was, its rapid evolution an outgrowth of the "second wave" of feminism that arrived around 1960. This was the women's movement expressed through the pioneering work of such figures as Betty Friedan (1921-2006) and, in popular culture, the late Mary Tyler Moore (1936-2017). Here in Italy, the movement's essential ideology was echoed by proponents such as Carla Lonzi (1931-1982) and Oriana Fallaci (1929-2006).

In academe, the movement supported the advent of "social history" to complement, even supplant, the exclusively "political history" that had dominated historiography until that era. We may well debate the degree to which reginal biography could or should be considered part of a historiographical trend that sought to draw attention to the experience of "ordinary," and theretofore overlooked, people rather than "great women" and momentous events. However, the subfield of reginal biography has derived some stimulus from the wider field of women's history, certainly in nations where social history has prevailed as a pragmatic means for examining our past.

Retrospect permits us to discern a division or transition of sorts. Speaking broadly, the writings of historians such as Charles Haskins (1870-1937) about the Norman Kingdom of Sicily virtually ignored its queens, while those of John Julius Norwich (1929-2018) at least considered their influence. Today, works such as this book seek to approach history with an eye to both its political and social contexts, without choosing one over the other, instead viewing them as two sides of the same coin or perhaps two facets of a multifaceted gemstone. Not only are we concerned with a queen's public persona expressed in charters and decrees (the political history), but with the everyday situations and challenges she faced, as well as the culture, art and religion that colored her life (the social history), which were exceptionally sophisticated in the polyglot Kingdom of Sicily.

The wider effects of second-wave feminism as a social phenomenon and shaper of attitudes are the subject of analysis, criticism and even deconstruction, some of it rather complex; here the author is simply recognizing the movement's beneficial impact in prompting historians to research and publish more about medieval women. Ideally, the study of queens and other prominent women would be seamlessly integrated into the general study of history.

Through biography we can come to know the suppressed, forgotten voices seeking to be heard, not as a doctrine or manifesto but as an expression of the unsung women who were always among us, even when we did not see them. Apart from feminism, the writing of reginal biography has been influenced, to a greater or lesser extent, by literary movements such as modernism (Virginia Woolf) and narrative journalism (Tom Wolfe).

As perspectives about independent, single women have evolved over time, so have our views of queens, especially regents. Largely gone are the tautology, atavism and condescension that characterized many of the biographies of medieval queens written (usually by men) before the middle of the twentieth century. Nowadays, these historical women, and studies about them, are more often accorded the gravitas they deserve, with proper attention paid to the facts and implications of the gender disparity that typified medieval life.

The last few decades have seen the flowering of insightful, sophisticated scholarship of a kind that reveals the true nature of European medieval queens as figures far more powerful, influential and multidimensional than what was formerly presented in print. Rather than offering us a strictly revisionist paradigm, the diverse *corpus* of work (much of which is published firstly in English) emerging from such study affords us the opportunity to complete or complement prior research, which tended to overlook the importance of women generally. Viewed in that context, books like this one are part of a wider trend.

Despite such progress, the fact remains that very few studies or biographies of value have been published (even here in Italy) which do justice to the women whose stories are told in this volume. Contrarily, overstatement can be a risk. In cases where scarcely enough is known about a queen to write even a brief chapter, *qui nimis probat nihil probat,* "she who proves too much actually proves nothing."

To reiterate an earlier observation, if few Sicilian queens were overtly glorified or disparaged by historians, it is because most were ignored altogether. By contrast, scholarly compendia such as Alison Weir's recent *Queens of the Conquest* bring us biographies that revise some longstanding perceptions regarding England's Norman queens, about whom much has been published over the centuries, an earlier example being Agnes Strickland's epic series *Lives of the Queens of England* of 1840.

Our field touches several areas: Sicilian studies, women's studies, monarchical studies, multiculturalism, and more. Although our focus is queens, the more general status of all women into the middle decades of the thirteenth century merits our attention. This is not simply "gender politics" or "identity politics," nor can it be defined merely as a dialectic reaction to the centuries-long views that instinctively and automatically glorified patriarchy, usually at the expense of the female half of the population.

If a case can be advanced that the populations of parts of what is now Italy boasted higher general literacy in the twelfth century than in the nineteenth, one could likewise be postulated that many of the women (besides queens) in these places had greater personal rights in the middle of the thirteenth century than they did in the middle of the twentieth. As the existing medieval evidence for this is, by its very nature, exiguous, such a thesis, however tenable, is never easy to quantify or prove.

Certainly, the rights of Italian women into the twentieth century were abysmal compared to those enjoyed in an earlier age when females were accepted to Salerno's distinguished medical school (Trota), protected in law by the Constitutions of Melfi, commanded troops (Sichelgaita), governed nations (Margaret), oversaw construction projects (Judith), and could bring cases for divorce and rape.

That chess, a game introduced in Sicily by the Arabs, finds the queen as the most versatile piece on the board seems appropriately emblematic of the significance of the reginal role. Yet for centuries historians generally overlooked the function of queens, even regents, in medieval society.

Pitfalls

Because our study involves the queens of a specific part of Europe, a few words about past studies in this unique place are in order, just as they would be if our focus were England or anywhere else. The difference is that the essential character of English historiography is generally known, whereas the idiosyncrasies encountered in Sicilian historical studies are little known outside Italy.

Only a few readers — mostly Sicilians — need to consider these observations at length.

In this volume we shall avoid the "Sicilianist" views that taint many works published (in Italian) by scholars here in Sicily. A single, commonplace example is sufficient to illustrate the effects of this kind of provincialism, which is hardly unique to a single part of the world.

Local historians like to refer to the *curiae generales* called by Roger II in 1130 as Sicily's first "parliament," in this way claiming antiquity over the English parliament established during the next century. Lacking legislative authority, these early "great councils" of Sicilian barons were, in reality, nothing like true parliaments.

In former times, such a meeting of barons was sometimes referred to colloquially as a *parlamentu,* a Middle Sicilian word which in its most common parlance was synonymous with *conversation* (compare *pinsamentu,* meaning an idea or plan).

The first Sicilian parliament, facilitating the baronial election of Frederick of Aragon as King of Sicily, began in late 1295. Aside from developments like the Magna Carta (in 1215), the inception of an effective parliament in England is generally dated to 1258; interestingly, it was prompted by baronial opposition to the support of a proposed papal-sponsored invasion of Sicily by King Henry III, whose late sister, Isabella, had been a Sicilian queen.[12]

It must be said, in the interest of fairness, that we Sicilians are not alone in accepting erroneous "facts" about medieval history. Historical clichés abound in many populations.

It falls to the historian, using an evidentiary model based on sound epistemology, to correctly revise the more serious, widespread errors, which may be rooted in ethnocentrism, nationalism or sexism. It is logic, not blind iconoclasm, that should guide these efforts.

Dearth of Sicilian Reginal Studies Explained

That there is a dearth of reliable biographical work published about Sicily's medieval queens is an inconvenient truth. A few specialized papers published in Italy during the last century focus on such things as the monasteries endowed by Sicily's regents. The first scholarly biography of Roger II was published in English only in 2002.

In English, the first detailed biographies of Joanna and Isabella "Plantagenet" were published in the middle of the nineteenth century.[13] The author's biography of Joanna's mother-in-law, Margaret of Navarre, is the first book (in any language) written about that queen regent. The first substantial biography written in Italian about a Sicilian queen was Domenico Forges Davanzati's eighteenth-century study of Helena Angelina of Epirus and her children.

A few reasons for the absence of a Sicilian reginal canon are worth mentioning, *pro forma* and succinctly, because the reader deserves at least a perfunctory explanation for why there are so many biographies about Margaret's contemporary and *consuocera* (co-mother-in-law), Eleanor of Aquitaine, yet only one book on the woman who was, arguably, Sicily's most important queen.

As we have seen, the greatest impetus for reginal studies derived from the more general women's movement that blossomed in the years after 1960 in the United States, Canada and the United Kingdom, with early effects in Scandinavia. This initial wave of social, economic and intellectual change arrived with some delay in Italy, where it was little more than a ripple. Consequentially, a few decades passed before the scholarly study of queens, or of any Italian women, gained much momentum in this country.

There are, however, other reasons for the absence, some rooted in phenomena that occurred a century before the birth of the women's movement that began around 1960.

With the unification of the Italian peninsula, along with Sicily and Sardinia, into a nation in 1860, histories of most of the former kingdoms that comprised the new state were suppressed in the public mind in an attempt to focus on Italy as a whole. This subtle but real censorship discouraged the publication of modern biographies of monarchs like Roger II and his grandson Frederick II. The trend, which only worsened under Fascism, was aggravated by a development mentioned earlier.

As we have seen, the Norman-Swabian Kingdom of Sicily was the subject of warped historiography long before the nineteenth century. Unfortunately, the successful efforts of the Guelphs in disparaging Frederick, and to a lesser degree even his Norman grandfather, the two greatest medieval monarchs in what is now Italy, resulted in problematical, if unforeseen, consequences. Most obviously, the pertinacious defamation of these kings that festered for centuries left the hapless Italians without a credible medieval hero when unification finally arrived. Spain embraced El Cid, France had Louis IX and Joan of Arc (and Hugh Capet and Charles Martel), Germany claimed Charlemagne and then Frederick II. Conversely, the Italian unificationists' feeble attempts to elevate a few medieval Savoys to this illustrious pantheon met with dismal failure, for none of those rustic counts could rival the intellectual and political stature of Roger and Frederick, whose achievements in Europe and the Mediterranean eclipsed anything that could be mustered by other Italian rulers of the Middle Ages.

Roger and Frederick were both "native sons" born in Italy, yet the chief biographies about them published in Italian before the present century are translations of works from German, French and English.

Freedom of expression finally arrived in Sicily in 1943 with the Allies, who granted Italian women the right to vote just in time for the referendum that ousted the monarchy three years later.

In succeeding decades it became possible, for the first time since national unification, to publish books and papers about Sicily's medieval golden age as a sovereign kingdom without risking the censorship that poisoned intellectual life in the erstwhile dictatorship. A conference was held on Frederick II in 1950, followed by one on Roger II in 1954, both in Palermo.

At that postwar juncture, however, other beasts reared their ugly heads to threaten the field of reginal studies. The Italian academy was never very meritocratic. Sadly, *raccomandazioni* (preferments), nepotism, cronyism and plagiarism are still commonplace, prompting many of the nation's best minds to seek academic careers abroad, where they find greater opportunities.[14]

In tandem with these conditions, a lingering misogyny prevails, hence the paucity of women professors until recently. Of the twenty-four papers presented in December 1972 at the first truly international conference held in Palermo on the Normans in medieval Sicily, exactly one was authored by a woman.[15] By comparison, the British academy already boasted female medievalists specialized in the Norman era of the calibre and renown of Evelyn Jamison and Marjorie Chibnall. That fields such as Women's Studies are all but unknown in Italian universities reflects the wider status of women in Italy.[16]

Equally disquieting is the ubiquitous survival of bizarre "Italian" views of history unduly influenced by Catholicism on the one hand and rather extreme political movements, from left to right, on the other. One also sees this in the distorted reporting of international events by the Italian press.

INTRODUCTION

Because conformity is the rule among Italian academics, these various phenomena transcend the field of medieval royal biography. Understandably, teachers and professors, being employees of the Italian state, are reluctant to contradict what has long been taught as "fact," even where it is a vestige of Fascist propaganda.[17]

The endogamy of Sicily's professoriate nourishes a complaisance bordering on sycophancy, ensuring a long life for tired clichés like the "parliament of 1130," which one hears parroted by teachers and tour guides.[18]

We need not wade into deeper waters than these. The author shall leave that to others.[19]

Clearly, however, all of these factors influence historiography, determining whether monographs about certain subjects are published in Italy.[20] The cumulative effect of this situation is that very little of legitimate scholarly value has been written by Italians about Sicily's first few medieval queens.[21]

This is anomalous, for we expect the first, lengthiest, most significant biography of a historical queen to be written at a reasonably early date in the country where she was crowned. Would it not seem strange to us if the first biography of Elizabeth I of England, who died in 1603, were written in Italian and published four centuries later?

Whatever its causes, for the biographer the dearth of previous biographies is at once daunting and liberating, for while it obviates the need for an exhaustive study of the sketchy secondary literature about the queens' lives, it imposes upon the historian the responsibility of defining how these women's stories should be evaluated and presented, setting the stage for subsequent work on the topic by others. Future biographers may choose to embrace the outline of a first biography or to deconstruct it, but they cannot ignore it.

Until now, the absence of a compendium such as this one meant that any reader interested in learning about these women collectively had to consult numerous works or rely on the (often inaccurate) information available on the internet.

Lost Kingdom

As we have said, the Kingdom of Sicily was politically divided in 1282, despite some later monarchs who ruled the peninsular part of it (which became the Kingdom of Naples) in successive centuries continuing to call themselves kings or queens of *Sicily*, whether they actually controlled the island or not.[22] Yet the twin crowns were sometimes borne on the same royal head in what historians call a "personal union," and in 1816, under the House of Bourbon, both realms were united to form the Kingdom of the Two Sicilies, its very name a reminder that in the thirteenth century rival monarchs in Palermo and Naples claimed the Mediterranean's largest island. It was the Bourbons who were displaced by the Savoys in 1860.

In reading about the queens of a country that has long lacked a monarchy, one risks losing a sense of historical continuity because there is no living point of reference to link the past to the present.

Has anybody in living memory actually met a Queen of Sicily? Yes, and this volume includes an interview with a princess of Sicily's last royal dynasty. The appendix on Queen Maria Sophia, who died in 1925, is an unusual excursus relevant to the continuity of a very general concept of queenship in Sicily over the centuries, and also to the fact of the kingdom itself surviving almost until our times.[23] That a woman of her dynasty had become Queen of Sicily in 1250 lends a certain conjunction to this. Unexpected in a book about medieval queens, Maria Sophia's story is a reminder that for many centuries monarchy was thoroughly woven into the social fabric of Sicily, much as it was elsewhere in Europe. She was the last woman in a long continuum.

Ultimately, it was the cataclysm of the Second World War that brought an end to monarchy in Italy, beginning with catastrophic military defeats in Africa and Russia but soon reaching the very doorsteps of ordinary Italian citizens. That discourse lies beyond the scope of this work, but for its dire consequences one need only consider that the first major Allied bombing run over Palermo, in February 1943, destroyed most of the structures behind Piazza Magione, in the process killing nearly a hundred civilians and severely damaging a splendid church erected during the twelfth century. Many deaths followed as the carpet bombing continued for months.

As a sobering footnote, in 1947 her misadventures earned dystopic Italy the dubious distinction of becoming the first nation to admit committing crimes against humanity (in places like Ethiopia).[24] The atrocities perpetrated at home and abroad in the name of Italy's monarch assured the beggared kingdom's descent into the darkest depths of infamy.

By 1950, a new wave of Italians was emigrating, seeking a chance at a better life in the United States, Canada, Britain, France, Germany and Australia. Sixty years later, there were more Italian-born Italians in greater London than in the city of Bologna.

Amidst postwar misery and bitter memories, few Italians were openly nostalgic for the monarchy, and for the next two generations most schools avoided the subject of Fascism altogether, teaching about Italian history as it unfolded up to 1920 but no further. In view of eclectic political currents, antipathy toward the very institution of monarchy did little to encourage the study of royalty here in Italy throughout the remainder of the twentieth century. Yet the last two decades have witnessed a growing interest in the history of the House of the Two Sicilies as well as our earlier dynasties.[25]

That royalty, monarchy and aristocracy are becoming anachronistic concepts need not concern us except where this makes it difficult for readers of later generations to appreciate the social subtleties intrinsic in such institutions. Understandably, ideas like "legitimacy" are scarcely even marginal in modern society, with its births-outside-marriage and even the redefining of marriage, along with anonymous gamete donation and other developments unimagined by our medieval forebears.

Two of the Sicilian kings mentioned in this volume, Tancred and Manfred, were born "illegitimately."

Queens and queenship are essential to the indelible identity, indeed the dignity, of a kingdom, or even an ex-kingdom, and its people past and present. Everything about the first queens of Sicily is indispensable to the cultural heritage of southern Italy. Queenship, with its mystique and customs and trappings, is one of the elements that makes the place and its people unique. The same principle would be just as valid were we considering the consorts of the high kings of Ireland or the emperors of Japan, not only because being the highest-ranking woman in a hereditary monarchy entails special responsibilities but because each place has its own historical norms, ideas that make it Sicilian, Irish or Japanese. Or Ethiopian or Russian or Chinese. It may be a special coronation rite or a certain kind of crown, or the national language. This is what makes each society something unto itself and not identical to others. Its medieval queens, or our remembrance of them, is one of the things that makes southern Italy *Sicilian* or *Neapolitan,* and not simply, generically "Italian" or "European." Our queens are part of us.

Though southern Italy is no longer a sovereign kingdom, the legacy of our queens is a subtle but real element of what contemporary anthropologists sometimes call "cultural sovereignty," the prerogative of a people to explicate its own cultural identity based on its communal historical knowledge and patrimony accrued over many generations. Reflecting, in its most rudimentary form, the intrinsic right of a population to define itself rather than to let outsiders define it, this need not lead to political discord. In its essence, it is simply the God-given right of each of us to tell our own story.

Through the following pages this Sicilian legacy endures.

Definitions

The usage of certain terms brings us medieval connotations, some unique to the Kingdom of Sicily.

A *dower* was land given to a bride by her husband (for our queens this was Mount Saint Angelo in Apulia), whereas a *dowry* was held by the bride as a gift from her father and perhaps given to her husband at marriage.

A *monastery* was a community of monks, while an *abbey* was a larger monastery overseen by an abbot or (for nuns) an abbess. A *cathedral,* for which Italians sometimes prefer the word *duomo,* was the seat of a bishop, while a *basilica* was a church (though not necessarily a large cathedral) having a certain status in canon law; Palermo's Magione is a basilica even though it is not very large.

Under Roger I the island of Sicily was a "great county." In theory, a *principality* or *duchy* encompassed numerous *counties* consisting of *baronies* composed of *manors*. In fact, certain principalities and duchies established by the Byzantines or Lombards before the Norman era (Amalfi, Capua, Gaeta), though smaller than the Normans' Duchy of Apulia, were prosperous and at times sovereign. By the twelfth century, some counties were larger than certain duchies. *Duke* finds its origin in the Latin *dux,* but the Longobards introduced the title of *gastald.*

The holder of a *manor* (or "fief") within a *barony* was typically an enfeoffed knight; in the Kingdom of Sicily the chief feudal roll was the *Catalogus Baronum*. The military (crusading) knightly orders were also present, having *preceptories* and *commanderies* where knights lived like monks. The feudal norms of the *Regnum Siciliae* were based on two distinct traditions (see note 197).

Titles like *familiaris* (royal counsellor), for which Sicily's Greeks preferred *archon,* as well as the Arabic *caïd* (chiefly a title of respect), had specific meanings. For *familiaris* the author uses *familiare*. Though it may share the same root, an *amiratus* was much more than an *admiral*.

At times the queens of Sicily found themselves involved with dominions having other customs and therefore different titles and ranks. We shall use the local nomenclature so that Greek *despots* and Arab *emirs* retain their native dignity. The Holy Roman Empire also had its own hierarchy and ranks.

A distinction is drawn between *serfs,* who were tied to the land, and other members of the peasantry.

Almost all of our contemporaneous sources are to be found in Latin, Arabic or Greek, those in Norman French or Middle Sicilian being rare. Certain Latin terms are open to interpretation depending upon context, where *castrum* may be a remote castle or a fortified town (see note 285). We find the term *comes* (count) more often than *baronis* (baron), with the latter sometimes inferred from context (though *seigneur* is used in French) when it refers to a landed noble who had several knights under his feudal authority. The word *miles,* sometimes *milites,* refers to a knight. In this volume *baronage* usually refers to landed nobles collectively, regardless of their rank as counts, barons or enfeoffed knights.

Ecclesiastical terms such as *archimandrite* have specific meanings in the Orthodox Church (the eastern church after 1054).

An attempt has been made to avoid the errors of past historians. Walter "of the Mill" owes his Anglice nickname to the belief that he was English (he was actually Norman) and that *offamilias,* which denoted his status as a *familiare,* referred to a mill. He became Primate of Sicily (see note 191).

The *tarì* was a small gold coin introduced by the Arabs. The *ducat* was a silver coin introduced by Roger II at Ariano in 1140. The *augustale* was a gold coin inaugurated by Frederick II with the Constitutions of Melfi in 1231. The various weights of the *follaris,* or *follis,* were copper.

In a few cases, *Sicilian* refers not only to the islanders but to all the inhabitants of the Kingdom of Sicily, though this potentially confusing usage has generally been avoided. *Sicily,* rather than terms like *Regnum Siciliae,* usually denotes the island alone.

Translations

Except where it is otherwise noted, all of the translations in this volume are the work of the author. In a few instances, they are the first translations of certain passages ever published in English.

Translating these sometimes gives birth to ideas. The author's translation of the *Ferraris Chronicle* made it possible for her to advance the theory of that codex being the first history of the Kingdom of Sicily, and not merely a chronicle or annal.

Dissemination

One never knows the precise extent to which a book will be distributed, especially in an age that finds electronic editions supplanting paper volumes in some quarters. Public and university libraries are by no means "obligated" to purchase works such as this one, and the publisher made an effort to keep the paperback edition's price affordable to students.

As some readers may know, there was initially no digital preview of this volume on the internet and no immediate publication of an ebook. This was to discourage, at least for a time, the copyright infringement and plagiarism (unattributed use of large passages of text verbatim) that, unfortunately, plague the academic environment.

Discovery

Some remarks about the structure of this work are appropriate.

The chapters of this book are chronological as well as topical because it is important to mention the major events that occurred during each woman's lifetime. Therefore, the conquest of Messina in 1061 is found in the chapter on Judith, and some observations about queenship and coronations are presented in the chapter on Elvira, Sicily's first queen.

The monographic biography of a single personage lends itself to the simple flow of history (what historians sometimes call its "chronology"), whereas in a book such as this one it is often necessary to revisit events already mentioned or to allude to those yet to occur at a future point in the narrative's natural chronology.

In other words, there are some instances of a certain queen's story overlapping that of her predecessor or successor. (See the chart following this introduction.)

The stories of Beatrice of Rethel and Joanna of England necessarily encompass their time as *queen mother* (Beatrice) or *queen dowager* (Joanna) because as young widows both lived long after their formal "reigns" (queenhood) ended, surviving into the reigns of their successors. For that reason, Beatrice's chapter inevitably deals with certain events that occurred *after* her tenure as queen consort because she lived into the reign of her contemporary and successor, Margaret. Beatrice, queen consort until 1154, died in 1185; Margaret, queen consort and then regent until 1171, died in 1183. At all events, an attempt was made to avoid excessive redundancy.

Because the genealogical charts are intended to show ancestry, kinship and marriage as simply as possible, such details as birth dates and even birth order are not always indicated. For visual clarity (and to avoid drawing lines that confusingly cross over other lines), an elder sibling may occasionally be placed where the reader would normally expect to find a younger one, or a first spouse positioned where the reader might reasonably presume to see a second one.

Some of the genealogical tables include coats of arms even where these were assumed after the lifetime of the countess or queen indicated. As the use of armorial heraldry in most of western Europe arrived in the second half of the twelfth century, it is clear that Elvira of Castile never saw the coat of arms later associated with her dynasty. The Hautevilles did not make use of a coat of arms or heraldic insignia as we understand the term; the blazon *azure a bend checky argent and gules* is apocryphal.[26]

The section of the bibliography dedicated to secondary literature lists works consulted which were found informative or at least relevant and therefore worthy of mention; it does not reflect an attempt to list every monograph or paper, whether useful or not. Hard-copy (printed) papers and studies were generally given precedence over those available exclusively in digital (electronic) format via websites.

Endnotes were chosen over footnotes because the former allow for quoting passages of text at greater length (notes 283 and 533) and tend to distract less from readability of the narrative. Observed the Italophile historian Sir Harold Acton, "The cult of the footnote, involving, at its apogee, a page crammed with encyclopaedic detail in small type to a solitary line of text, is no doubt a proof of diligence, but it may also be a tedious form of exhibitionism."

Amongst the topics treated rather fleetingly is cuisine. The author's book, *Sicilian Food and Wine,* considers something of Sicily's culinary history, with notes about its medieval iteration.

The crown shown on the title page is an adaptation of those worn by Elvira, Beatrice and Constance in the illuminated chronicle of Peter of Eboli completed early in the thirteenth century.

Some passages of text published in the following pages previously appeared in books or articles the author wrote and for which she holds the exclusive copyright. Likewise, a few maps, genealogical tables and photographs presented in this volume were first published in the author's *Margaret, Queen of Sicily* or *The Ferraris Chronicle*. Several previously appeared in *The Peoples of Sicily* or *Sicilian Studies*. While one seeks to publish completely original work at every turn, in certain instances there is no need to "reinvent the wheel." As this work is the result of years of research by the author into the history of medieval Sicily, it is logical that a few parts of it have already been published elsewhere in some form.

Most of the photographs that appear in this book were taken by the author during her numerous research trips around Europe. She appears in a few of them not to nourish her ego or to cultivate *protagonismo* but to establish scale, especially at medieval sites. She stands five feet, six inches (168 centimeters). The vast number of figures, maps and charts is exceptional for an academic monograph or even a popular history.

Except for scholarly citations, the opinions and positions expressed in this book are those of the author.

In consulting a reference work such as this one, the reader is entitled to know something of the author's background, which may inform views and biases. The author resides in Sicily and her ancestral roots are unabashedly Sicilian. She is not affiliated with any political party or organized movement. The costs (such as travel expenses) entailed in the research necessary to complete this monograph were borne by the author herself, not being defrayed by the publisher, a university, a foundation or any other source of funding.

As we have said, it is impossible to understand much about the lives lived by Sicily's queens without knowing something of Sicily itself. Let us meet the queens of the first Sicilian monarchy. First, let us visit the lands that became the Kingdom of Sicily.

QUEENS OF SICILY

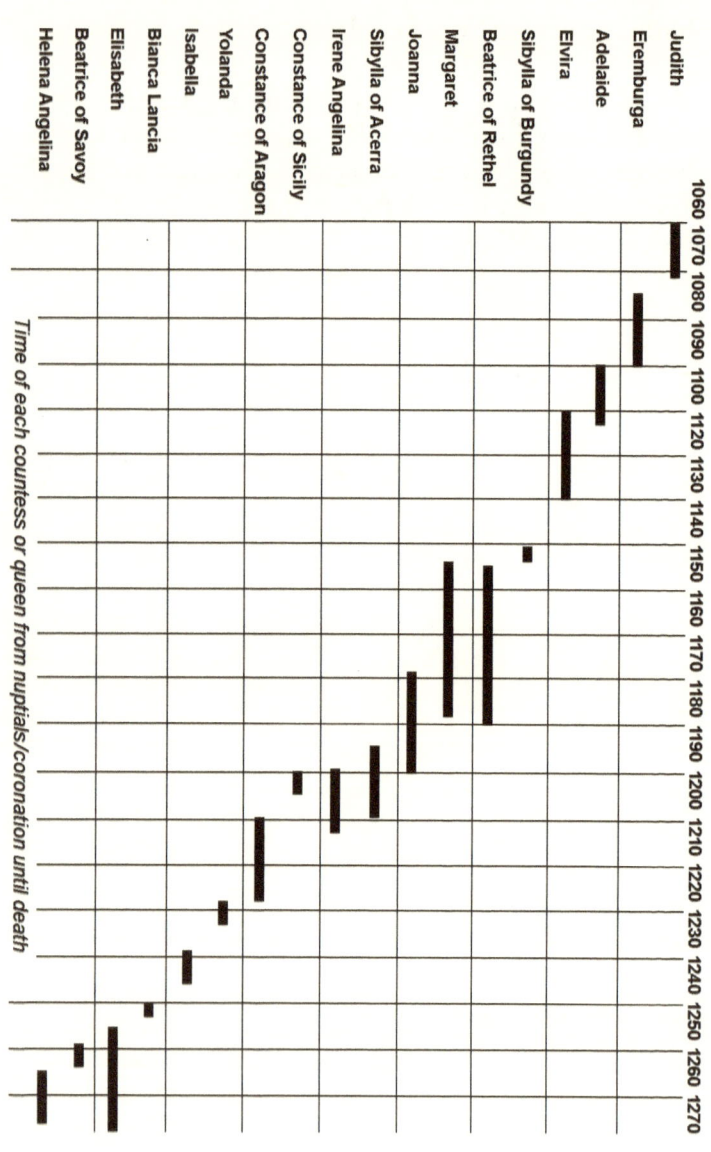

MAPS

Birthplaces of the Queens of Norman-Swabian Sicily

*Acre and Constantinople not shown

Acerra - Sibylla of Acerra
Acre* - Yolanda of Jerusalem
Agliano - Bianca Lancia
Angers - Joanna of England
Arta - Helena Angelina of Epirus
Autun - Sibylla of Burgundy
Chambery - Beatrice of Savoy
Constantinople* - Irene Angelina
Evreux - Judith of Evreux
Gloucester - Isabella of England
La Guardia - Margaret of Navarre
Landshut - Elisabeth of Bavaria
Lisbon - Constance of Aragon
Montferrat - Adelaide del Vasto
Mortain - Eremburga of Mortain
Palermo - Constance of Sicily
Rethel - Beatrice of Rethel
Toledo - Elvira of Castile

Regnum Siciliae: The Norman-Swabian Kingdom of Sicily

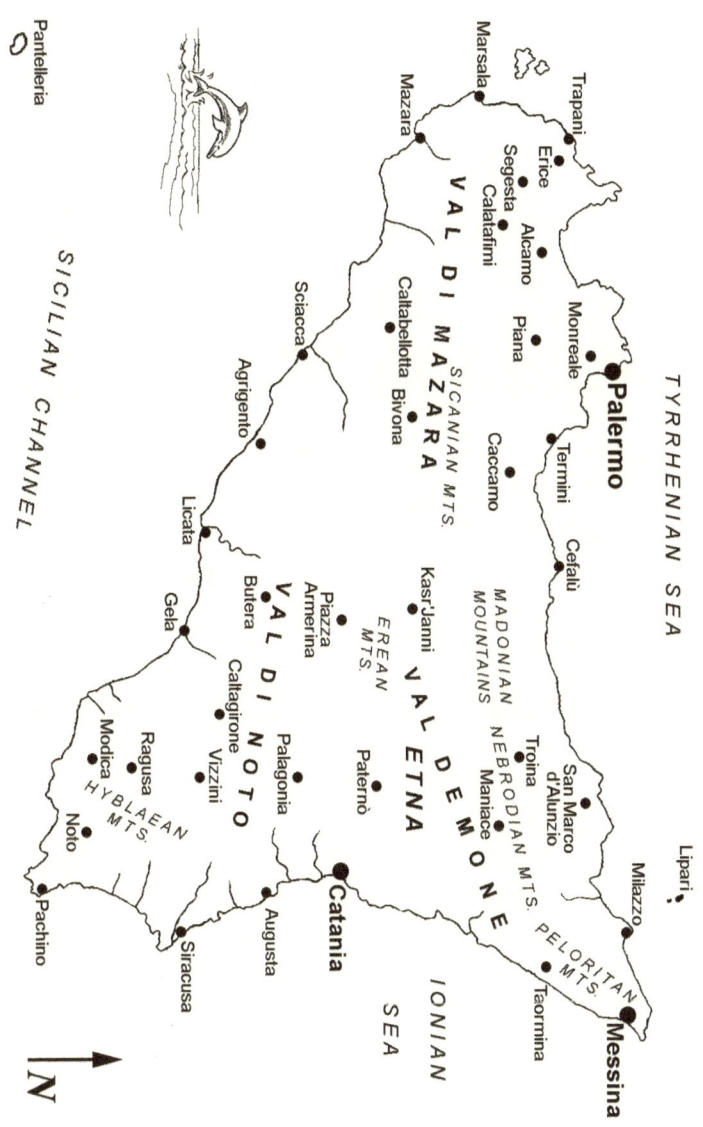

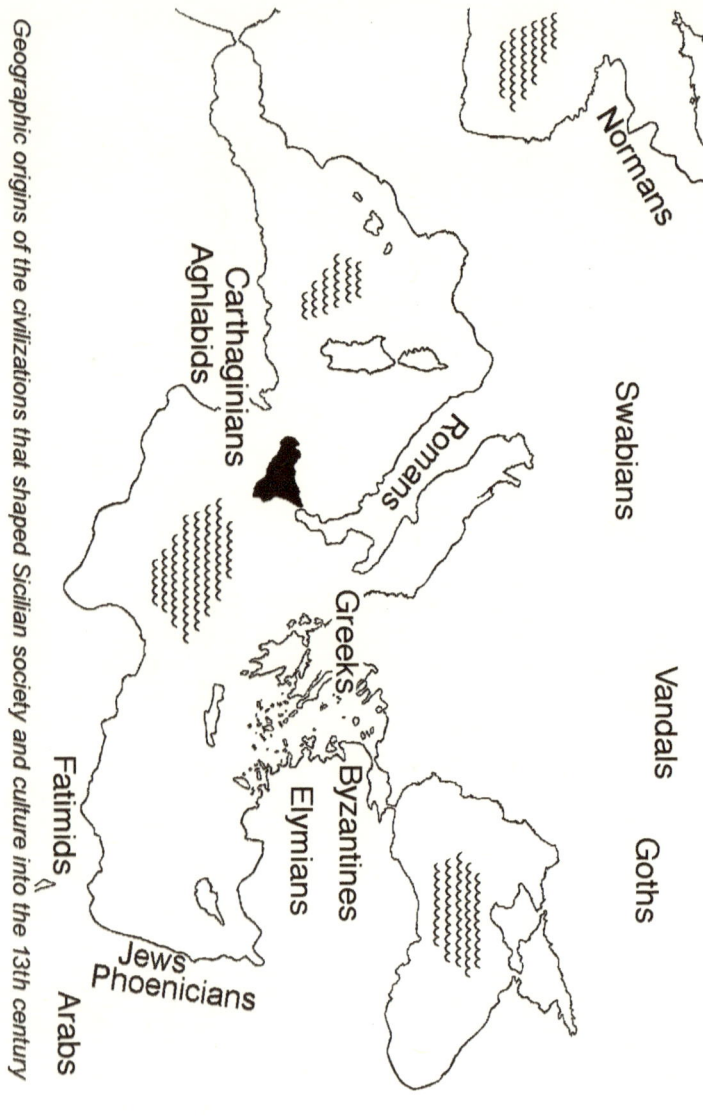

Geographic origins of the civilizations that shaped Sicilian society and culture into the 13th century

MAPS

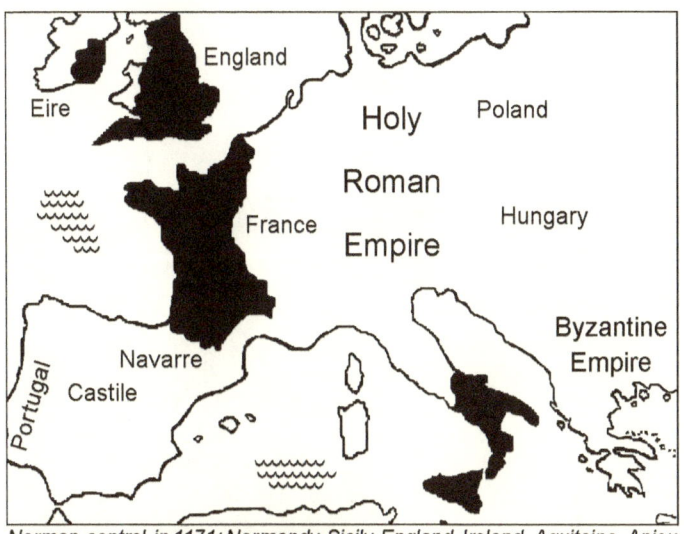

Norman control in 1171: Normandy, Sicily, England, Ireland, Aquitaine, Anjou

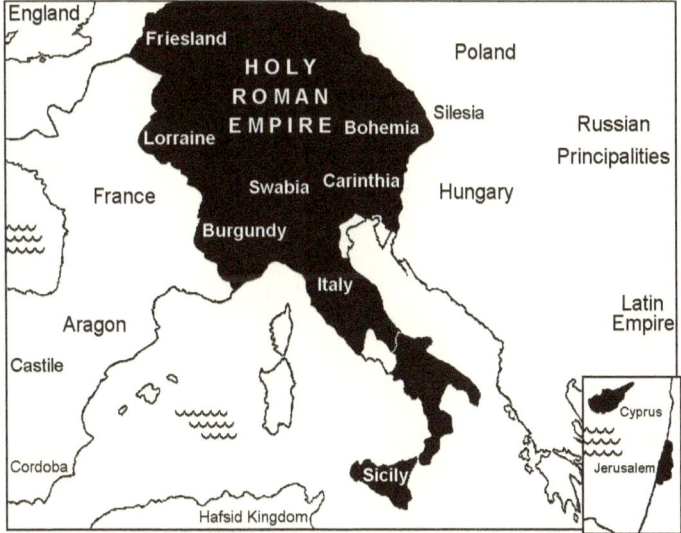

Greatest extent of Hohenstaufen dominion under Frederick II - 1229

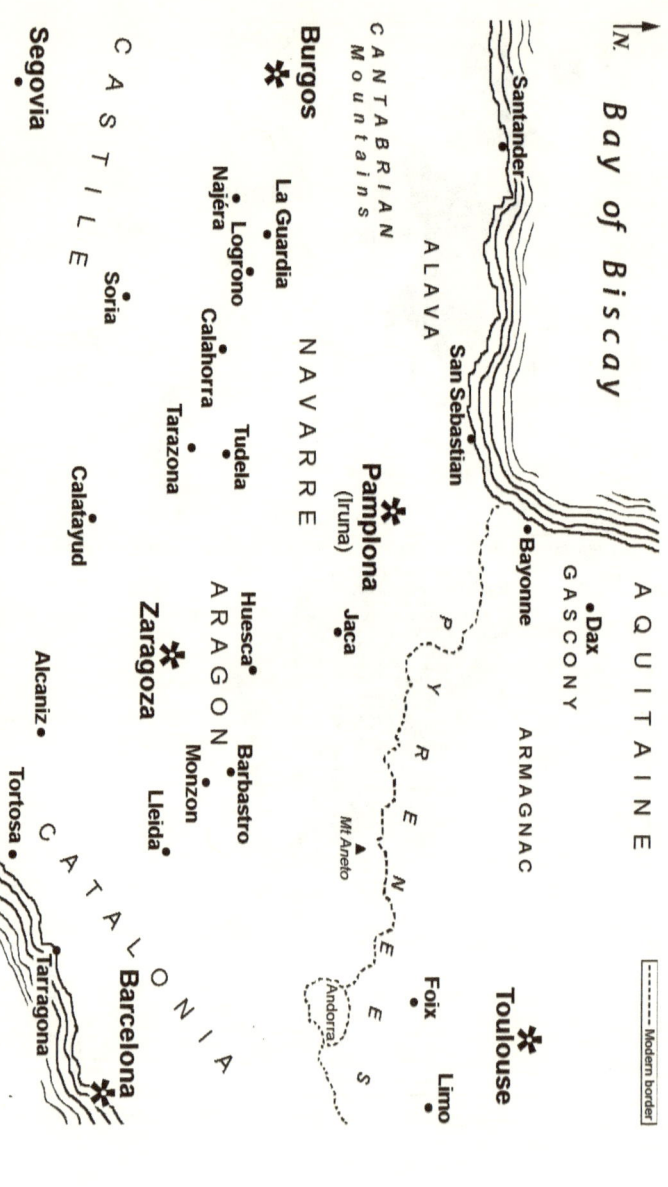

Regions and Jiménez dominions in northeastern Spain

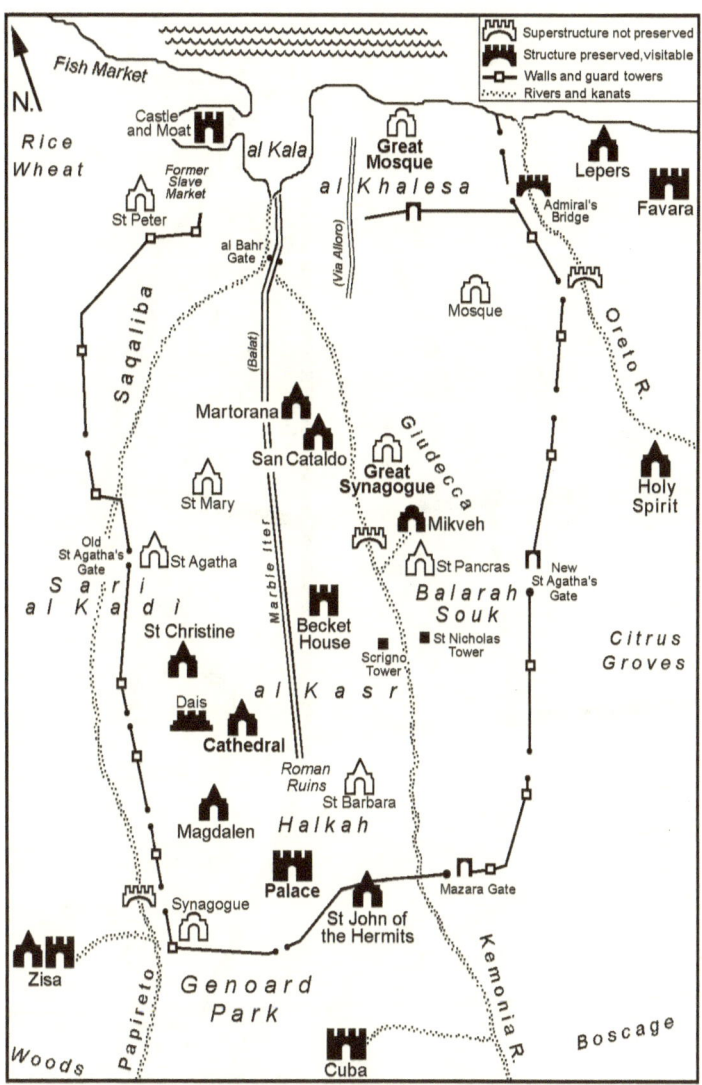

Palermo around 1180

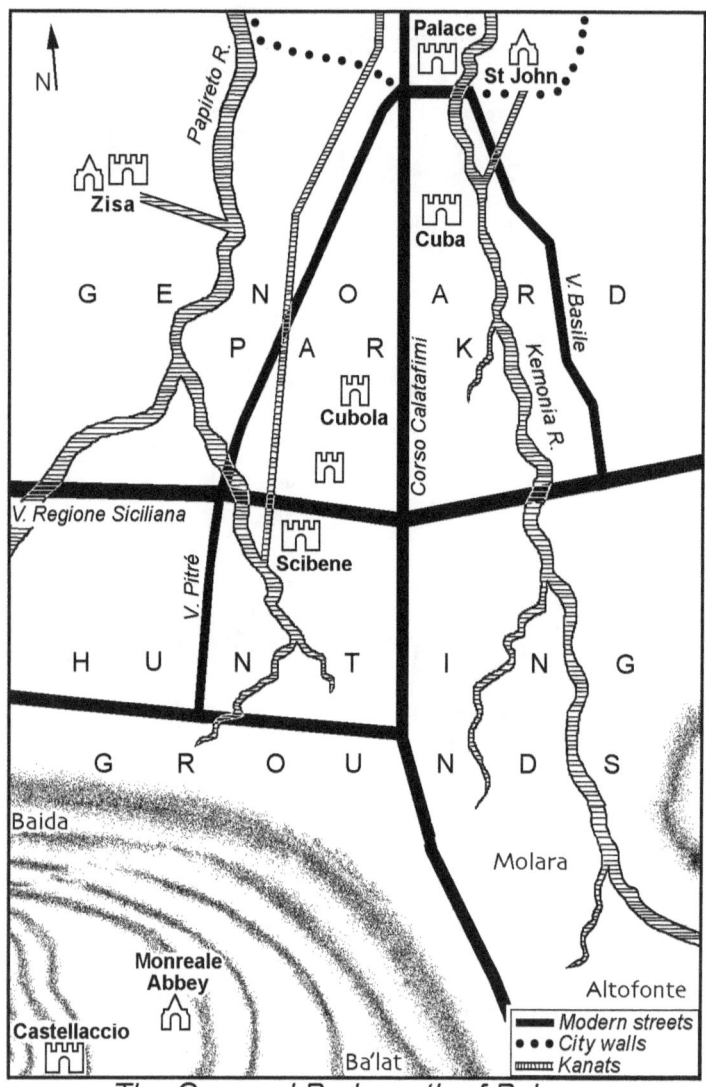

The Genoard Park south of Palermo

MAPS

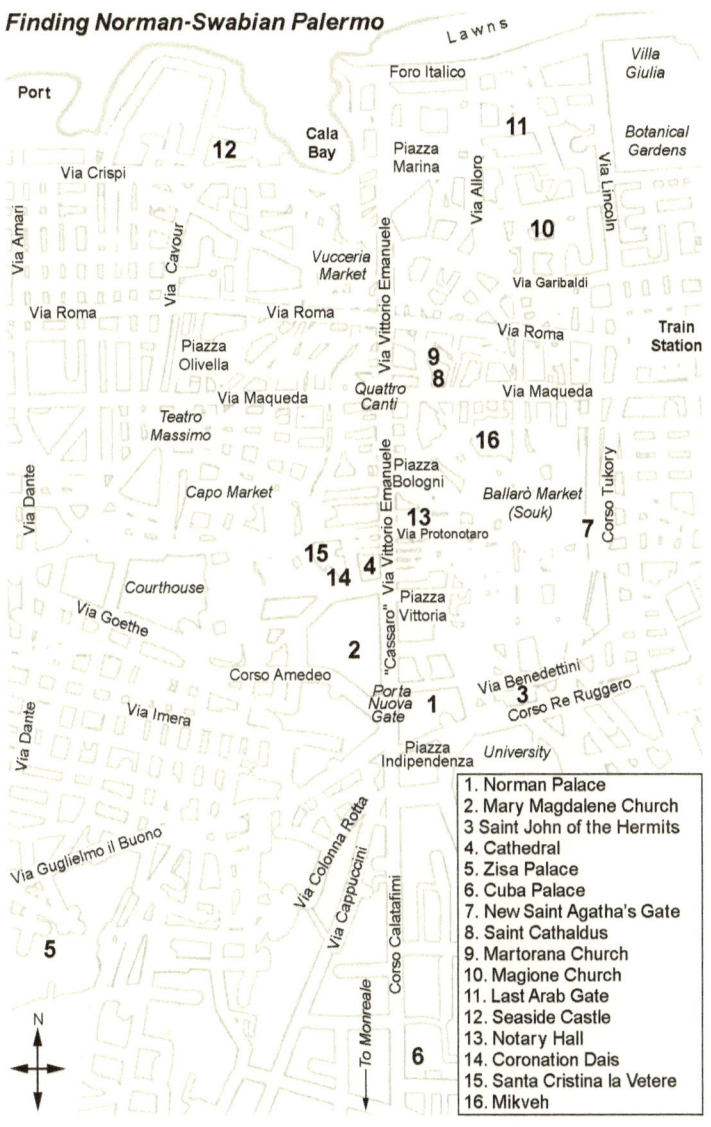

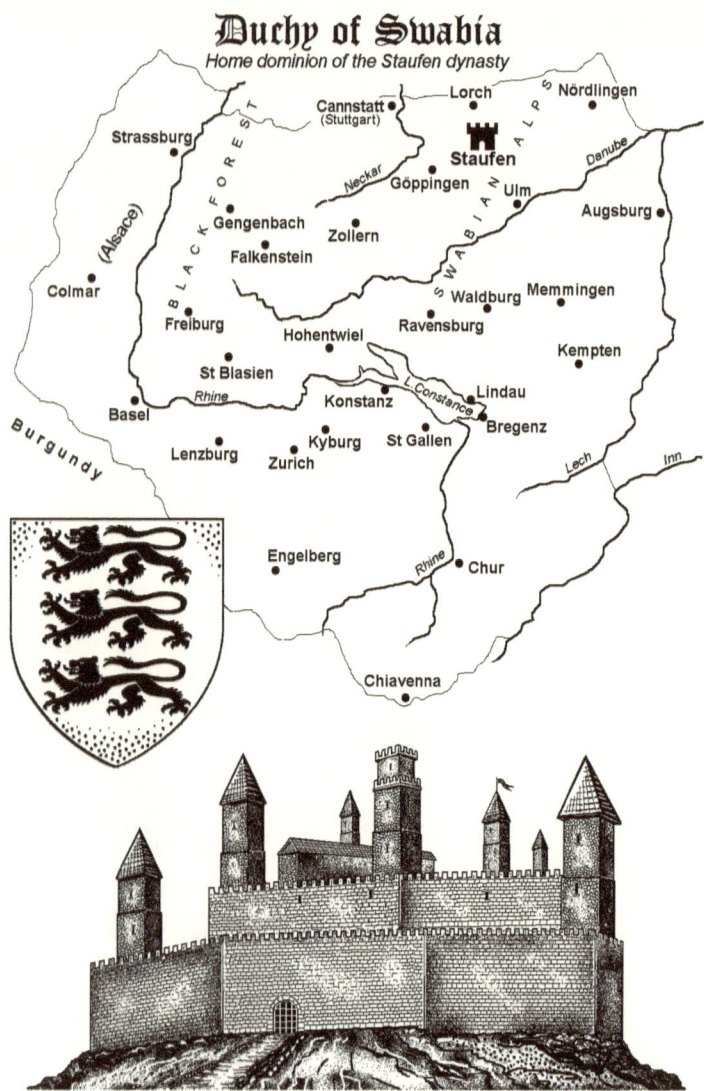

Hohenstaufen Castle in the 13th century

MAPS

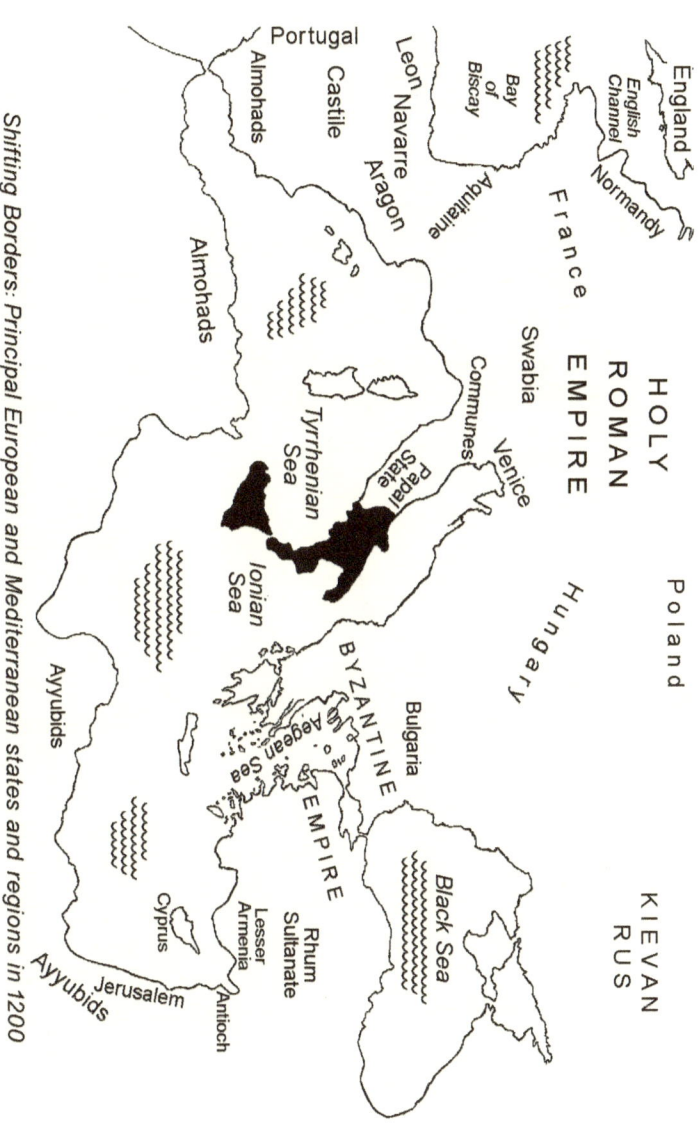

Shifting Borders: Principal European and Mediterranean states and regions in 1200

Jewish Districts of Syracuse and Palermo

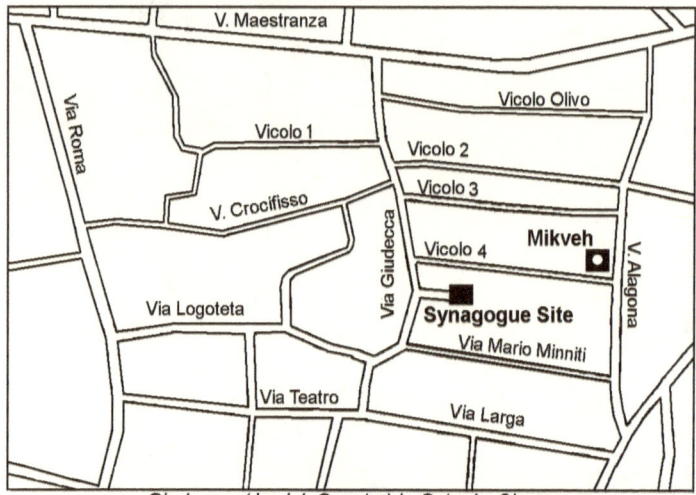

Giudecca (Jewish Quarter) in Ortygia, Siracusa
Great synagogue site is St John's Church. Mikveh at Via Alagona 52.

Palermo's Jewish Quarter, Souk (now Ballarò Market) and Kemonia Spring
Great synagogue site is San Nicolò da Tolentino Church. Mikveh under Jesuit cloister.

MAPS

Sicily's Jewish communities in the Middle Ages

Trilingual street sign at the site where Palermo's chief synagogue stood until 1493 (off Via Calderai)

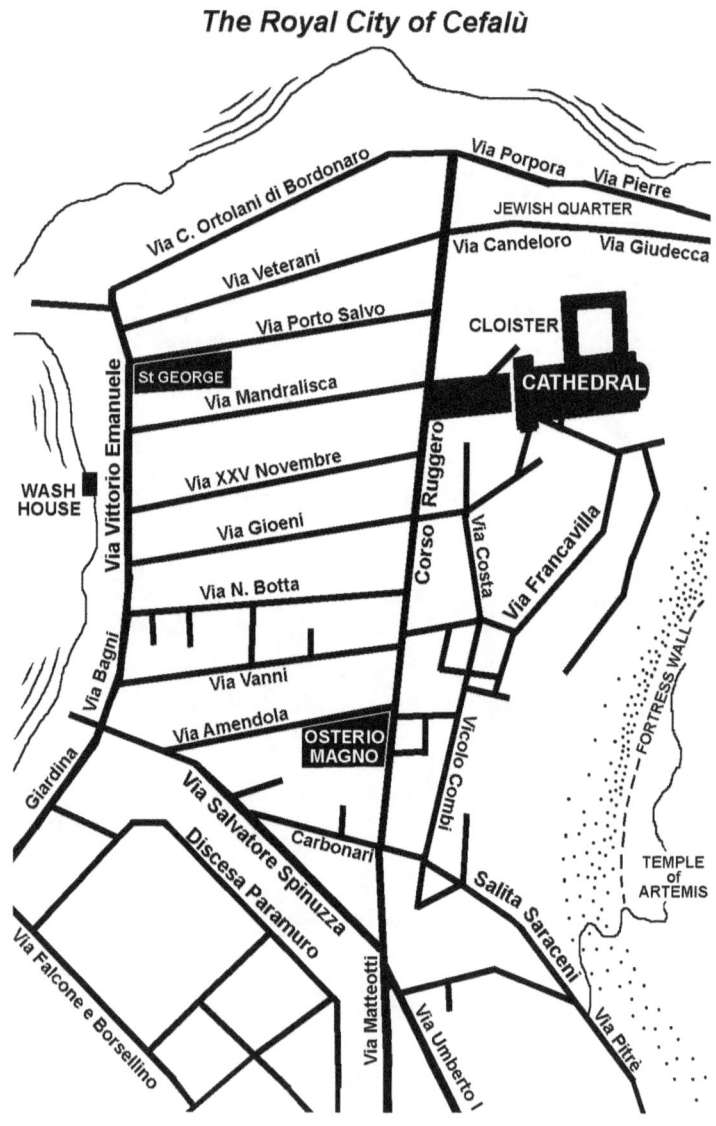

The Royal City of Cefalù

Chapter 1
BACKSTORY

It was never just an island.

At 26,711 square kilometers (10,313 square miles), Sicily is larger than Wales and slightly smaller than Massachusetts, but more mountainous than either. Majestic Mount Etna, Europe's largest active volcano and greatest natural wonder, rises to a variable 3,329 meters (10,922 feet) above sea level. The island's next highest peak is rocky Pizzo Carbonara (at 1,979 meters), in the Madonian Mountains visible from the environs of Palermo; like Etna, it is covered by snow for part of the year. Mount Soro, in the greener Nebrodian range, stands at 1,847 meters.

In addition to Sicily, the kingdom we shall encounter in these pages embraced most of peninsular Italy south of Rome, its territory more or less coterminous to that of ancient *Magna Graecia*. The temples standing at Segesta, Paestum and elsewhere are a silent testament to this Greek legacy.

The most northern point of the mainland territory was around Ancona (nominally part of Apulia in Norman times) on the Adriatic side and Terracina, in the southern part of what is now Lazio (essentially the ancient Latium) on the peninsula's Tyrrhenian side.

Except for a few notable plains, such as the area around Lecce in southern Apulia in the heel of the Italian boot, most of this part of Italy is mountainous.

There are a number of impressive chains, like the Sila of Calabria and the Gran Sasso of western Abruzzi, that are part of the Apennine range for which Italy is famous. The highest peak is Corno Grande near Teramo in Abruzzi, at 2,912 meters. Of course, the most famous mountain in the southern part of the peninsula is Vesuvius, the ominous volcano that casts its shadow over Naples. It is 1,281 meters high. Like Etna, it boasts a very long recorded history useful to geologists.

This peninsular part of the kingdom extended over an area of approximately 85,000 square kilometers (32,819 square miles); for comparison, Scotland is around 80,000.

The entire kingdom (the peninsula plus Sicily) was around 112,000 square kilometers which, as a point of reference, may be compared to England's 130,000.

For now, we shall focus on the island of Sicily.

Neolithic Sicily

The island boasts a few dolmens and cave drawings, but the earliest distinct civilization identified with Sicily is that of the indigenous Sicanians, whose forebears built Europe's first megalithic temples on Malta before 3500 BC (BCE). Impressive as it was, this was not the first achievement of its kind.

That distinction belongs to Göbekli Tepe, near Urfa, formerly Edessa, in Anatolia (Turkey), where the first such structures known to us were erected around 9000 BC. The cave drawings at Addaura, outside Palermo, and Levanzo, in Sicily's Aegadian Islands, have been dated to approximately the same era. Indeed, the cave paintings on Levanzo are the oldest such art in Italy.

By way of comparison, Stonehenge, in England, and Egypt's earliest pyramids were probably erected around 2800 BC.

Clearly, the Proto Sicanians of Malta and neighboring Gozo were fine builders for their era, standing at the vanguard of architectural technology, but they also invented a precursor of the wheel, a development destined to change the course of history. This apparatus was a stone carved into a ball and positioned into the semicircular groove of a larger, square stone.

The shore of the Gulf of Palermo was probably the site of a Sicanian village. Farther eastward along the coast, the foundation of a Sicanian temple, later modified by the Greeks, stands atop the rocky mountain overlooking Cefalù.

In antiquity, Sicily was an idyllic refuge of forests populated by deer, boar, hare, hedgehogs, wolves, foxes and striped cats, along with storks, the purple swamp hen and the northern bald ibis. Sparkling streams full of fish meandered through lush meadows. Mount Etna dominated the east, overlooking the scenic Nebrodian, Peloritan and Madonian ranges, where fir trees reached like spires toward the heavens. The Nebrodian Mountains take their very name from *nebros,* the Greek word for the deer that thrived there. Eagles and hawks soared above them, while grouse populated the bush lands of the foothills. Wild artichokes grew in the fields.

That the island is very different today is the result of rampant deforestation — which began in earnest with the Roman demand for grain but worsened in the Middle Ages with the need for timber for ship building — and overpopulation, as well as poor land management for the last few centuries. There is far less precipitation, and the average annual mean temperature is higher.

The Bronze Age

The inception of Sicily's Bronze Age, characterized by the use of copper tools, can be dated to around 2500 BC (BCE). By 2000 BC, Mycenaean and Late Minoan (Cretan and

Aegean) cultures were present in isolated eastern localities of Sicily, especially near the Ionian coast, and by this time Malta's last temple builders, identified with the Tarxien Culture, had left Malta, with some perhaps settling in southeastern Sicily, in effect returning to the land of their ancestors. The Ausonians, an Italic people, traded with the Aeolian islanders and other communities in the northeast, around Messina.

It was probably the Mycenaeans or Minoans who planted the first domesticated olive trees in Sicily, and a Kalamata cultivar from this era has been genetically identified.

Here dates are imprecise, but at some point not long before 1200 BC the indigenous Sicanians had been joined by the Italic Sikels in the east, and the Elymians, of Anatolian origin, in the northwest. These three societies seem to have coexisted peacefully, though our knowledge about them is sketchy at best. Sicily's name comes to us from the gentilics for two of these early civilizations, hence *Sicania* and *Sikelia*. By this time, the Iron Age had already begun in the Greek world.

Greeks and Phoenicians

The Phoenicians, who are identified with the Biblical Canaanites, probably founded Carthage around 840 BC (BCE). Within a few decades, the Phoenicians and Greeks began to colonize Sicily as part of their burgeoning empires.

Of course, there were Phoenician influences long before this. Their alphabet, the basis for the lettering systems of Greek and Latin, is the most obvious example. Some of the art they left in Sicily bears Egyptian motifs.

The Phoenicians established emporia in the island's west, especially at Motya (Mozia), Solunto and Zis (now Palermo).

For its unusual geographical position in a plain at the mouths of rivers surrounded by rocky mountains near a coast, Palermo might be compared to Malaga (the ancient Malaka), a city founded by Phoenicians during the same era. Sicily and Andalusia share rather similar topography and agriculture.

The Greeks founded colonies at Naxos (near Taormina), Agrigento, Catania, Selinunte, Hymera, Messina, Gela and, most importantly, Syracuse (Siracusa). The Elymians, whose major cities were Egesta (Segesta) and Eryx (Erice), readily assimilated with the Greeks.

Compared to the Elymians, the Sicanians had far less affinity with Greek culture but seem not to have actively resisted to a great degree. The Sikels, on the other hand, fought a series of battles against the Greeks, and the last isolated pockets of Sikelian resistance were defeated only around 450 BC.

When Phoenicia fell to the Chaldean (Neo-Babylonian) Empire in 612, Carthage, in what is now coastal Tunisia, became the Phoenicians' major city. With the emergence of Carthage as perhaps the wealthiest and most powerful metropolis in the Mediterranean, the Greeks turned their attention to this potential adversary. What followed was a complex series of wars over several centuries involving a tangled web of alliances with participants as far away as Persia. In 480 BC the Carthaginians (exhorted to fight the Greeks by Xerxes of Persia who had won victories in Greece) were defeated by Gelon of Syracuse at the first Battle of Hymera east of Palermo. The Persians, meanwhile, were defeated at the Battle of Salamis.

A few years later, in 474, the Syracusans won a decisive naval victory over the Etruscans at Cumae, but the Etruscans' Latin successors, the Romans, would one day pose a far greater threat to Greek hegemony. Visiting Syracuse some eight decades later, Plato suggested Sicily as a potential model for his utopian society, an idea that must have flattered the proud *Siceliots,* as Greek Sicilians were known.

Raging from 431 to 404, the Peloponnesian War was particularly bitter, leading to the Athenians' invasion of eastern Sicily where, fortunately, the Syracusans defeated them in 413.

Another Carthaginian war broke out in Sicily, lasting from 346 to 341. Following an ephemeral peace, there was a Carthaginian incursion into a few Greek-controlled areas in 311. Not without reason, the Siceliots were tiring of incessant problems with their contentious Punic neighbors.

In 310, the Greeks under Agathocles invaded some Carthaginian territories of the African coast. A treaty signed in 306 established the Halycos (Platani) River as the Greco-Punic boundary in Sicily.

The Greeks of antiquity endowed civilization with a priceless body of literature, philosophy and law. Greek culture has given us Sophocles, Aristotle, Plato, Aesop and (in Sicily) Archimedes, Empedocles, Theocritus, Philistus, Stesichorus, Timaeus, Aeschylus and Diodorus Siculus.

Sicily boasts a number of Greek temples, such as those at Segesta and Agrigento, and large theatres at Taormina, Siracusa and Segesta (the theatre at Agrigento is being excavated). Unlike Greece's white Parthenon, these are constructed of brownish local stone, but they are equally impressive.

Sicily was not their only territory. The Greeks colonized much of southern Italy, which they ruled for almost as long as they controlled Sicily. After a few centuries, the Italic peoples challenged their power. Fending off the Etruscans was not too difficult, but the burgeoning society of Rome, in Latium, posed a greater threat.

Roman Sicily

On the pretext of curtailing the Carthaginians' influence in northeastern Sicily, the ambitious Romans invaded in 264 BC (BCE). The Punic Wars, which would continue for another century, were essentially a territorial power struggle rather than an ideological conflict, but the enmity was real.

The Siceliot city of Syracuse, still the island's largest metropolis, made a tenuous peace with Rome. However, during a successive Punic War, the Syracusans reneged on this agreement by siding with the Carthaginians. This decision provoked an invasion by Rome. When Syracuse fell in 212 BC, Archimedes, the greatest scientist and engineer of his age, was killed. Much of Sicily's Greek culture died with him, yet Greek remained the island's chief vernacular language.

Although the Romans imposed heavy taxes, Sicily, the first Roman province, flourished. Public order was occasionally punctuated by slave revolts, but the long Roman period was essentially a peaceful and prosperous one for Sicily. Indeed, the island emerged as an important crossroads in the sprawling Empire. Yet historians' references to it as "the bread basket of the Roman Empire" may manifest a slightly exaggerated perception, even though (as mentioned above) the Romans deforested many areas to make room for wheat cultivation.

In 70 BC, Cicero prosecuted Verres, the province's corrupt governor, who fled following the great orator's opening argument.

Lasting from 27 BC until AD (CE) 180, the *Pax Romana* was a prosperous interlude, yet it saw Jesus put to death around AD 33.

Paul of Tarsus preached in Syracuse *en route* to Rome to stand trial around AD 59. At this early date, the Romans generally viewed Christianity as little more than a nuisance, an eccentric sect of Judaism.

Before long, the new religion came to be viewed as something more troublesome, at least from what was then the prevailing Roman point of view. Christians were regarded with raw contempt. Saint Agatha was martyred in 251 and Saint Lucy suffered the same fate some fifty years later during the rule of infamous Diocletian, who excelled at persecuting Christians.

Lucy's death in 304 came at the end of a long and wicked trend. Armenia, at the Empire's eastern fringe, had made Christianity its official religion three years earlier, and the Emperor Constantine, whose rule began in 306, brought about a more tolerant treatment of Christians. In 313, his Edict of Milan legalized the open practice of the new religion. In 325 the Council of Nicaea established a uniformity in the faith's fundamental precepts, and it was the Empire's official faith by 380. Before long, even some foreign peoples beyond the Empire's frontiers began to adopt Christianity. This included the Vandals and Goths.

In 395, following the death of Theodosius I, the Roman Empire definitively split into Western ("Latin") and Eastern ("Byzantine") administrations. Sicily began in the West but would vacillate between the two. Seven years later, the capital of the Western Empire was transferred from Rome to Ravenna. Eastern administration was based at Constantinople, the former Byzantium.

It was probably around this time that the Doric temple of Athena, at Syracuse, first began to be used as a church, though the architectural conversion occurred later. Now the cathedral, its pillars are still visible.

Myriad influences combined to weaken the mighty Empire, whose decline cannot be attributed to just one or two factors. In the event, Sicily was one of the last provinces to fall to external elements.

Vandals, Goths and Longobards

In 378, a Roman army was defeated at the Battle of Adrianople, now Edirne in European Turkey, by the ravenous Goths, a Germanic people who had been forced into Roman territory by the migrating Huns. Clearly, circumstances were changing, even if bureaucrats in Constantinople and Rome were initially reluctant to acknowledge the political implications of the debacle that took place at this outpost.

When the Vandals, Sueves, Burgundians and other tribes crossed the Rhine in 406, the "Great Invasion" had well and truly begun. Alaric's Visigoths sacked Rome four years later.

In 429 the Vandals occupied the Roman province of Africa, within striking distance of Sicily. An invasion in 440 led to mass raids in Sicily, but the Vandalic incursions were halted by the Byzantines in 441.

What followed was a series of migrations and invasions. Attila's Huns invaded northern Italy in 452. Following the pattern established by the Visigoths, the Vandals sacked Rome in 455, returning to Sicily in a long series of raids in 461. By 468 they were masters of the island. The Christianized Vandals left most of the existing administration in place but destroyed the synagogue of Syracuse.

Odoacer deposed the last Western Roman Emperor in 476, and the beginning of the Middle Ages is usually dated from this time. The Vandal king Genseric, meanwhile, concluded a "perpetual" peace with Constantinople.

In 491 the Ostrogoths achieved complete control of Sicily, ousting the Vandals, who retreated to their kingdom in Tunisia.

While most of the peoples who conquered ancient and medieval Sicily left something of value behind, the legacy of the Vandals and Ostrogoths is more difficult to quantify, apart from some genes for blondish hair and blue eyes. Their rule defined a brief interlude bridging the gap between what are now identified as the ancient and medieval epochs.

The Ostrogoth leader Theodoric the Great managed to keep his people unified against the Byzantines. His death in 526 brought an end to decades of peace.

Ascending the Byzantine throne as "Roman" Emperor in 527, Justinian already had his eye on Italy. Nobody in Constantinople seemed willing to assent to a jewel — and a territory of strategic importance to commercial shipping — like Sicily remaining in Ostrogoth hands.

In a series of bloody battles from 533 to 535, the Byzantine Greeks under Belisarius defeated the Vandals in Tunisia and the Ostrogoths in Sicily, annexing both regions to the Byzantine Empire and assimilating these aggrieved Germanic peoples into it.

The Byzantine Empire could afford such campaigns. A vestige of this prosperity is the grand basilica dedicated to Saint Sophia, erected in Constantinople in 537. The world's largest church epitomized Byzantine wealth and culture.

Back in Italy, the tenacious Goths did not succumb easily. The Ostrogoth leader Totila raided Sicily in 550 in an attempt to reclaim it for his people. This was little more than a lengthy incursion. Totila's defeat by Byzantine forces at the Battle of Taginae two years later signalled the end of Ostrogothic influence in Italy.

Following the Byzantine victories over the Ostrogoths in the bloody Gothic War, another Germanic people, the Longobards, invaded Italy *en masse* in 568, eventually reaching the south.

Coming to be called *Lombards* (and lending their name to a region of northern Italy), they handily confiscated rural areas, where they introduced something vaguely resembling rudimentary feudalism. The Byzantines, for their part, were generally content to rule the more important centers, leaving the rest for the Lombards, but over the next few centuries there were occasional conflicts. A decisive factor in Byzantine military campaigns at this time had little to do with strategy itself. For a generation or two, the problem was raising troops. An epidemic of bubonic plague in 541 decimated the population of the Byzantine Empire, rendering a reconquest of Italy all but impossible.

What soon emerged in southern Italy was a complex checkerboard of manorial and ecclesiastical dominions. Bari remained essentially Byzantine, while Salerno became the seat of a Lombard principality. Rome was held by the popes as the cornerstone of a pontifical state. The Greek influence was greatest in Apulia and Calabria; major Latin abbeys like Cassino and Cava answered to Rome.

Christianity was soon to lose its monopoly on the western world. Mohammed, the founder of Islam as its Prophet, was born in Mecca in 570.

The Byzantine Greeks

In 660, the Byzantine Emperor, Constans II, established his court at Syracuse with an eye to crossing into Calabria and invading the Lombard lands. This plan never materialized, and by the end of his reign eight years later Constantinople had, for the time being, given up any hope for such a conquest.

Now Latin, which appears never to have been the chief spoken language in the majority of Sicilian communities during the Roman era, was almost completely eclipsed by Greek, which was also the language of liturgy. Christianity would openly split only much later, with the Great Schism in 1054, but by the seventh century, with the distinctions between East and West little more than an arcane nuance, subtle differences were already growing between the two spheres of influence, namely Rome and Constantinople. (These would eventually provoke the Iconoclast Controversy.) For the present, however, there were greater differences between Christians, on the one hand, and Muslims on the other.

The Byzantine Empire, which was the medieval Greeks' continuation of the Eastern Roman Empire, survived in some form until 1453, when the Ottoman Turks finally took Constantinople. While there were inspired pockets of learning in Europe's monasteries as far afield as Ireland, until the eleventh century the greatest flowering of Christian culture was to be found in the Byzantine world.

The Arabs

Mohammed's death in 632 signalled a new onslaught. Despite divisive differences within Islam between what came to be known as the Shia and Sunni denominations, the Muslim Arabs conquered Carthage in 698, working their way westward and invading Spain in 711, seizing islands like Pantelleria. An Arab force was defeated by Charles Martel at Tours in 732, but this did not impede the general expansion of Islam. Syracuse, still Sicily's largest city, was attacked in 740 and again in 752.

Internecine disputes characterized the expansion. The Berbers, in particular, often resented the Arabian leadership. By 800 there were Berber traders in Sicily, particularly at Sciacca, Marsala and Mazara.

In 826, Euphemius, a Sicilian general disgruntled with the Byzantine Emperor Michael II, offered control of Sicily to the Aghlabids, the regnant dynasty of Ifriqiya (Tunisia), in return for political asylum. They accepted, but in the event Euphemius, who lent military support to the Aghlabids, was killed by Byzantine loyalists.

In July of the following year, the first major Arab-Berber incursion — over ten thousand troops, including some Persians, sailing from Tunisia — arrived under Asad ibn al-Furat, the general appointed by Emir Ziyadat Allah I ibn Ibrahim of Ifriqiya. Mazara was the first city to be occupied.

The facile first stage of the conquest belied difficulties to come. In September 831 Bal'harm (Palermo) was finally conquered by the Aghlabids following a year-long siege. This city was destined to become the capital of the Emirate of Sicily, but it took the better part of seventy years for the Aghlabids to bring all of the island, including the Greek areas of the east, under their control.

Peninsular Italy was not overlooked, and by 900 there was a small Arab trading settlement at the mouth of the Gagliano River on the Tyrrhenian near the town of Minturno. Lying near the papal domain, this was, arguably, Lombard territory, but Rome took an interest in it as the settlement grew in size over the next decade.

Meanwhile, in 909 the Fatimids had succeeded the Aghlabids in Tunisia and Sicily. It was to this new dynasty that the settlers on the Gagliano answered. In the spirit of Fatimid zeal, the settlers began to raid small towns in the immediate vicinity. At first they did so with impunity, exploiting the fact that the Lombards' dominion was little more than a loose federation of baronial estates lacking a large standing army. By 915, the papacy could no longer tolerate this nuisance. In that year, in a rare expression of unity, a joint army of Papal, Lombard and Byzantine troops attacked the Muslims and expelled them.

Back in Sicily, the Fatimids had problems of their own. As recently as 964, a battle was fought at the fortified Greek town of Rometta, near Messina, against a large force sent from Constantinople to bring Sicily back into the Byzantine fold, and this was a costly victory for the Arabs.

In medieval times, the ethnonym *Arab* came to refer to speakers of Arabic generally, and by the ninth century Islam was inextricably linked to Arab culture. The Koran was written in Arabic, and to this day translations into other languages are regarded as "interpretations" because the word of God was revealed to the Prophet in the Arabic language.

The arrival of the Arabs portended great changes in society. The Arabs instituted a period of religious tolerance, though giving precedence to Islam and converting a number of churches, including the cathedrals of Syracuse and Palermo, to mosques. They founded numerous towns, introduced Hindu-Arabic numerals and paper (from China), superior irrigation systems, and schools for girls as well as boys.

Mathematics and various sciences flourished under the Arabs; the word *algebra* itself comes to us from Arabic. While some of these ideas originated in India, China or Greece, it was the Arabs who refined and propagated them.

Agriculture was revolutionized. Sugar cane, rice, mulberries (for silk making as well as consumption), citrus fruits, cotton and various crops were cultivated. The basis of much of Sicilian cuisine was formed during this era. Halal and kosher dietary observances made their influence felt, a fact which may account for the dearth of traditional pork recipes.

Bal'harm became a marvelous city rivalled in its beauty only by Baghdad and Cordoba.[27]

The Fatimids ruled Sicily until 948 when, moving their center of power eastward, they entrusted the island to the Kalbid dynasty in a kind of suzerainty.

Like the Fatimids, the Kalbids were Shiites. The Aghlabids, conversely, were Sunnis who had introduced principles of Maliki law in Sicily. It has been suggested that this may have influenced English common law in the twelfth century when contact between Palermo and London was frequent.[28]

Jawhar al-Siqilli, thought to be a Sicilian, founded the Fatimid city of Al-Qahira (Cairo) in 976. Significantly, the Fatimids brought Sicily into a wide orbit of trade and prosperity extending from the Iberian peninsula to what is now Pakistan.

Like Sicily's Christians, who by the twelfth century found themselves divided between Byzantines and Latins, the Muslims were a diverse population. Not only were there Sunnis and Shia, but an Ibadi community flourished at Kasr'Janni (Enna) and perhaps elsewhere.

The Normans

On the Italian peninsula, Lombard power was on the wane, or at least less potent than it had once been. The Byzantine Greeks controlled southern Apulia and most of Calabria, the Lombards retaining much of the hinterland to the north and Salerno.

Chroniclers have suggested that by 1000 the Lombards of

Salerno were paying tribute to the Fatimids. Witnessing this extortion, some visiting Norman knights chased off the Arabs collecting it. Before long, this story goes, the grateful Lombard leader, Guaimar III, was employing Norman mercenaries.

Other accounts of the Normans' arrival in Sicily complement this.

In 1016, a band of Normans was employed by Melus, a Lombard lord who was trying to recapture the city of Bari, which he had seized from the Byzantines but then lost. Augmented by other Norman knights, this company joined the Lombard campaign.[29]

Following early victories against the catapan Leo Tornikios Kontoleon in the spring of 1017, a combined Norman-Lombard force suffered a decisive defeat at the hands of the catapan Basil Boioannes in the autumn of the same year.

Among Basil's troops were knights of the Varangian Guard, Norsemen (Vikings) in the service of Constantinople. The Normans were themselves the descendants of Norsemen who had settled on the Cotentin Peninsula, marrying women of the region that came to be called *Normandy*. Although they spoke a brand of French, the Normans in Apulia knew of their link to these distant Scandinavian cousins.

As knights errant, the Normans served the highest bidder. At Troia they briefly manned the garrison of the Byzantine catapan against whom they had fought.

Holding onto Apulia was one thing, but the Byzantine Greeks were seriously considering a reconquest of Sicily. With this objective in mind, they launched an invasion in 1038. These ambitions were quashed four years later, but not before George Maniakes occupied parts of eastern Sicily. His army was composed of Byzantines as well as Normans, Lombards and the Norse Varangian Guard under Harald "Hardrada" Sigurdsson, who went on to glory as King of Norway and defeat as invader of Saxon England. The Normans, more than the others, viewed Sicily as a place they might like to possess for themselves.

By now, the island was beset by the rivalries of jealous emirs. Separating it into four *qadits,* or administrative districts, in 1044, seemed not to help matters. In 1053, following the death of Hasan as-Samsam and the extinction of the Kalbid dynasty, three emirs divided control of Sicily's more important districts, but growing discord led to the eventual establishment of several minor emirates around the island over the next few years.[30] At least one emir decided to seek help further afield, and not necessarily from fellow Muslims.

The Normans established themselves at several towns in parts of Calabria, Lucania (Basilicata) and Apulia that were essentially Byzantine. Melfi was an important stronghold. Mileto, in Calabria, became the dominion and base of the many sons of Tancred, the lord of the small Norman town of Hauteville.

From Calabria, the Hauteville brothers began to eye the large island across the Strait of Messina. They wanted Sicily. Its capital, opulent Palermo, the richest city of what is now Italy, was the jewel in the crown.

Pope Nicholas II (Gérard de Bourgogne) also coveted the island. In 1059 he invested Robert "Guiscard," the eldest of the Hauteville brothers, as the *de jure* lord of Apulia, Calabria and Sicily. Rome, obviously enough, wanted the Muslims christianized, but she also wished to see Sicily's Greek "Orthodox" Christians under the papal yoke rather than Constantinople's ecclesiastical jurisdiction.

If the military conquest enjoyed papal support, the interests of the Hautevilles were more worldly than spiritual. The Normans wanted Sicilian territory as much as the papacy wanted its souls. Both would get what they wished for.

The unplanned result was a multicultural kingdom.[31]

Chapter 2
JUDITH OF EVREUX

Noted for its splendid Gothic cathedral, Evreux lies to the west of the Seine in what is now the department of Eure in Normandy. Here the local lords were a family descended from Richard I "the Fearless," the Duke of Normandy, who died in 996. To this grandson of the famous Norse warrior Hrolf (Rollo) is usually credited the introduction of manorialism in this part of France. Ruling first as counts and then dukes, Richard's family was the royal dynasty of Normandy.

Royal Lineage

One of Richard's sons, Robert, became Count of Evreux and Archbishop of Rouen as a rare "secular" prelate.

Around 1040, Robert's son, William of Evreux, wed Hawisa of Echauffour, the widow of his comrade Robert of Grandmesnil (Grantmesnil), who was felled in battle during a civil war between Norman factions over the royal succession of young William "the Bastard."[32] Like Robert of Grandmesnil, William of Evreux supported the Bastard.

Before her widowhood, Hawisa, the daughter of the Breton

lord Giroie of Echauffour, had already given birth to three sons and three daughters.[33]

By William she bore but one surviving child, a daughter named Judith, around 1042, who the chronicler Orderic Vitalis mentions in passing in telling us something of Hawisa's family.

Orderic tells us virtually nothing about Judith except for her eventual marriage.[34] He does, however, mention, that her elder half-brother, Robert of Grandmesnil (named for his father), took the habit of the Benedictine monks of Saint Evroul Abbey, a monastery endowed by Hawisa's family, around 1050.[35] This followed the young man's service for five years as an esquire of William the Bastard, after which he was knighted.[36]

Judith seems to have been born and raised at Evreux. It would be easy to dismiss her parents' marriage as the attempt of a knight to care for his fallen friend's widow, yet it seems that William and Hawisa were very much in love. Orderic recounts the story of William secretly taking a beautiful psalter from his father, the Archbishop of Rouen, and giving it to Hawisa, "to whom he was so much attached that he sought every means of pleasing her."[37]

Education of a Lady

What do we know of Judith's childhood in Evreux? Her education was not unlike that of the other ladies we shall meet.[38]

Medieval society distinguished between the privileged aristocratic lady, or noblewoman, and the ordinary "common" woman.

Aristocratic girls were educated, for the most part, in convents. Living with the nuns, they learned piety and devotion. Boys might spend a few formative years at the castle of a neighboring baron, where they would serve as pages and then esquires. Following his martial training, a boy of aristocratic parentage would be knighted around the age of twenty.[39]

Even the castle of a petty baron might assume the character of a royal court in miniature, and Judith's father was anything but a minor baron.

Many noblewomen were better-educated than their brothers.

Lessons included languages, especially Latin, and simple arithmetic, along with penmanship. The rudiments of botany and agriculture were studied. Poetry and theology were important. Parts of the Bible were studied, perhaps memorized. Some sense of canon law was inculcated into the children's minds. There might be a touch of music, and such studies as alchemy.

The children learned how to play chess, and the girls were taught to let the boys win.

Queens were inevitably sacrificed to kings, but there was a healthy respect for unpredictable knights, avaricious bishops and ambitious pawns. Royalty, the highest aristocracy, was mindful of the potential power of the nobility, the clergy and the common folk. The children were taught to appreciate the complexities of human nature as these were perceived in the medieval mind.

Horsemanship was important, even for a girl. This began with ponies and ended with palfreys. A knowledge of history, geography, genealogy, architecture, iconography and coinage was part of a young aristocrat's education.

The girls were taught how to recognize good fruit and luxurious fabric, and how to cook and weave. Even if a noble lady never had to butcher a goat or shear a sheep, her place as the directress of an important household made it necessary for her to be able to oversee those who did.

An unspoken but very real part of the education of a young lady involved learning about morality and responsibility. As she became an adult, she came to understand what was expected of her, something she must accept without question or complaint. The most important part of her role was easily summed up in two words: marriage and motherhood.

Damsel

When she was around fifteen, Judith met the youngest brother of a large family of siblings. Some nine years her senior, this knight hailed from a village to the west of Evreux, beyond hills, woods and pastures.

Hauteville, now Hauteville-la-Guichard, is said to have been founded by a Norseman named Hiallt around 920, less than a decade after Charles the Simple ceded Normandy to the Norse warlord Hrolf. Here one of Hiallt's descendants named Tancred sired many sons and a few daughters.[40] The youngest boy, Roger, was born around 1031; he barely knew his father, who died a decade later.

Because the Hauteville lands could not be divided into an infinite number of moieties among siblings, Roger, like most of his brothers, decided to venture to Italy as a knight errant. One of his brothers, Robert, who had already made a name for himself in the Italian south, was expecting Roger's arrival. This was not at all surprising, for Roger had been raised on tales of his older brothers' exploits in the land beyond the Alps.

Judith had occasion to meet Roger of Hauteville around 1055 during his travels eastward across Normandy, through Evreux and thence to Italy. While in this part of Normandy, he was one of many witnesses to an act of her half-brother, Robert, who became the abbot of Saint Evroul Abbey.[41]

Roger was described as tall, eloquent, and inclined to take decisions wisely following serious contemplation. He was kind to all, a sincere comrade, but also a formidable man-at-arms.[42]

The young knight was immediately smitten by the beautiful maiden, but as the landless son of a minor lord he had little to offer a young lady whose social status was comparable to that of royalty, or at least what passed for it in austere Normandy.[43] Here was the timeless story of an ambitious but, for the moment, comparatively poor man who longed to wed a beautiful girl born into a higher social station than his own. Judith, after all, was a second cousin of William, Duke of Normandy, with whom she shared a great grandfather, Richard the Fearless (see the genealogical table).

Normandy's feudal families were not unlike a loose network of clans. But even though there was no dearth of young suitors vying for pretty Judith's hand, neither was there any urgency in choosing one just yet. Social realities were complex, unpredictable, ever fluid, capable of changing from one month to the next. Friendships and alliances, even when sealed by bonds of blood, rarely enjoyed anything like permanence.[44]

Nevertheless, the Hauteville brothers' rise to power in southern Italy did not go unnoticed in Normandy. There was such a large, steady stream of young knights from Normandy to Italy that many families had a personal stake in these fortunes.

Vicissitudes

In Calabria, Roger found himself conquering territory alongside his brother, Robert "Guiscard."[45] Through these adventures, and despite fathering a son, Jordan, outside marriage, he never forgot the beautiful maiden he had met at Evreux.

Having renounced knighthood, another Robert, Judith's half-brother Robert of Grandmesnil, was formally elected abbot of Saint Evroul in 1059.[46] William, Duke of Normandy, confirmed this right to his erstwhile esquire, who brought the monastery into the Cluniac obedience.

During one of those periods of unrest that occasionally divided the baronage into warring factions, Abbot Robert found himself, along with many of his kin, opposed by his onetime lord, Duke William, the ruler of Normandy. In January 1061, the cleric departed for Rome to seek the aid of Pope Nicholas II in resolving this matter.[47] He also visited some of his kin in Apulia.[48] Upon returning, accompanied by papal legates, Robert witnessed a minor civil war in the countryside and learned that in his absence Duke William had appointed another abbot at Saint Evroul. In fact, Robert's return only enraged William. Clearly, Robert's tenure as Abbot of Saint Evroul had come to an end.

His kin in southern Italy had extended him an invitation to settle there. He now decided to accept it, taking an entourage of monks with him.

Judith and her half-sister, Anna, were in a convent in Ouche attached to Saint Evroul Abbey, south of Evreux, where, a moralistic Orderic Vitalis tells us, they had taken the veil. It seems more likely that Judith was simply living with the nuns and completing her education.

In the event, the two sisters did not hesitate to go with their brother to Italy. Wrote Orderic Vitalis, "Hearing that their brother Robert flourished under the temporal power in Italy, and finding themselves of small account and without support in Normandy, they went into Italy and relinquishing the veil gave themselves up with ardour to a worldly life, and both of them married husbands who were unconscious of their having taken the vows."[49]

For now, on their way toward Rome in the spring of 1061, Judith and her siblings were unaware of the events playing out farther south.

Messina

In the spring of 1061, while Judith and her siblings were making their way to Rome, Roger and his brothers were planning an invasion of Sicily, abetted by al-Timnah, a disgruntled emir.[50]

Such a campaign had been attempted months earlier. That effort ended in failure, with Norman knights on their ships forced back across the strait's rough wintery waters to Calabria. The only beneficial result came from a raid for booty along the Tyrrhenian coast to the west of Messina. In response, the Arabs sent ships from Palermo to patrol this area.[51]

This time, in late May, the Normans' sleek galleys, reminiscent of those of their Norse forebears, transporting men, horses and arms would arrive about six miles south of Messina, disembarking farther down Sicily's Ionian coast near Tremestieri. Each ship would cross the strait in the dead of night, landing in Sicily and then going back to Calabria to bring more troops. The men in this force were Normans as well as "Lombards" from southern Italy's feudal lands.

The Arabs expected an attack sooner or later, though from a more northern point directly across the strait, as before, hence their continued concentration of vessels in this area.

In the event, the undermanned garrison guarding Messina's seaside fortress was taken unawares, being unprepared for a ground assault from the south. By dawn, the Messinians, most of whom were Greek speakers, awoke to find their city, a springboard for trade as an important port, in Norman hands. Indeed, the fighting itself was brief and decisive. Most of the defenders were killed and few attackers injured.

Though the invading force of knights, footmen and archers consisted of several thousand, the fortifications were taken by an initial wave of a few hundred under the command of Roger, who advanced and attacked without waiting for Robert to arrive from Calabria.

The battle was followed by the pillaging typical of the Middle Ages, and the occasional rape. At least one Arab decided to kill his sister rather than risk her falling into the invaders' hands.

The victory gave Robert "Guiscard" Hauteville and his brothers a foothold in Sicily and absolute control over shipping traversing the Strait of Messina and most of the Ionian Sea. As it happened, the response from the emirs in other Sicilian cities was unimpressive. These jealous rulers were too busy nurturing their petty rivalries against each other to respond in a serious way to the arrival of the Normans. Yet their failure to send a large army to take back Messina did not mean they would give up their local emirates without a fight.

The extended campaign was to be a cumbersome enterprise not unlike the one prosecuted by the Arabs during the ninth century. Pursuing their objectives without delay, the Hauteville brothers, supported by a force of Normans and Lombards hungry for land, began a series of audacious incursions into the Nebrodian and Peloritan mountains. These were complemented by excursions into the heartland, as far as Kasr'Janni (Enna), a mountaintop stronghold that proved impregnable.

They set about erecting their first fortress in Sicily atop a rocky mountain overlooking the Tyrrhenian at San Marco d'Alunzio, once the site of an ancient Greek settlement and now a Byzantine monastery.[52]

At the outset, the Norman occupiers seemed tolerant of the people they encountered in the hinterland, whether Greek or Arab.[53] For now, conquest was the priority. Conversions would have to wait. Nevertheless, the Normans brought with them some Roman Catholic clerics, especially Benedictines.

Wife

Robert of Grandmesnil and his monks were to be given a monastery overlooking the Calabrian coast, near Nicastro, dedicated to Saint Euphemia. This reflected a subtle but determined papal effort to latinize those parts of Calabria which were traditionally Greek.

JUDITH OF EVREUX

Learning of Judith's arrival, Roger, who was at Troina in Sicily's Nebrodian Mountains, where he had spent Christmas, wasted no time going to her.

Our description of this comes from the chronicler Godfrey Malaterra, who states that, "a courier returning from Calabria bore the message that Robert, Abbot of Saint Euphemia, had brought with him from Normandy his sister, Judith, the granddaughter of Norman counts. The abbot invited Roger to come immediately to Calabria to marry the damsel. Roger was very excited to hear this. For a long time he had been in love with this beautiful maiden of noble lineage. He crossed into Calabria with alacrity to again see the girl he long desired. There he reached the Salina Valley, near San Martino. To the music of minstrels, he escorted his betrothed to Mileto to celebrate the solemn nuptials." This was in early January of 1062, as the wedding was likely celebrated immediately after the Epiphany.

"Having celebrated the wedding and spent some time with his bride," Malaterra tells us, "Roger did not forget that he still had much to do. He readied an army of knights, taking with him as his esquire a certain Roger sent by his brother. Then he left his young bride in Calabria, not allowing himself to be persuaded, let alone delayed, by her tears. He crossed over the strait into Sicily, penetrating inland."[54]

For a time, the monk Malaterra may have served at the abbey founded by Judith's brother. Partial though he may have been, he probably knew the people about whom he wrote. He was likely present at Judith's wedding.

The next few weeks found Roger fortifying castles like Troina, solidifying an alliance with those Arabs who supported the Normans, and enlisting the fealty of the people of towns like Entella and Petralia, thus extending Hauteville influence westward across the hinterland to a mountainous region fairly near Palermo.

Back in Calabria, his elder brother, Robert, was encroaching on some towns and revenues that, by prior agreement, belonged to Roger. Following a series of encounters in Mileto and Gerace, important Hauteville strongholds, the two brothers made peace. Unaware of this, Robert's wife, Sichelgaita, thinking herself to have been widowed during the fighting, fled to Tropea on the Tyrrhenian coast.[55] Although Judith may have been with her sister-in-law, who was a year or two her senior, it seems more likely that she was staying at her brother's abbey.

Sichelgaita, the daughter of the Lombard ruler of Salerno, was a remarkable figure in her own right who later became famous for leading troops on her husband's behalf.[56] In 1062, however, she was in her early twenties and the mother of two young children.

The solution to the Hauteville brothers' sibling rivalry, which risked becoming an internecine war, was to divide Calabria. With this, Robert went to tend to matters in Apulia. Roger returned to Sicily but this time he took Judith with him.

Soldier

Finding himself again in the Nebrodian Mountains, Roger set out to take control of several towns. At Troina, the Greeks, so we are told by Malaterra, seemed less enthusiastic about the Normans than they were during Roger's first incursion. Considering this, the Norman leader left his bride there with a small garrison which resumed work on the fortifications of the existing castle.[57]

Despite Judith's presence, the Greeks feared for their wives and daughters, with whom some of the knights flirted. Had he been present, Roger might have made an effort to discourage the young knights' more zealous attempts at seduction.

One day, while Roger was off besieging Nicosia, another Byzantine town, the people of Troina decided to attack the Norman knights at Troina and take Judith hostage.

The few knights acquitted themselves well enough against the mob, retreating with Judith and her ladies-in-waiting to some narrow streets. Fortunately, the Normans were able to send a messenger to Roger. At nightfall, they were still cornered but held their ground.

By the next morning, when Roger arrived with his contingent, the Greeks had been joined by some Arabs from nearby towns and erected barricades to restrict the Normans to one part of Troina.

The Normans' adversaries were well supplied with food and arms.[58] What soon confronted the knights was a force of nature, the coldest, snowiest winter of the last few decades.

In the frigid temperatures, Roger and Judith shared a mantle they used as a blanket, but there was not much to eat.

In Malaterra's words, "The young countess slaked her thirst by drinking water, but sated her hunger only with her tears and her slumber, having nothing to eat." It seems that the Normans eventually butchered their own horses and roasted the meat.

A few engagements were fought against the enemy. In one skirmish, Roger slayed several men with his sword despite his horse being felled by arrows. Then, showing no fear or urgency, he leisurely removed its saddle and strolled back to the Normans' secure quarter. The local people opposed to the Normans could not avoid noting the invaders' tenacity and courage.

The bitter stalemate dragged on for weeks that became months. Before long, snow accumulated on the narrow streets. As the temperatures grew ever colder, the Greek and Arab guards charged with watching the Normans' position at night began to consume wine in an effort to keep warm.

This gave birth to a strategy. Day by day, night after long night, the knights kept as quiet as possible, hoping to lull the guards into a false sense of security.

The ploy worked. One night, the knights left their position behind the timber barricades. A freshly-fallen layer of powdery snow muffled their footsteps into the part of town where the drunken guards were sleeping. It didn't take much to surprise them. Next, having overpowered the guards with minimal effort, the Normans took control of Troina in the violent confrontation that ensued.

With the city secured, its populace subdued, Roger ordered the execution of the ringleaders. Others were punished less harshly.

He then returned to Calabria to procure for his men, who had lost (or eaten) their mounts, some of the sturdy horses he favored. Judith, meanwhile, stayed at Troina and very diligently inspected the continuing work on the fortifications. She reassured the men that their efforts would be rewarded upon her husband's return.[59]

Countess

Roger continued to occupy lands, both Arab and Byzantine, in northeastern Sicily. As we have seen, his elder brother, Robert, had already ordered construction of a fortress on a rocky mountain at San Marco d'Alunzio.[60] This became the Hautevilles' base in Sicily, and remained a familial castle into the last years of the twelfth century.

Judith spent the next few years at San Marco. Here there was a small garrison, a monastery and a large crew of architects and builders working to ensure the castle's rapid construction.

Over the next few years, she gave birth to at least four daughters but, so far as we know, no surviving sons. Her known children were Matilda, Emma, Adelaide and another daughter who seems to have been named Flandina.[61]

In late 1071 Roger and Robert led a force by land and sea

to besiege Bal'harm (Palermo), Sicily's largest city. This was successful, but some time passed before Roger, now Great Count of Sicily, took up residence there, and he still had to subdue some Arab towns in central and southwestern Sicily. This meant that Judith and the children remained at San Marco and Messina for the next two or three years, with occasional visits to Palermo or Mileto.

Judith died of natural causes around 1076. She was entombed in her brother's monastery at Saint Euphemia, of which little remains today.[62]

QUEENS OF SICILY

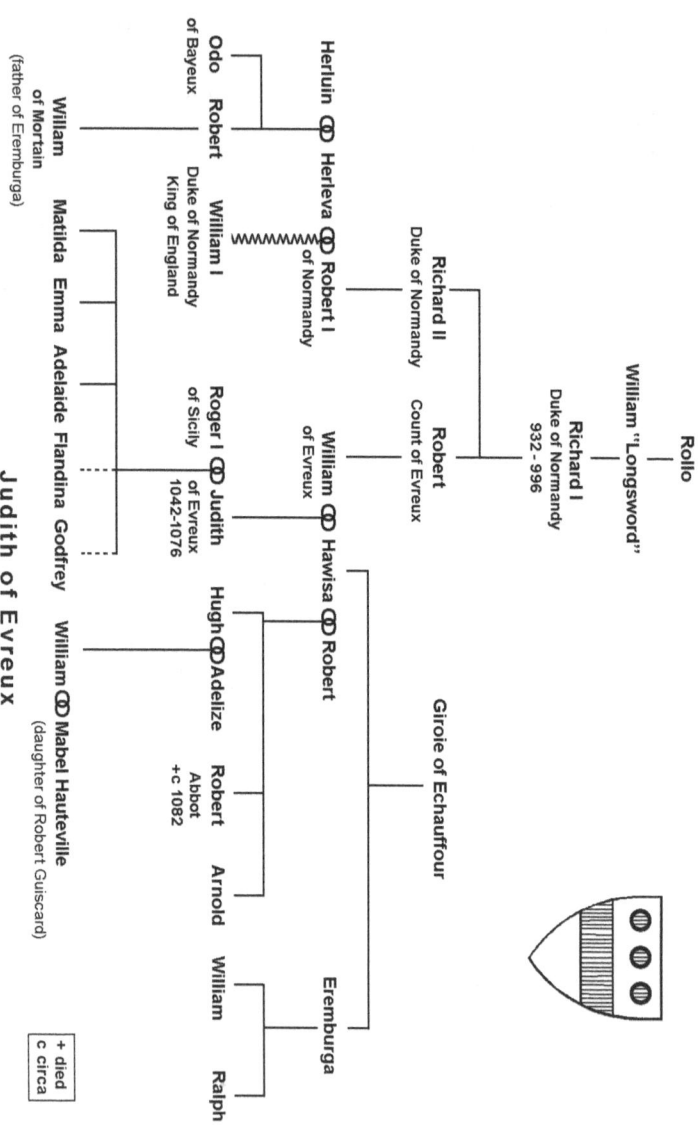

The author at a wall of the castle of San Marco d'Alunzio

Norman church built upon Roman temple at San Marco

Nebrodian Mountains viewed from San Marco d'Alunzio

Fresco icons from Greek church at San Marco d'Alunzio

In 1072, Palermo's great mosque had seven mihrabs like this one in Cordoba, a city to which it was compared.

Chapter 3
EREMBURGA OF MORTAIN

Around 1077, a young Norman noblewoman named Eremburga wed Roger, Great Count of Sicily, as his second wife. This was a daughter of William, Count of Mortain.[63]

Eremburga's father, William of Mortain, was a son of Robert, the half-brother of William the Conqueror, and Maud (or Matilda) Montgomery. Robert's brother, Odo of Bayeux, was likewise a half-brother of William the Conqueror.[64]

Mortain was a prosperous county in Normandy traditionally held by the region's dukes. In addition to this, Eremburga's father owned a number of estates in England.

Very little is known about Eremburga's childhood; indeed, we know less about her than we do about any other Sicilian consort of the Norman era. Born in Normandy around 1061, she was quite young when she married Roger, with whom she probably was not acquainted before her betrothal.

Motherhood

Bearing children — preferably males — was to be Eremburga's chief duty. Thus far, Roger had illegitimate sons but none born within marriage. More precisely, he had no legitimate sons known to have survived childhood, infant mortality being very high.

His continued attempts to subjugate the Arabs of southeastern Sicily kept Roger away from Palermo, the island's unofficial capital.

Eremburga, like Judith before her, spent most of her time at Messina and San Marco d'Alunzio, with occasional visits to Mileto in Calabria. She probably visited Palermo rather rarely.

She did not have to assume many administrative responsibilities. By now, Sicily was regarded as a great county, with Roger as its ruler. Robert, his elder brother, had designs on the Byzantine Empire which led to campaigns in Greece and the Balkans; he was content to leave Roger in Sicily.

The Arabs' Kasr fortress on high ground between Palermo's two principal rivers was being developed into Roger's protective stronghold. Here he left a strong garrison.

The palace was not without its charm, and an austere chapel was being built within its stout walls.[65]

Childbearing and child rearing became Eremburga's vocations. She gave birth to six children, if not more, and one may have been a boy.

The uncertainty arises from sparse records and the lack of precise identification of one or two of Roger's sons. Jordan was born outside marriage before Roger wed Judith. Another, Godfrey, seems to have been born during Roger's marriage to Eremburga but not by her, although he may have been the son of Judith of Evreux. Still another boy was named Godfrey, but we don't know that he was the son of Eremburga. A son of Roger named Mauger (Malgerio) is also known.

Eremburga gave birth to Matilda, Muriella, Judith, Flandina (assuming this was not the daughter of Judith of Evreux), Maximilla (or Constance), who wed Conrad II, King of Germany and Italy, and "Felicia," who married the King of Hungary.[66] Mauger may have been her son.

A Betrothal

For the most part, southern Italy was now unified under the Hauteville dynasty, with parts of it shared with families like the Drengot. Roger comfortably ruled Sicily, except for a few pockets of lingering Muslim resistance, as its great count. But there were familial matters to consider, even where these did not involve Eremburga directly.

It was time for Roger to forge alliances with rulers beyond Norman lands such as England. This, of course, would be attempted through dynastic marriages.

The late Judith's children were not the charge of Eremburga, but as the lady of the comital household and, in effect, a stepmother, she was closely apprised of events. A betrothal noted by Malaterra was that of Judith's daughter Matilda, herself not much younger than Eremburga.

First, a marriage was contemplated of young Matilda to Robert, Count of Eu and Lord of Hastings, who was many years her senior.[67] This idea was abandoned, apparently on the initiative of Robert himself.

Foreign rulers were beginning to take note of the Normans of Sicily and their emerging power. One of these was Raymond IV, Count of Toulouse, who in 1080 sent Roger emissaries bearing gifts and the request for his daughter's hand in marriage.

Born around 1041, Raymond, a widower, was about two decades older than Matilda. An ambitious man who already controlled much of southern France, he later became famous for his participation in the First Crusade and for capturing Tripoli, in what is now Lebanon. He would make a good ally.

Matilda was formally betrothed to Raymond, and a dowry was established, along with a marriage agreement. Malaterra describes the young bride as being so attractive that her beauty was known far and wide, and in a later entry he mentions that Emma, Matilda's younger sister, was likewise very beautiful.[68]

The chronicler offers few details regarding the betrothal itself or even the wedding ceremony. Nevertheless, his account is interesting, and significant for being the first description of its kind of a wedding of a maiden of the House of Hauteville in Sicily.[69]

One of the duties of Raymond's ambassadors was to meet Matilda and report to their lord regarding her beauty, health and intelligence, and perhaps something of her demeanor.

Raymond arrived in Sicily for the nuptials, and distributed gifts to the more important courtiers, amongst whom were Greeks and Arabs. Eremburga, as Roger's consort, may have received gifts, and she was probably present at the festivities.

Then Raymond sailed with his bride to Provence during the calm seas of summer.

We know little of Matilda's conjugal life or even her children, but she gave birth to no son that survived into adulthood. She died before 1094.[70]

Transition

Following a brief illness, Eremburga died in 1088 or early in 1089.[71] She was not yet thirty, but she had served her adopted country well.

Sicily's political situation was still unsettled. Certain cities, like Noto, were under Arab control even as prosperous Palermo was flourishing as the cornerstone of a multicultural society.

Like Judith, Eremburga was interred in Calabria. Her sarcophagus was placed in the church of the Holy Trinity Monastery at Mileto.[72]

EREMBURGA OF MORTAIN

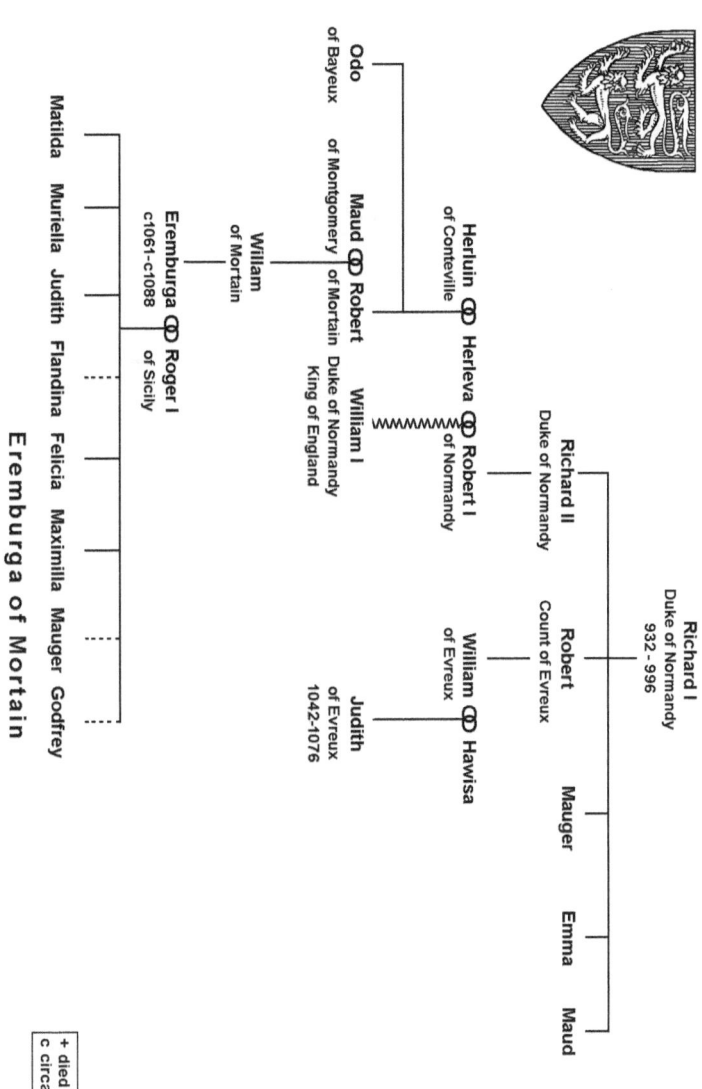

Built by emirs, the round tower of Palermo's sea castle was known to Eremburga. The gatehouse was erected later. This royal fortress survived intact until 1860.

Chapter 4
ADELAIDE DEL VASTO

In 1089, Adelaide of Incisa "del Vasto" of Savona married Roger, Great Count of Sicily. She was almost fifteen, and he was about fifty.

Ancestry

Little is known of the noblewoman's childhood in Montferrat, but her family's wealth was known far and wide.

Adelaide's natal family, the prosperous Aleramids, ruled lands in Liguria and Piedmont, strategic regions between the Frankish dominions once controlled by Charlemagne and the northern part of the Italian peninsula. The Aleramic dynasty itself was descended from William of Montferrat, a Frankish adventurer who arrived in the region around 888. The family takes its name from William's son, Aleram, who became a vassal of Otto I, Holy Roman Emperor, in 962.[73] For the most part, the roots of the feudal aristocracy of northern Italy, and hence many of Adelaide's ancestors, were Longobardic. The land itself was known for its vines, chestnuts and truffles; the rice for which it is now famous was probably introduced later.

Adelaide's father, Manfred, who was killed at a revolt in Savona in 1079, left his fertile estates to her brothers. Manfred's elder brother, Boniface, became the guardian of the orphaned children, including Adelaide, and emerged as one of the most powerful lords of northern Italy.

Adelaide barely knew her father, who died when she was about five years old, and her mother likewise seems to have been taken from this life while the girl was just a child.

Alliances

The Hautevilles regarded Liguria and Piedmont for their strategic value as a "bridge" into the part of Italy they controlled. Alliances to a powerful dynasty would prove opportune.

Adelaide's brother, Henry, wed Roger's daughter, Flandina. One of Adelaide's sisters married Roger's illegitimate son, Jordan. Another was betrothed to Roger's son, Godfrey, but the marriage did not take place because the young man was infected by leprosy before the nuptials could be celebrated.

Strategic considerations aside, Roger had more immediate concerns. By now, he had no living, legitimate sons to succeed him as heirs. His marriage to young Adelaide was intended to remedy this deficiency.

We do not know for certain that Godfrey was illegitimate, and he may have been a legitimate son of Judith or Eremburga, but as he was afflicted by leprosy he was considered unsuitable to rule.[74] (The possibility that two of Roger's sons may have borne this name creates confusion for genealogists.)

Adelaide's betrothal to Roger was approved by her uncle, Boniface, who sent her to Messina by ship in great pomp. The lavish nuptials were celebrated in Mileto, the Hautevilles' capital in Calabria. Palermo, the commercial and administrative center of the Normans' County of Sicily, was not yet its official capital city.

For the moment, Jordan was treated as if he were Roger's heir. Clearly, Adelaide was expected to bear children, preferably sons and preferably soon.

Roger was still suppressing Muslim revolts in southeastern Sicily. Because these geographically isolated disturbances were not seen to threaten the general peace, Roger was accompanied by Adelaide around the island.

Motherhood

In 1091, Noto, the last major Sicilian city in Muslim hands, surrendered to Roger. By then, Malta was also under his control; at Mdina he left administrative duties to the Arabs.[75] It was becoming clear that Troina, San Marco d'Alunzio and Messina would not suffice as the only points from which to control Sicily, but Roger was not quite ready to make Palermo its official capital despite the city's wealth and importance.

Ruling Sicily was not only a question of government. In keeping the Hautevilles' promise to the papacy, Roger was founding Latin abbeys around his island, and in some cases these supplanted existing Greek monasteries.[76] In Palermo, the cathedral long used as a mosque was converted back into a church shortly after the conquest of the city in 1072; the Greek (Orthodox) bishop, Nicodemus, was replaced by a Latin cleric, Alcherio, a decade later.

A century would pass before this latinization was anything like complete, but it was more than a matter of religion. Immigration also played a role. For example, some of Adelaide's Lombard kin were given fiefs in the Nebrodian Mountains in the northeastern part of the island, where they introduced settlers. This brought northern Italian linguistic influences to the local dialects.

In the other Norman dominions of Italy, Roger was instrumental in altering the balance of power. After the death of his elder brother, Robert Guiscard, two of the man's sons vied for power as his heirs. Roger supported the younger sibling, his nephew Roger Borsa, who emerged as the dominant force in Apulia. With papal and baronial assent, Guiscard's elder son, Bohemond, was given Taranto.[77] This brought an end to what otherwise might have become a major civil war in southern Italy, though a few rebellious vassals continued to resist the authority of Roger Borsa anyway.[78]

Adelaide maintained close contact with her kin and countrymen in Sicily. For the first time since the Battle of Messina thirty years earlier, Roger could address domestic concerns without worrying too much about open revolts.

Adelaide gave birth to a daughter, Matilda, around 1091.[79] Roger still needed sons. The year 1092 saw the death of Jordan, his illegitimate son, who until now was considered his heir.

Roger's wish for a son was granted with the birth of Simon in 1093. Another son, Roger, followed two years later. A girl named Maximilla (sometimes Matilda) was born around 1097.[80]

As a young mother, Adelaide concentrated her attention on her children, not on statecraft. Even so, she observed her husband's actions involving policy regarding the baronage, Sicily's urban populations and, of course, the church. In this, Roger was her mentor.

Catholicism was being introduced rapidly, feudalism and other traditional European institutions more slowly. Sicily's population was divided about equally between Muslims and "Greeks," with small Jewish communities in some localities. For now, the Normans were content with an equally polyglot system of administration and law.

Adelaide could not have been unaware of the internecine discord in the extended Hauteville family. Yet they were little different from any other medieval family in this regard. Fraternal dissension had been a fact of life since the days of Cain and Abel.

In 1095, Maximilla (or Constance), Roger's daughter by Eremburga, married Conrad II, the second son of the Salian prince Henry IV, Holy Roman Emperor. Ruling the Lombard and Piedmontese territories of the Holy Roman Empire, Conrad was King of Italy. This wedding was celebrated in Pisa. Malaterra mentions the union but not Maximilla's name. Sadly, the marriage was short-lived, as Conrad died six years later, aged just twenty-eight.

It is unlikely that Adelaide, who was busy raising her own children, was very involved with Maximilla's wedding.

In 1097 Felicia, another one of Roger's daughters with Eremburga, wed Coloman, King of Hungary.[81]

Malaterra notes that Adelaide was pregnant in 1098, without mentioning that she gave birth that year or the next. The pregnancy may have ended in a miscarriage, or the birth of a child who did not survive infancy.[82]

In May 1098 Roger found himself on the mainland besieging Capua alongside his nephew, Roger Borsa, in support of their kinsman, Richard Drengot. Years earlier, the Capuans had expelled Richard. With the help of the two Rogers and an army that included, among other forces, Arab archers from Sicily, Richard was quickly restored to power.

The immediate result for Roger was the lordship of Naples, and although this city was not yet as large as Salerno, Bari or Palermo, it was emerging as an important mercantile center. This meant that, in addition to Sicily and Calabria, Roger now controlled many of the Italian territories along the Tyrrhenian northward to Naples, even though Amalfi resisted.

Roger exploited this occasion to meet with Pope Urban II (Odo of Châtillon) to discuss a question involving ecclesiastical jurisdiction. Urban recognized Roger's civil authority in Sicily, and he had been instrumental in arranging Maximilla's marriage to Conrad, but a dispute arose when the pontiff decided to grant a bishop authority as his papal legate on the island. Now Roger was able to negotiate a unique agreement that allowed him, and henceforth his heirs, to nominate Sicily's bishops or approve the papacy's episcopal appointments.[83] This apostolic legateship was to become the envy of other European sovereigns, such as England's monarchs.[84]

Pope Urban had more immediate concerns, like the First Crusade he had initiated. Bohemond of Taranto, Roger's nephew (and half-brother of Roger Borsa), led a Norman contingent to the Holy Land, where he seized the city of Antioch. Unbeknownst to Adelaide, the Norman presence in Palestine would establish a rapport with the Frankish states, most notably Jerusalem, that would shape her destiny.

Sicily was becoming a springboard for the journey of crusaders *en route* to the Holy Land. Thanks largely to the Arabs of its cities, the island's economy prospered. However, the introduction of feudalism in rural areas found some Muslims and Greeks, deprived of their smallholdings, becoming serfs overnight.

When Roger died at Mileto, his favorite castle, in June 1101, Adelaide, at the age of twenty-six, became regent in the name of Simon, her elder son.[85]

Conrad, King of Italy, died the same year, and his widow, Roger's daughter Maximilla, returned to the land of her birth.

Regency

Adelaide was now faced with the task of governing Sicily, and raising her sons to rule it. Was she up to the task? The evidence suggests that she was.

One or two of Roger's sons by other women were still alive, and Adelaide seems to have taken careful steps to ensure the rights of her own two sons.[86] So far as we know, there were no overt contestations, no open conflicts arising from a half-brother's pretensions.

ADELAIDE DEL VASTO

Very little information is available about Adelaide's time raising her children. Young Roger seems to have suffered an ear infection in 1101, and one of Adelaide's first decrees is a charter issued in October of that year making a donation of four serfs, along with their families and property (including land) to the abbey of Saint Philip, in the Nebrodian Mountains, in gratitude for the boy's "miraculous recovery." Here we see the unabashed, sometimes ruthless, application of feudalism, as the same charter also grants the abbot additional lands, including vineyards confiscated from some serfs, presumably Arabs or Greeks, who had fled and were forcibly repatriated.[87]

Her son's illness, whatever it was, seems to have been rather severe, probably *otisis media* if not something worse. At the very least, it left a lasting impression on Adelaide, for she later made another donation to this monastery to commemorate Roger being cured. Undertaken eleven years later (in November 1112), and perhaps to mark Roger reaching the age of majority, this involved five named serfs ceded from the territory of the Hauteville demesne of San Marco d'Alunzio, with the proviso that henceforth all rights of justice and taxation over these men and their families was to remain exclusively under royal authority, exempt from any other civil jurisdiction. (Until then, the serfs may have enjoyed Adelaide's personal patronage and protection.)

There was no firm rule about the exact age at which a young heir reached the age of majority. Normally, he would be considered an adult at around fifteen. There were rites of passage. For example, the son of a baron or other feudal lord would be knighted at nineteen or twenty following several years as an esquire, though the son of a king, duke or count might be knighted sooner.

The realms Adelaide ruled in the name of her young son had to be governed well if his inheritance was to be preserved. Here there were political complexities.

Adelaide — in Simon's name — enjoyed the apostolic legateship in Sicily but she lacked the same privilege in mainland territories like Calabria. Therefore, her relations with the papacy were subtly different in Sicily and Calabria.

Whereas most of her counsellors in Calabria and northeastern Sicily were "Latins" (Normans and Lombards), Palermo and other important cities were administered by Greeks and Arabs. This included the treasury, the *diwan*. Most abbots were Greek Orthodox.

Contrary to what one might imagine, such a culturally eclectic environment did not pose a great threat to Adelaide's rule, for much had changed since the Normans' ordeal during that frigid winter at Troina four decades earlier. In practice, these non-Latin urban populations looked to their ruler to defend their interests against the zealous feudal baronage being introduced in rural areas. The comital bodyguard consisted of famously loyal Muslims.

The regent had few female peers to advise her. The intrepid Sichelgaita, widow of Robert Guiscard, was long deceased. Adelaide doubtless looked to her own siblings and cousins for advice, but she eventually made a certain Christodoulos, a Greek, her chief counsellor, entrusting him with day-to-day administration as *amiratus*. This title, sometimes *amiratus amiratorum,* from the Arabic *amir al umara* (emir of emirs), may be the origin of the modern *admiral,* but in Norman Sicily it was the highest official of the realm, outranking the chancellor.

One of Adelaide's stepdaughters, who may have been named Yolanda, married Robert of Burgundy, who seems to have become an advisor.[88] Whatever his status, he died a few years following his arrival in Sicily.

Initially, Adelaide chose to live with her children at San Marco d'Alunzio. Besides Matilda, Simon, Roger and Maximilla, there may have been a girl who did not live to see adulthood.

The town and castle of San Marco were about a hundred twenty kilometers (seventy-five miles) east of Palermo, and five hundred fifty meters (around 1800 feet) above sea level. Cicero famously observed that the corrupt Roman governor Verres refused to ascend these heights to extort payments from the town's citizens, the Aluntians, choosing instead to wait on the coast a few miles away whilst minions collected the money for him. The castle stood on the summit overlooking the town, with Greek churches nearby. A Catholic chapel was erected by the Normans upon the stylobate of the Temple of Hercules. In addition to its Greeks, San Marco had a thriving community of Jews engaged in silk making, and they probably produced fabric for the Hautevilles.

However, Adelaide's geographical power base was at Messina, from which she could keep an eye on her sons' Calabrian dominions across the strait, and it was in that city that most of her few extant decrees were issued. Preserved for centuries in monastic archives, a smattering of these charters were spared the fate of Messina's Arab-Norman castle, of which the last vestiges were destroyed by a catastrophic earthquake in 1908. (This was not a unique event. Over time, seismic activity has taken its toll across eastern Sicily and much of Calabria; only a single wall remains of the Hauteville castle at San Marco d'Alunzio.)

Adelaide made a serious effort to continue her husband's work to establish and endow Latin abbeys in Sicily and Calabria whilst assisting the efforts of the Greek communities to preserve their language and rite.[89] Her charters to the monasteries in the Nebrodian region were written in Greek.

Norman French was the chief vernacular of the Hautevilles and their feudatories. Simon and Roger also learned Latin, as well as some Greek and Arabic.

The next few years were remarkably — and fortunately — uneventful in the dominions Adelaide governed. The only major incident we know of is her suppression of an impromptu rebellion by some barons. This trial of nerves, which does not seem to have been part of a wider conspiracy, revealed who was loyal and who was not. Unfortunately, the fealty of the restless Norman baronage would frequently be called into question during the twelfth century.

Further afield, Bohemond of Taranto was ensconced at Antioch, while his half-brother, Roger Borsa, ruled Apulia and other parts of the Italian mainland.[90] Amongst the Hauteville rulers, fraternal feuds were avoided in favor of a tenuous peace.

Little of detail is known of Adelaide's time raising her children. Alexander of Telese refers to her as "a very prudent woman."[91] Orderic Vitalis, ever the cynic, would prove less generous in his appraisal.[92]

In his chronicle later commissioned by Matilda, Adelaide's daughter, Alexander alludes to a sibling rivalry, noting that Roger once taunted his elder brother, Simon, following a fight that ensued while playing a game of chance (flipping coins), stating that he, Roger, should rule Sicily and that Simon should instead become pope.[93]

In his next chapter, Alexander praises young Roger's piety, and also his generosity, explaining how the boy would give alms to poor men and pilgrims, and seek out his mother for additional coin when his funds were exhausted.[94] Were these the coins he won from his elder, pious brother?

Sadly, Simon died in September 1105 at the age of twelve. He was buried next to his father at Mileto. There is no evidence to suggest that he had already assumed any active duties as Sicily's count, but he may have been knighted.

This left Roger as his father's recognized heir.[95] Nonetheless, a few years would pass before the boy reached the age of majority.

Certain charters issued during this period refer to the regent and the young count with appellations such as "Adelaide and her son count Roger."

One of the reasons why rather few of Adelaide's charters survive is because some were written on paper rather than more durable parchment or vellum. The Arabs' introduction of paper facilitated correspondence, accounting and learning; the Sicilian population in Adelaide's time enjoyed a high rate of literacy, among women as well as men. One of her charters issued in Greek and Arabic in March 1109 ordering the people of Kasr'Janni (Enna) to respect the rights of a monastery under Adelaide's personal patronage is the oldest existing paper document in Italy and one of the oldest in Europe.

The very survival of this document (shown at the end of this chapter), which originally seems to have borne a royal seal, is remarkable considering that many similar paper charters were eroded by moisture within a decade; at one point Adelaide had to issue a vellum charter to replace one written on fragile paper first issued by her husband in 1099 assigning some serfs to the abbey of Saint Philip.

Other documents were lost to civil strife. That Adelaide was present at San Marco d'Alunzio in the autumn of 1109 is attested by a decree issued at the Hauteville castle to recapitulate the extent of the lands long held by a nearby abbey dedicated to Saint Barbarus, the original charter having been destroyed.

As Roger neared the age of majority, it became obvious that Adelaide would have to spend more time in Palermo. By now, a fortified palace built around four stout towers had been erected on high ground in the city's Kasr district. Overlooking a labyrinth of urban streets to the north and an extensive park to the south, it would be a secure residence, if not a home, for Adelaide and her children. Her late husband had left a garrison there, and another at the seaside fortress erected by the Fatimids about a mile away. The Latins were still a minority in the bustling metropolis, but several Catholic churches, besides the palace chapel, had been built for the city's growing Norman population.

This move to the west was more significant in the twelfth century than it might seem today; over time, the rivalry between Palermo and Messina took on a life of its own. The former city, mostly Arab, was the richer and more populous; the latter, still mostly Greek, was an important springboard to the Italian peninsula and the eastern Mediterranean. Neither Latin Salerno nor Greek Bari, important and impressive as they were, could compete with the two largest cities of Sicily. Indeed, Palermo was the most populated city in what is now Italy.

Both Bohemond of Taranto and Roger Borsa died in 1111, leaving young sons as their successors. This meant that their wives, respectively Constance of France and Adele of Flanders, became regents for boys who were not yet old enough to rule. In this sense, Adelaide was no longer alone as the regent of a young Norman heir, but her regency was nearing its end.

Alexander of Telese refers to Roger "reaching adulthood and being knighted."[96] This ceremony probably took place in 1112[97] in Palermo before numerous witnesses, and it was most likely Adelaide who knighted her son, who was now sixteen or seventeen.

Having reached the age of majority, Roger was now old enough to rule in his own name. He was Great Count of Sicily. Adelaide, who was around thirty-six, was no longer regent.

Queenhood

Adelaide was still beautiful, and even as a dowager she was very rich, for her son's dominions constituted one of the wealthiest realms in Europe. She did not go unnoticed, and in 1112, not long after Adelaide had ceded the effective rule of Sicily and Calabria to Roger, envoys arrived from

ADELAIDE DEL VASTO

Baldwin I, King of Jerusalem, seeking her hand in marriage for their sovereign. That the proposal was endorsed by Arnulf of Chocques, the Latin Patriarch of Jerusalem, lent it legitimacy.

Having arrived in the Holy Land with his brother, Godfrey of Bouillon, during the First Crusade, Baldwin of Boulogne was crowned the first King of Jerusalem in 1100. He was, of course, familiar with the late Bohemond of Taranto, who had ruled Antioch.

Baldwin, who was around fifty, had been married to Godehilde, a Norman noblewoman whose father, Raoul, fought alongside William the Conqueror at Hastings. Following Godehilde's death and his own coronation, Baldwin then wed Arda of Edessa, an Armenian. Little was publicly known of Arda's fate, though it was rumored that her marriage to Baldwin had been annulled or even that she was dead. Arda, who bore no surviving children, had not been seen in Jerusalem for several years; in fact, she was living in Constantinople.

Baldwin needed Adelaide's money. He instructed his emissaries to agree to any conditions she might stipulate. Roger was the official voice consenting to his mother's betrothal, and he had his own motives for doing so.

Adelaide's principal requirement was that any son she bore by Baldwin would be the undisputed heir to the crown of Jerusalem. If, however, she and Baldwin had no children, Roger would succeed Baldwin as king. These terms were agreed.

Adelaide — and her dowry — sailed for Palestine in the summer of 1113. Along the way, her flotilla survived a pirate attack followed by an unseasonal storm that blew her into hostile Muslim waters before finally arriving at Acre with great pomp. Here she was met by the enthusiastic Baldwin. The Sicilian galleys were laden with knights, arms, victuals, fine silk and, of course, plenty of silver and gold.[98]

Baldwin made sure to spend this wealth to pay men-at-arms whose stipends were long overdue, and to compensate barons whose estates had been lost to the Arabs.

Crowned Queen of Jerusalem, Adelaide took up residence in its royal palace but gave birth to no children. She effectively served as regent in Jerusalem while Baldwin was absent on a series of unsuccessful expansionist campaigns funded, at least in part, with what remained of her money. Adelaide had her own entourage. Indeed, a certain Pagano, who Baldwin appointed chancellor in 1115, had arrived with Adelaide, serving as one of her counsellors.

Adelaide was not pleased with what she saw in Jerusalem, where Patriarch Arnulf forbade Greek clerics to celebrate liturgy in their language at the Holy Sepulchre. The same prelate preached against the local Muslims. This was the antithesis of what Adelaide had known in multicultural Palermo, but there was little she could do about it.

When Baldwin, still childless, was stricken by a serious illness in 1116, it occurred to his nobles that his death might result in Roger of Sicily becoming their king, something nobody wanted. At this point the opportunistic Arnulf publicly proclaimed that Baldwin's marriage to Arda was still in force, never having been annulled.

Alas, Baldwin, who survived his illness, was exposed as a bigamist, and his friend the Patriarch Arnulf was revealed to be an accomplice in the treacherous scheme to lure Adelaide, and her dowry, to Jerusalem.

Seen by the people of Jerusalem as a usurper, Adelaide was now more unpopular than ever. Local popularity, however, was probably one of her lesser concerns.

Adelaide was livid, for she had been duped and defrauded. Even worse, as word of the scandal rapidly spread across Europe, she looked (and perhaps felt) like a high-priced harlot.

Pope Paschal II (Ranieri of Bieda) immediately deposed

Arnulf[99] but he also made it clear that Adelaide, now an estranged quasi-consort, could not long remain in Jerusalem.

Back in Palermo, Roger made his anger known. Not only had his mother been thoroughly humiliated, his chance of inheriting the Hierosolymitan crown had been thwarted.

Adelaide went to stay at Acre until matters could be sorted out, although the predicament was actually quite clear to her. In the spring of 1117, with her "marriage" to Baldwin annulled, the erstwhile Queen of Jerusalem sailed from Acre with a flotilla her son had sent to take her to Messina.

Whilst her own marriage was ending, her son's conjugal life was just beginning. Roger was to marry Elvira Jiménez, daughter of the King of Castile.

Orderic Vitalis disparaged Adelaide, but it is clear from his words that he knew very little about her.[100]

Retirement

There was no obvious role awaiting Adelaide in Sicily, where she retired to one of the nunneries under her patronage, the Holy Savior Convent, which her husband, Roger, had founded. This was located outside the town of Patti. It was a tranquil environment nestled between the coast and the foothills of the Nebrodian Mountains. Here Adelaide had her own small castle.

She found time to attend her son's wedding in Palermo during the autumn of 1117.[101] This was the first major royal event to be held in the capital.

Adelaide died peacefully at Patti on the sixteenth of April in 1118.

She is entombed in the medieval church dedicated to Saint Bartholomew which became the cathedral.[102]

QUEENS OF SICILY

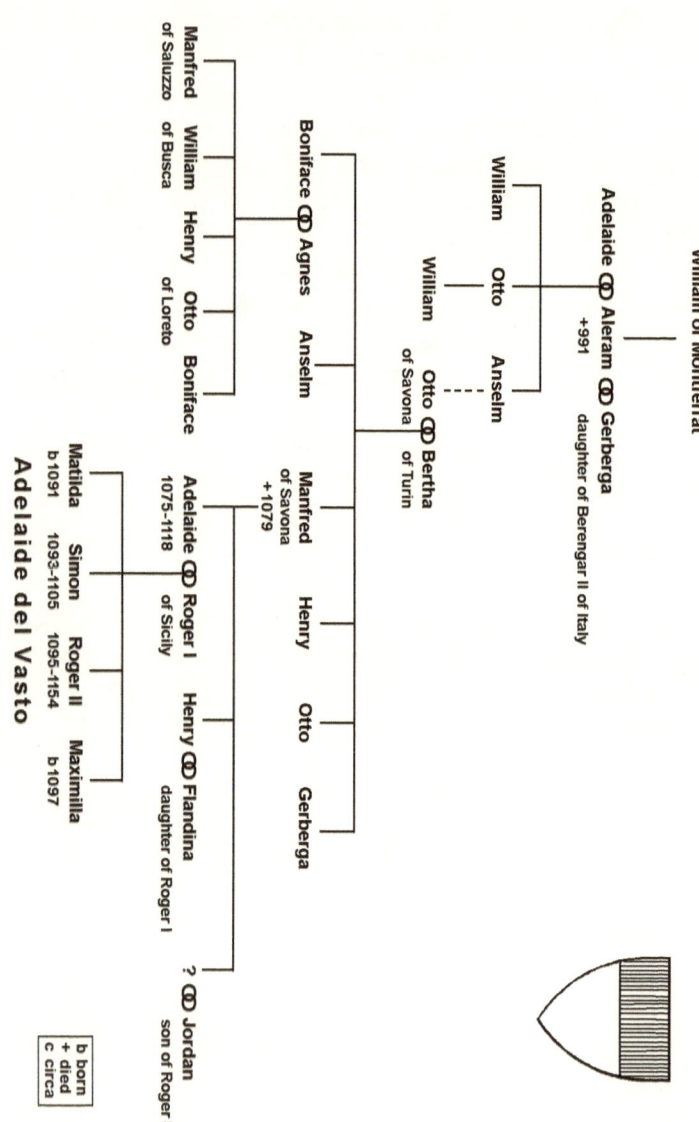

Adelaide del Vasto

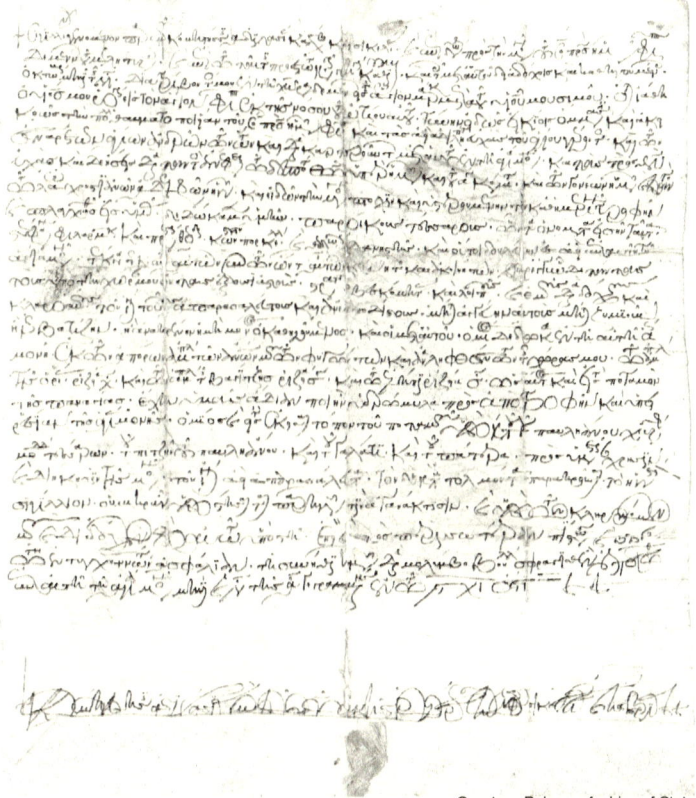

Courtesy Palermo Archive of State

This charter issued by Adelaide in Greek in 1101 cedes four serfs and their families to an Orthodox abbey in the Nebrodian Mountains as a donation in memory of the recovery of her son, Roger, from a severe ear infection. It is one of her first decrees, made just four months after the death of her husband. She made a similar donation for the same miracle in November 1112 around the time Roger II reached the age of majority.

This charter issued by Adelaide in 1109 in Greek and Arabic is the oldest surviving paper document in Italy and one of the oldest in Europe (only Spain has earlier exemplars). The damaged seal may be Adelaide's.

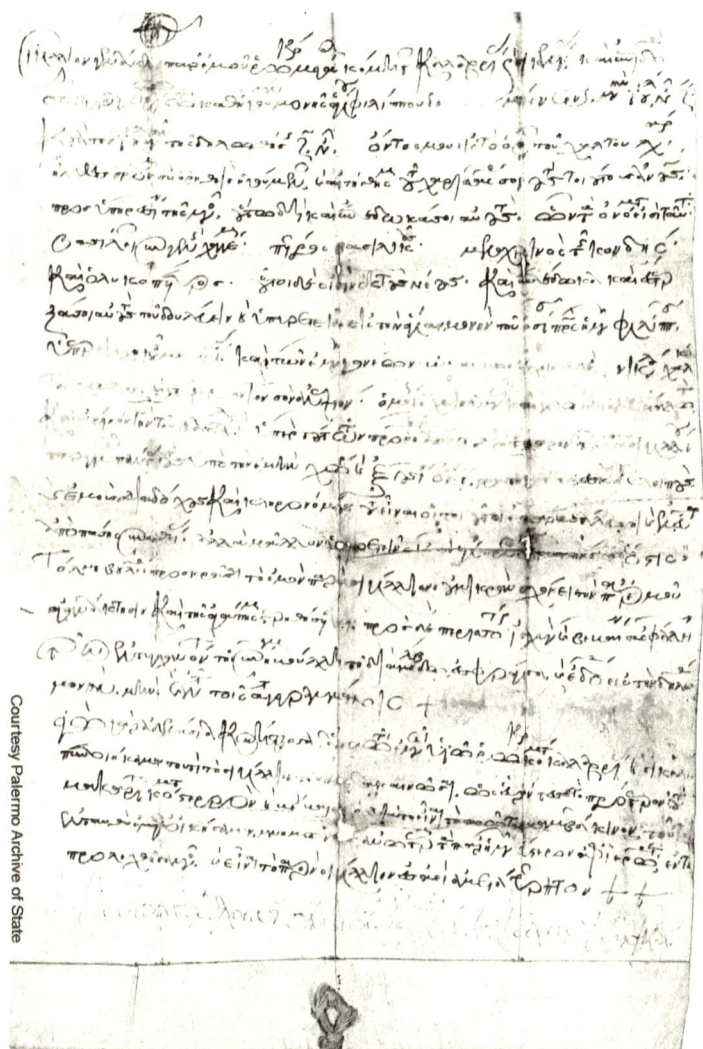

Adelaide issued this charter around 1110 to replace one that her husband had issued a decade earlier.

Adelaide's effigy and modern tomb at Patti

Palermo's royal chapel (now a crypt) in Adelaide's time

Chapter 5
ELVIRA OF CASTILE

Elvira Jiménez of Castile wed Roger II of Sicily in 1117 when she was around seventeen and he was twenty-two. Born in Toledo, she was the daughter of Alfonso VI "the Brave," King of Castile and Leon, by his fourth wife, Isabel, the former Zaida of Seville, a Muslim widow who was previously the monarch's mistress. Isabel was baptized when she wed Alfonso in 1089.[103]

Ancestry

Her mother, Isabel, died while Elvira was still a child. The young Elvira was raised amongst her half-siblings. One of these, her elder half-sister Urraca "the Reckless," succeeded as queen upon Alfonso's death in 1109, being his heiress. Urraca wed her cousin, Alfonso I "the Battler," King of Navarre and Aragon.[104]

Urraca was not too reckless to oversee Elvira's betrothal to Roger, although she probably left the details to her courtiers.[105] Thus began a connection between Sicily and Spain that would last for centuries, bringing the island nearer the Iberian orbit than the Italian one.

Sicily had much in common with the dominions of northern Spain, everything from the climate to the diversity of her peoples. In many ways, twelfth-century Palermo was not too different from the Spanish cities known to Elvira.

By the time Elvira was born at the dawn of the twelfth century, several branches of her father's Jiménez dynasty ruled much of northern Spain, the greenest part of the Iberian peninsula, vying for power with rival dynasties, both Christian and Muslim. The family's roots were Navarrese, and the Jiménez were closely connected to Pamplona, a multicultural city of Christians, Muslims and Jews.

The population of Toledo, Elvira's birthplace, was equally multicultural. Her mother, though christianized, had Arab roots. By now, however, Spanish *convivencia* was becoming ever more tenuous. The Christians were beginning to embrace the idea of the crusade, while the Moors were adopting *jihad*. Important cities like Zaragoza, in Aragon, were under Christian control one moment and Muslim dominion the next. Despite occasional truces like the union of Urraca to her kinsman Alfonso, the Jiménez cousins sometimes found themselves at odds with each other.

Motherhood

Elvira settled easily into her new life in Sicily and in 1118 she gave birth to a son named Roger.[106]

Another son, Tancred, was born the following year.[107] He was followed by Alfonso, who was named for Elvira's own father, in 1120.[108]

William was born in 1121.[109] He was destined to marry another Jiménez, Margaret.[110]

Giving birth, in rapid succession, to four healthy sons fulfilled Elvira's chief conjugal duty. However, she bore at least two more children.

A daughter, Adelaide (or Adelisa), named for Elvira's late mother-in-law, was born around 1127.[111] Henry was born in 1130.[112]

Elvira and Roger had at least one daughter who died in childhood.

Raising her children kept Elvira busy. Founding a family left little time for founding monasteries, and although she certainly passed some delightful months with her husband and children at San Marco d'Alunzio, Elvira was most often to be found at Palermo.

In 1127, William II of Apulia died childless, leaving Roger of Sicily the heir to the peninsular dominions of the Hauteville dynasty. His rapport with his late kinsman had sometimes been a stormy one, but Roger's dynastic rights were clear.[113]

There was initial resistance. Instigated by Pope Honorius II (Lambert Scannabecchi), Rainulf of Alife, the husband of Roger's sister Matilda, led some rebels. Yet the same pontiff soon recognized Roger's rights.

The Amalfitans had to be subdued, and Roger himself went to Apulia to confront other rebels, who swore their fealty to him. Further challenges to his authority would ensue over the next decade. Although the papacy was not yet convinced that a sole Hauteville should be invested with so much power, Anacletus II (Peter Pierleoni), who historians now regard as an antipope, proved sympathetic to Roger.

What Elvira thought about these events is not difficult to infer. Quite simply, she supported her husband and the dynastic rights of her sons. In his territorial ambitions Roger was assisted by George of Antioch, who years earlier had been a protégé of the *amiratus* Christodoulos in the service of his mother, Adelaide. Recent setbacks in northern Africa did not diminish Roger's influence in Italy.

George of Antioch was destined, within a few years, to be named *amiratus amiratorum,* succeeding the late Christodoulos.

To the Greeks this "emir of emirs" was "archon of archons." He would serve his lord well in the years to come.

For now, Roger sought to consolidate his power in a definitive way. He would found a kingdom.

The seed for this idea seems to have been planted by Roger's trusted counsellors, known as *familiares* (they are *archons* in Greek records), and the proponents included his uncle, Henry del Vasto.[114] A meeting of assenting barons[115] was convened at Palermo, where Roger and Elvira were crowned and anointed in Palermo's cathedral on Christmas 1130 by a bishop acting on the authority of Pope Anacletus.

Alexander of Telese described the ceremony and festivities at length, mentioning the silk vestments, plates and goblets of gold and silver, polychrome carpets in the palace, and the "countless" number of subjects that partook of the event.[116]

The girl from Toledo had become the first Queen of Sicily.

Sicilian Queenship

Her day-to-day activities changed little, but Elvira was now part of an elite European sorority, even if a few years were to pass before Anacletus' papal rival recognized the fact. Papal schisms were inconvenient indeed, yet frequent during the Middle Ages. This one left Roger's new royal status recognized by some sovereigns but ignored by others.

Here we see what became the pattern for Sicilian queenship. Based on Norman norms, it was to survive, in some form, into the nineteenth century, forging part of what became the identity of a people.

Coronation was a religious rite celebrated by a bishop. Existing chronicles note that certain queens were anointed with holy oil or chrism during the coronation ceremony. Alexander of Telese mentions anointing specifically, although referring to Roger rather than Elvira.[117] However, a record of a Siculo-

Norman reginal coronation survives.[118] During this ceremony, the queen was invested with regalia, anointed with oil, and then crowned and enthroned.

Rooted in longstanding Christian practice, Sicilian coronations were based chiefly on the "Roman-German pontifical," and the anointing was a normal part of these rites. This may be presumed even where it is not stated explicitly in a surviving chronicle.

Whether anointing itself entailed specific reginal rights and privileges depended on local tradition and law. In multifaith Sicily, for example, there are signs of what reflects, at the very least, a popular perception of the nature of kingship, and hence queenship. An example of this is an icon rendered in mosaic in Palermo's Martorana Church, erected by the faithful *amiratus* George of Antioch for the city's Greek community, depicting Roger, garbed as a Byzantine basileus, crowned directly by Christ, as if his authority to rule emanated from God Himself. Such an idea was not altogether unknown among Christian monarchs, all of whom reigned by divine right, and in Sicily it was enthusiastically embraced in Byzantine (Orthodox) circles as well as Latin (Catholic) ones.

The idea that a queen's anointing, rather than the *entire* coronation rite, entailed specific rights *ipso facto* was not codified in Sicilian law.[119] Nevertheless, anointing conferred a certain status in the eyes of the church. That being said, in the Norman-Swabian Kingdom of Sicily there were never "secular" (non-religious) coronations or quasi-morganatic marriages; those are essentially modern concepts. The nearest thing to this was the presumed marriage of Frederick II to his mistress, Bianca Lancia, who died before she could be crowned, resulting in the subsequent legitimization of their son, Manfred.

Obviously enough, the Sicilian monarchy was younger than those of the other Norman realms, specifically that of England, to which it is often compared. Its fundamental precepts, later expressed in the legal code known as the "Assizes of Ariano," though based on the venerable Code of Justinian, were promulgated only a decade after the coronation of Roger and Elvira.

Although Sicily's monarchy was rooted in Norman practices, albeit subtly colored by Byzantine and Fatimid influences, each of its queens confronted different challenges. In such an environment, what was the paradigm of Sicilian queenship?

The traditional position of a European medieval queen was prescribed by rather rigid practices reflected in such principles as those enshrined in Salic Law. Only rarely did she actually rule in her own right, even when she was the sole child of a king, her father, whom she succeeded. In such a case, the heiress's husband might rule in her name or by his right as her spouse, *jure uxoris*.

In the Norman-Swabian Kingdom of Sicily, the status of Constance, the daughter of Roger II, came closest to that of a true queen regnant. Indeed, some of her charters were issued in her own name and bearing her seal. The charters issued by others, most notably Margaret, in their own names did not usually concern matters of state; an interesting example (discussed later) was a charter she issued following her regency, merely to confirm monastic privileges.

Would that we could define early Sicilian queenship in precise terms that applied satisfactorily to each and every queen. Alas, the facts preclude convenient platitudes and insouciant pronouncements. Instead, we must be guided by context, which is intertwined with the nature and institutions of the Sicilian monarchy. Here an obvious example shall suffice.

Henry II of England and William I of Sicily each ascended his throne the same year, 1154, but the realities faced by the two monarchs and their queens, Eleanor of Aquitaine and Margaret of Navarre, were very different in terms of the economy, law and social practices in general. To cite a single factor, the King of Sicily enjoyed the apostolic legateship, a special status which permitted him to approve, or even appoint, bishops in his realm; the King of England could only envy this prerogative, which might well have obviated some of his own conflicts with ecclesiastical authority.

Sicilian queenship was nothing if not tempestuous, the perfect storm of circumstance, much of it difficult to forecast very reliably or analyze very precisely in retrospect.

Literature and common belief ascribe a certain "mysticism," even spirituality, to the state of a woman being a queen, or even a princess.

Whatever we construe from Roger's image in the Martorana mosaic and in the coinage he issued, the idea that the right to rule emanates from God originated long before the twelfth century, spawning what might be termed a supernatural, philosophical or religious view of kingship and queenship, and of monarchy (and feudalism) in general. While such concepts constitute the undercurrents of European medieval life, they need not be considered at length here except insofar as they conditioned royal power and the interaction of specific queens with their subjects.

It will be seen, for example, that Christian and Muslim views of Sicilian queenship differed somewhat, though not so much as one might intuit. As regents, both Elvira's mother-in-law (Adelaide) and daughter-in-law (Margaret) found themselves ruling a large population of Muslims, with few complexities engendered by that fact so far as we know. Indeed, Sicily's Muslims regarded these women as the guarantors of their most essential rights, which they feared might be usurped by the zealous Norman baronage. It was most often the Christians, not the Muslims or Jews, who challenged reginal authority.

Regalia

What did a Sicilian queen's crown look like?

The only surviving exemplar (shown on this book's front

cover) is that of Constance of Aragon, taken from her tomb. It resembles a kamelaukion.

In the *Liber ad Honorem Augusti,* the illuminated chronicle of Peter of Eboli, a court poet in the early years of the thirteenth century, the reginal crowns are quite similar to those of Roger II (visible in a noteworthy mosaic in the Martorana church) and his grandson, William II (seen in a mosaic in Monreale). Such drawings are generally consistent with other artistic references, though they differ from the representations seen on some seals and coins.

These Byzantine-style crowns were formed of a series of flat plates joined by hinges and mounted into a circular rim. (Though it is somewhat more representational than literal, the drawing on this book's title page was inspired by some renderings in Peter's chronicle.)

The crowns of Sicilian kings and queens shown in Peter's book are strikingly similar to the squarish imperial crowns worn by emperors and empresses in the *Historia Bizantina* completed by John Skylitzes some fifty years earlier.[120]

Into the thirteenth century, the court called upon Greek goldsmiths to create crowns and jewelry. In bringing these projects to fruition, it is no surprise that the Greek masters would be influenced by the same Byzantine traditions and methods that had shaped their profession for centuries, hence the distinctive kamelaukion of Constance of Aragon. Constance probably had several crowns, and it is quite possible that one or more of the others resembled the king's crown, being made of plates.

The design of the Sicilian crowns depicted by Peter of Eboli was not by any means unique. The *reichskrone* used at the coronations of most of the Kings of the Romans since the eleventh century has a similar construction, consisting of eight plates. Its preservation in the collection of the Hofburg in Vienna is fortuitous, for most medieval crowns were eventually smelted for their precious metal. With the obvious exception of the crown of Constance of Aragon, most Sicilian regalia was stolen from tombs centuries ago.

Although it is not, strictly speaking, regalia, the gold reliquary pendant of Queen Margaret is one of the most important personal possessions of a Sicilian queen to survive from the Norman era. There are also a few of Constance's rings bearing gemstones.

Queen Elvira

Following the coronation, King Roger II had to send troops led by George of Antioch to peninsular Italy to suppress another revolt by the Amalfitans, who refused to cede the castles in their region to royal authority. This was resolved but other vassals continued to rebel. Among them was Roger's brother-in-law, Rainulf of Alife. Matilda, Rainulf's consort, had sought the king's protection from an abusive husband.[121]

In May 1132, Roger himself led an army to the mainland. The king ended up fighting a series of battles across southern Italy, from Campania to Apulia. Grimoald Alferanites, a Byzantine leader who had seized power at Bari, surrendered to royal authority following a three-week siege. At Nocera, however, the monarch and his knights were forced to retreat.

Back in Palermo, Elvira was Roger's effective surrogate, even if daily administration was handled by the *familiares* and other courtiers. Her eldest son, Roger, now fourteen years old, was on the mainland with his father learning the craft of war firsthand.

With Grimoald dead and Rainulf swearing vassalage, the king returned to Sicily in August of 1134. Onerous as his expedition had been, it brought southern Italy firmly under his control, at least for now. Nevertheless, Pope Innocent II (Gregory Papareschi), in opposition to Pope Anacletus II, still refused to recognize Roger as king.

King Roger invested his eldest son, Roger, the heir apparent, as Duke of Apulia.

The next tangible attempt to undermine the king's authority would come from Lothair II, the Holy Roman Emperor, an ally of Pope Innocent, supported by John II Comnenus of Constantinople, who was eyeing Bari now that Grimoald was gone. Rainulf of Alife had already solicited Lothair's military support, but the emperor was not immediately prepared to provide it. The conflict with Lothair was thus still a few years away.

In Palermo, Roger fell ill late in the year. His illness seems to have been contagious, infecting the queen. Elvira died on Wednesday, the sixth of February in 1135.[122]

Her funeral was held in Palermo's cathedral. The entire city mourned her passing. The woman Alexander of Telese described as "devout and generous" was entombed in the chapel she founded, dedicated to Mary Magdalene in the cathedral.[123]

Roger's despair was palpable. His love for Elvira had been a true one.

So inconsolable was the king that he refused to leave the palace for months. This fostered the rumor that he was dead. For the next four months, he suffered what seems to have been a severe depression.

In an age of expedient dynastic unions, the marriage of Elvira and Roger was that rarest of rarities, a love match.

Interregnum

When she died, Elvira was just thirty-five, young even by the standards of her era. Her youngest child, Henry, was five.

In the coming years, Roger, now a widower, saw no reason to remarry. He had enough sons to ensure the succession, and they had no real need for a young stepmother.

Indeed, fifteen years were to pass before the king took another wife. The effect of this was that the Kingdom of Sicily, the *Regnum Siciliae*, lacked a queen.

This was the beginning of a reginal "interregnum."[124] To the extent that this was problematic, it was so because the populace of Palermo no longer had any occasion to see their queen, or even a princess of the royal family. The best they could hope for was a glimpse of one of Elvira's ladies-in-waiting visiting one of the city's souks. Adelaide, the daughter of Elvira and Roger, was barely ten years old, and she would soon be betrothed to a count in central Italy.

The presumption that King Roger was dead encouraged Rainulf of Alife and others on the mainland to again rebel against royal authority, now presumably vested in his eldest son, Roger. This was especially disturbing because these men had sworn fealty to the sovereign. Initially, the revolts were suppressed by the king's military forces, led by Warren (Guarin) the chancellor and John the *amiratus*, his governors for Campania and Calabria.

The king himself returned to the peninsula in early June 1135 to suppress the disloyal vassals. The next few years found the sovereign combating his detractors in southern Italy, where the rebels were aided by Emperor Lothair II, who led an invasion supported by Pope Innocent II.

In August of 1135, the king's two eldest sons, Roger and Tancred, were knighted. As his heirs, the former was already Duke of Apulia, and the latter was made Prince of Bari and Taranto.

Roger did not forget to reward those who had been loyal to Elvira. In a royal charter issued in April of 1136, the monarch granted to Adeline, the wet nurse of his son Henry, some land and serfs near the fortified town of Vicari.[125]

Tragically, Tancred, Prince of Bari and Taranto, died in 1138.

Law

By 1140, Anacletus II, the antipope, was dead and Innocent II had recognized Roger's status as king. A new coin, the *ducat,* reflected Roger's royal authority over the *duchy* of Apulia.

At Ariano, Roger promulgated a legal code, the "constitutions," that would unite his lands and his subjects. The two surviving codices of these *Assizes of Ariano* (see Appendix 1) were rediscovered only in the nineteenth century, and the chronicler Falco of Benevento, never a Norman apologist, famously mentioned Roger's introduction of the unpopular ducat at Ariano while ignoring the new legal code.[126]

Since the Normans' arrival, Sicily's legal system was essentially a patchwork of disparate codes, ranging from the feudal to the religious. Justice was uneven, if not arbitrary. Each citizen was judged by her own religion: Canon law, Maliki law, Halakha law. For the barons, there was Justinian's *Codex Juris Civilis* but also the Lombards' *Codex Legum Longobardorum*. What was needed was a legal code that could be applied universally without undue complexity or subjectivity, in the process bolstering centralized government whilst making the law essentially the same for everybody.

Apart from the legal principles themselves, clearly inspired by the Code of Justinian, this code asserted the king's role as lawgiver.

All subjects were equal in the eyes of the law, even if a few were "more equal than others." This was a European kingdom, after all, so justice was weighted in favour of the nobility and the Catholic Church. Barons and bishops could still mistreat almost everybody else, usually with impunity, but even *they* might be called to account for their actions every now and then.

Various offenses were addressed, particularly violent ones.

Arming a mob, thereby inciting riots, was a grave act. Bishops, like nobles, were accorded certain privileges. Among Christians, apostates and heretics lost their rights of citizenship *ipso facto*.

Rape was outlawed, though chiefly for nuns and virgins.[127] Treason was made a capital offense, Jews were forbidden the holding of Christian serfs, jesters were prohibited from blaspheming, simony was made illegal, fugitives were permitted asylum in churches. Sentences for crimes against public officials were to be taken seriously, taking into account that these acts were, in effect, affronts to the monarch himself.

The forgery and theft of documents were unequivocally capital crimes. Counterfeiting or clipping coins was outlawed. Royal approval was required for men born outside the nobility to become knights, judges and notaries. Infringement of royal estates was outlawed. Marriage was required as the basis for legitimacy of heirs. Adultery and prostitution were addressed, likewise kidnapping and robbery. Licensing of physicians was established. Overt corruption was not to be tolerated; judges who accepted bribes could be executed.

Many of these principles were already known, some from the time of Justinian, but Roger made them the law of the land.

The legal position of queens regent and consort was not addressed explicitly.

In such fields as commerce, we also find among the Arabs of Norman Sicily the application of an early form of common law, which soon vanished in Italy but survived in England. This reflects Muslim influences.[128]

Although the ecclesiastical point of reference of the Assizes was papal, Nilos Doxopatrios, an Orthodox cleric who arrived at Palermo about 1142, wrote a theological treatise expounding upon the traditions and prerogatives of the Orthodox Church.[129]

Heirs

The new legal code was not perfect, and neither was the king who issued it. However great his affection for Elvira, Roger was known to father children outside marriage. Around 1130 a bastard son named Simon was born; this boy was eventually made Prince of Taranto.

Around 1138, young Roger, Duke of Apulia, followed suit, fathering an illegitimate son, Tancred, with Emma, daughter of the Count of Lecce, whilst married to Elizabeth of Champagne.

Both Simon and Tancred were destined to play a role in the Kingdom of Sicily.

Elvira's thirdborn son, Alfonso, who was now Prince of Capua and Duke of Naples, died in 1144. Henry, her second son, died the following year.

The Second Crusade began in 1147, and Roger exploited this opportunity to attack the lands of the Byzantine Empire. Led by George of Antioch, this campaign was successful in bringing some Aegean territories under Sicilian rule. It was followed by conquests on the African coast in what are now Tunisia and Libya; this was not Roger's first incursion into that region. Successful as these exploits were, the king had problems closer to home.

The heir apparent, Roger, Duke of Apulia, died in the spring of 1148 (though the year is disputed), survived by his illegitimate son, Tancred of Lecce, but no legitimate heirs.[130]

This left William, Elvira's youngest son, as the sole heir in the line of succession. Until now, William had enjoyed a life of hunting, gaming and wenching. Now he was betrothed to Elvira's cousin, Margaret Jiménez, daughter of the King of Navarre.[131]

The dearth of legitimate heirs was a potentially dire predicament. Confronted with this, Roger decided to take a second wife who, it was hoped, might bear a few sons.

ELVIRA OF CASTILE

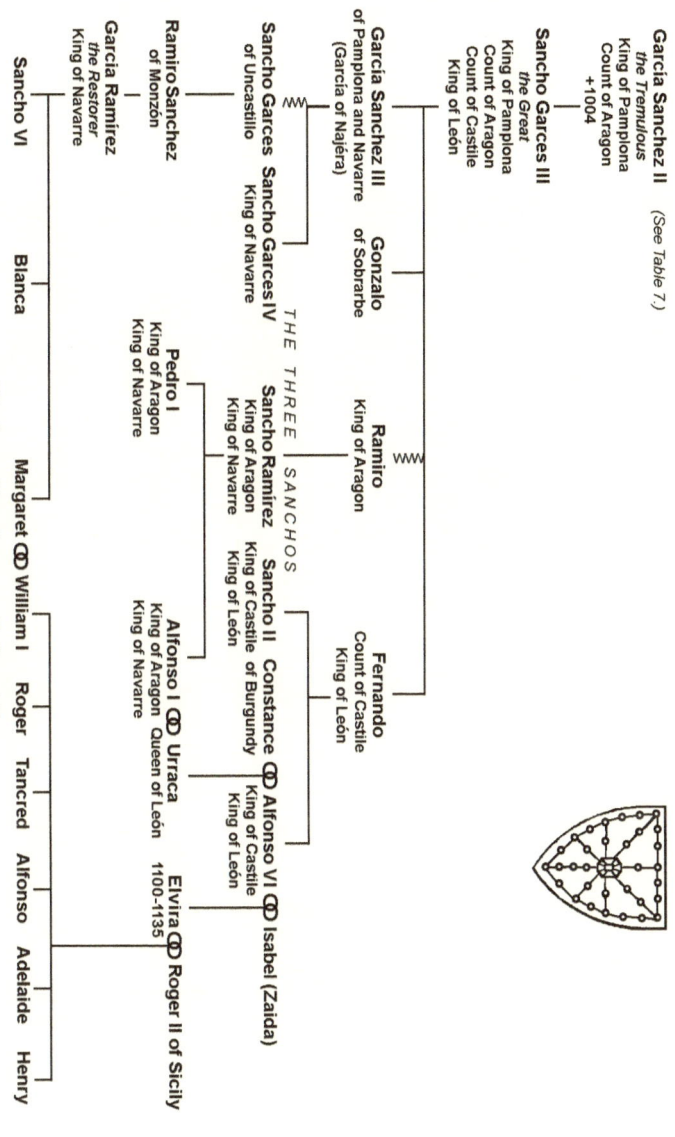

Elvira Jiménez of Castile

Courtesy Burgerbibliothek, Bern

Constance in the chronicle of Peter of Eboli, depicted wearing the crown that inspired the drawing on this book's title page. She holds Frederick II.

The chronicle of Peter of Eboli shows Elvira, Sibylla, Beatrice and Constance wearing the same type of Byzantine crown

Courtesy Biblioteca Nacional, Madrid

Sicilian coronations were similar to this one depicted in the Historia Bizantina, likely copied in Sicily when Elvira was queen. Even the crowns were similar.

Roger II depicted as a Byzantine basileus crowned by Christ in engraving based on mosaic in Martorana church, Palermo

Zaida (Isabel), thought to have been the mother of Elvira of Castile, was born at Seville. The Alcazar, though erected later, evokes the atmosphere of the city Zaida knew as a girl.

Chapter 6
SIBYLLA OF BURGUNDY

Sibylla of Burgundy was born in 1126 to Hugh II, Duke of Burgundy, and his consort, Felicia Matilda of Mayenne, possibly at Autun. A "middle child," she was the ninth of twelve children born to the couple. The first, Aigeline, was born in 1116, the last, Aremburge, in 1132. Sibylla was named for her patrilineal grandmother, who was of the same dynasty.

Ancestry

Sibylla's natal family was an illustrious one. Here were not rustic nobles or arrivistes but a cadet branch of the House of Capet, the ruling dynasty of France. Whilst Roger was erecting Sicily and southern Italy into a united kingdom, one of Sibylla's kinsmen was doing the same for Portugal, annexing sundry Iberian lands seized from the Almoravids to forge a nation and an identity that survive to this day.

For the first King of Sicily, the wider political advantages of the union were overwhelmingly obvious. Sibylla's immediate family, though based in southeastern France near what was then Swabia, boasted dynastic connections around Europe. At one point, they controlled more of what is now France than their Capetian kinsman, who was its king.

As she neared adulthood, the inception of which would have been the age of about fifteen years, the young woman could not have been ignorant of her family's importance. Her father's first cousin, Alfonso, had ruled Portugal as its count since Sibylla was just two years old, becoming its king in 1139. However, although she was raised on stories of his conquests, there is no evidence that Sibylla ever visited Portugal.

If Sibylla was betrothed "late" at the age of twenty-two, it may have been because her family had to arrange marriages for so many children, even though several eventually entered the religious life. It may even be that Sibylla herself initially chose to take vows and live in a nunnery a few years before Roger sought her hand.

One thing is certain. Sibylla of Burgundy was a true princess, and a suitable consort for any king.

Wife, Queen, Mother

When Hugh II died in 1143, he was succeeded by his son, Odo II, Sibylla's eldest brother, sometimes known as Eudes. It was Odo who undertook the betrothal of Sibylla to Roger II. The nuptials took place in Palermo late in 1148.[132]

By then, Roger had but one surviving legitimate son, William, who was about to wed Margaret of Navarre, thus providing the jovial Palermitans two royal wedding feasts in one year's time. It was no secret that the King of Sicily needed more male heirs, preferably legitimate ones, if the Hauteville line were to survive. Were his other legitimate sons still living, Roger, who had been a widower for many years, might never have remarried. The women of his harem offered him more than sufficient companionship and affection.[133]

At twenty-two, Sibylla was no child bride, and she must

have understood her marital duties. To Margaret, she would have seemed like an elder sister. Yet the two women could not have come to know each other very well, for Roger sometimes took Sibylla with him to peninsular Italy, leaving William to tend to royal administration in Palermo.

Little is known of the details of her betrothal to Roger, but Sibylla may have been the first Sicilian queen to receive lands in the *Regnum Siciliae* as part of her dower.

It wasn't long before Sibylla was pregnant.

In late July 1149, Eleanor of Aquitaine, the consort of King Louis VII of France, called at Palermo *en route* to her dominions whilst returning from the ill-fated Second Crusade. Her ship had been blown off course toward Africa whilst her husband's galley made it to peninsular Italy. Eleanor, who was ill, stayed in the capital for about a fortnight before traveling with Roger to Messina, thence to Lucania to meet Louis. (See note 446.)

Meanwhile, King Roger's second wife gave birth to a son, christened Henry, on the twenty-ninth of August. Sadly, the boy died early the next year.

By then, Sibylla was pregnant with another son. Most of this pregnancy was without incident. Then, near Salerno, the queen seems to have gone into labor prematurely, and this child was stillborn on September sixteenth 1150. Shortly thereafter, on the nineteenth, Sibylla died of complications from childbirth.[134]

She was entombed in the stately church of the Benedictine abbey of Cava nearby.[135]

It has been conjectured that Sibylla did indeed give birth to a child who survived infancy, a daughter who may have been Henry's fraternal twin, though the evidence for this is sparse.[136]

Sibylla's death, along with the loss of two infant sons in one year, was a sobering experience for Roger, but he did not spend long grieving in reclusion as he did following the death of

Elvira. Concerned about the succession, he crowned his heir, William, already Duke of Apulia, *rex filius* on Easter in 1151. Margaret was crowned with him.

This was an act of pure pragmatism. Though strongly identified with the Normans, the practice of crowning a son king during his father's lifetime was not unknown elsewhere in western Europe. Its purpose was to ensure that there would be no subsequent contestations, or at least none that were credible, regarding the heir apparent's right to rule.

Margaret of Navarre thus became Queen of Sicily, albeit in a largely symbolic sense, as her husband, William, was not yet a regnant sovereign but rather a "king-in-waiting." This made Margaret a "queen-in-waiting." Nonetheless, in view of Sibylla's untimely death Margaret was, for the moment at least, the only queen the Sicilians knew. By the end of the year, she was expecting her first child.

Meanwhile Roger, wishing to leave nothing to chance, took a third wife. Margaret's monopoly on Sicilian queenship had lasted but a few months. She would get another chance eventually, but for now she had to patiently wait her turn.

SIBYLLA OF BURGUNDY

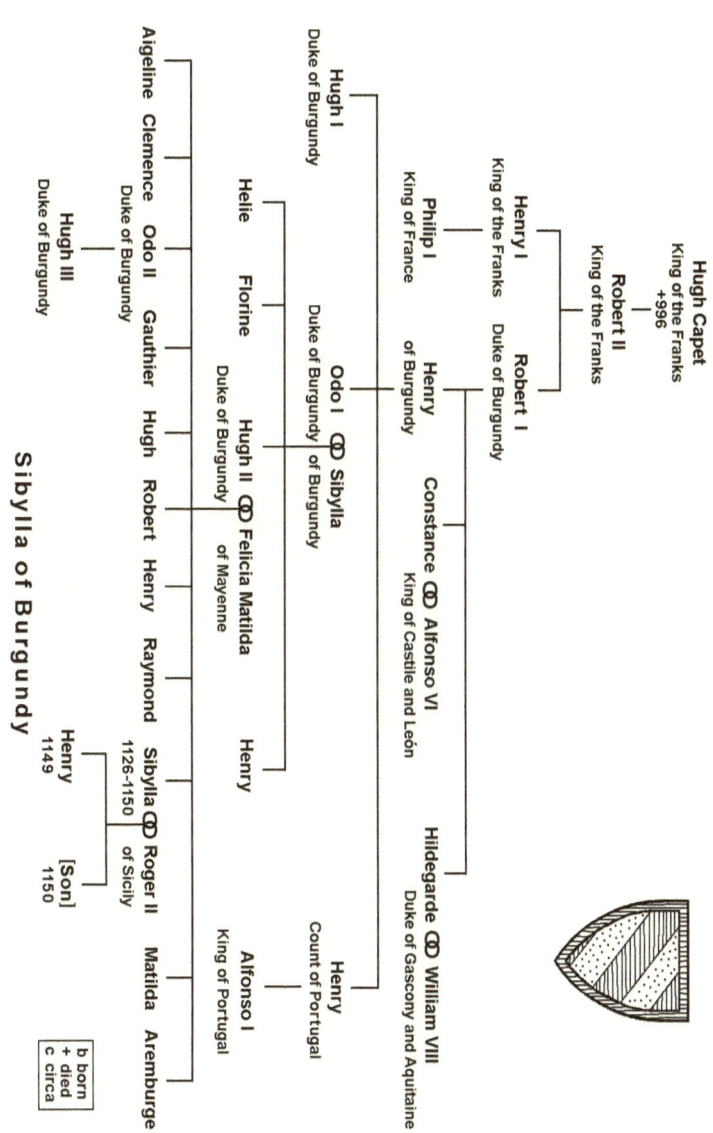

Sibylla was familiar with trilingual Greek-Latin-Arabic psalters such as the Harley Psalter (composed before 1153 in Palermo) used during mass in the royal chapel.

Apse and cupola of the Palatine Chapel

Martorana tower and Saint Cathaldus

Saint Cathaldus nave and apse

Chapter 7
BEATRICE OF RETHEL

Beatrice of Vitry of Rethel was born around 1132, the eldest of at least six children of Guitier of Rethel and his wife Beatrice of Namur.[137] Rethel was a forested feudal dominion in the Ardennes region straddling France and Belgium, bordering Namur. The charming town of Rethel, where Beatrice was raised, sits along the banks of the Aisne River.[138]

Ancestry

Beatrice's father, Guitier (Gunther, Ithier or Witer), was the son of Odo of Vitry and Matilda of Rethel. Little is known of Odo's lineage. As castellan of Vitry, to the south of Rethel beyond Reims, he was not exceedingly wealthy in his own right, but his wife, Matilda, was the sister of King Baldwin II of Jerusalem. Her family had held Rethel since the last years of the tenth century.[139] Clearly, Odo's social rank was not nearly equal to that of his wife.

Matilda herself came into possession of Rethel upon the death of her brother, Gervais, in 1124, when Baldwin showed no inclination to trek to the Ardennes from Palestine to claim it.

Odo and Matilda had four children but Guitier, as their only son, was their feudal heir.

Guitier thus inherited the county of Rethel from his mother's family. During Beatrice's childhood, however, her father had not yet succeeded to the lordship of Rethel, which was still held jointly by his parents, Odo and Matilda.

Queenhood

We know of no political motivation on the part of the Sicilian court for the marriage between Beatrice and Roger II. The sole purpose for the maiden's marriage to him was to provide an heir. Nonetheless, Guitier is unlikely to have lamented the fact that his daughter was marrying a powerful monarch.

The betrothal of Beatrice to Roger was undertaken early in 1151. The wedding was celebrated in Palermo on the nineteenth of September. Beatrice was around nineteen years old, marrying a man old enough to be her father.

The surviving manuscript of the chronicle of Peter of Eboli shows an illumination of Roger and Beatrice riding separate horses. The queen is depicted with light brown hair and wearing a Byzantine crown similar to her husband's.

Roger was still preoccupied with fathering a son, but not long after his wedding to Beatrice his daughter-in-law, Margaret, who was just two or three years younger than the new queen, gave birth to a boy christened Roger. This bolstered Margaret's prestige but did nothing for that of Beatrice. Strictly speaking, both women were queens yet only one had produced an heir to the throne.

Virtually nothing is known of Beatrice's rapport with Margaret, but they were destined to coexist in Sicily for decades. If they viewed each other as rivals, there is no surviving evidence of it.

Motherhood

It is possible that Beatrice fell pregnant almost immediately. She may have had a miscarriage or two. Roger's frenetic diplomatic and military activities continued, as ever, and these seem to have limited his time with Beatrice in Palermo.

In 1152, Frederick Barbarossa was crowned King of Germany (formally "King of the Romans"), and with this he began eyeing the imperial crown. By the Treaty of Konstanz negotiated with Pope Eugene III (Bernardo Pignatelli da Pisa) in March of the following year, he promised to support the papacy at all costs, even if it led to war with the King of Sicily. Although Roger had bolstered Eugene's position in the past, even sending his chancellor Robert of Selby to suppress a rebellion in Rome in 1149 so he could return after having been expelled by the citizenry, the pontiff again found himself exiled from the city; Frederick now offered to suppress the rebels. Pope Eugene's death in July 1153 did not quell Barbarossa's ambition to invade southern Italy. The pontificate of Eugene's successor, Anastasius IV (Corrado Demetri della Suburra), was brief, ending in late 1154.

Widowhood

Beatrice was nearly a month pregnant when Roger died in February 1154 at the age of fifty-eight. On November second she gave birth to a red-haired daughter named Constance.

By then, William was King of Sicily, with Margaret as queen consort, having been re-crowned on Easter. This left Beatrice as "queen dowager."[140]

The death of the first King of Sicily signalled the end of an era. William showed little of the sagacity or pragmatism of his father, and before long Roger's wisest advisors, perhaps feeling unappreciated, departed the court. Notable among the emigrés were the Englishman Thomas Brun, accorded the title *caïd* by Sicily's Arabs, who returned to the land of his birth to serve in the exchequer of King Henry II, and Abdullah al Idrisi, the court geographer.

Beatrice chose not to remarry, remaining instead in Sicily to raise her daughter.

Though frequently present in Palermo, Beatrice spent much time at the Hauteville castle in San Marco d'Alunzio, far from court intrigues and baronial unrest. Did she ever seek the companionship of a lover? We do not know.

She seems to have avoided public life. There is virtually no mention of her in chronicles or charters for the remainder of her days. A rare exception is her name appearing in a letter sent by Pope Alexander III (Rolando Bandinelli) in 1170 to Henry of France, Archbishop of Reims, ordering the prelate to act in favor of Stephen of Rethel, the cathedral's rector, who was Beatrice's nephew. Stephen had appealed to his aunt to ask the pontiff to intervene on his behalf.

In the event, an isolated case of her helping a kinsman is scarcely sufficient for us to judge the queen a "power player."

For a number of years, Beatrice's daughter, Constance, lived the celibate life until she was called upon to wed an imperial heir to seal the peace of the *Regnum Siciliae* with the Holy Roman Empire. In 1184, Constance, whose story awaits us in a later chapter, was betrothed to Henry Hohenstaufen, a son of Frederick Barbarossa. She and Henry were wed, and crowned, in Milan the following year.

Beatrice died on March thirty-first in 1185.[141] In death, she was placed in the Magdalene chapel of Palermo's cathedral alongside Elvira, but as construction soon began on a new basilica she was removed to the church of the same name nearby.[142]

BEATRICE OF RETHEL

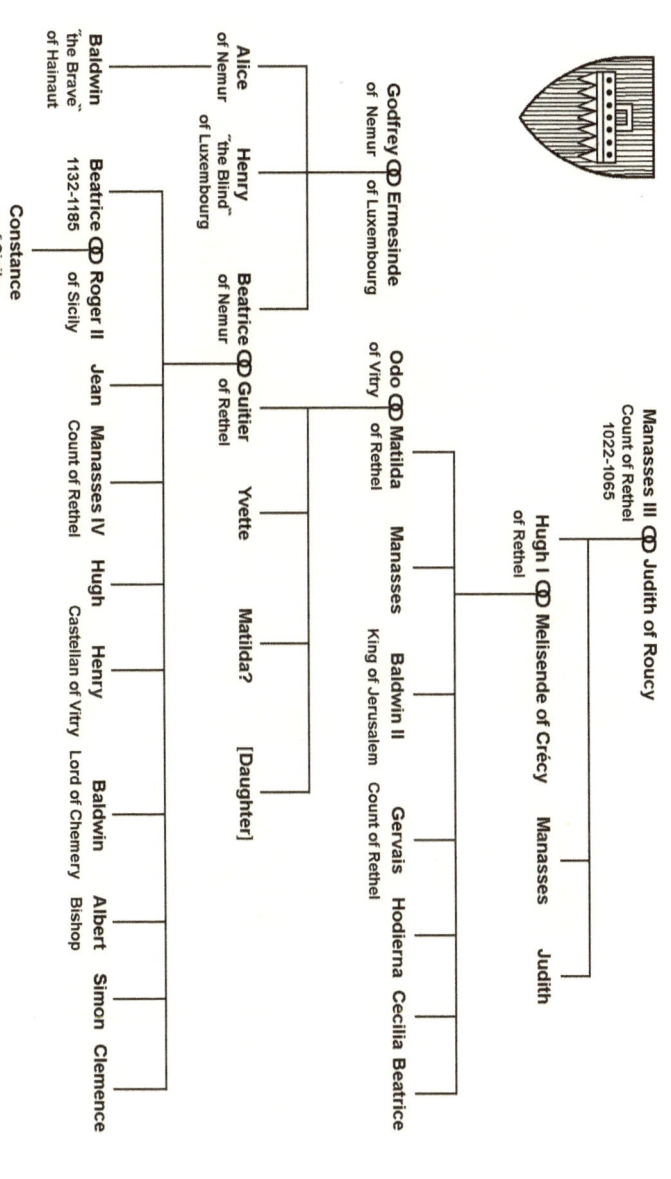

Beatrice of Rethel

Medieval Sicilian languages in a Norman tombstone dated 1148 (Latin, Hebrew, Greek, Arabic) displayed in the Zisa Palace (Palermo): the polyglot linguistic heritage of Sicily under the Normans and Swabians

Pisan Tower of the Norman Palace

Cloister of Saint John of the Hermits, a Benedictine monastery

At her coronation, Beatrice of Rethel was anointed with a gold spoon similar to this one used in Norman England

Chapter 8
MARGARET OF NAVARRE

Margaret Jiménez of Navarre, the youngest of three siblings, was born in 1135 at La Guardia, a small, high, fortified town overlooking the verdant valleys of La Rioja, a region known today for its robust red wine and reddish soil.[143] Her father, García Ramírez, had nearly finished restoring Navarre to its rightful position as a sovereign kingdom on a parity with her jealous neighbors Aragon and Castile, a status which it had been denied for decades.[144] For this his countrymen accorded García the flattering appellation "the Restorer."[145] Thus young Margaret's mother, a Norman lady named Margaret of l'Aigle, as the spouse of a triumphant warrior king, became a queen consort. In fact, her dowry, which included the prosperous multiconfessional town of Tudela, contributed much to her ambitious husband's consolidation of Navarre.[146]

The royal family was soon acclaimed at Pamplona, Navarre's historical capital, where they took up residence in a dilapidated castle in need of restoration. It was at Pamplona that Margaret, the future Queen of Sicily, spent her childhood.

Little is known of the youth of Margaret and her siblings, Sancho and Blanca, but with their father's accession to kingship they became royalty destined to marry royally. Margaret's story bequeaths us a very special treasure. Thanks to the survival of two detailed chronicles written by men present at the Sicilian court, we know far more about Margaret of Navarre than we do about any other Sicilian queen considered in these pages (therefore what follows is this book's lengthiest chapter).

Unlike any other queen of the High Middle Ages in what is now Italy, Margaret, as regent, emerged as the most powerful woman in Europe and the Mediterranean. In a land of intrepid women, she is the quintessential queen. Her legacy is a tangible one, for she has left us the greatest medieval church to be seen in southern Italy: Monreale.

Nonetheless, there was nothing in Margaret's childhood to foreshadow her greatness.

Basque Princess

The Basques of Navarre regarded Margaret and her sister as princesses, as indeed they were, but the Jiménez (or Ximénez) dynasty itself was not Basque; their geographic origin is not precisely known, even though some of their kings are entombed at Nájera, not far from La Guardia. At the dawn of the twelfth century, the extended family controlled most of northern Spain: Navarre, Aragon, Catalonia, Castile, León.[147] Unfortunately, they had spent much time warring among themselves.

The most infamous case of this chronic fratricide was the War of the Three Sanchos, which broke out in 1065 amongst the three Jiménez cousins who ruled Navarre, Aragon and Castile, each monarch named Sancho for the same grandfather, namely Sancho III "the Great" of Pamplona. This bizarre conflict was rooted in disputes over the empire left by Sancho III to his sons upon his death three decades earlier.

García Ramírez was born into a comparatively poor, illegitimate branch of the Jiménez family, his father's father having been born outside marriage.

Unfortunately, García's father, Ramiro, died too soon to offer much to the young, ambitious knight, who had to literally fight to carve out a niche for himself.

García Ramírez was not the first of his ancestors to establish his reputation on the battlefield. His mother's father was none other than Rodrigo Diaz of Vivar, known to posterity as *El Cid,* who fought for Castile in the War of the Three Sanchos and from whom young García seems to have inherited much of his warrior spirit.[148] This served him well.

As we have seen, Margaret was a distant cousin of Elvira of Castile, the Jiménez princess who had wed Roger II of Sicily.

Margaret's first language, which her mother spoke to her, was Norman French. The l'Aigle lands of her mother's father (Gilbert) were in lower Normandy, and the Perche family of her mother's mother (Juliana) held lands in a county that straddled the regions of Normandy and Maine. Margaret was schooled in Latin and she probably spoke some Basque, which was unrelated to these other languages. The aristocratic vernacular of her homeland was Navarro-Aragonese. She certainly heard Arabic, but we do not know that she learned to speak much of it before coming to Sicily.

Childhood

Margaret's childhood was a complicated one.

Her mother, having inherited estates from a Norman uncle, Rotrou of Perche, who had subjugated Tudela and a few other pieces of northeastern Spain, was important in her own right.[149] Margaret of l'Aigle was a remarkable woman whose name appears on several charters, and they reflect what seems to be a faithful rapport with the man she married.

As early as 1135, we find a royal decree confirming the privileges previously granted to Pamplona's diocese, stating that the new sovereign is acting *cum consilio et auctoritate uxoris mee Margarite regine,* "on the advice and with the consent of my wife Queen Margaret."[150]

A similar formula appears in several subsequent decrees. Of particular note is a charter relative to the city of Tudela.[151] Issued in 1138, it assigns to the Bishop of Pamplona the Church of Saint Mary at Tudela, "with all the assets therein appertaining to Moors and Christians."[152]

Although she was a politically astute force whose influence was key to her husband's success, Margaret of l'Aigle is all but ignored by historians, perhaps for a bitterly unpleasant incident that poisoned her marriage.

Even after the restoration of the Kingdom of Navarre, García Ramírez often found himself traveling around the realm and beyond. True, most medieval monarchs had to constantly reinforce their authority, but King García also had kinsmen who were trying to encroach upon Navarre's borders.

Fortunately, the king had a wife who could oversee matters in Pamplona during his absences. Unfortunately, about the year 1139, he returned from one of his trips around the kingdom to find her pregnant with another man's son. This boy was christened Rodrigo in honor of the glorious *Cid,* even though that great knight was not, in reality, the child's ancestor. Rodrigo's illegitimacy was never much of a secret. He was effectively disinherited by García.[153]

Yet Rodrigo remained close to his half-sister, Margaret, and was destined to play a role in Sicilian history.

Writing about him at the Sicilian court a few decades later, the chronicler Romuald of Salerno described Rodrigo, who the Sicilians took to calling "Henry," simply as *Henricus naturalis frater,* "Henry the natural brother" of Margaret of Navarre.

The words of Hugh Falcandus were more venomous: *Rex navarrorum nunquam filium suum vel esse credidit vel dici voluit, indignum existimans eum quem mater multorum patens libidini vulgo concepisset, regis filium appellari.* "The King of Navarre never considered him his son, nor did he wish him to be called such, for it would be disgraceful if this boy conceived by a woman notorious for her sexual liaisons with various men were identified as the son of a king."[154]

To justify this unflattering comment, Falcandus further explains that the information was provided by the Navarrese who accompanied Rodrigo to Sicily.[155] Of Rodrigo's name, Falcandus reports that *Roderic* was "abhorrent, derided by the Sicilians as unknown and barbaric, so the queen decided that he should be called Henry."[156]

Margaret of l'Aigle did not have to bear her disgrace for very long. She died in May 1141.[157] Whatever her foibles may have been in life, in death her funeral in Pamplona's splendid cathedral was one befitting a queen. The celebrant was Bishop Sancho, the same man who had crowned her six years earlier.

In June 1144 García Ramírez took as his second wife Urraca, who was only twelve. She was the illegitimate daughter of his ally King Alfonso VII of Castile. This union was meant to resolve a short-lived but potentially catastrophic conflict with Alfonso. The marriage, happy or not, would strengthen the bonds between Navarre and Castile.[158]

Urraca[159] was about the same age as Blanca, so the young bride was hardly a "stepmother" to the daughters of King García Ramírez. They may not have been too accepting of a very young woman who they probably perceived more as a sister than their father's wife. Some semblance of such attitudes existed even in the twelfth century.

Another complexity was Urraca's social, and even dynastic, position. Because this girl was now queen, Blanca and Margaret had to defer to her rank and status. Much had changed since the death of the mother of the two young sisters just a few years earlier.

For Sancho, as heir apparent, the new situation was less severe. Whatever he thought of Urraca, or she of him, his dynastic position was assured. At this point in his young life, he was already being taught about geography and politics, as well as the importance of dynastic marriages arranged with both in mind.[160]

In truth, we know virtually nothing about the intricacies of the relationship of Blanca and Margaret with their father's second wife, who eventually gave birth to a daughter.

Though remarried, García Ramírez had not put his first wife completely out of his mind. In August 1145, he seized a synagogue at Estella (Lizarra) which was to be converted into a church that would be ceded to Pamplona's diocese in memory of the late queen, *pro anima uxoris Margarite regine,* as well as the souls of himself and his entire family.[161]

Blanca and Margaret saw their father only rarely during these years. Ever the warrior king, he occupied Tauste in 1146. Though located very near the border, it was claimed by Aragon, and García's father-in-law, Alfonso of Castile, intervened to negotiate an immediate end to what might have sparked a war between Navarre and Aragon.

A few towns in La Rioja, on the southern fringe of Navarre, had already been lost to Castile. Although none were very important economically, at least two had sentimental value. The Jiménez kings rested at Nájera, and García's daughters were born at La Guardia. Nevertheless, García Ramírez had consolidated his power and re-established a kingdom. Navarre was finally at peace with her neighbors, at least for now.

Betrothal

The Kingdom of Pamplona, as it was still known officially, was beginning to attract the attention of kings further afield, and it was time to find suitable husbands for the Jiménez sisters.

Here age conferred precedence. Negotiations began for Blanca to marry into the family that ruled Catalonia from Barcelona on the other side of Aragon, a dynastic union meant to neutralize the more zealous machinations that emanated from Zaragoza every now and then.[162]

Late in 1148 there arrived at Pamplona several noblemen and a bishop sent from Palermo by Roger II, the King of Sicily.

The Sicilian ambassadors were seeking the betrothal of Margaret to King Roger's son. One imagines the heart of the young princess being filled by equal parts of exhilaration and apprehension.

Rotrou of Perche had died too soon to be involved in the marriage negotiations, although he may have spoken to García Ramírez about the possibility of one of the girls marrying into a Norman family, but his son, Margaret's cousin, was to play a role in Sicilian history.[163]

It was proposed that Margaret marry William, who we met in a previous chapter. He was fourteen years her senior.

There was a certain urgency in the wedding arrangements because by this time the Sicilian royal family found itself, rather unexpectedly, with a dearth of heirs to the throne, William's elder brothers having died. Roger now had only one legitimate son and no legitimate grandsons.[164]

The ambassadors wanted to see the girl, and perhaps even speak with her. Was she reasonably intelligent and well-educated? Was she pretty enough to become their queen? Most importantly in view of the dynasty's present predicament, was Margaret of childbearing age?

The precise details of Margaret's betrothal and dower are not known to us, but we do have a well-documented example that offers us some insight into what it was. This is the betrothal of Joanna of England to Margaret's son in 1176.[165] By then, such things had changed very little.

With her father's consent, Margaret was betrothed to William and given a few months to prepare for her voyage to Sicily.

In the late spring of 1149, she said good-bye to her father, sister and elder brother. She would never see them again.

Setting off for Sicily, Margaret was accompanied by a few ladies-in-waiting, a few nobles, a bishop or two, a small company of knights and perhaps two dozen servants and other retainers. In all, there were at least sixty people traveling in Margaret's entourage. A dozen or so were destined to remain with her in Sicily.

Undertaken in early summer, the first leg of the journey (see the map at the end of this chapter) would take them across Aragon and Catalonia to Barcelona, through lands ruled by Christians or friendly Moors. From there, they would follow the coast from Girona, passing Perpignan, Marseille, Toulon and other cities along the French coast. Around Nice, they would board a flotilla of galleys sent by the King of Sicily, for Navarre had no fleet to speak of.

The ships would follow the Italian coast to Naples, and thence to Messina and finally Palermo. This maritime route along the coasts ensured that the travelers were always in friendly waters.

A faster, direct route from Barcelona to Majorca to Sardinia and then Sicily would have entailed a far greater risk of the flotilla encountering pirates. The ships of the Sicilian navy could very effectively respond to such a threat, but there was always the danger of a galley or two being lost. Natural hazards posed another danger. Whilst the Mediterranean was usually serene by May, storms were unpredictable, so it was better to stay fairly near the coast.

At Palermo, where she was acclaimed by ecstatic crowds,

Margaret met the man she was to marry. William had medium brown hair and brown eyes, essentially the same coloring as Margaret.

The wedding was celebrated in the Palatine Chapel of the opulent royal palace, where the couple took up residence.

Norman Palace

Margaret's new home was a palace set on high ground between the city of Palermo to the north and the vast Genoard park to the south. She could see both from the arched windows of her residence on the top floor of one of the stout, square towers.[166] Beyond a cityscape of golden limestone buildings, where the cupolas of stately churches and mosques stood out like the bulbous caps of freshly-sprouted mushrooms, was the azure Tyrrhenian. On the other side, looking past the verdant Genoard, with its trees and streams, Margaret could see rocky mountains.[167] Beyond the mountains were more mountains.

Multicultural Palermo was not unlike the polyglot environment Margaret had known in Pamplona and Tudela. Sicily's landscape, agriculture and cuisine were vaguely similar to Navarre's.[168]

Crowning a hill in Palermo's Halkah district, the palace was fortified, its massive crenelated walls built to withstand an attack from any direction, yet its interior was far more luxurious than any castle Margaret or her Navarrese ladies-in-waiting had ever seen.

There were walls covered with ornate mosaics depicting the peacocks and palm trees of the Genoard. The designs themselves were simple yet sophisticated, combining traditional Byzantine workmanship with Islamic symmetry, so one encountered such elements as twin leopards rendered in profile, facing each other. For the most part, the background of the mosaic designs was a vast sea of gold tiles. One wall of a room used as a kind of throne chamber and office by Margaret's father-in-law was covered in these tiny golden tiles of uniform lustre.[169]

The capitals of the stone columns were carved into ornate Fatimid motifs inspired by local creatures and plants. Here a Sicilian lizard creeping across an acanthus leaf could wind his tail into a knot.

The walls of some rooms, including the royal sleeping quarters, were covered by tapestries of velvet in colors ranging from the deepest crimson to a light pastel green. Silk drapes concealed some of the windows. Oil lamps were suspended from the vaulted ceilings by seemingly endless chains.

Margaret was accustomed to tables made of wood. In Palermo's palace the top of every table was a polychrome field of pieces of inlaid marble formed into unidentifiable yet pleasing motifs. These too were Fatimid. The floors bore some of the same geometrical designs, only larger.

The Muslims at court said that Palermo's palaces and mosques were similar to those of Baghdad and the cities of Andalusia.

The palace had two chapels. The austere older chapel known to Adelaide (see the photograph in Chapter 4), served as the crypt of a newer one built by Margaret's father-in-law.

The newer chapel, where Margaret and William were wed, boasted a wooden muqarnas ceiling replete with painted designs and figures of such things as people playing chess. Spreading his arms across the apse was an imposing icon of Christ Pantocrator rendered in mosaic, similar to another at Cefalù's cathedral up the coast. Here the Byzantine and Fatimid traditions met.[170]

Motherhood

Desperate for more heirs, Margaret's long-widowed father-in-law, King Roger, married a young woman, Sibylla of Burgundy (see Chapter 6), who died in September of 1150, leaving behind no surviving children. William was still Roger's only legitimate heir.[171]

The king then wed Beatrice of Rethel (Chapter 7) in autumn of the following year.

It may be that Roger did not view William as the ideal successor.[172] Nonetheless, the king ensured that he was crowned *rex filius* in April 1151. For a few fleeting months, until Roger's marriage to Beatrice, Margaret was Sicily's only living queen as the consort of the newly-crowned William. This status ended when King Roger wed Beatrice late in 1151.[173] By that time, Margaret had more immediate concerns. She was pregnant with her first child.

Back in Spain, her father had died, leaving her brother as King of Navarre.

Her sister, Blanca, had fared well. After her planned Catalonian marriage failed to materialize, she was wed to Sancho, the son and heir apparent of Alfonso VII of Castile. In order to ensure the succession, Sancho, like Margaret's husband William, had already been crowned, thereby making Blanca a queen consort.

In 1152, Margaret gave birth to a healthy boy christened Roger.

Producing an heir surely enhanced her prestige at court and throughout the *Regnum*. The birth confirmed her fertility, and a male child, naturally, was seen as the better result. Sicily needed future kings more than it needed royal princesses. William and his father had good reason to be happy.

In the eyes of her father-in-law and her subjects, who were granted two days of celebration to mark the prince's birth, Margaret, at seventeen, had proven her worth. With luck, she would bear more sons.

Court life was as rich intellectually as it was materially. The

Sicilian court boasted some great minds.

Maio of Bari, who succeeded the Englishman Robert of Selby, was an efficient chancellor, effectively the kingdom's "prime minister." English-born Thomas le Brun managed the royal treasury using Hindu-Arabic numerals. Abdullah al Idrisi was busy mapping Sicily and other territories and constructing a planisphere of a round Earth. It is clear that Roger was able and willing to delegate a great deal of the realm's daily administration to trusted officials.[174]

Although William assisted his father in the running of the *Regnum,* we have only vague impressions of what his precise responsibilities were. Despite his saturnine temperament, he was not remiss in his conjugal duties, and in 1153 Margaret gave birth to a second son, who was named Robert.

Did Margaret and William have any daughters? We know of none, but it is a distinct possibility.

In truth, we don't even know the names of all the daughters of Roger II.[175] That is hardly surprising since chroniclers usually noted the existence of a royal daughter only when she was betrothed to an important king or prince. Likewise, the birth of a child of either sex who died in infancy was rarely recorded. There were only two chroniclers present in Sicily who were close enough to the court to even learn of such events, and neither Hugh Falcandus nor Romuald of Salerno mention a daughter of Margaret and William.[176]

Margaret may have wished for a daughter or two, but her husband desired sons. So did her father-in-law.

In February 1154, King Roger II died in Palermo of natural causes at the age of fifty-eight.[177] He was survived by his pregnant wife, Beatrice of Rethel.

William automatically became regnant King of Sicily and Margaret became the realm's unequivocal queen consort.

This royal succession, as it happened, was painless and uncomplicated, but it belied great challenges to come.

Queen Consort

Roger had wished to be buried at the cathedral in Cefalù, a splendid church that he founded. Instead, his porphyry sarcophagus was placed in Palermo's cathedral. His successor's decision was challenged but never changed.[178]

Roger had proven himself a remarkable ruler. Not without reason, Sicily's first king is cited by historians as a paragon of intellect, one of the greatest monarchs of Europe's High Middle Ages, his court a multifaith, multilingual center of European and Mediterranean cultures.[179] In forging a kingdom, he united southern Italy into a cohesive state while forming Sicily's diversity of peoples into something resembling a single nation. The Kingdom of Sicily would survive, in one form or another, into the nineteenth century.

First, however, it had to survive the reign of Margaret's husband, King William I.

William I was re-crowned and anointed in Palermo on Easter in the presence of hundreds of barons and ecclesiastics. The same public ceremony saw Margaret crowned and anointed with her husband.[180]

It was true enough that Roger had defined the *Regnum* on his own terms. That was necessary considering its polyglot roots. The Greek, Arab and Norman populations each had their own concepts of kingship.

The first King of Sicily had to bring his people together while defending his territory. It would be prudent for William to continue the policies of his father.

But even in death Roger himself cast a very long shadow. He was an intellectual, a humanist whose court cultivated intellect, even brilliance. What is more, he was able to inspire the people he led. Any heir, however competent, would encounter considerable difficulty in succeeding so great a figure. Those at court understood this.[181]

So did Margaret. She would have to be much more than William's wife. Necessity and circumstance made her his advisor. Whether he would accept her advice was another matter altogether.

In early November Beatrice, Roger's widow and now "queen dowager," gave birth to a daughter christened Constance.[182]

By now, William had more urgent duties to address than celebrating the birth of a half-sister. Encouraged by the new pope, Adrian IV (Nicholas Breakspear), the recently-crowned Holy Roman Emperor, Frederick I "Barbarossa" was planning an invasion of the Kingdom of Sicily.[183] Manuel Comnenus of Constantinople, whose Byzantine Empire had been invaded by King Roger, was willing to cooperate in this effort, perhaps by attacking Apulia by sea while Barbarossa attacked the northern part of the *Regnum* by land. A major war was very possible, and for William it would be a defensive conflict.

Yet he seemed prepared for it. With the baronage united in Palermo at his coronation, William had appointed Maio of Bari his privileged *amiratus*, the "emir of emirs," naming a new chancellor.[184] He also used the occasion to grant Loritello to Robert of Bassonville, a cousin who had been divested of other feudal lands by King Roger.[185] Maio was loyal, but Robert was to prove much less so.

At the head of an army of some five hundred knights, Robert of Loritello[186] exploited the prospect of Barbarossa's planned invasion to lead a rebellious faction of the baronage against William.

The Italians have an old saying rooted in the Middle Ages: *Parenti serpenti!* "Relatives are snakes." Robert was a good example of this. Indeed, he seems to have wanted the throne for himself.[187]

The fighting began with William's unsuccessful siege of Benevento, a papal enclave within the territory of the *Regnum*.

This was led by Asclettin, who was a trusted general as well as chancellor, while William himself returned to Palermo in April 1155 to his family.

This now included a third son, William's namesake.[188]

King William now made his firstborn son, Roger, the Duke of Apulia, a title reserved to the heir apparent.

Meanwhile, unable to take Benevento but hoping to intimidate Pope Adrian, Asclettin attacked a number of towns on the southern fringe of the Papal State. This gave Adrian a pretext for excommunicating King William. Excommunicated or not, at least the king was back in Palermo to spend time with Margaret and the children.

By June, when Barbarossa was crowned Holy Roman Emperor, his German knights and barons were beginning to make it clear to their leader that they had no intention of participating in his plan to march southward into the Kingdom of Sicily in the middle of the torrid, mosquito-infested summer. This did not entirely discourage Robert of Loritello, William's disloyal kinsman, who was soon receiving troops and gold from Manuel of Constantinople. Robert began to use Apulia as a base from which to launch occasional attacks northward and westward into other regions of the peninsular part of the *Regnum*.

William wanted to respond to these attacks but he fell ill late in 1155. Margaret and the court physicians cared for him. What struck William was probably a very debilitating, viral pneumonia. His absence from public life led many to think he had died.

By spring of the following year, he was strong enough to ride to the Sicilian town of Butera to quash a revolt there. Then he headed to Messina, where a large army and navy were waiting to accompany him to the mainland.

Asclettin was royally chastised for his poor tactics against the rebels. William had never been very enthusiastic about this former cleric, who he now ordered jailed.[189]

With the imposing force assembled in Sicily, William himself would go to Apulia to excise the cancer infecting his kingdom.

The royal army, with its knights and archers, made its way across Calabria to Taranto, along the way gaining strength through the support of loyal barons and eliminating token resistance. The navy reached the port city of Brindisi, whose coastal fortress had been resisting a long siege by the rebels.

The warrior king had returned.

Victory came easily. The traitors were punished, some put to death. Bari, which had fallen to Byzantine control with the collusion of its citizens, many of whom were Greek, was largely destroyed, although its major churches were left unscathed.

William then led his army westward to Salerno and other cities in the Campania region around Naples. Robert of Loritello was not beheaded but exiled; he found refuge at the court of Frederick Barbarossa, whose aborted invasion of the *Regnum* he had supported.

Clearly, anybody who ever thought William incompetent or weak had underestimated him.

Margaret was not one of the doubters. Yet she understood that her husband was inclined to delegate authority whenever he could. This was shown by his appointment of Maio as a kind of "super minister" and his reliance on Asclettin to fight battles that he, as king, should have prosecuted himself. It was good to have competent ministers, but relying on them completely was ill-advised.

Peace Restored

Lacking support in view of humiliating military defeats, zealous Pope Adrian was chased out of Rome by an angry populace. He took refuge at Benevento, which William besieged. In June 1156, with this papal city on the verge of starvation, Adrian negotiated a truce. Here William was represented by Maio of Bari, and Adrian by Roland of Siena, a learned cardinal fated to become Pope Alexander III. Archbishop Hugh of Palermo was also present, accompanied by Romuald of Salerno. The young scribe who composed the text of the Treaty of Benevento[190] was Matthew of Aiello, a notary destined to play a greater role at court.

The Sicilian monarch remunerated to the pontiff a tribute pledged by his late father, and the papacy finally, unequivocally recognized William as King of Sicily. The apostolic legateship, the right of the sovereign to approve the appointment of bishops, was confirmed for the island of Sicily.

William's excommunication was lifted. In Sicily, Palermo was erected to a metropolitan see, with other bishops on the island suffragan to it. Archbishop Hugh became the Primate of Sicily.[191] That is to say, he was the most senior prelate of the entire Kingdom of Sicily, outranking the bishops of Salerno, Bari, Capua, Syracuse and Messina.

Frederick Barbarossa regarded the treaty as an affront because it effectively nullified his own, prior alliance with Pope Adrian, but for now the Holy Roman Emperor was not in a position to invade the *Regnum* as he had hoped. William's ministers also concluded a treaty with Genoa, one of the kingdom's most important trade partners.

Barbarossa was soon facing his own rebellion by the vassals and cities of northern Italy.[192] William, on the other hand, found himself at peace with the papacy and most of the northern Italian communes.[193]

Margaret's inner peace was shattered late in 1156 when news arrived that her sister, Blanca, had died in August while giving birth to a second child, who died with her. Naturally, Margaret had longed to see her beloved sister again someday, if only one last time, even if she knew that a journey back to

Spain was unlikely. Sicily was where she belonged, and she had better make the best of it.

Blanca was buried at Santa María la Real in Nájera. Her sarcophagus (shown at the end of this chapter), regarded as a supreme twelfth-century European expression of emotions in sculpture, depicts a mourning female figure. It has been suggested that the woman represented is Blanca's sister-in-law, Sancha, but it may be her sister. If the weeping figure is not Margaret, it could just as easily have been. The following year, Sancha also became Margaret's sister-in-law, and Queen of Navarre, when she wed her brother, Sancho "the Wise."

In 1158, Margaret gave birth to a fourth son, Henry. The same year, the King of Sicily named his secondborn son, Robert, Prince of Capua, a title reserved to the prince who was second in line to the throne. Roger, the eldest son of William and Margaret, was already Duke of Apulia.

William had every reason to be content. His family was growing, and following some raids in what is now Greece a treaty was negotiated with the Byzantine Empire.

For Margaret, tranquility was a luxury. With four young children to raise, advising her husband on matters of government was not her only job. During the long absences of William and Maio, the Palermitans looked to their queen for leadership.

By the end of 1159, it seemed clear that William was about to lose his last outposts in northern Africa. This was an economic misfortune.

Whether for lack of inspiration in Sicily or for greater opportunities abroad, the court's greatest minds had left. Thomas le Brun went to England, where he ended up as the almoner for King Henry II. Idrisi left for his native land.[194]

It would happen that most of the challenges confronting Margaret and William over the next few years were to come from domestic quarters.

Baronage

Court intrigues were no novelty, either in Italy or anyplace else. But in Sicily they bore the mark of peculiar conditions. The Bariots and other Greeks in Apulia might rebel if instigated by forces in the Byzantine Empire. The Arabs in northern Africa may have decided against Norman rule. It was disquieting whenever any group in the kingdom's multicultural mosaic thought itself mistreated.

However, the real problem came from the baronage, itself a privileged, even overprivileged, feudal class woven from everfraying threads into a coarse piece of fabric that could rarely decide whether it was linen or silk. The rebellion led by Robert of Loritello had shown that even a richly-enfeoffed royal cousin could not be trusted to uphold his oath of fealty. The barons' faux obeisance to the king fooled nobody.

Unlike their brethren in England, the first Norman barons of Italy were, for the most part, mercenaries born into Normandy's minor families. Generations after their arrival in Italy, some families still harbored resentment that the Hautevilles, once ordinary knights errant like themselves, had become kings.

In 1159, Margaret welcomed at court her young cousin, Gilbert. She saw to it that he was invested with the wealthy county of Gravina near Bari. Gilbert's father, Bertrand, was an illegitimate son of Margaret's generous great-uncle, Rotrou of Perche, the man who had given Tudela to her mother as a dowry.

At first, Gilbert seemed to be trustworthy, aloof of local politics, but before long the words of the native barons began to cloud his judgment.

Sicily's barons were an untamed lot. Even as they acquired manors and serfs, there were those among their number who rarely seemed content with the great wealth the conquest of southern Italy had brought them and their families. Now, a century after the Battle of Messina, they were little more than a noisy pack of hungry hounds, and there is evidence to suggest that they were envious of the island's mercantile classes, especially the Muslims of Palermo.

Here the flower of chivalry bore the malicious spore of bigotry, if not racism.

Most barons were wealthier than most merchants. The difference was that while a baron's wealth, based on agriculture, was difficult to conceal, a trader could hide his coins in a purse buried in a shallow hole beneath the floor of his house, thus evading taxation.

The Hautevilles had given a great number of manors, or fiefs, to the knights who accompanied them to Sicily in 1061. During the last years of his reign, King Roger sought, with the help of the treasurers of the royal *diwan*, to make the heirs of these barons accountable for their feudal duties. Usually this meant military service, and a large barony might be expected to provide several knights. Training and outfitting a knight was costly, but scutage, the payment of money in lieu of military service, was still unknown in southern Italy.

Although a baron or enfeoffed knight could elevate an esquire to knighthood, he could not do so merely at whim. Apart from the many years of martial training required, the postulant had to meet certain conditions set forth in the statute *De Nova Militia,* "Dubbing Knights," of the Assizes of Ariano. Most notably, the young man had to be born into a family of knightly status. Only an act of royal grace could supersede this prerequisite.[195]

In the Kingdom of Sicily the record of the barons and enfeoffed knights, not only their names and manors but their feudal obligations, was compiled in a roll analogous to England's *Domesday Book,* the *Catalogus Baronum.*[196]

Here such terms as *baronage* and *baronial* refer to the landed nobility generically, but there existed a feudal hierarchy in the Kingdom of Sicily by 1160. In Margaret's time, there was little distinction between princedoms (like Taranto) and dukedoms (Apulia), each of which might consist of several large counties (such as Mandra). A county comprised a number of baronies; within a barony there were usually a few manors (fiefs). Naturally, the actual size and wealth of such territories varied greatly.

The manorial system was held together through vassalage. The knight enfeoffed with a manor swore fealty to the baron from whom he held it. The baron, in turn, swore fealty to the count, and so forth. Ultimately, every vassal of the *Regnum Siciliae* owed fealty and homage to the king, who held some lands directly.[197]

Despite feudal bonds, baronial revolts were disturbingly frequent. Sometimes they arose when a renegade in a place like Loritello or Butera incited some of his neighboring barons to challenge royal authority. It was never too hard to concoct an unfounded justification as a pretext for open conflict. The instigators knew that loyalty was the foundation of the barons' relationship to the crown. They also knew that loyalty could often be purchased.

Some grievances with the crown were motivated by little more than personal grudges, and the resulting violence spelled the difference between life and death.

Tragedy

In the last days of 1159 Margaret's son Robert, the Prince of Capua, died during one of those illnesses that claims the lives of young children. The boy was entombed in the chapel of Mary Magdalene attached to the cathedral, within sight of the palace.[198] Grief-stricken by the death of a son who was not yet seven years old, Margaret was unaware of the plotting of a growing number of dissentients beyond the Strait of Messina.

The unruly barons could hardly be trusted under the best of circumstances. By 1160, their cauldron of discontent was boiling over. Here their scapegoat was not the king but his chief minister.

If not overtly arrogant, Maio of Bari was certainly confident in his own abilities. He exercised great control not only in the daily function of government but over policy, and despite successes like the Treaty of Benevento he was blamed for obvious failures like the recent loss of Mahdia, Sicily's last African stronghold, to the Almohads.[199]

Perhaps it was Maio's privileged position at court that rankled some of the barons.[200] Much of the venom directed at him grew out of envy. Not surprisingly, exiled Robert of Loritello was a leading detractor.

Nevertheless, it seems that at least a few baronial grievances were justified. If even a fraction of what nasty Hugh Falcandus wrote about him is true, Maio was avaricious, lecherous, publicly disdainful of William, and guilty of torturing and blinding some of the rebels taken prisoner in Apulia following the revolts a few years earlier. Romuald of Salerno is kinder, or at least less strident.

There seems to have been a nugget or two of truth to some of the allegations against Maio, yet William trusted him, and so did Margaret.

Of course, an attack on Maio was an *ipso facto* attack on William, and even on Margaret. The barons knew this.

They also knew that King Roger had died leaving the coffers of the treasury full. Land was good but gold was better. There was enough gold and silver in Sicily's treasury to buy a small country or two, perhaps even three or four, or to equip a navy to invade Africa and take back Mahdia.

For one of the barons the grievance with Maio of Bari was to become violently personal.

Rebel Baron

Matthew Bonello held lands around Caccamo and Prizzi, as well as some estates in Calabria. Overlooking a fertile valley to the east of Palermo, Caccamo was dominated by a large castle built during Arab rule and expanded by the Normans. Bonello, who was not yet forty, was engaged to marry the young daughter of Maio of Bari.

Bonello's future father-in-law trusted him enough to send him to mainland Italy to assuage the doubts of some barons who were sufficiently disgruntled with Maio to have sent missives to the king requesting the minister's removal. In Calabria, Bonello began to wander astray, first by courting a beautiful heiress[201] and then by heeding the words of Roger of Martorano, one of Maio's most vocal detractors.[202] Among the malicious malcontents was Gilbert of Gravina, Margaret's cousin.[203]

All kinds of things were being said. The campaign against Maio was a dirty one. It was even alleged that he had tried to kill Archbishop Hugh of Palermo by poisoning, and that Matthew of Aiello, Maio's protégé, had attempted to bribe the newly-elected pope, Alexander III, into deposing King William.[204]

Margaret herself was not immune to vicious rumors. According to Falcandus: "Voices flew around Sicily, one sometimes contradicting the other, saying that Maio had shown some of his confederates several crowns and other regalia, insinuating that the queen herself had sent him these objects from the palace. It was believed, in fact, that everything took place with her consent, linked as she was to Maio by bonds of undignified familiarity. However, many people thought these rumors false."[205]

The power of innuendo to shape public opinion cannot be underestimated, and this inexpungible passage is the source of a persistent perception about Margaret's moral character that has survived eight centuries, painting her as unfaithful.[206] Yet there is no evidence to implicate her in Maio's actions, and Falcandus himself tells us that the rumor's veracity was sometimes questioned. Indeed, the allegation about the crowns being purloined from the royal treasury was later debunked.[207]

Maio was warned that a conspiracy was afoot and that Bonello might be involved. However, he found himself reassured by the denial of his future son-in-law, who went so far as to request that the wedding be celebrated even sooner than had originally been planned. This led the older man to set aside any lingering doubts.

The baronial conspirators planned the assassination fastidiously. As they saw it, the killer had to be somebody who could get close to Maio without arousing suspicion. Bonello was the ideal candidate.

Saint Martin's Day, the feast on the eleventh of November that marked the end of autumn, was approaching.[208] The days were getting ever shorter, the nights ever cooler. It was as good a time as any to commit a murder. Bonello would not act alone.

Street Crime

In 1160, the day before Martinmas fell on a Thursday. Around dusk, not long after the sun had descended behind the mountains surrounding the city, Maio of Bari and a small entourage paid a visit to Archbishop Hugh[209] at Palermo's archiepiscopal palace, which was located next to the cathedral. In the group was Matthew of Aiello.

After some time, the group left the archbishop's residence. By now it was completely dark and a bit chilly. For some, it would get colder still.

Maio and his cortege had made their way to Old Saint Agatha's Gate, where there was an imposing wall, beyond which the ground sloped toward the bed of the Papyrus River, whose waters had been diverted through a subterranean *kanat*.[210]

Here the ambush took place. Bonello sprang upon Maio, slaying him with a sword. At the same time, his squad of knights attacked Maio's companions. One of them, the notary Matthew of Aiello, was wounded but managed to escape with the others.

Matthew Bonello and his company of rogues immediately fled the city, riding at full gallop to the castle at Caccamo in the dead of night. Back in Palermo, a crowd of exultant citizens dragged Maio's corpse along the streets. The vigil of Martinmas had just become more festive than usual.

So great was the tumult that it could be heard from the palace. The festivities seemed to be getting out of hand, and William demanded to know what was happening. It wasn't long before he was informed. The king immediately sent guards into the labyrinth of streets and squares to prevent a general insurrection. He had the presence of mind to dispatch some men to protect Maio's home to ensure that the dead man's family was not harmed.

If William was angry, Margaret was livid, expressing her rage in no uncertain terms. Her worst wrath was directed at Bonello and his accomplices, who by now were well on their way up the coast.[211]

Margaret's reaction was crystal clear. Beyond his initial response, however, William acted with uncertainty, perhaps for the first time in his life. From the comfort of his window in a high tower of the palace, he could see the jubilant behavior of the Palermitans.

The scene was disturbing. William's subjects seemed happy to be rid of Maio. The people who had lit bonfires for the vigil of Martinmas were now dancing around the flames to celebrate the death of a tyrant. This suggested to the king that the man he so long defended was indeed despised by many.

Matthew Bonello, though a fugitive, had popular support. In the present climate, arresting the defiant baron would be an operation fraught with peril. Where there was one rebellious vassal there were usually others as well.

Margaret entertained no such doubts. She wanted the perpetrators punished.

Court Intrigues

The true extent of Maio's guilt will never be known. At first, William was reluctant to accept the tales of corruption he heard about the dead man. This changed with the discovery of royal crowns in a chest found in Maio's possession; did Maio's delusions of grandeur lead him to think he could wear them himself?

In truth, the crowns were not royal property but gifts Maio was planning to give the sovereign.[212]

As inquiries were made, it became clear that some of the accusations made against Maio had been based on exaggerations while others were rooted in reality. Damning revelations came from those in his family who worked as his assistants; his son and brother confessed to Maio's explicit acts of wrongdoing, such as the payment of bribes to ecclesiastics with money pilfered from the royal treasury. A Calabrian bishop, Erveo of Tropea, confirmed this by reimbursing to the king the money received from Maio, and then some.

Matthew Bonello was granted clemency for the murder based on the macilent pretext that Maio had deceived the king. With this, the baron returned to Palermo, where he was received at the palace by William and acclaimed by the people. If unpersuaded by Bonello's feigned sincerity, the king did not have to be convinced of his influence among both the baronage and the populace.

Margaret seems to have entertained suspicions about

Bonello. As if her own doubts were not enough, the palace eunuchs warned her of his amoral ambition.[213]

Some eunuchs were servants, scribes or cooks, and a few were advisors. One of their chief duties at the palace was guarding and managing the harem.

Matthew Bonello remained dangerous, and his audacity increased with each passing day.

Unbeknownst to the king, the late Maio had permitted his intended son-in-law to defer payment of a debt due the crown of sixty thousand gold tarì, an extremely large sum.[214] Advised of this, the king now demanded remittance of these monies from Bonello and his guarantors.

As the winter months passed, Bonello found himself invited to court ever less frequently. This implicit admonition he blamed on Adenolf, the chamberlain, who had been a friend of Maio.[215] With the recent death of his ally Archbishop Hugh, Bonello's own friends at the royal court were ever fewer.[216] The arrogant baron correctly inferred that the king, supported by Margaret, was trying to marginalize him.

Not willing to accept his diminished position, Bonello began to conspire with other barons. There were always a few malcontents about, but this time he didn't have to look beyond the putrid fruit of the Hauteville family tree, where covetous serpents concealed themselves among the leaves.

It was easy to enlist the support of one man who had a particularly large axe to grind with the King of Sicily. He was Simon, William's half-brother. This illegitimate son of King Roger harbored a grudge against William for divesting him of Taranto some years earlier.

Another conspirator was Tancred, Count of Lecce, a wealthy city in Apulia.[217] Young Tancred was William's nephew, being the illegitimate son of his elder brother, Roger, who died in 1148.

Being born outside marriage may have made Simon and

Tancred dynastically illegitimate, but in the eyes of many their role in the conspiracy legitimized the plot against King William I, for here were two of the king's nearest blood relatives acting against him.

For good measure, Gilbert, Margaret's cousin, joined the plot. Here was the supreme affront, for whatever could be said of William's treatment of Simon and Tancred, Margaret had treated Gilbert with nothing but respect.

Clearly, Bonello was not lacking in ambition, and now his target was not an emir of emirs but the man on the throne. In the first days of March in 1161, he convened a secret meeting at his castle in Caccamo to finalize his plans.[218]

What followed was an object lesson in how to execute the overthrow of a medieval monarch in his own household.[219]

Because the royal palace was heavily guarded, it was necessary to enlist the cooperation of two key figures if the plot were to have any hope of success. The palace castellan, the chief saboteur recruited, controlled the entrances. The guards' captain commanded some three hundred men and oversaw the jail. Enticed by coin, both were convinced to betray their king, leaving no more obstacles to the plan being set in motion.

Every step of the plan was worked out in minute detail, calling upon the knowledge and expertise of each player. For example, Simon, who had spent his childhood in the palace, was familiar with its corridors and chambers, as well as the maze of passages known only to those who lived there. This meant that he could help the others find the king.

The rebels' belief that their plan may have already been revealed to William forced Simon and Tancred to act prematurely, without waiting for Bonello to arrive in Palermo.

Since the murder of Maio of Bari, Margaret saw that her husband was unmotivated to do much except meet with his *familiares,* his trusted counsellors.

Palace Coup

Thursday, the ninth of March, probably seemed like any other day in late winter. There was still a trace of snow on the rugged summits of the mountains visible from the towers of the palace, but wild asparagus was sprouting in the countryside, where the almonds were blossoming in shades of pink and white. Easter was around the corner, and William spent an early hour of daylight at liturgy in the chapel, where he was joined by Margaret and the children.[220]

The conspirators took advantage of this time to enter the palace, reach its dungeon and free all of its prisoners. By the time the royal family left the chapel, the rebels were already on their way to the Pisan Tower, the king's inner sanctum. Margaret and the children went to the royal apartments to begin the day's lessons, while William headed toward his chamber accompanied by Henry Aristippo, the archdeacon of Catania, who had replaced Maio of Bari. An intellectual, Henry was one of the few advisors the king still trusted.[221]

Nearing the chamber he used as an office, William was walking down a narrow corridor with Henry when the pair saw half a dozen men striding toward them, brusquely and unannounced. It was unusual to see soldiers carrying swords and daggers in this part of the palace. The king did not yet know what had transpired whilst he was at holy mass. Who were these men?

Either William's eyes deceived him, or it was Tancred of Lecce and Simon of Taranto. The king's first reaction was instinctive anger that these two undesirable kinsmen had been granted entry into the palace. What were they even doing in Palermo? This dastardly duo couldn't have overpowered the palace guards by themselves.

But William quickly realized that his immediate problem was far worse than the arrival of uninvited guests within the castle walls. With the two princes were irate nobles who, until a few minutes earlier, had been imprisoned in the palace dungeon. The mere fact of this confrontation meant that William's predicament was dire indeed.

Unarmed, and unaccompanied by a military escort, William glanced down the corridor behind him, thinking he might find a guard or two at the other end of the hall. If he acted quickly enough he might even slip into a secret passage to his tiny armory, where he kept swords and daggers. Outnumbered, he and Henry considered running but thought better of it.[222] They were seized by the intruders. After haranguing the king, the rebels demanded his abdication.

But now the group turned from regnal politics to unbridled thievery. Leaving the king under guard in one of the tower's rooms, the men, led by Simon, made their way into those chambers where money, regalia, rings, precious gemstones and silver vases were kept. Joined by the castellan and other traitors, they looted the premises. Some stole royal robes. Others hurled handfuls of glittering gold tarì coins out the windows to a boisterous crowd that was gathering below, seeking in this way to buy the Palermitans' loyalty.[223]

Some preferred the pleasures of the concubines in the harem to material wealth.[224] Each rebel plundered according to his own taste. Here was the epitome of rape and pillage.

Henry Aristippo, though an ordained deacon, worshipped at the same altar of debauchery as the others. He abducted a few girls for himself and kept them at his house, where he set up his own little harem.

Margaret and a few servants were in a room with the children. It wasn't long before some rebels arrived to ensure that they didn't leave.[225]

Confined to a chamber on the fourth floor of the Pisan Tower, William was left alone to think about a course of action. The rebel cabal posted a guard outside the door but the room had a window from which the king could shout down onto the square for help. If anybody heard, nobody responded.[226]

Meanwhile, the knights of Bonello's beastly cohort gave chase to the eunuchs, most of whom had fled the palace at the first sign of danger.[227] As part of their plan, the revolt's ringleaders had already found sympathizers beyond the palace district to join the riot, and a number of knights, swords in hand, left the seaside castle to murder some escaped eunuchs they found in the streets.[228]

The violence didn't end with the eunuchs and concubines. A great number of Muslim shopkeepers, along with those collecting taxes in the building that housed the *diwan,* or those walking along the streets, were killed by the same knights who had massacred the eunuchs.

When many of these Muslims, who Maio of Bari had disarmed the previous year, realized the extent of the knights' assault, they made for the part of the Sari al Kadi district outside the city wall, beyond the Papyrus River. They were pursued by the Christians, but the fighting reached a stalemate because the aggressors had trouble attacking the defenders in the narrow alleys. In this way, the knights were repelled and the butchery minimized.[229]

Not content with the mayhem they had wrought, the leaders of the revolt incited the citizens to build a bonfire into which they tossed a great number of records. Not surprisingly, this included the tax rolls listing the barons' feudal obligations.[230]

The queen and her ladies-in-waiting could see the smoke and chaos from a palace window, even if they couldn't make out every skirmish taking place in the streets below. It was one thing to observe an isolated riot, but here was the better part of one of Europe's largest cities in utter turmoil.

Violent as the revolt was, regicide was not precisely what

Simon and Tancred had in mind. What they wanted most was a friendly monarch they and Bonello could control.

Early in the afternoon, the two princes entered the chamber where Margaret and her three sons were sequestered. The rebels demanded that her eldest son, Roger, Duke of Apulia, who was then nine years old, don some regal robes and then go with them to the stables. Seeing that she had no choice, Margaret complied with this request.

In late afternoon, the two renegade princes set young Roger upon a pony and led the boy around the streets of Palermo, presenting him as the new king to the cheering crowds.[231] Walter, young Roger's tutor, addressed the people, holding forth on how King William was a tyrant that now had to be replaced.[232] Young Roger was proclaimed king.[233]

That night, the rebels secured the palace, allowing nobody to enter. The next day, Friday, they repeated Thursday's spectacle, again parading Roger around the city. This failed to placate everybody, and there were isolated skirmishes between Muslims and Christians which led to a number of Arabs being killed, their shops looted.

By Saturday, Matthew Bonello still had not arrived at Palermo. There were those in the populace who began to question recent events, wondering why the crowned King of Sicily, whatever anybody thought of him, was still being held prisoner, and why the rebels' killing and pillaging should be justified. And anyway, who had appointed Simon and Tancred to act as kingmakers?

Increasingly worried about the atmosphere in Palermo, Tancred rode with several other rebels to Mistretta, in the Nebrodian Mountains, to confer with Bonello. Simon, meanwhile, was beginning to entertain serious thoughts of having himself crowned.

Goaded by several clerics, a large group of local men took up arms and stormed the palace, threatening to besiege it with ladders and towers unless the rebels freed King William.[234] Simon and the other conspirators held out initially but finally complied. They went to William, who promised to grant them safe conduct if he were freed. Once released, the king spoke to the populace from a tower window.

When the crowd demanded that the rebels be executed, William announced to his subjects that their loyalty to him was more than sufficient to satisfy any need for justice or reprisal. With entente thus achieved, Simon and his henchmen rode off to Bonello's castle at Caccamo.

The crisis was over, but in the commotion a stray arrow hit young Roger, who was standing near a window, mortally wounding him. He was dead within hours.[235]

Condolences were expressed by many who had once despised the king, but Margaret was inconsolable. She had lost her second child.[236]

Survival

Following a period of mourning, William met with local leaders to reassure them.

Bonello had not given up his ambition to unseat the king. Having assembled another rebel force, he marched toward Palermo from Caccamo, but he retreated as some of the king's galleys arrived from Messina with reinforcements.

The defiant baron was eventually coaxed to the palace, where he was arrested. Some Palermitans protested this, but Bonello died in a dungeon within the palace walls late in 1161. Sporadic revolts around Sicily were suppressed.

If the king could not tolerate open rebellion, he could make a sincere effort to mend his tattered ties with the barons by addressing their grievances. One of his measures in this direction was the restoration of the right of feudal inheritance to the sons of vassals killed in royal service.[237]

William exiled Tancred and Simon, who went to the eastern Mediterranean, where they could go on pilgrimage in the Holy Land or render service as mercenaries in Constantinople.

Gilbert of Gravina, the queen's cousin, was pardoned at Margaret's urging even though he had participated in the hellish folly that cost her the life of her son. William ordered him back to Apulia to respond to some raids by Robert of Loritello.[238]

In the aftermath of recent events, William was left with very few people he could trust. He pardoned the notary Matthew of Aiello, who set about compiling a feudal tax roll to replace the *Catalogus Baronum* destroyed by the rebels. The king was suspicious of the intellectual deacon Henry Aristippo, who had raided the harem, although he chose not to punish him.

He could trust Margaret. With the loyalty of the realm's highest officers left in a nebula of doubt, William more frequently turned to his wife for counsel, even reassurance.

After Christmas, the king swept through eastern Sicily and onto the mainland with a large army to quell some isolated disturbances that could not be left to the limited military resources of Gilbert of Gravina. William left Margaret in Palermo as his effective surrogate until he returned in the summer of 1162.

She was assisted by an Arab eunuch named Martin, a convert to Catholicism who undertook retaliations against people thought to be the king's adversaries. Caïd Martin was especially hostile to Christians.[239] Henry Aristippo, the lecherous deacon, was apprehended, deprived of his mini-harem, and cast into a dark dungeon to die.

We do not know how influential Margaret was in these bloody reprisals. Did she instigate them? Had she, like her sister queens confronted by adversity, become a she-wolf? Having seen a son killed in connection with the revolt of the previous year, she was embittered. Whilst the king was away, she and Martin did what her husband was unwilling, or at least less willing, to do. If Margaret did not personally order the reprisals, she certainly knew of them. Perhaps she relished them. Here was the dark side of her personality.

Ruling the Kingdom

When he returned to Palermo, William fell into his old habits. He still preferred passing his time in the Genoard to the pleasure of Margaret's company. A new coterie of concubines was lured, or coerced, to serve in the harem. The Christian king seemed to enjoy the life of a baptized sultan.[240]

The status of Palermo's Muslim Arab population had suffered in the recent riots. For the first time since the Normans took the city in 1071, its Muslims had been attacked in large numbers by Christian knights. This doubtless prompted many to consider abandoning Islam.

Religious freedom, women's rights, prostitution, slavery, forced castration. All were important issues. Of course, in the twelfth century none of these things were viewed from the same perspectives as the sensibilities that color our times. Even if it were argued that the presence of eunuchs and harems reflected what were essentially Muslim practices inherited from the emirs who once ruled Sicily, William was unwilling to alter this aspect of the society over which he reigned.

By the end of 1162, the king was again ceding day-to-day administration to others. Martin was joined by Richard Palmer and Matthew of Aiello.

An event the next year served to remind Margaret of the dangers still lurking around every corner, even within the palace walls.

Following the revolt led by Simon, Tancred and Bonello, the king had transferred important prisoners to a jail outside the palace.[241] However, a few were still in the palace dungeon enclosed by thick Phoenician walls.[242] It was only a matter of time before these men were moved to another jail, such as the round tower of Palermo's seaside castle.

Lacking any hope for being released, several prisoners convinced the guards to free them. With this accomplished, they made for a gate leading out of the palace. Their escape was foiled by the castellan, who quickly went through the gate, closing it from the outside and trapping the fugitives within the palace's curtain wall.

Next they entered the base of one of the towers, thinking they might find the king on one of the upper floors. Instead, they ended up in the room where young William and his brother, Henry, usually met for their lessons. Fortunately, the boys' tutor, Walter, had whisked the two to the safety of the bell tower as soon as he heard the commotion. Margaret was in a chamber upstairs and unaware of what was happening.

Martin managed to lock the escapees in a large room, where they were all killed. The knaves' lifeless bodies were literally thrown to the dogs, and the corpses were forbidden a burial.[243]

Perhaps at Margaret's urging, William ensured that henceforth no prisoners were to be jailed in the palace, even temporarily.

Overlooking the Kala harbor and protected by a moat, the sea castle was far more secure than the palace dungeon. Its master, sadistic Robert of Calatabiano, had made the fortress infamous for torturing the prisoners kept there.

His fief was on the other side of Sicily, near Catania, but Robert used his position to accrue wealth through corrupt means everyplace on the island. With the collusion of Caïd Martin, several avaricious justiciars[244] would bring fraudulent charges against men whose estates they desired. The accused would be released only upon paying substantial bribes, or ceding a manor or two. This extortion seems to have touched many innocent Sicilians, but William was probably unaware of it.

Apart from these chronic abuses, the *Regnum* was peaceful. Indeed, the king had told his three chief counsellors to avoid disturbing him unless it was absolutely necessary.[245]

For her part, Margaret was occupied with raising her two sons. By now, she gave little thought to her husband's habits and whims. Martin and his ilk, like Maio of Bari years earlier, concealed their corruption.

Building Bridges

Whilst an effort was undertaken to build bridges with the Muslims, the construction of churches and palaces continued in earnest. By 1164, new monasteries and castles were springing up around Sicily in an unprecedented number.[246]

In the capital a few noteworthy edifices besides the royal palace and its chapel were already standing. (Here it may be best to focus on those which have survived until the present day.)

The "admiral's bridge" over the Oreto was built on the orders of George of Antioch, who also built the Martorana Church. San Cataldo was erected under the auspices of Maio of Bari. The original Mary Magdalene chapel, built by Queen Elvira next to the cathedral, was already standing; it is where Margaret's sons were buried.

Beyond the Genoard, in the vast hunting grounds in the mountains, a chapel dedicated to Saint Michael the Archangel was erected at what is now the town of Altofonte; next to it was a royal hunting lodge. This meant that William could spend a few days at a time hunting in the woodlands without having to return to Palermo to attend mass.

In the former slave district was the church dedicated to Saint Peter. One wonders whether its congregants ever heard an occasional scream from a prisoner being tortured by Robert of Calatabiano in the sea castle nearby.

At least two of the emir's palaces were still standing. Located in the Genoard, the Scibene[247] was expanded following William's reign. The Favara, in what is now the Brancaccio district, was a favorite place for William, Margaret and the children to pass the torrid days of summer. Both had tiny lakes fed by springs.

The House of Hauteville was like a castle built of sand. A single wave of discontent could carry it away. If that happened, the monarchy would endure, but under the crown and aegis of another family. By now, the dynasty into which Margaret had married had ruled Sicily for a century, and as kings for just thirty-four years. Margaret herself was not quite thirty.

Legacy of William I

In 1165, the king ordered his architects to draw up plans for a new palace to be erected in the Genoard. The Zisa took its name from the Arabic *aziz*, "splendid" or "beautiful," a word that survives in the Sicilian language as *azzizare*, "to make attractive." It was William's wish that this palace set amidst lakes and greenery might surpass the splendour of those of his father.[248]

The greater part of the Zisa was built in a short time. Margaret was not involved in this project.

The year 1166 began well enough, but in March the king was struck by a terrible bout of dysentery. This illness seemed to have passed when a relapse made William suspect that his end was near. Seeking to settle his affairs to avoid contestations should he die, he formally decreed his elder son as his heir. He took the step of appointing Richard Palmer and Matthew of Aiello as *familiares*, trusted counsellors, to assist in governing the *Regnum*. The *familiares* would become a leitmotif in the government of the Sicilian kingdom.

Significantly, the moribund monarch named Margaret "keeper of the entire realm." Regent.[249]

King William I of Sicily expired in May at the age of forty-six.[250] He was buried in the palace chapel.[251]

At the age of twelve, Margaret's son was now King William II of Sicily. He was crowned by Romuald of Salerno in Palermo's cathedral.[252]

The girl born in Navarre had endured adversity after adversity to become, in her thirty-first year, queen regent of one of Europe's most important kingdoms. She was now the most powerful woman in Europe and the Mediterranean.[253]

Margaret's life until this point had been little more than a haphazard apprenticeship for what lay ahead of her.

Queen Regent

The spring of 1166 found the path before Margaret obscured by a fog of incertitude. The regent may not have known exactly what to do, but her actions show us that she had very definite ideas about what *not* to do, and she probably wished to avoid what she and others regarded as the mistakes of her late husband.[254]

Young William II was as prepared for the transition to kingship as a boy his age could be. Was Margaret ready for regency?

Every scrap of information known to us suggests that she was. When her husband was absent from the capital, Margaret, the progenitrix of the next monarch, was the political point of reference for a city wealthier and more influential than most European kingdoms. During one of these absences, she probably colluded with Caïd Martin to eliminate some of the king's opponents. For the final years of her husband's reign, she had a say in certain aspects of royal government.[255] It is abundantly clear that William I, particularly during his last few years on the throne, did not care very much for "hands-on" administration of the *Regnum Siciliae*. His complacency was disturbing.

Margaret spent very little time mourning the death of her

husband, if she was even inclined to shed more than a few tears for the man from whom she seems to have been estranged for the last few years. Instead, she immediately plunged into the business of running the kingdom. In this she had little choice, for the appearance of a power vacuum would be even worse than the effect of poor decisions.

Her initial actions, though not unheard of in the annals of European medieval history, were unusual enough to make people stand up and notice her. Margaret's intent, of course, was that the subjects should ascribe these sage decisions to their young sovereign, William II.

There was no model, no guide to follow except perhaps some of the policies of her father-in-law, the fondly-remembered Roger II. The royal sisterhood, such as it was, found itself with a dearth of sisters. In England, headstrong Eleanor of Aquitaine, wife of Henry II, was influential but wielded little power of her own; in Normandy the decisions of Eleanor's mother-in-law, Maude, reflected the policies of Henry II. Margaret had very little contact with such female contemporaries during her regency, certainly none that would permit her to garner any advice from them.[256] In the event, the social fabric of the Kingdom of Sicily was far more complex than what existed in these other regions.

Some of her husband's unfinished undertakings had to be completed. For the most part, that meant wrapping up construction of the Zisa palace and similar projects.

Building a solid foundation for her son's power was a far greater challenge, and there was no time to lose. Margaret needed a base of support and she needed it now. In an absolute monarchy the sagacious use of power was absolutely necessary.

If there was a framework for Margaret's authority, it was millennial European tradition and the kingdom's Assizes of Ariano.

Using Power

The queen could not afford to be indifferent. Reasoning that bloody revolts were the progeny of dissent, she sought to eliminate their root cause. She beguiled the restless baronage by redressing their unvoiced grievances. Her stratagems were simple.

The first decrees Margaret issued in the name of her son were intended to still troubled waters and to encourage loyalty toward the new monarch. These took several forms, all quite pragmatic.[257]

The justiciars seem to have applied the law arbitrarily, meting out justice as they saw fit but ever influenced by the king's mentality. This sometimes resulted in overzealous prosecution and excessively harsh sentences even for minor transgressions. A disturbing degree of corruption permeated officialdom.

To reconcile such matters, Margaret released a great number of prisoners from the kingdom's jails, including those on islands such as Lipari. Mostly men, some were barons to whom she restored lands that had been confiscated by William I, albeit usually with good cause when this was a punishment for treason. She forgave the debts of most of the prisoners she released.

Through a further act of clemency, the queen repealed the exile imposed on a number of barons who had openly rebelled. They were permitted to return to the *Regnum* and claim their former lands, which in most cases had been confiscated.

She began to grant property to nobles but especially to the monastic orders. As we shall see, her granting of lands to monasteries increased over time.

Margaret abolished certain taxes that had been levied in recent years, particularly the "redemption fees" which had become a burden in Apulia and in the area around Salerno and Naples.[258] She made it clear that such taxes were not to be collected in the future.

The queen was not seeking the subjects' unctuous obedience; their compliance with the law and a smidgen of loyalty to the crown would be sufficient.

Her sobriety of thought distinguished her. Presented in a velvet glove, Margaret's policy concealed an iron fist.

Familiarity

She appointed the eunuch Caïd Peter, the head of the royal diwan, as her chief *familiare,* telling Richard Palmer and Matthew of Aiello that henceforth they had to answer to him. Neither Richard nor Matthew accepted this blissfully, but for now there was nothing they could do about it.

In appointing her own team, Margaret was choosing her own approach to government. But the ubiquitous court intrigues did not cease just because the queen was asserting her authority.

It didn't take long for some bishops to begin trying to convince Peter that Richard Palmer was planning to kill him. Yet Peter was reluctant to act against Richard despite the insistence of the bishops that he do something.

Obviously, the intended target of this episcopal scheming was Richard Palmer.

With him removed, Gentile Tuscus of Agrigento or one of the other bishops could take his place. Gentile, in particular, was unabashedly ambitious; he had always behaved as a sycophant around William I but grew disillusioned when Richard, who was closer to the king, thwarted his proposals for various projects. According to Falcandus, one of the plotters was Romuald of Salerno. Matthew of Aiello, who also began to believe that Richard should perhaps be removed from power but still respected him as a colleague and peer, preferred to use his own methods to achieve the task.

Falcandus wrote that one of the pretexts for the antipathy

towards Richard Palmer was his Anglo-Norman origin. Gentile and his unsavory ilk probably inferred that as an "outsider" Richard would never be easily manipulated. As the last Englishman at court, he was the only obvious obstacle to them taking control.

Caïd Peter, they thought, could be dominated more easily. An Arab convert to Catholicism, he had once served as a naval commander.

Margaret herself did not cultivate a great liking for Richard Palmer, but she refused to dismiss him.

There was a reason for her resentment. When her husband was alive, the queen had sought support from Richard for some of her proposals, only to receive from the pompous cleric cynical and condescending missives.[259] His arrogant comportment led Margaret to believe that he hated her, and she was probably right. But for now she preferred marginalizing Richard to removing him altogether.[260]

Meanwhile, Gilbert of Gravina, Margaret's cousin, having been advised of young William's accession to the throne, and Margaret's regency, made his way to Palermo. Couriers arrived at Palermo with this news when Gilbert was still at Messina, a few days away.

Gilbert was already the acting governor of the mainland part of the *Regnum*. Now he sought to displace Caïd Peter, the chief *familiare*. He may have thought his cousin weak, yet her word alone had saved his hide from serious punishment for conspiring with Bonello a few years earlier. Arrogant Gilbert came to believe that he had been rewarded for his own merits; in reality, his "success" was little more than the product of nepotism. Quite simply, he was the queen's cousin. If King William I exiled his own kinsmen, Simon and Tancred, he certainly would have had Gilbert exiled or killed.

The arrival of Gilbert imposed a temporary delay on the plans of the bishops to remove Richard Palmer from power.

The company of knights traveling with Gilbert was not sufficient to attack Palermo, but it made an impression on Gentile of Agrigento and the other plotters. Richard Palmer also took note, and warned Gilbert about the conspirators. The queen's cousin reassured Richard of his support.

Caïd Peter's faction, being loyal to Margaret, was not closely allied to any of the others. These men publicly commended Gilbert for having raced to Palermo to support his kinswoman. In private, however, they sought to convince the queen of her cousin's ambition to rule the kingdom. Their caveats were unnecessary, as Margaret already knew enough about Gilbert's character, or lack of it, to ascertain his objectives.

One day, Gilbert spoke to her in private audience, though in the presence of Caïd Peter. Here Gilbert defended Richard Palmer, spoke against the court eunuchs, and suggested that changes be made at court.

Margaret affirmed her faith in the people at court and her general agreement with the organization her late husband had put in place. She offered her cousin a place as *familiare* under Peter. This enraged Gilbert, who found it offensive to be offered a position beneath that of a palace eunuch. He launched into a diatribe, ranting that Margaret's prestige in Apulia was abysmal, and before long his utterances degenerated into a series of vicious personal insults against his cousin.

Tears of disillusion gathered in the eyes of the woman who had done so much to help a wayward kinsman of low birth. But the queen stood her ground throughout the tirade.[261]

Having thoroughly berated his cousin, Gilbert stormed out of the palace but he did not leave Palermo. He began to contemplate ways of eliminating the chief *familiare*.

Peter surmised that Gilbert's knights could be divided into two groups.

The enfeoffed knights were landed barons of the peninsular part of the *Regnum* who served Gilbert and the crown as part of their military obligation. Looking toward their own interests, these barons preferred to see Gilbert appointed chief *familiare* in Peter's stead.

Most of the mercenary knights, on the other hand, were indifferent about such matters. Led by a salaried constable, Richard of Mandra, they need only be paid for their service; it was not a feudal obligation on their part. Before long, they would return home, which for many of them was someplace beyond the Alps.

At Caïd Peter's suggestion, the queen enfeoffed Richard of Mandra with the County of Molise, which included wealthy baronies like Boiano and Venafro.[262]

Not only did Margaret know how to sew together a patchwork of supporters, she knew how to sow the seeds of dissent among those who chose to oppose her. Woe betide her antagonists.

The formal investiture of Richard with his prosperous county was an ostentatious event, and the first public occasion of its kind over which Queen Margaret presided. Here the entire nobility could see the use of royal power.

Gilbert and his followers were rankled by the elevation of Richard of Mandra, now Count Richard of Molise. There was nothing they could do to stop a feudal investiture, which was a royal prerogative, but they now conspired in earnest to kill Peter.

Thinking his position untenable and his life endangered, Caïd Peter departed Palermo under cover of night, taking a chest of gold tarì with him. He sailed to Africa, where he renounced Christianity, to which he had converted in youth, to embrace Islam anew under his original name, *Ahmed*.

It was rumored that Peter had taken some crowns and other regalia with him. The queen refuted this nonsense but to clear the air she summoned the barons, bishops and court officers present in northwestern Sicily to an audience at the palace.

It wasn't long before the meeting degenerated into a heated exchange, with Gilbert of Gravina insulting Peter and Richard of Molise defending him. In defense of Peter's honour, Richard challenged to trial by combat any baron present who persisted in defaming the absent *familiare*.

The argument descended to the level of personal insults, with Richard calling Gilbert a coward unworthy to lead royal troops.

These fighting words were precisely the kind of opening Gilbert was waiting for, and the two men squared off, swords drawn. Fortunately, some knights intervened to separate them before anybody was hurt.

Margaret ordered the two counts to desist, and they retracted the stream of invective they had unleashed upon each other. But their mutual acrimony remained, and Gilbert began a covert campaign to sully Richard's reputation.

Realpolitik

Now, only a few months into her regency, Margaret found herself confronted by a stark choice. Either she could somehow marginalize her cousin or she could have him arrested and exiled, or perhaps executed.

Gilbert's altercation with Richard of Molise had shown just how difficult it would be to subdue him. The queen wished to do so without her actions appearing to be motivated by hatred for her cousin. How could she accomplish such a feat?

The *familiare* Matthew of Aiello was responsible for reading correspondence that arrived at court from around the *Regnum*. Seizing on rumors that Frederick Barbarossa was again planning an invasion of southern Italy, Matthew had such a letter forged stating that the threat was imminent.[263] He read this message to an assembly of barons.

This gave Margaret a credible pretext for sending Gilbert

back to Apulia.²⁶⁴ She flattered her cousin by telling him he was the best man to raise an army and defend that part of the kingdom. To reinforce his authority in the region, she made him governor of Apulia and Campania. Gilbert suspected there may be trickery behind his appointment to this mission, but open insubordination would make him an enemy of the court. Besides, he had already come to understand that, realistically, there was little more he could do to facilitate his ambitions in Palermo. Mollified, he departed for Apulia with his son, Bertrand.

Gilbert's audacious pretensions to influence at court were yet another confirmation that royal authority was likely to be challenged, especially when it was vested in a woman, and that the instigators would make use of any means at their disposal to tip the balance of power in their favour.

Although the actions of Gilbert and the bishops were not aimed solely at the Arabs, be they Muslim or Christian, the tenor of the insults directed against Peter reflected a subtle religious bigotry.

In place of Caïd Peter, Margaret promoted Richard of Molise to *familiare*. Unlike his predecessor, Richard was a decisive man who commanded his own little army. This struck fear into his opponents.

With Gilbert gone, the bishops resumed their efforts to subvert the position of Richard Palmer. This movement was led by Cardinal John of Naples, the papal envoy.[265]

It was not with unbridled enthusiasm that Margaret countenanced the obnoxious, condescending Richard Palmer as a *familiare* at court. Apprised of this, John suggested to the queen a plan not unlike the strategy that was so effective in prompting Gilbert's recent *exeunt*.

Richard Palmer was bishop-elect of Syracuse. During Margaret's regency this episcopal see was vacant and therefore depended directly from the Holy See.[266] It will be remembered that episcopal appointments in Sicily had to be confirmed by the monarch as the pope's apostolic legate, but here there was no hindrance as Margaret wholeheartedly supported Richard's consecration.

If he were summoned to Rome to be consecrated, Richard would consequently have to assume his duties in Syracuse, his designated diocese, on the other side of Sicily. Naturally, this meant he could spend less time at court in Palermo. Margaret liked this idea as much as she disliked Richard.[267]

The plan was set in motion, and before long[268] John was at the palace standing before Margaret, young King William, the *familiares,* several bishops and sundry barons reading the papal command to all of Sicily's bishops-elect to present themselves in Rome for consecration so as to regularize their positions. As a separate announcement, John added his own condition that the bishops-elect must comply with the papal directive within a certain date.

Richard Palmer craftily agreed to the papal order to be consecrated while refusing to accept any separate, additional conditions imposed by John of Naples. The aspiring prelate thus rejected the deadline. This abnegation was debated at length but resulted in an impasse.

Whilst Richard Palmer's obvious reason for the delay was to avoid abandoning the seat of power at court, he may have harbored an ulterior motive as well. Syracuse enjoyed great prestige as the oldest diocese of the *Regnum,* and arguably the oldest in western Europe, but Richard aspired to more. If he could swap his appointment to Syracuse for Palermo, he would emerge as the most powerful person in the kingdom after the regent herself.

Margaret would have to devise another way to distance Richard Palmer from her inner circle. Word had reached the court that he was beginning to speak against her openly in public. That was something she could not tolerate, for a lack of respect of the regent's decisions might weaken the subjects' loyalty to their queen.

Cardinal John of Naples did not give up trying to get Richard to Rome, and the latter knew he could not forestall consecration forever. So Richard Palmer appealed to another Richard, namely his fellow *familiare* Richard of Molise, who enjoyed the queen's confidence, to aid his cause.

There was no way to force a change in policy, but the pope's envoy might be tricked into providing Molise a platform from which to defend Palmer. This tactic was to prove effective. At a subsequent audience at court, John of Naples responded negatively to requests that he delay the consecration deadline, prompting Richard of Molise to reproach him for threatening to enforce an order that would absent an important counsellor from royal service.

The cardinal responded that Richard Palmer would be free to return to Palermo following his consecration by Pope Alexander. But now John's resolve offended the queen's sense of authority.

Perhaps annoyed that a papal prelate presumed to challenge her prerogative by ordering a *familiare* away from Palermo, Margaret stood up and declared that, "The presence of the archbishop-elect is needed at court, so for now he cannot leave. He can depart in another moment when circumstances permit."[269]

What persuaded the queen to change her mind? Perhaps Margaret was made privy to the tactic of Richard of Molise before the gathering took place, and had reason to think she should make a point of her own by reminding those present that she was in charge. Her decision had the additional benefit of placing Richard Palmer in her debt, in the eyes of others if not his own. Henceforth his public criticism of her would ring hollow. Whatever motivated Margaret, people would remember her willingness to take a decision long after they had forgotten its rationale or even what the decision was about.

The extemporaneous pronouncement had the desired effect of imparting to her subjects the notion that the queen was to be respected.

Divorce Court

Because the monarch was the judge of final appeal, all kinds of cases came before Margaret. Some were rooted in personal dilemmas.

Not long after the incident involving Richard Palmer, a man named Richard of Sai arrived at court accompanied by his wife, who he wished to divorce in order to marry Theodora, a girl who happened to be the niece of Alfano, archbishop of the important diocese of Capua, north of Naples.

Descended from a Norman family, Richard of Sai was captain and master constable of Apulia. His deeds over the last decade had shown him to be steadfastly loyal, even more faithful than Margaret's cousin Gilbert who held authority in the same region. Richard's wife was a noblewoman, sister of Bartholomew of Parisio.

Margaret's first decision was to reward Richard by enfeoffing him with Fondi, a county that had belonged to a deceitful vassal who was now exiled.[270] That was the simpler task, but it showed the queen's willingness to enforce her authority even in unpleasant matters.

A divorce could be just as bitter, and embittering, as the attainder of a disloyal baron. The crown permitted divorce, but because the couple seeking legal separation was Christian, rather than Muslim or Jewish, their case had to be referred to the ecclesiastical authorities.[271] The queen instructed the *familiares* to ask the prelates to convene a hearing so that both husband and wife could present their cases. Indeed, the cardinals present at court were accustomed to adjudicating divorces.[272]

Beyond purely legal questions, these matters bore with

them all kinds of wickedness. Despite her uncle being a high prelate, Theodora was regarded as a sexual libertine, whether she was actually promiscuous or not. The mere fact of a woman taking up with a married man was sufficient "justification" for her to be branded a whore.

For her part, Margaret did not seem to hold an opinion of this case strong enough to dissuade her from giving a prosperous town to a loyal subject like Richard of Sai. In a stance redolent of modern sentiments, she was more concerned about Richard's professional life than his adultery.

Like many divorces, this one engendered certain complexities, and perhaps a touch of dishonesty. As the ecclesiastical council would not be satisfied with a vague lament such as adultery to justify dissolving a marriage, Richard of Sai had to come up with a convincing legal argument.

His chief witnesses were two knights who claimed to have seen Richard, some time before his marriage, conducting a romantic affair with a pretty cousin of the woman he eventually married. This would seem to violate the law regarding affinity, a legal form of kinship acquired through marriage "in law," which defined such relationships as a brother-in-law or sister-in-law.[273]

Witnesses for Richard's wife accused the two knights of perjury, claiming they could demonstrate that the two men had lied. Some of these witnesses, being cousins of Richard's estranged wife, felt their kinswoman had been maliciously slandered by her husband's very allegations. But their chief legal argument was that the statute regarding affinity simply did not apply to this case because Richard of Sai had never actually been married to his wife's cousin, with whom he claimed to have had sexual relations.

In this last affirmation they were correct. In strictest terms, the prohibition of affinity should only be applied if a man were actually married to a woman and later sought to wed her sister or cousin.

Cardinal John of Naples wanted to bring the case to a rapid conclusion. At the same time, he hoped to curry favour with Richard of Sai. He made the witnesses swear an oath on their words, he granted the divorce and, as was normal in such settlements, he made the ex-spouses vow not to engage in sexual relations with each other henceforth.

Not every prelate was happy with the decision rendered by John of Naples, for it did not conform to canon law. Ubaldo Allucingoli of Ostia (later Pope Lucius III), one of the men who negotiated the Treaty of Benevento a decade earlier, felt that his fellow cardinal had been compromised ethically through bribery. Other prelates also criticized John. When they asked him if they could apply a similar sentence in like cases, he arrogantly responded that his decision did not establish a legal precedent, and that anyway it was his personal perquisite to do what they could not.

Nobody ever accused John of Naples of lacking an ego. In any case, Richard of Sai was now free to wed Theodora.

Marriage Proposal

Divorces were not the only conjugal questions arising at court. When Manuel Comnenus, the Byzantine Emperor, learned about the death of the Sicilian monarch, he reasoned that the regent would be easier to deal with than the late king. Perhaps an actual alliance could be arranged.

Along with his condolences, he sent ambassadors from Constantinople bearing his proposal that young William II marry his daughter, Maria "Porphyrogenita" (so nicknamed because she was "born to the imperial purple") who, as Manuel's only child, stood to inherit an empire that included part of Asia Minor and the Balkans.

After consulting with her son, the court prelates and the *familiares*, Margaret decided to delay responding to this seductive offer whilst confirming the peace treaty her husband had negotiated with Manuel some years earlier.

Although she did not refuse the betrothal proposal altogether, Margaret needed time to consider its complex stipulations. Having wed at so young an age herself, she probably saw no reason for her son to marry too soon.[274]

This would not be the only decision the queen was obliged to make regarding members of her immediate family and their marriages.

Arrival of Rodrigo, Margaret's Brother

Having heard that Margaret was regent, her half-brother, Rodrigo (who we met earlier), arrived at Palermo with a large contingent of Navarrese knights. She probably summoned him for additional protection at court, but his knights errant were little more than opportunists. Margaret encouraged Rodrigo to change his name to *Henry,* which the Sicilians found more acceptable and pronounceable.[275]

Falcandus describes him as rather fat and ugly, of dark complexion, prone to gambling and lacking in eloquence; boorish, even vulgar.

Margaret had not seen Rodrigo/Henry since he was a child. She did not know him, or his personality, very well, but she may have been warned about his habits.

As her experience with Gilbert had proven, kinsmen could be troublesome. These men were best kept at a distance, and Margaret knew a good place for her wayward sibling.

The queen enfeoffed her younger brother with the prosperous County of Montescaglioso, near Taranto, and several towns in Sicily, namely Noto, Sclafani and Caltanissetta. She also provided him with enough coin to support himself in a dignified manner during his initial travels.

First he spent some time in Palermo, entranced by its souks

and atmosphere. Never had he or his knights seen such a magnificent metropolis.

Then, having squandered most of the money his sister gave him, Henry of Montescaglioso (as he shall now be called) made his way to his new county on the mainland, stopping first to inspect his Sicilian manors.

Along the way to Montescaglioso, he had to pass through Messina. This port city, a springboard for European merchants, pilgrims, knights and pirates on their way to and from the eastern Mediterranean, was infamous for its vice and debauchery, attracting charlatans, beggars and prostitutes. To an inveterate gambler like Henry, the attractions of this place, a kind of medieval "Las Vegas on the Ionian," were irresistible.[276] If Palermo was a city of arrant luxury, Messina was an urban jungle of shameless sin.

News of Henry's impromptu sojourn got back to Margaret, who ordered him, as his sovereign and his older sister, to cross the Strait of Messina and make his way to Montescaglioso. It was summer and he had best reach his estates in time for the harvests.

Almost as an afterthought, Margaret arranged for her brother to marry Adelaide, one of the daughters of her late father-in-law, King Roger II.

Arrival of Stephen of Perche

The government was served well enough by the *familiares* Richard Palmer, Matthew of Aiello and Richard of Molise, with the treasury overseen by Caïd Martin and the palace by its chamberlain Caïd Richard. Of course, these were not the only important courtiers; archdeacon Walter, the tutor of Margaret's sons, was considered important enough to witness royal charters.[277]

But personal ambitions threatened to create fissures in this façade. Matthew wanted to become grand chancellor of the realm, while Richard Palmer envisaged himself as Archbishop of Palermo. Richard of Molise was the most trusted of the *familiares*, and the one most likely to receive the political favours he requested.

Beyond the complexities engendered in the personalities of these men, Margaret saw potential problems in the existing organization of the *Regnum*. No longer a neophyte, she decided, as a matter of policy, to appoint councils of ecclesiastics to manage diocesan lands where there were no serving bishops, thus removing this power from the authority of bailiffs, who were easily corrupted.

The queen felt that she needed intelligent, trustworthy counsellors at her court. She knew that some of her kinsmen were more reliable than Gilbert and Henry, but there were too few of them she had ever had occasion to meet.

At this point she sent a letter to her cousin, Rotrou, who had recently been made Archbishop of Rouen.[278] There was a precedent in presuming to ask such a favour of him. Some years earlier, as Bishop of Evreux, Rotrou had sent Walter to Palermo to serve as the tutor of Margaret's sons. This was the same Walter who sheltered the children in the bell tower when some prisoners escaped the palace dungeon, the same Walter who served as a deacon of Cefalù. It was Walter who she sent to Rouen bearing her letter to Rotrou.

Margaret requested that her cousin might send to Palermo either Stephen of Perche or Robert of Neubourg, intellectuals known for their integrity.

It so happened that Stephen was already in Italy, where he was visiting Gilbert of Gravina, the son of his brother. Stephen and his company intended to go to the Holy Land, perhaps on pilgrimage, but made their way to Palermo when summoned.

In September, Stephen of Perche arrived in Palermo accompanied by the theologian Peter of Blois and thirty-six knights, esquires and friars. Here he was greeted by the Sicilian *familiares,* barons, knights and bishops, who escorted him to the palace to meet his cousin.

Margaret greeted him warmly, receiving him in audience in the crowded presence of her courtiers. Here, invoking memories of her childhood and the kinsman who gave the town of Tudela to her parents, she made a portentous pronouncement that she wanted heard by the entire court:

"Here I see myself finally achieving what I have ardently desired. To the sons of the Count of Perche I owe the same honour one accords a brother. The work of their father, in truth, gave my own father his kingdom. It was the Count of Perche who granted to my mother as his niece, and thereby to my father, a dowry of vast lands conquered in the face of great dangers and prolonged effort from the Muslims of Spain. You need not be surprised that I regard his son, Stephen, my mother's kinsman, as if he were my brother, welcoming him with joy the moment he arrives here from faraway lands. I desire and command that all who declare good wishes to me and my son will sincerely respect and honour Stephen. From your kind treatment of him, I will infer the depth of your fealty and affection toward us."[279]

These were royal words, regally spoken in Norman French, which Falcandus tells us was *quae maxime necessaria esset in curia,* "necessary for those at court to know."

What Margaret needed as much as fealty and good wishes was a loyal advisor and confidant who answered directly to her. At this point, she was not contemplating the replacement of any of the *familiares,* but simply adding Stephen to their number. This, of course, presumed that Stephen himself wished to remain in the Kingdom of Sicily.

The riches they saw in Palermo were beginning to make some of his knights think that settling here might not be such a bad thing. Normandy and England were austere by comparison, and with the onset of winter the men began to cultivate an appreciation of Sicily's climate and delights that transcended olives, dates and artichokes.

As 1166 drew to an end, it was clear that Queen Margaret had shown her mettle to all and sundry.

Power

The barons, ecclesiastics and courtiers promised to accord Stephen of Perche the reverence he deserved, even if, in the deepest depths of their hearts, some of them may have harbored resentment toward a visitor they viewed as an interloper. Despite the warm reception at court, Stephen expressed a certain reluctance to linger in the *Regnum* very long.

The attractions of Palermo were plainly evident. Anybody arriving from elsewhere in Europe was struck not only by its size but by its cosmopolitan ambience. If Messina was Las Vegas, here was New York or Tokyo.

The queen was too busy with the work of ruling the kingdom to partake in Palermo's pleasures. Most of her routine duties were indeed rather banal; a charter of March 1167 finds her acting in the transfer of ecclesiastical property in Palermo.[280]

Speaking to her newly-arrived cousin, Margaret made the point that he would prosper here, where his companions could expect wealth and opportunities far greater than what awaited them beyond the Alps.[281] Peter of Blois, for example, could presume an appointment as the young king's tutor, a position which would permit him plenty of time for his writings.

Stephen discussed the queen's proposal with the companions who had accompanied him to Italy with the intention of thence proceeding to the Holy Land. Not all of them need remain, but it was hoped that some would choose to stay. Among those persuaded to live in Sicily, at least for a few years, were Odo Quarrel, a canon of Chartres, and erudite Peter of Blois.

Grand Chancellor

It wasn't long before Stephen of Perche told his cousin, the queen, that he and most of the men in his company had decided to remain in the Kingdom of Sicily. Wasting no time, Margaret announced that she had appointed Stephen as her grand chancellor, with authority over the *familiares* and the rest of the court.[282] He would be the queen's sword and shield.

Not all at court were enthralled by this appointment, but it was supported by an important cardinal who happened to be in Sicily on his way to France. This was William of Pavia, a papal diplomat whose presence was urgently required in England, where a dispute had broken out between King Henry II and the Archbishop of Canterbury, a London-born prelate of Norman lineage named Thomas Becket. Cardinal William would first stop in France, where Becket was living in self-imposed exile.

The intrigues at the Sicilian court were tame compared to the storm raging beyond the English Channel.

The Queen of Sicily had too many problems of her own to find much time to contemplate the implications of this foreign dispute at any great length, but she knew that familial connections were intertwined across the Norman realms. One of Margaret's kinsmen, Richard of Aigle, held lands in Sussex, where in happier times he went hawking with Thomas Becket.

At an audience with Margaret, Cardinal William expressed how worried he was about two of the exiled archbishop's nephews who had been expelled from England. Could they, he wondered aloud, stay in Sicily until Henry permitted them to return to their homeland?

Yes, said the queen. A letter sent to the queen from Thomas Becket thanks Margaret for her kindness.[283]

Meanwhile, Stephen, as grand chancellor, set about governing the kingdom on his cousin's behalf. Margaret made it clear that all matters concerning administration should be submitted to him. Naturally, the other *familiares* were displeased by this, for it had the intended effect of restricting their access to the queen and their influence in the kingdom.

Outwardly, the prelates seemed to like Stephen. Before long, Romuald of Salerno, who had been Archbishop of Palermo for five years (see note 216), ordained him a subdeacon. Soon the other bishops, acting on Romuald's suggestion, unanimously supported a decision to consecrate Stephen as Archbishop of Palermo and therefore Primate of Sicily, the first among equals in the island's ecclesiastical hierarchy.

This permitted Romuald, who was also Archbishop of Salerno, to focus on his duties as a papal diplomat. However, as Romuald surely knew, Stephen's imminent consecration, which could be years away, created new complexities in the power structure.

At least two clerics at court were eyeing the appointment. Walter, a deacon of Cefalù and the royal tutor, may have seemed the more likely candidate, but Richard Palmer, the bishop-elect of Syracuse, was equally ambitious. Romuald's manoeuvre thwarted their ambitions.

To Romuald — and perhaps even to Margaret — naming the same man to the highest civil and ecclesiastical offices of the realm may have seemed like a good idea.

One of Stephen's first acts as chancellor was to appoint his friend Odo Quarrel as the master of his household. Just as it was necessary to go through Stephen to get to the queen, anybody seeking to reach Stephen needed Odo's consent and cooperation. The problem with this was that Odo's temperament was ill-suited to a secular environment beyond the walls of a monastery. Odo was given to greed, even extortion. He was easily bought, if for a high price.

Stephen's generosity, on the other hand, was beyond question and he was inclined to treat people fairly. Until Stephen's appointment as chancellor, Richard Palmer drew a hefty salary for his services at court. As these duties diminished, so did his salary. In practice, this money was paid from the taxes levied upon a number of hamlets which belonged to the crown rather than a baron or abbot.[284] Stephen permitted the *familiare* to exchange these small settlements for two wealthier villages, not only compensating Richard's loss of remuneration but actually increasing his earnings. One town would be held by Richard *ex officio* only during his tenure as *familiare*, whilst the other was his to keep and someday hand down to his heirs.[285]

Margaret voiced no objection to this *quid pro quo*. Indeed, it reflected her policy of granting counties and baronies to loyal subjects.

Although Romuald himself was instrumental in bringing about Stephen's eventual consecration, if only to foil the ambitions of other likely candidates, before very long he began to entertain grave misgivings about his decision.[286] He had sought to acquiesce to Margaret's desire to spare her court the constant intrigues of the *familiares* and prelates, but the concentration of so much power in one man was risky.

Appointing Stephen chancellor was at least rational. Conversely, electing him archbishop was part of an attempt to attenuate the power of the omnipresent prelates. This annoying problem need not have existed. The cardinals and bishops should have been tending to matters elsewhere instead of conniving in the capital. Once appointed to a diocese, a bishop belonged in his bishopric serving the needs of his flock, not in Palermo stirring up trouble.[287]

Corruption

Avarice was ubiquitous, but many of the grievances against the chancellor were petty complaints rather than affairs of state. Some of the resulting incidents were nothing short of bizarre, and it is fortunate that Margaret didn't have to deal with them herself.

Many nobles and prelates from other parts of the *Regnum,* even distant regions bordering the papal lands, had to make their way to the court to have important charters notarized, or witnessed. It was customary to pay for this service, although the payment was in the nature of an honorarium or gratuity rather than a fixed fee. There was no schedule of fees, the clients paying what they thought was commensurate with the service rendered.[288]

Notaries did not simply witness documents; some were officers akin to what we now call a *barrister* or *attorney,* empowered to draft charters, contracts and treaties, and even to defend legal cases before a justiciar.[289]

A Palermitan notary named Peter, a kinsman of the *familiare* Matthew of Aiello, was rarely content with what was offered him and asked for much more. Such avarice was not aberrant, but the norm.

Refusing to pay the honorarium Peter demanded, several clients went together to Stephen, complaining not only about the high fee requested by Peter but the time the greedy notary required to seal a document.[290] Stephen immediately referred the drafting and notarization of the documents in question to another notary present at court, who completed the work that same day.

It didn't take long for Peter to realize that people who habitually requested his services in the past were no longer doing so. He inferred that his regular clients were going to another notary. If he couldn't entice them to be his clients he would coerce them into it.

Of course, he wasn't the only greedy notary in the capital. Accompanied by some like-minded colleagues, he undertook surveillance of the streets his former clients had to traverse when leaving the offices of the competing notaries who charged lower fees. One day the angry notaries and a squad of thugs violently confronted the clients, beating and insulting them, and confiscated their notarized documents, tearing the charters to shreds and smashing the wax seals affixed to them.[291]

Apprised of the incident, Stephen summoned the perpetrators to court. Among those ordered to appear was Peter, the instigator, who was thrown in jail following a perfunctory but fair hearing during which he readily admitted his guilt.

Richard Palmer took the occasion to denounce Peter's arrest as illegal and unreasonable. He scornfully affirmed, as if it were true, that in Stephen's native France the law might be enforced in this manner but not here in Sicily. According to Richard, the notaries, having great influence at court, did not deserve to be punished so harshly.

The chancellor was more than a little irritated by the belligerent tone of this criticism, especially coming from somebody for whom, just three days earlier, he had guaranteed the income of two wealthy villages. He was especially annoyed that Richard voiced his vociferous criticism in public instead of speaking to Stephen privately.

Rather than respond to this public insult, embittering as it was, the chancellor ordered that Peter be immured in a dungeon until a suitable sentence could be considered against a man capable of threatening the peace of the realm and thereby offending the dignity of the sovereign. But a few days later, acting on the request of the *familiares,* Stephen freed Peter, punishing him by rescinding his right to exercise the profession of notary.

To discourage future incidents of this kind, the chancellor

fixed a limit on what notaries could charge for specific services.[292] Finding the profession a closed caste, he permitted the licensing of a number of new notaries, opening the ranks of this profession to many qualified men who, until now, had been unjustly excluded.

The notaries weren't the only officials adept at the unchecked abuse of power. The provincial and civic bailiffs[293] were likewise out of control, inclined to impose illegal fines on the people under their authority. Most of these monies found their way into the bailiffs' own coffers. This occurred in cities and other territories under royal jurisdiction, as opposed to the feudal lands held by barons.

Stephen's success in curtailing this profusion of abuses earned him the respect of the common folk. He instituted what today would be called an "open-door" policy. This meant that ordinary people could ask for justice. Men and women arrived at court in droves from every part of the *Regnum* seeking writs against their oppressors. So great was their number that there were scarcely enough notaries to draft their complaints or justiciars to hear their cases.

Some viewed Stephen as "an angel sent by God," whilst others extolled the kingdom's new golden age.[294] There were still others, however, who saw in the chancellor a perpetual nemesis.

The Calatabiano Case

It was becoming apparent that, as grand chancellor, Stephen could not be corrupted. Besides this, he was now designated to become the premier ecclesiastic of the realm, something that only enhanced his moral authority. Indeed, it made him something of a "super enforcer" of the law, both religious and secular.

Aware of his power, some Palermitans prevailed upon the

chancellor to rule on the position of Christians who had apostatised and embraced Islam, perhaps covertly. It was claimed that the deception perpetrated by these converts was encouraged by the eunuchs, many of whom were themselves christianized Arabs of dubious religious conviction.

But the reality was rarely so simple. Some of the alleged "apostates" had begun their lives as Muslims, converted to Christianity as young adults, and then, after much contemplation and soul-searching, returned to the Islam of their parents.[295] This was not exactly the same thing as a person raised as a Christian abruptly becoming a Muslim.

This nuance seemed to escape Stephen, who began to prosecute the "apostates" zealously. Such a policy did not endear him to Sicily's Muslims.[296] Only judiciously should modern ideas be applied to medieval circumstances, but there was a perceptible conflict between Stephen's position as chancellor, from whence he represented all the subjects of the realm, and his status as a prelate who spoke only for its Catholics.[297]

If Margaret was not yet *au courant* of Stephen's "apostate policy," she learned of it with the emergence of a specific case.

This involved Robert of Calatabiano. When we last encountered him, he was ensconced in Palermo's seaside castle, where he tortured prisoners and exacted bribes. His proclivity for violence and bribery had gone unpunished because the palace eunuchs concealed his misdeeds from royal eyes.

When it became obvious that Stephen's religious zeal was more than a mere gesture, a number of people took advantage of the situation to step forward to accuse Robert of Calatabiano of being a closet Muslim, a secret apostate. And that was only the tip of the iceberg.

Now Robert stood accused of everything from extortion to theft to murder. His accusers even claimed that he had forced Christian women and boys into prostitution at a private brothel frequented by Muslims. There was no telling where delusion ended and truth began, but the veracity of the allegations was presumed by many, including Stephen and the pope.[298] The people clamored for justice.

Unlike most of the other cases brought before Stephen and his justiciars, this one involved a high official, a great number of alleged victims and monstrous sums of money. Moreover, Robert was well-connected. In former times he was protected by Caïd Peter, who had fled the court and gone to Africa. He now enjoyed the friendship of the influential palace eunuchs. This helped him at the royal court but hurt him in the court of public opinion, for most of the eunuchs were christianized Arabs whose alleged collusion lent credibility to the hypothesis of the private brothel and sexual abuse by Muslims.

The case against Robert of Calatabiano ended up before Margaret.

Here the eunuchs begged the queen to grant clemency to the accused, who they declared to be the victim of malicious slander. They further claimed that the fugitive Caïd Peter was the culpable party because it was he who had ordered, even coerced, Robert to steal and kill.

Stephen saw how difficult the case was, effectively pitting the populace and the public interest against the eunuchs and even the *familiares*.

Margaret likewise found herself in a trying predicament. She wanted to support the majority of her subjects without alienating her government. Attempting to appease both sides was like walking a tightrope without falling into the abyss.

Without actually defending Robert, she asked her chancellor to reduce the number and severity of the charges being brought against the murderous sadist. When Stephen balked at this, she used her authority to overrule him, and ordered him to desist in prosecuting Robert for allegations lodged against him by individuals.[299] This did not exclude crimes against the crown and the Catholic Church.

Margaret made it understood that she wanted an example made of Robert. She did not, and could not, condone his ungodly behavior. Yet her stance implied that, despite the gravity of his crimes, she did not wish to see him become a symbolic "martyr" for the *familiares,* eunuchs, bailiffs and barons.

Without contradicting the queen directly, the chancellor responded that the best he could do was to suspend prosecution of Robert for civil charges. This would exclude offenses that might result in capital punishment. It seemed like a pragmatic compromise.

Privately, Stephen told his royal cousin that he would resign from his positions if she ever again undermined him as she had during this legal case.

He made it clear that for crimes in ecclesiastical jurisdiction Robert would be tried by a jury of bishops. This addressed perjury firstly, followed by incest and adultery, leaving aside larceny, robbery, murder, rape and corruption.[300]

It could be argued that this legal remedy was slightly flawed because, according to the Assizes of Ariano[301] enacted by King Roger, perjury and adultery were civil crimes. One presumes that, in the first instance, they would be prosecuted by justiciars rather than bishops, even though they were also ecclesiastical offenses in the Roman Church.

The verdict was announced at a later audience. To the extent that it did not mete out a death sentence, the *familiares* and eunuchs were satisfied, if not entirely content.

Robert of Calatabiano was flogged before a jeering crowd. His property was seized, and he was sentenced to a prison term in the same castle where he had tortured so many innocent men.

On the way to the seaside fortress, the condemned man was to be paraded along Palermo's main streets as his crimes were announced to the multitude, but the bishops thought better of this plan when they saw how many angry people were gathered in narrow passages from which to pelt Robert with stones. Things were getting out of hand. The sword-bearing knights guarding the prisoner on all sides could barely restrain the relentless crowd, intent as it was on stoning the man to death.

At that point a more circumspect approach was suggested. It was decided to hold Robert behind a wall of the cathedral until the crowd dispersed. A few days later he was taken to the jail in the seaside castle. Clearly, the rumors of the prisoner bribing his way out of confinement were greatly exaggerated.

He died following some sporadic bouts of torture.

The common folk were happy to learn of the tyrant's fate, but others were less pleased by it. Robert's trial and punishment had the effect of cautioning the great of the realm that they too could be penalized for their crimes. This only exacerbated their dislike of Stephen of Perche.

In central Italy, meanwhile, Pope Alexander III was defending papal territory against a major incursion by Frederick Barbarossa. Margaret sent funds to assist the besieged pontiff, who was forced to leave Rome. In the event, it was not papal military might but an epidemic among his imperial troops that drove Frederick out of Italy. This eliminated any foreign threat to Margaret during the regency. Most of her detractors were in the *Regnum* itself.

Defamation

Until now, the magnates were reluctant to speak ill of the queen except perhaps through whispers about her poor choice of a chancellor. Whilst Margaret, in the interest of keeping the peace, might attenuate the prosecution of a corrupt castellan like Robert of Calatabiano, she was far less likely to tolerate overt treason against her son or herself. Margaret's rule as regent was absolute.[302]

If it were difficult to find fault with Stephen of Perche, his detractors might invent flaws they could easily attribute to him and perhaps even the regent. Palermo was a rumor mill; conditions favored the wide and rapid diffusion of hearsay.

Margaret knew this as well as anybody. A revolt fomented by rumors had claimed the life of one of her sons. However majestic its wonders, Palermo's vicissitudes had shown that the city was no magical "Camelot on the Tyrrhenian."

Although the kingdom's magnates did not savor the idea of taking orders from a woman, something to which they were unaccustomed, they knew that it was only a matter of a few years before William reached the age of majority. In the meantime, however, the chancellor could do much to delimit the scope of their power. He had already shown what he could achieve in the space of just one year.

It was easy enough to contrive rumors about "corruption" at court, and the agitators knew that vague allegations of wrongdoing, however outlandish, were difficult to refute very convincingly. Simple reasoning would dictate that the burden of proof lies with the person asserting a claim, for it is easier to show that something happened than to prove that it did not, but by Margaret's time the epistemology enshrined in the Socratic method was all but forgotten. Facts were whatever the hate mongers wanted them to be.

Besmirching the queen's name would not be a very simple matter.

Somebody at court — so it was said — noticed the queen smile at the chancellor in a way that "somebody" deemed to reflect undue familiarity, even intimacy. "She devoured him with her eyes, and it was feared that an illicit love was hidden behind the guise of kinship," wrote Falcandus.[303]

Lacking any legitimate grievance against the regent, some men resorted to the centuries-old practice of defaming a woman as promiscuous or adulterous.

This technique for attacking medieval queens was not terribly original, nor even too unusual. In Margaret's time, accusing a queen of having a sexual affair with a highly-placed courtier was something of a cliché.[304] The path before many a woman was strewn with such innuendo.

The attacks directed at Stephen emanated from several quarters. The eunuchs despised him for imprisoning their ally Robert of Calatabiano. The barons resented him because most of the largesse and influence they monopolized in the past were now going to Stephen's friends. Sicily's most prominent Muslim, Abu'l Kasim, disliked the fact that his rival, Caïd Siddiq, Palermo's wealthiest Muslim, had become one of Stephen's advisors.

Little could be done to pacify those bemoaning the lust they thought revealed itself in Margaret's eyes, but Stephen sought to allay the laments that reached his ears.

Injury

Although his efforts were earnest, Stephen's reputation was not helped by an incident that seemed to reflect an overzealous surveillance of his adversaries.

One of the men suspected of stirring up dissent was Matthew of Aiello, the *familiare*. When it was observed that he was sending more letters than usual across Sicily to his brother, John, an influential prelate in Catania, an attempt was made to intercept some of the couriers carrying these documents.[305] This mission was entrusted to Robert of Bellisina, whose men attempted to apprehend a messenger who was returning to Palermo.[306] While the courier bearing a letter from John got away, his colleague was caught. This man resisted arrest and was wounded.

Matthew soon learned of the incident. Finding himself under suspicion, he decided to act.

Not long after the incident involving Matthew's courier, Robert of Bellisina fell ill with a grave fever. A physician named Salernus[307] was recommended to administer a cure. Knowing Salernus to be a close acquaintance of Matthew, who had undertaken to get him appointed as a judge in the city of Salerno, Stephen sagely refused sending him to Robert. Instead, he ordered another doctor to treat him.

Concealing his movements from the chancellor, Salernus visited Robert several times. Nevertheless, the sick man failed to recover and soon died. Stephen was sad to learn of Robert's death.

The condition of the corpse was disturbing. Robert's hair fell out and patches of his skin separated from his muscle tissue. This suggested to some that poisoning had killed him, but to be certain the chancellor asked a team of physicians led by Romuald of Salerno[308] to begin a medical investigation.

Those who had been close to Robert of Bellisina confirmed that Salernus had offered him a liquid, but what was in the potion?

It so happened there was living proof of its toxicity. A friend of Robert's showed the investigators a hand bearing a wound from a haemorrhage that erupted when, out of view of Robert and the servants, this man had poured the same liquid on his own palm, thinking to test it in this way before ingesting it.

Another witness, a notary named William, informed the investigators that a man in the employ of Matthew of Aiello often approached him to ask about Robert.

Thus informed, Stephen of Perche met with the *familiares,* Romuald and others, who agreed that the chancellor should summon Salernus for questioning.

Initially, the man denied ever administering a medicinal syrup to Robert of Bellisina but recanted this mendacious testimony when confronted by witnesses. Then he claimed to have given Robert innocuous rose water made by Justus, a local druggist. However, when interrogated, this apothecary swore that he had sold nothing to Salernus during the four weeks prior to Robert's death. It was clear that Salernus was not telling the truth.

The next day, the high justiciars of the court convened an audience. Under interrogation, Salernus responded to their queries in a desultory way, offering no exculpatory evidence.

He was found guilty of murder, the justiciars ordering his death and the confiscation of his property. Had Salernus decided to cooperate with the investigation by divulging the name of his fellow conspirator, the justiciars might have been inclined to grant him clemency, commuting his sentence to prison time and sparing his life. However, he could not be persuaded to disclose this information.

Margaret was advised of the trial and sentence but played no part in it. If Matthew of Aiello were involved in some way, the incident was indeed disconcerting.

The fate of Salernus, unlike that of Robert of Calatabiano a few weeks earlier, was not important enough politically to warrant royal intervention. What is more, the evidence against Salernus was overwhelming.

As the weeks passed, there would be greater challenges to face.

Margaret's Brother Returns

It will be recalled that for his steadfast loyalty Richard of Molise (Mandra) was granted a large county and made a *familiare*. This irritated his Apulian peers, who managed to turn Margaret's brother, Henry (Rodrigo) of Montescaglioso against this man he barely knew. The pretext was that Richard was abusing his power, while Henry, as the regent's brother and the young monarch's uncle, deserved a lofty position at court.

Henry's arrogance was nourished by the support of the company of Spanish knights who came to Italy with him, their number augmented by others who had recently arrived from Navarre. With these knights and several influential barons[309] allied with him, he crossed from the mainland to Sicily with the intention of intimidating Margaret, Stephen and the *familiares* into acceding to his demands. If he knew that Gilbert of Gravina, who was his second cousin, had already failed in trying to achieve the same thing, it made no difference to him.

Advised of Henry's arrival at Messina, the *familiare* Richard of Molise met with Stephen of Perche to warn the chancellor that these interlopers must not be granted any standing at court, even if it were necessary to subdue them through armed confrontation.

Stephen was no great admirer of Richard of Molise, but the last thing he wanted was to see blood spilled in the city. Acting prudently, he sent to Henry a letter written on the queen's authority ordering him to come to the capital but without his confederates, who were to remain at Termini Imerese, about midway between Palermo and Cefalù.

Meeting with Henry, Stephen was able to convince him to ignore the complaints of the Apulian barons. As the queen's brother, he had obtained much and might be further rewarded if he were loyal to her. Henry made peace with Richard of Molise, who he had been led to view as a rival.

Margaret was angry about her brother's insubordination on the mainland, where for months he had failed to follow her orders, but the chancellor managed to broker a reconciliation between the siblings. Henry went so far as to promise obedience in the future.

With this familial truce achieved, Stephen summoned the vassals who had come to Sicily with Henry and were waiting at Termini up the coast. At court, they reaffirmed their fealty once they realized that their plan had failed. One amongst them, Bohemond of Manopello, who was distinguished for his exceptional intelligence, established a sincere friendship with the chancellor.

Henry also became very friendly with Stephen. This displeased those who were conspiring to obtain power.

Having failed to achieve their ends through force of arms, these malcontents now sought to dissuade Henry's friendship with Stephen through words. They strove to convince his most trusted Spanish knights that befriending the chancellor was not in their noble lord's interest. Here they resorted to what they thought were effective methods, telling the knights that Stephen was having an incestuous relationship with the queen.[310] They went further, implying that Henry was naive, seeing as he was the only person at court unaware of this (alleged) liaison between Stephen and Margaret.

Henry was not wise. Indeed, he was credulous and rather easily duped. Nevertheless, at first he was disinclined to believe what he heard about the affable chancellor and the queen, people he knew and respected.

He changed his mind when the rumor's imagined accuracy was reinforced by the very people who, unbeknownst to Henry, had hatched it in the first place.[311] This led him to forswear his loyalty to Stephen of Perche, believing the worst about his own sister. With this, the queen's brother joined the plotters.

Ubiquitous Disloyalty

Henry of Montescaglioso was not alone. Within the palace walls, Caïd Richard, the chamberlain, who despised Stephen, was convincing ever more men-at-arms, from knights to archers, to join the plot against the chancellor.[312] Most of this he achieved through simple bribery.

Stephen was vaguely aware of this. He organized a fifty-man bodyguard that included many French knights, never going anywhere in Palermo without a company of at least twenty or thirty armed men.

One may argue the degree to which the hatred directed at the chancellor also reflected baronial resentment of the queen he served but, in the worst scenario, Stephen's death would certainly weaken Margaret's position. It would also spawn chaos at court. The *familiares* might remain loyal, but there was no way to tell where the unrest would end.

Margaret had already seen violence aplenty.

Stephen reasoned that confronting the conspirators at this point might be preferable to waiting for them to make the first move. For now, he lacked much evidence against any of them, yet he didn't want to give them more time to prepare a rebellion that could lead to a civil war.

If, as he had been informed, there were plotters like Caïd Richard within the palace walls, that made the capital itself potentially dangerous.[313]

Disturbing as this was, expediency alone suggested that it may be best to address the problems growing outside the confines of Palermo. Whatever they were doing on the island, the more egregious offenders garnered their most effective support in Apulia, where royal authority was entrusted to a cadre of men whose loyalty sometimes seemed dubious, among them Margaret's kinsmen Gilbert of Gravina and Henry of Montescaglioso. The queen therefore contemplated an inspection tour of the mainland during the spring. If nothing else, her appearance would remind any doubters of her authority throughout the realm, not only on the island of Sicily.

The strategic key to the kingdom was Messina, whose harbor was at least as important, both commercially and militarily, as the port of Palermo. From there, it was easy to follow Calabria's Ionian coast by land or sea to Taranto and then Bari.

With this in mind, Stephen proposed that the queen spend the approaching winter at Messina. The city wasn't really very far from the capital. A relay of couriers on fast steeds made it possible to get a letter to or from Palermo in three full days.

Margaret liked the idea of spending some time at Messina, where there was a fortified royal palace near the coast.[314] Her extended presence might even discourage some of the city's infamous vices.

Regardless of whether the queen ultimately decided to travel to Apulia, bringing the court to Messina from time to time was rooted in geographical reality. More than half the *Regnum* was in peninsular Italy, and for anybody coming from Apulia, Calabria, Campania, or even more distant Abruzzi, a journey to Messina was far more convenient than riding another four or five days to reach Palermo after crossing into Sicily.

In September, Stephen summoned his kinsman Gilbert of Gravina to Messina, explaining that the court planned on passing the winter there.

The October of 1167 was rainier than usual, and the *familiares* used this as an excuse to try to dissuade the queen's departure during this season. Stephen was undeterred, ordering that the coastal roads to Messina be prepared for the arrival of young King William and the royal family.

In early November, word was received that the pope had ratified the nomination of Stephen as Archbishop of Palermo. The prelates of the kingdom swore their fealty to him as their primate, and Romuald intended to consecrate him in a solemn ceremony in the capital's cathedral. Yet Stephen was never actually consecrated as planned.[315]

Stephen, like the queen, often tended to minutiae, such as confirming the privileges of the Benedictine monastery of Saint John of the Hermits near the palace.[316]

The weather improved by Martinmas, and on the morning of Wednesday, the fifteenth of November, the royal party set out for Messina. The chancellor left an army of knights behind to guard the capital; these men were loyal to Stephen.

Caïd Richard, as the chamberlain, was left in charge of the palace, but couriers seeking to consign letters to the queen and chancellor knew where to find them.

Accompanied by the chancellor, high justiciars and some notaries, along with a large company of knights, the queen visited a number of towns *en route* to Messina. This included the fortress of San Marco d'Alunzio, where Beatrice, the widow of King Roger II, was living with her young daughter Constance. Although young King William was about the same age as Constance, the girl was his aunt.

The queen and her family finally arrived in Messina at the very end of November.

Reginal Wisdom

A number of nobles were waiting for Margaret at Messina. One of them was Robert of Caserta.[317] This loyal count had heard that his cousin, William of San Severino, whose exile had recently been lifted, had convinced Margaret to restore his former lands to his possession.

Accompanied by several advocates, Robert petitioned the court requesting a revision of this decree on the basis that, in fact, certain lands now held by William legally belonged to the former. The reasoning for this was that in an earlier time William's father had come to possess them illegally through the use of force. In other words, these lands had never belonged to William by law.

Margaret wanted to rule justly. Although she understood Robert's complaint, the queen did not wish to alienate William by diminishing his property and wealth.

William had earned Stephen's trust; the chancellor considered him loyal. On the other hand, there were doubts in Stephen's mind about Robert's fealty. Nevertheless, there was no point in offending this man to the degree that he might be encouraged to join the kingdom's malcontents.

Acting on Stephen's advice, the queen gave Robert of Caserta, who seemed to have the stronger case, the lands he requested, compensating William of San Severino with other manors. She imposed the condition that this decision was final, and therefore the matter would never again be brought before the court.

The ecclesiastical sphere, as always, was full of complexities, even conflict. Margaret granted a charter to Nicholas, the Archbishop of Messina, confirming his episcopal rights following a local dispute in which the prelate's authority had been challenged.[318]

The next matter brought before the queen involved local taxes. King Roger had given the city certain privileges and tax exemptions, only to rescind these measures later. The rights later confirmed by his son seemed insufficient compensation for those that had been revoked.[319] Seeking to encourage Stephen to reinstitute these rights, the Messinians offered him bribes. The chancellor categorically rejected the gifts proffered him but convinced Margaret to bestow anew the rights once granted by her father-in-law. This seemed like a good way to earn some respect from the local people.

Stephen's strategy was effective. By December, there was always a crowd of subjects at court seeking justice. The people came from Calabria, eastern Sicily and elsewhere in the *Regnum*. The scene was not unlike what had occurred a few months earlier in Palermo, when the chancellor instituted his "open door" policy and began to assail corruption. The queen herself addressed very few cases, usually those involving important prelates and nobles, but every decision was rendered in the name of her son, King William II.

Richard of Aversa

Seeing that the queen and chancellor were just, a delegation of Messinians came forth to denounce the abuses of Richard of Aversa, their city's governor.[320] Here the long litany of accusations was similar to that advanced against Robert of Calatabiano. Richard was said to have committed every kind of crime, often through accomplices acting as his proxies. The jeremiad included murder, robbery, thievery, even arson. It was said that the governor had illegally confiscated houses and vineyards. The people claimed that he excelled at bribing justiciars. Debauchery and adultery were not overlooked. If even a fraction of the allegations were true, Richard was the busiest man in the kingdom.

Stephen of Perche suspected that a few of the accusations might well be true, but he sought to control the governor rather than subject him to the rigors of a formal trial.

Having believed that the queen's presence augured well for them, the Messinians resented this procrastination, offended that everybody else in the kingdom obtained justice whilst the crimes perpetrated in their loyal city were neglected. Some leaders wrote out the grievances against the governor on signs they attached to long poles, displaying these during a raucous protest in front of the palace.

The Christmas season had already begun, but the clamoring crowd convinced Margaret that she had to resolve this matter here and now. Without hesitation, she commanded Stephen to accept the Messinians' petitions. He referred the case to the high justiciars, ordering them to begin an inquest, specifying that a hearing be held during the next few days.

The subsequent trial revealed that Richard of Aversa was unambiguously guilty of a great many offenses. He was imprisoned and his property was confiscated. Having left the trial to the justiciars, Margaret and Stephen now remonstrated with Richard, and there was no vocal opposition to the verdict except perhaps from the condemned man and his family.

To say that this decision bolstered local esteem for Stephen would be an understatement. The people loved him. Just as importantly, the subjects sang the incessant praises of their queen. Margaret felt that, at long last, she was paving the way to a peaceful kingdom for her son.

It was finally time to celebrate Christmas. These festivities, with their endless liturgies, extended into early January, culminating with the Epiphany.

Management Style

The subtle contours of Margaret's policy were being shaped by pragmatism. She was not rewriting her late husband's script, merely editing it into a form resilient enough to survive into the first few years of her son's majority. She wanted to hand him a kingdom as free of disquietude as a medieval realm could be. In this she was selfless.

What emerges from a sober analysis of the first phase of the regency is an approach to governing that was meant to eliminate abuses whilst maintaining the essential organization of the monarchy. The three *familiares* represented the feudal (Richard of Molise), governmental (Matthew of Aiello) and ecclesiastical (Richard Palmer) spheres.[321] The high justiciars were a kind of "supreme court," whilst the other justiciars were, essentially, district judges. Constables, bailiffs (governors), ecclesiastics (bishops and abbots), and vassals (counts and barons) administered specific territories. All reported to the regent and chancellor, although prelates answered to the pope for strictly ecclesiastical matters. The legal code, the Assizes of Ariano, provided a juridical, and even social, framework for the Kingdom of Sicily, and the rights of religious minorities were guaranteed.

In contrast to the smaller, less important realm of her brother, Sancho "the Wise" of Navarre, Margaret's *Regnum Siciliae* placed her on an economic and political parity with Henry II of England and Frederick Barbarossa.

However, whereas Henry and Frederick were waging their own jurisdictional or territorial battles with the papacy, Margaret was friendly with Pope Alexander III. Her "foreign policy" (to use a modern term) was solid, and solidly beneficial to her subjects.

At home, the treasury was administered well, and the greater number of subjects were happy to see corrupt men removed from power. Serfdom was not as widespread here as it was in many other parts of Europe.

The three "feminine estates" were virgin, wife and widow, defining women by their relationship to men. The most influential Christian women were abbesses; these nuns were well-educated. The Muslim and Jewish women of the *Regnum* were, for the most part, just as literate as the nuns.[322]

Rare indeed was the woman who managed a small manor, let alone a barony, rarer still the woman who practiced medicine.[323]

Margaret was resolute in her conviction that the kingdom should be ruled a certain way, but her approach was much more than an instinctive reaction to the way her husband had ruled.

At a formative stage in his life, young William was learning by example as he attended royal audiences. Procedures and principles were explained to him. Unlike most young European monarchs, he was being taught not only by male tutors but by the woman who ruled in his name. This was highly exceptional in 1167, and it was one of the things that made William II an exceptional monarch.

There is nothing to suggest that Margaret was unduly harsh, but there can be no doubt that she was unafraid to wield the absolute royal authority she held in her slender hands. At least a few criminals and traitors reluctant to live righteously under her rule died by it.[324] Anybody who presumed to break the law with impunity simply because there was a woman on the throne had best think again.

Falcandus tells us that there were subjects who resented the "Spanish woman," but there is no evidence to suggest that Margaret ever attracted much opprobrium from the common folk who, on the contrary, literally cheered when oppressive tyrants like Robert of Calatabiano and Richard of Aversa were tried and punished. The most obstreperous naysayers were to be found among the aristocracy.

Bad Blood

By the middle of January in 1168, the majority of Messinians seemed content. Unbeknownst to the queen, however, Henry of Montescaglioso, her troublesome half-brother, was up to his old tricks. In this he was abetted by Bartholomew of Parisio, whose sister, it may be recalled, was once married to Richard of Sai, the man granted a divorce on questionable grounds in order to wed a woman reputed to be a harlot. Bartholomew's conniving may have had less to do with the perceived slight against his sister than with his own maneuvering to achieve greater power for himself through his close alliance with Henry. Not only did Bartholomew exercise a certain influence over some Messinians, a number of Calabrians present in the city to greet the young king were party to his covert machinations.

No attempt at rioting was made during the Christmas season that had just ended, but it would transpire that Henry was contemplating a more specific operation, for which public disorder was merely a diversionary tactic.

Bartholomew was to some degree discouraged by the arrival of Gilbert of Gravina, Margaret's cousin, with a formidable company of a hundred well-armed knights. It was precisely to avoid potential dissension that Stephen of Perche had summoned Gilbert to Messina. Gilbert, of course, was Stephen's nephew.

Both were Norman to the core, and here was the root of yet another potential problem, for in recent weeks the French knights present in unruly Messina had taken to treating the local people[325] with contempt, frequently insulting them.

Bartholomew wanted more than an insurrection. He and his minions incited Henry to plan the assassination of Stephen, thinking that the chancellor's death might pave the way for the queen's half-brother to seize power. To that end, Henry solicited a certain Roger, a local justiciar, to join the plot. Roger feigned collaboration but secretly advised the chancellor of Henry's homicidal plan a day before it was to be set in motion.

Stephen instructed Roger the justiciar to behave with Henry and Bartholomew as if nothing had changed; in the meantime he informed the queen of the situation, advising her to act without delay.

News of the murder conspiracy upset Margaret greatly. Its implications were myriad. Here was gross disrespect by a man toward his own sister, who had helped him in every conceivable way. Beyond that, he was a traitor to the kingdom she ruled in the name of her son.

The queen knew she had to act if this kind of thing were to be discouraged throughout the *Regnum*, but she found it, at the very least, distasteful to mete out justice to her own brother. More immediately, Henry had to be punished to dissuade others who might still attempt to carry out the assassination even after its chief plotter and beneficiary was unmasked.

Margaret Jiménez might consider clemency for her stupid brother, but Margaret, Queen Regent of Sicily, enjoyed no such prerogative.

Henry's Trial

The queen needed a strategy. First, she would convene a

formal trial. Either Henry would be found guilty, or he would admit to his crimes of his own volition. Either way, he would then be expected to cooperate by identifying the other conspirators. If he were reluctant to name them, some time in a castle jail might loosen his traitorous tongue. Dungeons were cold this time of year.[326]

Margaret had Henry arrested, and ordered Stephen to summon the high justiciars, *familiares,* bishops and nobles who were to hear the case. The hearing took place ten days later under heavy guard.

Even though Henry himself was in custody, most of his co-conspirators were still at large; they posed a very real risk. In his opening statement, the accused man decried the value of his "paltry" income from the County of Montescaglioso. An aggrieved Henry wanted Taranto, even though that strategic port city was traditionally reserved to a member of the royal family. At the very least, he felt entitled to some wealthy lands in eastern Sicily.

Ridiculous as this demand was, it did not lack for a pretext. If refused these prosperous lands, Henry hoped to more plausibly justify his hatred of Stephen of Perche for forcing the queen's half-brother into penury.

In response, Gilbert of Gravina thundered that Henry had tried to use the implicit threat of military force to coerce the queen into giving him lands which, had he behaved better in the first place, might have already been in his possession. He accused the queen's half-brother of deception, stating that the man should not, by right, hold any lands in the kingdom. He then excoriated him for being a spendthrift whilst oppressing the peasants on his estates. Gilbert went on to cite Henry's foolish suggestion that Margaret fortify castles in his manors and hide money there against the future possibility that William II might not always be loyal to his own mother. He spoke of how Henry tried to manipulate young William into thinking that Margaret was somehow damaging the king and the kingdom, and how the boy responded (to Henry) that in distrusting his own mother he would also have to distrust her brother. Gilbert spoke of how Henry accused him, Gilbert, of disloyalty. He asked Henry what fault he found in Stephen so grave that it justified assassination.

Gilbert concluded by saying that Henry, despite his maudlin appeal to justice, deserved no lands in the Kingdom of Sicily. As a traitor, he deserved to be deprived of his property, along with his very life.

When Henry vehemently denied organizing any conspiracy to kill the chancellor, Roger the justiciar was brought in to testify, affirming the details of the plot. Henry's testimony became even more unseemly as he lost his temper and accused Roger of betraying a promise to collaborate in the conspiracy. Here the accused man contradicted himself, for just a few minutes earlier he had adamantly denied plotting to kill the chancellor.

In this way Henry condemned himself with his own words. He was ordered detained in the palace, where the trial had taken place.

Before long, word reached Stephen that Henry's company of knights was assembling at the condemned man's residence in the city, and that many Messinians were taking up arms in expectation of a riot, or even a battle. The chancellor ordered his own knights, and those of Gilbert of Gravina, to guard the palace. Armed men were dispatched into the streets to restore order by assuring the populace that there was no need for alarm.

Whilst Henry languished in jail, his knights[327] were ordered to surrender their weapons and immediately cross into Calabria, with the caveat that any men who failed to comply with this royal command would be imprisoned immediately. Deprived of their swords, daggers and shields, the downtrodden knights made their way to the port and traversed the strait.

Having heard about what had occurred over in Sicily, the local Greeks[328] saw the opportunity for plunder and a touch of vengeance. An angry mob assaulted the disarmed men, leaving them with little more than the clothes they were wearing. The beaten knights made their way northward but many died in the frozen forests of the Sila Mountains.

Back in Messina, an attempt was made to identify Henry's most pernicious partisans. One of these men who approached the chancellor and voluntarily confessed was temporarily exiled whilst his lands were entrusted to an abbot friendly to the queen.[329] Another, conversely, was imprisoned because he came forward only after the identities of the chief conspirators had already been divulged by Margaret's incarcerated half-brother.[330] Under interrogation, and with no immediate hope of release, Henry had seen fit to disclose most of the plot's details.

Some at court propounded that Stephen of Perche pardon most of the offenders, even if many of the plotters clearly merited death or, at the very least, lengthy imprisonment. Gilbert of Gravina suggested otherwise. He had his own reason for this.

Richard of Molise Accused

Richard of Molise, it may be remembered, had nearly come to blows with Gilbert of Gravina, the queen's cousin, during an argument about the flight of Caïd Peter to Africa. At Richard's urging, Matthew of Aiello successfully managed to have Gilbert sent away from the court on the pretext that he was needed on the peninsula to fend off an impending invasion by Frederick Barbarossa. True, Barbarossa did eventually make his way into papal territory, but he was forced to withdraw before invading the Kingdom of Sicily. Nevertheless, duplicitous Gilbert, who was envious of Richard's rank as *familiare,* had never forgotten this affront. His enmity was at least explicable.

At a royal audience, Bohemond of Manopello[331] accused Richard of having covertly supported the recent conspiracy. At first, Margaret found this absurd, but if her own brother could not be trusted, then who could she trust? On the other hand, Bohemond was a confederate of her brother.

For his part, Richard of Molise vigorously denied the ludicrous allegation that painted him as a miscreant, challenging to trial by single combat anybody who accused him of such a flagrant betrayal.

Further accusations followed, intended, more than anything, to erode Richard's credibility in the eyes of the queen. Their substance was that he continued, illegally, to hold the County of Mandra, as well as some royal towns around Troia. To this the *familiare* responded that Mandra had been entrusted to him temporarily by Caïd Peter and the Troian towns by Turgisio, that region's chamberlain. Turgisio, who was present, refuted this.

An impromptu jury led by the high justiciars, but excluding Matthew of Aiello, the other *familiare* present, then conferred to discuss the charges against Richard. This was not entirely proper but Margaret and Stephen did not object to it. In any case, the queen was the ultimate judge in the matter.

The sanctimonious "judges" decided that Richard held Mandra and the Troian towns legally so long as Caïd Peter guaranteed his possession, but effectively lost this tenure as soon as Peter fled the *Regnum*. Richard protested this casuistry, saying that justice was being corrupted, but Stephen did not wish to contradict a jury led by high justiciars. The travesty of justice that condemned Richard bore all the hallmarks of a vengeful show trial for which the verdict had already been determined.

The accused nobleman was not allowed to exonerate himself. Instead of his accusers being required to prove his guilt, Richard was expected to prove his innocence.[332]

The *familiare* was arrested, and imprisoned in the castle on the rocky mountain overlooking Taormina to the south of Messina.

A number of others were condemned for being directly involved in the conspiracy. Most, like Bartholomew of Parisio, were imprisoned. Walter of Moac demanded trial by combat, and this duel was scheduled.[333]

Henry of Montescaglioso was imprisoned at Reggio in Calabria. Stephen ordered Odo Quarrel to hold him there until he could be taken to Spain. Margaret had decided to send him to the court of her brother, King Sancho, at Pamplona, with a thousand ounces of gold. The plan was for seven galleys under Odo's command to take Henry as far as Arles. From there, the fickle prince could make his way overland to Spain.

In exchange for Gravina, Gilbert requested the affluent County of Loritello. If this discouraged the return of Robert, its exiled holder, so much the better, at least from Gilbert's point of view. Stephen granted this request, which angered the residents of Loritello who had hoped that Robert might one day return to them.

It had been an awful winter. How many more like it could Margaret hope to survive?

Palermo

Margaret's presence in Messina had reminded the people of her power, but this was little more than a bittersweet victory. Now she really did not know who to trust. Like her kindred sovereigns, she was learning that royal authority was tenuous, and dangerous for whoever held it.

The regent found time in early March to grant the Agrò forest to the Most Holy Savior abbey.[334] These lands had belonged to a Greek Orthodox monastery, and the number of such communities was dwindling while those of the Roman Catholics increased. The queen also exempted a monastery from an import tax[335] and ceded the manor of Rahal el Melum Rameth, near Milazzo, to the nunnery of Santa Maria delle Scale[336] of Messina, in the care of Antiochia, its abbess.[337]

Following a visit to inspect Santa Maria delle Scale, where a royal chapel was consecrated, Margaret and her sons left Messina on the twelfth of March. On the way to Palermo, they stopped at a number of coastal towns. The most important was Cefalù, where they were welcomed by the bishop, Boson of Gorron, who very much wanted the bodies of Roger II and William I to be entombed in his cathedral. The royal party arrived at Palermo on the twentieth.

Conspicuously absent from the entourage was Richard of Molise, the *familiare* now imprisoned at Taormina on the other side of the island. Whatever he thought of his fellow *familiare*, Matthew of Aiello, who had spent the winter with the royal party at Messina, had made no effort to defend him. There was a certain logic to this, regardless of the working relationship that had existed between the two men. Quite simply, Matthew now had one less peer with whom to share his power.

We do not know if Margaret had misgivings about Richard's sentence; the evidence against him was flimsy indeed, but she never abjured her contention that he was guilty. She needed an exegesis. More importantly, she needed allies, and if, as Richard claimed, his loyalty to the queen had never faltered, Margaret made a grave error in permitting him to be incarcerated. In choosing not to exercise her moral authority, she had renounced it. What is more, she alienated a *familiare* who otherwise would have remained one of her most steadfast allies.

Margaret found herself somewhat more isolated than she had already been, even if this reality was not immediately obvious. But she knew that her trial by fire had not yet ended, and she had three more years to serve as regent before William reached the age of majority.

Disloyalty was rampant. The *familiare* Matthew of Aiello, the chamberlain Caïd Richard and Bishop Gentile of Agrigento perceived a changed situation now that Gilbert of Gravina and his large contingent of knights were no longer present to bolster the power of Stephen of Perche, the chancellor. The absence of Richard of Molise, who also commanded some knights, only reinforced their belief that Stephen was underprotected and could now be overthrown.

As usual, there were pretexts for the claim that the chancellor was acting inappropriately. One of the more credible among these was that the Frenchman[338] to whom Stephen had given the Sicilian lands of the late Bonello was mistreating the local people. This allegation bore a grain of truth because only the people classified as serfs, be they Arab or Greek, were obligated to remit the kind of taxes[339] the French baron was collecting.

Deceptively, the complaint painted Matthew, Richard and Gentile as defenders of the populace despite their disdain for the common folk. Unfortunately, in rendering judgment in the matter Stephen relied on the advice of two French counsellors[340] rather than Sicilians knowledgeable in local law.

The traitorous triumvirate wasted no time contemplating an attack on Stephen, conspiring to kill him on Palm Sunday, the Sunday before Easter.[341] Their scheme called for him to be struck down whilst leaving Palermo's cathedral with the royal cortege.[342]

Obviously, the assassination plot required the participation of a certain number of accomplices if it were to be successful. The chief conspirators were adept at stabbing somebody in the back verbally, but the task of doing so literally, with a real sword, was assigned to a professional. In the event, the plan was aborted after several knights involved in it were arrested and divulged some of its details.[343]

For now, Stephen's detractors sought wider support for their cause. One of their tactics presented itself in the reaction of Stephen's counsellors to the French baron's taxation on peasants. Exploiting this, the trio disseminated the rumor that the populace of the entire *Regnum* would soon be subjected to these taxes, which until now were unheard of.

It didn't take long for Stephen to determine the source of these detrimental rumors. He suspected that Matthew of Aiello might be the mastermind of the most recent defamation scheme. Matthew was summoned to court, where he was formally accused of treason. Unable to defend himself against such an accusation, the *familiare,* who was also high notary of the realm, was summarily incarcerated. The chroniclers differ slightly in their assessments of Matthew's character.[344]

The chancellor didn't stop with Matthew of Aiello. Stephen wanted to arrest Caïd Richard, who he felt certain was involved with Aiello in the disinformation campaign that was eroding his prestige.

But here Margaret drew the line, forbidding the arrest of the palace chamberlain.[345] The most that Stephen achieved was having Richard confined to the palace and prohibited from communicating with his company of knights.

Daily Life

By 1168, Margaret found herself in the midst of ruling and, for the most part, governing a kingdom of more than two million people.[346] What was a typical day like for the most powerful woman in Europe?

She usually woke up early and attended matins in the palace chapel with her sons and a few ladies of the court. Some days this was followed by liturgy (mass) in the palace chapel or in one of the nearby churches, such as the Mary Magdalene chapel, where two of her sons were buried. Then she would have breakfast. Commoners might consume one or, with luck, two meals per day, but royalty sometimes had three.

During the morning, the queen met in audience with the chancellor, the *familiares,* the bishops, the high justiciars or other courtiers. Except for Stephen of Perche and a few trusted advisors, private meetings were rarely granted. She issued decrees and dictated letters.

The children, meanwhile, studied with their tutors. Margaret saw them again at lunch, which was the main repast of the day.

After lunch, the queen might return to the chamber where she met with the court in the morning. Here she could convoke additional audiences or read the letters which had arrived during the day. By now, it was more likely that William, the young monarch, would be present at some of these meetings.

If she were inclined to visit the Genoard park with her children, or take them to one of the city's souks, she would probably do so in the afternoon.

Margaret had very little free time, but she probably spent it reading. It is probable that her vision was still good. She was in her thirties, rather slender and quite fit.

In the evening the family might have a third meal, something less substantial than lunch. On some evenings Margaret and the children attended vespers. There was time for leisure on Sunday.

The queen and her children might occasionally venture beyond the environs of Palermo, to places that were only a day's ride away, but their stay in Messina for four months was exceptional.

Margaret was rarely alone. She was almost always accompanied by ladies-in-waiting, typically damsels in their twenties, and perhaps a nun or two. We do not know the names of these women, but it is possible that there were youngish Norman or Navarrese cousins among them. Palermo's palace was not merely a royal residence; it was the kingdom's administrative center, and at any time at least a hundred people were there. One encountered guards, chamberlains, notaries, scribes, sundry courtiers and visitors, servants, cooks, tailors and the occasional monk. The staff still included a few eunuchs, but during Margaret's regency the maidens of the harem were relegated to such tasks as weaving.

The royal family's living quarters, as we have seen, were in the Pisan tower, the only tower that has survived *in toto* (if much altered) until our times.

We know of no female advisors in the queen's intimate circle, certainly not by name. Indeed, we have only sparse information to suggest who was in that circle except for counsellors such as Stephen of Perche. However, it seems likely that there were a few female intellectuals among Margaret's close friends. Some may have been slightly older. In this connection, it should be borne in mind that Margaret's contemporary, Henry II of England, was only two years her senior; many of Margaret's royal advisors, like his, were forty or fifty years old. These avuncular figures were a priceless asset.

The extent of a queen's isolation from her people depends on the nature of the kingdom itself, and even the woman's personality. Here it must be remembered that Palermo was one of Europe's largest cities, so Margaret need only stroll a few steps from the palace to meet many of the people she ruled.

Agrigento

It wasn't long before Gentile, the Bishop of Agrigento, realized that the plan to discredit Stephen, and perhaps even kill him, had been foiled. What was worse, the other two conspirators in his malevolent trio had been removed from circulation.[347] Gentile, despite his name, was anything but gentle. So profound was his perfidy that even a local manifestation would satisfy it, if only temporarily.

Gentile was one of the prelates who spent more time in the capital than in his own bishropic. Now he found a reason to justify his presence in Agrigento. Accompanied by a few knights, he headed there covertly, traveling along obscure roads.

There was a reason for such secrecy. Bedevilling as certain prelates were, the queen had come to prefer having the more troublesome bishops in Palermo, where she could keep an eye on them.

The Agrigentans themselves rarely lamented Gentile's prolonged absences. Its timeless Greek temples attested to the city's survival over many long centuries. If the most heinous tyrants of antiquity had failed to break Agrigentan will, the local bishop hardly stood a chance of doing so.

Suppression was not always in Gentile's interest. Early in April of 1168, his strategy consisted chiefly of manipulation. Many of the people in the towns around Agrigento were recent converts from Islam.[348] The ardor of these new Catholics led a good number of them to embrace Christianity just as zealously as they had professed the Muslim faith of their ancestors, and they held bishops in high esteem.

Resorting to the usual tropes, Gentile sought to exploit his flock's confidence in him. He impudently announced that Matthew of Aiello had been imprisoned illegally, and that Stephen of Perche planned to usurp royal authority by marrying Margaret.

In his crazed rantings, the bishop underestimated the Arabs' loyalty to the queen, whilst straining credulity. In Agrigento and the surrounding manors he convinced nobody. Open rebellion was the last thing anybody wanted.

Within days, those at court noted Gentile's absence; perhaps they missed his habitual tirades and chronic gossip. Margaret sent to the bailiff of Agrigento a justiciar[349] bearing an order for the bishop to report to the royal court at once, accompanied by the same justiciar.

Back in Palermo, Gentile faced a hearing. There was no dearth of witnesses to offer evidence against him, and their testimony was unassailable. His treachery exposed, he was held in custody, but the punishment of a prelate was more appropriately handled by the pope. To that end, the queen sent a letter to Pope Alexander soliciting a response to the situation. Meanwhile, Gentile was escorted to the royal fortress at San Marco d'Alunzio, where he was detained pending a papal reply.

Any hope of a successful conspiracy or rebellion might have ended with Gentile's arrest. It so happened that troubles in northeastern Sicily began to take on a life of their own, threatening the peace of the entire *Regnum*. Most of this can be attributed to one man, Odo Quarrel.[350]

Messina

Just days after sending Bishop Gentile to San Marco, Stephen had to contend with problems created by Odo. It may be recalled that Odo Quarrel was supposed to accompany Henry of Montescaglioso, Margaret's bothersome brother, to France.

The chancellor was annoyed to learn that his assistant was still in Messina long after he was scheduled to depart. Knowing something of Odo's avarice, Stephen hastily dispatched a letter tactlessly ordering him to set sail within three days, telling him to forget exploiting Messina for his own gain.

Odo had embarked on a scheme to exact his own tax from ships leaving Messina, or simply passing through its straits, on the way to the Holy Land. This was tantamount to extortion, and it enraged the Messinians, as well as the merchants and pilgrims. But the abuses didn't end with Odo himself.

Some of his French companions, who were given to getting drunk as they wandered aimlessly through the city's streets, entered a gaming house and began to insult the men gambling there. At first the gamblers, fearing reprisal from the chancellor if they responded to the aggressors, tolerated the unprovoked abuse. Finally, unable to further endure the pejorative words of the foreigners, they beat the men.

When news of this incident reached Odo's ears, he summoned Andrew, the city's governor, and demanded that the gamblers be apprehended immediately and brought to him. Andrew demurred, suggesting that any punishment be delayed until the local populace was more tranquil; he explained that in recent weeks the Messinians had been growing restless as the result of rumors, so it might be imprudent to arrest the gamblers at this moment. Seeking a conciliatory tone, the governor stopped short of excoriating Odo. Vilifying the chancellor's assistant directly would hardly be politic; indeed, it could have dire consequences. For now, comity and appeasement might be more effective than bitter words. Having witnessed, just months earlier, the demise of his predecessor, Richard of Aversa, Andrew thought it possible to catch more flies with honey than with vinegar.

Odo's approach, on the other hand, was to swat any fly that crossed his path. Known for his intolerance and short temper, the haughty mandarin bristled that the supposed influence of peasants did not concern him. The prosecution of these men would serve as a deterrent for others.

Given no choice, Andrew went to the house where the altercation had transpired. The crowd of men gathered there had no intention of being scolded. They began to assault the governor, who quickly mounted his horse and fled amidst a flurry of stones being hurled at him.

The Messinian gamblers and their friends were speakers of Greek. The "Latins" of the city, along with foreign merchants who were there on business, had other grievances, such as Odo's tax on shipping. These men incited the Greeks, saying, among other things, that Queen Margaret had married Stephen of

Perche, and that young King William was in danger, if indeed he was not already dead. The governor and his judges were reluctant to enforce order for fear of provoking a general riot.

Within days, news of the unrest engulfing Messina and its purlieus reached Margaret back in Palermo.

Before pandemonium ensued, the queen took the uncommon step of composing a letter to be read publicly at Messina. Issued jointly in her name and that of her son, the king, it sought to assuage the Messinians' fears, exhorting the people to remain loyal to the sovereign and his officers. It explained the reasoning behind the recent decisions against Bishop Gentile, Caïd Richard and Matthew of Aiello, and how Stephen ensured that the three conspirators were not punished too harshly despite the gravity of their treason. Margaret's missive was not intended to prompt panegyrics for the queen or her chancellor; it was only meant to placate the vast swath of society that was getting ready to rebel against royal authority. The final passage reassured the people that Queen Margaret and King William were well and unharmed.

Unfortunately, nobody but the governor and his judges (and Hugh Falcandus) ever learned the contents of the royal letter.

Andrew called the people together at the new cathedral. Here, as the governor procrastinated reading the letter aloud, rumors circulated among the crowd. Existing falsehoods were embellished and new ones were created. By the time Andrew finally began to read the letter, his voice was drowned out, lost in a sea of shouts and screams. The unruly horde had been carried away by a wave of imaginative lies: Stephen of Perche had been crowned king. William was dead, his younger brother besieged at Palermo's seaside castle. Geoffrey, the brother of Stephen of Perche, was coming to Sicily to marry Constance, the young daughter of King Roger II, and rule in her name.

Finally, a self-appointed leader enjoined the people to assassinate Odo Quarrel, suggesting that they then liberate the queen's brother, Henry of Montescaglioso, who, the man said, had always been benevolent to the Messinians. Andrew, whose purview it was to maintain order, implored the mad mob to abandon these ideas, but his words went unheeded.

Wasting not a moment, the people assaulted Odo's house, which was adjacent to the royal palace. This initial attack failed, and Odo managed to escape to the palace, which an angry crowd surrounded once it became known that he was inside.

At the harbor, some of the people armed themselves, commandeered seven galleys, boarded the ships and crossed the strait to Calabria, where the royal chamberlain[351] permitted the Messinians to enter the gates of Reggio. There a local crowd escorted them to the fortress where Henry was imprisoned.

The knights guarding this castle attempted to defend it by tossing stones upon the intruders, who nonetheless persisted in demanding that Henry be freed. The knights refused, declaring that they would hand the prisoner over to the Messinians only if ordered to do so by a competent authority. The rebels accepted this proposal, crossed back to Messina, and returned with James the Innkeeper, the man who the chancellor had sent to outfit the galleys that were to take Henry to France. The knights were expecting a judge, if not the governor himself; at the same time, there was only enough food in the castle to last three days. They reluctantly acceded to the Messinians' demand.

As soon as Henry of Montescaglioso was freed, he crossed over to Sicily, where he was acclaimed by the Messinians.

The revolution had begun.

Odo's Demise

A few days were to pass before detailed reports of the most recent events at Messina arrived at the court in Palermo during the middle of April 1168.[352] For now, Henry of Montescaglioso had seized control of one of Europe's most important cities, a key to shipping and a gateway to the eastern Mediterranean. Ironically, the Messinians were not supporting Henry out of affinity for him so much as the belief that he was their best hope of supporting the monarchy which they believed had been threatened. The unsubstantiated rumors of the young king's death led the people to embrace his uncle.[353]

The people wanted odious Odo Quarrel, dead or alive. For the moment, he was still in the royal palace near the sea. The castellan responsible for protecting the palace was reluctant to turn him over to an angry horde, but he cooperated with Henry, who sent a squad of men with a notary to take an inventory of Odo's possessions, and especially the money he had accumulated from his illegal tax.

At this point Odo was taken into custody. During the night he was removed from the palace, placed on a boat, and transported to the old seaside castle[354] near the harbor, where he was imprisoned. The more astute Messinians suspected that Henry was protecting Odo to ensure that the corrupt cleric, being the assistant and close friend of the chancellor, might intervene on the rebels' behalf with the royal court, whoever was running it. At the very least, as a hostage Odo would make an effective bargaining chip in the negotiations Henry envisaged with Margaret.

The best way to avoid this, the leaders of the avenging mob reasoned, was simply to eliminate Odo, but nobody said anything about killing him.

Instead, the throng demanded that Henry consign Odo to them for corporal punishment. Here they made mention of the grave offenses the treacherous man had perpetrated against the monarch he served, and against the people of Messina. Reluctant as he was to comply with this request, Henry thought it impolitic to defy the popular sentiment of people whose support he may yet need.

Odo had already been divested of his money and precious gems, so no harm was seen in placating public desires.

Therefore, the queen's half-brother permitted the mob to attach the tyrant's feet to a sturdy donkey that then dragged him naked down the streets. Some scraped skin, along with a few superficial bruises inflicted by a mild cudgelling, would ensure that Odo emerged from the experience chastened but essentially unscathed. This scenario, terrible as it is to the modern mind, was not altogether unorthodox in the twelfth century. Henry intended to throw the man into prison following the macabre spectacle. The premise behind this reprisal was that a generous dose of humiliation might serve Odo well.

Henry was expecting little more than a token gesture that would satiate the public appetite for justice.

But that is not what was delivered. The queen's half-brother had neglected to recognize the fact that he was witnessing the excessive response of an unruly crowd, not a sentence, however harsh, meted out by a justiciar and supervised by guards.

Before long, Odo was stabbed to death. Then his body was chopped into pieces. His head was placed at the end of a lance and paraded along the city streets. It was this savage spectacle that set the stage for what was to come.

Seized by an uncommon furor, the Messinians began running amok, killing any men they could find in the city who hailed from beyond the Alps. In this they were motivated in large measure by a loathing for French knights like those who had arrived with Odo Quarrel and harassed the gamblers a few days earlier. Even here, the splenetic mob's frenzy was misdirected, for there were many German, French and English merchants and pilgrims in Messina who had nothing to do with Odo of Quarrel or the chancellor he had served.

Henry put an abrupt end to this wanton violence by announcing that anybody who committed murder would be tried and summarily punished. Clearly, there was a method to Henry's madness. Indeed, he was not mad at all.

Military Operations

Undaunted, Margaret considered a response to the burgeoning rebellion led by her half-brother. She was told that a number of knights could be mustered hastily from Palermo and some towns to the east. They could be sent along the Tyrrhenian coast toward Messina. Even though the April rains might hamper the knights' advance somewhat, it was fortunate that these coastal roads had been widened and repaired on the chancellor's orders the previous autumn.

The immediate problem was a question of numbers. At the very least, the size of such a force would have to be sufficient to dissuade the Messinians from rebelling further. For this a full-fledged army was required, and that would take time.

Henry's advisors surmised the royal court's reaction, even if they suspected that King William himself might be dead. They had to defend the areas to the west of Messina, and for that they needed Rometta.[355] This fortified city straddling the Peloritan Mountains overlooked the Tyrrhenian coast near Milazzo, where there was a seaside castle. Controlling it was a paramount strategic necessity because any troops arriving by land from Palermo had to pass through this area.

Rometta had no baron; it was a royal town where the castellan guarded a small fortress. Most of the inhabitants were speakers of Greek. A few promises[356] were sufficient to dislodge the castellan, and the Messinians left a small garrison at Rometta's castle. The next operation would be far more onerous.

Its objective was Taormina, where Richard of Molise was imprisoned in a castle atop a rocky mountain overlooking the Ionian Sea far below. The town was famously impregnable, being one of the last strongholds in Sicily to fall to the Normans during the previous century.[357] Bearing this reality in mind, Henry led an army of Messinian knights and archers to Taormina as furtively as he could, along obscure mountain passes.

The element of surprise worked to the attackers' advantage, and the town was subdued with minimal effort. The problem was the fortress; here their efforts were repulsed.

Like Rometta, this was a royal town. Matthew, the castellan, defiantly refused to relinquish his prisoner. He could not be enticed, bribed or intimidated. But perhaps he could be persuaded.

Exasperated, Henry sent the brother of Matthew's wife with entreaties. This man begged the castellan, his brother-in-law, to release the prisoner, saying that he should think of the lives of his sister, nieces and nephews, who were being held hostage in Messina pending Richard's release. Matthew was unmoved, responding that, as a question of honour, he would not capitulate, even if the cost of refusal was his own life or that of his sister.

Matthew's brother-in-law finally took another approach. He persuaded the jailer, with whom he was acquainted, to free Richard while Matthew was asleep. This led to a skirmish and the death of the castellan. With this, Henry's forces took the castle.

Henry of Montescaglioso and Richard of Molise now controlled a strategic chunk of Sicily. Significantly, the northeastern region was the gateway to the peninsular part of the *Regnum*.

The two men had never been very fond of each other, but politics makes strange bedfellows.[358] Margaret's half-brother had always been troublesome, even disloyal. Richard, on the other hand, had been imprisoned following a trial motivated by little more than envy; his loyalty to Margaret had never wavered, and he probably did not deserve the fate that befell him.[359]

Henry and Richard might share doubts about Margaret's wisdom in acquiescing to their imprisonment, but this was overshadowed by their visceral hatred of Gilbert of Gravina and Stephen of Perche.

Back in Palermo, Stephen was alarmed at the fall of Taormina and the release of Richard of Molise, a competent warrior. An immediate response was necessary, but this was not forthcoming with any urgency, for there was an unforeseen impediment at court.

One of the figures at larger European courts, such as Sicily's, was the astrologer, something of a cross between a sorcerer and an astronomer. The most sophisticated among them came from the Muslim lands, and in Palermo astrologers were probably part of the Arabs' *dar al-hikma,* or "house of wisdom," a secular place of learning. The study of astrology found its way into other fields, such as meteorology and agriculture.

One of the era's better known astrologers was Adelard of Bath, who visited Sicily and then introduced the Muslims' knowledge of astronomy and geometry to England, where he served as the tutor of a young Henry II.[360]

Not surprisingly, there were astrologers among William's teachers.[361] Peter of Blois, the chief tutor, did not object to the young king learning about the zodiac, the stars, comets, eclipses and the phases of the moon, and neither did Margaret. The boy was developing a serious interest in astrology, and it was indeed considered a science in the twelfth century, when it was distinguished from astronomy little more than alchemy was differentiated from chemistry. Seen in its best light, astrology was usually thought to complement religion rather than contradict it.

Margaret herself may not have been very interested in astrology, but her son, who was present at ever more meetings, was growing obsessed with it. Therefore, it was not surprising that the young monarch turned to astrologers to determine a good time to attack the rebels in Messina.[362]

Here the queen was left with little choice. Even if she thought the horoscope useless, by mitigating the influence of the court astrologers she would be casting doubts upon their legitimacy. Worse, she would be seen to be contradicting, even chastising, her son before the eyes of his subjects. This may explain why she did not act, but her indolence delayed action when every passing day was crucial. The result was grave inefficiency at a moment when nothing short of a timely response would suffice.

The *Regnum* risked a civil war.

If Stephen of Perche could not immediately attack Henry and Richard, he would attempt to cripple them logistically. Because the rocky hills around Messina yielded little grain, the city's ravenous demand was usually satisfied with wheat from Calabria; that source was not viable this year because the region had suffered a preternaturally meager harvest the previous autumn. Knowing this, the chancellor cut off the supplies from Catania, whose plains produced plenty of grain.

Requiring a large army, the chancellor sought allies on the island to participate in the postponed military attack. The Lombard towns[363] expressed their unequivocal support for the queen. Between knights, footmen and archers, these communities alone could raise an army twenty thousand strong.[364] These loyal subjects encouraged Stephen to act soon, and he assured them that a day had been chosen to march on Messina. He did not mention that the day had been selected by astrologers.

Henry and Richard were more than capable of leading an army. Killing was their stock in trade. By now, they may have known that William and Margaret were alive and well. If so, the fact did not dissuade them. What they really wanted was to topple Stephen of Perche from his lofty perch. Then they would deal with Gilbert of Gravina.

With the widening dissent, Roger of Gerace, one of the barons who had conspired with Bishop Gentile of Agrigento but escaped notice, saw an opportunity to further his interests. To that end, he rode to Cefalù to solicit the support of Boson, its bishop, who controlled the royal city on the Tyrrhenian coast and was known to be one of Stephen's critics. Although Boson was, in principle, amenable to supporting the Messinians, there was little he could offer them materially, for the chancellor had already stationed a garrison of knights in the mountaintop citadel that overlooked the cathedral and town. From this vantage point, it was possible for sentinels to guard the coast for many miles; on a clear day one could see the volcanic Aeolian Islands to the northeast.

This made it obvious to the insurgents that the mobilization of troops to be used against them was proceeding, however sluggishly. Rapid as the rebels' advance had been thus far, its success was by no means assured. Fortunately for Henry and Richard, some allies of like mind were working toward the same objective on another front.

Crown Immunity

Like Richard of Molise, the *familiare* Matthew of Aiello had been imprisoned following a trial on the basis of sketchy evidence. Were both arrests no more than a ploy by Stephen of Perche to eliminate the two men most likely to challenge his authority? This we shall never know.[365]

What emerges from the scant facts known to us is the distinct possibility that, as chancellor, Stephen of Perche was occasionally overzealous, even unwise, inclined to paint several men with the same scornful brush. Whilst Margaret's capricious half-brother merited discipline for his treason, the *familiares* had never shown themselves to be overtly disloyal, nor had they ever confessed to their purported guilt. Had Stephen succumbed to hubris? Some thought so.

The rebels' hatred was never targeted directly at Margaret except through surreptitious rumors. Perhaps they viewed the queen as a victim of Stephen's thirst for power. Of course, Henry, Richard and Matthew wanted to slake some ambitions of their own; they sought control. Apart from that, however, there was no common thread running through the motivations of Stephen's detractors. The men shared no philosophy or political view significant enough for the chroniclers to record. They were, quite simply, European Christian men of their time. That they resented the presence of somebody they viewed as a usurper of their perceived birthrights reflected little more than nastiness nurtured in the depths of the mind.

"The queen can do no wrong." Crown immunity is a modern legal concept rooted in medieval practice. It was one of the fundamental principles underpinning the lengthy reign of England's Queen Victoria, and the even longer reign of Britain's next queen regnant, Elizabeth II. Another legal doctrine that survives in England is appointment, dismissal or even incarceration "at the queen's pleasure." In the Kingdom of Sicily this principle was enshrined in the Assizes of Ariano, which confirmed royal authority as the ultimate law of the realm. This idea had existed long before the twelfth century; no medieval monarch of Europe ruled without it, and there is nothing to suggest that Margaret ever abused her reginal rights.

Margaret and the young king were unimpugnable, indeed untouchable. They were not simply "above the law." They themselves were the final arbiters of the law. Anybody brazen enough to openly defame the monarch or regent risked permanent incarceration, even death.

The rebels knew this. It was a sacrosanct fact of life, and it meant that any maneuvering against the chancellor would have to result in a "surgical strike" against him, and against him only, were it to bear fruit. This was not just a question of law. A handful of knights and barons could not hope to control a city the size of Palermo if things turned violent. The loyalty of the people was, first and foremost, to the sovereign; Bonello's revolt had shown the bedlam that could break out when the populace rebelled against the rebels.

As a purely military operation could be haphazard, the rebels resorted to trickery within the palace walls, where Matthew of Aiello was being held prisoner.

Matthew's incarceration was something more akin to "house arrest" than conventional captivity. His imprisonment in the royal palace did not confine him to a jail; indeed, the palace dungeon no longer served that purpose. Since the deposed *familiare* was not isolated, he communicated with people in the palace. In this way, he learnt of the revolts in northeastern Sicily and the recent transfer of some men in Stephen's elite corps of bodyguards to Cefalù and other strategic towns.

It so happened that the royal castellan, Ansaldo, a close ally of Stephen of Perche, was absent from his post, confined by illness to a high floor in another tower of the palace. This gave Matthew an opportunity to convince the man's colleague, Constantine, to enlist the majority of the palace personnel to assassinate the chancellor on an appointed day.[366] The plan was for them to attack Stephen and the two close associates, Roger of Avellino and John of Lavardin, who arrived with him most mornings at a certain gate.[367]

The threshold of the palace, at least in theory, was a kind of Rubicon; within its walls no visitors, not even knights, were allowed to carry swords and daggers.[368]

As there were, in total, some four hundred men between servants and guards, this diabolical strategy stood a good chance of success.[369]

Opportunism was rife in Palermo, where it took very little for some greedy ruffians in the Kasr district near the palace and cathedral to agree among themselves to attack whichever faction seemed more likely to be overpowered once the expected fighting began. Ideally, from their warped point of view, this would be Stephen, whose death would permit the criminals to pillage the wealth of gold they thought was kept in his house.

Umpteenth Plot

Stephen suspected that something was afoot; there usually was. Ansaldo confirmed that there was a plot against the chancellor, and that a large number of people seemed to be involved thus far. Stephen's life was in danger. The castellan went on to counsel his friend to go to a fortified town of the hinterland that he could use as a base. From such a place, he could summon the troops he needed from the Lombard[370] towns and any other localities where the fealty of the populace had not yet been compromised.

Ansaldo suggested that Stephen depart the capital immediately, paying no heed to the date established by the astrologers to march on the enemy. In this way, he could assemble a force without delay. Then the young king could join him.

Was Margaret's presence presumed? Probably.

Ansaldo's plan was essentially sound, but Stephen of Perche did not follow through on it. Instead, he took the advice of some of his French knights, and particularly that of Robert of Meulan.[371] These men advised him against leaving the king in Palermo, believing the capital to be safe. The fundamental flaw in this counsel was that these men-at-arms, being foreigners, had no idea of the degree to which the Palermitans were capable of conspiring. Many secrets lurked in the shadows cast by the palace walls.

The day finally dawned for the attack planned on Stephen.

That morning found a few of the murderous servants waiting just inside the gate the chancellor usually entered. Upon arriving, Stephen was expected to step through with two or three trusted associates, leaving his company of armed knights outside the wall.

But this morning he did not arrive.

Somehow, Odo, the master equerry, the man responsible for the horses stabled within the palace's curtain wall, had found out about the plan. Early in the morning he went to Stephen's house to alert him.

Having been warned of the plot, the chancellor dismissed the knights waiting outside his house to escort him to the palace. Several of his friends remained with him.

As soon as he learnt of this, Constantine, the traitorous assistant of the palace castellan, ignited a rebellion by sending a large number of servants into the city with orders to incite the populace against the chancellor. Claiming that Stephen was about to abscond from Palermo by sea with chests of gold belonging to the king, the servants goaded the citizens into taking up arms and encircling Stephen's house.

Nearby, Hervé "the Florid," who was resented not for his loyalty to Stephen but because he was a braggart, and Roger of Avellino were trotting their horses outside the palace. A large mob attacked the two. Hervé was struck off his horse and stabbed to death with swords. Roger rode into the flat area south of the city gate at the edge of the Genoard.[372] Here the crowd was about to assault him with lances when King William, who had heard the noise, suddenly appeared at a window and ordered the people to desist, threatening them with punishment if Roger was harmed.

The events unfolded with an uncommon fury as a frail decorum devolved into chaos. Partaking in the rebellion were the chancellor's most vociferous critics, whose steady stream of gossipy propaganda spurred hundreds of ordinary Palermitans to join them just as the rabid Messinians had acted against Odo Quarrel. The stark difference was that Odo's sins were real, whilst most of those attributed to Stephen had been crafted by fabulists animated by vested interests to remove him from power, by force if necessary. The chancellor's denouement, the rebels hoped, would be fast and fierce.

From a tower window, Margaret could see the violence enveloping the Kasr district. Fearing the worst should the insurrection sweeping the city go unchecked, she ordered Roger of Avellino to be taken to the seaside castle in the Kala, where he could be protected and assist in its defense.

Meanwhile, the crowd at Stephen's house was growing larger by the minute. Among these people were the royal longbow archers who, Falcandus tells us, were never the last to arrive at riots when there was any chance for lucre to be had.[373]

Stephen had left the protection of his residence to Simon of Poitiers. This man-at-arms placed knights and foot men around the perimeter of the house's wall, but the crowd's sudden onslaught threatened to overwhelm them.

Seeing that the situation was critical, the chancellor moved quickly to escape with a few trusted friends[374] into the bell tower of the church adjacent to his house, along with several other French knights. Amongst them was Robert of Meulan, who just a few days earlier had advised Stephen to remain in Palermo because a revolt in the city seemed unlikely. Overconfident Robert might live to eat his presumptuous words, but first he had to survive the present peril. It was turning into a long day.

To better see what was happening, Margaret ascended the steps along a narrow passage to the roof of the Pisan Tower. Much of her view of the streets below was blocked by the low buildings.[375] But she could see the bell tower where Stephen and his companions had taken refuge, and the scene didn't look good.

William was with his mother. The young king was learning

firsthand the form a rebellion could take in a large city. It was a sober lesson in the reality of ruling a kingdom.

Accompanied by a brave company of knights, Roger of Tiron, the high constable, made his way to the bell tower and assailed the most aggressive attackers.[376] But he and his men were overwhelmed by the onslaught of the armed mob and forced to retreat.

Meanwhile, the mob attacked Stephen's house even more truculently than before. The knights besieged within its walls fought back just as ferociously.

With the collapse of public order, Matthew of Aiello and Caïd Richard were able to leave the palace unopposed. The pair ordered the servant musicians to go sound horns and drums outside the chancellor's house. Summoning the people to battle in this way was a royal prerogative, so another segment of the populace, consisting of Muslims as well as Christians, assuming that the signal had been given on the queen's orders, arrived to reinforce the assault.

Margaret and William could see that the violence was concentrated in the area around Stephen's house and the church next to it. The palace, though by now largely abandoned by the guards, was not under attack. What the queen and her son were witnessing was unchecked street fighting on an unprecedented scale. Numbering fewer than a hundred, the loyal knights did their best to defend the chancellor and themselves against thousands.

The fighting at the house was intense, but in the end the edifice was overrun by rioters who gained entrance to it through a passage from the church next door. This led to the knights at the house being taken prisoner by rebels led by Constantine, the disloyal castellan who had instigated the disorder in the first place.

With the chancellor's house finally taken, the crowd could focus its efforts on the bell tower, where Stephen and his company continued to defend themselves. Having reached an impasse, the rioters began to consider ways to overcome the resistance, perhaps by building a siege engine to attack the tower, or simply by piling wood and igniting a fire whose heat would force the structure's porous bricks to crumble.

Margaret was now desperate. She wanted the people to desist. Something had to be done, and right now.

Not without grave misgivings, the queen proposed that she and William leave the palace to go speak to the people. Matthew of Aiello forestalled this, explaining that all the arrows and stones flying about made an unannounced public appearance too risky.[377] His words were not devoid of reason, for safety was indeed a factor to consider; Margaret remembered how an earlier revolt had claimed the life of one of her sons. Nonetheless, Matthew's words conveniently camouflaged the fact that the young king's presence would almost certainly convince the Palermitans to cease the hostilities, which were initiated earlier in the day on the pretext of a royal order.

Margaret may not yet have known how the revolt had begun, but she probably had her own suspicions about who instigated it, and she saw the violent results.

By the end of the afternoon, the conspirators were beginning to succumb to some fears of their own. A problem appeared just as the sun began to disappear behind the rugged mountains to the south of the city. The crowd was likely to disperse at dusk, with no guarantee that even a few of the fickle Palermitans would remain to prevent the chancellor and his knights escaping in the darkness. Short of imprisoning Margaret and her sons, it would be impossible to prevent the young king from emerging to address his subjects the next day; indeed, the people might even demand it, just as they did during Bonello's revolt years earlier.

All along, the rebels' objective had been to eliminate Stephen of Perche, yet they had failed to overpower him. In seeking to checkmate their nemesis, they had achieved nothing more than a sour stalemate. It was time to negotiate. This was done in the king's name, if not with his willing consent.

In the haggard twilight, the voice of reason emerged from the smouldering embers.

If he agreed to leave, Stephen would be guaranteed safe conduct out of the realm. He and the men who had come with him from France would be supplied armed galleys to take them to whatever land they wished, and the Sicilian barons with him in the tower could retain their estates in the *Regnum*. Stephen's mercenary knights were given the choice of continuing their service to the king or accepting passage to a place of their choosing. These terms were accepted. The deposed chancellor and a small company would sail to Jerusalem[378] via Constantinople.

Caïd Richard, Matthew of Aiello, Richard Palmer, John of Malta and Romuald of Salerno jointly gave their word that the conditions of the agreement would be respected. The next morning, after bidding his cousin a sad farewell, Stephen renounced his status as Palermo's archbishop-elect and boarded his galley, setting sail on a westward course around Sicily. The only encumbrance proved to be a problem with his galley that forced him to purchase another vessel at Licata. Before long he was in the Holy Land.

Queen's Counsel

Stephen's departure may have left Margaret melancholy, but she had little time to dwell on her sorrow. She needed solid advice. Unfortunately, it was not forthcoming from any quarter except, perhaps, the feckless astrologers or a handful of sycophants. Having placed so much faith in one man, the queen had alienated some who otherwise might have been more willing to take up her cause. Peter of Blois, the royal tutor, was a worthy confidant, but he left shortly after his friend Stephen.

A few days after Stephen of Perche departed, Henry of Montescaglioso arrived in Palermo's harbor with a score of armed galleys. Accompanying him were Bishop Gentile of Agrigento, who he had freed from San Marco d'Alunzio, and his ally Richard of Molise.

Margaret was anything but gratified to see these three again. Most of all, she abhorred seeing her half-brother.

The queen was coerced into appointing a number of *familiares*. The list included the notary Matthew of Aiello, the archdeacon (and royal tutor) Walter, Caïd Richard, Bishop Gentile of Agrigento, Richard Palmer, Bishop John of Malta, Archbishop Romuald of Salerno, Roger of Gerace, Richard of Molise and, worst of all, Henry of Montescaglioso. The only consolation in having ten headaches instead of two or three was that they might fight enough among themselves to permit Margaret to serve as an effective referee. The doctrine of *divide et impera* would serve her well.

Collectively, these *familiares* represented the most important elements of the ruling class, namely the baronage, the bureaucrats and the clergy. In principle, this might provide political stability.

A certain faction of historians has taken to referring to this expanded group of *familiares* as a "council of regency," a characterization predicated on the belief that the queen's authority suddenly evaporated under the torrid Sicilian sun. There is a morsel of truth in this. However, it was rare for more than four or five of these men to be present at court at the same time.[379] Margaret was still the nexus of power in the Kingdom of Sicily.

A complementary theory, little explored until now, is that the effect of the "council," whatever its initial intent, was to give a voice to the baronage. Here, arguably, we see the first seeds of representative government, which eventually took root at the end of the next century with Sicily's first parliament.[380] Although it cannot be compared to England's

Magna Carta, which was a formal charter of baronial rights, the "council" certainly gave the nobles a greater influence at court than they otherwise could have expected.[381]

In the other great Norman realm, King Henry's Assize of Clarendon introduced certain rights that, in a perfect world, could redress perceived injustice of the kind claimed by Sicily's rebellious baronial element. Trial by jury, novel disseisin and other elements of what came to form the foundation of common law[382] might well have been instituted in Sicily. This may have obviated the very premise of some complaints because it is quite likely, based on what little we know, that Matthew of Aiello and Richard of Molise would not have been found guilty had their cases been heard by a competent jury.

Continuously forced to respond to immediate challenges to her authority, Margaret had little time to address fundamental legal questions. Even if she did, some subjects might well have questioned her prerogative, as regent, to bring about substantial changes in her son's name. At all events, if it became known that certain principles of a hypothetical Sicilian common law were indeed inspired by notions derived from the Maliki School, as a few modern juridical scholars[383] have suggested, the more bigoted Christians would have resented the statutes for their Islamic origin. By the time Margaret became regent, there weren't even many erudite scholars left at court to advocate for new laws.

Apart from the crisis that saw the expulsion of Stephen of Perche, grave as it was, there was very little to stimulate the queen to effect sweeping additions to the existing law. Unlike the English king, whose actions were motivated in part by a jurisdictional "turf war" with the Catholic Church, Margaret's relationship with the papacy was consolidated by such things as the apostolic legateship. For now, the Assizes of Ariano[384] would have to suffice, and Margaret would have to endure an expanded cadre of *familiares*.

The first act of the newly-appointed *familiares* was to expel Gilbert of Gravina (and Loritello) from the *Regnum*. Sensing that she had no choice, Margaret agreed to this, however reluctantly.[385]

She drew the line at their request to attaint or exile Hugh of Catanzaro, a kinsman of Stephen of Perche.[386]

Falcandus tells us that the *familiares* relented for two reasons. On the one hand, Hugh was violent and unpredictable, and therefore capable of waging an insurgency against them; on the other, the *familiares* wished to mitigate the queen's anger.[387]

Apart from Margaret's feelings and Hugh's belligerent temperament, the *familiares* had good reason to fear the Count of Catanzaro. Unlike Stephen's other companions, who had few ties to the Kingdom of Sicily, Hugh had a link to it that was worth fighting for. The large chunk of Calabria he controlled was held by right of his wife, the heiress Clementia, who once flirted with Matthew Bonello. Hugh had enough resources, and enough support from the Calabrian baronage loyal to his wife's family, to raise a formidable army of his own.

After the first few chaotic months, the power of the *familiares* was more like a placid pond than a raging river. But even a docile lake can be dangerous for those unable to swim. Fortunately, Margaret knew how to survive in perilous waters, and she refused to let herself drown in her own tears.

As individuals, some of the *familiares* wielded considerable influence at court. Matthew of Aiello ensured that John, his brother, was consecrated Bishop of Catania as planned. This took place in July.[388]

The queen restored to Richard of Molise the prosperous lands he had held until his imprisonment.

Henry of Montescaglioso was finally granted his wish for more territory when he was invested with the Principate, a large county that included territories around such cities as Salerno and Avellino. The queen reasoned that this concession, ludicrously generous as it was, would keep her half-brother far away from the royal court. Margaret's only modicum of satisfaction in this gesture came the moment Henry made submission by kneeling before her and William to swear fealty to the monarch.

The *familiare* Walter, archdeacon of Cefalù, had no hope of being consecrated bishop of that diocese so long as Bishop Boson[389] was alive, and he was hardly content to serve exclusively as rector of the palace chapel. Almost as soon as Stephen had left the *Regnum*, overbearing Walter began seeking supporters who might endorse his appointment as Archbishop of Palermo. He reassumed the role of royal tutor held until recently by Peter of Blois, soon emerging as the most important *familiare*.

By the autumn, exiled Robert of Loritello learnt of recent events. For months, he had been sending Margaret letters requesting that she lift his exile. Reasoning that he might reclaim his old manor now that Gilbert of Gravina was no longer in the *Regnum*, he began sending insistent letters to the regent asking for it back. Margaret had to think about this.

She was busy dispatching correspondence of her own, to such people as Thomas Becket, who had sent letters to the queen[390] and to her chancellor[391] thanking them for providing hospitality to his nephews.

Not surprisingly, Richard Palmer corresponded with his countryman. Ostensibly acting on behalf of the King of France but perhaps at Margaret's urging, the Archbishop of Canterbury asked Richard to intervene to recall Stephen of Perche to Sicily.[392] Richard, of course, wished to keep Stephen as far away as he could.

By the end of 1168, a certain calm had been restored to the kingdom. Margaret's authority had diminished slightly, but hers was still the most powerful voice in the *Regnum*.

Statecraft

By early 1169, it was clear that the regency would be a solitary duty. The queen regent found herself without familial peers to assist her.

She decided to permit Robert of Loritello, her son's distant cousin, to return from exile; this might bring him into her camp. Other problems were more complex.

In the wake of the resignation and departure of Stephen of Perche, the chancellorship was not filled and the archbishopric of Palermo was vacant. The queen's failure to make these appointments might elicit subtle dissent in certain quarters. No matter.

Hoping, however wistfully, that her cousin might someday return and reassume his former post, Margaret saw no immediate need to appoint another chancellor. Not being eager to see the concentration of power in one courtier, the *familiares* voiced no objection to this lacuna.

As the Archbishop of Palermo was, *ex officio,* the Primate of Sicily, a position that brought with it its own privileged place in the kingdom's power structure, the queen, at least for the moment, saw no urgency in advancing any names for it. For now, reticence was a trait that might serve her well.

The taciturn regent would have her way eventually. It would be best for her political detractors not to view her silence to imply consent.

Walter

As the royal tutor, Walter, who was also the rector, or dean, of the palace chapel, spent more time at court than any other *familiare*. He even had a tiny office in the palace. Although he never became chancellor, Walter was, effectively if unofficially, the chief *familiare,* and we find his signature as the first witness in many royal decrees.

Like Stephen, Walter had been sent to Sicily by Margaret's kinsman Rotrou of Rouen. However, having arrived earlier than, and separately from, Stephen and the hated French knights, Walter never came to be closely associated with them in the public mind. Spared the bitter animus directed at them, he was not expelled with the others.

Archbishop Walter[393] may not have been a close friend of Stephen, but neither was he an enemy. In any case, he never defended him with much vigor, and in the end he added his voice to the opposition.

With Stephen of Perche and Peter of Blois gone, Walter was the best advisor Margaret could expect to find, even if he would never be a trusted confidant. The queen bore the indelible memory of how years earlier, during the revolt that claimed the life of her son, Walter was one of the opportunists who exploited the public sentiment of the moment to advocate the abdication of her husband.

Tireless were his efforts to garner enough support to justify being elected the capital's archbishop. Before long, he renounced his position in the diocese of Cefalù to be appointed archdeacon of Agrigento, a more important see.[394] This suggests a certain amity with Gentile Tuscus, Agrigento's bishop.

Falcandus claims that Walter attempted to gain the appointment as Archbishop of Palermo by paying a violent mob to frighten the local clergy into supporting him. The queen hoped Pope Alexander III would refuse to ratify this election on the grounds that Stephen, having renounced his archiepiscopal status under duress, was still archbishop-elect.

The chronicler contends that Margaret sent Peter of Gaeta, subdeacon of the papal curia, seven hundred gold ounces to give the pope to encourage Rome's support.[395] This account, if truthful, implies that the regent's actions were tantamount to bribery. In this she was not alone, for the baronage, which endorsed Walter, made its own entreaties to the pontiff, along with a bribe even more substantial than Margaret's.

After contemplating the situation, the pope decided to confirm the election of Walter who, by February, had already begun to behave as if he were archbishop, witnessing charters with that title and celebrating liturgy in the cathedral.[396]

Pope Alexander kept the gold Margaret had sent him but, seeking to spare her feelings, he delayed sending Walter's charter of appointment to Palermo. Margaret was not happy about losing so much gold in a nugatory effort, but by now she had more urgent matters to address.

Natural Disaster

Early in the morning of the fourth of February 1169 a violent earthquake shook eastern Sicily and southern Calabria. Its epicenter was near the city of Catania, which it all but levelled.[397] Some fifteen thousand Catanians perished. Most of the people in Lentini were killed. There was damage from Messina down to Syracuse. Castles crumbled at Modica and other towns, and from Taormina the snow-capped summit of Mount Etna was observed to sink somewhat.[398]

Lending the catastrophe an apocalyptic air was its occurrence during the vigil of the feast of Saint Agatha, Catania's heavenly patroness. The city's cathedral was dedicated to her, and its collapse[399] crushed Bishop John of Aiello, the brother of Matthew the *familiare,* along with forty-five monks inside for matins.

Margaret and her sons made their way to Catania to comfort the people as best they could. Here William spoke publicly in his first official address to his subjects: "Let each of you pray to the God he worships. He who has faith in his God will feel peace in his heart." Such words reflected William's kind disposition to all the Abrahamic faithful he ruled.[400]

Nothing could portend such a catastrophe, let alone explain it. To the medieval mind, a disaster of this magnitude could be nothing less than an act of a wrathful God. Some thought it foretold even worse cataclysms to come. In a letter to Richard Palmer, Peter of Blois expressed the opinion that the earthquake was God's vengeance.[401] According to Falcandus, there were people who believed that Stephen of Perche, said to be at the court of Constantinople, might return, flanked by Robert of Loritello and a faction of the baronage, to take control of the court.

This speculation ended when news arrived that Stephen had died in Jerusalem, where he was buried with full honours in the Templars' chapter house.[402]

With this, Margaret realized there was no purpose to be served in crying over spilt milk. She would have to face her destiny alone.

Generations

Three years earlier, when the Emperor of Constantinople proposed betrothing his daughter to Margaret's son, the queen's reaction was tepid. The young king was now fifteen; he would reach the age of majority in two years.

Recent events had shown that he was becoming a decisive young man, intelligent and confident. The time had come to begin the search for an appropriate wife for him.

The Byzantine proposal, interesting as it was, did not appeal to the queen. Her affinity for Norman society prompted her to look northward. She was not the only one in her family to entertain such a notion.

Alfonso VIII of Castile, the son of her beloved sister Blanca, was making overtures to Henry II of England to marry one of the English king's daughters. Alfonso was the same age as William, but his life thus far had taken a far more cumbersome course.

Margaret's brother-in-law, Sancho III of Castile, died in 1158, just two years after Blanca, leaving young Alfonso as an orphan in the care of what became a succession of Castilian noblemen. Warring factions fought over custody of the young king. It saddened Margaret to learn that her brother, the King of Navarre, exploited this tragedy to seize some border territories that belonged to Alfonso, who was his late sister's son. This included La Rioja, where Margaret and Blanca were born.

As much as Margaret may have wanted to help her nephew in Castile during the hardships facing him, there was little she could do. She probably had hoped that her half-brother, Henry of Montescaglioso, a knight errant by nature, would have returned to Spain with his men, perhaps to end up fighting at young Alfonso's side, but that was not to be.

Out of necessity, Alfonso had come of age and was now ruling a kingdom with the support of some loyal barons who did their best to look after him, advise him and defend his interests. Quarrels among the Castilian baronage and a chronic conflict with Sancho, the King of Navarre, made this a fruitless task.

Margaret learned that Matilda, one of the daughters of Henry II and Eleanor of Aquitaine, had recently wed the Duke of Saxony. There were two princesses left, and Leonor (Eleanor), the elder, was not yet eight years old. Despite the girls' tender years, however, it could not hurt to make a discreet inquiry. Margaret wasn't seeking promises, only possibilities.

Golden Rule

For the moment, she had to rule the *Regnum*. This entailed establishing policy when necessary, but more often confirming feudal grants, founding monasteries and, of course, protecting the rights of all the subjects. She had little time to think about those who had left. The eunuch and onetime *familiare* Caïd

Peter, for example, was now an admiral in the service of Abu Yaqub Yusuf, the Almohad emir. It will be remembered that once he left Sicily Peter reassumed his original name, Ahmed; to this he had since added the surname *es-Sikeli,* "the Sicilian."

In February, the queen permitted Matthew of Aiello to establish a tax-exempt monastery on his property in Palermo. The salutation of this charter, which is typical of those issued during the regency, refers to "William, benevolent King of Sicily, Duke of Apulia and Prince of Capua, with Lady Margaret his Queen Mother, resplendent in their great and glorious royal generosity."[403]

Several such charters survive. Another example, dated May 1169, confirms the rights to an abbey in northeastern Sicily formerly granted by John of Aiello, Matthew's brother, the late Bishop of Catania. This monastery, which seems to have been uninhabited by this time, once housed Byzantine monks.[404]

These charters reveal something of the form the court had assumed. Caïd Richard was the master chamberlain, assisted by Caïd Martin, the royal chamberlain. The *familiare* Matthew of Aiello was high notary. Richard of Molise was also present.

Stephen's death removed the last theoretical impediment to Walter's formal appointment as Archbishop of Palermo, and Pope Alexander formalized it by decree in June.[405] Margaret then had to endure attending the petulant prelate's consecration in Palermo's cathedral in late September.[406]

Walter convinced her to appoint his brother, Bartholomew, as a *familiare,* but the archbishop's avarice did not stop there. He also prevailed upon the queen to concede to him the feudal rights of the mills of the manor of *Bur-Ruqqad,* or Brucato, as well as other lands.[407]

Margaret had her own way of reminding pompous Walter that the Kingdom of Sicily wasn't his personal theocracy. This involved adding a layer of power to the court hierarchy. She appointed Matthew of Aiello, the *familiare* and high notary, her vice chancellor. This was a slightly ironic title as there was no high chancellor for him to serve under. Nevertheless, it sent the clear signal that the *Regnum* was a monarchy, not a dictatorship, and that Margaret was still in charge.[408]

By Christmas, Henry II had expressed his consent to the marriage of his youngest daughter, Joanna, to King William. This was not a formal, binding decision, and Joanna was just four years old, so the wedding was still some years away, but the English monarch's agreement was a hopeful sign. Without delay, the queen sent ambassadors to discuss the matter with the pope.

By the beginning of 1170, there was peace and stability in the kingdom, whilst the treasury, the *diwan*, was as rich as ever. Margaret may have found Walter and his ilk overbearing, if not downright obnoxious, but she managed to achieve a tolerable coexistence with them. More important than her needs was the necessity of rebuilding Catania and the other localities destroyed during the previous year.

To the north of the kingdom's border, Pope Alexander III spent a good part of his pontificate exiled from the city of Rome, which was a hotbed of unrest rooted in the ambitions of Frederick Barbarossa and the occasional antipope. The pontiff resided instead at Benevento, Gaeta and Anagni. Gifts like the gold he received from Margaret and the Sicilian barons the previous year made this exile bearable.

In January, the pontiff received as Margaret's ambassadors Robert of Loritello and Richard Palmer, whose brief it was to seek approval for the idea of the marriage of William to Joanna, the youngest daughter of King Henry of England. These emissaries were more reliable than others the queen might have sent; Robert was distant kin to her son and Richard was English by birth.

At England's royal court, like Sicily's, life proceeded unhindered despite political complexities. King Henry's dispute with Thomas Becket, who Pope Alexander supported, had yet to be resolved.

The Sicilians were anything but oblivious to what was transpiring in England, and the matter was doubtless discussed, if only perfunctorily, by the two Sicilian ambassadors and the pope. It did not impede the negotiations, but Becket himself was displeased, personally offended by what he viewed as disloyalty on the part of the two emissaries, with whom he was familiar, and perhaps even Margaret. In a letter to Ubaldo, Bishop of Ostia, he wrote that, "Even the King of Sicily, in whose dominions you live, has been promised the daughter of the King of England if he will join in effecting our ruin."[409]

That criticism was misplaced and simply erroneous. Margaret was merely seeking to secure a marriage for her son. Like many, she hoped for a resolution to a conflict that had already dragged on for years. Thomas Becket further asserted that Richard Palmer was offered the bishopric of Lincoln, as if this were comparable to the importance (and climate) of Syracuse, if he supported King Henry politically and financially.[410] There seems to be no basis for Becket to have believed such a thing; most of the money he mentions would certainly have to come from the treasury of the *Regnum,* and that would require Margaret's approval.

Margaret supported Becket[411] whilst Matthew of Aiello, who was now her vice chancellor, was inclined to endorse King Henry's views. Yet the Kingdom of Sicily took no official position in the dispute, and during the summer of 1170 the Archbishop of Canterbury and the King of England seemed to reach a compromise.

As the months passed, the queen continued the business of running a kingdom. As always, the greater number of decrees she issued in her son's name dealt with feudal and ecclesiastical rights. Typical of these is a charter of October, in which she granted a hermit monk of the Byzantine tradition a small manor and the rights to a mill.[412]

Margaret's improvised strategy of "divide and conquer" was beginning to achieve its desired result. Archbishop Walter viewed Matthew of Aiello as a rival, and their rapport was sometimes difficult. Over time, however, the two men developed a reasonably efficient working relationship.[413]

By the Christmas season of 1170, it seemed as if the marriage agreements of William II to Joanna of England and that of his cousin Alfonso VIII of Castile to her elder sister, Leonor (Eleanor), would soon be confirmed.

The English monarch hoped to benefit from these unions. Princess Leonor's marriage to Alfonso would provide Henry more security along the southern border of Aquitaine and other regions he ruled by right of his wife. Joanna's marriage to William would more closely link England, Normandy and Henry's various French lands to the affluent Kingdom of Sicily.

Little account was taken of love, at least not before the fact. Henry's daughters would be expected to embrace the husbands chosen for them, just like Margaret herself had done many years earlier.

For his part, Alfonso wanted support from King Henry, whose lands extended to the Pyrenees, to offset the territorial ambitions of his avaricious uncle, Sancho of Navarre. By surrounding Navarre in this way, the young King of Castile hoped to restrict Sancho's expansion into Castilian territories beyond La Rioja.

Margaret's motives were more nuanced. She had no lofty political or economic objectives in arranging her son's marriage to Henry's daughter, but closer ties with Henry and his dominions on the continent would not be unwelcome.

These incipient wedding plans were torn asunder by an event that occurred in the last days of December. Thomas Becket was murdered in Canterbury by four of Henry's knights.

Reginal Duties

Nothing in the first days of 1171 marked the year as beginning very differently from any other.[414] Queen Margaret passed the Christmas season with her sons, as always. There were no serious conflicts within the *Regnum,* and no foreign threats. The seasonal snow on the mountains beyond Palermo was a reassurance that some things never change. The queen was at the pinnacle of her power.

There was still time to find William a suitable bride. Indeed, another offer soon arrived from the Emperor of Constantinople. This reiterated his proposal of several years earlier. His daughter was still available, although no longer his universal heiress as a son had been born since he last tendered Margaret a proposal that William wed Maria "Porphyrogenita." This time, Margaret decided to accept the offer.[415]

As the most influential *familiares,* Matthew of Aiello and Walter the Archbishop of Palermo worked together well enough for a later chronicler to describe them as "two firm pillars" supporting the Kingdom of Sicily.[416] That portrayal may well have reflected popular sentiment.

Now, at the age of thirty-six, Margaret could begin to think about retiring from the most important public role of her life. Her elder son, the heir, was nearing seventeen, the age of majority.

For the moment, her time was consumed by such tasks as rendering "extraordinary" decisions in matters referred to her. Most cases involving bishops were addressed by the queen rather than by a civil authority such as the justiciars. In March, Margaret restored to Gentile, Bishop of Agrigento, a mill of which, according to a surviving charter, the prelate had somehow been defrauded.[417] Other decrees defended the rights of Muslims and Jews.

By 1171, the composition of the population of the realm Margaret ruled in her son's name could be identified by religion in a general way. The Jews were the only religious minority of note in the peninsular part of the Kingdom of Sicily. On the island of Sicily, perhaps one in four subjects were Muslim, and no more than one in ten were Jewish.

God and Country

The world around her was undergoing one of those subtle shifts that alters the form, if not the spirit, of religion every now and then.

To the south of Sicily, a Sunni family succeeded a Shia dynasty. The death of the last Fatimid caliph brought changes to the African lands running along the Mediterranean all the way to the Red Sea. Cairo, the family's capital, had been founded not long after the Fatimids made their way to Egypt from Tunisia.[418] In September 1171, Saladin, a Kurd, established what was to become a new ruling house. His Ayyubids, who had a natural religious affinity for the Sunni Abbasids of Baghdad, were intent on asserting their power around Jerusalem. Islam spanned three continents, influencing regions from Spain to what is now Pakistan.

The Christianity of some regions on the fringe of Europe was being brought into line with Rome's customs and rites. After a band of English knights had occupied part of Ireland, King Henry, not wishing to see them establish a rival kingdom on the island, reminded them that he was their lord. He and a large invasion force would land in Ireland in October. Pope Alexander approved the conquest of Eire so long as Henry encouraged its people to embrace the same liturgy and traditions as the Catholic Church in England, setting aside certain distinctively Celtic practices. The same pontiff made an effort to more firmly integrate the people of Finland into Rome's fold.

In Sicily, as we have seen, the Christians were becoming ever more Latin. Margaret was eyeing some abandoned Greek monasteries on the eastern side of the island with a view to establishing Roman Catholic houses for the religious orders, especially for nuns.

Building churches was becoming something of a competition, a kind of medieval one-upmanship, in Norman Sicily. Great churches were the mega-tall skyscrapers of their day. Maio of Bari built San Cataldo as his private chapel to challenge the Martorana of George of Antioch next door; Matthew of Aiello built Saint Mary of the Latins in the Saqaliba district and later endowed the Magione in the Khalesa quarter, while Walter wanted to leave his mark on Palermo with a new cathedral. Each power player had his own "pet project."

As queen, Margaret had the resources to beat the boys at their own game. That's how she would spend her retirement.

Acumen

Was Margaret a competent leader, perhaps even an exceptional one? The quality of leadership depends greatly on context, and especially the challenges one faces, as much as personal ability. Difficult as Margaret's regency was, it would have been far more arduous, indeed potentially catastrophic, if it involved anything like repelling a large military invasion such as the one attempted, and aborted, by Frederick Barbarossa. The challenges from prelates in Sicily were nothing like the ideological war of words between Henry II and Thomas Becket, and as Margaret's regency was ending Henry stood on the threshold of an internecine squabble that would degenerate into armed conflict against his own sons.

It could be argued that the scheming, conspiring efforts to undermine the queen's authority were more difficult to respond to, and defeat, than a transparent military or juridical attack. There can be no doubt that some of the verbal barbs launched in Margaret's direction were, by their very nature, misogynistic, intended to exploit a woman's perceived vulnerabilities in an age that saw very few females in positions of leadership.

Viewed from such a perspective, Margaret's regency cannot

be regarded as anything less than a success. Not every decision she made was unflawed, but perfection is not the measure of great leadership. Triumph in the face of adversity is what makes good leaders great.

And what of the populace? Did the people view their queen regent as a leader they could support?

What scant indications exist tell us that they did. Looking at the minorities, Islam flourished despite many conversions to Catholicism, and the Jews were protected.

The few major revolts were not upheavals motivated by widespread injustice but, rather, rebellions instigated by aristocrats. The ringleaders of the revolt that led to the exile of Stephen of Perche negotiated with the chancellor precisely because they feared that by nightfall the Palermitans they had incited to riot would abandon the effort and return to their humble hearths.

A unique occasion occurred in the middle of 1171 when one of Margaret's most famous countrymen, the rabbi Benjamin of Tudela, visited Sicily. It was the last noteworthy event of her regency.

Queen Mother

Margaret was no longer regent. Inevitably, the day arrived for William, who was now an adult, to act independently of her. In the early days of May in 1172, the king and his young brother, Henry, who was then twelve, left with a large entourage for Taranto, where they were to meet Maria "Porphyrogenita" of Constantinople, to whom William was betrothed the previous year.[419] This was the first time that Margaret's sons left their mother's presence for more than a day or two, and it was to prove a fateful journey.

It had been agreed with Manuel Comnenus of Constantinople that his daughter would arrive with several galleys and a number of emissaries, knights, ladies-in-waiting and servants. A legation of Sicilian ambassadors had visited the Byzantine court to ensure that Maria, who was nearly two years older than William, was sufficiently healthy, intelligent and attractive to become Sicily's queen consort.

With the birth of her half-brother, Alexius, Maria was no longer Manuel's universal heir to the Byzantine throne, but she was just as eligible as any other princess to become William's bride, for her father's empire was an important ally. Unstated was another aspect of the union that was not to be overlooked.

In the event of the childhood death of her brother, who was not yet three, Maria would again become Manuel's heiress, an eventuality that might well open the door for William to claim the Byzantine Empire by marital right. This possibility did not escape Manuel or, for that matter, any other monarch whose interests touched Mediterranean shores, especially Frederick Barbarossa.

William waited at Taranto for about ten days. Presuming a timely departure from Constantinople, there was no immediate explanation for a delay in Maria's arrival. The seas were calm this time of year. The route of her flotilla would take Maria through the Aegean, following the Greek coasts into the Ionian to Corfu and then to Apulia.

Not wishing to spend too much time idly waiting, William left a company of prelates and nobles at Taranto to receive Maria while he and his brother went to pray at the sanctuary of Saint Michael on Mount Gargano, a site very important to the Hauteville dynasty.[420] They then went to Barletta for a few days.

As the days passed, it became obvious that Maria was not going to arrive. An armed flotilla sailing through friendly coastal waters did not risk an attack by pirates, and there were no storms, so the royal court could only conclude that Manuel Comnenus had reneged on his word. If that matter were not grave enough, the event itself left William greatly dismayed. The young man had expected to meet the woman who would be his wife. Instead, he departed Apulia without so much as an explanation for her failure to appear.

Receiving word of the incident, Margaret was equally frustrated. More than once, Manuel of Constantinople had proposed the union of his daughter to her son, finally committing to it formally, only to abandon the idea now. Not only was this annoying, it was highly offensive to royal dignity. It was enough to anger any mother.

The lack of an explanation, or indeed any communication, from the Byzantine court only added insult to injury.

Lost Prince

From Apulia, William and his company headed to the western side of the peninsula. Before long, he was passing through Benevento. At this point, young Henry began to complain of illness.

The king thought it best to send his brother to Salerno. Not only did that city have a good medical school and exceptional physicians, it was a convenient port from which to embark for Sicily.

Matthew of Aiello and Archbishop Walter remained with William. Despite their concern for Henry, both *familiares* wanted to be as near to the king as possible.

From Salerno, young Henry returned by sea to Palermo accompanied by a small retinue. During the sea voyage, his physical condition did not improve.

In Sicily, the illness only worsened. Henry died in the middle of June.

Having visited Capua, William soon headed to Salerno, where the royal galleys were waiting to take him to Sicily. He embarked without further delay and set sail for his capital.

Upon reaching Palermo, William learned of his brother's death. He did not take it well.[421]

The people of Palermo attended yet another royal funeral. Margaret was beside herself with grief. The long arm of death had snatched three of her sons from this earth.

But the political repercussions of Henry's premature passing transcended even a mother's anguish. Henry's death brought with it dynastic ramifications that could change the course of history.

The young prince had been first in line to the throne. Now there were no legitimate male heirs in sight.

Constance, the posthumous daughter of Roger II, became heiress presumptive. It will be remembered that she was around William's age, even though she was his aunt.

If Constance were to marry, her husband might rule in her name *jure uxoris,* by marital right. Until now, Constance's mother, Beatrice of Rethel, had made no effort to find the girl a husband, and neither had Margaret. Thus far, married life did not seem to interest her.

Finding William a wife to produce heirs was more important than ever.

A proposal came from the Holy Roman Empire when ambassadors representing Frederick Barbarossa offered the hand of his daughter, Beatrice Hohenstaufen.

This German offer was not accepted, but neither was it immediately refused. The issue was complex.

Margaret and William both knew that Pope Alexander and Frederick Barbarossa had yet to negotiate a peace with each other. Jeopardizing Sicily's rapport with the papacy was not a good idea.

After careful contemplation, William refused to wed Frederick Barbarossa's daughter. The rebuke, accompanied as it was by William's refusal to negotiate a new treaty with the Holy Roman Emperor until the papal dispute was resolved, enraged Barbarossa.

Other monarchs were more willing to cultivate good relationships with the papacy, if only out of expediency. In England, Henry II reached what seemed like an accommodation with Pope Alexander III in the wake of the Thomas Becket assassination.[422] Could this serve to resuscitate the abandoned betrothal of Henry's daughter to Margaret's son?

Matronage

Between mourning for her lost son and fretting over the future of her last living child, Margaret had a great deal to think about. If she confronted depression, she did not succumb to it.

The canonization of Thomas Becket in February 1173 only served to remind her of the earlier tragedy that ended in her English friend's martyrdom, and her dashed desire for William to wed young Joanna of England.

Faced with uprisings in France instigated by his own sons, King Henry could be forgiven for ignoring the subject of the betrothal of his daughter to the King of Sicily.

Letters from the English king advised fellow monarchs of developments in his realm. One such letter arrived at Palermo. Margaret encouraged William to respond amicably.[423] She probably gave very little thought to Henry's insolent sons. It was his daughter, Joanna, who interested her; the queen was beginning to think it possible to salvage the plan for the young princess to marry William.

At some point in 1173, Margaret ventured into northeastern Sicily. She visited Beatrice of Rethel and Constance before trekking into the Nebrodian Mountains to inspect the monastery being built at Maniace.

None of these royal dames ever traveled with anything less than a company of knights, esquires, grooms, ladies-in-waiting, servants, and perhaps a friar and scrivener. At the bare minimum, that meant no fewer than twenty people.

We know rather little of the sense of sisterhood that existed among Margaret, Beatrice and young Constance, but there was now a dearth of legitimate Hauteville males. Despite the ambitions of the *familiares* who governed the *Regnum* from one day to the next, dynastic power rested firmly in the hands of William and Margaret.

Margaret enjoyed a unique status as queen mother. Several charters relating to the monasteries she founded in the Nebrodian Mountains cite her authority exclusively.[424] We find, for example, the phrase *dominae Margaritae gloriosae reginae matri,* without William being mentioned explicitly[425] Within a few years, Maniace became a vast network of holdings outside the ecclesiastical jurisdiction of the Archbishop of Messina, ceded to the authority of the abbot of Monreale.[426]

This is not to suggest that anything like a "mini-kingdom" was ruled by Margaret in northeastern Sicily once her son reached the age of majority. However, using the royal castle at San Marco d'Alunzio as her base, she exercised her authority with a certain degree of autonomy.

As queen mother, Margaret's most ambitious project, apart from finding her son a suitable bride, was to assist him in founding a large Benedictine abbey at Monreale, overlooking Palermo. This was viewed as young King William's effort to compete with Walter, Palermo's archbishop, and to demonstrate his independence from his former tutor. Monreale Abbey, which soon became the seat of its own archbishopric, was autonomous; much like the abbey at Cava, near Salerno, from whence some of its first monks were recruited, it was outside the local ecclesiastical authority.[427]

Walter had long sought to wield his influence over the young monarch, who still yielded on occasion. Amongst the few royal charters that survive from these years is one that permits Walter, as the Archbishop of Palermo and chief *familiare,* to try adulterers in his archdiocese.[428] Adultery is an example of something that was a crime in both ecclesiastical law and in the civil law enshrined in the Assizes of Ariano. Too few cases are known in Palermo for us to ascertain exactly how this archiepiscopal authority was applied in practice, although Walter's jurisdiction included Roman Catholics, not Muslims, Jews or Greek Christians.

Margaret's involvement in such matters is not known, but it seems that she acted as her son's advisor for several years after he reached the age of majority and began to rule in his own right.

Walter was much chagrined to hear about royal plans to build Monreale.[429] He wanted funding for his own enterprise, an expansion of Palermo's cathedral, something he eventually obtained.[430]

Monreale epitomizes the syncretic art and architecture that flourished during Sicily's Norman era. The church's impressive Byzantine mosaics, which include a large Pantocrator overlooking the earliest public image of Thomas Becket, cover most of its walls, a mosaicry area more extensive than that of any other church in Italy (even Saint Mark's in Venice). A fountain in the cloister, and the exterior of the church's apses, are of Fatimid design. The detailed, sculpted capitals of the cloister's columns reflect Provençal and Norman influences.[431]

Monreale was not William's only major project.

One of the people that Margaret, as regent, had permitted to return from exile was Tancred of Lecce, the illegitimate grandson of Roger II who had participated in the Bonello revolt. During the middle of 1173, William decided to entrust the wayward prince with commanding a fleet to support a Fatimid uprising in Egypt against Saladin's ambitious Ayyubid government, which had designs on the Holy Land. This expedition did not meet with success, but Tancred and his fleet returned to the kingdom, where the bastard prince was destined to be favored by fortune.

News eventually reached the Sicilian court that William's cousin (Margaret's nephew), Alfonso VIII of Castile, was to marry Leonor (Eleanor), the daughter of Henry II, in view of the English monarch's formal reconciliation with the papacy. This opened the door to renewed negotiations for the betrothal of Leonor's younger sister, Joanna, to William.

The betrothal was confirmed in 1176 and the nuptials were celebrated in Palermo early the following year (see the next chapter). On this occasion, one of the gifts sent to Margaret, probably from Joanna's mother, Eleanor of Aquitaine, was a pendant containing some relics of Thomas Becket (see Appendix 2).

Margaret was now a mother-in-law.

In July 1177, Romuald of Salerno represented William at the negotiations that culminated in the Treaty of Venice.[432] This brought peace between the papacy and the Holy Roman Empire. Abandoning his support of an antipope, Frederick Barbarossa recognized Alexander III as pope whilst regularizing his relations with papal allies like the northern Italian communes and Sicily.[433]

South of the Alps, the chief effect of this heretofore elusive treaty was a rare era of peace over the next few years. For the Kingdom of Sicily, it meant domestic security throughout William's reign.

Yet the *Regnum*, like other European kingdoms, had its shortcomings. Manorialism was a fact of life, and Monreale's abbot, being the feudal lord of a chunk of the Sicilian hinterland analogous to a vast barony, was beginning to act the part of a zealous baron. When several Muslims, not wishing to accept their status as his serfs, left the territory only to be repatriated, the perfervid prelate made the men swear on the Koran never to leave again, for they were tied to the land.

In 1183, when William was making one of his periodic tours of the peninsular part of the *Regnum*[434] with his courtiers, the two queens, Margaret and Joanna, were left in charge at Palermo as the *de facto* "governors" of Sicily in the king's absence.[435]

Margaret, who was now forty-eight, spent the next few months at Palermo and in a palace next to Monreale's church. The summer was as warm as ever.[436]

On Sunday, the thirty-first of July, she attended liturgy. It would be her last time, for that night she went to sleep, never to awaken.[437] We do not know what claimed her life, only that it ended.

A few days later, her funeral at Monreale was attended by thousands who hiked up the mountain to commemorate their queen. The chief celebrant was the Archbishop of Monreale.

Here, in the cathedral she loved, lies one of Sicily's most beloved women.

Her epitaph[438] is eloquent in its simplicity: "Here in regal dignity lies Queen Margaret, distinguished by her noble spirit, the consort of a king, the mother of princes, the regent for King William II the son she bore. Commended to Heaven on the Feast of Saint Peter in Chains, in the year one thousand one hundred and eighty-three. Amen."

QUEENS OF SICILY

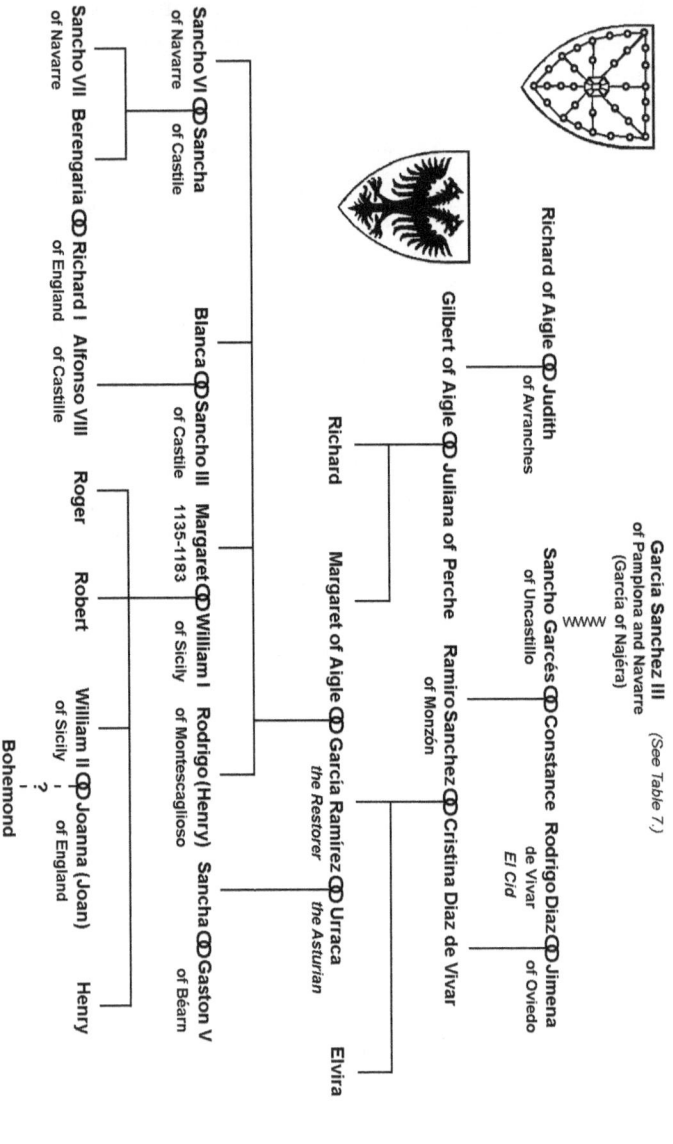

Margaret Jiménez of Navarre

The author at the site of La Guardia Castle, where very little remains of the fortress where Margaret was born. This tower became part of an abbey.

Pamplona Cathedral: Margaret's father and brother rest in the royal crypt in the center of the nave. The Gothic structure replaced a Romanesque church.

Blanca's sarcophagus at Nájera (top) depicts her death in childbirth. The sobbing female figure on the left may be Margaret.

Tudela (now Tudela de Navarra), town of Benjamin who visited the court of King William II near the end of Queen Margaret's regency.

Margaret's Journey to Palermo

Feudal charter issued by Margaret to Walter, Archbishop of Palermo, in the name of her son, King William II, in 1169, a rarity as very few charters issued during her regency survive. The seal was designed in deep red ink, a common practice in Sicily during this period. The charter on the following page appears to be granted in the queen's name.

Margaret's charter of November 1171 in Latin and Greek confirming privileges granted by Roger II to abbeys in the Nebrodian Mountains

In this charter issued in March 1168 (the date was later altered) in William's name, Margaret's name is also indicated as she was regent.

✝HIC REGINA IACES REGALIB
EDITA CVNIS: MARGARITA TIBI
NOMEN · QVOD MORIBVS VNIS:
REGIA PROGENIES PER REGES
DVCTA PROPAGO: UXOR REGIS
ERAS: ET NOBILITATIS IMAGO:
SIT AC EAM QVIBVS IPSA NE-
PLES PRECONIA MVNDV: REGE
W. SATIS E PEPERISSE SECVNDV
✝VND ETES CENTV·DECIES V·IIETII
BVS ANNIS: POST hOMINEM XP·M·
MIGRAS NECIS ERVTA DAMPNIS:
LVX EA QVA POPVLIS DANT PETRI
FESTA CATENE: hIS TE DE NEBVL
TVLIT AD LOCA LVCIS AMENE ✻

Margaret's epitaph and sarcophagus at Monreale

Fatimid fountain in Monreale's cloister

Pantocrator overlooking other mosaic icons in the apse of Monreale Abbey. The second figure from the right of the Fatimid lattice window is Thomas Becket.

Margaret refused a request to entomb King Roger II in Cefalù's splendid cathedral

Chapter 9
JOANNA OF ENGLAND

Joanna of England was born in October of 1165 to Eleanor of Aquitaine, the queen consort of King Henry II of England, at Angers in Anjou.[439] Whilst Eleanor was giving birth to their seventh child, Henry was back in England, possibly with his mistress.[440] He would not see his newest daughter until spring of the following year, when he returned to the continent to assert his authority and to suppress a few barons who were rebelling against his wife's sovereignty over some lands in her personal dominions. On Easter, Henry also met with Louis VII of France, his wife's ex-husband.[441]

It was Joanna's fate to be born into a tempestuous family during a tumultuous time in the history of what later came to be called the "Angevin Empire," the exonym referring collectively to the lands ruled by Henry, from England and part of Ireland southward through Normandy, Maine, Brittany, Anjou and Aquitaine, thence embracing lands as far as the foothills of the Pyrenees. During the course of Joanna's childhood, the marriage of her parents would be marked by estrangement and her brothers would rebel in a military campaign against her father, whose ideas about law and government fueled a chronic, fatal feud with England's premier prelate.

The lives of Henry, Eleanor and their sons Richard "Lionheart" and John "Lackland" are fodder for England's most memorable medieval saga. The story of the colorful "Plantagenet" dynasty brings us everything from connubial squabbles and filial betrayal to crusades to constitutions to the Magna Carta.

Parentage

This is not mere retrospective embellishment, for by no means were Joanna's parents passive figures in history. To the contrary, they did much to shape the society of their time and our modern perceptions of it. To Eleanor we owe certain notions of medieval reginal motherhood and power, to Henry the fundamental tenets of common law that form the basis of principles enshrined in Britain's "unwritten" constitution and, to this day, the legal framework of nations influenced by such ideas, notably the United States, Canada, Australia and India.

Henry's control of continental territories beyond Normandy, effectively half of what is now France, led to conflict and war; his incursion into Ireland spawned consequences that would span many centuries. Rooted in questions of law and jurisdiction, his feud with Thomas Becket, the Archbishop of Canterbury, had little immediate effect in English society but it was, arguably, a seed that germinated, centuries later, into one of the pretexts for the establishment of the Church of England.[442]

Henry II "Curtmantle" became the undisputed King of England in 1154 following a dynastic controversy that led to what in English history is appropriately called "The Anarchy." This was essentially a civil war.[443] His claim to the throne was inherited through his mother, Maude (Matilda), herself one of the most powerful women in Europe and the daughter of Henry I "Beauclerc," fourthborn son of William the Conqueror.[444]

Thus Henry II was Norman on his mother's side. His father, through whom he inherited lands in France, was Geoffrey V, Count of Anjou, who died in 1151. For this reason, Henry and his descendants are usually referred to in British historiography as *Angevins.* The term *Plantagenet,* though known, became popular somewhat later.[445]

Henry's only wife, graceful Eleanor of Aquitaine, was about a decade older than the young king. As the heiress of the prosperous Duchy of Aquitaine, she was much desired. She wed, firstly, Louis VII of France in 1137. The marriage cannot be said to have been a happy one.

There may be some truth to the belief that the youthful bride was indecorous, even audacious, and ten years later she accompanied her husband on the misadventurous Second Crusade. At Constantinople, the chronicler Nicetas Choniates praised her beauty.

Eleanor's sea voyage back to France was hindered by Byzantine assaults, and unforeseen storms blew her ship off course, possibly as far as the African coast, but she eventually made it to the port of Palermo at the end of July in 1149, ill but safe. Her husband's galley, meanwhile, had landed in Apulia. King Roger II accompanied Eleanor to the mainland, where she was united with her husband. The two kings met at Potenza in late August. Roger then had the royal couple and their suite escorted to Tusculum to meet the pope.[446]

At Tusculum, Eleanor and Louis prevailed upon Pope Eugene III to grant an annulment of their marriage based on the pretext of close consanguinity through what was actually rather distant kinship. This was ridiculous considering the frequent marriages between royal cousins; it seems more likely that Louis was simply disappointed that Eleanor had produced two daughters[447] but no sons, for it was stipulated upon their marriage that he could not rule Aquitaine *jure uxoris* and that the duchy would be inherited only by a male heir. Nonetheless, the annulment was granted and in 1152 Eleanor wed the King of England, by whom she bore sons, beginning with William, who died young, and Henry, who lived into adulthood.[448] The most significant result of this union, apart from the births of Henry's successors Richard and John, was that Aquitaine henceforth fell under Plantagenet rule. A great deal has been written about Eleanor, much of it flattering.[449]

Childhood

Images of Joanna depict her as a pretty blonde.[450] Her childhood may be viewed as privileged, even by the royal standards of her time. Whereas her two elder half-sisters, Marie and Alix (Eleanor's daughters by Louis VII), remained at their father's court, Joanna and her two "full" sisters enjoyed the benefit of a close relationship with their mother. Every scrap of evidence suggests that Eleanor was a loving mother.[451]

Marie and Alix were not Joanna's only half siblings, as Henry II fathered illegitimate children, notably Geoffrey of York and William Longespée.

Joanna's full siblings were William (who died young in 1156), Henry the Young King (who died in 1183), Matilda (Maude), Richard "Lionheart," Geoffrey, Leonor (Eleanor), and John "Lackland," who was born the year following Joanna.

Eleanor did not often see her eldest two daughters from her first marriage. Their father, Louis, may have brought them to visit her at Angers when he went there to meet Henry in April 1166, but this is not known with certainty.

Most of what we know of Joanna's childhood comes to us through our knowledge of her strong-willed mother's actions and movements.[452] Indeed, Eleanor and her three daughters by Henry were back in England by the end of 1166, where John was born at Oxford.

Joanna's grandmother, the remarkable Maude, died at Rouen in 1167. By then, Henry's interminable quarrel with Thomas Becket was in full vigor.

Thomas Becket

Few ecclesiastics of England's Middle Ages have been the subject of as much study as Thomas Becket, whose eloquent epistles fill many volumes, painting a punctilious portrait of his personal character and his theological views. No discourse on the concepts of national sovereignty, ecclesiastical authority or the separation of church and state is truly complete without at least a perfunctory consideration of the unholy feud between King Henry II of England and his onetime ally, Thomas Becket, Archbishop of Canterbury.[453]

A cosmopolitan education abroad led Thomas to the service of Theobald, Archbishop of Canterbury, where he became known as a learned and pragmatic man, more thinker than scrivener. In 1155, Theobald recommended him to become the chancellor of newly-crowned Henry II.

This post involved collecting monies owed the crown, whether from barons or bishops. Thomas performed his duties efficiently, bringing order to the royal accounts. He and the king become good friends, passing much time together hunting, conversing and drinking. Thomas was Henry's closest confidant, perhaps even something of a mentor.

Henry believed that justice should be available to all his subjects, and that some semblance of equality could prevail under the law. True, there were barons and there were serfs, and a feudal order that kept every man in his place (with little thought given to women), but the long civil war he witnessed as a boy convinced the king that just laws could bring about a fundamentally just society.

Thomas Becket agreed with these principles, at least initially. Amongst their prominent proponents were Richard of Luci, the chief justiciar (England's highest judge), and Ranulf of Glanville, the erudite scholar who succeeded him.[454]

With Henry's introduction of civil (secular) tribunals, a law emerged that was "common" throughout England. Decisions might establish precedent, ensuring consistency in the prosecution of the same crime in different parts of the realm.

Henry's common law[455] did not completely supplant existing principles. Nonetheless, the new laws forever changed the face of England's juridical landscape.

An obvious obstacle to universal enforcement was that in England, as in most of Europe, the church was, in effect, a "state within a state" governed by its own laws. Not only did the church control much property, about one in five subjects was under ecclesiastical jurisdiction, either as a cleric, nun or serf.

Upon Theobald's death in 1161, Henry saw the appointment of his friend, Thomas, as Archbishop of Canterbury, and therefore Primate of England, as a way of introducing his tenets of law into the ecclesiastical sphere. Thomas, however, had other ideas. As archbishop, he began, unexpectedly, to take traditional papal positions on the issues so important to the king. The Constitutions of Clarendon enacted in 1164 became a particular bone of contention, though not the only one.

Seeking a pretext to remove Thomas from power, Henry accused him of malfeasance allegedly committed during his tenure as chancellor. The king summoned the archbishop to appear at a great council at Northampton to answer these charges. When convicted, Thomas stormed out of the trial and fled to France, where he obtained sanctuary from King Louis VII.

In 1166, with Thomas in exile, Henry enacted the Assize of Clarendon. Very little of this dealt with ecclesiastical authority. Rather, it transferred much power from the barons to the royal judges. Trial by jury was instituted based on an evidentiary model, replacing such methods as compurgation, an accused person being released if a certain number of his friends swore that they believed him, and trial by single combat, a knight duelling an opponent to decide his case.

Henry took reprisal against the prelate's family, which he exiled, and (as we have seen) eventually two of Becket's nephews were granted hospitality by Queen Margaret in Sicily.[456]

By 1167, Pope Alexander III was actively intervening in the dispute through the diplomacy of one emissary after another. Whilst he agreed with Thomas in principle, the pontiff saw no point in allowing the controversy to drag on for years.

A meeting between the king and the archbishop east of Paris early in 1169 resolved nothing, ending with both men parting in exasperation.[457]

Even little Joanna occasioned Becket's consternation. It was during 1169 that he wrote the letter (quoted in the previous chapter) to Ubaldo, Bishop of Ostia, criticizing King William II of Sicily for seeking Joanna's hand in marriage.[458]

Henry was just as obdurate as Becket. He arranged for his eldest son, Joanna's brother Henry, to be crowned *rex filius* by the Archbishop of York, whose see contested Canterbury for primacy in England. This was meant to humiliate the exiled Becket, as everybody knew that the privilege of coronation belonged to Canterbury alone. The coronation took place in June 1170.

Becket's reaction was to excommunicate the Archbishop of York, along with the bishops of London and Salisbury who assisted him in crowning Prince Henry, the Young King.[459]

Convinced that the elder Henry had gone too far, Pope

Alexander confirmed Becket's excommunications of the bishops and others. Fearing that an interdict on England might be the next misfortune to befall his reign, the king met with Thomas in France in late July. The exile formally ended and the two tacitly agreed to ignore, for now, the myriad jurisdictional complications arising from the Constitutions of Clarendon and other legislation.

Thomas Becket returned to England in early December. Henry was distressed to learn that his erstwhile friend refused to lift the excommunication of the Archbishop of York. Worse yet, the archbishop excommunicated other subjects in what seemed like an attempt to test Henry's resolve, if not his laws.

Seeing Henry's displeasure, four of his knights went to Canterbury to confront the archbishop. There, in the cathedral, they struck down Thomas Becket with their swords at the hour of vespers on the evening of Tuesday, December twenty-ninth.

Henry repudiated this heinous act, disavowing any responsibility for it. Yet the assassins, though publicly condemned, went unpunished except for banishment from the court and excommunication, rather painless penalties.

Education of an English Princess

By then, Joanna was living with her mother in the Maubergeonne Tower at Poitiers, where Eleanor held court and maintained a large household. It seems that the young princess and her brother, John, also spent some time with their mother at Fontevrault, an abbey under Eleanor's patronage.

Earlier in 1170, Joanna's sister, Leonor, had traveled to Castile to wed Alfonso VIII, the nephew of Queen Margaret of Sicily.[460]

News of Becket's death shook England, and before long the cause for his canonization was opened. Eleanor was one of the many to venerate the murdered archbishop. Joanna, at the tender age of five, came to think of him as a saint.[461]

Her father spent the first months of 1172 prosecuting an invasion of Ireland he had begun the previous year, not wishing for the island to fall under the exclusive control of a few of his vassals who had already occupied parts of it. The campaign extended Henry's influence to the Irish lands, which would remain under English control for centuries. The month of May found the king at Avranches, where he was absolved of guilt in his erstwhile friend's murder. Then he went to Caen to meet with a council of bishops and reiterate what he had professed at Avranches, effectively abrogating most of the crown rights he had asserted against ecclesiastical authority during the past few years.[462]

Henry was with Eleanor and their younger children at Chinon for Christmas.[463] This was a rare occasion for Joanna, now seven, to see her father. The outward tranquility in Joanna's family was to prove fragile.

In February 1173, Eleanor, her husband and their younger children were present at the Council of Limoges.[464] Thomas Becket was canonized the same month, and his cult spread rapidly across Catholic Europe. Other matters brewing in Henry's realms were far less seraphic.

A conflict emerged between Henry II and his eldest living son, Prince Henry (the Young King), who was wed to Margaret, a daughter of Louis VII of France. As the heir of Eleanor, who held Aquitaine and other lands in her own right, the younger Henry thought of these dominions as his birthright. This was reasonable.

Joanna and John were still children, yet their father was already brokering their marriages. Negotiations for the marriage of Joanna to William II of Sicily recommenced now that her father's predicament with the papacy was resolved. It would be a few years before this could be concluded.

In seeking a suitable wife for John, Henry took the liberty of adding three castles (Chinon, Mirabeau, Loudun) to the boy's patrimony to sweeten the English proposal of the young prince to wed Alice, a daughter of Humbert III of Savoy; this count ruled part of southeastern France but did not yet have a son. Humbert's interesting offer was made through an ambassador Henry met, probably at the Council of Limoges at which Eleanor was present, but it is unclear whether the queen herself attended this meeting.[465]

As the three castles were in Eleanor's territory, her husband's action was viewed as an infringement.

In reality, it was precisely the kind of pretext that Louis VII and a number of nobles might exploit to break the grasp of Henry II on half of France.[466]

Their effort was encouraged, indeed incited, by Eleanor, whose rapport with her consort had been sour for years, and still more so following Becket's assassination.

Young Joanna was about to witness a conflict between what were literally warring spouses.

Prince Henry enlisted support by promising lands in his mother's extensive dominions to various noblemen. This was, for the moment, an effective political strategy, even if it would lead to the dismemberment of what he stood to inherit.

What followed was a war that pitted Eleanor and her three sons against her husband for eighteen months. In the spring of 1173, the supporters of Prince Henry made an incursion into Normandy.

Henry II advised a number of European monarchs of the dire situation, receiving a letter from, amongst others, King William II of Sicily.[467]

Having left Poitiers, Eleanor was captured by her husband's forces and sent to him at Rouen, his headquarters. By spring of the following year the fighting had reached England.

In July of 1174, Eleanor and her two youngest children

were taken by Henry II to England. Placed under guard at Sarum Castle, in Salisbury, the Queen of England and Duchess of Aquitaine was now a captive in all but name.[468]

Henry, meanwhile, did penance at the tomb of Saint Thomas Becket at Canterbury.[469]

The king soon managed to defeat his enemies in England. When Henry returned to Normandy he was able to obtain the surrender and submission of his three rebellious sons. Joined by Louis VII, they reached a peace in late September 1174.

Henry forgave his progeny but not his wife, who he kept under house arrest. Eleanor, Joanna and John resided at Sarum until early 1176.[470]

There was a family gathering at Winchester for Easter that included Eleanor's adult sons (Henry, Geoffrey, Richard) and her estranged husband.[471] Around this time, or soon afterward, Joanna took up residence at that city's castle.[472] Eleanor was still under house arrest.

There is nothing to suggest that the two youngest children's lives were in any way disturbed or their education interrupted.[473] As ever, Eleanor was a loving mother.

Joanna was the only daughter of Henry and Eleanor who was not yet married; Matilda had wed Henry III "the Lion" of Saxony in 1168 and Leonor, as we have seen, had married Alfonso VIII of Castile in 1170.

Betrothal

In the spring of 1176[474] some ambassadors arrived from the Kingdom of Sicily seeking the hand of Joanna for William II. Henry received them at Westminster.[475]

William's mother, Margaret, may have sympathized with the suffering of her sister queen, but she could not let Eleanor's plight interfere with plans to finalize the dynastic marriage proposed years earlier.[476] The two queens lived in very different realities. One of the differences was that Eleanor had four living sons, whereas Margaret had only one, and William needed a bride.

Margaret's influence was not entirely unknown in English circles. A few years earlier, she had intervened with the pope to forgive the excommunicated Bishop of Salisbury for that prelate's defiance of Thomas Becket.[477]

We know far more about the details of the betrothal of Joanna of England to William of Sicily than we do about the great majority of royal unions negotiated in Europe during the twelfth century. So complete are the surviving records of it that the event, as it has become known to us, is the very archetype of its era.

To achieve her objective, Margaret turned to a trusted prelate, Rotrou of Rouen, the kinsman who had sent Stephen of Perche to her court years earlier. Rotrou offered to go to England to meet with Henry. Accompanying him were two bishops, Elias of Troia and Arnolf of Capaccio, along with a faithful nobleman and justiciar, Florio of Camerota. With a company of knights and servants, these four ambassadors reached England early in April 1176.

There was never really any doubt that Henry would consent to this marriage; he had already agreed to its conditions a few years earlier. In the meantime, of course, he had also approved the betrothal of another daughter to Margaret's nephew, the King of Castile.

Nonetheless, the King of England followed the formality of meeting in council with the prelates and high nobles of his court to grant his royal assent before sending William's ambassadors to meet Joanna at Winchester.

Considering Joanna's tender years, this was a precocious betrothal even by the standards of the twelfth century; the girl was six months shy of her eleventh birthday.

At Winchester, the ambassadors were permitted to meet

the young princess. Her beauty and poise were obvious enough. The men were curious about the girl's health and intelligence.

Communication was no obstacle, as Joanna spoke Norman French. The men asked her a few questions. Having heard something about the fiery temperaments of her mother and father, they were probably at least a little interested in Joanna's personality.

The ambassadors overwhelmingly approved of Joanna.

Brooking no delay, they made their way back to London to discuss the betrothal details with the king. There they explained that the affianced Joanna would receive a large dower that included, among other lucrative manors, the wealthy county of Mount Saint Angelo, with the coastal towns of Siponto and Vieste, all in Apulia.[478]

Rotrou of Rouen was present, along with Cardinal Hugh Pierleoni, the pope's permanent ambassador to the English court. Henry's next step was to send his own ambassadors to Palermo to convey his personal greetings to William, his future son-in-law.

Meanwhile, the Sicilian ambassadors, Elias, Arnolf and Florio, remained in England as Henry's guests whilst Joanna prepared for her voyage. They would accompany her to Sicily. The princess and her ladies-in-waiting would be ready to depart in four months.

Henry visited his daughter during the middle of August to wish her well, and to remind her of the importance of the role she was about to assume.[479]

Joanna's father was known for his volatility. For that matter, so was Eleanor. Yet Joanna, as the youngest daughter of parents who, though vigorous, were no longer youngish themselves, seems to have been privileged with the benefit of their experience. Whereas Eleanor had instigated three of her sons to rebel against their father, her three daughters were subjected to little more than the usual effort to ensure marriages that were politically advantageous. That was seen as the girls' contribution to the family. The Plantagenets, of course, were not just any aristocratic family but one of Europe's most powerful dynasties.

Joanna could not have known her father very well. The record shows that she saw him only rarely. As a king he achieved much, and much has been written about his reign. Some of it is still debated. His success as a father is even more debatable. The most serious conversation Joanna ever had with him was almost certainly the one they had just before her departure from England.

Neither of Eleanor's marriages was a happy one, but there is no sign of her inner anguish coloring her treatment of her three daughters by Henry, and it is difficult to discern in the known historical record any evidence that she favored one girl among them. By most accounts, Richard was her favorite son.

Though she would be crowned in a far country, Joanna, as we have said, spoke her husband's language. Different as they were, the Plantagenet and Hauteville courts shared at least that much.

Joanna had never been to London. Even if she had seen that city, there was little there or elsewhere in her parents' dominions to prepare her for what she was about to encounter in the flourishing kingdom beyond the Alps.

It was hard to say whether the new alliance of England with Sicily would yield any tangible advantages to the former beyond increased trade, but that was quite enough. Besides, Henry had announced his intention of going on crusade, an endeavor for which having an ally in the central Mediterranean might prove useful, just as it did for Eleanor when she was returning from her own adventure in the Holy Land.

The Journey to Sicily

In October, Henry received a letter[480] from William thanking him and setting forth some details of Joanna's journey.

One imagines Eleanor offering a few words to Joanna explaining what to expect in Sicily.

The day of the departure eventually arrived. Joanna embraced her mother, Eleanor, knowing she might never see her again.[481] Her retinue then set out for Sicily with a large company of prelates and nobles. With them Henry sent his future son-in-law gifts of fine horses, clothes, gold and silver, and precious vases.[482]

The royal party included Archbishop Richard of Canterbury and Bishop Geoffrey of Ely, along with Bishop Giles of Evreux and Hugh of Beauchamp.

Among the travelers was Hamelin of Warenne, King Henry's half-brother. Not all of these clerics, courtiers and kinsmen would accompany Joanna all the way to Sicily. Some would go only as far as Saint-Gilles, on the French coast, where a flotilla of Sicilian galleys would meet Joanna. Elias of Troia, Arnolf of Capaccio and Florio of Camerota, being William's ambassadors, were to travel with the company to Palermo.

Joanna, of course, was the youngest of the travelers, and one of the few women. On the leg of the journey over land, the large royal party, with its many wagons, traveled much more slowly than a pair of couriers or a company of knights would have ridden over the same distance.

Having crossed the English Channel, the company was met in Normandy by Joanna's eldest brother, Henry the Young King, who accompanied them to Poitiers. From there, her brother Richard escorted the company southward through Aquitaine, which he had inherited from his mother.

In late November, Joanna and her suite arrived at Saint-Gilles, where twenty-odd Sicilian galleys were waiting for them. She had just celebrated her eleventh birthday.

Unfortunately, the two galleys bearing precious gifts that William had sent his father-in-law were lost at sea. This was reported by Bishop John of Norwich, one of Henry's returning ambassadors, who described a terrible voyage from Messina to Saint-Gilles.

Leading the Sicilian flotilla were Alfano, Archbishop of Capua, Richard Palmer, Bishop of Syracuse, and Robert, Count of Caserta. Most of the royal retinue embarked, but Richard of Canterbury and Geoffrey of Ely returned to England to report to Henry that the first part of the journey was successful.

The galleys set out along the Italian coast, occasionally stopping along the way. The waters of the Tyrrhenian, the same sea that had claimed the galleys carrying gifts for King Henry, were choppy this time of year. Joanna was unaccustomed to sea travel. She suffered a bout of sea sickness that necessitated stops along the coast more frequent that what had been planned. (See the map of Joanna's itinerary at the end of this chapter.)

Joanna and her suite finally reached the waters of the Kingdom of Sicily. They disembarked at Naples to celebrate Christmas and give Joanna a few days' rest. At this point it was decided to travel over land, stopping at Salerno and Calabria. This took longer than an itinerary by sea, but it was less injurious to Joanna's physical condition. It also offered the advantage of affording her a glimpse of the peninsular part of the *Regnum*. Naples was gradually increasing in population and importance, while Salerno, with its splendid cathedral and palace, was one of the kingdom's most important cities.

Royal Wedding

When Joanna reached Palermo in early February 1177, William was waiting for her at one of the city's eastern gates. It was nearly nightfall when Bishop Giles of Evreux presented her to the King of Sicily. Joanna mounted a palfrey and rode with William through a city lit by lamps and torches. Exultant crowds hailed the couple and their endless entourage.

Accompanied by her ladies-in-waiting and servants, the bride-to-be was received by Queen Margaret at the Zisa palace[483] on the other side of the Genoard.

On Sunday, the thirteenth, Joanna was wed to William in the chapel of the royal palace beneath the benevolent gaze of the Pantocrator. Here she was crowned and anointed Queen of Sicily.[484]

On this occasion, according to Romuald of Salerno, William was crowned for the second time, *in cappella sua desponsavit, et se et eam gloriose coronari fecit, et solemnes de illa nuptias celebravit.* The nuptials and twin coronations were performed by Archbishop Walter, who could finally enjoy the satisfaction and prestige of having crowned a king.

Back in England, Henry and Eleanor received a report of the magnificent event. The only disappointment was the loss of the two galleys transporting gifts for Henry and, perhaps, for Eleanor.

The dynastic marriage formed an esoteric link between the mothers of the spouses. We Italians use the word *consuocera* (co-mother-in-law). The term describes the relationship between two mothers whose children have wed each other. The marriage between William and Joanna made the two queens, Margaret and Eleanor, *consuocere.*

One of the gifts Joanna brought for her mother-in-law was the gold reliquary, formed into a pendant, bearing relics of martyred Thomas Becket. This was made on the initiative of Reginald of Bath, but it may have been sent to Margaret at Eleanor's urging.

Three Queens

The Kingdom of Sicily now had three queens. There was Beatrice of Rethel, the "queen dowager," the widow of Roger II. There was Margaret, the queen mother. Then there was young Joanna, the newly-crowned queen consort, who was not yet even a teenager. As heiress, Constance, the daughter of Beatrice, was a potential queen.

There was no telling when Queen Joanna might bear children. For the moment, she was little more than a child herself. Joanna and her ladies-in-waiting may have spent the next year or two living at the Zisa before the young queen took up residence with the king and consummated her marriage.

As we have seen (in the last chapter), the Treaty of Venice of 1177 brought with it a period of peace to the Kingdom of Sicily.

Monreale Abbey was William's greatest architectural feat but it was not his only one.

Amongst the many projects undertaken was construction of a palace similar in style to the Zisa. Situated on the opposite side of the Genoard, near the Kemonia River not far from the road leading through the park to Monreale, the Cuba, being surrounded by a lake, was somewhat smaller than the Zisa but equally impressive. Like the Zisa, the Cuba, which takes its name from the Arabic *qubba*, "cupola," is still standing.[485] Boccaccio mentioned it in his *Decameron,* where it is a setting in the sixth story of the fifth day.

By 1179, with the *Regnum,* the central Mediterranean and northern Italy pacified, it was possible for Joanna to contemplate a future devoid of serious hardship. The young queen's chief duty was obvious enough: William needed a son.

It is possible that during 1181 or 1182 Joanna gave birth to a child, rumored to have been named Bohemond and to have died in infancy. However, only one chronicler reports the event, and he was not in Sicily. Robert of Torigni, a Norman, was the abbot of Mont Saint-Michel and godfather to Joanna's sister, Leonor. Significant as his chronicles are, Robert's statement about Bohemond's birth is probably inaccurate.[486]

It is highly possible that King William could not produce

heirs.[487] One would have expected Joanna to fall pregnant by the age of sixteen or seventeen.[488]

In a report corroborated by Arab sources, Robert of Torigni also tells us that the same year, 1181, saw the arrival in Palermo of an embassy from Tunisia that confirmed a decade-long treaty with the Kingdom of Sicily. The impetus for this trade accord was an event that occurred two years earlier, when a Sicilian fleet encountered a floundering ship taking the daughter of the Almohad caliph to her wedding to a Muslim emir and returned the girl to her grateful father.[489]

Passages

Pope Alexander III, known for his part in mitigating the feud between Thomas Becket and Henry II, died in August 1181. His most lasting achievement was the reformative Third Lateran Council, largely a dilatory attempt to curtail corruption and make the papacy more efficient. Many occupants of the See of Peter were wicked misanthropes. Pope Alexander, a devout man of God, was the exception. His successor was Ubaldo Allucingoli, long a fixture at the Sicilian court; this octogenarian took the name Lucius III. Perhaps not surprisingly in view of his age, Lucius was a bit of a reactionary, but his pontificate was destined to last just four years.

Except for sending a fleet to the island of Majorca[490] as part of a half-hearted Christian effort to oust the Muslims, William's military exploits during this period were few. Most of his time was occupied with domestic affairs. Elsewhere, however, events transpired that had a subtle ripple effect on the Kingdom of Sicily.

In April 1182, the Greek populace of Constantinople erupted against the many Italian merchants in the city.[491] Few of the victims were Sicilian; most were Genoan or Pisan. Thousands of Roman Catholics were attacked and killed indiscriminately. Not even the papal ambassador was spared. This prompted William and other European monarchs west of the Adriatic to contemplate an invasion of the Byzantine territories.

Queen Margaret died the following year.

Virtually nothing is known about Joanna's time as queen consort, except that she bore no children. In the spring of 1184, she went with William to Calabria to comfort its population following a destructive earthquake powerful enough to force the collapse of Cosenza's cathedral.

It is quite possible that Joanna introduced the troubadour tradition in Sicily. At the very least, its introduction coincided with her arrival. This was characterized by the use of a vernacular language. Although the spoken language of the Sicilian and English courts was Norman French, Joanna's mother tongue, which she learned in childhood from Eleanor, was actually Occitan, the *langue d'oc*. Her influence was likely an impetus at the Sicilian court for the use of a local vernacular, Middle Sicilian, in decades to come.

Jubayr

In December of 1184, the traveler bin Jubayr was shipwrecked at Messina, where he was given hospitality by an Arabic-speaking King of Sicily. His Sicilian travels took him westward by ship, with stops at Cefalù, Termini, Solunto and finally Palermo. Following a week in the capital, he departed by land for Trapani, passing Alcamo along the way.

Among many other details, he describes several castles which no longer exist. He refers to a military fleet under construction; these were probably galleys for William's planned invasion of Greece.

In Palermo he found a city of gardens and streets in a metropolis that combined "the benefits of wealth and splendor," comparing it to Cordoba. He mentioned its limestone buildings, its springs and its rivers.

Jubayr remarked that the Christian women dressed with much the same modesty as their Muslim sisters, and wore scarves or veils; his description leads us to infer that many of them spoke Arabic.

He also described the Martorana Church, and specifically its bell tower (perhaps higher then than now). He observed that the city of Messina was predominantly Greek Orthodox, with a dwindling Muslim community. Some of his comments are cryptic. He mentions a tax on Muslims, without making clear whether this tax was also levied upon Christians and Jews.

It is obvious from his writings that Jubayr was devout in his Sunni faith, perhaps even something of a dogmatist. But the winds of religious intolerance and change were gathering force, and perhaps that is what he concluded from what he saw in Sicily, where he might have hoped to see more Muslims. A number of mosques had already been converted to churches to accommodate the growing number of Muslims becoming Catholic.[492]

Jubayr's record is useful in establishing the continuity of the Palermitan cultural atmosphere over the centuries. It is, in effect, a link in a chain. Mohammed ibn Hawqal, a merchant from Baghdad with a penchant for geography, described an Arab-Byzantine Sicily in the time long before Idrisi and Jubayr, and a capital just as prosperous.

Jubayr also visited Jerusalem and other places, and wrote about these.

Decisions

Virtually nothing is recorded about Joanna over the next few years, though much is known of her husband's reign.

In 1184, William arranged the marriage of his aunt, Constance, to Henry, a son of Frederick Barbarossa. This may have reinforced Sicily's bonds with Germany, but any child of Constance would be a Hohenstaufen, not a Hauteville. The queen dowager Beatrice of Rethel, Constance's mother, died a few months after the betrothal.

Joanna was now the only Queen of Sicily.

In 1185, while Constance was making her way northward to marry[493] Henry Hohenstaufen, William launched an invasion of the Greek lands to the east of the *Regnum,* something he had been considering ever since the Byzantine massacre of the Latins at Constantinople a few years earlier. Leading this incursion was his bastard kinsman, Tancred of Lecce, along with Margaritus of Brindisi, an able admiral. The Sicilian advance toward Constantinople was stopped by Emperor Isaac Angelus Comnenus, with whom William made peace four years later.

When Saladin captured Jerusalem late in 1187, the only military opposition to arrive from Europe was the Sicilian fleet led by admiral Margaritus. The next year, Margaritus relieved the Knights Hospitaller, who were besieged by Saladin at their large fortress, Krak des Chevaliers.

With other Christian kings, William was already contemplating a Third Crusade to take back the Holy City.

Widowhood

When King William II of Sicily died without children in November 1189, his aunt Constance was his designated heir.[494] The baronage, not wishing to see the *Regnum* fall into the hands of the Holy Roman Emperor, had other ideas. Led by the chancellor, Matthew of Aiello, the rebellious barons crowned illegitimate Tancred of Lecce as King of Sicily. This choice was supported by Pope Clement III (Paolino Scolari), who feared any union of the Kingdom of Sicily with the Holy

Roman Empire. For now, there was nothing Constance or her husband could do about the coronation.

Joanna might have rallied forces to oppose Tancred, but for whom? She had no son of her own to claim the throne usurped by Tancred, while Constance, in whose name such a campaign would be prosecuted, was too far away to support such an effort. For now, Constance herself was childless. The grave predicament lacked a clear resolution.

Joanna's father, Henry II of England, died in the same year as her husband. Henry was succeeded as king by his son, Joanna's brother Richard, who liberated his beloved mother from confinement.

Tancred knew not what to do with Joanna, but he harbored no doubts about her wealth. He confiscated her dower lands in Apulia, along with whatever other reginal assets he could find, and restricted the queen's movements, placing her under guard in Palermo, probably at the Zisa palace.

His reasons for these actions were several. The motive for confiscating Joanna's property was simple enough. As to the queen's confinement, Tancred's major concern was that Joanna, who openly supported Constance's claim to the throne according to the late William's wishes, might instigate an insurrection against him. Part of Tancred's rationale was that his own wife, Sibylla of Acerra, was now Queen of Sicily, and thus entitled to the dower.

The lady from England may have seemed isolated, but Tancred had overlooked, or at least underestimated, a very important element: Joanna's crusading sibling.

Joanna is Freed

The Third Crusade occasioned the visit of King Richard I "Lionheart" of England and King Philip II "Augustus" of France to Messina in 1190 *en route* to the Holy Land.[495] The

English fleet had sailed around the Iberian peninsula to arrive in the Mediterranean.

Consisting of more than a hundred vessels, Richard's fleet arrived at the Sicilian city in the middle of September ahead of its lord, who undertook the last leg of the journey over land, working his way down the Italian peninsula.[496] Philip and his French force arrived at Messina a day or two after the English.

Richard was delayed for another week in Calabria, where some local peasants took him to task for claiming a falcon that was theirs.[497] This bizarre incident near Mileto would be all but insignificant except that it may have informed the king's condescending opinion about the local folk and his subsequent actions toward them. Across the strait, his people were not welcomed very cordially by the Messinians.

At Messina the French were received by the populace no more kindly than the English, but it was the latter under Richard that decided to take the city following a series of skirmishes in which Philip initially sided with the Messinians.

This was achieved in a single assault, with plenty of rape and pillage in its wake, although Richard sagely put an end to the violence before it led to mass carnage. Philip and the French disapproved of the occupation, if only because they felt deprived of their share of the plunder, and protested. Fortunately, the two kings brought matters under control before their armies began a major battle against each other.[498]

Walter of Coutances, Archbishop of Rouen, who was traveling with Richard, threatened to anathematise whomever did not restore to the Messinians the silver taken from them.

With Messina occupied, Richard sent a party of trusted emissaries, led by Hugh III of Burgundy and Robert of Sablé, to Tancred's court to demand compensation for losses to the crusaders resulting from the Messinians' aggression.

More importantly, they also conveyed Richard's explicit demand that his sister be freed immediately and her dower lands restored, along with the portion of her late husband's money due her. On his sister's behalf, Richard further demanded a golden throne to which she was entitled, along with two dozen silver goblets and plates. For himself he wanted a golden table, a silk pavilion large enough to cover two hundred knights seated at dinner, and some ships and provisions.[499]

The fact that the English king had just conquered one of the kingdom's largest cities "in less time than a priest could chant matins" lent an implicit gravity to this request.[500] Seeing that Messina was impossible to repossess, Margaritus of Brindisi, Tancred's trusted admiral, abandoned it as soon as he could.

Farther north, Constance and her husband were attempting an invasion of the *Regnum* to claim the Sicilian throne. Joanna, as we have seen, supported Constance. Whether or not Richard seriously considered a conquest of Sicily on Constance's behalf, which was well within his army's capability, Tancred probably understood the scope of the English king's military might.

Nonetheless, although the King of Sicily immediately took steps to free Joanna, he stalled for time regarding the dower and money on the pretext that he first had to consult with his advisers. In this he may have been secretly encouraged by Philip, whose trust in Richard was beginning to wane.

Tancred's delay in paying Richard emboldened some Messinians, who began to obstruct English supply ships whilst cooperating with the French, who had curried favor with the local leaders. However, Tancred and his subjects relented when Richard began the construction of a castle called *Mategriffon* on a hill overlooking Messina, a gesture that suggested he might be willing to stay in Sicily for a while.

In late September, Joanna was freed, released to her brother's protection. She traveled by galley from Palermo to Messina, where Philip, a widower, was entranced by her beauty.

For her safety (from the Messinians but perhaps also from Philip), Joanna was lodged at the monastery at Bagnara, across the strait in Calabria, where Richard left a small garrison to guard her. With this in mind, he had already ordered his engineers to fortify the abbey founded a century earlier by Roger I.[501]

Richard's rapport with Philip, who had supported him in a series of battles against his own father, was growing strained, especially after Richard called off his planned marriage to Philip's half-sister, Alys. The English king was now planning to wed Berengaria of Navarre.

Tancred eventually paid Richard twenty thousand gold ounces for Joanna's dower. Another twenty thousand was paid to accommodate Richard's other requests, though according to one chronicler this was ostensibly a dowry for Tancred's daughter, Elvira, to wed Richard's young nephew, Arthur of Brittany, whom Richard had declared heir presumptive to the English throne. This betrothal was never finalized; the contract for Elvira's dowry may have been little more than a ploy by Richard to justify his theft of Joanna's money.

Joanna's dower lands in Apulia were not restored to her, and Richard never gave her much of the remuneration remitted to him by Tancred.[502]

Richard accepted an invitation to meet Tancred at Catania, where the two monarchs made peace, sending a copy of their treaty to the pope. Then Richard returned to Messina and Tancred to Palermo. Much to the chagrin of the Messinians, the English and French armies wintered in Sicily.

On Christmas, Joanna attended Richard's lavish feast at Mategriffon.[503] Philip of France, who was present, was already admiring the widow's beauty with an eye to marrying her.[504]

In March 1191, Philip set sail for Palestine while Richard crossed the strait to Calabria to meet his mother, Eleanor, who arrived with his fiancée, Berengaria of Navarre.[505] Eleanor, who had lived through much since her previous visit to Sicily four decades earlier, had not seen her youngest daughter in fourteen years. In the event, she stayed into the first days of April before returning to England, stopping *en route* to visit the pope, leaving her daughter and future daughter-in-law at Messina to proceed to the Holy Land.

On Crusade

In early April, Richard sent Joanna and Berengaria ahead of him to Palestine with a small flotilla while he tended to some final preparations before setting sail with his main fleet a few days later.[506] Among many other tasks, he destroyed most of Mategriffon, the castle he had built of timber and stone to keep an eye over the Messinians.[507]

Along the way to the Holy Land, the large galley transporting Joanna and Berengaria was blown off course by a violent storm. The ladies and their retinue found themselves off the coast of Cyprus.[508] Richard landed at Rhodes, where he spent a few days recuperating from an illness while Philip was already at the Siege of Acre. Before long, Richard's fleet was sailing again.

Anchored in deep water near the port of Limassol, the galley carrying Joanna and Berengaria waited for several days in late April while some pilgrims from other ships went ashore. Unfortunately, these pilgrims were attacked, robbed and imprisoned.

About a week later, the ruler of Cyprus, Isaac Comnenus, a kinsman of the Byzantine Emperor of the same name, began to coax the ladies and their entourage into coming ashore. They were on the verge of accepting when Richard's fleet arrived and routed the Byzantine force, constraining Isaac to come to terms.[509]

On the twelfth of May, with Cyprus under his control, Richard wed Berengaria at Limassol, where she was crowned Queen of England.[510]

Now Isaac, safely ensconced in a castle, demanded that Richard leave Cyprus and began waging a campaign against him. This consisted of little more than a series of skirmishes, but it took the king a fortnight to conquer the entire island. He then deposed and imprisoned Isaac whilst leaving his own men in charge of Cyprus.

Joanna and Berengaria arrived at Acre on the first of June, joined by Richard two days later following his engagement and defeat of a Saracen vessel.[511]

The besieged city capitulated in July. With this, the crusading kings established contact with Saladin through emissaries. On July twenty-first, Richard brought his wife and sister into the city, lodging them in its palace.[512] Ten days later, Philip returned to France to confront domestic problems, leaving Hugh of Burgundy in charge of the French troops.

The Arab chronicler Baha ad-Din tells us that two Catholic attendants in Joanna's service who were converts from Islam escaped to the Ayyubid camp, where they embraced their former faith and were received by Saladin.[513]

Having waited a month for a reply from Saladin, on August twentieth Richard ordered the execution of over two thousand Muslim prisoners. Saladin retaliated by killing his Christian prisoners.

In early September, the Christians won an important battle at Arsuf. The crusaders' victory forced Saladin to the negotiating table. He sent his brother, Al-Adil ("Saphadin"), to meet with Richard.

Incredibly, one of Richard's proposals was that as part of a peace agreement his sister, Joanna, should marry Al-Adil and the couple could then rule Jerusalem together. The very thought angered Joanna.[514] This unorthodox idea was discarded after perfunctory discussion about the incompatibility of the hypothetical spouses, although Richard reportedly put forward the name of his niece, Eleanor of Brittany, after

Joanna refused to be bartered. The Muslim chronicler from whom the account comes suggests that neither Saladin nor his counsellors sincerely believed that Richard was serious in advancing the idea.[515]

After the negotiations failed, Richard pressed on to Ascalon, which he fortified. A series of battles fought in 1192 culminated in September of that year with a compromise that gave Christian pilgrims and clergy access to Jerusalem. Under the circumstances, which had been reached only through much bloodshed, little more could be expected of either the Christian "Franks" or the Muslim Ayyubids.[516]

The Voyage Home

On Michaelmas, the twenty-ninth of September, the two queens, Joanna and Berengaria, boarded a galley at Acre and their flotilla set sail for Italy, where Stephen of Turnham accompanied them to Rome to see Pope Celestine III (Giacinto Bobone).[517] With them was the daughter of Isaac Comnenus of Cyprus; this princess, whose name is not known to history, became Richard's ward and joined the English court following the deposition of her father.

Richard and the crusader fleet departed Palestine on Saint Denis Day, October ninth. Forewarned that enemies instigated by the Count of Toulouse planned to ambush him in southern France, the king landed at Corfu on the eleventh of November, and from there he sailed up the Adriatic to Aquileia. At this point he decided to travel over land, incognito, with a small band of knights. This seemed simple enough, and Richard made his way through the Alpine lands of his brother-in-law, Henry "the Lion," Duke of Saxony and Bavaria, husband of his sister Matilda, without incident.

Just before Christmas, however, Richard was identified and captured in Vienna by Leopold V, Duke of Austria, who incarcerated the English king at Dürnstein Castle. Leopold felt his grievances with Richard were legitimate, but this treatment of a fellow sovereign and crusader was a violation of law that earned him immediate excommunication. (Richard's incarceration is considered in Chapter 12.)

Now fearing what might befall them if they traveled through German territory, Joanna and Berengaria remained at Rome with Pope Celestine for six months. Eleanor, meanwhile, raised money to ransom Richard even as her younger son, John, was conspiring with Philip of France to undermine his authority and take his lands.

In late 1193, Joanna and Berengaria finally left Rome accompanied by Cardinal Melior, traveling over land to Pisa, thence to Genoa. At Marseille the two queens were received with honor by Alfonso II, the King of Aragon, who ruled Provence. He escorted them to the border of the dominion of his neighbor Raymond V, Count of Toulouse, who then accompanied the ladies and their large suite northward through his dominions toward Poitiers.[518] Although Raymond might have considered treachery against Richard, his despised feudal overlord, he would not imperil two ladies.

Raymond's son, who succeeded him the following year as Raymond VI, may have first met Joanna when she was traveling to Sicily seventeen years earlier. Now he had a chance to converse with the widowed queen as well as the daughter of Isaac Comnenus of Cyprus.[519]

The younger Raymond had been married twice but had no sons. He was now seeking another consort.

Richard's release from imprisonment in February 1194 left him free to confront the zealous ambitions of his brother, John, who had run amok for the last few years and was now abetted by Philip of France. After restoring his position in England, Richard went to Normandy, where he and Philip fought a series of battles interspersed with occasional truces.

War was not the only blight. These were difficult times, and much of Europe was stricken by plague and a famine.

Joanna was safe with her mother when Philip of France sought her hand in 1195.[520] After this proposal was rejected by Richard and Eleanor as politically unsuitable Philip wed Ingeburga of Denmark.

Back in Palermo, Tancred had died and Constance was now queen, with her husband, Henry VI, ruling in her name. The Hauteville dynasty was extinct but Constance had recently given birth to a son who would be its heir as the grandson of Roger II.

Motherhood

At Richard's prompting, which probably need not have been very adamant, Raymond VI of Toulouse agreed to marry Joanna. This was accepted.[521] The nuptials, attended by Richard, Berengaria and Eleanor, were celebrated at Rouen in October 1196.[522] One imagines entertainment at the feast given by troubadours singing in Occitan.

This marital union brought an end to a lengthy, if sometimes subtle, conflict between two regions and ruling families. The rulers of Aquitaine had long acted as the overlords of the counts of Toulouse. As part of the marriage agreement, Richard renounced his hereditary claim (through his mother) to sovereignty over the County of Toulouse in favor of Raymond. Although he failed to restore to his sister the money from her lost Sicilian dower, Richard now offered the counties of Agen and Quercy to Raymond as Joanna's dowry.

Joanna took up residence with her husband at Narbonnaise Castle in the city of Toulouse. The marriage seems to have been a happy one, at least at the beginning. A son, the future Raymond VII, was born at Beaucaire in July, followed by a daughter, Joan, the next year.[523]

343

We find the couple celebrating Easter with Richard and Berengaria at Le Mans in 1198.[524] The next year found Joanna pregnant with a third child.

Despite this apparent bliss, a dispute soon emerged between Joanna and her husband. Its cause remains inexplicable, but whatever it was, the matter became divisive enough to leave the couple separated, both geographically and emotionally.[525] At some point early in 1199, Joanna stopped receiving monies from Raymond, although it is difficult to contemplate this as the root of the problem, as if the couple were at odds over finances and nothing else. Perhaps it had something to do with religion.

The County of Toulouse was a complicated place to rule. Joanna's husband was reluctant to persecute the Cathars of his realm, whose peculiar religious practices led to their condemnation as heretics. Raymond's tolerance was destined to earn him feudal enemies and papal censure but, in fairness, it is difficult to imagine him singlehandedly defeating a spiritual idea through coercion or force of arms, even if he were ever inclined to resort to such tactics. Joanna's view of the Cathars is not known, although as a devout Catholic she probably did not condone their practices, and there is no convincing evidence that Raymond, despite his sympathies, ever joined the sect.

Whatever differences Joanna may have had with her spouse, she took a strong position against her husband's detractors, whose violence might destabilize the county. One of these men, William, the feudal lord of Saint-Félix, seems to have embraced Catharism, or at least used it as a pretext to defy Raymond's comital authority.

For reasons that are not entirely clear, a pregnant Joanna, in the spring of 1199, led the siege of Les Cassés, near the city of Toulouse, where some of these rebels had taken a stand. Her hopes of success were quashed when some of her own subjects began undermining her by surreptitiously arming the rebels and supplying them with victuals. Then the traitors committed arson, covertly setting fire to her army's encampment.[526]

Barely escaping the blaze, Joanna abandoned the siege of Les Cassés and made her way northward, ostensibly to seek the help of her brother, who was besieging Chalus, in Aquitaine southwest of Limoges.

Did Joanna want Richard's military advice, or was she merely using this as a pretext to escape her husband's court? Chalus was just a few days away, but Joanna's pregnancy, perhaps coupled with the heavy spring rains, delayed her arrival.[527]

In the meantime, Richard had been struck in the shoulder by a crossbow arrow. The wound itself was not grave, but it appears that part of the dart's iron tip remained lodged in the flesh after a surgeon extracted the shaft, and gangrene set in.

Richard died on April sixth with his mother by his side, although his wife, Berengaria, was not summoned. Whilst the king himself forgave the crossbowman, it would happen that Joanna could not find it within herself to do the same.

On her way to meet Richard, Joanna was notified by a courier of her brother's death. Already in a foul temper as a result of the recent betrayal of her own people, and bitter about the shortcomings of her marriage, she was left even more sullen about the loss of her brother than she might have been in other circumstances. Her experience at the siege she was forced to lift at Les Cassés was, in itself, more than sufficient to bring out her contempt for rebels.

Joanna continued her trek northward through forests and across streams. It wasn't long before one of Richard's allies delivered the arbalester into her hands. Without hesitation, she ordered the man tortured to death for having committed the unconscionable felony of regicide.[528]

Then she went to Niort to meet her mother. Like her daughter, Eleanor was presently traveling, but for the last few years she had been living mostly at Fontevrault, the large abbey under her patronage.

The recent weeks had seen a great deal of incessant traveling for a pregnant woman, but Joanna rested for a month or so at Fontevrault. Eleanor left her daughter there in late April before she herself went to Poitiers.[529]

Although Joanna had visited this splendid abbey as a young child, it is unlikely that she still remembered it very clearly from all those years ago. It was probably during this tranquil sojourn that she began to seriously consider becoming a nun, notwithstanding the fact that she had a husband and two young children back in Toulouse.

Eleanor soon requested Joanna's presence. By July, mother and daughter were both at Rouen with John, who had succeeded his elder brother as king.

In late August, King John gave Joanna, who had fallen gravely ill, three thousand silver marks as compensation for the monies from her Sicilian dower never fully repaid by the late Richard, plus another hundred marks.[530]

She used some of this money to endow Fontevrault Abbey. At Rouen, despite being married and pregnant, Joanna was permitted to take the veil, *consecratam presente matre sua et Abbate de Torpeniaco*, "consecrated in the presence of her mother and the Abbot of Turpenay."[531] This made her one of the abbey's nuns, even if she was not fated to return to the abbey.

The original manuscript no longer survives, but along with Joanna's last will the text of the endowment of Fontevrault dated September 1199 is the only known record of any of her charters.[532]

Her will, which reflects Joanna's generosity not only to the church but to the people dearest to her, is the quintessential example of this kind of royal testament.[533] Significantly, it addresses matters in her personal fiefs.

On September fourth, Joanna died at Rouen whilst giving birth to a boy, believed to have been christened Richard, who died shortly thereafter.[534] Initially entombed in Rouen Cathedral, she was then, on Eleanor's initiative, taken to Fontevrault to be interred there.[535] Joanna of England, Queen of Sicily and Countess of Toulouse, reposed peacefully at Fontevrault next to her mother Eleanor, her brother Richard, and her two sons[536] until the last decade of the eighteenth century, when revolutionaries despoiled the royal tombs, casting out the mortal remains, defacing the effigies and vandalizing the carved epitaphs.

The queen's maids-in-waiting, her lifelong friends Alice and Beatrice, took the veil as nuns at Fontevrault.

Joanna's effigy was subsequently lost but she was fondly remembered as the Queen of Sicily.[537]

QUEENS OF SICILY

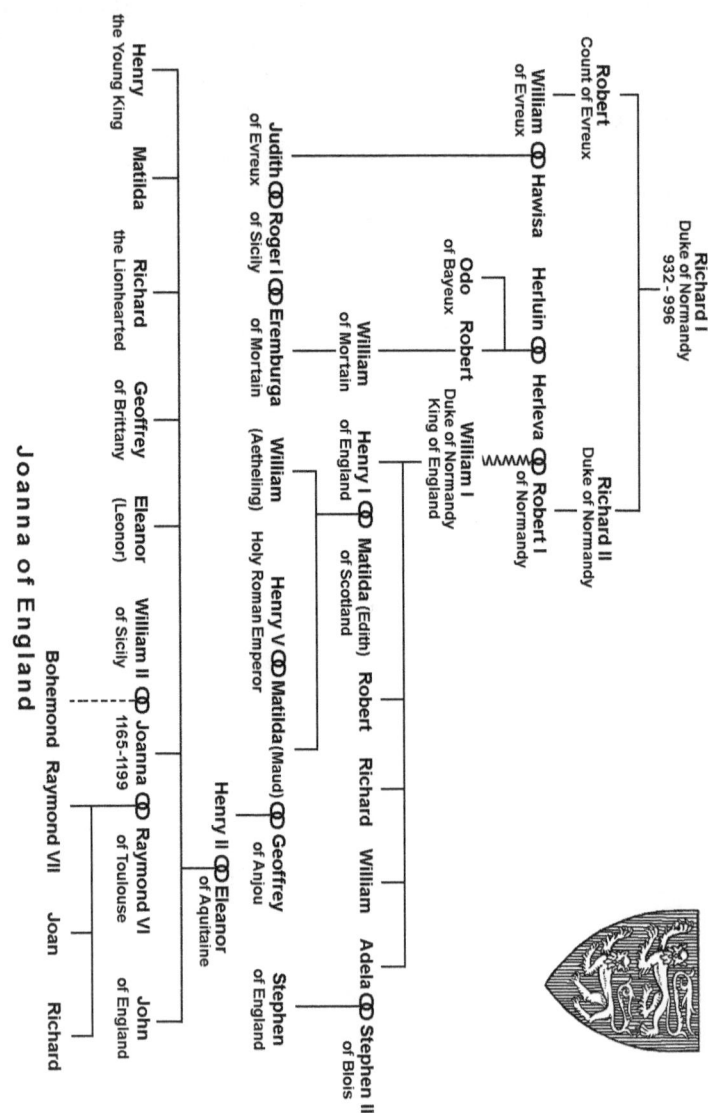

Joanna of England

Icon of Thomas Becket in mosaic at Monreale

Canterbury Cathedral: Thomas Becket was venerated by Joanna, and his nephews were granted refuge in Sicily during their exile from England.

The author in a Romanesque corner of the abbey at Canterbury little changed since the days when Thomas Becket lived there

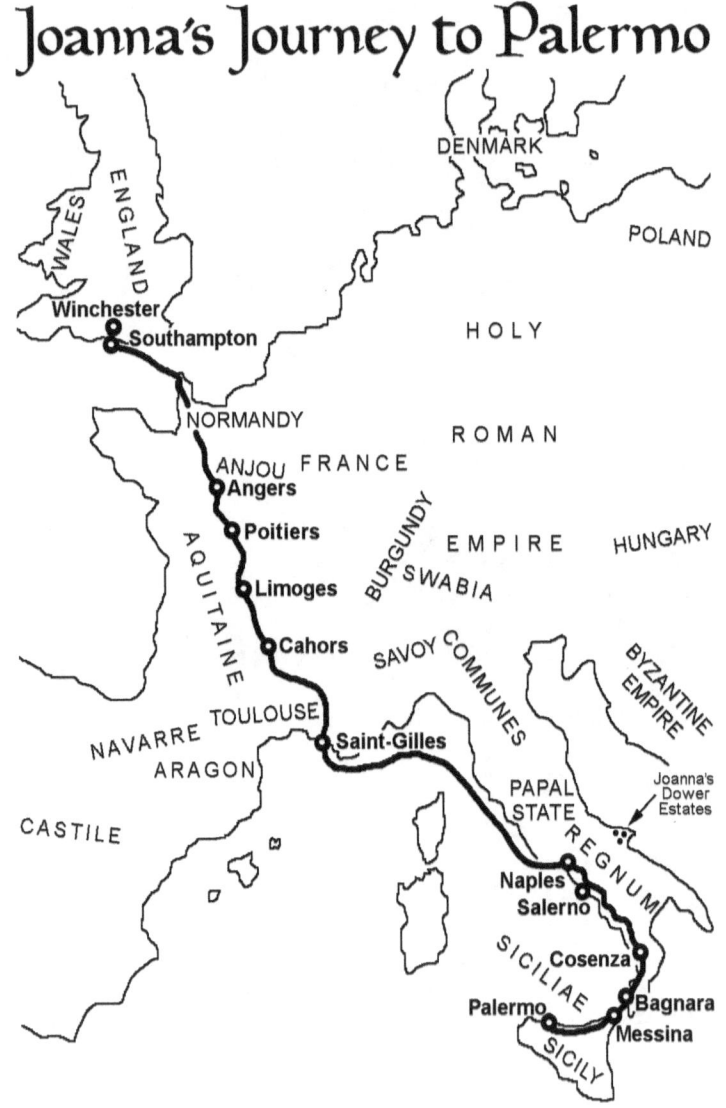

Before her wedding, Joanna was lodged in a certain palace in Palermo, probably the Norman-Arab Zisa in the Genoard.

Joanna and her brother, Richard Lionheart, greet Philip Augustus of France at the Siege of Acre in this copy of the history of William of Tyre written in French during the 13th century. Joanna is depicted with blonde hair.

The seal Joanna used later in life

Fontevraud Abbey: Joanna and her parents rest in this church near Chinon in the Loire region.

Site of Thomas Becket's murder in Canterbury Cathedral

Chapter 10
SIBYLLA OF ACERRA

Sibylla of Acerra was born at Acerra in 1153 to Rainald, holder of sundry manors, and Cecilia, daughter of Robert of Acerra, a noble having ancestral roots at Mayenne in Anjou, not far from Normandy.[538] Rainald's father was Lando IV, who held the county of Aquino and its environs until he was divested of those lands in 1137 in favor of the abbey of Cassino by the Holy Roman Emperor.

Rainald's lineage through his father's family was Lombard; he was descended from a long line of gastalds who ruled large territories comparable to counties. By the time Sibylla was born, her mother's family was wealthier and more influential than that of her father.

Youth and Motherhood

When Cecilia's elder brother, Roger, who had infamously supported Matthew Bonello in the treasonous revolt against King William I, died without heirs in 1167, Acerra and other lands were inherited, through her, by her son, Richard. This was Sibylla's elder brother.

During the reign of King William II, Richard of Acerra was a comrade-in-arms of Tancred of Lecce, the bastard grandson of King Roger II.

Tancred had a checkered past. With Richard's uncle, the late Roger of Acerra, a younger Tancred had been a co-conspirator of Matthew Bonello and Simon of Taranto in the plot against William I (see Chapter 8).

It was probably Richard who arranged the marriage of his sister to Tancred.

By the time Sibylla wed Tancred around 1170, her new husband had been "rehabilitated" by William II, whose mother, Margaret, as regent, had permitted the onetime rebel to return to the kingdom following a few years of exile. Tancred seems to have been reformed, for he led successful military missions on behalf of William and never questioned the young king's authority.

Tancred was about fifteen years older than his bride. His fiercest critic, the chronicler Peter of Eboli (who may never even have seen him), described Tancred as short and ugly, and that unflattering description has endured in the public mind even though it may have been more figurative than literal.[539]

Tancred's character was more complex than his appearance. Despite having participated in the Bonello revolt years earlier, at around the age of twenty-two, he matured to become something of a pragmatist. Indeed, Tancred came to be known as a reliable counsellor and competent military leader. No longer an eccentric Hauteville kinsman, he was an asset to the sovereign he served.

From Sibylla's point of view, marriage to a bastard prince was probably at least as desirable as marrying a count or baron. Tancred, of course, held the prosperous Apulian county of Lecce, along with sundry other lands inherited from his mother, Emma, daughter of Achard of Lecce.

During the next decade, Sibylla resided chiefly at Lecce and later at Palermo, though her precise movements are not known. As the typical "military spouse," she sometimes followed her husband, mostly around Apulia. Her presence was not always required at Lecce, where her mother-in-law, Emma, could oversee local affairs. Tancred spent ever more time at court as one of William's chief military counsellors, or leading missions to the eastern Mediterranean with fleets that departed from ports in Apulia.

Sibylla and her husband invested in the town of Lecce, erecting such structures as the Benedictine monastery of Saints Nicholas and Catald. In this they may have been inspired by the efforts of Margaret and William in founding Monreale and other abbeys in Sicily. Another example was Tancred's grandfather, Emma's father Achard, who had founded the nunnery of Saint John the Evangelist, where Emma herself later became the abbess.

In 1175, Sibylla gave birth to a boy named Roger. Three daughters followed: Elvira, Constance (sometimes Cecilia), Veldrade (or Madonia). A second son, born around 1185, was christened William.

Precious little is known about Sibylla's life during the reign of William II and her husband's service to that monarch. Details of her relationships with Margaret, Joanna and Constance during these years remain enigmatic. Sibylla's children were not considered royalty, yet there would be times when they were the only young children at court related to the royal family. They were educated as though they were royal princes and princesses.

Despite the circumstances of her husband's birth, Sibylla's life was not lacking in prestige. As a soldier, her husband earned the respect of the court, clergy and baronage; in Lecce he was esteemed as a feudal lord and patron of the church. Tancred emerged as one of the most powerful men in the kingdom. As his wife, Sibylla bathed in this reflected glory.

Queen

At the death of William II in 1189 there were no living, legitimate Hauteville heirs to succeed him as king.

As we have seen, William had named his aunt, Constance, as his heir apparent. She still had no children, but if she ever bore a son, he would be a Hohenstaufen, not a Hauteville. As King of Germany, and perhaps Holy Roman Emperor, this child could end up ruling much of Europe. In this hypothetical scenario, the Kingdom of Sicily might well become a German monarch's secondary dominion, perhaps ruled from afar.

This was a very real concern. Serfs, merchants and monks might be largely indifferent to such subtleties, but for the courtiers and barons local rule was usually preferable to foreign rule.

The *Regnum Siciliae* had no parliament in the twelfth century, yet the baronage, instigated by Matthew of Aiello and other influential counsellors once loyal to William, now found it expedient to crown any Hauteville male they could find rather than leave the path to ruling the kingdom open to another dynasty.

The barons' decision may have reeked of treason, and some observers might well have viewed it as an affront to the late king's memory, but there was sound reasoning behind it.

The papacy had its own reason for supporting the barons against Constance. The last thing any pope wanted was to see his papal dominions sandwiched between imperial lands to the north and Sicilian territory to the south, both ruled by the same sovereign.[540]

Tancred and Sibylla were crowned in Palermo in January 1190. They thereby became the king and queen of Sicily *de facto* if not, strictly speaking, *de jure*.

Not without reason, some viewed Tancred as a usurper. However, though illegitimate by birth, he had long been recognized as a Hauteville. Legitimate or not, he was a grandson of Roger II. Nobody doubted his parentage.

Whether his being a male, albeit born outside marriage, outweighed the fact of Constance being the legitimate daughter of one king and the designated heir of another, is fodder for debate. At all events, it would be inappropriate to describe Tancred as anything other than the King of Sicily, for he enjoyed the assent of the church and the barons, as well as diplomatic recognition by most other European sovereigns. Moreover, he actually ruled the kingdom.

Sibylla, the girl from Acerra, was Queen of Sicily.

Constance had other ideas, and some in the *Regnum* shared them, particularly on the mainland. There Roger of Andria led a resistance that sought to enthrone Constance, or perhaps even himself.[541] On the peninsula, Tancred's interests were defended by Richard of Acerra, Sibylla's brother, who managed to capture and kill Roger of Andria.[542]

Back in Palermo, circumstances led Tancred and Sibylla to take measures that otherwise would have been unthinkable. William's widow, Joanna, was detained. Knowing her late husband's wishes, she supported Constance's claim to the throne. If one person on the island of Sicily could topple Tancred from his tenuous perch, it was Joanna.

For now, Tancred named his son, Roger, heir apparent as Duke of Apulia, and the Messina mint was soon coining *follari* bearing their names.

Conflict

The next two years saw a series of battles, some little more than skirmishes, especially in the areas around Naples, Salerno, San Germano (Cassino) and Capua. Sibylla remained in Palermo while Tancred responded to these matters. Initially, he delegated his military duties to his brother-in-law Richard of Acerra and the trusted Margaritus of Brindisi.

William had died unexpectedly. For lack of time and money,

Constance and her husband responded to Tancred's gesture with the largest force they could muster at the moment. It was substantial but not overwhelming.

Following the death of his father, Frederick Barbarossa, Henry VI was crowned Holy Roman Emperor in Rome in April 1191. He wanted Pope Celestine III to nullify Tancred's pretension to the throne. Immediately after the imperial coronation, the couple hastened southward with an army to claim Constance's birthright.[543] (For more on Constance's experiences see Chapter 12.)

Later the same year, when the army of Richard Lionheart encamped at Messina for a few months *en route* to the Holy Land, Tancred was forced to release Joanna to her brother, with whom he made terms. (See the previous chapter.) This was when Tancred may have promised one of his daughters, probably Veldrade, to Arthur of Brittany, but the marriage never came to be.

While Joanna was freed, Constance was captured at a siege near Salerno.[544] Though a prisoner, she was soon received with full honors by Tancred at Messina before being taken under guard to Palermo.

Tancred requested that Sibylla assume the care and custody of Constance, to the point of the two dining together and living in the same quarters of the palace.[545]

Sibylla protested this idea. In response, Tancred told her to consult Matthew of Aiello, which she did. According to Peter of Eboli, she complained to Matthew about her husband's poor judgment.[546]

Sibylla disapproved of Tancred's diplomatic treatment of Constance, and although the two women were known to have bickered, her protest was caused by more than clashing personalities. She did not wish to see Constance treated in any way that might be construed by the populace as lending legitimacy to her rival claim to the throne. Not surprisingly, Constance had sympathizers in her native city.

At the very least, Sibylla wanted Constance incarcerated in a real prison. She may have even preferred that the empress simply be put to death, but this Tancred chose not to do.

At Pope Celestine's insistence, Constance was liberated in 1192.[547] Having survived her ordeal, she returned to Swabia, leaving military matters to her husband.

Thinking of the future, Tancred found time to have his son, Roger, crowned *rex filius* and then married at Brindisi to Irene Angelina, daughter of the Byzantine Emperor Isaac Angelus of Constantinople (see the next chapter). Sibylla does not seem to have been present for these nuptials, though Emma may have been.[548]

Transition

Fate conceded the newly-wed King Roger little time to enjoy conjugal life, for he died in December 1193 aged about eighteen, leaving Irene Angelina a young widow.

Whilst on the mainland, Tancred himself fell ill. He returned to Sicily, where he died in February 1194, leaving Sibylla as regent for young William.

Just before his death, Tancred seems to have crowned his younger son, William, who was about eight years old, *rex filius*.[549]

Sibylla's regency for her young son would prove ephemeral, and only a few of her decrees survive, but their appellation was not unlike the formula Margaret employed during the majority of William II. We find, for example, the phrase *domina Sibilla gloriosa regina matre*.[550]

There were few capable leaders left to assist the queen and her son; an aged Matthew of Aiello had died the previous year. The defense of the kingdom fell, first and foremost, to intrepid Margaritus of Brindisi, who was married to an illegitimate daughter of King Roger II.

By August 1194, Henry VI had conquered Naples. He was in Palermo by November, when Margaritus surrendered the city's sea castle to the invaders.

In the meantime, Sibylla had sent her son and daughters to Caltabellotta Castle for safety. She seems to have remained in Palermo to defend the city.[551] Following this exercise in futility, the deposed queen was made to attend Henry's coronation on Christmas. The emperor, now King of Sicily *jure uxoris,* was about to become the father of a boy born to Constance on the mainland.

He had promised Sibylla a comfortable "domestic exile" at Lecce, even offering her son the County of Taranto. Alas, this offer was too good to be true. At a meeting of barons at the royal palace a few days later, Henry publicly accused Sibylla and several prominent nobles, including Margaritus, of plotting a conspiracy to overthrow him. This was likely nothing more than a pretext to eliminate potential opponents. They were summarily arrested and sent to Germany.[552]

Young William was blinded and castrated, then made to disappear following a year or two of imprisonment at Hohenems Castle.[553]

With revenge in season, Sibylla's brother, Richard, was executed as a traitor for having supported Tancred against Constance. Tancred's remains, along with those of the son he crowned, were cast out of the Magione church erected by Matthew of Aiello. The royal tombs were destroyed as part of an effort to erase every trace of both father and son.[554]

Wasting no time, Henry betrothed Irene Angelina, the young widow of Sibylla's son Roger, to his brother, Philip of Swabia.

Legacy

Sibylla and her daughters were detained at a convent in Hohenberg.

A certain disorder arose in the Holy Roman Empire in the wake of Henry's death in September 1197. The next year the new pope, Innocent III, protested Sibylla's imprisonment just as his predecessor had objected to the detainment of Constance by Tancred a few years earlier. He threatened excommunication and interdict.

In the meantime, in 1198 Sibylla and the girls escaped the nunnery.[555] They made their way to France, where they were received with honor at the royal court. Constance, Sibylla's onetime nemesis, died later that year.

At a meeting convened at Melun, King Philip II of France agreed to betroth Elvira, Sibylla's eldest daughter, to Walter III of Brienne, an enterprising lord. This wedding, attended by Sibylla, was celebrated in 1200.

By now, as both Henry and Constance were gone, the Kingdom of Sicily was haphazardly administered, with several zealous courtiers given to squabbling amongst themselves. It was time to seize an uncommon opportunity. Sibylla and her son-in-law solicited Pope Innocent III for his approval of an ambitious effort to take back the *Regnum*.[556]

The following year, Walter, accompanied by Elvira, made an incursion into the Kingdom of Sicily in an attempt to occupy Lecce and Taranto *en route* to fight in the Fourth Crusade.[557] Presumably, Walter would leave Elvira with a strong garrison at Lecce or Taranto while he departed for Palestine. This invasion, which (according to dubious accounts) was financed in part by the King of France, enjoyed papal support because it might dislodge young Frederick, the orphaned son of Constance and Henry, from the Sicilian throne. However, while Innocent approved Walter's claim to Lecce and Taranto as Elvira's birthright, he did not condone an outright conquest of the entire kingdom. The invasion's total success ultimately proved elusive when Walter was killed in 1205.[558] A son, also Walter, was born to Elvira following her husband's death.

Another of Sibylla's daughters, Constance, wed Peter Ziani, who became the Doge of Venice in 1205. Valdrada, Sibylla's youngest surviving daughter, married Jacob Tiepolo, who became Duke of Crete in 1212 and Doge of Venice seven years later.

Sibylla died in March 1205.[559] If nothing else, she had the satisfaction of having survived both Henry VI Hohenstaufen and Constance Hauteville, whose Sicilian reign proved just as ephemeral as Tancred's.

SIBYLLA OF ACERRA

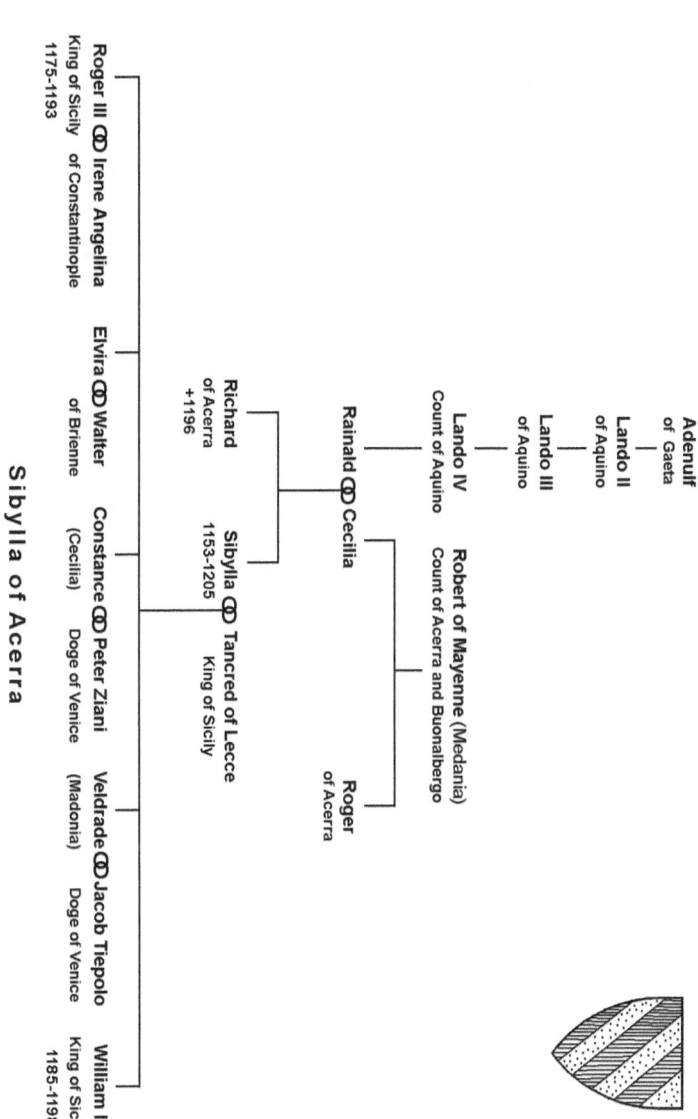

Sibylla of Acerra

Built for the Cistercians, the Magione was the resting place of King Tancred and then a church of the Teutonic Knights

Some Coins of the Norman-Swabian Era

"Scyphate" ducat of Roger II

"Lion's face" follaris of William II

Fatimid tarì   *Tarì of Roger II*

QUEENS OF SICILY

Sibylla (top and bottom) and Tancred (center)

Chapter 11
IRENE ANGELINA OF CONSTANTINOPLE

Irene Angelina of Constantinople was born in that city around 1179 as the second daughter of the Byzantine Emperor Isaac II Angelus Comnenus and his first consort, Irene Palaeologue. Though descended from an illustrious dynasty, Isaac did not inherit the throne but claimed it in 1185 through a popular revolt against an unpopular ruler, his kinsman Andronikos.

Childhood

Irene had an elder sister, Anna, a younger brother, Alexius, and two younger half-brothers, Manuel and John. Her mother, of whom little is known, ended up in a nunnery, and in 1186 Isaac wed Margaret of Hungary who thus became Irene's stepmother.

Isaac was not always at peace with Sicily's Norman rulers, who had designs on his Byzantine Empire. In 1186, his generals defeated an invading force led by Tancred of Lecce and captured Richard of Acerra, who we met in the last chapter.[560]

None of this touched Irene and her sister growing up at the imperial court in an opulent city, where they were sheltered from most of the world's ugliest ills. Constantinople was a prosperous metropolis whose importance, large population and great wealth rivalled those of Baghdad and Palermo. Whereas some of the women destined to become Sicilian queens, like Richard's sister Sibylla of Acerra, were raised in feudal towns, Irene spent her girlhood in a cosmopolitan, metropolitan environment. Unlike the others whom we have met, she was not originally Roman Catholic but Greek Orthodox.

Marriages

Emperor Isaac, whose empire included lands across the Ionian from the Kingdom of Sicily, wanted peace with his western neighbor. By 1191, with a crown on his head and an aunt in Germany challenging his right to it, Tancred of Lecce found it expedient to cultivate alliances wherever he could, be it east or west. Having obtained recognition of his royal claim by the kings of England and France, and betrothing his daughter to a Plantagenet prince, he looked to the east.

Not long after he crowned his firstborn son, Roger, *rex filius* as his heir apparent, Tancred began negotiating to marry him to one of Isaac's daughters. Irene, who was about four years younger than Roger, was the logical candidate.

Isaac and his counsellors assented to this, and in 1192 Irene arrived with a flotilla at Brindisi, where she was wed to Roger.[561] As Roger's wife, Irene was anointed queen.

This marriage did not last long, since Roger died in December of the following year. With this, Irene took up residence in Palermo's royal palace. In late 1194, she was captured by Henry VI, who claimed the Kingdom of Sicily in the name of his wife, Constance (see the following chapter).

Unlike her mother-in-law Queen Sibylla, Irene was not viewed as either a threat or an annoyance. She had no child who might claim the throne, and she was young and beautiful.

Whilst Sibylla and her children were taken prisoner and exiled to Germany, Irene was betrothed to Henry's younger brother, Philip of Swabia.[562] Irene's sister, Anna, wed Roman, the ruler of Galicia and much of what is now Ukraine.

This rarified moment found four women living who were, in one way or another, queens of Sicily: Joanna, Sibylla, Irene, Constance.

Born in imperial Pavia, Philip Hohenstaufen, the youngest son of Frederick Barbarossa, was about two years older than Irene. He abandoned a career in the church to support the ambitions of his brother, Henry, who he accompanied on the Italian campaigns that restored the Sicilian crown to Constance.

It was in Italy that Irene was introduced to Philip, but it was clear that she would eventually have to travel to Swabia to take up residence at the family seat, Hohenstaufen Castle. At first, the wedding was postponed due to Philip's demanding responsibilities.

Henry ceded Philip the control of Tuscany as its margrave in 1196. Following the death of his brother, Conrad, Philip became Duke of Swabia the next year.

The wedding of Irene to Philip was celebrated outside Augsburg in May 1197. Swabia's forested Alpine, and very Catholic, environment was quite different from Greek Constantinople and sunny, multicultural Sicily, but Irene seems to have adapted to it well enough. Her name must have seemed too Greek to the Swabians, who took to calling her Maria, but the *minnesinger* Walther von der Vogelweide described her in flattering terms as "a rose lacking a thorn, a dove lacking in deceit."[563] His words imply that Irene was not given to the machinations that tainted many a queenly heart. Descriptions of her husband by other contemporaries were not always so kind.

Irene enjoyed a period of bliss as a new bride, and she was soon pregnant with her first child. It was the calm before the storm.

While in Italy in September of 1197, Philip heard of Henry's untimely death in Messina. Anticipating difficulties from the restless nobles of the Holy Roman Empire, he hastened to Germany to defend the position of his late brother's young son, Frederick.

Motherhood

Philip hardly had time to revel in the birth of his daughter, Beatrix, at Worms in the spring of 1198, for a faction of the imperial aristocracy was now supporting the dynastic claim of the rival House of Welf to rule Germany and the Holy Roman Empire in the person of Otto of Brunswick. In response to this, and in view of the reluctance of the German elector princes to accept his nephew, a young boy living far away in Palermo, as their king, Philip had himself elected and crowned. Irene was crowned with him at Mainz in September 1198.[564]

Christmas 1199 saw Irene, Philip and little Beatrix at Magdeburg, within striking distance of Otto's lair. This lavish feast was commemorated by Walther von der Vogelweide as a form of propaganda for Philip.

It would take more than sugary words to convince the supreme pontiff. Pope Innocent III was openly supporting Otto against Philip in an attempt to break the Hohenstaufen hold on Germany, northern Italy and the Kingdom of Sicily. Even Philip's offer to betroth little Beatrix to one of Innocent's nephews failed to erode the pope's resolve.

Irene sometimes traveled with her husband as he tried to keep the Hohenstaufen dominions united, and she gave birth to another daughter, Maria, in Tuscany in the spring of 1201. A third daughter, Kunigunde, was born a year later.

The Hohenstaufens needed sons but none were forthcoming following the deaths of two boys, Reinhald and Frederick, in infancy.

IRENE ANGELINA OF CONSTANTINOPLE

In 1201, Alexius, Irene's brother, arrived at the court to solicit Philip's help in restoring his father, Emperor Isaac, to the throne, perhaps as part of the Fourth Crusade now being planned. Isaac had been deposed by his belligerent brother, Alexius III, six years earlier. It was only with the help of crafty Pisan merchants that Irene's brother, who was also held captive, managed to escape his wicked uncle.

Irene was doubtless influential in helping her brother to garner western European support for a campaign to oust her uncle and restore her father. Philip wished to assist his brother-in-law, who promised to heal the schism between the Christians of east and west if placed on the Byzantine throne.[565]

Thus in 1203 the Fourth Crusade was diverted to Constantinople. Tragically, it resulted in a horrific bloodbath perpetrated by the Latin Franks against the Byzantine Greeks. This led to the establishment in Constantinople of a "Latin Empire" that flourished for the next few decades at the expense of Byzantine sovereignty and culture. Philip was not directly involved in this debacle, even if his efforts to assist his brother-in-law were a key factor in the crusaders' decision to go to Constantinople.[566] Instead, he was forced to remain in the German lands to challenge the pretensions of his ambitious rival, Otto of Brunswick.

A fourth daughter, Elisabeth (sometimes Beatrice), was born to Irene and Philip at Nuremberg in the spring of 1205.

In June 1208, Irene and Philip went to Bamberg to celebrate the wedding of his niece, Beatrice of Burgundy. For reasons that are still debated, an unarmed Philip was stabbed and killed by the count palatine Otto of Wittelsbach of Bavaria, who was mentally unstable. Otto's violent temper was known in royal circles, and a few years earlier Philip had terminated the betrothal of one of his daughters to the mad count.[567]

Irene, who was pregnant, returned to Hohenstaufen Castle, where she died giving birth on August twenty-seventh to a stillborn daughter posthumously named Beatrix.[568] The erstwhile Queen of Sicily was interred at Lorch Abbey, traditional burial site of the Hohenstaufen sovereigns.[569] Her mortal remains can no longer be identified but a tombstone carved in 1898 preserves her memory.

Irene's daughters were placed in the nominal care of their cousin, Frederick II, whose counsellors betrothed them to princes.[570]

IRENE ANGELINA OF CONSTANTINOPLE

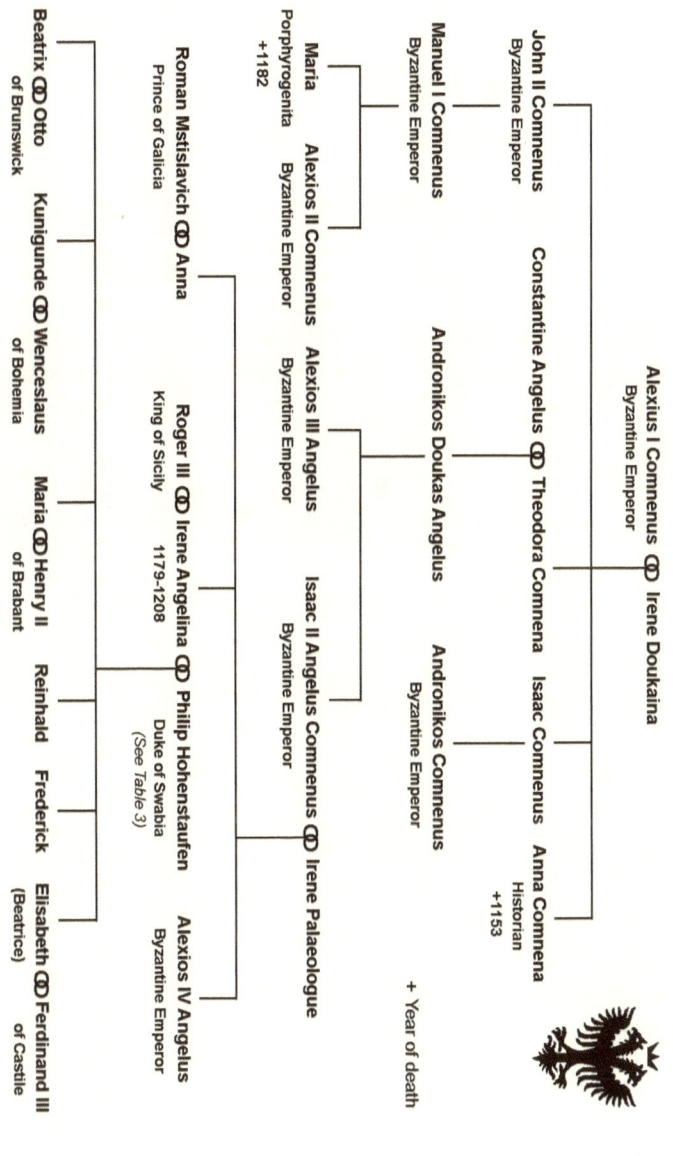

Transept, towers and apses of Palermo's cathedral, where many Sicilian kings and queens were crowned

Irene Angelina's daughter, Elisabeth (sometimes Beatrice), was betrothed to Ferdinand III of Castile. She is entombed at Seville in Europe's largest Gothic cathedral, where a mosque stood. The bell tower was once a minaret.

Irene Angelina's first husband, Roger III, was interred in the Magione but his remains were removed

Chapter 12
CONSTANCE OF SICILY

Constance of Sicily was born in Palermo on the second of November 1154 to Beatrice of Rethel, the third wife of the late Roger II, who had died in February. Following Constance's birth, Beatrice (who we met in an earlier chapter) decided to raise her only child in Sicily. The girl was intelligent, perhaps precociously so, her head topped by a mane of distinctively red or "strawberry blonde" hair.

Thus far, we have glimpsed this singular queen, who represents a bridge between two great dynasties, through the eyes of her mother or from the perspective of her sometime rival Sibylla of Acerra. The time has come to meet Constance Hauteville of Sicily on her own terms.

Child

Constance passed her first few years at the royal palace in Palermo at the court of her half-brother, William I. Although Beatrice saw no immediate reason to leave the cosmopolitan city, there is no mention of the mother and daughter during this period, not even in otherwise detailed accounts of the Bonello revolt.

Around that time, and certainly thereafter, Beatrice and Constance occasionally resided at the Hauteville castle at San Marco d'Alunzio. Compared to the intrigues of chaotic Palermo and its court, this was a serene environment in which to raise a daughter. In removing Beatrice from power struggles, it kept her and her daughter aloof of politics.

Following her birth, we next hear about Constance explicitly in 1168, when a revolt at Messina spawned the wild rumor that Stephen, the controversial chancellor appointed by Queen Margaret, planned to depose young William II and in his stead crown his own brother, Geoffrey of Perche, with Constance as consort.[571] This suggests that Constance, who was nearing the age of fourteen, was still living with her mother, either at Palermo or at San Marco. A chronicler writing many decades later states in passing that at a certain point William's patrilineal aunt "lived at the palace in Palermo"[572]

Damsel

Around 1170, instead of being affianced to a suitable prince, Constance may have gone to live in a nunnery. If so, it is most likely that this was one of the convents in the Nebrodian Mountains near San Marco under the patronage of Margaret, the queen regent.[573]

Despite the presumption, perpetuated by later writers, that Constance became a nun, there is nothing to suggest that she actually took vows. It is merely a possibility.

In fact, no contemporaneous evidence is known that confirms Constance's presence in an abbey. The very idea may have originated much later in the mind of Dante, and it has been embraced by modern scholars based on the unsupported belief that the princess received a papal dispensation to marry.[574]

Nevertheless, it is true enough that circumstances argue for the possibility that Constance lived in a convent, for why was she not betrothed at an age when most royal princesses were paired with appropriate husbands?

At this moment, the House of Hauteville had a dearth of daughters who might marry foreign kings and facilitate dynastic alliances. If only out of a sense of duty, Constance would be expected to do this when called upon.

We may well speculate about the forces that motivated Constance's choice to delay marriage. Perhaps she was indeed religiously devout to the exclusion of conjugal life and motherhood. It may be that she found court life unappealing, even distasteful. It is possible that she did not particularly enjoy male company or the prospect of marriage. Her choice may have been rooted in personal questions of gender or sexuality. Whatever the reason, it was probably her own decision, not one thrust upon her, for the "conventional" choice would have been marriage.

The death of Henry, Prince of Capua, in 1172 left no closely-related, legitimate heirs in the royal line of succession. Although the fact does not yet seem to have been proclaimed publicly, Constance became, through genealogical happenstance, the heiress presumptive of her nephew, William II, who still was not married. Nonetheless, there does not seem to have been any effort made to convince Constance to marry at that time.

Neither Constance nor her mother had any kind of official role at the Sicilian court, though they were doubtless present for William's wedding to Joanna of England in February 1177. For now, that was the extent of their dynastic obligations.

The rapport between Constance and William seems to have been a good one. At the least, there is nothing to suggest any kind of rivalry or antipathy between the two, or between their mothers.

Five months after his wedding to young Joanna, William

sent a delegation led by Romuald of Salerno to confirm the Treaty of Venice formalizing peace with the Holy Roman Empire. Frederick Barbarossa's ambassadors then visited Sicily, where they may have met Constance.

It is difficult to say with certainty that the idea of betrothing the princess to one of Barbarossa's sons was already being formulated; his son Henry was only twelve. A few years earlier, however, the emperor had offered his daughter's hand to William, thus making it clear that he grasped the value of dynastic unions as a political tool.

By around 1182, efforts were being made to realize such a union. Although the sycophantic chronicler Richard of San Germano later ascribed this initiative to Walter, Archbishop of Palermo, it is difficult to contemplate that nobody else was long considering it, either at the Hauteville or Hohenstaufen courts.

Leaving Walter aside, the degree to which William and his other *familiares* understood the dynastic implications of their decision has long been a point of debate among scholars.[575] Matthew of Aiello seems to have foreseen a potential problem in a dynastic union. At the time, it was probably presumed that Joanna would bear a son or two soon enough. Boccaccio later mentioned the political effects of Constance's marriage in the succinct chapter dedicated to her in his *De Claris Mulieribus*.[576]

Wife

A few years were to pass before the wedding arrangements were finalized. Perhaps William and his mother wanted to ensure that the treaty signed at Venice led to a lasting peace before they committed Constance to the marriage. As if to sweeten the deal made with the Hohenstaufens, the King of Sicily provided Constance with the most lavish dowry seen in Europe for at least a generation. Here was a public display of power.

The betrothal was finally announced at Augsburg on the twenty-ninth of October in 1184. With this, William undertook to provide his aunt with more than what was necessary, for apart from the trousseau of silk and furs there were several chests full of gold tarì coins.[577]

Sadly, Constance's mother, Beatrice of Rethel, died in March 1185, a few months after Henry's mother, another Beatrice, the Countess of Burgundy.

In the summer of that year, William II sailed with his aunt and her suite on a royal flotilla to Salerno, where knights, nobles and many servants were waiting with wagons, destriers and a hundred fifty sturdy mules to transport the princess and her precious dowry. William accompanied Constance as far as Rieti, where the endless train of courtiers and equines arrived in late August. From there, an imperial delegation escorted the princess and her large company northward. She may have met her future father-in-law at Foligno before proceeding to Piacenza and Pavia, and thence to Milan.

At that city, Constance and Henry were wed and crowned in the basilica of Saint Ambrose on Tuesday, the twenty-first of January 1186.[578] Now a widower, Frederick Barbarossa was the only parent of either spouse to be present.

Whatever ambivalence the Milanese ever had about imperial rule, this rare event gave them an excuse to celebrate for several days.

Troublesome Kin

Constance took up residence with her husband at Trifels Castle, in the Palatine Forest (not to be confused with Hohenstaufen Castle in Swabia). Unfortunately, Henry was often absent due to his imperial responsibilities.

Her geographic isolation did not prevent Constance's involvement in political affairs, especially where these concerned her own family. In 1188, she successfully intervened with her husband and father-in-law on behalf of her cousin, Baldwin of Hainaut, to retain Namur when an attempt was made by another kinsman, Henry of Luxembourg, to deprive him of it.[579] The resulting settlement brought an end to what was quickly escalating into a small civil war.

Disconcerting as that reality was, an even more disturbing incident involved the same Baldwin of Hainaut and his first cousin Albert of Rethel, Constance's uncle, three years later.

The bishops of Liège enjoyed temporal influence as princes of the Holy Roman Empire. When Baldwin's political rival, Henry of Brabant, managed to get his own brother, Albert of Louvain, elected to this important episcopal see, Baldwin refused to recognize him based on the pretext that the electee was under the canonically-required age and that the election had been rigged.

Baldwin then had a group of canons under his power elect his kinsman, Albert of Rethel, to the bishopric.

This time, Constance's best efforts to help Baldwin were fruitless. Seeking to avoid controversy, her husband, who was acting as imperial regent while his father, Frederick Barbarossa, was away on crusade, simply nominated a third candidate, Lothar of Hochstaden. This left Albert of Rethel marginalized.

In the meantime, Albert of Louvain went to Rome to press his claim. There Pope Celestine consecrated him a bishop.

Returning to the diocese that was now his, Albert was met near Reims by three knights who convinced him to ride with them near the city. During the ride, they ferociously struck the prelate in the head with their swords, killing him.[580]

This atrocity, with its eerie similarity to the murder of Thomas Becket two decades earlier, exacerbated the factional division between the princes of this region of the Holy Roman Empire and provoked a reaction against Lothar of Hochstaden, who was soon excommunicated.

Many suspected Constance's husband of, at the very least, failure to act properly in his treatment of Albert of Louvain, and some suggested that he ordered the killing.[581] Here again was an analogy to the Becket case, which found Henry II of England accused of complicity in the assassination of the Archbishop of Canterbury by four of his knights. Like Thomas Becket, Albert of Louvain came to be venerated, though not as widely, and was later canonized.

Although Constance was not involved in Albert's murder, the incident was a sobering lesson in the use and misuse of power.

Baldwin was not Constance's only troubling kinsman. By now, she and her husband had more serious matters to address that required their attention south of the Alps.

Following the untimely death of Constance's beloved nephew, William II, in 1189, Tancred of Lecce managed to obtain enough baronial and ecclesiastical support to get himself crowned King of Sicily early the next year despite the fact that Constance was the late monarch's lawful and designated successor. (This was considered earlier; the events described in the next few pages intersect the lives of three other Sicilian queens, namely Joanna, Sibylla and Irene, each accorded her own chapter.)

Henry VI had pressing domestic concerns to address; his dynasty's longstanding Welf rival Henry the Lion, Duke of Saxony, was making incursions into imperial territories and was threatening the Hohenstaufens' reign. His father, Frederick, was still away on crusade. Undertaking a military expedition to the Kingdom of Sicily was the last thing Henry wanted to do at this moment, but he had little choice as his wife's fundamental dynastic rights were at stake.

The papacy, for its part, was not enthusiastic about Tancred, of all people, ruling half of Italy, but neither did it want Henry to have control of it.

The Hohenstaufens' status and prestige derived chiefly from their position as emperors. Apart from that, they were not very different from a dozen other influential German families. Swabia, their ancestral realm, was not Germany's largest or wealthiest region. Impressive as it was, the Holy Roman Empire was essentially a confederation of German hereditary principalities conjoined to some prosperous, semi-independent cities in northern Italy. To the west, the "Angevin Empire" was a patchwork of historically sovereign kingdoms and dukedoms that happened to be ruled by one dynasty, the Plantagenets. France was a fraction of the kingdom it would later become. In an age of shifting borders and equally unstable loyalties, the Kingdom of Sicily forged by Constance's father from a loose conglomeration of Norman duchies and counties was larger than almost any single realm of western Europe; it was also one of the wealthiest. Keenly aware of these facts, neither Henry or his consort could afford to lose it. To Constance, of course, the *Regnum Siciliae* was more than a source of wealth or power; it was a sacred birthright.

Constance's Kingdom

Constance's support in the peninsular part of the kingdom was encouraging but not sufficient, and the first months of Tancred's reign brought a series of setbacks there. The island of Sicily and most of Calabria were under the usurper's complete control.

Even in the best of circumstances, raising a large army could take a year or more. Fortunately, the imperial couple could readily muster one by diverting some of the forces already engaged to fight Henry the Lion in Saxony and Bavaria. A treaty being negotiated with him obviated the need to use this army in Germany.

Constance would accompany her husband on an expedition

to her homeland. Nevertheless, as Frederick Barbarossa had seen, an invasion of southern Italy could be a formidable task.

In May 1190, Henry sent a large advance force led by Henry "Testa" of Kalden[582] southward while he stayed in Germany to settle succession questions arising from the recent death, on crusade, of his imperial vassal Louis III of Thuringia and to conclude the treaty with Henry the Lion.

Before Henry and Constance departed for Italy, news arrived at court that Frederick Barbarossa had died in Asia Minor in June 1190. Since the imperial crown was now Henry's as Frederick's heir, it was opportune for him to go to Rome to claim it from the pope. That this was on the way to Naples and Salerno meant that two birds, coronation and conquest, could be hit with one stone. One objective would prove easier to achieve than the other.

Along the way to Rome, Constance and Henry met Eleanor of Aquitaine and her future daughter-in-law, Berengaria, at Lodi, near Milan, in January 1191. The two ladies were going to Sicily to meet Richard Lionheart, who stopped at Messina *en route* to the Third Crusade.[583] (See chapter 9.) Told of Constance's plight, Eleanor lent a sympathetic ear, and even witnessed a charter being issued by Henry, but she could not know that her son was about to recognize Tancred's right to the Sicilian throne. Eleanor's true opinion about the Sicilian dispute is not known. As we have seen, her daughter Joanna, widow of William II, supported Constance and opposed Tancred.

By the time Henry and Constance were to be crowned, a new pope had just been elected as Celestine III (Giacinto Bobone). This pontiff's only initial request was to be ceded the city of Tusculum, a wish Henry granted.[584]

The imperial coronation of Henry and Constance took place on Easter Monday in 1191. Constance was now an empress.

There was little time for rejoicing. It was imperative that the rightful Queen of Sicily reclaim the *Regnum Siciliae* at the earliest opportunity. Despite the couple's entreaties, Pope Celestine III, even after crowning the new Holy Roman Emperor, was reluctant to issue a declaration nullifying Tancred's coronation as King of Sicily. What could not be achieved through diplomacy might be accomplished at the point of a sword or two.[585]

The emperor viewed his prospects of success with a healthy dose of pragmatism. At Cassino he demanded, and received, a pledge of loyalty from the monks.

Capua and Aversa submitted to Constance's authority readily enough. With the help of Pisan and Genoan navies, Henry besieged Naples, but Margaritus of Brindisi successfully defended the city.

Now an old, familiar beast reared its ugly head as an epidemic swept through the imperial army, prompting its withdrawal. Henry himself was infected but recuperated. He accepted the invitation of the Salernitans to leave Constance, who had fallen ill from the torrid summer temperatures, in their city with a small garrison as a sign of her sovereign authority and his solemn promise to return. As Salerno boasted one of the best medical schools in Europe, there were competent physicians present to cure her.

The queen's presence was significant as Salerno was the largest city of the peninsular part of the kingdom, and Constance was lodged in its royal fortress, Terracena. Henry's presence was required back in Germany so he could address the kind of domestic problems that only the emperor could resolve.

Having survived the imperial siege and forced Henry to withdraw, the unsavory Neapolitans exploited this moment to score a cheap victory. Some nobles led by Nicholas of Aiello, the son of Tancred's chancellor Matthew, contacted the Salernitans, claiming that Henry was dead and encouraging the citizens to attack Constance at her stronghold in order to prove their loyalty to Tancred. Fearing a bloody reprisal by Tancred for having negotiated with Henry, the Salernitans complied with this demand.

The empress herself suspected that her husband might be dead. She attempted to negotiate with the besiegers but the best she could obtain from their leader, her distant (and obviously disloyal) kinsman, Elias of Gesualdo, was safe conduct for the knights of her garrison. This surrender left her a prisoner of Tancred, the bastard king.

Making his way out of the kingdom, Henry, who was still ailing, was at Cassino when he received news of his wife's capture. Enraged, he took hostages at San Germano, the town beneath the abbey, but did not draw blood. After he departed the *Regnum,* several of his vassals remained behind to wage a piecemeal war in isolated parts of Apulia and Lucania. If nothing else, this served to remind Tancred that his power on the mainland was neither absolute nor uncontested.

Constance would not forget the treachery of Nicholas of Aiello and the others, but for now she was to be taken by galley to Sicily. What was most important, for the moment, was that she lived to fight another day. It was becoming crystal clear that claiming her crown, no less sitting on her father's royal throne, was going to be an exercise in perseverance.

The Empress of the Holy Roman Empire and Queen of Sicily donned regal attire and let herself be escorted to the port of Salerno.

By the time Constance arrived at Messina late in 1191, Richard Lionheart, who had spent several months in the city before departing for the Holy Land in the spring (see Chapter 9), had recognized Tancred as King of Sicily. Like so many other irksome annoyances of recent months, that affront would not be forgotten. For the moment, however, the woman from Palermo had to confront more immediate challenges.

At Messina, Constance was brought before Tancred. She was thirty-seven, her captor fifty-three. If Peter of Eboli is to be believed, Constance was slender and stately, Tancred short and ugly. Though they may have met in the past, it is unlikely that they ever exchanged many words with each other. Their terse conversation as it is recounted in Peter's verse chronicle lends us an impression of the queen's reasoning:

"Was the entire world not enough to satisfy you?" Tancred asked. "Why do you desire my lands? Know that God will judge us fairly for what we do, and take his wrath upon those who take the law unto themselves. Fate has delivered you into my hands because you inflicted injury upon my kingdom. As we have seen, your husband, who was ill, has retreated."

"Do not forget what I am saying to you now, Tancred," Constance replied. "Before long, your rising star shall turn against you, just as my star has fallen upon me. Destiny cannot be changed. I do not seek your kingdom but that of my father, which is mine by right. Are you Roger's son? Not by any means. I am the king's heiress because I am his legitimate child by my mother. The legal rights of both my parents bequeath me the realm you presently hold as a usurper. You have not yet confronted the man who shall obtain these lands for me by the sword. What laws and oaths gave you the realm that appertains to me? It was only the benevolent grace of King William that permitted you to keep even Lecce."[586]

Having uttered these defiant words, Constance, as self-assured and dignified as ever, engaged in no further conversation with Tancred. She was sent to Palermo, where she resided with Tancred's wife, Sibylla, who did not relish the task of being a gaoler. (See Chapter 10.) Constance was treated well, though Sibylla probably wanted to kill her.

Back on the mainland, meanwhile, the towns that had recently submitted to Constance's authority were being taken back, one by one, by Tancred's vassals.

At Henry's urging, Pope Celestine used the threat of excommunication to persuade Tancred to release his imperial prisoner to papal custody.[587] Tancred's only real condition for consenting to this request was that the papacy recognize his claim to the Sicilian throne.

In June 1192, Constance was accompanied to Messina, and then onto the mainland, by Giles of Anagni, a cardinal, who was the papal chancellor.

The papal entourage escorting Constance was intercepted at Ceprano, just inside papal territory, by some imperial knights led by Roffred of Liri, a cardinal who was formerly the abbot of Cassino. The loyalty of this Benedictine, who had been imprisoned briefly for supporting Tancred, was for the moment reasonably secure because his brother, Gregory, was being held hostage by Henry in Germany. Constance was soon reunited with her husband at Trifels Castle.

Little is known of Constance's conjugal rapport with her husband. Arguably, the absence of children early in their marriage might suggest a lack of affection or intimacy. Whatever the case, Henry was adamant in his intent to conquer his wife's kingdom, if not her heart.

The Return

By the autumn of 1192, it was clear to Constance and Henry that determination alone would not be enough for a proper conquest of the *Regnum Siciliae*. A serious campaign would require a massive investment, perhaps more money than they could generate through taxes and other sources of revenue. Not only had they been defeated in Italy, their prestige had suffered for the recent assassination of Albert of Louvain, mentioned earlier.

An opportunity was to present itself from unexpected

quarters. Not only would it be lucrative, it would satiate Constance's desire for justice in view of her poor treatment at the hands of certain parties.

Specifically, this involved Richard Lionheart, King of England. After the deaths of Henry's father and brother on the Third Crusade, Leopold, Duke of Austria, hastened to Palestine to assume command of the imperial contingent while Henry undertook the campaign against Tancred in Italy. Following the capture of Acre, Leopold expected the same courtesy as that accorded the other sovereigns present. Instead, Richard ordered the duke's banner removed from its staff alongside the others flying atop the city's ramparts. Enraged at this affront, Leopold and his knights decamped and immediately returned home.

This, of course, was not the only criticism directed at Richard, who was rarely reluctant to offend his peers. By the time the aggrieved duke complained to the emperor about the banner incident, Henry was already nurturing his own grievance against Richard based on the English king's support for Tancred's claim to Sicily.

One of Richard's sisters was married to Henry the Lion, who was a thorn in the emperor's side, but this was not the only reminder that familial alliances were endlessly complex. Conrad of Montferrat, the recently murdered King of Jerusalem, was a cousin to both Henry and Leopold. Richard, a vocal opponent of Conrad, with whom he had quarrelled, was suspected of complicity in the assassination of this fellow monarch.[588] Naturally, this matter was far more grievous than Richard's refusal to fly a comrade's flag.

In December 1192, Richard Lionheart, whilst returning from the Third Crusade, was captured by Leopold, who confined him at Dürnstein Castle. Henry probably approved of this.

At Speyer in March of the following year, Richard was

transferred to Henry's custody and taken to Trifels Castle, where he was accused of murdering Conrad of Montferrat. The Holy Roman Emperor demanded a ransom of a hundred fifty thousand silver marks to release the King of England.

Following much effort to raise this sum to defray the cost of a "king's ransom," Richard's mother, Eleanor, came to remit the monies. It was the second time she and Constance met, and the younger woman had yet to sit upon the throne that was hers by hereditary right. Richard was finally released in February 1194.[589]

By now, Tancred and his elder son, Roger, had died. The Kingdom of Sicily was being ruled by Tancred's widow, Sibylla, as regent for her younger son, William. (See Chapter 10.)

With the imperial treasury replenished by English silver to defray the expenses of a major military campaign, it was time to launch a serious effort to restore the Kingdom of Sicily to Constance.

By the time Henry set out for the Kingdom of Sicily in May 1194, Constance was pregnant.[590] Her condition would restrict her participation but not her courage. If necessary, she would stay behind in papal territory whilst Henry fought his way into the northern part of the *Regnum*.

By August, Henry's army had reached Naples, which fell easily. The city of Salerno was sacked and vandalized in retribution for the disloyalty its citizens had shown in consigning Constance to Tancred three years earlier. Word of this pitiless reprisal preceded Henry as he advanced further into the *Regnum*. The emperor expected resistance but encountered virtually none as he and his surrogates subdued Apulia, Lucania and Calabria over the next few months. At times, the kingdom seemed undefended.

November found Henry in Palermo where, predictably, there was more fighting than what had been seen in the other cities. Nevertheless, this siege was a brief one.

It was time to mete out justice. The most important *familiares* of Sibylla, Tancred's widow, were exiled. Prominent among them was Nicholas of Aiello, who had instigated the attack on Constance at Salerno that led to her capture. Others, such as Eugene of Palermo, a Greek, were viewed as apolitical and thus spared following a brief imprisonment. On the mainland, Richard of Acerra, Tancred's brother-in-law, was eventually found and executed.

Sibylla and her children were exiled (see Chapter 10), and Irene Angelina, the widow of Tancred's elder son, was betrothed to Henry's brother (see Chapter 11).

Mother

On Christmas in 1194, Henry had himself crowned King of Sicily in Palermo Cathedral by right of his wife.[591] He now ruled more territory and more people than any other monarch in Europe.

The next day, Constance went into labor in the March of Ancona. At the town of Jesi, she ordered her attendants to erect a pavilion where she could give birth in view of numerous witnesses, mostly clerics and courtiers. Her worry was that the maternity of a quadragenarian who had not yet given birth during nine years of marriage might later be placed in doubt by naysayers. Her son was christened Frederick.

On that day the torch that lit the flame of the Sicilian monarchy was passed from the Norman Hautevilles to the Swabian Hohenstaufens. The survival of the *Regnum Siciliae* founded by Constance's father was assured.

With this, Constance entered two parallel phases of her life, motherhood and effective queenhood. In March of the following year, she was crowned Queen of Sicily at Bari following her husband's first major meeting of the baronage.

In outward appearance, Constance's queenship was not too

different from that of any other heiress of royal rank whose husband ruled *jure uxoris* on her behalf. However, if not precisely a queen regnant, Constance was the nearest thing to it in Sicily's Norman-Swabian era.

The daily operation of the kingdom did not change any more than it had when Tancred assumed power following the death of Constance's nephew, the fondly-remembered William II. Its fundamental laws and institutions remained in place. There was no ideological transformation, and no serious attempt by Henry to integrate the Kingdom of Sicily into the Holy Roman Empire as if it were a German duchy. Frederick's grand inheritance would be a personal union, not a political one. This was significant because the *Regnum Siciliae* was a "centralized" monarchy with a unitary legal code rather than a conglomeration of duchies and counties. The political complexities of the Holy Roman Empire need not concern us at length, but the simple reality was that no one German monarch, even the ruler of a large dominion like Saxony or Bavaria, became King of the Germans and then, if he were fortunate, emperor, by hereditary right alone; he needed the approval of the elector princes and bishops.

As soon as he had reached Palermo, and without immediately notifying his wife, Henry withdrew much money from the treasury. Just as significantly, he enfeoffed some German barons in Sicily and installed the faithful Teutonic Knights in Messina and Palermo. In the capital, he gave this chivalric order the Magione, a splendid church (still standing) erected by the late Matthew of Aiello for the Cistercians, as soon as the tomb of Tancred housed there was destroyed. Commanderies were also established in Apulia.

The Teutonic Order was founded in Palestine a few years earlier under the patronage of Henry's late brother, Frederick of Swabia. Unlike the knightly orders of the Hospital and the Temple, which were multiethnic and independent, the

Teutonic Knights, though ostensibly autonomous, were closely linked to a specific culture and dynasty, the German Hohenstaufens.

Experience had taught Henry and Constance that the very thought of trusting the baronage and populace of the *Regnum* was fraught with risk. Here, on "foreign" soil, the German knights and barons were unlikely to rebel against one of their own.

This policy of germanification led to Sicily's Muslims, whose numbers were already diminishing, being excluded from government.

Henry's attempt — in his own way — to calm a sea of potential Sicilian troubles was successful at first, and it seems to have met with Constance's approval. The most turbulent waters were those bubbling up from the murky flow of the Tiber. Thanks to Constance's delivery of a healthy boy, the papacy's worst fears had come to pass. In an undercurrent destined to shape papal policy for the next seven decades, there was now a male heir to the powerful realms that engulfed the lands ruled by the pope. From London to Kiev, temporal sovereigns took notice of the power that bisected Europe in a line extending from the North Sea to the central Mediterranean.

By June, Constance was in Palermo issuing decrees in her own name and under her own seal as Queen of Sicily.[592] Her surviving charters reflect the typical duties undertaken by a monarch as the court of final appeal in matters involving baronies, manors, abbeys and serfs.

As if one empire were not enough, Henry began eyeing the Byzantine Empire to the east. He was also contemplating a crusade. Neither ambition was to be realized.

For now, he had more than enough on his plate. It was nearly as challenging for Henry to rule the combined territories of the Holy Roman Empire, the northern Italian communes and the Kingdom of Sicily as it was for his contemporary, Genghis Khan, to control the vast, growing Mongol Empire to the east. Henry's family was much smaller than that of his Asian counterpart; appropriately, he delegated some duties in Italy to his only surviving brother, Philip of Swabia.

Knowing that the pretensions of the rival Welf dynasty could rekindle themselves at any time, Henry sought to consolidate his young son's position in Germany. As empress, Constance understood the importance of this. At Frankfurt in 1196, young Frederick was elected King of the Germans (or "King of the Romans"), a status that qualified him, under imperial law, to be crowned king and then emperor. Some important electors in other regions dissented.

The empire was not the only realm where rebellion could erupt, and the next year found Henry back in the *Regnum Siciliae,* where he had to quell a baronial revolt. Accustomed to the comparative laxity of administration under William II and Tancred, these barons, joined perhaps by some Arabs, resented Henry's rigidity and tax increases. Constance may have shared their view, though not their decision to start a violent rebellion.[593]

Henry's untimely death at Messina on the twenty-eighth of September 1197 made Constance the regent for young Frederick. Henry was interred in Palermo's cathedral in a tomb of porphyry befitting his imperial rank. Fate left his widow little time to dwell on her loss.

In retrospect, little can be discerned about Constance's marriage. Husband and wife seem to have had rather different ideas regarding taxation and finances, and slightly contrasting temperaments about the use of power. In some ways, Constance may have had a greater affinity for the common folk, especially her people, the Sicilians. But here wanton speculation would be useless.

Regent

Ruling from Palermo, Constance could control the Kingdom of Sicily, but grasping the reins restraining the headstrong German princes was another matter altogether.

Even as arrangements were being made for his brother's funeral, Philip raced to Germany in an attempt to defend Frederick's rights there (see the previous chapter). This was a daunting task.

Now, as regent, Constance was exercising the sovereign rights of her son.[594] She had an efficient chancellor in Walter of Palear.

Most of Constance's day-to-day duties were rather ordinary, even banal. The education of her son was a paramount concern, naturally, but there were competent tutors to tend to this. The boy was to be taught several languages, including Arabic and some Greek, and an appreciation of the diversity of cultures that made his kingdom unique.

Constance had to think about more than her son's education, and on Saturday, the seventeenth of May 1198, the three year-old was crowned King of Sicily in Palermo Cathedral. Hopefully, this would ensure his dynastic rights in the Kingdom of Sicily.

By then, Philip, Frederick's uncle, hoping to placate imperial elector princes reluctant to embrace administration by the mother and courtiers of a boy king in another country, had already had himself elected King of the Germans. In September, he was crowned at Mainz. At this juncture there was little choice, for some German princes were already throwing their support behind the rival Welfs. Constance's reaction to her brother-in-law's decision is not known, but she certainly understood the complexities facing the Hohenstaufens in Germany.

With this in mind, she tacitly, though not explicitly, renounced her son's imperial claims by omitting any mention of these at his coronation or in subsequent charters. By no means was this a formal abdication of Frederick's inherent dynastic rights. Rather, it was a pragmatic effort to permit his uncle, Philip, to defend that inheritance in any way possible while avoiding the ire of a pope who felt threatened by Hohenstaufen power in Italy.

This permitted Constance, as queen, to focus on local problems. Relying upon the expertise of local advisors, she sent most of her late husband's counsellors back to Germany. Those enfeoffed in the *Regnum* remained. In at least one case this was problematic.

Markward of Anweiler, a courtier of Henry, who had generously granted him lands in the northern marches of the *Regnum,* came forth claiming to possess the "genuine" will of the late emperor making him, and not Constance, the regent of the kingdom. This, the vassal affirmed ridiculously, was because Frederick was not actually born of Constance. The queen responded to this nonsense by banishing Markward from the kingdom.[595] Unfortunately, he would eventually return to foment still more chaos.

Now the dearth of Hohenstaufen males was proving just as problematical as the shortage of Hauteville heirs had been during Constance's childhood. Showing uncommon foresight, the queen made certain provisions for her son's future. Most importantly, she named Pope Innocent III the young king's guardian in the event of her death.[596] This would have made the pontiff the *de facto* regent of the Kingdom of Sicily until Frederick reached the age of majority. As Frederick's guardian, the pope was to receive thirty thousand gold tarì per year.

Constance also renounced the apostolic legateship enjoyed by her Norman forebears, though some of her successors asserted this privilege.

By the autumn of 1198, the queen was already thinking about a bride for her son, perhaps a sister of Peter II, the young, recently-crowned King of Aragon.[597]

It is quite possible that Constance's immediacy in addressing these matters was motivated by a persistent illness which led her physicians to make a pessimistic prognosis of her chances for survival. On the other hand, she was the last of her house, and personal experience had taught her the importance of establishing matters involving dynastic succession in a clear, unequivocal fashion that would leave such details beyond later contestation.

Constance died in Palermo on the twenty-seventh of November in 1198. Her legacy is one of certitude, rectitude and fortitude. Constance has come to be regarded as the very avatar of Sicilian queenhood.

Frederick

Her son's childhood was not destined to be simple or even very happy. Pope Innocent appointed Cencio Savelli, the future Honorius III, as Frederick's principal tutor. Philip, the boy's uncle, permitted arrogant Markward of Anweiler to invade the kingdom and oust Walter of Palear, the chancellor and acting regent, from power. Fortunately, Markward died in 1202. Then William of Capparone, another German, served as the effective regent until 1206. In that year, Walter of Palear became Frederick's personal guardian through the efforts of Dietpold of Schweinspünt, the warrior who had defeated and killed Walter of Brienne a few years earlier (see Chapter 10). Upon reaching the age of majority in 1208, Frederick began to recruit some of his own counsellors.

By then, a marriage was already being arranged for the young Sicilian sovereign to an older, wiser woman who might become his advisor as well as his consort.

Constance of Sicily

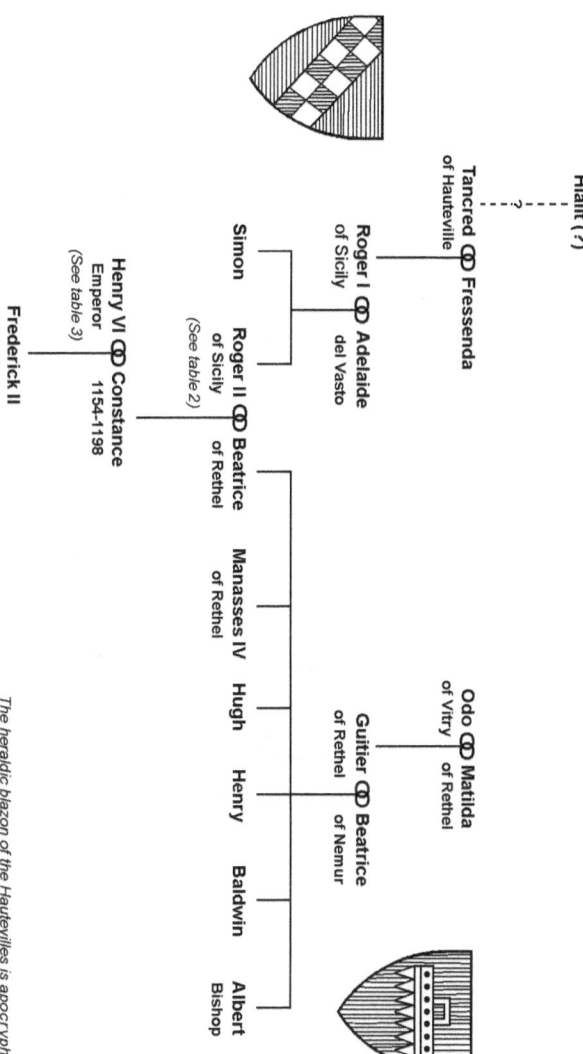

The heraldic blazon of the Hautevilles is apocryphal, created long after the dynasty's reign in Sicily.

On 15 April 1196 Constance issued this charter under her own name and seal, ceding authority over some serfs (named in the decree) to a certain jurisdiction. Here she is referred to as Roman Empress and Queen of Sicily.

Constance received at Salerno by the city's nobles (chronicle of Peter of Eboli)

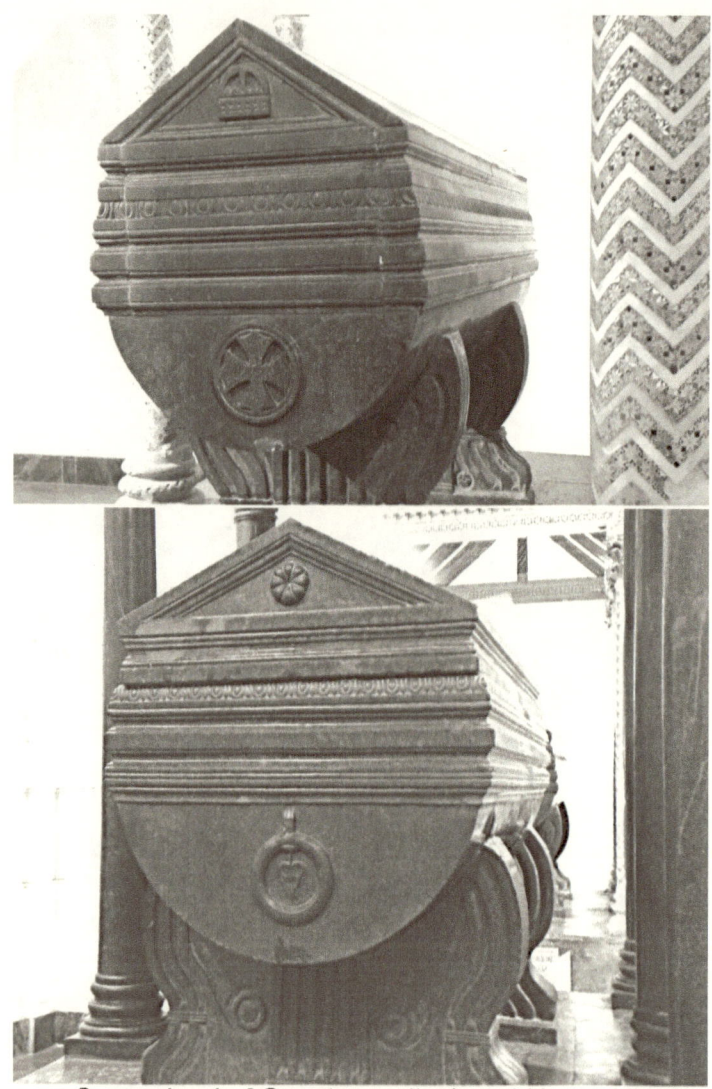

Sarcophagi of Constance (top) and Henry VI

As queen regnant, Constance used her own seal (top). As regent, Margaret used her son's seal (shown is the version drawn in red ink).

The Cubola, one of the few pavilions in the vast Genoard park to survive from the Norman era until our times, is a sight with which Constance was familiar.

Chapter 13
CONSTANCE OF ARAGON

Constance of Aragon was born in Lisbon in 1179 as the eldest daughter, and second-oldest child, of Alfonso II, King of Aragon, who was also Count of Barcelona, and Sancha of Castile. Her Sicilian marriage, though brokered by Pope Innocent III as the guardian of a young Frederick II, was the fruit of earlier efforts by the king's late mother, the last Hauteville, to arrange a match with one of Alfonso's younger daughters.[598]

Parentage

Constance's father was descended in the male line from the Bellonid dynasty founded in the eighth century by a certain Bello of Carcassone, who was thought to be of Visigothic ancestry. Her father's mother, Petronella, who was Queen of Aragon in her own right, bore the same Jiménez roots as Elvira of Castile and Margaret of Navarre, two queens we met earlier. (See table 7.)

Alfonso cultivated political alliances with monarchs whose lands bordered his Iberian dominions, hence his friendship with Richard Lionheart.

Sancha, Constance's mother, who also boasted Jiménez lineage, was an independent-minded woman, and doubtless an early influence on her eldest daughter. Owing to a dispute with her husband over some estates she had inherited from her father, King Alfonso VII of Castile, Sancha led a force in 1177 to seize some lands that formed part of her dowry, in effect fighting a war against her own spouse.

Constance spent her childhood in Zaragoza and other inland towns, but mostly in coastal Barcelona, northern Spain's gateway to most of Europe.

This magnificent city on the Mediterranean was the cornerstone of a burgeoning confederation, the "Crown of Aragon," destined to become a thalassocracy that would one day expand its power as far as Sicily, laying the cornerstone of what later became the Spanish Empire. In Constance's time it comprised little more than the Kingdom of Aragon and the neighboring County of Barcelona (Catalonia) united under her ambitious father. By 1200, the city of Barcelona was arguably the most important Spanish locality under Christian control.

Constance had seven siblings, namely Peter (later Peter II), Alfonso, Leonor, Raymond, Sancha, Ferdinand and Dulcia. She seems to have been especially close to Alfonso, who was one year her junior.

First Marriage

Following the untimely death of her father, aged just thirty-nine, in 1196, Constance was betrothed, on the orders of her elder brother, now reigning as Peter II, to Emeric, King of Hungary. Recently enthroned, Emeric was seeking a closer rapport with the kingdoms to the west, and Pope Innocent III was instrumental in helping him to find a suitable bride.

As a dower, Emeric gave Constance two counties and

thirty thousand gold ounces. Marriage would take her to a court and an environment very different from what she had known as a child.

The nuptials were celebrated in 1198.[599] The next year, Constance, now a crowned queen, gave birth to an heir, Ladislas.[600]

Like the Crown of Aragon, Hungary was an expanding realm. Constance's husband was already an experienced monarch. Years earlier, Emeric's father, Bela III, had him crowned *rex filius* and then appointed him to govern Croatia and Dalmatia. Hungary was Catholic, while the Byzantine territories bordering it were Orthodox.

The greatest challenge Emeric confronted during his reign was not division in the church but violent dissent within his own family, as his younger brother, Andrew, coveted the crown for himself. Emeric placated his envious sibling by making him the duke of Croatia and Dalmatia, a duty that kept the troublesome prince far away from Esztergom, the Hungarian capital. Nevertheless, Emeric eventually had to place his defiant brother under arrest.

After Emeric died following a lengthy illness in November 1204, his young son, already crowned *rex filius* in August of that year, ascended the throne as Ladislas III, with Andrew as regent. It wasn't long before Andrew reneged on the solemn promise he had sworn to the moribund Emeric to respect the boy's rights.[601] Not surprisingly, he confiscated the young king's inheritance kept at Pilis Abbey, despite being warned by the pope to protect royal assets.

Learning that Andrew was trying to assassinate his young nephew, Constance fled with Ladislas to Vienna, where she received the protection of her husband's cousin, Duke Leopold VI, even in the face of Andrew's boisterous threat to invade Austria.[602]

Regicide was not the only thing on Andrew's mind; his fleeing sister-in-law had managed to take with her the monetary part of her dower. As a widow, she was entitled to a pension of twelve thousand silver marks in addition to the gold she received at marriage.

Sadly, young Ladislas died in exile in May 1205 following a grave illness, and was entombed at Székesfehérvár Basilica.[603]

This tragic event changed the course of the widowed queen's life, for she was now isolated from the Hungarian court, where Andrew was crowned.[604] Constance returned with her small entourage to Aragon, where she took up residence with her mother in the royal convent at Sigena. Her sojourn there was not to last long.

Second Marriage

When Constance's brother, Peter II, was re-crowned by Pope Innocent III in 1205, the pontiff exploited the occasion to discuss the possibility of a marriage between the king's widowed sister and Frederick II.[605] By 1206, with Constance living in Aragon, it was decided that an older woman might be a good choice for the young Sicilian sovereign. Peter had his own reasons for concluding this marital agreement.[606]

In 1208, as the result of negotiations by Innocent, the widow was betrothed to Frederick II of Hohenstaufen, King of Sicily and would-be Holy Roman Emperor, whose mother we met in the last chapter.[607] Constance was never to see her own mother again, for Sancha died in November.

The marriage agreement stipulated that Constance would receive a dower consisting of Mount Saint Angelo and the nearby towns, the same lands once conceded to Queen Joanna. Additionally, she would have Taormina and a number of smaller fiefs in Sicily.[608]

Departing Aragon in early June 1209, Constance was accompanied to Sicily by her brother, Alfonso, and a company of five hundred knights. She was wed at Messina in August.[609]

As Frederick was barely fifteen years old, Constance could almost have been his mother. Her experiences in life thus far had left her sober, if not taciturn. Her wisdom transcended her years.

There wasn't much time for celebrating.

Hegemony

The murder of Frederick's uncle, Philip of Swabia, in 1208, opened the way to the Welf claimant, Otto of Brunswick, to be crowned Holy Roman Emperor in the autumn of 1209. Riots forced him out of the eternal city but did not dissuade him from further adventures in papal Italy.

Otto's loyalty to the papacy was far from absolute, and he could not resist reclaiming papal lands that had once been imperial fiefs. Encouraged by easy victories at Ancona and Spoleto, and abetted by Frederick's disloyal German vassals on the northern fringe of the *Regnum,* he soon launched a successful military expedition into Apulia, eventually making it as far as Calabria.[610]

Constance had brought with her a large contingent of five hundred knights accompanied by their supporting esquires and troops. The prowess and fealty of these men was beyond cavil. Their very presence encouraged the submission of barons on the island who otherwise might have proven reluctant to restore crown lands usurped during Frederick's minority.

Unfortunately, many of the Aragonese and Catalonian knights fell prey to a fatal epidemic. The illness also claimed the life of their leader, Constance's beloved brother, Alfonso. In view of this tragedy, the remaining Spanish knights returned to their homeland.[611]

Thinking his position ironclad, Otto, who was now in possession of most of the peninsular part of the realm, arrogantly demanded that Frederick recognize him as an overlord in the peninsular part of the *Regnum*. When Frederick ignored this demand to pay homage, the invader claimed these regions outright. Otto's march on Rome to attempt to constrain papal concessions to a proposed imperial prerogative to appoint bishops prompted Innocent to excommunicate him late in 1210.

Before confronting Otto, Frederick had to get his own house in order. Acting on his wife's advice, he dismissed Walter of Palear, who was now Bishop of Catania, from the chancellorship, although the prelate was later reinstated at the pope's urging.

Back in Germany, the high nobility was growing tired of Otto's behavior, and at the Diet of Nuremberg in 1211 a vocal faction elected Frederick their king with Innocent's assent. This resulted in the emperor's withdrawal from Italy with his tail between his legs, leaving most of the occupied territories under Frederick's control. Otto may have presumed that his short-lived marriage to a Hohenstaufen lady would bolster his position.[612] If so, he was sorely mistaken.

Amidst this unrest, Constance gave birth to a son, christened Henry, in 1211.

If Frederick were to reclaim the peninsula and accept the German crown, the first order of business was to raise an army. There were also political considerations.

It seemed ironic that the pope, normally opposed to rule of the lands surrounding papal territory by a sole monarch, would now acquiesce to such a situation. The arrangement was accepted on the condition that Frederick's newborn son become King of Sicily whilst Frederick himself became Holy Roman Emperor.

With young Henry thus crowned, Frederick tended to further diplomatic details that might put Pope Innocent's mind at ease. For example, he reiterated his late mother's renunciation of the apostolic legateship.

In the spring of 1212, Frederick sailed with a flotilla and a modest force to Gaeta, north of Naples, from whence he would trek northward.

School

He left Constance in Sicily as his regent, effectively his surrogate or governor. Whilst Frederick and his company of knights were wending their way toward the Alps and into Germany, avoiding cities allied with Otto, Constance addressed daily affairs and cared for her infant son. She could not have helped thinking about Ladislas, the son she had lost years earlier, but this was a new life in what must have seemed like a different world. Indeed, the queen could finally exercise a modicum of control over her own affairs.

What was life like at Constance's Sicilian court?

As a strategic base, the queen generally preferred Messina to Palermo because it facilitated closer contact with the mainland.[613] Yet in 1212, while Frederick was attending Christmas mass at Speyer's magnificent cathedral, Constance and Henry attended the liturgy at Palermo's equally impressive basilica, the largest church in Italy south of Rome.[614]

Constance issued a number of charters jointly in her name and that of her young son, with the formula "Constance, Queen of the Romans, Queen of Sicily, together with Henry, King of Sicily, her son." Most of these decrees involved ecclesiastical matters.[615] The queen lent her personal patronage to the abbey at Fiore in Calabria's mountainous Sila region.

Frederick's personal interests generally ran more toward the scientific sphere. He welcomed the presence of scholars like Michael Scot, a gifted mathematician, reprising the intellectual splendor the court enjoyed in the time of Frederick's grandfather, Roger II.[616]

Frederick himself was to become known as the most brilliant European monarch of his generation. His scientific legacy is a book on falconry.

Norman French was no longer the Sicilian court's vernacular language. A new tongue, Sicilian, had emerged over the last few decades.

Poets like Cielo of Alcamo and Giacomo of Lentini composed poetry in this language, and so did Frederick. The Sicilian School embodies the oldest Italian vernacular.[617]

Cielo's *Contrasto* (which appears in this volume with a translation) is the longest poem written in Middle Sicilian, which differs markedly from the modern Sicilian language one occasionally hears today, just as Chaucer's Middle English differs from the English spoken in our times. The *Contrasto* is a classic example of a dialogue of courtly love expressed by a knight seeking the affection of a noble damsel. It evokes the spirit of chivalry, with its minstrels, troubadours, tournaments and heralds.

Sicily was undergoing a linguistic and literary evolution. The Muslims were ever fewer, and as they converted to Catholicism they embraced the Sicilian language, to which they brought Arabic influences. The latinization of the Greeks was insidious, a subtle matter of the clergy being Latin where formerly there were only Byzantines. The gradual transition from Orthodoxy to Catholicism brought with it the use of Latin in liturgy and, by the thirteenth century, Sicilian for everyday conversation. In Sicilian one finds words that are etymologically Latin, Greek, Arabic, German and French, as well as Lombardic.

Constance's marriage was for now a distant one, at least geographically. While Frederick was away, she kept up a regular correspondence with her friends and family abroad.

Her husband's long absences did not bode propitiously for conjugal life. In reality, Constance could never have come to know Frederick extremely well, for they passed little time together. Even so, historians generally agree that she was the favorite amongst the women he married.

If Frederick missed his wife, his travels did not deprive him of female company. In his time away from Constance, he fathered a number of children outside marriage.[618]

Constance never met any of these children or their mothers. Yet she would have been naive to ignore the likelihood of their existence. It was part of royal marriage. What is more, there was still a harem in Palermo's palace.

Empress

Frederick's coronation at Mainz in December of 1212 made Constance Queen of the Germans, if only in the eyes of some. It would take a few more years for her husband to consolidate his power in Germany, where he did not yet enjoy the support of all the elector princes and bishops. The enmity between the rival factions that came to be known as Ghibellines (Hohenstaufen advocates) and Guelphs (Welf proponents) continued in earnest, complicated by occasional wars emanating from other quarters.[619] One of these conflicts, the Anglo-French War, led to the disastrous defeat of Otto of Brunswick at Bouvines in 1214 by a French army led by King Philip II, effectively ending Welf military power and quashing Otto's aspirations to greatness.

In 1213, Constance convinced the papacy to grant her brother, Peter, a Catholic burial even though he died fighting against the church in one of the Albigensian wars (see note 611).

A coronation at Aachen in July 1215 left little doubt of Frederick's status as King of the Germans, and the death of his perennial rival, Otto of Brunswick, isolated and abandoned, three years later, left the younger man unopposed.

In June 1216 Nicholas of Aiello, Archbishop of Salerno,

and his brother, Richard, visited Constance's court to show their allegiance to Frederick and to ask forgiveness for supporting Otto a few years earlier.[620]

With his position consolidated, Frederick summoned Constance to Germany. She and young Henry set out from Messina with six galleys in July 1216, reaching Nuremberg in December.[621] Their route took them through Capua, where Constance berated Bartholomew, the Bishop of Chieti, for his dispute with the pope, and then through Bologna and Cremona.

In Germany, she accompanied Frederick in his travels from place to place. Despite Aachen's symbolic significance, the Holy Roman Empire had no actual, permanent capital, so Frederick was forced to travel frequently to show himself and assert his authority. There is little doubt that Constance advised her husband in the matters confronting him, but we know nothing about what she said.

The couple set out southward for Rome in August 1220. Frederick and Constance were crowned emperor and empress by Pope Honorius III in November of that year. While in Rome, Constance expressed to the pontiff her firm refusal to cede her Hungarian dower to King Andrew, her former brother-in-law, who had solicited papal intervention in the hopes of retrieving the gold.

Following the coronation in Rome, Constance traveled with Frederick to Capua.

Frederick decided to tighten his grip on the barons, who had run amok during his minority and in some cases even supported an invader. The king pursued an effort to update the Assizes of Ariano, the legal code instituted by his grandfather, with promulgation of the Assizes of Capua now and the Assizes of Messina the next year. These were intended to amend Roger's code rather than to replace it altogether. This represented an attempt to accrue more power to the crown.

Frederick acceded to a papal request to go on crusade;

though years would pass before he could depart, he sent a fleet to Damietta. In a gesture the papacy found less enticing, he had young Henry elected King of the Germans.

After visiting Capua and Cassino with Frederick, in January 1221 Constance and her son spent a month at Sessa Arunca, a fortified town north of Capua. Frederick stayed with them for a few days before going to Capua with his counsellors. Once his business in the region was done, the family continued on to Apulia.[622]

Constance, Frederick and Henry reached Messina in May. They then went to Catania.[623]

The royal family stayed in eastern Sicily until July. From Catania, they then set out for Palermo at the end of that month, stopping for a few days in Caltagirone. They were in Palermo by the middle of August.[624]

In November 1221, they traveled to Agrigento, and from there to Catania, where they celebrated Christmas. In early 1222 Constance remained in Catania while Frederick went with Henry to Apulia and then Naples and Capua.[625] At Anagni the emperor met the pope.

Although he was only eleven, Henry, as the heir apparent, would soon have to learn the art of statecraft. This trip with his father would be useful. It was the kind of paternal mentorship that Frederick had never had.

A localized revolt by the Muslims of Jato, near Palermo, brought Frederick back to the island in May, when he was met by his wife at Messina and probably left Henry with her.[626]

Frederick was at Jato when Constance died at Catania on the twenty-third of June 1222.[627] A funeral was celebrated in Catania, with a second one held in Palermo, where the Queen of Sicily, Queen of the Germans, Holy Roman Empress and Queen of Hungary was entombed. In death, she wore rings befitting a queen, and a splendid jeweled crown of Byzantine design.

QUEENS OF SICILY

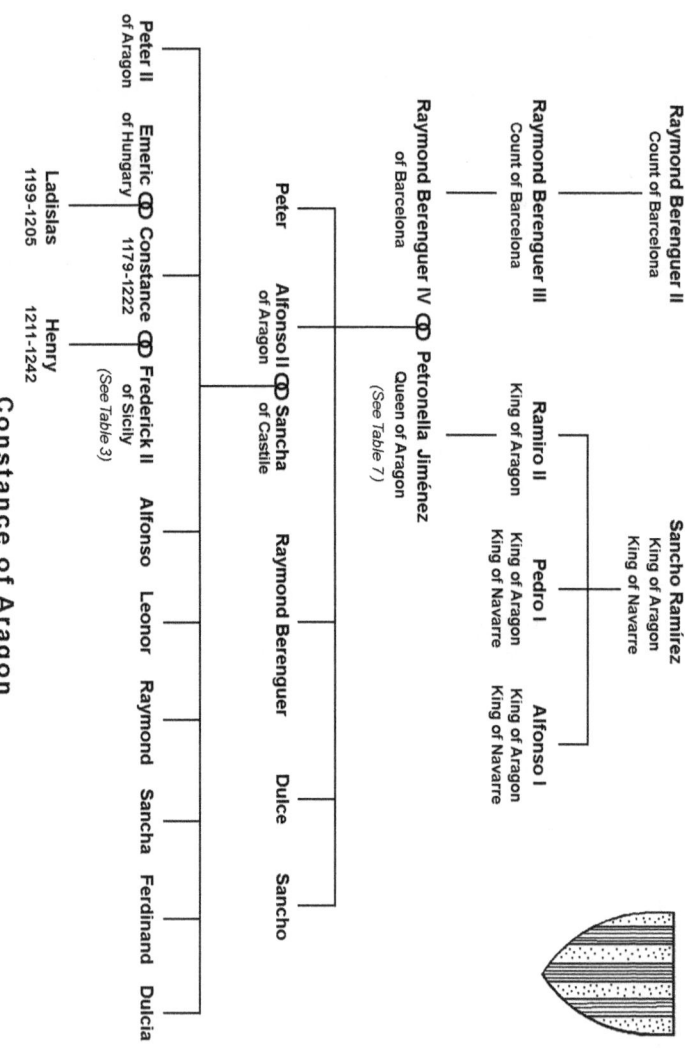

Constance of Aragon

Lisbon Cathedral, where Constance was baptized

Though born in Lisbon, Constance spent part of her childhood in Aragon, probably at the Aljaferia Palace in Zaragoza, built by the Moors.

Constance lived for a time at Barcelona's royal palace.

Silver endotaph placed in the tomb of Constance of Aragon recording details of her life and death as queen and empress

Chapter 14
YOLANDA OF JERUSALEM

Yolanda of Jerusalem was born in Acre late in 1212 to John of Brienne and his wife, Maria of Montferrat, Queen of Jerusalem. Maria's death shortly after her daughter's birth left young Yolanda, sometimes Isabella, as Queen of Jerusalem by *jure sanguinis,* hereditary right.[628] Though John was crowned with Maria in 1210 and is usually referred to as the "King of Jerusalem," this was essentially a courtesy title. He was, more exactly, Maria's consort; during his wife's lifetime John was, at best, a co-ruler. Maria's untimely death left John as Yolanda's regent.[629] By the time Yolanda was born, Jerusalem wasn't even much of a kingdom, and she never set foot in the holy city for which it was named.

Prelude

The realm Yolanda was meant to inherit was founded in 1099 as a tangible result of the First Crusade. The Kingdom of Jerusalem was a Roman Catholic, European contrivance which, at its greatest extent, included most of Palestine. To its north were the neighboring states of Tripoli and Antioch, founded by crusaders, and Cilicia (Lesser Armenia), established by Christian refugees fleeing Seljuk expansionism. In 1192 Cyprus became the seat of a similar monarchy. Knightly orders like the Templars and Hospitallers also held small pockets of sovereign territory.

The kingdom's first century of existence found it ruled by a series of dynasties having ancestral roots in or near what is now France, and French was the court language. Though succession to the crown was hereditary, approval by a council of nobles was necessary for a king to rule.

Holy to all three Abrahamic faiths, the city of Jerusalem was lost to Saladin in 1187, and in the wake of the Third Crusade the Frankish monarchy was re-established at Acre in 1192. John's actual dominion included Acre as the kingdom's capital, the city of Tyre, and some coastal territories. This is where Yolanda spent her childhood.

Though not royal, John's family was not without its lustre. His father, Erard, was Count of Brienne and a military leader of the Third Crusade. John's elder brother, Walter, whom we met in Chapter 10, wed a daughter of Tancred of Sicily and invaded the *Regnum*.

It was with the approval of the Hierosolymitan baronage that John married Maria, the daughter of Queen Isabella I of Jerusalem (daughter of King Amalric) and Conrad of Montferrat. Ruling lands in Piedmont and Liguria, the dynasty of Montferrat was the ancestral family of Adelaide del Vasto (see Chapter 4), who wed an early King of Jerusalem in a disastrous marriage.

Childhood

Yolanda's childhood in Acre was a rose with a few thorns.

In 1214, John married Stephanie, heiress to Lesser Armenia. Stephanie, who did not like Yolanda, gave birth to a son two years later. Not enough is known about her for us to ascertain whether Stephanie was a truly wicked stepmother, but her son's birth may well have exacerbated any resentment she cultivated toward Yolanda.

Only death itself could bring an end to Yolanda's queenship. Stephanie knew this.

John was one of the leaders of the ill-fated Fifth Crusade, and he was chosen to rule Damietta after the besieged town fell to his Franks in 1219. He soon departed for his own lands, planning to go to Cilicia to claim his wife's birthright as heiress of Lesser Armenia.

When Stephanie died unexpectedly, it was rumored that her husband had beaten her to death for attempting to poison young Yolanda.[630] In any case, the death of Stephanie's son mooted the pretext for John's claim to the Armenian throne.

While it resulted in a tenuous truce, the Fifth Crusade ultimately failed to achieve its objective of restoring the city of Jerusalem and other territories to the Christians. Even if the Hospitallers and Templars retained some of their castles and estates, Damietta and the other Egyptian lands were lost to the Ayyubids.

Back in Europe, Pope Honorius III was already advocating a crusade to re-occupy Jerusalem. This was music to John's ears, for a successful restoration would, presumably, increase his power and prestige.

Marriage

The reality was slightly more complicated. To entice support, it was decided to exploit young Yolanda as a lure. By 1223, with Frederick II a young widower, the kingmaker in Rome was casting an eye his way.

Although the sporadic outbreaks of unrest amongst Sicily's diminishing Muslim population were a concern, Frederick did not oppose Islam on ideological grounds. Indeed, it could be argued that he was not the ideal candidate to lead a holy war against the Ayyubids. True, he had already made the commitment to go on crusade, but his duties in his own vast realms had not yet permitted him to embark for Palestine.

There was something slightly tawdry in John hawking the hand of Yolanda, a very young queen, to the highest bidder. Yet what is known of him suggests that John was an eternal opportunist, continuously formulating one scheme or another, always seeking a royal heiress to wed in the hope of placing a crown on his own head. In the event, what he was doing was hardly atypical of the time.

Yolanda's fate was decided during a meeting at Ferentino in March 1223 that John held with Frederick and Honorius.[631] The papal view was that the marriage agreement was predicated on Frederick's promise to go on crusade. With less justification, John seems to have inferred from the meeting that a successful crusade would make him the *de facto* governor of the city of Jerusalem whilst his daughter resided in Europe with her new husband. Frederick clearly expressed the position that he would undertake such a crusade only as King of Jerusalem by right of Yolanda. Thus each man entertained a slightly varied, personalized perception based on his own objectives. In the spirit of the times, any views that might be held by Yolanda, the young woman whose destiny was the subject of the negotiations, were considered inexistent, if they were considered at all. Around the time Frederick was negotiating for Yolanda's hand, he fathered a child, Frederick "of Antioch," born to a woman whose identity is debated.

Following further negotiations, the wedding was arranged. To avoid the kind of controversy that might arise afterward, the pope granted a dispensation from the canonical impediment of the spouses' distant kinship; Yolanda and Frederick were third cousins.[632] The ceremony would be celebrated, in the first instance, by proxy two years later.[633]

That is because Yolanda had not yet reached the age usually required for marriage, and she was far away in Acre. Frederick wanted to ensure that she was already his wife before he set foot in her kingdom. There was no point traveling there for a wedding, returning to Italy, and then undertaking a costly second voyage to Palestine for the crusade. Apart from this, he was busy in his own dominions, founding a university at Naples and planning a major meeting of imperial vassals. John, meanwhile, went to Burgos, where he wed Berengaria of León, the sister of King Ferdinand III of Castile.

In August 1225, Henry of Malta, a Sicilian vassal, set sail from Brindisi for Acre with a flotilla of twenty galleys to transport Yolanda to the Kingdom of Sicily following her impending wedding. At a ceremony in Acre's Holy Cross church, she was wed to Frederick, and a jeweled ring sent by him was placed on her finger.

Immediately after this ceremony, the Patriarch of Jerusalem, with the assent of the high nobles of Jerusalem, crowned her their queen. This was followed by two weeks of celebration.[634]

Accompanied by some leading nobles of Jerusalem and a company of knights of the trusted Teutonic Order, Yolanda then began her journey to Apulia, stopping *en route* at Cyprus to visit Alice, her aunt.

In early November she was met at Brindisi by her father and Frederick.[635] The nuptials, and Yolanda's coronation as Queen of Sicily and Holy Roman Empress, were held in the city's cathedral. A lavish feast, which in our time might be called an "after party," followed for several days in Oria Castle, where many of the guests were lodged.

The bride was barely fourteen years old. The chronicler Ernoul recounts that the morning following the nuptials John found his daughter in tears. Yolanda explained to her father that the previous night Frederick had abandoned her in favor of an impromptu tryst with her pretty cousin, one of the ladies-in-waiting.[636] Even if the story was woven of little more than a few strands of court gossip, it reflects a widespread perception that the spouses had little natural affinity for each other.

Conversely, the rumor that soon after the wedding Frederick began to shun his father-in-law, is at least supported by subsequent events.

Here was the epitome of a marriage of dynastic convenience. Sadly, there is nothing to suggest that there was ever much affection between Yolanda and her husband, a man eighteen years her senior accustomed to the company of mistresses.

Later in November, Frederick's son, Henry, married Margaret, the daughter of Leopold VI of Austria, at Nuremberg. This too was a forced dynastic union; Henry was fourteen and Margaret was twenty-one.

Queenhood

Almost immediately, Frederick was styling himself King of Jerusalem.[637] This reflected the status he claimed by *jure uxoris*. If John, his father-in-law, found this offensive, there was nothing he could do about it.

In January 1226, while traveling with Frederick in Apulia, Yolanda issued a decree confirming privileges to the Teutonic Order.[638] By February, the royal couple was at their palace in Salerno.[639] This sojourn was rather exceptional, as Yolanda did not travel much with her husband around the kingdom and the imperial lands. In March, Frederick left Yolanda at Salerno. While he trekked northward to the imperial cities of Italy, she sailed to Sicily.

Though her husband did not make a serious attempt to expose Yolanda to public life, he remained as visible as ever, holding an imperial diet at Cremona in the spring of 1226.

Yolanda may have given birth to a daughter late that year, probably in Palermo. If so, the girl apparently did not live into adulthood.

By now, the differences between Frederick and his father-in-law were clearly apparent.[640] This must have had an effect on Yolanda.

Frederick was back in Apulia in November 1226, and crossed over to Sicily in January of the following year.[641] Yolanda probably met him at Messina.[642]

The queen's chief responsibility was to bear children, hopefully males, and before long she was again pregnant. Much to the pope's annoyance, and perhaps even Yolanda's, the crusade to Jerusalem was endlessly delayed.

By the late spring of 1227, Frederick was with his wife in Apulia, where he was overseeing construction of a fleet to sail to Palestine. In the middle of August he was with Yolanda at Otranto, where he left her to go to Brindisi, where his crusader army was gathering.[643]

On the thirtieth of April 1228, Yolanda died at Andria after having given birth to a boy christened Conrad.[644] She was entombed in that city's cathedral. Her funeral was attended by many magnates of the kingdom present for a meeting with Frederick at Barletta.

It seems unlikely that Yolanda ever had any great passion for the king she wed or the kingdom he ruled.

The tales told of Yolanda's life hardly inspire envy for the girl nearly poisoned to death by a hateful stepmother, or the young woman betrayed by an unfaithful husband on her wedding night.

Yolanda's son, Conrad, was raised at court and survived into adulthood, destined for kingship.

Postlude

Following a few false starts, the Sixth Crusade began. By

September of 1228 Frederick was in Acre, the birthplace of the woman who gave him the crown of Jerusalem.[645]

Frederick's army consisted almost exclusively of knights from his own dominions. In the Holy Land he achieved a ten-year truce with the Ayyubids without fighting a war. One of the conditions of the agreement was to make Jerusalem into what was, in effect, an open city. Frederick had himself crowned there in February 1229.

In June, Frederick returned to Italy to find his father-in-law ravaging his lands in southern Italy with papal approval.[646] It didn't take long for Frederick to take back these territories and expel John.

John finally got a crown of his own when he became the Latin emperor of Constantinople, where a Catholic monarchy had been established following the disgraceful Fourth Crusade.

In 1231, with his eldest son acting as his surrogate in Germany, Frederick issued a new legal code, the Constitutions of Melfi, for the Kingdom of Sicily. Although it did not bring about certain important rights (like trial by jury) established by England's Magna Carta, Frederick's statutes reiterated the fundamental principles encapsulated in his grandfather's Assizes of Ariano, such as the criminalization of certain forms of rape. After Frederick's time the laws formulated at Melfi gradually, decade by decade, fell into disuse; rape did not again become a felony in Italy until the twentieth century. The right to a speedy trial was likewise discarded in Italy over successive centuries, as law and bureaucracy became ever more complex, contradictory and inefficient.[647]

Frederick did not immediately remarry, but his relationship with a Piedmontese noblewoman named Bianca Lancia brought him a son and a daughter. Manfred, born of this union around 1232, may have been his favorite son.

Frederick remained a widower until 1235.

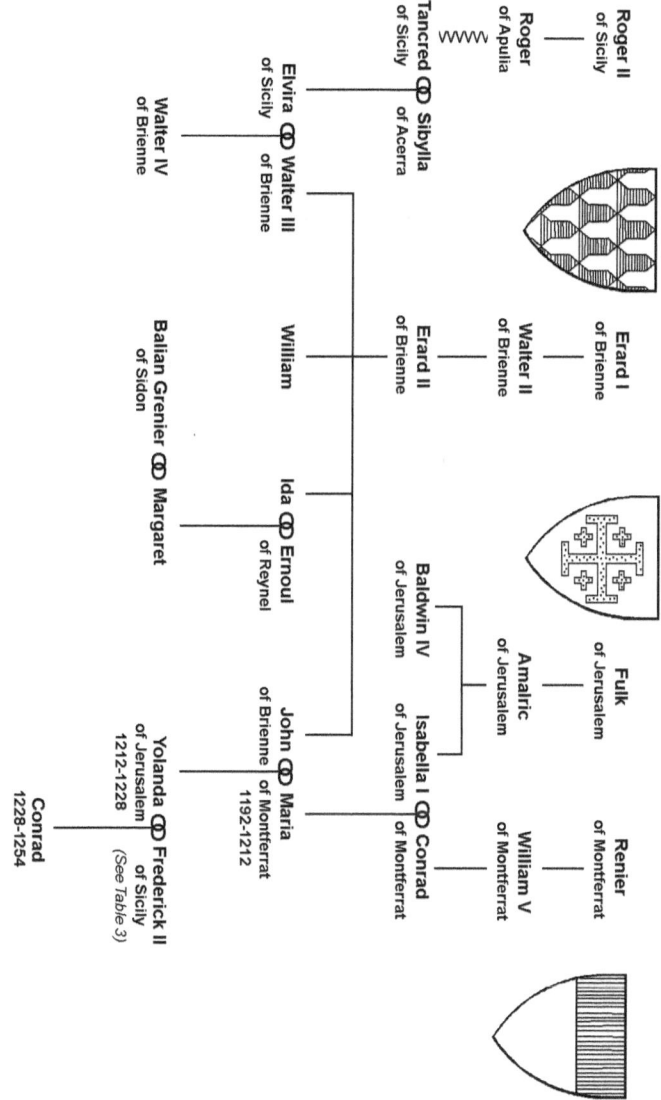

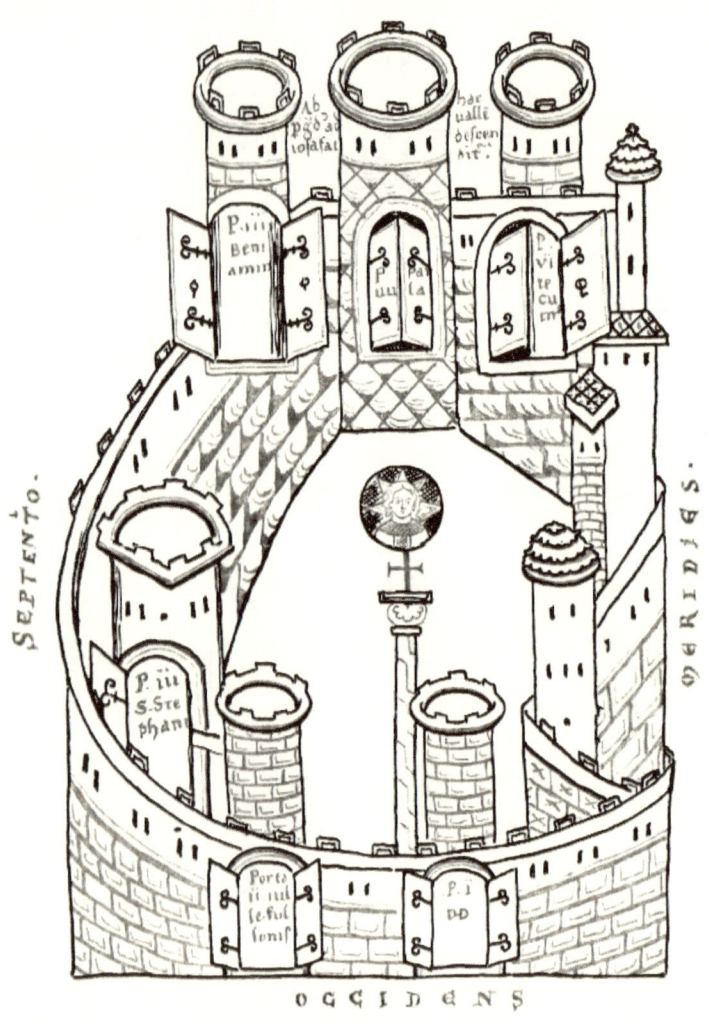

Yolanda's Inheritance: Jerusalem drawn around 660 by Arculf, a monk from what is now France

Chapter 15
ISABELLA OF ENGLAND

Isabella of England was born at Gloucester late in 1214 to King John "Lackland" of England and his second wife, the beautiful Isabella of Angoulême, as the fourth of five children. Her father's sister was Joanna, who became Queen of Sicily as the wife of William II. The given name shared with her mother was usually recorded in contemporary Latin records as *Ysabella* rather than Elisabeth.[648]

By most contemporary accounts, John and his wife both had volatile tempers, and what little is known of the marriage of Isabella's parents suggests that it was often stormy. In the year Isabella was born, John confined her mother, under guard, to house arrest for flirting with a servant. The queen was kept in the bedchamber of Isabella's elder sister; the man accused of this impropriety was summarily judged and brutally tortured.[649]

Fortunately, Isabella and her siblings were too young to understand much of what they may have witnessed of these conflicts.

Childhood

Isabella never truly knew her father, who died in 1216 at

the age of forty-nine. Apart from his untimely death, it is not surprising that John had little time for his children. The last years of his reign were an era of civil strife and economic decline. He had lost control of prosperous Normandy, Anjou and Poitou as a result of the disastrous Anglo-French War, the same conflict that deprived his ally Otto of Brunswick, onetime rival of Frederick II, of his imperial power. It was this defeat that prompted the English baronage to rebel against their king and demand the rights outlined in the Magna Carta, John's greatest contribution to posterity.[650]

Isabella was the second of three daughters born to her parents. After John's death, her elder brother became king as Henry III, with valiant William Marshal as regent and protector of the realm. Not long afterward, when Isabella was six years old, her mother crossed the channel to oversee her ancestral lands in Angoulême and married Hugh X of Lusignan.[651] Learning of this, the king's council threatened to confiscate the widowed queen's dower lands.

It would be reasonable to argue that the first duty of Isabella of Angoulême, as queen mother, was to raise her five children by John and perhaps lend a hand to stabilize the English realm in a difficult time. In France, the dowager Queen of England was to give birth to nine children by her second husband.

These unforeseen circumstances left young Isabella separated from her mother, to be raised in England.[652]

Over the next few years, she and her siblings resided in a succession of castles in the south of the country. They celebrated Christmas at Winchester in 1219.[653] By then, Isabella already had her own little retinue, including her nurse (nanny), Margaret of Biset, a noblewoman who seems to have taken a maternal interest in the young princess, and a bodyguard.[654]

After William Marshal, who famously defended young King Henry from a French incursion into England, died in 1219, his duties as regent were assumed by Hubert de Burgh, with the assistance of Stephen Langton, Archbishop of Canterbury. Isabella was present for her brother's coronation at Westminster in 1220.

Her elder sister, Joan, who had returned from France, was soon married to Scotland's monarch, while her younger sister, Eleanor, was betrothed to a son of William Marshal.

A clause in Joan's betrothal to Alexander II, King of Scots, offered him the hand of Isabella should Joan not become available, but in the event there was never any reason for it to be effected.[655]

Damsel

Before long, Isabella was the only one of the three daughters of the late King John still at the English court, and efforts were afoot to find a suitable husband for her. In 1225, a marriage was considered for her to the son of Frederick II.[656] This was Henry, who had already been crowned King of Sicily and King of the Germans. The proposed marriage did not come to pass, and Henry was wed to Margaret of Austria later that year.

Henry III of England came of age in 1227.

In 1229, following further effort to find her a suitable husband, Isabella, still a maiden, went to live at Marlborough. By November 1231 she was at Gloucester, where she stayed for a few months. (Over the next few years she occasionally moved between these castles.) She lived with several friends, effectively ladies-in-waiting, such as a certain Katherine, who left Isabella's "court" to marry. The Close Rolls record that the royal tailor purchased a fur cape for Isabella at a fair in Saint Edmondsbury at the king's command. For Christmas that year, Henry gave his sister three silver plates and salt dishes. Throughout the year, he would frequently send her venison and wine.[657]

By summer 1232 the pretty princess was again living at Marlborough, where she had her own household and chaplain and rights to total revenue of the locality's lands. In 1234 she took up residence in the Tower of London whilst her brother lived at the Palace of Westminster two miles away. Here again she had her own household and a small court, and Henry ensured that she was supplied with fine wine and other necessities.

Although these accommodations were more than spacious, much of the Tower seen today was erected or rebuilt after Isabella left. Her brother became known for his ambitious building projects in the Gothic style, exemplified by the expansion of Westminster Abbey.

With Isabella were her former nanny Margaret of Biset, now a faithful confidant, her ushers (and perhaps bodyguards) Alfred Aloet and Roger Pilet, and a cook named Jordan. There was also a chaplain. Present were at least two ladies-in-waiting, each a few years older than Isabella, and the guards stationed at the castle. There were servants such as maids and grooms and a small cooking staff for Jordan. In all, Isabella's household consisted of at least a dozen attendants. Here in London a few, such as the tailor, may have been shared with her brother, who was continuously sending her gifts, such as almonds (then a rarity in England).[658]

The fact of Isabella, from the age of sixteen or seventeen, living independently with her own little royal court lends itself to perplexity. Failure to explain it has led one or two historians to speculate that she was somehow imprisoned; that theory does not bear scrutiny. Nonetheless, Isabella's independent lifestyle was indeed something of an anomaly for its time, especially for a single woman and even for a princess. Regardless of social rank, few women of such tender years were privileged by freedom of this kind.

Henry's feud with France left little time to search for a suitable husband for his sister amongst the fellow monarchs who were friendly to him. He had not even found himself a wife, although his courtiers had a candidate in mind.

Henry's forthcoming marriage to Eleanor of Provence reflected an attempt at support from southern France, where Gascony and other lands were under threat from the French crown. This was a useful alliance. In a parallel development, Eleanor's sister, Margaret, had just wed Louis IX of France, with whom Henry was negotiating a tenuous peace. That the two kings, who were cousins, would now become brothers-in-law might aid this effort at detente.

In early 1235 a credible opportunity presented itself for Isabella's betrothal, and in the spirit of the times its scope was typically geopolitical. It was decided to use Isabella to seal a friendship with an ally who ruled the empire to the east of France.

Marriage

Frederick II was still a widower. His mistress, Bianca, had recently given birth to a boy and a girl, but what he really needed were a few more legitimate sons. That, of course, required marriage. Frederick enjoyed a good diplomatic rapport with the kings of both England and France even if, for the moment, he was contested in Germany by his own son, Henry.

It seems to have been Frederick, with papal approval, who initiated the marriage proposal. This marriage uniting dynasties on both sides of his kingdom so frightened Louis IX that Pope Gregory IX (Ugolino di Segni) had to write him as if in reassurance that it posed no menace. Nevertheless, the King of France had good reason to fear this formidable alliance capable of attacking, and defeating, him on opposite fronts.[659]

Whatever the outcome of Frederick's efforts at peace, be it with his heir apparent or fellow sovereigns, a closer relationship with a dynasty of northwestern Europe could not be a bad thing. Most of the details of the marriage agreement were worked out by Frederick's chancellor, Peter della Vigna, who visited England to meet the princess before committing his lord to the match.[660] In a visit redolent of the sojourn of the Sicilian ambassadors meeting with Henry II to see Isabella's aunt, Joanna, during the previous century, Peter and his suite were received in February 1135 at Westminster by the king.

Isabella's brother then took three days to consult with his counsellors before approving of the proposed betrothal. With this achieved, he summoned Isabella to come to court. The visitors immediately approved of her. They presented her an engagement ring from Frederick, and details of the dowry of thirty thousand marks were agreed upon with Henry. To generate this sum, Isabella's brother would have to levy a tax on hides. The Irish were also taxed. A third of the total amount was remitted immediately from the exchequer. This money would be spent on the efforts of Henry's new brother-in-law to rein in the imperial communes of northern Italy. As Queen of Sicily, Isabella's dower would include Mount Saint Angelo and the estates near it.[661]

Planning the wedding entailed endless details. A few of Isabella's ladies-in-waiting and attendants would go with her to Germany, but they would not stay with her, instead returning to England. Her faithful nurse and confidant, Margaret of Biset, was provided a pension, along with the attendants Alfred Aloet and Roger Pilet, and the cook, Jordan.[662]

An appropriate trousseau was assembled.[663] This included a jeweled crown but also a wealth of cloth and furs, with a few tailored items. There were fourteen long dresses, several of silk, and a few capes. There were two beds with blankets and linen. Henry did not overlook his brother-in-law, to whom he sent six regal robes. Frederick, in turn, sent Henry some fine horses. The company of twenty attendants, plus the servants, traveling with Isabella also received splendid robes.[664]

In early May a grand farewell feast was held for Isabella at Westminster. In late June, she departed England for Germany on ten galleys. The detailed description by Roger of Wendover is an exercise in eloquence.[665]

"In the month of February of 1135 two Templars, with some enfeoffed knights and other special ambassadors, came to the king at Westminster, charged with letters, sealed with gold, from the emperor Frederick, soliciting the hand of the English king's sister, Isabella, in matrimony. They reached the king on the twenty-third of February, and begged for an answer to the letters and the request, that they might announce the king's decision to their lord with all haste. The king then held a careful deliberation with the bishops and nobles of his kingdom for three days, when they all, after duly considering the matter, unanimously agreed that the lady should be given in marriage to the emperor, and on the twenty-seventh of February the king gave his answer agreeing to the requested alliance. The emissaries then asked permission to see the lady, and the king sent some trustworthy messengers to fetch his sister from the Tower of London where she was carefully guarded. The messengers conducted her with all honour to the king at Westminster where she appeared before the emissaries of the emperor. She was a lady in her twentieth year, beautiful to look upon, adorned with virgin modesty, and distinguished by her royal dress and manners.

"After they had refreshed their sight for some time with gazing on the lady, they decided that she was most worthy in all respects of the imperial couch, and confirmed the marriage on the soul of the emperor by oath, presenting her with a wedding ring in his name. After they had placed it on her finger they proclaimed her Empress of Rome, all exclaiming, 'Long live our empress!' They then sent messengers with all haste to inform the emperor of what they had done. Immediately after Easter, Frederick sent the Archbishop of

Cologne and the Duke of Louvaine with a large array of nobles into England to bring the empress to him with due honour, and to complete the marriage ceremony, in order that it might be consummated.

"There was such a profusion of ornaments at this marriage that they appeared to surpass kingly wealth. For the empress herself a crown had been most elaborately constructed out of pure gold adorned with jewels, and on it were carved likenesses of the four martyr and confessor kings of England, to whom the King Henry had especially assigned the care of his sister's soul. She shone forth with such a profusion of rings and gold necklaces, and other splendid jewels, with silk and thread garments, and other like ornaments, which usually attract the gaze and excite the desires of women even to covetousness, that they appeared invaluable.

"With bridal garments of silk, wool, and linen, she was so well supplied that it was difficult to say which would be most likely to attract the emperor's affections. Her bed was so rich in its coverlets and pillows of various colours, and the various furniture and sheets made of pure fine linen, that by its softness it would invite those lying in it to a delightful slumber. All the drinking cups and dishes were of the purest gold and silver. What seemed superfluous to everyone, all the cooking pots, large and small, were of pure silver. And to take the management and care of all these, some of the attendants of the court were assigned to wait on the empress and her family in kingly custom.

"After being supplied with these and many other gifts by her brother and receiving a dowry from him, the lady Isabella remained under the care of the Bishop of Exeter, and Ralph Fitz Nicholas, the king's seneschal, and other noblemen of his household, and attended by noble dames and damsels, who, being all skilled in courtly manners, would suffice to wait on and escort the empress.

"After he had thus arranged matters the king, on Saint John's day, held a solemn festival before the Latin gate at Westminster in company with the Archbishop of Cologne and the emperor's other ambassadors. On the day following they all took the road towards the borough of Dartford accompanied by the king with a harp train of earls and barons. The king had also procured for the lady, in honour of her as empress, a number of horses remarkable for their various colours and of gentle paces, which bore their riders with a delightful gentleness, without annoying them by the motion of their feet; the trappings and saddles too, gilt and carved, were of such a variety, and the bridles and reins so elaborately worked in gold, that they set off the rider as well as the horse.

"They proceeded through the city of Rochester and arrived at the abbey of Feversham, and starting from thence they went to Canterbury to perform their devotions to the archbishop and martyr, Thomas Becket. After fulfilling their religious duties, they proceeded to the port of Sandwich to the number of about three thousand knights. From that port the empress and the Archbishop of Cologne, with the noblemen and ladies appointed as her suite, embarked on the eleventh of May, and put to sea under full sail. It was not, however, without weeping that the brother and sister, the king and empress, parted."

Frederick, meanwhile, was making his way across his Holy Roman Empire, where he was suppressing revolts stirred up by his son, to Worms, where the rebellious heir submitted himself to paternal judgment.

Isabella and her large company were received at Antwerp with great enthusiasm. Here again we have a grandiose description by Roger of Wendover.

"After a voyage of three days and nights they entered the mouth of the river Rhine, and after a run of a day and night up that river, they arrived at Antwerp, a city under the imperial jurisdiction. On their landing at this place they were met by an immense army of armed nobles, who had been sent by the emperor to act as a guard to the empress, to keep vigilant watch round her person day and night, for it was reported that some of the emperor's enemies, who were in alliance with the French king, were planning to carry off the empress, and prevent the wedding.

"The royal company was also met by all the priests and clergy of the adjacent districts in solemn procession, ringing bells and singing songs of joy, and with them came all the best masters in every sort of music with their instruments, who accompanied the empress with all kinds of nuptial rejoicings during her journey of five days to Cologne."

Once she reached Cologne, where the crowds were ecstatic to see her, Isabella and her large entourage waited for Frederick's son to be tried at Worms before riding southward to that city.[666] Roger of Wendover described this with unabashed perspicuity.

"When Isabella's approach became known at Cologne there went out to meet her, with flowers, palm branches, and in festive dresses, some ten thousand of the citizens. A few mounted Arabian steeds, and put them to full speed and engaged in jousting with one another. Accompanied by these rejoicing crowds the empress proceeded through the principal streets of the city, which had been decorated in every manner for her arrival. On learning that everyone, and especially the noble ladies of the city, who stood in the balconies, were desirous of seeing her face, she took her scarf from her head for all to get a glimpse of her, for doing which every one praised her, and after they had gazed at her gave her great commendations for her beauty as well as her humility. She then took up her abode outside the walls of the city on account of the noise therein, and there awaited the emperor's instructions."

Weeks were to pass, for it was at Worms that Frederick would wed his third wife. In the event, an observer might be forgiven for being unable to decide which spectacle was more impressive, the younger Hohenstaufen lying prostrate as a supplicant before the elder one, or the grandest royal wedding seen in these parts for decades.

Finally, "the Archbishop of Cologne and the Bishop of Exeter, with the other nobles of her suite then set out on their way to the emperor, and, after a journey of seven days brought the empress to him amidst all kind of nuptial pomp and rejoicing.

"She was received on her arrival with joy and respect by the emperor, who was beyond measure delighted with her beauty, and the marriage was solemnized at that place on Sunday the twentieth of July, and although her beauty pleased the emperor at first sight he was much more pleased after marriage. After the nuptial festivities had continued for four successive days, the Bishop of Exeter and the rest who had attended the empress thither, obtained leave from the emperor and returned joyfully to England, taking with them as presents from him to the English king, three lions with other costly presents which were scarce in the countries of the west. The emperor also promised to assist King Henry against the King of the French."[667]

Roger of Wendover, who died not long after the events he described, was not the only one to leave us an account of the magnificent wedding. Local German chroniclers, as eyewitnesses, also wrote about it.[668] These accounts are all essentially consistent with each other. The exception is Matthew Paris; it is difficult to know what to make of his claim that, heeding the advice of the court astrologers, Frederick abstained from joining Isabella in bed on their wedding night.

There is no doubt that the people of Worms talked about the events in their city in the summer of 1235 for years to come, but Isabella's wedding was meant to be more than a solemn ceremony followed by a few days of celebration. It was a bold display of power and wealth by two of Europe's most important sovereigns. In particular, it was a not-so-subtle reminder of the strength of the empire ruled by Frederick Hohenstaufen, an intellectual leader sometimes loved but perhaps more often loathed. Louis IX of France, who felt threatened by this power, was destined for sainthood, Frederick for repeated excommunication. The former saw crusading and piety as ends in themselves, whilst the latter viewed such things as means to an end. Historians might read much into this, going so far as to speculate about idealism versus pragmatism, but in 1235 it was difficult to argue with a man who had just had his own son and heir dragged off to jail in chains for opposing policies that some viewed as repressive, even draconian. Whatever Frederick's opponents thought of him, they grudgingly respected him, especially now that he was at the apogee of his power.

After the feast the newlyweds went to Mainz. By December they were at Haguenau.[669] As Holy Roman Empress, Queen of Sicily and Queen of the Germans, Isabella of England was now much more than a Plantagenet princess, but her first duty was to produce children.

Frederick maintained a continuous correspondence with his brother-in-law. The subject of these letters ranged from the emperor's excommunication to Henry's chronic conflicts with the French king, among other matters.[670] We cannot know how much of this, if anything, Frederick discussed with his wife.

Frederick left Isabella in Germany while he crossed the Alps to subdue some Lombard towns. He probably sent her to stay for a few months at Trifels, the imperial fortress in the Palatine Forest, where Isabella gave birth to a daughter, Margaret, late in 1236 or early the next year.[671] The empress was in Italy by August 1237.

Around this time, Isabella received a letter from her

brother. The previous year, safe conduct had been granted to one of Frederick's clerks, accompanied by a messenger, for travel in England and Ireland. This messenger or another was charged with the mission of conveying a personal letter from Isabella to Henry. The response, probably taken to the continent by the same messenger, is Henry's only known letter to his sister. It belies little of the sincere affection that existed between the siblings. Not much can be inferred from this, but it is just possible that Isabella had expressed to her brother a certain disillusionment with her marriage.[672]

At Ravenna in February 1238 she gave birth to a boy. Christened Henry, he was named for Frederick's father or Isabella's grandfather.[673] Nobody seemed bothered by the fact that Frederick's elder son of the same name was rotting away in prison, all but forgotten. The same year, Enzio, who seems to have been Frederick's oldest surviving illegitimate son, was wed in Sardinia.

Isabella resided at Andria, in Apulia, from September 1238 until December of that year, when she went to Palermo. In February and March of 1239 she stayed at Noventa while Frederick was at Padova. By February 1240 she was at Castel dell'Ovo, the imposing coastal fortress of Naples. The next year she was again with her husband visiting, if not besieging, the imperial communes bordering the papal lands.

A Kept Woman?

In motherhood, Isabella appeared in public rather rarely, and no record survives of her attending any formal ceremonies. As we have seen, she was often separated from her husband while he trekked around northern Italy to keep the imperial communes in check. The Italians were not the only ones on his mind; in 1241 a Mongol army attempted to invade the eastern reaches of the Holy Roman Empire.

An incident that occurred during the same year has given rise to speculation, which has become something of a trope, that Isabella was kept in seclusion. It is a supposition that may bear a morsel of truth.

Though Frederick was still King of Jerusalem, the city did not long stay in Christian hands following the end of the ten-year truce he had made with the Ayyubids. The Barons' Crusade led by, amongst others, Isabella's brother Richard of Cornwall, reclaimed the holy city, leading to its control by Franks for the next few years. Returning from the crusade during the summer of 1241, Richard stopped in Sicily, where he landed at Trapani, hoping to find Frederick and Isabella at Palermo. Informed that they were still in northern Italy, he continued northward.

Richard reached his brother-in-law, in whose name he had claimed Jerusalem, at Faenza.[674] It seems that Frederick initially brushed aside Richard's wish to visit Isabella, who was in the first trimester of pregnancy and perhaps unwell. Finally, after a few days of waiting, he made a formal request, to which Frederick acceded. The esteemed Earl of Cornwall was then accompanied to meet his sister, the Queen of Sicily and Holy Roman Empress. Not much can be gleaned from this episode, and accounts of it vary.[675]

In correspondence with Frederick, Isabella's other brother, King Henry III, expressed dismay that she did not participate in public ceremonies and was not often seen wearing a crown. In his many letters, the chancellor Peter della Vigna, who was often present at court and had negotiated Isabella's marriage, scarcely mentions her.[676]

A concise but curious entry by Matthew Paris for the year 1240 mentioning "the rising hopes of Isabella" seems to refer to a recent improvement in her relationship with her husband.[677] This, of course, implies that there was improvement to be made, and that Isabella's situation was known beyond the court. Matthew's source is not identified, but being farther from imperial circles than Peter della Vigna afforded him the privilege of candor without fear of reprisal.

Did Frederick wish to keep his third wife isolated from public life? What little evidence is available suggests that he did. Even were that the case, Isabella's existence was hardly tantamount to imprisonment.

The true measure of Frederick's personality must be based not only on his exceptional intellect and astute statecraft but on his apparently overzealous reactions to offense. Frederick's harsh, lengthy imprisonment of his eldest son indicates a degree of intolerance, and perhaps even an emotional need to control his social environment. It seems slightly excessive even for an absolute monarch ruling during the thirteenth century. Such a mentality may well have extended to his marriage with Isabella.

There was clearly a difference between Frederick's relationship with his first wife, Constance, who was older than him and served as his *de facto* regent for Sicily, and his other wives, Yolanda and Isabella, younger women less experienced in affairs of state. This, of course, was the norm, for medieval princesses were rarely trained in how to run a kingdom.

Ever in need of legitimate sons, Frederick seems to have desired that Isabella focus on bearing and raising children. Despite her frequent separation in distance from her husband, she was pregnant almost every year of her marriage.

Peace

Isabella died at Foggia on the first of December in 1241 giving birth to a child who did not survive.[678] She was entombed at Andria in the same church as Yolanda of Jerusalem.

Her dying wish was that her husband and her brother should remain friends.[679] That they did.

Following Frederick's death, Isabella's son, Henry, was governor of Sicily during the reign of his elder half-brother, Conrad. He died in 1254. Her daughter, Margaret, wed Albert II, Margrave of Meissen. She bore five children before her death in 1270.

ISABELLA OF ENGLAND

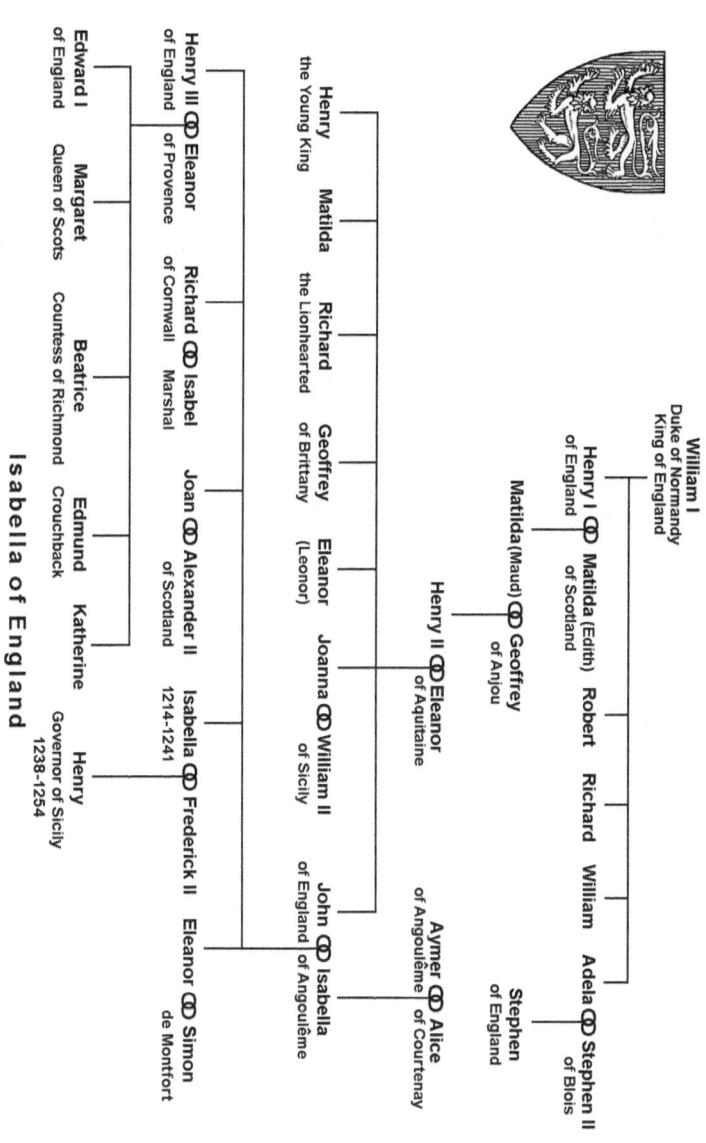

Isabella of England

Saint John's Chapel in the Tower of London

Chapter 16
BIANCA LANCIA

Bianca Lancia of Agliano was born around 1210 into a noble Piedmontese family thought to have shared the Aleramic lineage of Adelaide del Vasto. Her paternity is much debated, but her father was probably Boniface of Agliano. Her surname, literally *lance,* derives from the nickname given to Manfred of Busca, Bianca's putative grandfather, a lance-bearer of Frederick Barbarossa. Bianca's mother may have been Bianca Maletta, a noblewoman.

Bianca met Frederick II about 1225 during his travels around Italy. Although her family was Piedmontese, and Bianca may have been born at Agliano, the town of Arce, near Frosinone, has also been suggested as her birthplace because it seems she spent part of her childhood there. She had several siblings.

After the death of Frederick's second wife, Yolanda of Jerusalem, Bianca gave birth to three of the monarch's children, namely Constance, Manfred and Yolanda. Frederick did not immediately marry Bianca because a politically opportune union was preferred over marriage to the daughter of a noble but less important family.

Frederick's relationship with Bianca lasted for a number of years, throughout his marriage to Isabella of England. It may partly explain why he sought to isolate his third wife from public affairs. We do not know that Isabella ever learned of Bianca, but it is distinctly possible that she did.

Queen Bianca

She was more than an occasional mistress. Frederick seems to have truly loved her. Bianca was cared for, and as Frederick's mistress she may have resided occasionally in Apulia, if not Sicily. Her kinsmen were later granted fiefs on the island. Upon marriage, Bianca was given the traditional reginal dower of Mount Saint Angelo.

Although the chroniclers Bartholomew of Nicastro and Salimbene de Adam mention Bianca, two sources nearer to her in time offer the earliest known information about her marriage to Frederick. Matthew Paris states that she wed Frederick shortly before her death *circa* 1247.[680] Though the Englishman was sometimes given to bias, even hyperbole, his statement here seems accurate. There are also references to Bianca's family in a chronicle about her son, Manfred, completed a few years after Matthew's entry by a person connected to the royal court.[681]

That her son's marriage in 1247 refers to him simply as "Manfred Lancia," with no indication of his illustrious paternity, suggests that Bianca and Frederick were not married until the following year. However, Manfred was soon recognized officially as Frederick's son and inherited Bianca's dower lands in 1250.

There is a dearth of royal charters issued by Frederick that refer to Bianca even implicitly, and she has become the subject of highly conjectural, esoteric scholarship.[682]

Bianca's status as queen brings us to a timely consideration of two topics, coronation and legitimacy, which, though taken for granted in the thirteenth century, are today occasionally the subject of scholarly debate. Whilst there were general European norms based on longstanding practice and law, in large measure these matters were framed by the usage of each kingdom, sometimes even varying somewhat by dynasty within the same realm over time, and either one could be the subject of a lengthy treatise.

Coronation

There is no evidence that Bianca was ever actually crowned. The most we can reasonably presume is that Frederick gave her a ring when he married her. Of course, she received a dower.

As we saw earlier, the queens of Sicily were anointed with holy oil or chrism at coronation. This was the norm in this kingdom, and it was the practice even in cases, such as that of Margaret, of a woman crowned before her husband's succession; William I was crowned *rex filius* after his marriage to Margaret, when she was crowned with him. With good reason, Sicilian chroniclers frequently use the terms "anointed" and "crowned" interchangeably, often preferring the Latin verb *ungere* (anoint) when writing about these rites. We have a surviving record of a Sicilian reginal coronation *ordo* of this period (see Appendix 6).

With the sole exception of Constance Hauteville, who was the nearest thing the *Regnum Siciliae* had to a queen regnant during its Norman-Swabian era, coronation confirmed the status of queen consort, which depended from marriage.

That is to say, it is true enough that the king's wife became queen *ipso facto* based on her marriage to him, but coronation was the solemn, quasi-sacramental religious rite that confirmed it, usually in a very public way, in the eyes of the church. With the exception of Bianca, Frederick's wives were crowned at marriage.

Royal prescription (by William II) having the force of law, bolstered by the simple physical fact that legitimate male heirs were absent, made Constance, King Roger's daughter, as the eldest surviving blood kin in the male (Hauteville) line, the *de jure* Queen of Sicily upon her nephew's death even though she was not yet crowned and did not immediately rule her kingdom. It was ecclesiastical and baronial assent that made Tancred of Lecce the *de facto,* though perhaps not *de jure,* King of Sicily. The Kingdom of Sicily is not the only place to have experienced civil war as the result of conflict between these two principles. From Tancred's case arises still another concept.

Legitimacy

The papacy eventually found Bianca's marriage to be sacramentally valid but did not sanction it as canonical for the purpose of dynastic succession. Leaving aside the theological complexities intrinsic in that position, the question of legitimacy was not out of place.

In Europe nowadays the terms mean little outside regnant royal families and arcane fields such as heraldry, but in the Middle Ages an obvious distinction was made between "legitimate" children and "natural" ones, the latter ("bastards") being those born outside marriage. A further distinction within bastardy was sometimes drawn between the "adulterine bastard," a child of parents who (being wed to other people) were not free to marry at the time of the child's birth, and a simple bastard.

The state of bastardy bore with it a certain social stigma, but this was alleviated considerably when the bastard's father was a king who recognized the child as his own. Such "recognition," however, did not necessarily constitute legitimization *per se* or bestow a place in the line of royal succession.

A monarch could legitimize a child born to a knight or baron outside the sanctity of matrimony, but on canonical grounds a pope might refuse to confirm the decision of a king to legitimize his own progeny born of an adulterous union. Normally, an adulterine bastard was not legitimized by his parents' subsequent marriage.

Although close consanguinity constituted canonical grounds for nullifying an otherwise valid marriage, in most cases the children already born of such a union were not thereby considered illegitimate.

Legacy

In view of these tenets and others, a strong case can be made that Bianca's marriage to Frederick, despite its unusual circumstances, made her his queen consort. A further case, *arguendo*, could be made that her children were thereby legitimized, in the popular mind if not the papal one. This is relevant because, as we shall see, one of those children eventually became King of Sicily.

By the time Frederick wed the dying Bianca, Henry, his eldest, long-imprisoned son born of Constance of Aragon (not to be confused with the boy of the same name born to Isabella of England), was deceased. This left Conrad, the son of Frederick's second wife, Yolanda of Jerusalem, as the heir apparent.

It was Conrad who immediately succeeded as King of Sicily and King of the Germans upon Frederick's death of natural causes in Apulia in 1250. Filling his father's shoes would not be easy; it might not even be possible.

Matthew Paris famously described Frederick as *stupor mundi*, "the wonder of the world."[683] It was Frederick's astute rule that permitted the golden age of the Kingdom of Sicily to flourish beyond its formative Norman era and into the thirteenth century. As an avid patron of the arts, letters and sciences, he was the most intellectual European ruler of his time. Dedicated to Bianca's son, Manfred, who features in its pages, Frederick's treatise on falconry is unique as a major scientific work authored by a medieval European monarch.

Important though it was, Frederick's code of laws, the Constitutions of Melfi, was not destined to shape the legal landscape so significantly as the Magna Carta. Whilst the former reflected an autocrat's initiative the latter was the expression of rights demanded by, and granted to, an angry baronage, a caste modern commentators have seen fit to identify with "the people." Over time, John's law was reiterated by his successors, its principles later propagated as far away as Australia and America. Within a few generations of his death, Frederick's law was all but forgotten.

In spite of his political differences with the papacy, Frederick was its defender, yet Islam, Judaism, and the vanishing vestiges of Eastern Christianity enjoyed protection during his reign. Truer to science than religion, the man himself was not zealously pious. Here was a true intellectual. The term "freethinker" might well have suited him.

Great as his achievements were, Frederick's personality left much to be desired. Nonetheless, strength of will permitted him to grasp the reins of the dominions inherited from his ancestors, marshalling their peoples into a time of prosperity despite chronic papal meddling. In certain ways, the challenges Frederick faced, and usually overcame, were far more daunting than those thrust upon contemporaries like Henry III of England and Louis IX of France.

The Middle Ages were an epoch that saw the status of women defined largely, indeed predominantly, by men. In no environment was this patriarchy more obviously entrenched than the world of royalty and monarchy, where even the most enlightened king could be a repressive husband and cruel father.

Could they be resurrected and queried, Frederick's first and last wives, Constance and Bianca, might have much good to say about him. The words of his two middle spouses, Yolanda and Isabella, would probably be less edifying. The views of his many children would be eclectic indeed, though some barely knew him well enough to formulate any opinion at all.

Much that we could say about Frederick's character is necessarily based more on context than hard fact. However prone he might be to offend somebody's sensibilities, he rarely insulted anybody's intelligence. He seems to have been the kind of man who did not suffer fools gladly.

Frederick's rule epitomized the eternal adage that it was acceptable for adversaries to despise a man so long as they feared him.

QUEENS OF SICILY

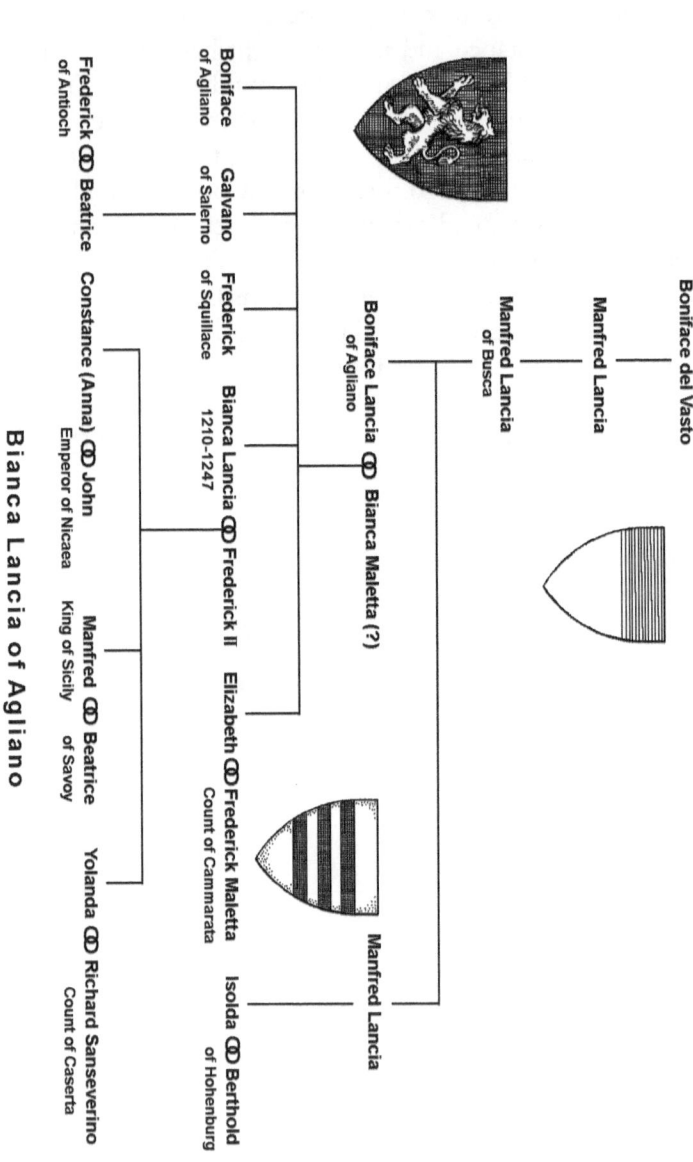

Bianca Lancia of Agliano

Chapter 17
ELISABETH OF BAVARIA

Elisabeth Wittelsbach of Bavaria was born at Trausnitz Castle in Landshut around 1227 to Otto II "the Illustrious," Duke of Bavaria, and his wife Agnes of the Palatinate. The Wittelsbachs had ruled Alpine lands since the early years of the tenth century, emerging as one of the most important dynasties of what is now Germany. True to her father's nickname, most of Elisabeth's recent ancestors were as illustrious as her earlier forebears.

Otto II was the son of Ludwig (Louis) I "Kelheimer" Wittelsbach of Bavaria and Ludmilla of Bohemia. Agnes, his consort, was born into Germany's powerful House of Welf, sometime contenders for the imperial crown, her father being Henry V "the Elder" of Brunswick. The mother of Agnes, her namesake Agnes of Hohenstaufen, was a daughter of Conrad of the Rhine, himself a son of Frederick "the One-Eyed" of Swabia and hence a half-brother of Frederick Barbarossa.

Wife

Elisabeth thus shared the Staufen lineage of the man she married.[684] By the time she wed Conrad, son of Frederick II and Yolanda, at Vohburg early in September 1246, Elisabeth had already been betrothed to Frederick of Austria.[685] That earlier betrothal was aborted in view of her father, Otto, supporting Frederick II, whom he had once opposed, since 1241.

Elisabeth's marriage to Conrad was, of course, a synergistic convenience, for it brought the Wittelsbachs into the most important family of Europe whilst providing the emperor a steadfast ally in a time and place of unsteady alliances.

By the time Elisabeth married him, Conrad had already been crowned King of the Germans and King of Italy. He had succeeded as *de jure* King of Jerusalem upon his mother's death (see Chapter 14). Conrad was initially raised in Italy; not until he was made Duke of Swabia, in 1235, did he set foot in what is now Germany. In that year, his fate as a European ruler was sealed by the deposition and imprisonment of his elder half-brother, Henry (Frederick's son by Constance of Aragon), once the heir apparent, who died in 1242.

Elisabeth's precise year of birth remains an object of speculation, but she was nearly twenty when she married Conrad, who may have been a few months her junior. Groomed to succeed his father, Conrad had already been given responsibilities in the administration of imperial lands in Germany and, to a noteworthy degree, northern Italy.

Although she often traveled with her young husband, Elisabeth also spent much time at Trifels, the imperial castle. As this was near Bavaria, the residence afforded her much contact with her family. Her father assumed the role of an informal confidant and advisor to Conrad.

If the early years of her marriage found Elisabeth living in her husband's shadow, that was about to change.

Queen

When Conrad succeeded his father, Frederick II, as King

of Sicily upon the death of the latter in 1250, Elisabeth became Queen of Sicily. As far as we know, she had not yet given birth to any children who survived infancy; she may have suffered miscarriages.

There is no secure knowledge to suggest that Elisabeth ever set foot in the Kingdom of Sicily. Considering her exalted status in Germany, through ancestry as well as marriage, she may not have viewed her Sicilian queenship as a very consequential status in itself. Nevertheless, she doubtless understood the significance of this realm to her husband's dynasty.[686]

To Conrad, the Sicilian crown was of paramount importance, and in 1151, after having put down a revolt in Germany, he departed for Italy to enforce his dynastic rights, which, as ever, were being challenged by a papacy bent on undermining the power of the Hohenstaufens. Papal hegemony in the *Regnum Siciliae* was being contested, with fair success, by Conrad's half-brothers Manfred, the son of Bianca Lancia (see the previous chapter), and the younger Henry, the son of Isabella of England (see Chapter 15).

In March 1252, Elisabeth gave birth to a boy, Conrad, known to history as Conradin, or "Conrad the Younger." Messengers were promptly dispatched to Apulia to notify her husband of the birth of an heir.

Sadly, Elisabeth's husband, the elder Conrad, died in Lucania (Basilicata) in May 1254, a victim not of arms but of malaria.[687] He was lawfully succeeded by young Conradin, who remained in Swabia with the widowed Elisabeth.

Elisabeth initially accepted her late husband's appointment of her countryman, Berthold of Hohenburg, as young Conradin's regent, Manfred having at first declined to accept this responsibility. It wasn't long, however, before Berthold renounced this onerous burden in favor of Manfred.[688]

Over the next few years, consequently, Manfred acted as the boy's regent in the *Regnum*. The death of young Henry Hohenstaufen, who was briefly governor of the island of Sicily, left Manfred leading the military campaign to defend the dynasty's interests; meanwhile, Enzio of Sardinia, one of the late Frederick's illegitimate children, was imprisoned in northern Italy. In 1255, Frederick of Antioch, another illegitimate son of Frederick II, died of illness in Apulia while supporting Manfred.[689]

Two years later, tireless papal intrigues led to Richard of Cornwall, the once-loyal brother-in-law of the late Frederick II, being elected King of the Germans, though it proved difficult for him to enforce his authority. This was part of a papal attempt to marginalize young Conradin. Another papal machination would lead to Richard's nephew, Edmund "Crouchback," being advanced as a claimant to the Sicilian throne if his father, Henry III of England, remitted enough money to Rome, an action vociferously contested by the English baronage.[690]

Despite their best efforts, there was little that Elisabeth or her natal family could do about any of this, with her beloved husband gone and her brother-in-law fighting to defend the dynasty's rights beyond the Alps in the Kingdom of Sicily. The late Conrad had not been crowned Holy Roman Emperor, and the diminishing hopes of restoring Hohenstaufen authority rested with the rights of an infant.

Sensing that he could better defend the *Regnum* in his own name than as the regent of a boy in Germany, and perhaps believing young Conradin to be dead, Manfred had himself crowned King of Sicily at Palermo in 1258.

Second Marriage

The following year, Elisabeth wed Meinhard of Gorizia, a man a decade younger than her who held lands in Tyrol. This union would further Wittelsbach influence, thereby shielding the family from the power of whichever dynasty eventually seized the imperial crown now that the Hohenstaufens seemed unlikely to continue as emperors.

Her young son, meanwhile, was placed in the care of the Bishop of Konstanz, though often residing at the court of Elisabeth's brother, Ludwig. If not precisely abandonment, this arrangement was by no means the ideal manifestation of maternal affection.

Elisabeth was to bear six surviving children by her second husband: Elisabeth, Otto, Albert, Ludwig, Henry, Agnes.

Her relationship with Conradin was not subsequently a very close one. She saw him only rarely over the next few years. In 1267, mother and son saw each other for the last time before the young man departed for Italy to reclaim the *Regnum* lost the previous year in the wake of the Battle of Benevento.[691]

In August 1268, Conradin's army was defeated at the Battle of Tagliacozzo, an event that spelled the end of the Hohenstaufen dynasty. The new King of Sicily was the victor, Charles of Anjou, the unsaintly younger brother of saintly Louis IX of France. Conradin, aged sixteen, was summarily executed in Naples.

Yet there was lingering sympathy for the last legitimate Hohenstaufen heir. It was later written that, "many were convinced that the local monks, whether out of devotion, or pity for his mother, or for the sake of prayers or money, secretly exhumed Conradin's remains and consigned these to his grieving mother."[692]

Heart-wrenching as the death of her eldest child must have been, Elisabeth viewed these developments from a distance. She assumed patronage of the Carmelite basilica of Saint Mary in Naples, where Conradin was entombed.[693] In Tyrol, she and her second husband established the Cistercian monastery at Stams, where Elisabeth was interred following her death in October 1273.

Elisabeth's time as Queen of Sicily was a brief one during a chaotic era. The same could be said of her modern Wittelsbach kinswoman, the last queen, who stepped into this role six centuries later (and who is profiled in Appendix 7).

Over the centuries, some have attributed Elisabeth's earnest patronage of the Stams abbey to her wish to commemorate Conradin. It is a fitting legacy.

ELISABETH OF BAVARIA

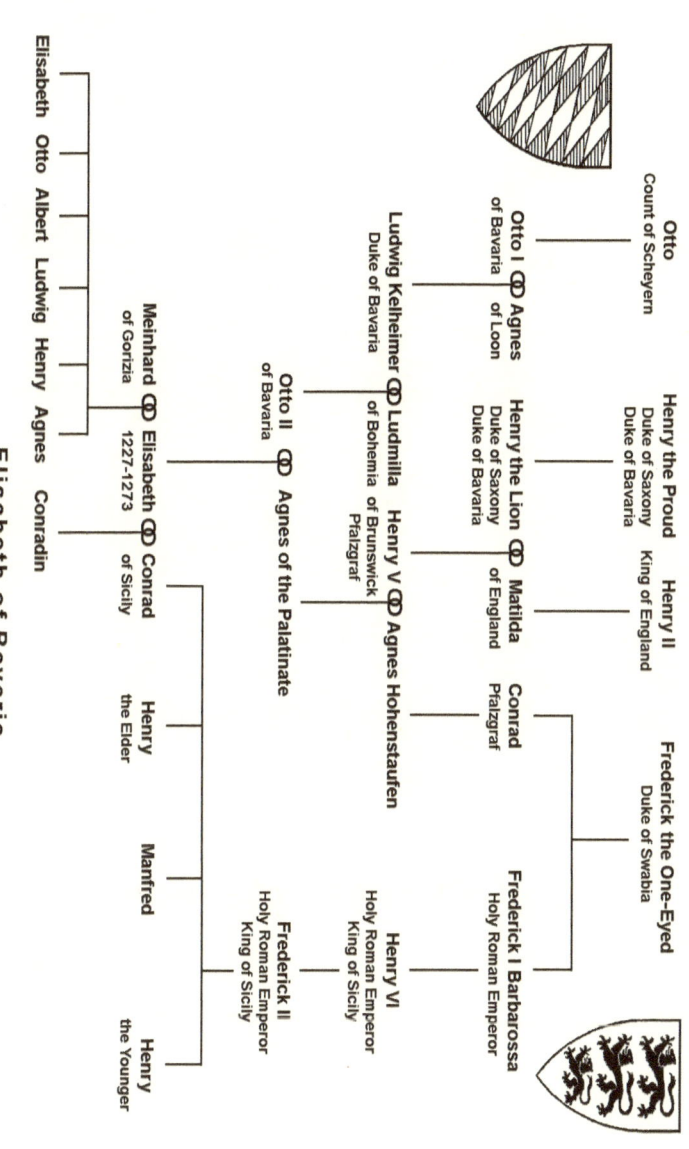

Elisabeth of Bavaria

Seal of Elisabeth of Bavaria

Chapter 18
BEATRICE OF SAVOY

Beatrice of Savoy was born around 1221 to Amedeo IV, Count of Savoy, and his first wife, Margaret (Anna) of Burgundy. The Savoy family, which can be identified as early as the eleventh century, ruled a region in the southeastern corner of what is now France, eventually establishing their capital at the fortified town of Chambery.

The Savoyard dominions did not extend to the sea but toward the mountains. The family's political influence derived from their control of strategic Alpine passes as vassals of the Holy Roman Emperor, and through opportune marriages they sought to extend their influence into areas bordering their native Savoy.

In keeping with this expansionist policy, Beatrice was betrothed, in 1223 while still very young, to Manfred III del Vasto, Marquis of Saluzzo, holder of several territories in the Piedmont region of Italy. Manfred, who was descended from the family that ruled Montferrat, shared the ancestry of Adelaide del Vasto, Bianca Lancia and Isabella of Jerusalem, whom we met in earlier chapters. He was at least fifteen years older than his bride.[694] In addition to a pretty, well-bred young wife, he received her dowry of a thousand silver marks. Beatrice's sister, Margaret, wed Manfred's cousin and feudal ally, Boniface II of Montferrat.

Wife

Beatrice's nuptials were celebrated around 1235, producing four children, namely Alice, Thomas (who succeeded his father as marquis), Margaret and Agnes. Agnes was born in 1245 a few months after Manfred's death the previous year.

With this, the widowed Beatrice was betrothed to another Manfred, the son of Frederick II and Bianca Lancia, in 1247. There was no urgency, as Manfred was only around fifteen; Beatrice was about ten years older and probably much wiser. The details were finalized the next year, and Beatrice then traveled southward to meet her young husband, leaving her children behind in Piedmont.[695]

This arrangement was not quite as harsh as it sounds to modern ears, since the children were placed in the care of Margaret, Beatrice's sister, whose husband, Boniface, assumed regency of the marquisate until young Thomas reached the age of majority.

Beatrice's wedding ceremony took place at Vercelli's splendid basilica late in 1248.

Beatrice was granted a "widow's pension" of a thousand marks. Manfred Hohenstaufen brought to the marriage far more than her first husband ever could have offered. Though the precise degree of kinship between Beatrice's first and second husbands, the two Manfreds, is unknown, it must have been quite distant; at the nearest, the two men were fourth or fifth cousins.

As a dower, Beatrice — or her father — received many manors in Piedmont, along with the rights to fortify some of these, marking the Savoys' first major territorial acquisition in that region.[696] The marriage itself was part of an imperial effort to take firm control of this strategic area known for its chestnuts and truffles.

It seems that Manfred Hohenstaufen had not yet been legitimized through the marriage of his parents.[697] Nevertheless, his paternity was known, and the union was clearly intended by Beatrice's father to curry favor with his overlord, the Holy Roman Emperor. It yielded a daughter, Constance, in 1249. By that time, Manfred had been legitimized. Beatrice could therefore take comfort in the fact of having given birth to a royal and imperial princess.

This was the most illustrious marriage the rustic Savoys ever could have hoped to attain.

In the aftermath of Frederick's death in 1250, Beatrice accompanied her husband across the peninsular part of the *Regnum Siciliae* as he fought to preserve his dynasty's position in the face of papal aggression. She is mentioned in passing by the chroniclers Jamsilla, Bartholomew of Nicastro and Saba Malaspina. Only one of these chroniclers, "Jamsilla," who alone of the three writers cultivated Ghibelline sympathies, is likely to have met her, as he traveled with Manfred and was probably a courtier.[698]

Following King Conrad's untimely death in 1254 (see the previous chapter), Manfred became regent for his young nephew, Conradin. By then, it is possible that Beatrice and Manfred began to live apart, at least for some periods. The evidence for this is sparse and somewhat subjective.[699] We cannot know with certainty that it reflected an estrangement between the spouses.

An incident is known that may have irritated, even enraged, Beatrice. Although it occurred after 1254, it exemplifies the kind of thing that might have provoked a conjugal rift a few years earlier.

Hoping to earn his way back into Manfred's favor following

some petty betrayals, the imperial courtier Berthold of Hohenburg (who we met in the last chapter when he renounced the regency of young Conradin) proposed that Beatrice's daughter, Constance, wed Ganar, his nephew.[700] There is no evidence that Manfred seriously considered this idea, though he may have feigned interest in it. Nonetheless, Beatrice probably found the notion disturbing because, as a Savoy wed to a Hohenstaufen, she likely had greater aspirations for her daughter.

In 1258, based on the belief, or perhaps merely the pretext, that Conradin was dead, Manfred had himself crowned King of Sicily.

Queen

Thus did Beatrice become a queen, although she did not live long enough to savor her reginal rank. We do not know the precise date of her death, but evidence suggests that it occurred during 1258. Jamsilla notes, though without mentioning Beatrice, that Manfred's coronation took place in August of that year. Significantly, Saba Malaspina refers to her as "Queen Beatrice."[701] Manfred remarried in June 1259.

In 1262, her daughter, Constance, was betrothed to Peter III, son of the King of Aragon.[702]

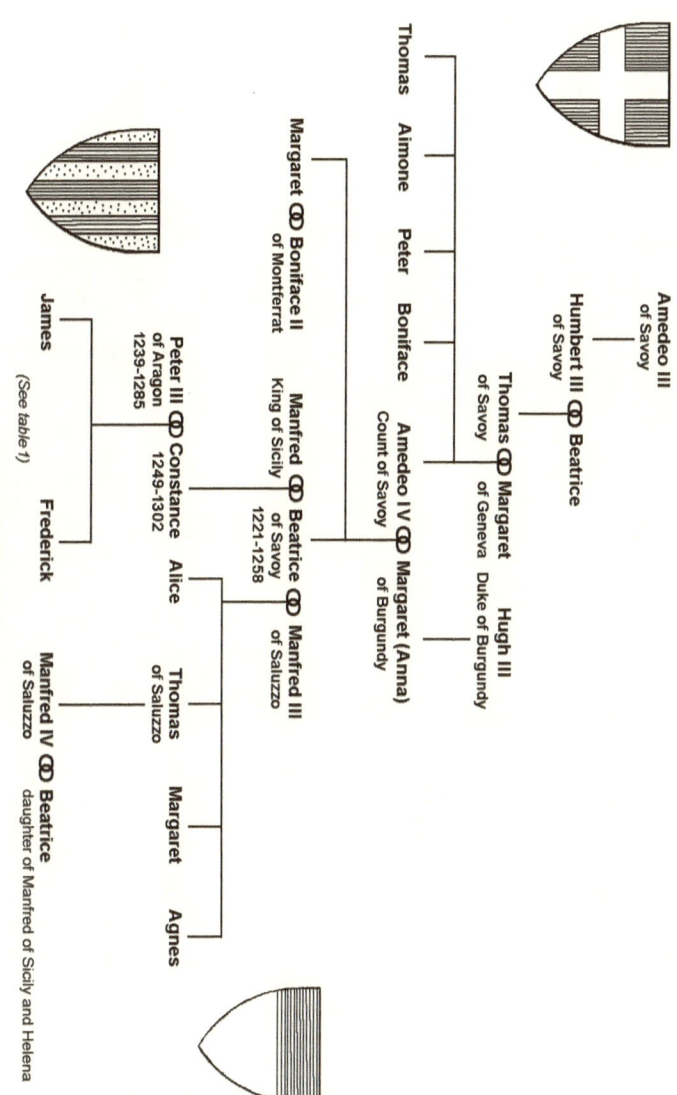

Beatrice of Savoy

Beatrice's daughter, Constance, consort of Peter III of Aragon, was crowned Queen of Sicily in 1282. She rests in Barcelona's splendid Gothic cathedral.

Chapter 19
HELENA ANGELINA OF EPIRUS

Helena Angelina Doukaina of Epirus was born in the Despotate of Epirus, probably in Arta, the ancient Ambracia, in 1242 to Michael II Comnenus Doukas and his wife Theodora Petraliphaina, a lady later venerated as a saint. Michael's dominions included parts of what are now Greece, Albania and Romania preserved as the western vestiges of the Comnenus dynasty's Byzantine Empire that fell to the Franks (Latins) following the Fourth Crusade. A kindred Greek dynasty ruled the northern part of Asia Minor from Nicaea. Michael held regions such as Thessalonika and Thrace. Some Greek ports were controlled by the Venetians, while Constantinople and its environs were held by the Courtenays, a cadet branch of the French House of Anjou. Helena had a sister, Anna, and a brother who eventually succeeded her father.

Beginning in the eleventh century, the Hautevilles had made a number of incursions into the Byzantine lands, and King Tancred of Sicily wed his son, Roger III, to one of Helena's distant cousins, Irene, whom we met in Chapter 11. These efforts reflected more than a need to increase trade and territory; they were an attempt to challenge Venetian and Muslim influence in the eastern Mediterranean. These politics were inherited by the Hohenstaufens, and Manfred of Sicily sent a force into the Albanian part of Michael's dominion.

Marriage

Helena does not seem to have known her father very well, but he was not beneath brokering her marriage to a westerner, Manfred, in order to solidify a tenuous peace with a neighbor and former enemy. The rapport between the two monarchs as in-laws made them tenuous allies, united against Venice and Rome. Doges and pontiffs were not Michael's only concern. The despot was also contemplating the advantage of having an ally like the King of Sicily in the event of an attempt to seize Nicaea from Michael VIII, his Greek "frenemy" to the east in Asia Minor (see the map at the end of this chapter), a military conquest that might lead to his own assumption of the Byzantine imperial crown.

Michael furnished his daughter with some dowry lands in the northern part of his realm, along with Corfu, Buthrotum (near Vlore) and Kaninë, and sent her with eight galleys in late May 1259 across the Adriatic to Apulia to wed a man a decade her senior.[703] Despite Helena's lack of choice in the matter, she was probably told something about the man she was to marry.

Of all Frederick's sons, Manfred was most like his father. Highly educated, he continued his father's role as a patron of the arts and sciences. Thanks to Manfred's uncommon intellect and competent leadership, little had changed in the cultural life of centers like Palermo, Salerno, Bari and Messina since the death of Frederick II. Though ever fewer in number, the Muslims were still permitted to govern their own communities at places like Lucera. The Constitutions of Melfi were still the law of the land.[704]

The nuptials were celebrated at Trani's cathedral in early

June of 1259. Manfred was permitted to keep the Albanian territories he had occupied around the important city of Durres, and to claim Helena's dowry, which included Vlore. He also took control of several smaller towns that were part of Helena's dowry.[705]

Motherhood

Helena followed Manfred in his travels around the *Regnum,* and initially spent some time in Palermo. Here she may have occasionally attended liturgy at the Martorana, the city's most important Greek church, just a ten-minute stroll from the royal palace.

In 1260, Helena bore a daughter christened Beatrice. The following year Frederick was born. In late April 1262, perhaps while at Naples, she gave birth to a boy named Henry. At some time during the next two years another son, Enzio (Anselm), was born.[706]

In the summer of 1261, the city of Constantinople fell to the forces of Michael VIII of Nicaea, thus bringing an end to the Latin Empire based there for the better part of six decades. The newly-elected pope, Urban IV (Jacques Pantaléon), was already acutely aware of the diminishing papal influence in the east, having been the Latin Patriarch of Jerusalem for several years, but his more immediate target was Manfred.

In spring or summer of 1262, Helena saw to the details of the marriage of her stepdaughter, Constance, to Peter of Aragon.[707] The maiden then departed for Barcelona.

The *Regnum* was ably ruled by Manfred and administered by competent men like John of Procida, who had served Frederick II.[708] As there were few Hohenstaufens left, Manfred was assisted in his efforts by his trusted Lancia kinsmen. The greatest threat to the kingdom's security emanated from Rome, where the French-born pope began plotting to install a dynast of his choosing on the Sicilian throne, the name of the English candidate, Edmund, having been withdrawn.

The most obvious candidate, or at least the one most willing to submit to overbearing papal control if chosen, was Charles of Anjou, the younger brother of Louis IX of France. This was the choice preferred by Urban's successor, Clement IV (Guy Foucois), a widower and formerly the secretary of Louis IX. Following his election as pope in France in 1265, Clement made his way to Italy incognito and sought to bring to fruition his plans to defeat Manfred. The new pontiff resided, for the most part, at Viterbo as the city of Rome supported Manfred. The cauldron of conflict between Ghibellines and Guelphs was reaching an alarming temperature.

Trials

They may have been unaware of the more intricate details of the papal machinations, but Helena and the others at court learned that Clement crowned Charles at Rome in January 1266. Charles brought with him a large army. With this, the Guelphic supporters of the papacy finally had an advocate to champion their cause using more than words.

Following a series of cat-and-mouse skirmishes, the armies led by Charles and Manfred confronted each other in a pitched battle along the Calore River near Benevento on February twenty-sixth 1266. The muddy terrain of winter was the worst environment for such an encounter.

Helena did not witness the fighting, as she and her children were kept in safety in a rare position.

Manfred acquitted himself well, valiantly leading charges into the heat of battle. His Arab archers were among the world's finest, and many of his knights were equipped with rudimentary plate armor, a recent military innovation. The armies seem to have been matched fairly closely in size, with over four thousand knights and light cavalry on each side, and Manfred's archers probably outnumbered those of Charles. Were it not for a series of mishaps and setbacks, the day would have been Manfred's. Tragically, Manfred did not survive that February day, and his defeat spelled not only the end of his dynasty but a turning point in Italian history.[709]

The widowed Helena initially took refuge with her children at Lucera. This Muslim city was the home of the largest Islamic community remaining in Italy, subjects fiercely loyal to the House of Hohenstaufen. But Lucera was only one city against many that would soon fall to the Angevins. It was immediately clear that Helena could not remain in the *Regnum* unprotected. She made her way to Trani to sail for Epirus with her children. Unfortunately, this plan was dashed by a sudden storm.

Captured at Trani in early March, Helena was separated from her sons and imprisoned. Her daughter accompanied her but her sons were kept at Castel del Monte, in Apulia, for the next three decades.

Helena was soon brought before Charles of Anjou at Lagopesole, near Potenza, where the new king tried to coerce her to cede her dowry lands to him. Beyond the strategic value of these territories, possessing them in this way would have legitimized Charles in the eyes of sovereigns besides his brother and the pope. The point was moot, as Helena's father repossessed these localities and her brother, who was soon to succeed him, refused to renounce them.[710]

Instead of betrothing Helena to his sometime supporter Henry of Castile, as some courtiers suggested, Charles confined her in the castle of Nocera, near Salerno, beginning in the middle of March 1267.[711] The next year saw Manfred's nephew, Conradin (who we met in Chapter 17), defeated at the Battle of Tagliacozzo and executed.

Helena's life at Nocera was reasonably comfortable. Charles

allocated forty gold ounces per year to maintain her small court, declaring in a charter of July 1269 that he did not wish for the deposed queen to want for anything.[712] He confirmed this expenditure the following year.[713]

Charles established his royal capital at Naples, visiting Palermo only occasionally. He went to the city in 1270 for the funeral of his brother, Louis, whose heart was placed in Monreale's cathedral as a sign of the Angevin presence.

We do not know Helena's precise date of death, but it was probably in February 1271. In March of that year her ladies-in-waiting were set free. The next year, Beatrice was transferred to a prison in the Castel dell'Ovo of Naples.[714] Helena was interred at the abbey of Cava, near Nocera, though no sign of her tomb remains.

Aftermath

What of Helena's children? Their fate was decided in 1282 by the War of the Vespers, which forced Charles to divert his military resources to an ill-fated effort to suppress an uprising in Sicily instead of invading the Byzantine lands to restore Latin (Catholic) control in Constantinople as he had planned. Supported by King Peter III of Aragon, who ascended the Sicilian throne by right of his consort, Manfred's eldest daughter Constance, the Sicilians forced the separation of their island from the rest of the kingdom. This gave birth to the phrase "Two Sicilies," as both Charles of Anjou and Peter of Aragon claimed the Sicilian crown, one from Naples and the other from Palermo.

In connection with this, Beatrice was liberated from the Castel dell'Ovo of Naples in 1284 through the efforts of her elder half-sister, Constance. The Vespers conflict found Charles "the Lame," heir of Charles of Anjou, taken prisoner, and freeing Beatrice was in the nasty king's interest if he wished to see his own son set free (though there is evidence to suggest that the elder Charles was sometimes indifferent about his eldest son's fate). This was a prisoner exchange.

In 1286, before marrying Manfred IV of Saluzzo, Beatrice renounced her dynastic rights to the Sicilian crown.[715]

Despite their efforts to assist Beatrice, it is clear that Constance and her husband, Peter of Aragon, now King of Sicily *jure uxoris,* thought better of demanding the release of her three brothers; this was to avoid possible contestations to the claims of their own sons in the future.[716] In 1299, Charles the Lame, who as king was nearly as petulant and vindictive as his namesake, transferred Helena's sons to the Castel dell'Ovo.[717] Frederick and Enzio died there a few years later, but Henry lived until 1318.

For the next few generations, the queens of Sicily were the consorts of the Aragonese dynasts who ruled the island or the wives of the Angevin kings of Naples who claimed it.

QUEENS OF SICILY

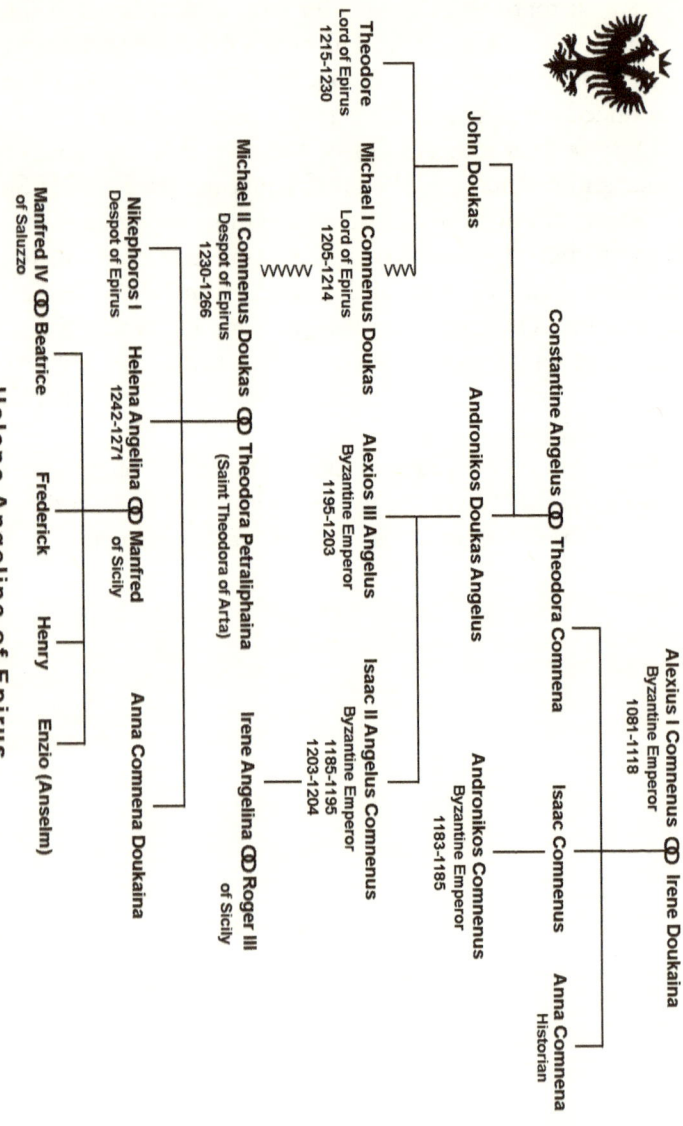

Helena Angelina of Epirus

Helena's Byzantine Heritage

St Francis, Palermo, built when Helena was queen

EPILOGUE

Constance Hohenstaufen, through her marriage to Peter III of Aragon, brought the Sicilian crown into the Spanish orbit, where it would remain for the next few centuries. Yet, as early as her coronation in Palermo Cathedral in 1282, an attempt was made to keep the Sicilian and Aragonese crowns separate. This met with mixed success over time because, in effect, the island of Sicily became part of the burgeoning thalassocracy called the "Crown of Aragon."

Constance and Peter had six surviving children. Upon Peter's death in 1285, the Kingdom of Sicily, now separated from the peninsular Kingdom of Naples, was inherited by the couple's secondborn son, James, while Aragon went to their eldest son, Alfonso. At Alfonso's death without heirs in 1291, James succeeded him as king of both Aragon and Sicily, something the Sicilian baronage, not desiring to be ruled from afar, had hoped to avoid. A few years later, the island's first true parliament elected Frederick, the younger brother of James, as Sicily's sovereign, crowning him in Palermo Cathedral as King Frederick III.

As a result, Constance, still in her forties, had to witness a brief conflict between her sons. The wider conflict, the War of the Vespers, ended officially with the Peace of Caltabellotta signed in 1302, a few months after Constance's death. Constance, the last Hohenstaufen heiress to wear the Sicilian crown, is entombed in Barcelona's Saint Eulalia Cathedral.

Papal plans were already being conceived with the intent of uniting Sicily to the mainland through dynastic marriages between the Aragonese dynasty and the Neapolitan Angevins. Thus did Eleanor, a daughter of Charles II of Naples (Charles "the Lame" of the previous chapter), wed Frederick III of Sicily in 1302.

Both dynasties defined their rights by the Hohenstaufens, one by defeating them at Benevento and Tagliacozzo, the other by descent, through Constance, from Manfred, son of the great Frederick II. Sicilian queenship did not immediately change outwardly, but the island, despite its centralized position, was deprived of its former lustre, becoming somewhat isolated.

Never again would Sicily enjoy the greatness she had known during the Norman-Swabian golden age. Her prosperity waned. The multicultural court vanished. Palermo no longer attracted the best and the brightest from around Europe and the Mediterranean. A Latin monoculture came to dominate life. The island itself suffered as ever more forests disappeared, their timber used to build Aragonese galleys, the denuded land then exploited to produce wheat for export. Fewer rivers flowed. Over time, the deer and boar were hunted to extinction. Taxation became crippling. When the Renaissance flourished, Sicily was all but ignored.

In the wake of these changes, being Queen of Sicily, ever a mark of prestige, no longer engendered the realities that once existed under the Hautevilles and Hohenstaufens.

This was, in every way, the passing of an era.

Queenhood is an eternal triumph, a crowning glory that unites the sisterhood of the ages.

GENEALOGICAL TABLES

QUEENS OF SICILY

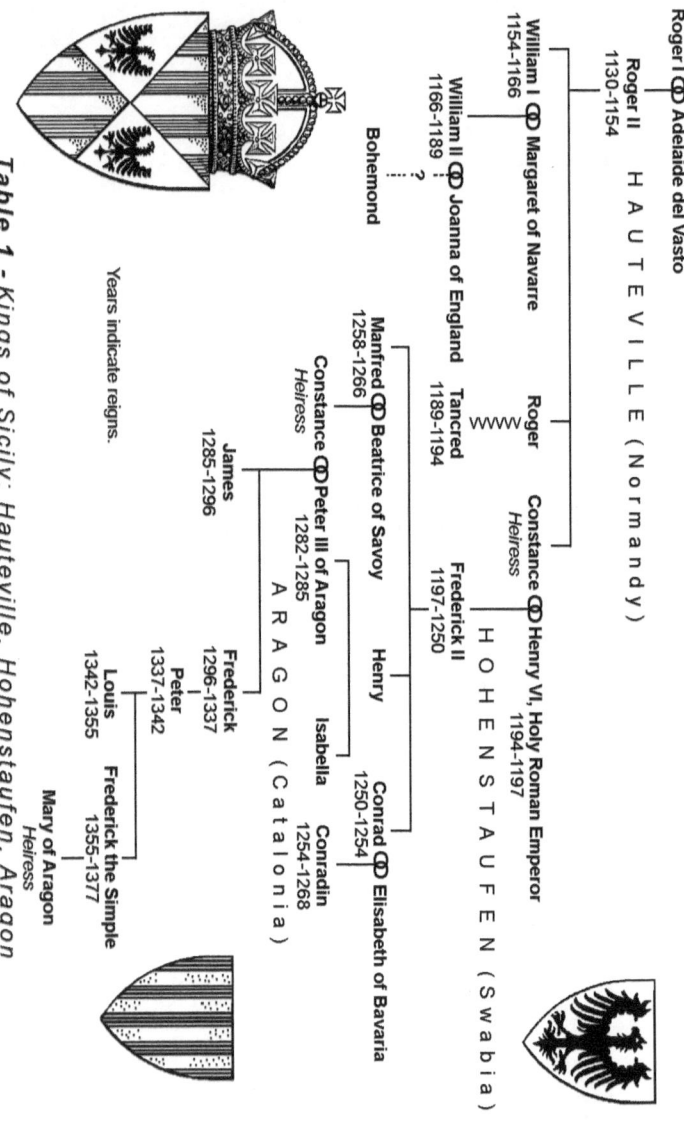

Table 1 - *Kings of Sicily: Hauteville, Hohenstaufen, Aragon*

GENEALOGICAL TABLES

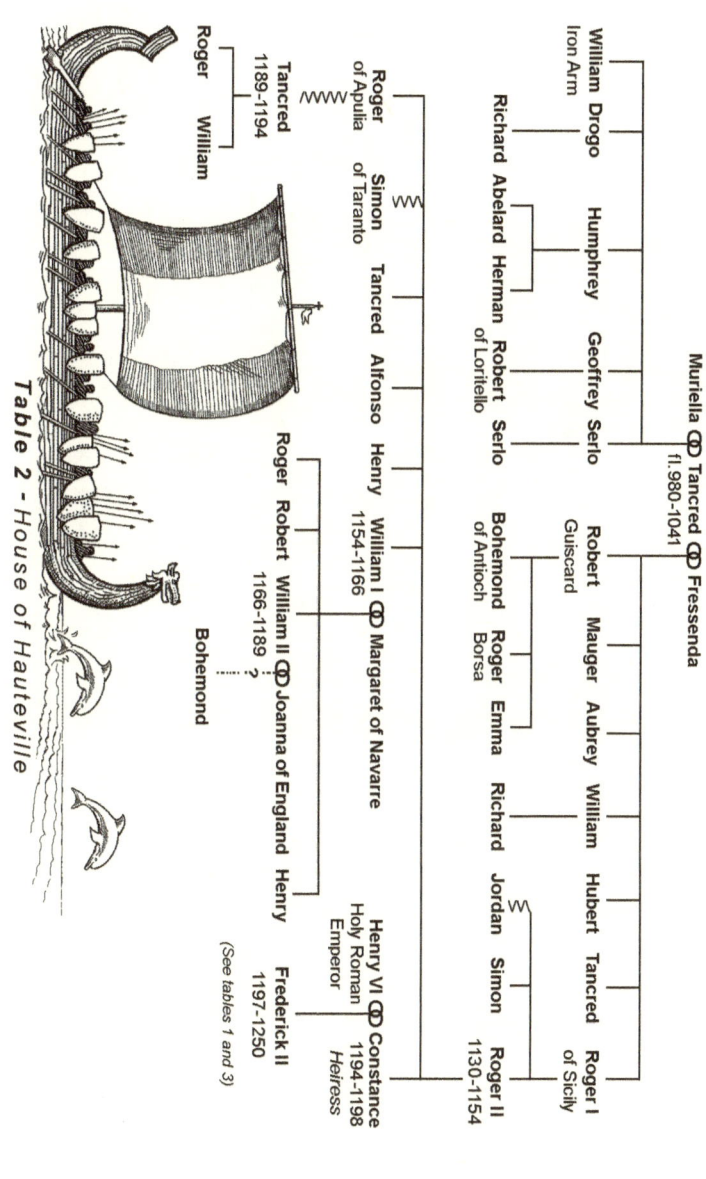

Table 2 - *House of Hauteville*

Muriella ⊕ Tancred ⊕ Fressenda
fl.980-1041

- William Drogo Humphrey Geoffrey Serlo
  Iron Arm

- Richard Abelard Herman Robert Serlo
  of Loritello

- Roger ⌇ Simon Tancred Alfonso Henry William I ⊕ Margaret of Navarre
  of Apulia   of Taranto   1154-1166

  - Roger
    1189-1194
  - Tancred
  - William
  - Roger Robert William II ⊕ Joanna of England Henry
                   1166-1189
                       ?
                   Bohemond

- Robert Mauger Aubrey William Hubert Tancred Roger I
  Guiscard   of Sicily

  - Bohemond Roger Emma Richard Jordan Simon Roger II
    of Antioch Borsa   1130-1154

                                                   Henry VI ⊕ Constance
                                                   Holy Roman 1194-1198
                                                   Emperor   Heiress

                                                   Frederick II
                                                   1197-1250

(See tables 1 and 3)

QUEENS OF SICILY

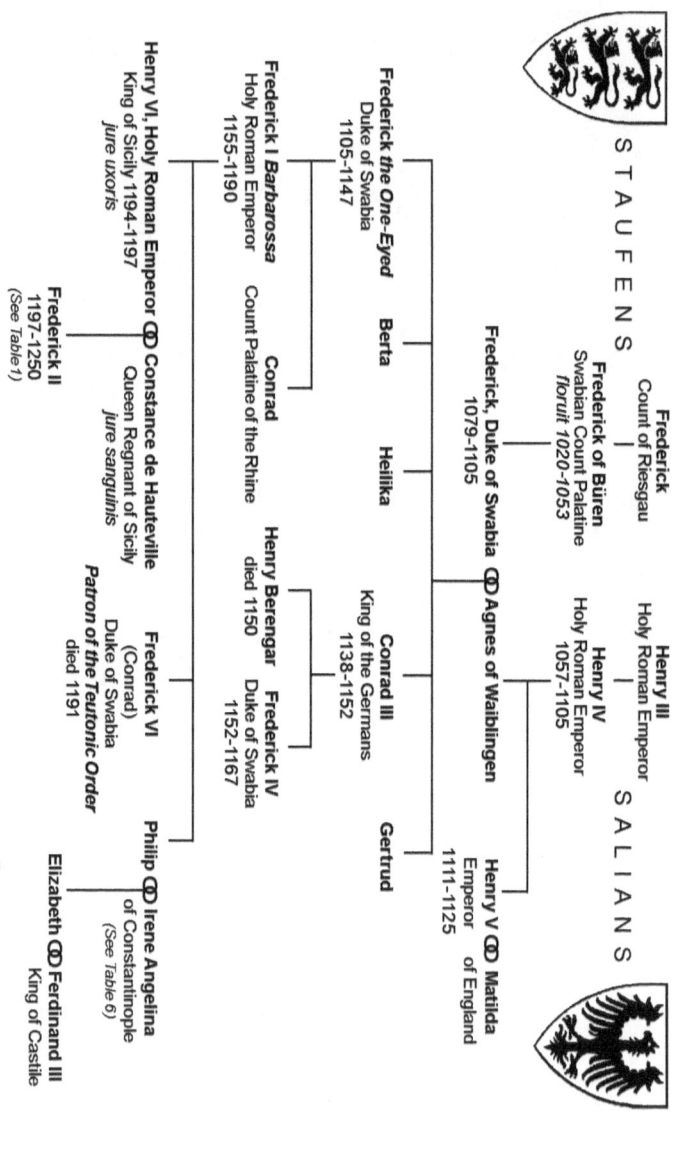

Table 3 - *Hohenstaufen Origins: Swabian Ancestors of Frederick II*

GENEALOGICAL TABLES

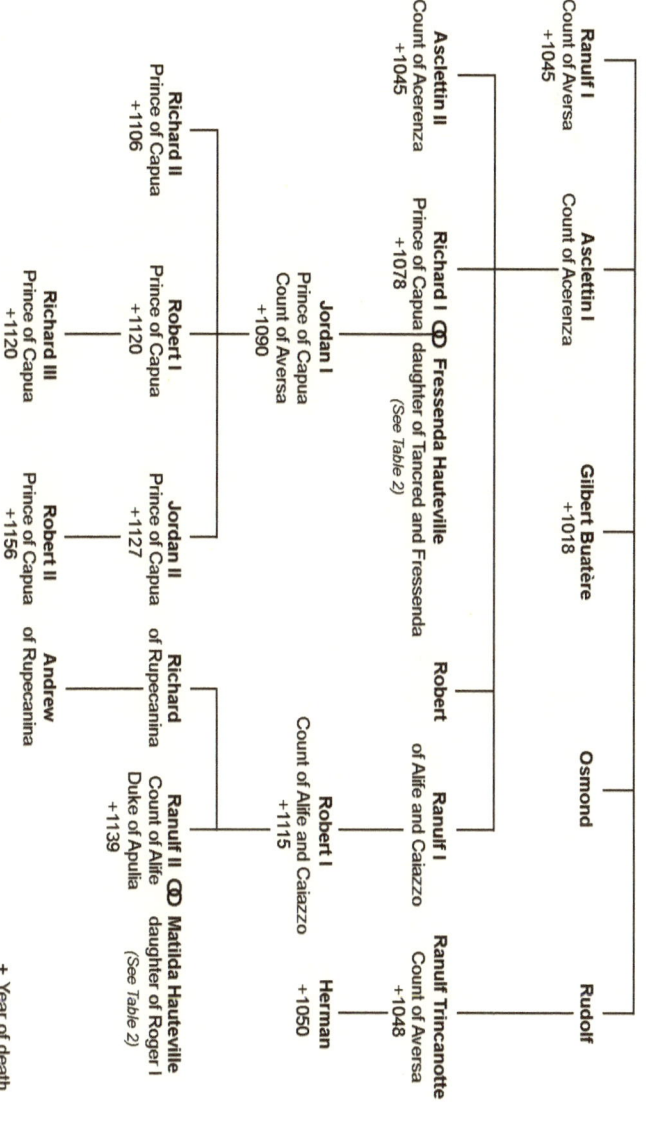

Table 4 - *Drengot Dynasty of Capua and Aversa*

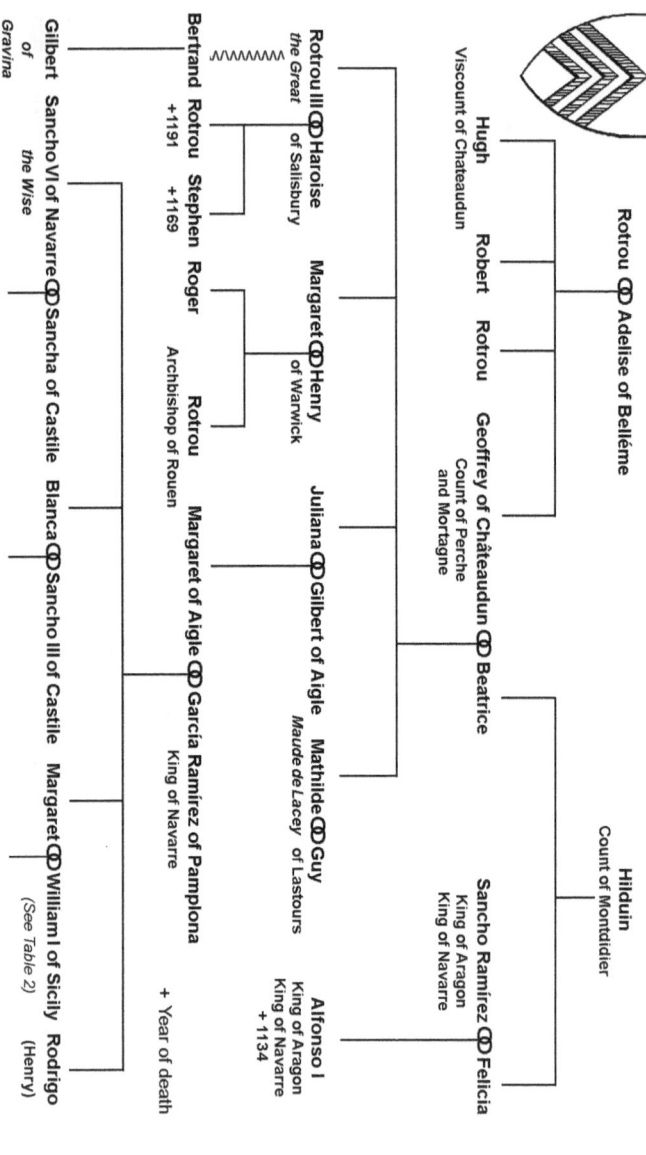

Table 5 - Perche Family of Normandy and France

GENEALOGICAL TABLES

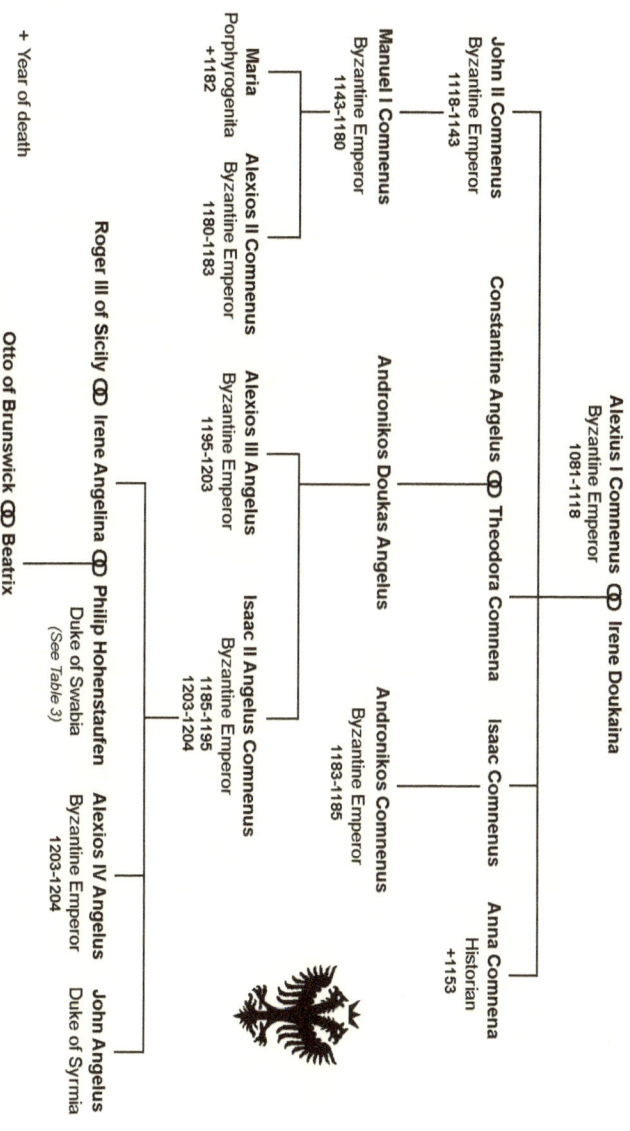

Table 6 - *Comnenus Dynasty of Constantinople*

QUEENS OF SICILY

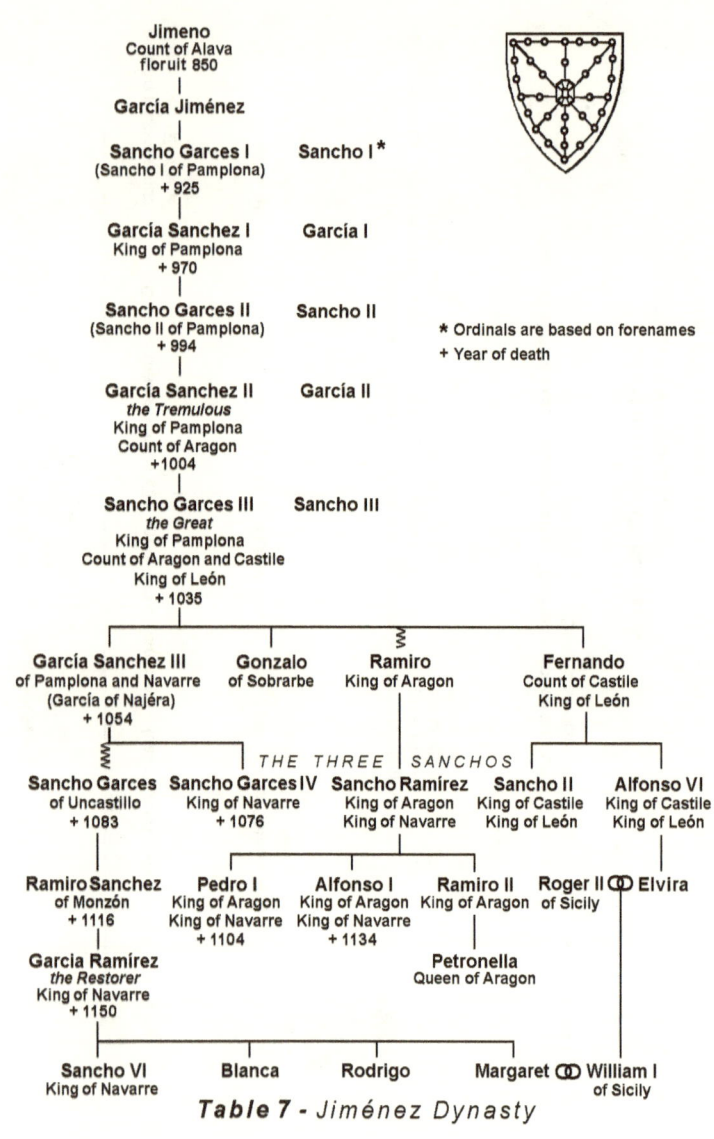

* Ordinals are based on forenames
+ Year of death

THE THREE SANCHOS

Table 7 - *Jiménez Dynasty*

TIMELINE

This succinct chronology is intended merely as a general framework to lend context to the history and events recounted in the preceding pages. It is not meant to present in detail those events that occurred during this period, or to substitute the narrative text in this monograph.

Kalbid-Fatimid Period

998-1019 - Rule of Jafar al-Kalbi in Sicily under Fatimids. Construction of Favara palace in Palermo is attributed to this emir.

1000 - Norse civilization in northwestern France (Normandy) assimilates with local culture. Approximate period of Norse landings in Newfoundland.

1002 - Defeat of al-Mansur ibn Abi Aamir (Almanzor) leaves most of Navarre and Catalonia in Christian hands.

1004 - Fatimids establish large library and *dar al-hikma* (house of wisdom) in Egypt.

1008 - Fatimids re-establish diplomatic relations with China.

1016 - Norman knights first participate in battles in Italy. First Turkish raids in Armenia.

1018 - Bulgarian lands conquered by Byzantines, who also defeat Italians (Lombards) at Battle of Cannae, in Apulia, where many Norman knights are felled.

1019-1037 - Rule of Ahmed al-Akhal in Sicily.

1035 - County of Aragon becomes a kingdom.

1037-1040 - Rule of Sicily by Abdallah Abu Hafs, usurper.

1038-1042 - Byzantine forces of George Maniakes briefly occupy parts of eastern Sicily; army includes Greeks, Normans, Lombards, and Norse Varangian Guard under Harald Sigurdsson Hardrada, later King of Norway (killed in battle in England in 1066).

1040 - Hasan as-Samsam begins his rule in Sicily; deposed in 1044.

1042 - Birth of Judith of Evreux (approximate year). Normans establish Melfi as their Italian capital.

1044 - Sicily divided into four qadits. Rivalry among emirs worsens.

1045 - Zirids of Tunisia rebel against Fatimids to unite with Abbasids of Baghdad. Cathedral of Gerace (Calabria) consecrated.

1053 - Following death of Hasan as-Samsam and extinction of Kalbid dynasty, three important emirs divide control of Sicily: ibn al Hawas at Kasr' Janni (Enna), ibn al-Timnah at Syracuse and Catania, Abdullah ibn Hawqal at Trapani and Mazara. Normans defeat Lombards at Battle of Civitate.

1054 - Great Schism between eastern and western Christianity. Sicilian Christians initially remain "eastern" (Orthodox). Supernova observed by astronomers in Asia; becomes Crab Nebula.

1055 - Seljuk Turks occupy Baghdad.

1056 - Agnes of Aquitaine regent of Holy Roman Empire until 1061.

1057 - Tunisia invaded by Banu Hilal of Arabia, with Zirid lands reduced in size.

1060 - Unsuccessful Norman attack in coastal northeastern Sicily.

Norman Period

1061 - Birth of Eremburga of Mortain (approx. yr.). Battle of Messina. City and parts of Nebrodian and Peloritan region occupied; permanent Norman presence in Sicily.

1062 - Judith of Evreux marries Roger I.

1065 - Kingdom of Castile founded. Seljuk Turks invade Georgia.

1065-1067 - War of the Three Sanchos among three Jiménez cousins ruling Castile, Navarre and Aragon.

1066 - Battle of Hastings leads to complete Norman conquest of Saxon England. Battle of Messina forms partial pattern of this invasion of an island from a continent. (Some Norman knights fight at both battles.)

1071 - Normans attack Palermo; Norman invaders are led by Robert of Hauteville, Arab defenders by Ayub ibn Temim. Byzantines lose Battle of Manzikert to Seljuk Turks.

1072 - Battle of Palermo ends in January with Norman occupation under Roger and Robert of Hauteville. Greek Orthodox Bishop Nicodemus removed from authority over Christian community.

1074 - Birth of Adelaide del Vasto (approx. yr.). Seljuk Turks seize Jerusalem from Byzantine control.

1075 - Investiture Controversy begins as conflict between Papacy and Holy Roman Emperors.

1076 - Death of Judith of Evreux.

1077 - Eremburga of Mortain weds Roger I (approx. yr.). Excommunicated Henry IV, Holy Roman Emperor, does penance at Canossa.

1078 - Arab poet ibn Hamdis leaves Sicily.

1079 - Frankish settlement begins along Way of Saint James in northeastern Spain.

1081 - Suppression of revolt led by self-appointed "emir" Bin al Wardi (Bernavert) at Catania; another of his revolts is quashed at Syracuse in 1085.

1083 - Roger I appoints Latin (rather than Orthodox) Bishop of Palermo and Gallican Rite is introduced in new churches.

1084 - Bruno founds Carthusian Order in Germany.

1085 - Alfonso VI of Castile seizes Toledo from Moors.

1087 - Ibn Hammud, Emir of Kasr'Janni (Enna), last major Arab stronghold in Sicily, surrenders to Normans; Noto falls in 1091.

1088 - Death of Eremburga of Mortain.

1089 - Adelaide del Vasto weds Roger I.

1091 - Byzantine Greeks defeat Pechenegs at Battle of Levounion.

1094 - El Cid conquers Valencia.

1095 - Roger II, future King of Sicily, is born. Pope Urban II preaches First Crusade.

1096 - First Crusade begins; some Norman knights participate under Bohemond of Hauteville (later Prince of Antioch), brother of Roger I.

1097 - Odo of Bayeux, younger brother of William the Conqueror, dies in Palermo *en route* to the Crusade while visiting Roger I.

1098 - Roger I, as Great Count of Sicily, becomes apostolic legate, with right of approval over bishops. Cistercian Order founded in France.

1099 - Crusaders conquer Jerusalem. Death of El Cid in Spain.

TIMELINE

1100 - Birth of Elvira of Castile (approx. yr.). Crusaders control Palestine in the wake of the First Crusade and crown Baldwin first King of Jerusalem.

1101 - Roger I, Great Count of Sicily, dies, succeeded by Simon, his eldest living, legitimate son, who is still a minor. Roger's consort, Adelaide del Vasto is regent.

1104 - Alfonso I "the Battler," a cousin of García Ramírez, becomes King of Aragon and Navarre.

1105 - Roger II succeeds his elder brother Simon (1093-1105) as ruler of Sicily under Adelaide's regency.

1108 - Bohemond of Antioch becomes vassal of Byzantine Emperor.

1109 - Bertrand of Toulouse occupies Tripoli (Lebanon).

1112 - Roger is knighted (this ceremony marks his age of majority and sovereign authority following regency under his mother).

1113 - Adelaide weds Baldwin I of Jerusalem. Order of Saint John (Knights Hospitaller) based in Palestine chartered by Pope Paschal II. Establishes commanderies in Sicily and later (in 1530) receives Malta from Charles V, King of Sicily and Holy Roman Emperor.

1117 - Elvira of Castile weds Roger II of Sicily.

1118 - Death of Adelaide del Vasto.

1119 - In Spain, Alfonso the Battler takes control of Tudela from Moors. Knights Templar founded in Palestine.

1120 - Council of Nablus establishes legal code for Kingdom of Jerusalem.

1121 - Betrothal of young Margaret of l'Aigle to García Ramírez. Presumed year of birth of William I of Sicily.

1122 - Concordat of Worms between Papacy and Holy Roman Empire.

1123 - First Lateran Council forbids Roman Catholic clerics wives or concubines; until now Catholic priests were permitted to marry before ordination. Rotrou III "the Great" of Perche takes possession of Tudela.

1125 - Christian army defeats Seljuk Turks at Battle of Azaz.

1126 - Birth of Sibylla of Burgundy.

1128 - Portugal declares independence from León, which recognizes its monarch, Alfonso Henriques, in 1143.

1130 - Roger crowned first King of Sicily (known henceforth as "Roger II"). Elvira becomes first Queen of Sicily. On royal orders Saint John of the Hermits, an Orthodox monastery in Palermo, is ordered rebuilt as Benedictine abbey, completed in 1148. Palatine Chapel rebuilt to present form during this period.

1131 - Cathedral of Cefalù erected.

1132 - Birth of Beatrice of Rethel (approx. yr.).

1135 - Death of Elvira of Castile in Palermo; birth of Margaret of Navarre. García Ramírez crowned King of Pamplona. Beginning of "Anarchy," a civil war over royal succession, in England.

1136 - Construction of Saint-Denis near Paris; Gothic movement begins.

1138 - Death of Anacletus II ends papal schism (which began in 1130); Innocent II universally recognized as Pope. Major earthquake around Aleppo.

1139 - Second Lateran Council, convened by Pope Innocent II, makes celibacy mandatory for Roman Catholic priests, reiterating a canon established in 1123 but not widely enforced. Innocent recognizes Roger II as King of Sicily.

1140 - Roger II promulgates Assizes of Ariano, introduces ducat.

1141 - Death of Margaret of l'Aigle, mother of Margaret of Navarre.

TIMELINE

1143 - Martorana Church (Palermo) built in Norman-Arab style for Greek Orthodox community by George of Antioch. Nilos Doxopatrios, Orthodox cleric, authors a theological treatise supporting the Eastern Church. Legal principles expressed in Assizes of Ariano are in force by this time.

1145-1148 - Second Crusade; participation by Sicilian knights is limited.

1147 - Almohads displace Almoravids in northwestern Africa and southern Spain.

1148 - Sibylla of Burgundy weds Roger II.

1149 - Eleanor of Aquitaine calls at Palermo; Margaret of Navarre weds William II.

1150 - Death of Sibylla of Burgundy. Death of King García Ramírez, father of Margaret; accession of Sancho VI of Navarre.

1151 - Beatrice of Rethel weds Roger II. William I of Sicily crowned *rex filius*.

1152 - Birth of Roger, first son of Margaret and William.

1153 - Birth of Sibylla of Acerra. Birth of Robert, second son of Margaret and William. End of "Anarchy" in England. First Treaty of Konstanz between Papacy and Holy Roman Empire to prevent Byzantine conquests in Italy.

1154 - Death of Roger II; birth of his daughter, Constance of Sicily. Reign of King William I begins. *Book of Roger* completed by court geographer Abdullah al Idrisi. Accession of Henry II in England.

1155 - Birth of William II, third son of Margaret and William I. Birth of Alfonso VIII of Castile, son of Blanca (Margaret's sister). Frederick I "Barbarossa" Hohenstaufen crowned Holy Roman Emperor.

1156 - Death of Blanca, Margaret's sister. Treaty of Benevento between Papacy and Kingdom of Sicily.

1158 - Birth of Henry, fourth son of Margaret and William. Thomas le Brun (Thomas Brown), treasurer at William's court, returns to England to reform exchequer of Henry II, thus influencing European accounting principles.

1159 - Death of Robert, secondborn son of Margaret and William. Arrival in Sicily of Gilbert of Gravina, Margaret's cousin.

1160 - Mahdia, last Norman stronghold in North Africa, is lost.

1161 - Matthew Bonello leads revolt of Norman barons, resulting in death of Roger, firstborn son of Margaret and William. Rhum Sultanate makes peace with Byzantine Empire.

1165 - Birth of Joanna "Plantagenet" of England to Eleanor of Aquitaine and Henry II. Design and construction of Zisa palace begin in Palermo.

1166 - Death of William I; reign of young King William II begins under Margaret's regency. Arrival in Sicily of Rodrigo (Henry), Margaret's half-brother.

1167 - Margaret appoints her cousin, Stephen of Perche, chancellor.

1168 - At Messina, Margaret oversees trials of Rodrigo (Henry) and others. Stephen of Perche deposed and expelled.

1169 - Major earthquake in Catania and southeastern Sicily. Walter becomes Archbishop of Palermo.

1170 - Sibylla of Acerra weds Tancred of Lecce (approx. yr.). Thomas Becket murdered in Canterbury Cathedral.

1171 - Margaret's regency ends when William II reaches age of majority. Benjamin of Tudela visits Sicily. Saladin deposes Fatimids, establishes Ayyubid rule.

1172 - Death of Henry, Margaret's fourthborn son. Planning and construction begin on Monreale Abbey.

1173 - Thomas Becket canonized.

1174 - Sicilian fleet led by Tancred of Lecce attacks Alexandria.

1175 - William II signs treaty with Venetians. Henry II of England signs treaty with Irish.

TIMELINE

1176 - Betrothal of Joanna of England to William II. Byzantines lose much of Anatolia to Seljuk Turks.

1177 - Joanna of England marries William II. Treaty of Venice between Pope and Holy Roman Emperor.

1178 - Sicilian treaty with Holy Roman Empire. Romuald Guarna of Salerno leaves Sicily.

1179 - Birth of Constance of Aragon. Birth of Irene Angelina of Constantinople (approx. yr.). Third Lateran Council convened by Pope Alexander III.

1181 - Sicilian treaty with Tunisia. Pope Alexander III dies.

1182 - Massacre of the Latins in Constantinople.

1183 - Death of Margaret of Navarre. Monreale becomes archdiocese.

1184 - Major earthquake in Calabria. Bin Jubayr visits Sicily. Construction of Palermo's new cathedral.

1185 - Death of Beatrice of Rethel. William II invades Byzantine lands.

1186 - Constance, daughter of Roger II, weds Henry VI, future Holy Roman Emperor.

1187 - Saladin captures Jerusalem. William II sends fleet to Palestine.

1189 - Death of William II. Richard I "Lionheart" crowned King of England.

1190 - Tancred of Lecce crowned King of Sicily. Richard Lionheart, brother of Queen Joanna of Sicily, occupies Messina with Philip II of France for several months *en route* to Third Crusade. Death of Frederick I "Barbarossa," Holy Roman Emperor; succeeded by Henry VI.

1191 - Joanna of England, widow of William II, goes on Third Crusade. Henry VI and Constance defeated in attempted invasion of *Regnum,* with Constance captured. Construction of Magione church (Palermo) by Matthew of Aiello.

1192 - Irene Angelina weds Roger III, who dies the following year. Constance is rescued. Isabella I crowned Queen of Jerusalem.

1193 - Death of Saladin.

1194 - Death of Tancred of Lecce; Constance becomes queen, gives birth to son, Frederick II. Holy Roman Emperor Henry VI arrives in Palermo and rules by right of his wife, Constance.

Swabian Period

1195 - Constance crowned Queen of Sicily.

1196 - Joanna, widow of William II, weds Raymond VI of Toulouse.

1197 - Henry VI dies; Constance becomes regent for Frederick II. Irene Angelina weds Philip of Swabia. Basilica of Saint Nicholas (begun in 1089) consecrated in Bari.

1198 - Death of Constance; she is survived by her son, Frederick II. Constance of Aragon weds Emeric of Hungary. Teutonic Order founded under Hohenstaufen patronage.

1199 - Death of Joanna of England at Rouen.

1204 - Constance of Aragon widowed in Hungary. Latins ("Franks") sack Constantinople during Fourth Crusade, establishing "Latin Empire."

1205 - Death of Sibylla of Acerra.

1206 - Mongols unite under Genghis Khan (Temujin), who conquers large parts of Eurasia.

1208 - Death of Irene Angelina of Constantinople.

1209 - Constance of Aragon weds Frederick II.

1210 - Birth of Bianca Lancia (approx. yr.). Francis of Assisi meets Pope Innocent III; founds Order of Friars Minor (Franciscans). Albigensian

Crusades begin. Birth of John of Procida, later counsellor of Frederick II. Otto IV invades Italy.

1211 - Constance gives birth to Henry, eldest child of Frederick II.

1212 - Birth of Yolanda (of Brienne) of Jerusalem.

1214 - Birth of Isabella of England.

1215 - Magna Carta in England. Dominic of Osma (of Caleruega, Spain) founds Order of Preachers (Dominicans or "Blackfriars"), confirmed by Papacy in 1216.

1217 - Cleric and scientist Michael Scot (born 1175) translates *On the Sphere* by the Arab astronomer Al-Bitruji (or Alpetragius), who died circa 1204. Fifth Crusade begins.

1220 - Frederick issues Assizes of Capua.

1221 - Birth of Beatrice of Savoy (approx. yr.). Frederick issues Assizes of Messina.

1222 - Death of Constance of Aragon.

1223 - Following execution of Arab rebel leader Morabit in Sicily (in 1222), thousands of Muslims from Iato area, who had revolted with their leader Ibn Abbad (or Benaveth), are deported to Lucera and other towns in Apulia. Many Muslims have already converted to Catholicism. Jews from occupied Jerba (in Tunisia) invited to Sicily. Transfers of Muslims to mainland Italy continue until around 1246.

1224 - University of Naples founded by Frederick II.

1225 - Yolanda of Jerusalem marries Frederick II.

1226 - Frederick II summons Imperial Diet of Cremona.

1227 - Birth of Elisabeth Wittelsbach of Bavaria (approx. yr.).

1228 - Yolanda dies giving birth to Conrad.

1229 - Frederick II, accompanied by Saracen guards and Italian and German knights, goes on Sixth Crusade as King of Jerusalem. Signs peace with Ayyubids without war.

1230 - Upon his return from Jerusalem Frederick suppresses Templar preceptories in Sicily and defeats John of Brienne in Apulia.

1231 - Constitutions of Melfi become legal code for Kingdom of Sicily under Frederick II.

1233 - Cathars of France persecuted as heretics by first Inquisition.

1235 - Isabella of England weds Frederick II.

1240 - Cielo of Alcamo composes poetry in Sicilian language. First of a series of major revolts by Sicilian Arabs, including some Christian converts, but Frederick retains trusted Saracen guards and court officers.

1241 - Isabella dies giving birth. Mongol-Tatar army of Batu Khan arrives in central Europe after having sacked Kiev. Leads to foundation of "Golden Horde."

1242 - Birth of Helena Angelina of Epirus.

1244 - Fall of Jerusalem to Khwarazmian forces.

1245 - First General Council of Lyon convoked by Pope Innocent IV.

1246 - Elisabeth of Bavaria weds Conrad, son of Yolanda and Frederick II.

1248 - Bianca Lancia marries Frederick II shortly before her death. Beatrice of Savoy, a widow, weds Manfred, son of Frederick II. Crusade to Egypt by Louis IX of France.

1250 - Death of Frederick II. Elisabeth of Bavaria becomes queen as consort of Conrad.

1252 - Elisabeth gives birth to son, Conrad (Conradin). Papal bull *Ad Extirpanda* institutes use of torture on heretics in Inquisition.

TIMELINE

1254 - Death of Conrad; Manfred, natural but legitimized son of Frederick, becomes regent for his young son (Conradin). Death of Pope Innocent IV.

1255 - Manfred is excommunicated by Pope Alexander IV but reclaims much of southern Italy from papal control.

1258 - Manfred crowned King of Sicily. Beatrice of Savoy crowned, dies. Baghdad falls to Mongols.

1259 - Helena Angelina of Epirus weds Manfred. Widowed Elisabeth of Bavaria marries Meinhard of Gorizia.

1261 - Byzantine Empire restored when Constantinople falls to Greek (Nicaean) control.

1262 - Constance, daughter of Beatrice of Savoy and Manfred, weds Peter III of Aragon.

Angevin Period

1266 - Charles of Anjou (brother of Louis IX of France) becomes king of Sicily following defeat and death of Manfred at Battle of Benevento. Establishes capital at Naples.

1268 - Young Conradin, a (legitimate) grandson of Frederick II and last male Swabian claimant, is executed following defeat at Battle of Tagliacozzo.

1270 - Following Eighth (Tunisian) Crusade, funeral of Louis IX of France at Monreale, where his heart is preserved; canonized in 1297.

1271 - Helena Angelina dies in captivity; Charles of Anjou captures some of her dowry lands in Albania and Epirus.

1273 - Rudolf of Hapsburg becomes king in Germany; his dynasty will succeed Hohenstaufens as Holy Roman Emperors.

1281 - Angevin forces defeated by Byzantine troops in Albania and Greece.

Aragonese Period

1282 - Constance, daughter of Beatrice of Savoy and Manfred, crowned Queen of Sicily following Vespers revolt that expels Angevin French from Sicily and makes Peter III of Aragon its sovereign. Neapolitan invasion of Constantinople (to restore "Latin Empire") is aborted as military resources must be diverted to Sicily.

1285 - Deaths of Charles I of Anjou and Peter III of Aragon, succeeded by their sons.

1298 - Death of John of Procida, chancellor of Frederick II and Manfred.

1300 - Destruction of Lucera by Charles II and conversion of its Muslims; end of Islam in Italy.

1302 - Death of Constance, daughter of Beatrice of Savoy and Manfred of Sicily. Peace of Caltabellotta treaty signed between Aragonese and Angevins.

Appendix 1
ASSIZES OF ARIANO

This is the *corpus* of law of the Kingdom of Sicily in force until 1231, when it was supplanted by the Constitutions of Melfi. Taking a cue from the Code of Justinian whilst definitively asserting royal authority in specific areas, the Assizes established generally uniform jurisprudence, whereas until the first decades of the twelfth century cases were often decided (based on the subject's religion) according to Canon, Maliki or Halakha law, and sometimes by *judicium dei,* "the judgement of God," of which trial by ordeal is the most obvious example.

Clearly, the Assizes transcended certain Norman and Longobardic norms whilst permitting the preservation of others (see note 197).

By no means was this a purely "secular" legal code, as church law continued to be applied in many cases. The Assizes represented a concrete step in the Normans' latinization of their Kingdom of Sicily. In addition to Islamic and Judaic legal principles, certain Byzantine (Orthodox) Christian precepts were now subjugated to those of Rome. Evidence suggests that a few vestiges of common law remained in daily life, particularly among the Muslim population (see note 128).

This legal code was not, in the strictest sense, a "foundation charter," but it clearly reflected the unifying jurisdiction established with the sovereignty of Roger II. It cannot, however, be compared directly to the laws formulated by Henry II in England.

The Assizes were most likely drafted in 1140 (their traditional date) or shortly thereafter, a decade following Roger's coronation and establishment of the *Regnum Siciliae*. Their connection with the town of Ariano is uncertain.

Unsurprisingly, the code does not clearly address the role of the queen, either as consort or regent, matters left to traditional practice and law. There was no Queen of Sicily in 1140. As Roger was a widower when the Assizes were drafted, there was no reginal input.

There exist fine published translations of the text into Italian, French and English. Here, for the benefit of jurists and latinists, and to avoid ambiguity in interpretation, is the original text of both extant manuscripts; these were copied decades after Roger's reign.

Codex Vaticanus Latinus 8782 has forty-three statutes (clauses), or "assizes," and a preface. This is probably the more faithful to the original document. A later manuscript, *Codex Casinensis 468,* is abbreviated in form but includes seven additional statutes. Both codices were rediscovered during the nineteenth century.

That the contemporary chronicler Falco of Benevento mentions Roger's controversial introduction, at Ariano, of the ducat but not the new legal code suggests to some scholars that the Assizes were issued somewhat later and elsewhere. Moreover, the fact that the Assizes of Capua of Frederick II were deemed necessary in 1220 might lead a skeptic to question the application (or dissemination) of the earlier Assizes of Ariano. Thus far, a manuscript copy of the Assizes of Ariano dated to circa 1140, if it survives, has yet to be discovered.

Yet modern historians seem to have known of the Assizes,

sometimes mentioned as "Roger's laws," long before the nineteenth century.

The following texts incorporate minor stylistic editing, such as full words in place of abbreviations. Numeration of the statutes in the second codex was added by the author.

Codex Vaticanus 8782

Dignum et necessarium est o proceres si quod de nobis et universi regni nostri statu meritis non presumimus; a largitate divina gratia consecuta recepimus; divinis beneficiis quibus valemus obsequis respondeamus, ne tante gratie penitus ingrati simus. Si ergo sua misericordia nobis deus pius prostratis hostibus pacem reddidit, integritatem regni, tranquillitate gratissima, tam in carnalibus quam in spiritualibus, reformavit, reformare cogimur iustitie simul et pietatis itinera, ubi videmus eam et mirabiliter esse distortam. Hoc enim ipsum quod ait, inspiramentum, de munere ipsius largitoris, accepimus, dicente ipso: per me reges regnant et conditores legum decernunt iustitiam. Nichil enim gratius deo esse putamus, quam si id simpliciter offerimus, quod eum esse cognovimus, misericordiam scilicet atque iustitiam. In qua oblatione regni officium quoddam sibi sacerdotii vendicat privilegium.

Unde quidam sapiens legisque peritus iuris interpres, iuris sacerdotes appellat. Iure itaque qui iuris et legum auctoritatem per ipsius gratiam optinemus, eas in meliorem statum partim erigere, partim reformare, debemus et qui misericordiam consecuti sumus in omnibus eas tractare misericordius, interpretari benignius, presertim ubi severitas earum quandam inhumanitatem inducit. Neque hoc ex supercilio quasi iustiores aut moderatores nostris predecessoribus in condendis legibus interpretandisve nostris vigiliis arrogamus, set quia in multis delinquimus et ad delinquendum et ad delinquendum procliviores sumus, parcendum delinquentibus cum moderatia nostris temporibus apta conveniens esse censemus.

Nam et ipsa pietas ita nos instruit dicens: Estote misericordes sicut et pater vester misericors est.

Et rex et propheta: Universe vie domini misericordia et veritas. Et proculdubio tenebimus, quia iudicium sine misericordia erit ei qui iudicium fecerit sine misericordia.

Volumus igitur et iubemus ut sanctiones quas in presenti corpore sive promulgatas a nobis, sive compositas nobis facimus exhiberi, fideliter et alacriter recipiatis.

I. De legum interpretatione

Leges a nostra maiestate noviter promulgatas pietatis intuitu asperitatem nimiam mitigantes mollia quodam moderamine exaucuentes; obscura dilucidantes, generaliter ab omnibus precipimus observari, moribus, consuetudinibus, legibus non cassatis pro varietate populorum nostro regno subiectorum, sicut usque nunc apud eos optinuit, nisi forte nostris his sanctionibus adversari quid in eis manifestissime videatur.

II. De privilegio sanctarum ecclesiarum

Noverint ergo omnes nostre potestati subiecti, quoniam in voto nobis semper fuit, et erit, ecclesias dei pro quibus dominus Ihesus sanguinem suum fudit, protegere, defensare, augere modis omnibus, sicut et proienitores nostri consueta liberalitate, id ipsum facere studuerunt, ideoque multa et innumera beneficia a deo consecuti sunt semper in melius. Itque sacrarum ecclesiarum res omnes et possesiones in nostra post deum et sanctos ejus custodia collacatas atque commissas ab omnibus incursibus malignantium, gladio materiali nobis a deo concessas defendimus et inviolatas custodimus; principibus, comitibus, baronibus et omnibus nostris fidelibus commendamus, scituri, quod nostrum decretum quisquis violare voluerit, nostram se sentiat ledere majestatem.

III. Monitio generalis

Monemus principes, comites, barones, maiores atque minores, archiepiscopos, episcopos, abbates, cunctos denique qui subditos habent cives, burgenses, rusticos, sive cuiuscumque professionis homines, eos humane tractare, misericordiam adhibere, maxime cum debitum adiutorium conveniens et moderatum valent ab ipsis quos habent subditos, postulare. Gratum enim deo faciunt, et nobis maximum gaudium, cuius potestati atque regimini divina dispositio, tam prelatos subdidit quam subiectos. Quod si fuerit neglectum, nostram spectabit sollicitudinem male factum in melius reformare.

IV. De rebus regalibus

Scire volumus principes nostros, comites, barones universos archiepiscopos, episcopos, abbates, quicumque de regalibus nostris magnum vel modicum quid tenet, nullo modo, nullo ingenio, possit ad nostra regalia pertinens alienare, vel vendere, vel in totum vel in partem minuere, unde iura rerum regalium minuantur, aut subvertantur sive aliquod etiam dampnum patiantur.

V. De sanctarum reliquiarum venditione

Sanccimus nemini licere martirum, vel quorucumque sanctorum reliquias vendere, vel comparare. Quod si presumptum fuerit, nondum pretio numerato nichil ets consecuturus si venditor emptorem voluerit convenire. Si autem numeratio facta est, emptori repetitionem non esse, fiscum vero vendicare. Nostram spectabit providentiam temeritatem contrahentium cohercere, et ubi decuerit, reliquias cum consilio antistitum collocare.

VI. De confugio ad ecclesiam

Presente lege sanccimus per loca regni nostri omnia deo propitio in perpetuum valitura nullos penitus, cuiuscumque condicionis de sacrosantis expelli ecclesiis, aut protrahi confugas, nec pro his venerabiles episcopos, aut yconomos exigi, que debentur ab eis qui hoc moliri aut facere presumpserit, capitis periculo, aut bonorum omnium ammissione plectendis. Interim confugis victualia non negentur. Sane si servus, aut colonus, aut servus glebe se ipsum subtraxerit domino, vel furatus res ad loca sancta confugerit, cum rebus quas detulit, domino presentetur, ut pro qualitae commissi subeat ultionem, aut intercessione procedente restituatur et gratie. Nemini quippe ius suum est detrahendum.

VII. De privilegiis ecclesiarum non violandis

Si venerabilis ecclesie privilegia cuiscumque fuerint temeritate violata dolove suppressa commissum iuxta dampnositatem ecclesie compensetur. Quod si non sufficiat ad condempnationis mulctam, regis iudicio vel officialium arbitrio committetur. Nichilominus pro qualitate commissi regis providentie, vel officialium arbitrio subiacebit.

VIII. De episcoporum privilegio

Episcopus ad testimonium non flagiterur, nisi forte in causis ecclesiasticis, vel publicis, cum necessitas, aut regis auctoritas postulaverit. Presbiteri non cogantur corporale sacramentum in negotiis exibere; diacones, subdiacones et infra positos altari sacri ministros, ab obsequiis sordidis alienos esse precipimus; presbiteros tantum non etiam ceteros omnibus angariis personalibus prohibemus.

IX. De illicitis conventiculis

Conventiculam illicitam extra ecclesiam in privatis edibus celebrari vetamus, proscriptionis domus periculo imminente, si dominus eius in eam clericos novam vel tumultuosam conventiculam celebrantes, susceperit non ignarus.

X. De ascripticiis volentibus clericari

Ascripticios sine voluntate et assensu eorum quorum iuri subditi sunt, et potestati, nullus episcoporum ordinare presumat, neque de aliensa parrochia, per litteras commendatorias secundum canonum instituta, vel ab episcopo, vel a proprio capitulo. Hii quorum ascripticii sunt, si quod premium pro data licentia consecrandi suscepisse convicti fuerint, huiusce ascriptii perdant qui dedit pecuniam ab ordine cadat, fisco vero cum omnibus rebus suis vendicetur. Solent sancto voto atque proposito sanctis occasionibus pravitas se ingerere, et dei servitium atque ecclesie ministerium perturbare. Ne ergo sinistrum aliquod aliquando possit nostris institutionibus obviare, si forte in rure vel in vico ecclesia assignatos habuerit sacerdotes quibus decedentibus sint alii (subrograndi et) domini ruris vel vici super ascripticiis, episcopo fieri subgorationem negaverint, presertim cum ex ipsis ascripticiis persona ydonea ab episcopo expectatur, dignum nostre clementie videtur, atque iustissium ad iustam petitionem ecclesie ascripticiorum dominum iure cogendum; filii vero decedentis presbiteri ad asripticiorum condicionem reddatur omni occasione remota.

XI. De raptum virginum

Si quis rapere sacratas deo virgines aut nondum velatas causa iungendi matrimonium presumpserit, capitali pena feriatur, vel alia pena quam regia censura decreverit.

XII. (sic)

Iudeus paganus servum christianum nec vendere, nec comparare audeat, nec ex aliquo titulo possidere seu pignori detinere. Quod si presumpserit, omnes res eius infiscentur, et curie servus fiat. Quem si forte ausu vel nefario vel suasu circumcidi vel fidem abnegare fecerit, capitali supplicio puniatur.

XIII. De apostatantibus

Apostantes a fide catholica penitus execramus, ultionibus insequimur, bonis omnibus spoliamus, a professione vel voto naufragantes legibus coartamus, succesiones tollimus, omne ius legitimum abdicamus.

XIV. De ioculatoribus

Mimi et qui ludibrio corporis sui questum faciunt, publico habitu earum virginum, que deo dicate sunt, vel veste monachica non utantur, nec clericali; si fecerint verberibus publice afficiantur.

XV. De pupillis et orphanis

Pupillis et orphanis pietatis intuitu, multa privilegia priscis legibus confirmata pro qualitate temporum quibus absolverint in ultimo delegamus nostri iudicibus ubi iactura tollerabilis non est, favorabiliter commendamus. Mulieribus nichilominus ubi non modice lese sunt, propter fragiliorem sexum, legum equitatem sectantes tam per nos, quam per officiales nostros ex pietatis visceribus subveniendum decrevimus, sicut decet et oportet.

XVI. De indigne anelantibus ad sacerdotum

Nemo sacerdotum dignitatem pretio petere audeat, contumeliam pro premio reportaturus et penam, mox ut fuerit propria petitione detectus. Ille enim honore se privat, qui inpudenti fronte, velud importunus expostulat.

XVII. De sacrilegiis

Disputari de regis iudicio, consiliis, institutionibus, factis non oportet. Est enim par sacrilegio disputare de eius iudiciis, institutionibus, factis atque consiliis et an is dignus sit quem rex elegerit, aut decernit. Multe leges sacrilegos severissime punierunt, set pena moderanda est arbitrio iudicantis, nisi forte manufacta templa dei fracta sunt violenter, aut dona et vasa sacra, noctu sublata sunt, hoc enim casu capitale est.

XVIII. De crimine maiestatis

Quisquis cum milite uno vel cum pluribus, seu privato scelestem inierit factionem aut factionis dederit, vel susceperit sacramentum, de nece etiam virorum illustrium, qui consiliis et consistorio nostro intersunt, cogitaverint et tractaverint, eadem severitate voluntatem sceleris qua effectum puniri iura voluerunt, ipse quidem ut pote reus majestatis gladio feriatur, bonis eius omnibus fisco addictis; filii vero eius nullum unquam beneficium sive a nostro beneficio seu iure consensum optineant. Sit ei mors solacium et vita supplicium. Quod si qiusquam de factiosis mox sine mora factum detexerit, veniam et gratiam mox sequatur. Crimen majestatis post mortem rei etiam incipit et tractatur; rei ù memoria condempnatur, adeo ut quicquid contraxerit, fecerit, statuerit, a die criminis nullam habeat firmitatem; set omne quod habuit, fisci iuribus vendicetur. Hoc crimine qui parentem purgaverit, eius successionem meretur. Hoc crimine tenentur omnes, quorum consilio fugiunt obsides, armantur cives, seditiones moventur, concitantur tumultus, magistratus necantur, exercitus deseritur, ad hostem fugitur, socius proditur, dolo malo cuneus discinditur, bellis ceditur, ars desolatam relinquitur, sociis auxilium denegatur, cetaraque hujusmodi sicut regii consilii explorator, summissor et publicator, et qui susceperit hospitio hostes regni, et ductum prbeuerit non ignarus.

XIX. De nova militia

Divine iustitie consentientes probanda probamus contrarium refutamus. Sicut, enim, nullatenus exasperandi sunt boni, ita beneficiis non sunt fovendi mali. Sanccimus, itaque tale proponentes edictum, ut si quicumque novam militiam arripuerit, contra regni nostri beatitudinem, atque pacem, sive integritatem, militie nomine et professione, penitus decidat, nisi forte a militari genere per successionem duxerit prosapiam. Idemque statuimus de sortientibus qualiscumque professinis ordinem, ut puta si vel auctoritatem iudicii optinuit, sive notariorum officium, ceterisque similibus.

XX. De falso

Qui litteras regias aut mutat aut quas ipse scripsit notho sigillo subsignat, capitaliter puniatur.

XXI. De cutendibus monetam

Adulterinam monetam cudentibus, vel scienter eam accipientibus, penam capitis irrogamus, et eorum substantiam publicamus; consentientes etiam hac pena ferimus. Qui nummos aureos vel argenteos raserint tinxerint, vel quocumque modo imminuerint, tam personas eorum, quam bona omnia publicamus.

Ubi questio falso inciderit, diligens inquisitio mox sequatur, argumentis, testibus, collatione scripturarum, et aliis vestigiis veritatis. Non solum accusator probationibus honeretur, set inter utramque personam iudex sit medius, ut omnibus que competunt exquisitis, demum sententiam ferat. Capitali post probationem supplicio secuturo si id exigat magnitudo supplicii, vel alia pena pro qualitate delicti.

XXII. De falso instrumento

Qui falso instrumento nesius utitur, falsi crimine non punitur. Qui falsitatem testibus astruxerit, falsi pena cohercetur.

XXIII. De abolitione testamenti

Amator testamentorum, publicorum instrumentorum, celator, delator, perversor, eadem pena tenetur. Si quis patris testamentum deleverit, ut quasi ab intestato succedat, patris hereditate privatur.

XXIV. De officialibus publicis

Qualitas persone gravat et relevat penam falsi. Officiales reipublice, vel iudicis qui tempore amministrationis pecunias publicas subtraxerint, obnoxii crimini peculatus, capite puniantur, nisi regia pietas indulserit.

XXV. De bonis publicis

Qui sua negligentia bona publica deperire, vel minui permiserit, in persona propria et rebus suis, constituetur obnoxius, et hoc prospectu pietatis rege. Qui sciens furantibus assensum prebuerit, eadem lege tenetur.

XXVI. De coniugiis legitime celebrandis

Quoniam ad curam et sollecitudinem regni pertinet leges condere, populum gubernare, mores instruere, pravas consuetudines extirpare, dignum et equum visum est nostre clementie, quandam pravam consuetudinem, que quasi clades et lues huc usque per diuturna tempora, partem nostri populi perrependo pervasit edicti nostri mucrone decidere, ne liceat vitiosas pullulas de cetero propagare. Absurdum quippe moribus repugnans sacrorum canonum institutis, christianis auribus inauditum est, matrimonium velle contrahere, legitimam sobolem procreare, indivisibile vite consortium alligare, nec dei favorem et gratiam nuptis nuptiarum in stabulis querere, et tantum in Christo et ecclesia ut dicit apostolus sacramentum confirmandum per sacerdotum ministerium creare. Sancimus itaque lege presenti deo propitio perpetuo valitura, volentibus omnibus legitimum contrahere matrimonium necessitatem imponi, quatinus post sponsalia nuptias celebraturi sollempniter quisque pro suo modulo seu commodo, limen petant ecclesie sacerdotum benedictionem post scrutinium consecutum anulum ponat, pretii postulationique sacerdotali subdantur, si volunt futuris heredibus successionem relinquere.

Alioquin noverint ammodo molientes contra nostrum regale preceptum, neque ex testamento, neque ab intestato se habituros heredes legitimos, ex illecito per nostram sanctionem matrimonio procreatos. Mulieres etiam dotes, et aliis nubentibus legitime debitas non habere. Rigorem cuius sanctionis, omnibus illis remittimus, qui promulgationis eius tempore, iam matrimonium contraxerunt.

Viduas vero volentibus ducere, huius necessitatis vinculum relaxamus.

XXVII. De adulteris

Generali lege presente sancimus pietatis intuitu, cui viscera tota debemus, quotiens a nostra provisione et ordinatione iura regentibus accusatio adulterii aut stupri fuerit presentata, oculo non caligante personam despicere, condiciones notare, etates et consilium animi investigare, si deliberatione vel consultatione, vel lubrico etatis proruperint, ad facimus, vel prolapse sint. Utrum earum fortuna tenuis sit an torosa, petulantia stimulate fuerint, an dolore maxime materiali. Ut, his omnibus perquisitis, probatis vel manifestis, non de rigore iuris, set de lance equitatis, super commissis excessibus, lenior vel asperior sententia feratur. Sic, enim, perfecta iustitia divine iustitie respondebit. Nam nec nos poterit illa divina sententia: in qua mensura mensi fueritis remetietur vobis.

Legum igitur asperitate lenita, non ut olim gladio agendum, set rerum ad eam pertinentium confiscatio inducetur, si filios legitimos ex eo matrimonio violato, vel alio non habuerit. Periniquum est successione quippe fraudari, qui nati sint eo tempore quo thori lex legaliter servabatur. Aut viro traenda est, nullatenus ad vite periculum servituro, set ultionem thori violati, nasi truncatione, quod sevius et atrocius inducitur persecuturo. Ultra enim, neque viro, neque parentibus sevire licebit. Quod si vie eius noluerit in eam dare vindictam, nos huiusmodi maleficium non sinemus inultum, precipimus publice flagellandum.

Qui coram se spectante, vel arbitrio, permittit cum ganeis suam coniugem lascivire, non facile poterit vero iudicio accusare. Viam quippe mechandi aperit, qui cum possit prohibere consentit.

Quamvis uxorem suspectam quis habeat, eum lenocinii non dapnamus. Quis enim alieni thori iure inquitet quietem. Quod si patenter deprehendimus quempiam habere uxorem questuosam, dignam nostris temporibus mox sequimur pene vindictam, eum quoque pena infamie condempnamus. Femine penitus, et adulterii et stupri severitate iudiciaria prestentur immunes, quas vilitas vite dignas legum observatione non credit.

XXVIII. De eodem

Que passim venalem formam exhibuit, et vulgo prostitutam se prebuit, huius criminis accusationem ammovit. Violentiam tamen ei ingeri prohibemus, et inter boni testimonii feminas, ei habitationem vetamus. Adulter, adultera simul accusari non possunt, alter singulariter est accusandus, et rei exitus expectandus. Nam si adulter defendi poterit, mulier est secura, nulli ulterius responsura. Si vero fuerit condempnatus, tunc demum mulier accusatur.

Lex delectum non facit, quis primum conveniri debeat. Set si uterque presens est, vir conveniendus est primum.

Repudium in accusatione est semper permittendum; neque violentia seu detentio est adhibenda.

XXIX. De lenocinio

Lenas sollicitantes alienam scilicet castitatem genus criminis pessimum, tamquam ipsas adulteras puniendas presente lege sanccimus. Matres virgines filias venalicias proponentes, et maritalia federa fugientes, ut lenas ipsas persequimur, scilicet ut nasus ejus abscidatur. Castitatem enim suorum viscerum vendere inhumanum est et crudele. Quod si filia se ipsam tamen prostituerit, mater vero solummodo consentit, iudicum arbitrio relinquatur.

XXX. De violatione thori

Si providentia rege celsitudinis nullo modo patitur inter regni nostri militem baronum nostrorum quemlibet alterius castrum invadere, predas committere, cum armis insurgere, vel inique fraudari, quin pro commisso bonorum omnium iactura ipsum afficiat, quanto amplius dampnandum censemus si compatris et vicini thorum violare presumpserit. Intolerabile prorsus de iure videtur. Sanccimus itaque si de tali facto nobis aliquando fuerit proclamatum, manifestum fuerit, vel probatum, bonorum omnium mulctatione plectendum. Si maritus uxorem in ipso actu adulterii deprehenderit, tam uxorem, quam adulterum occidere licebit, nulla tamen mora protracta.

XXXI. De adulterio

Lex maritum lenocinii pena cohercet, qui uxorem in adulterio deprehensam, retinuerit, adulterumque dimiserit, nisi forte sine sua culpa ille diffugit.

XXXII. De desistendibus ab accusatione

Qui post crimen adulterii intentatum uxorem receperit, destitisse videtur ab accusatione ideoque suscitare qustionem ultra non poterit.

XXXIII. De iniuriis privatis personis illatis

Quod iuri et rationi est consentaneum satis iure cunctis est gratum, et quod a ratione equitatis dicrepat, universis ingratitudinem representat. Nulli igitur mirum si quod in homine deus carius et dignius posuerit, cum negligitur atque despicitur, et inprobo iudicio vilipenditur, sapiens et honestatis amicus rationabiliter indignatur.

Quid enim absurdius quam equa lance pensari ubi iumenti cauda decerpitur, et ubi honestissimi viri barba depilatur.

Pro suggestione ergo populi nostro regno subiecti atque supplicatione legum suarum ineptitudinem cognoscentis hanc legem et edictum proponimus. Ut cuicumque de popularibus excusato, tamen et deliberatione barba fuerit depilata, reus talis commissi pena huiusmodi feriatur solidis aureis scilicet regiis sex; si vero in rixa factum fuerit, sine deliberatione et studio, de eisdem solidis III.

XXXIV. De iniuriis personis illatis curialibus

Observent diligentissime iudices, ut in actione iuriariarum, curialium dignitatem personarum considerent, et iuxta personarum qualitatem sententiam ferant, eorum scilicet quibus fiunt, et eorum qui faciunt, et quando ubi temeritas presumitur, et iuxta qualitatem personarum sententiam ferant; ipsis autem facta iniuria, non ad ipsos dumtaxat, set etiam ad regie dignitatis spectat offensam.

XXXV. De mederi volentibus

Quisquis ammodo mederi voluerit, officialibus et vicibus nostri se presentet, eorum discutiendus iudicio. Quod si sua temeritate presumpserit, carcere constringatur, bonis ejus omnibus publicatis. Hoc autem prospectum est, ne quilibet nostro regno subiecti periclitentur imperitia medicantum.

XXXVI. De plagiariis

Qui sciens liberum hominem vendiderit hac pena legitima teneatur, ut ex bonis suis venditus redimatur; ipse vero maleficus curie nostre servus sit, bonorum suorum residuo publicato. Quod si non poterit redimi, pro servo tradatur parentibus venditi, bonis eius curie addictis. Quocumque autem venditus redeat, maleficus curie servus fiat, fillis etiam post hunc casum nascentibus subiectis curie perpetue servituti.

XXXVII. De siccariis

Qui aggressorem vel latronem in dubio vite discrimine constitutis occiderit, nullam ob id factam calumpniam metuere debet.

XXXVIII. De infantibus et furiosis

Infans sine malignitate animi et furiosus si hominem occiderit, non tenetur. Quia alterum innocentia consilii, alterum fati infelicitas excusat.

XXXIX. De fure

Nocturnum furem qui occiderit, impune ferat si aliter comprehendi non potuerit, dum modo clamore id fiat.

XL. De incendiariis

Qui dolose domum incenderit capitis pena plectatur, velud incendiarius. In maleficiis voluntas spectatur non exitus; nichil enim interest occidat quis an mortis causam prebeat.

XLI. De precipitatoribus

Qui de alto se ipsum precipitat, et hominem occiderit, et ramum incautus prohiciens, non proclamaverit, seu lapidem ad aliud iecit, hominemque occidit, huic pene non succumbit.

XLII. De poculo

Mala et noxia medicamenta, ad alienandos animos, seu venena quis dederit, vendiderit, habuerit, capitali sententia feriatur. Poculum amatorium, vel aliquem cibum noxium, quisquis instruxerit, etiam si neminem leserit, impunis non erit.

XLIII. Si iudex litem suam fecerit.

Iudex si accepta pecunia reum quem criminis et mortis fecerit, capitis periculo subiacebit. Si iudex fraudulenter atque dolose sententiam contra leges protulerit, auctoritate iudiciaria inrecuperabiliter cadat, notetur infamia, rebus eius omnibus publicatis. Quod si ignorantia a iuris sententia oberraverit, ferens iudicium pro simplicitate animi manifesta, regie misericordie et providentie subiacebit.

Codex Casinensis 468

Leges a nostra maiestate noviter promulgatas, generaliter ab omnibus precipimus observari, moribus, consuetudine, et legibus non cassatis, nisi forte nostris his sanctionibus adversari quid in eis manifeste videatur.

1. De privilegiis ecclesiarum

Primo itaque iura sanctarum ecclesiarum, res omnes et possesiones earum in nostra post deum et sanctos ejus custodia collacatas ab omnibus incursibus malignantium, gladio materiali a deo nobis concesso defendimus et inviolatas custodimus; quisquis hoc nostrum decretum violare voluerit, nostram senserit ledere maiestatem.

2. Ut domini subiectos humane tractent

Monemus, princeps, comites, et barones, omnesque dominos, subiectos humane tractare, misericordiam adhibere, maxime cum debitum adiutorium et moderatum et conveniens volent ab ipsis, quos habent subiectos, postulare.

3. Ut regalia non minuantur

Quicumque de regalibus nostris magnum vel modicum quid tenet, nullo modo, nullo ingenio possit ad nostra regalia pertinens donare, vendere, vel alienare, vel in totum vel in partem minuere.

4. De sacrosanctis ecclesiis, et episcopis, et clericis

Sancimus nemini licere sanctorum reliquias vendere vel comparare. Sancimus sub capitis periculo nullos penitus cuiuscumque condicionis de sacrosanctis ecclesiis expelli aut protrahi confugas; nec pro his venerabiles episcopos vel iconomos exigi que debentur ab eis; nec ipsis confugis interim victualia negentur. Servus vero, colonus, seu gleba servus, subtrahens se domino, vel furatus res ad loca sacra confugiens, cum rebus quas detulit domino presentetur.

Privilegia ecclesiarum inconcussa serventur. Episcopus ad testimonium non flagiterur, nisi forte in causis ecclesiasticis vel publicis, et cum summa necessitas, aut regis auctoritas postulaverit. Diaconos et subdiaconos et infra positos altari sacri ministros, ab obsequiis sordidis, alienos esse precipimus. Presbiteros vero tantum non etiam ceteros ab angariis personalibus prohibemus.

5. De illicitis conventiculis

Conventiculam illicita extra ecclesiam in privatis edibus celebrari vetamus.

6. Ne servi vel ascripticii clericentur

Ascripticios sine voluntate eorum quorum iuri subditi sunt, nullus episcoporum ordinare presumat. Iudeus, paganus, servum christianum, nec compare audeat nec ex aliquo titulo possidere.

7. De ioculatoribus

Mimi et mime, et qui ludibrio corporis sui questum faciunt, publico habitu veste monachica, vel clericali non utantur; quod si fecerit, verberibus publice afficiantur.

8. De raptu

Si quis rapere sacratas virgines, aut nondum velatas causa iungendi matrimonium presumpserit, capitali pena feriatur.

9. De apostatis

Apostatas insequimur ultionibus, bonis omnibus spoliamus. A professione vero naufragantes seu voto legibus coartamus, succesiones tollimus, omne ius legitimum abdicamus.

10. De pupillis et orphanis

Leges que pro pupillis et orphanis faciunt relevamus. Mulieribus lesis ex pietatis visceribus propter fragiliorem sexum subveniendum decrevimus sicut decet, et quatenus oportet.

11. De sacrilegis consiliis

Disputari de regis iudiciis, consiliis, institutionibus et factis non oportet; talis disputatio par sacrilegio computatur. Multe leges sacrilegos severissime punierunt, set pena moderata est arbitrio iudicantis, nisi forte manu facta templum dei fractum est violenter, aut dona et vasa sacra noctu sublata sunt, hoc enim casu capitale est.

12. De crimine maiestatis

Quisquis cum milite uno aut pluribus seu privato villano scelestam inhierit factionem aut factionis dederit vel susceperit sacramentum, de nece etiam virorum illustrium, qui consiliis et consistorio nostro intersunt, cogitaverint et tractaverint, eadem enim severitate voluntatem sceleris qua effectum puniri iura voluerint, ipse quidem ut pote reus majestatis gladio feriatur, bonis eius fisco addictis. Filii vero eius nullum unquam beneficium sive a nostro beneficio seu iure confertum optineant;sit ei mors solacium et vita supplicium. Quod si quisquam de factiosis mox sine mora factam detexerit, et premio a nobis et honore donabitur.

Is vero qui usus fuerit factione, si vero tamen incognita adhuc patefecerit et conciliorum archana absolutione tantum ac venia dignus habebitur; sic tamen, si suis assertionibus veri fides fuerit opitulata, laudem maximam et premium a nostra clementia consequetur; alioquin capitali pena plectetur.

Crimen maiestatis post mortem rei etiam incipit et tractatur, et rei memoria condempnatur adeo ut quicquid contraxerit, fecerit, statuerit, a die criminis nullam habeat firmitatem; hoc crimine qui parentem purgaverit, eius successionem meretur.

Hoc crimine tenentur omnes quorum consilio fugiunt obsides, armantur cives, seditiones moventur, concitantur tumultus, magistratus necantur, exercitus deseritur, ad hostem fugitur, dolo modo cuneus scinditur, socius proditur, bellis ceditur, arx desolatur vel relinquitur, sociis auxilium denegatur, cetaraque huiusmodi, ut regii consilii explorator, sive missorum publicator et qui susceperit hostes regni hospitio, vel ductum prebuerit non ignarus.

13. De jnjuriis curialium

Observent iudices diligentissime, ut in actionem injuriarium curialium personarum dignitatem et qualitem eorum quibus illate sunt, et eorum qui faciunt, et quando, et ubi, huiusmodi temeritates presumuntur, et sic ferant sententiam; quia non ad ipsos dumtaxat, sed ad regie dignitatis spectat offensam.

14. De crimine falsi

Qui litteras regias aut mutat, aut quas ipse scripsit notho sigillo subsignat capitaliter puniatur. Qui falso instrumento utitur nescius, falsi crimine non punitur.

Adulterinam monetam cudendibus vel scienter eam succipientibus, et utentibus, penam capitis irrogamus, et eorum substantiam publicamus; consentientes etiam, hac pena ferimus.

Qui nummos aureos vel argenteos raserit, tinxerit, vel aliquo modo minuerit, tam personas eorum, quam bona omnia publicamus.

Qui falsitatem testibus astruxerit falsi pena coherceantur.

Motor testamentorum publicorum, instrumentorum celator, deletor, perversor, eadem pena tenetur.

Si quis patris testamentum aboleverit, ut quasi ab intestato succedat, patris hereditate privetur.

Qualitas persone gravat et relevat penam falsi.

15. De coniugiis

Sancimus lege presenti, volentibus omnibus legitimum contrahere matrimonium necessitatem imponi, quatenus post sponsalia celebraturi nuptias sollempniter quisque pro modulo suo seu quomodolibet limen petat ecclesie, sacerdotum benedictionem post scrutinium consecuturum anulum ponat, preci postulationique sacerdotali subdantur, si voluerint futuris heredibus successiones relinquere. Alioquin amodo molientes contra regale nostrum edictum, neque ex testamento neque ab intestato, habituros se legitimos filios heredes ex illicito matrimonio per nostram sanctionem noverint procreatos; mulieres etiam aliis nubentes legitimas dotes debitas non habere. Viduas vero volentibus ducere hoc necessitatis vinculum relaxamus.

16. De crimine adulterii

Generali lege sancimus quotiens nostra provisione et ordinatione iura regentibus accusatio adulterii vel strupi fuerit presentata, oculo non caligante personas despicere, condiciones notare, etates et consilium animi investigare, si deliberatione, consultatione, vel lubrico etatis proruperint ad facinus vel prolapse sint, an dolore maxime maritali; ut, his omnibus perquisitis, probatis vel manifestis, non de rigore iuris set de lance equitatis super commissis excessibus levior vel asperior sententia proferatur. Sic enim profecto iustitia nostra divine iustitie respondet.

Legum igitur asperitate lenita, non ut olim gladio agendum, set rerum ad eam pertinentium confiscatio inducetur, si filios legitimos ex eo matrimonio violato vel alio non habuerit. Iniquum enim est eos successione privari, qui nati sunt eo tempore quo thori lex legaliter servabatur. Aut viro tradenda est nullatenus ad vite periculum servituro, set ultionem thori violati nasi truncatione quod sevius et atrocius inducitur persecutor; ultro enim nec viro nec parentibus sevire licebit. Quod si vir eius noluerit in eam dare vindictam, nos maleficium huiusmodi non sinemus inultum; precipimus igitur publice flagellandum.

Qui coram se spectante, vel arbitrio permittit cum ganeis coniugem suam lascivire non facile nostro iudicio poterit accusare. Viam quippe peccandi mechandi aperit, qui cum possit pohibere consentit.

Quamvis uxorem suspectam quis habeat, quamvis famosam, si tamen fidem habet, eum lenocinii non dampnamus; quis enim iure thori alieni inquietet quietem. Quod si patenter deprehendimus quempiam habere incestuosam uxorem, dignam mox sequemur pene vindictam; eum quoque pena infamie condempnamus.

Femine penitus et adulterii et stupri prestentur immunes iudiciaria severitate, quas vilitas vite dignas legum observatione non credidi, sicut ministre caupone.

17. De meretricibus

Que passim formam venalem exhibuit, et vulgo prostitutam se prebuit, huius criminis accusationem amovit; violentiam tamen ei ingeri prohibemus, et inter boni testimonii feminas habitare vetamus.

18. De accusatione adulterii

Adulter et adultera simul accusari non possunt, alter singulariter est accusandus, et rei exitus expectandus; nam si adulter defendi poterit, mulier est secura, nulli ulterius responsura. Si vero fuerit condempnatus, tunc demum mulier accusatur.

De crimine adulteri pacisci non licet, et par delictum accusatoris prevaricatoris et refugientis veritatis inquisitionem. Qui autem pretium pro comperto stupro accepit, pena legis Julie de adulteriis tenetur. Crimen adulterii maritum retenta in matrimonio uxore, inferre non posse nemini dubium est.

Lex delectum non facit, quis primum debeat conveniri, set, si uterque est presens, vir convenendus est primum. Repudium in hac accusatione pretermittendum, neque violentia seu detentio adhibenda.

19. De officialibus rei publice

Officiales rei publice vel iudices qui in tempore amministrationis pecunias publicas subtraxerint, obnoxii crimine peculatus, capite puniuntur, nisi regia pietas indulserit.

Qui sua negligentia bona publica deperire vel minui permiserit, et in persona propria et in rebus suis constituetur obnoxius; et hoc prospectu regie pietatis.

20. De furtis

Qui sciens, furanti sinum prebuit, eadem pena tenetur.

21. De crimine lenocinii

Lenas sollicitantes alienam castitatem genus criminis pessimum tamquam ipsas adulteras puniendas, presenti lege sancimus.

Matres virgines filias venalicias proponentes et maritalia federa fugientes, ut lenas ipsas persequimur, scilicet ut nasus earum abscidantur; castitatem enim et virginitatem suorum viscerum vendere inhumanum est et crudele; quod si filia se ipsam tamen prostituit, mater vero tantum consentit, iudicis arbitrio relinquetur.

Crimen lenocinii contrahunt, qui deprehensam in adulterio uxorem in matrimonio tenuerit, non qui suspectam adulteram habuerunt.

22. De eodem

Si providentia rege celsitudinis nullo modo patitur inter regni nostri limitem baronum nostrorum quemlibet alterius castrum invadere, predas committere, cum armis insurgere, vel inique fraudari, quin pro commisso bonorum omnium ipsum iactura afficiat; quanto amplius dampnandum censemus, si compatris vel vicini thorum violare presumpserit quis intolerabile prorsus de iure videtur. Sancimus itaque si de tali facto nobis aliquando fuerit proclamatum, et manifestum fuerit vel probatum, bonorum omnium mulctatione plectendum.

23. De vindicta adulterantium

Si maritus uxorem in ipso actu adulterii deprehenderit, tam adulterum quam uxorem occidere licebit, nulla tamen mora protracta. Lex maritum lenocinii pena cohercet, qui uxorem in adulterio deprehensam retinuit, adulterumque dimisit; nisi forte sine sua culpa ille diffugerit.

24. De desistentibus ab accusatione

Qui post crimen adulterii intemptatum uxorem receperit, destitisse videtur, ideoque suscitare questionem ultra non poterit.

25. De plagiariis

Qui sciens liberum hominem vendiderit, hac pena legitima teneatur, ut ex bonis suis venditus redimatur; ipse vero maleficus curie servus sit, bonorum suorum residuo publicato; quod si ex rebus ipsius redimi non poterit, pro servo tradatur parentibus venditi, bonis eius curie addictis; quocumque autem casu venditus redeat, maleficus curie servus fiat, filiis etiam post hunc casum nascentibus subiecti sint curie perpetua servitute.

26. De sicariis secundum legem corneliam

Qui aggressorem vel latronem, in dubio vite discrimine constitutis occiderit, nullam, ob id factum, calumpniam metuere debet. Qui aggressorem ad se venientem ferro repulerit, non homicida set defensor salutis est.

Nocturnum furem qui occiderit, impune feret, si aliter comprehendi nequiverit, si modo cum clamore id fiat.

Infans sine malignitate animi et furiosus si hominem occiderit, non tenetur; quia alterum innocentia consili alterum facti infelicitas excusat

Nichil interest occidat quis, an mortis causam prebeat.

In maleficiis voluntas spectatur non exitus.

Qui de alto se ipsum precipitat et hominem occidit, qui ramum incautus deiciens non proclamavit, seu lapidem aut aliud deiecit hominemque occidit, huic pene succumbit.

27. De incendiis

Qui dolose domum incenderit, capitis pena plectetur velut incendiarius.

28. De noxiis medicaminibus

Poculum amatorium vel aliquem cibum noxium quisquis instruxerit, etiam si neminem leserit, impunis non erit.

29. De eisdem

Mala et noxia medicamenta ad alienandos animos, seu venena qui dederit, vendiderit, habuerit, capitali sententia feriatur.

30. De iudice depravato

Si iudex accepta pecunia reum quemlibet criminis et mortis fecerit, capitis periculo subiacebit.

Si iudex fraudulenter atque dolose sententiam contra leges protulerit, auctoritate iudiciaria inrecuperabiliter cadat, notetur infamia, rebus eius omnibus publicatis. Quod si iuris ignorantia a iuris sententia aberraverit, ferens iudicium pro simplicitate manifestum regie misericordie subiacebit.

In maleficiis voluntas spectatur non exitus.

31. De arripientibus novam militiam

Quicumque novam militiam arripuit contra regni nostri beatitudinem et pacem sine integritate militie nomine et professione penitus cadat, nisi forte a militari genere per successionem duxerit prosapiam.

32. De tironibus

Nullus tiro ga aut veteranus aut censibus obnoxius ad militia accedat.

33. De iniuriis privatorum

Cuicumque de popularibus ex consulto tamen et deliberatione barba fuerit depilata, reus soldorum aureorum VI regalium pena condempnetur; si vero in rixa factum fuerit, sine deliberatione, solidorum III.
Vel iumenti cauda decerpitur.

34. De fugacibus

Si quis temerario ausu presumpserit bona in quiete et tranquillitate regni habita, cum pro ipso laborare expedit, labores fugiendo obmittere, omnia bona sua dominus eius habeat, et illius persona curie assignetur.

35. De seditionariis

Si quis in exercitu seditiones, iurgia seu aliud fecerit, uti exercitus noster turbetur, persona eius cum omnibus suis bonis mercedi curie subiacebit.
Si quis ficte vel fraudulenter ad magnum exercitum non venerit, seu, postquam venerit, ab exercitu sine licentia curie recesserit, capitalem subibit sententiam, vel in manibus curie tradetur, ut ipse et eius heredes culusti fiant.

36. De mordisonibus

Comperit nostra serenitas infra regni nobis a deo concessi fines quorundam immanitate clandestina incendia, tam in urbanis quam rusticis prediis, perpetrari, arbores quoque et vites furtim cedere. Proinde hac edictali pragmatica sanctione in perpetuum valitura deo propitio sancimus, ut si quis amodo de hujusmodi reatu fuerit appellatus, si suspectione careat et eius conversatio per bonorum testimonia illibata consistat, pro tenore veterum legum, aut cuiuscumque loci consuetudine se expurget. Si vero tanti reatus non levis suspitio de eo fuerit, vel preterite vite sue probrosus cursus extiterit, opinionemque eius apud bonos et graves dehonestaverit, de calumpnia prius actore iurante, non ut actenus set ceteris super hoc legibus sopitis et moribus, igniti ferri subeat iudicium. Predicti denique criminis confessus aut convictus, dampno prius lese partis de eius facultatibus resarcito, vite sue periculum, vel membrorum suorum privatione pro bene placito maiestatis nostre incurret.

37. Que sit potestas justitiarii

Sancimus ut latrocinia, fracture domorum, insultus viarum, vis mulieribus illata, duella, homicidia, leges parabiles, calumpnie criminum, incendia, forisfacte omnes, de quibus quilibet de corpore et rebus suis mercedi curie debeat subiacere, a iustitiariis iudicentur, clamoribus supradictorum baiulis depositis, cetera vero a baiulis poterunt definiri.

38. De intestatis

Nuper ad nostri culminis pervenit audientiam quod cum aliquis burgensium vel aliorum hominum civitatum intestatus decedit, sive filii ex eo existant sive non, res eius ad opus curie nostre capiebantur, quod admodum maiestati displicuit et grave tulimus.

Nos itaque, ex solita nostre benignitatis gratia, hanc pravam consuetudinem penitus resecare volentes, precipimus, ut, si quis burgensium vel aliorum, qui in ipsa civitate devenerit, intestatus decesserit, si ex eo filius vel filia exiterit, ipse sui patris heres existat, et tertia pars omnium rerum eius pro ipsius anima erogetur.

Si vero nulli filii ex eo existant, tunc proximiores eius tam ex linea ascendentium et descendentium quam ex latere venientium, qui de iure ei succedere debent, heredes existant, si de feudo vel de servitio non fuerit, tertia tamen parte rerum suarum pro defuncti anima distributa.

Si autem filius vel filia ex eo nullus exiterit, vel alius tam ex linea ascendentium quam et descendentium, vel ex latere venientium, qui de iure ei succedere debeat, tunc etiam tertia parte omnium rerum suarum ut dictum est integre pro defuncti anima prestita, residuum ad opus curie nostre capiatur.

Si vero cum herede seu sine herede testatus decesserit, ultima eius voluntas in integrum observetur.

39. De excessu prelatorum et dominorum

De prelatis autem ecclesiarum sic a regia munificentia statutum est, ut in his tantum ab hominibus suis adiutorum exigant, vidilicet, pro consecratione sua, cum ad concilium a domino papa vocantur, pro servitio exercitus nostri, si quando in exercitu servierint, vel si vocati fuerint a rege vel missi, pro corredo nostro si quando in terris eorum nos hospitari vel corredum ab eis recipere contigerit. Et in his tantum casibus a prelatis omnibus, comitibus, baronibus et militibus moderate secundum facultates hominum suorum audiutoria exigant et accipiant.

40. Rescriptum pro cleris

De eo autem quod male interpretatum est videlicet quod de nostre maiestatis constitutione villani non audeant ad ordinem clericatus accedere, sine voluntate et assensu dominorum suorum, ita statutum est, quod si aliquis villanus est et servire debet personaliter intuitu persone, ut sunt ascripticii et servi glebe, et alii huiusmodi, qui non respectu tenimentorum vel alius beneficii servire debent, set intuitu personarum, que persone eorum sunt obligate servitis isti quidem, sine assensu et voluntate dominorum suorum ad ordinem clericatus accedere nequerunt. Illi vero, qui non intuitu personarum set respectu testimentorum vel aliquorum beneficiorum que tenent servire debent dominis suis, si voluerint ad ordinem clericatus accedere, liceat eis etiam sine voluntate dominorum suorum, prius tamen renuntiatis his que tenent a dominis suis.

Dignum et necessarium est opere[t] siq[ue] de nobis et uniu[er]si regni n[ost]ri statu mentus n[ost]ro p[re]sumim[us]. a largitate diuina q[uantum] c[on]secuta. recepim[us] diuinis beneficiis q[ui]b[us] ualem[us] obsequiis resp[on]deam[us]. ne tante gr[ati]e penitus ingr[a]ti sim[us]. Sig[?] sua m[iserico]r[di]a nob[is] d[eu]s p[er] p[ro]strat[is] hostib[us] pace reddidit. integritate[m] regni. tranq[ui]llitate gratissima. t[a]m in carnalib[us] q[uam] in sp[irit]ualib[us] reformaui[t]. reformare cogimur iustitie simul et pietatis itinera. u[t] uideri eam et mirabilit[er] e[ss]e distortam. h[oc]. n[on]. ip[su]m q[uod] air. inspiram[?]. de munere ip[s]i[us] largitoris accepim[us]. dicente ip[s]o. p[er] me reges regnat. et c[on]ditores legum decernu[n]t iustitiam. Hic. n[on]. gr[atu]m d[e]o e[ss]e putam[us]. q[uod] s[uu]d s[i]b[i] p[re]s[en]t[em] offerim[us]. q[uod] eum e[ss]e cognouim[us]. m[iseric]iam. s.

Beginning of the text in the Vatican codex

Appendix 2
MARGARET'S PENDANT

The only contemporary image of Margaret of Navarre known to us, which may indeed be a merely symbolic representation, is a gold reliquary pendant (a color photograph appears on this volume's back cover) made by skilled goldsmiths in Canterbury, a center of this craft. This was given to her by Bishop Reginald of Bath, whose name appears on it: "Bishop Reginald of Bath consigns this to Queen Margaret of Sicily." Clockwise, beginning from the cross at the middle-top of the border, this Latin inscription on the obverse reads: ISTUD REGINE MARGARETE SICULORUM TRANSMITTIT PRESUL RAINAUDUS BATONIORUM.

Seven tiny relics of Saint Thomas Becket were once preserved under a crystal. These are described in the inscription on the reverse side: DE SANGUINE SANCTI THOME MARTYRIS DE VESTIBUS SUIS SANGUINE SUO TINCTUS DE PELLICIA. DE CILITIO. DE CUCULLA. DE CALCIAMENTO. ET CAMISIA. "Of the blood of Saint Thomas Martyr. Of his vestments stained with his blood: of the cloak, the belt, the hood, the shoe, the shirt."

The majuscule characters are typical of the ecclesiastical engraving and inscriptions of the twelfth century; the lettering rendered in mosaic in the epitaph above Margaret's tomb in Monreale is very similar (see the photograph in this book).

Bishop Reginald "Fitzjocelin" (de Bohun) of Bath, whose ambivalent relationship with Thomas was described by Herbert of Bosham, probably presented this pendant to Margaret on the occasion of her son's marriage, in 1177, to Joanna, the daughter of King Henry II of England.

Becket was murdered in late 1170. He was canonized in 1173. Fashioned between 1174 and 1176, the gift was probably an acknowledgment of Margaret's support for Becket, specifically for giving refuge to his kinsmen in Sicily, and for her support of the Church generally. There is debate as to whether the image depicts Margaret being blessed by Reginald, or by Becket himself, though the latter is the majority view among scholars.

Measuring 5 x 3.1 x .7 centimeters (nearly two inches in height), the pendant is exceptional for the mere fact of its preservation. The great majority of English goldsmiths' work of this period was melted down over the centuries. Hallmarks were not used in the twelfth century; the gold purity of the pendant is approximately twenty-two karats, which is slightly less than that of gold coins minted during the same period.

The engraving is quite similar in style to various drawings and illuminations of its era. For comparison, particular reference is sometimes made to those of the unfinished Winchester Bible, and specifically its Ecclesiastes (folio 268 recto). Forming the pattern of what were to be painted illuminations, the manuscript's drawings resemble the lines of the pendant's figures.

Margaret is shown bowing slightly for the bishop's blessing. Her gaze seems to be fixed on something she is holding in her hands, perhaps the reliquary itself. Not much can be inferred from this simple representation except that Margaret is depicted as rather slender and statuesque, nearly as tall as the prelate invoking the benediction (Thomas Becket was taller than average).

Long and tortuous has been the reliquary's journey from Canterbury to Palermo and then around Italy, finally crossing the Atlantic during the middle years of the twentieth century. It is now part of the collection of the Metropolitan Museum of Art in New York, where it is usually displayed in the Treasury gallery at the Cloisters Museum in Fort Tryon Park in Upper Manhattan, catalogued under accession number 63.160. Part of a significant bequest made in 1963 to the museum by Joseph Pulitzer (1913-1993), who acquired it from the Italian collector and art dealer Piero Tozzi, it was first described at length by Thomas Hoving (op.cit.) in 1965.

A photograph follows on the next page.

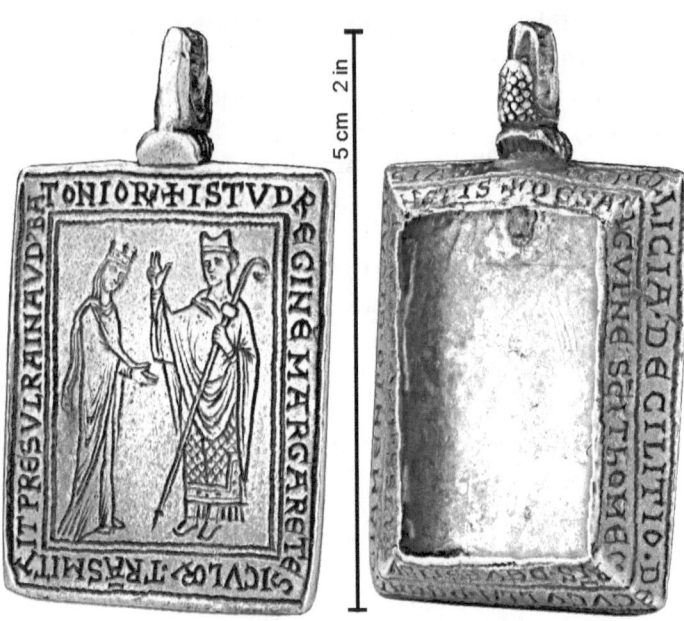
Courtesy Metropolitan Museum of Art

Detail of unfinished illumination in the Winchester Bible

Appendix 3
JOANNA'S BETROTHAL

In addition to the notes by Romuald of Salerno, we have descriptions of Joanna's betrothal and marriage written by several English chroniclers. Beyond providing the details of how Margaret and her advisors found a bride for William II, these texts, more generally, offer insight into royal betrothals of the twelfth century, including Margaret's, with special reference to the Kingdom of Sicily.

From the Chronicle of "Benedict of Peterborough"

Here the description of Joanna's betrothal from the chronicle of "Benedict of Peterborough" (written by Roger of Howden) is presented in English, with the rubrics (headings) from the surviving manuscripts, and especially the Cotton Manuscript, thus *De adventu nunciorum regis Siciliae* for the first section and *Carta regis Willelmi regis Siciliae de dote uxoris suae* for the last one.

Arrival of the Ambassadors of the King of Sicily

Meanwhile [April 1176], there landed in England the bishop elect [Elias] of Troia and the bishop [Arnolf] of Capaccio, with count Florio of Camerota, ambassadors of King William of Sicily. Accompanying them was archbishop Rotrou of Rouen, kinsman of the King of Sicily.

They went to meet King Henry at London, petitioning the monarch to betroth his daughter, Joanna, to their sovereign, William. Before responding to this request, Henry convoked in London his bishop [Gilbert Foliot] and other high prelates and knowledgeable counsellors of the realm. Accepting his counsellors' advice, he sent William's ambassadors to Winchester to see if the girl might be acceptable.

The King of England Betroths his Daughter to King William of Sicily

The ambassadors of the King of Sicily, mentioned earlier, went to see the girl, and they very much approved of her. To conclude the agreement, they then went to see her father, and the papal legate, cardinal Hugh Pierleoni, and the archbishop of Rouen.

With this, King Henry commanded John, bishop of Norwich, Paris, archdeacon of Rochester, Baldwin Bulot and Richard of Camville to travel on his behalf to the court of William, King of Sicily, with Elias of Troia bearing the message that he [Henry] granted to him the hand of his daughter in marriage.

At the same time, the other ambassadors [Arnolf and Florio] remained in England as King Henry's guests until Joanna's departure.

Peace Between the Archbishops at Winchester

On 15 August, the feast of the Assumption of Mary, King Henry arrived at Winchester, where he held a council. Here a reconciliation was reached between Richard, archbishop of Canterbury, and Roger, archbishop of York. The monarch also visited his daughter, Joanna, before her departure for Sicily.

The council ended with concord achieved among the prelates. Archbishop Richard of Canterbury and bishop Geoffrey of Ely readied themselves to accompany the daughter of King Henry to Saint-Gilles, where a galley sent by King William, to whom she was betrothed, would meet them.

With King Henry and King William having exchanged ambassadors, Joanna prepared for her voyage.

King Henry sent Joanna off unhurriedly, with the dignity befitting her, to meet Henry the Younger, her brother, in Normandy. The King of England made gifts to the King of Sicily of horses, clothes, gold and silver, and precious vases.

There Henry the Younger came to meet his sister, conducting her with the greatest honour to the County of Poitiers of his brother, Richard. Thenceforth, Richard escorted Joanna through the lands he held [Aquitaine and Anjou]. Then the girl traveled to Saint-Gilles with Richard of Canterbury, Geoffrey of Ely, Giles of Evreux, Hugh of Beauchamp, and Hamelin of Warenne, her father's half-brother.

In December [1176] Richard of Canterbury and Geoffrey of Ely, who had conducted King Henry's daughter to Saint-Gilles, returned to their episcopal sees in England.

Likewise John of Norwich, who had been dispatched to the court of King William of Sicily, returned to England. However, upon arriving with Paris of Rochester, he reported to Henry that during his voyage from Messina to Saint-Gilles he had encountered a storm, and two fine galleys carrying various, precious gifts from William had sunk.

Henry Receives Joanna's Dower Charter

The royal ambassadors consigned to King Henry [1177] the charter of the marriage settlement of his daughter, Joanna, who was given in matrimony to King William of Sicily. Here is what it said. [See the following section.]

From Roger's Annals

This is Henry Riley's eloquent, Victorian translation of the account of the wedding and the text of the marriage charter (and dower inventory) from the *Annals of Roger de Hoveden* (volume 1, pages 413-417) published in London in 1853. (One might note the Anglice "Howden" preferred by Doris Stenton, Frank Barlow and other scholars in more recent times.) Roger's *Annals* are complementary to Romuald's succinct description, translated in *Margaret, Queen of Sicily*. The chronicle of "Benedict of Peterborough" was most likely written by Roger of Howden, and the text of the dower document was compared to what is reported there (on folios 100-101 of the manuscript); minor corrections in orthography have been made to such details as the names of people and places.

In the year 1176 there came to England, from William, King of Sicily, [Elias] the bishop of Troia, the archbishop elect of Capaccio, and count Florio, as envoys to Henry, King of England, the father, and asked of him his daughter Joanna in marriage for William, King of Sicily, their lord.

A council upon the matter being accordingly held in London, the King, the father, with the consent of all the bishops, earls, and barons of the Kingdom, gave his daughter to the King of Sicily. And with this assent, the King [of England] first sent to the King of Sicily the bishop of Troia, John, bishop of Norwich, Paris, archdeacon of Rochester, Baldwin Bulot, and Richard de Camville, and in the meantime prepared for his daughter, Joanna, the things necessary for her equipment and journey. After these were all completed in a becoming manner, the King sent his daughter, Joanna, to be wed to William, the King of Sicily.

When she had arrived at Palermo, in Sicily, together with Giles, bishop of Evreux, and the other envoys of our lord, the King, the whole city welcomed them, and lamps, so many and so large, were lighted up, that the city almost seemed to be on fire, and the rays of the stars could in no way bear comparison with the brilliancy of such a light: for it was by night that they entered the city of Palermo. The said daughter of the King of England was then escorted, mounted on one of the King's horses, and resplendent with regal garments, to a certain palace, that there she might in becoming state await the day of her marriage and coronation.

After the expiration of a few days from this time, the before-named daughter of the King of England was married to William, King of Sicily, and solemnly crowned at Palermo, in the royal chapel there, in the presence of Giles, bishop of Evreux, and the envoys of the King of England, who had been sent for that purpose. She was married and crowned on the Lord's day before the beginning of Septuagesima, being the ides of February; and was with due honour endowed with the county of Mount Saint Angelo, the city of Siponto, the city of Vesta, and many other castles and places. Whereupon, the King of Sicily executed in her favour his charter, as follows:

The Charter of William, King of Sicily, which he executed in favour of Joanna, daughter of Henry, King of England, as to her dower

"In the name of the Father, and of the Son, and of the Holy Ghost, Amen. Amid the other blessings of peace, the nuptial tie binds and fastens most strongly the unison and the concord of human affairs; a rite, both venerable from the weightiness of its obligations, remarkable in the circumstances of its institution, and sanctioned by universal usage, from the beginning of the world and of time; of which the virtues and the comeliness, inasmuch as it has derived its origin from Divine institution, have neither contracted blemish from sin, nor have been sensible of any diminution by desuetude, through the lengthened ages of past time.

"Moreover, to this venerable and mysterious institution this honour is added, that the consent of the man and of the woman to enter matrimony typifies the sacramental bond of Christ and His Church. Being therefore led by the nature of this great and mysterious institution, and by veneration for the same, we, William, by the favour of the Divine grace King of Sicily, Duke of Apulia and Prince of Capua, do unite unto ourselves by the laws of matrimony and the bond of wedlock, with the Divine sanction and under happy auspices, the maiden Joanna, of royal blood, and the most illustrious daughter of Henry, the mighty King of the English; to the end, that her fidelity and chaste affection may produce the blessings of the married state, and that by her a royal offspring may, by the gift of God, hereafter succeed us in the Kingdom, which, both by reason of its endowment with all virtues, and of its title by birth, by the Divine grace, both may and ought to be raised to the Throne of this Realm.

"But, inasmuch as it is befitting our exalted position that so noble and illustrious an alliance should be honored with a becoming dower, by this present writing we do give, and as a dower, do grant to the before-named queen, our most dearly beloved wife, the county of Mount Saint Angelo, the city of Siponto, and the city of Vesta, with all the rightful manors and appurtenances thereof. We do also grant for her service, out of the manors of count Godfrey, Alesina, Peschiza, Bicum, Caprile, Barano, and Filizi, and all other places which the said count is known to possess as of the honour of the said county of Mount Saint Angelo. In like manner, we do also grant for her service, Candelari, Saint Clair, Castel Pagano, Bersenza, and Cagnano.

"We do also grant, that there shall be as of the honour of the said dower, the monastery of Saint Mary de Pulsano, and the monastery of Saint John de Lama, with all the manors which those monasteries hold of the honour of the aforesaid county of Saint Angelo — upon condition that the Queen, our aforesaid wife, shall always recognize all the rights of our heirs, who by our ordinance shall succeed us in the Kingdom, and shall do unto our said heirs, fully and unreservedly, all services for the aforesaid manors, according as the tenure in fee thereof shall require, and shall always observe her fealty to them.

"Wherefore, in remembrance of the said gift and grant, and for the inviolable establishment thereof, we have commanded this present charter to be written by the hand of Alexander, our notary, and, the golden bulla, our seal, being impressed thereon, to be confirmed with our said seal, and graced therewith.

"Unto which, by our command, the personages of our household and others have subscribed their names in manner following:

Walter, archbishop of Palermo.
Alfanus, archbishop of Capua.
Richard, bishop of Syracuse.
Bartholomew, bishop of Agrigento.
Reginald, archbishop of Bari.
Nicholas, first archbishop of Messina.
Ruffus, archbishop of Cosenza.
Theobald, bishop and abbot of New Saint Mary.
Robert, bishop of Catania.
Guy, bishop of Cefalù.
Elias, bishop elect of Troia.
Justus, bishop of Mazara.
Robert, bishop of Tricarico.
Peter, bishop of Caiazzo.
John, bishop of Potenza.
Robert de Bizino.
Robert Malcovenanz
Alexander Gupille
Matthew, royal vice-chancellor
Robert, count of Caserta.
Amphusus, count of Scrulac.
Jocelyn, count of Loret.
Hugh, count of Catanzaro.
Richard, count of Fundano, admiral.
Walter of Moac, admiral of the King's ship Fortunatus.
Aldewin of Candida, seneschal of our lord the King.
Berardus Gentili, constable of the palace of Messina.
Richard, keeper of the records in the royal palace.
Bamalis de Montefort, chief justiciar.
Persicus, chief justiciar of the royal court.
Frederick, justiciar of the royal court.

    Given at the flourishing city of Palermo by the hands of Walter, the venerable Archbishop of Palermo, Matthew, vice-chancellor of the King, and Richard, the venerable bishop of Syracuse, members of the household of our lord the King, in the year from the incarnation of our Lord one thousand one hundred and seventy-seven, in the month of February, being the tenth year of the indiction; and in the eleventh year of the happy reign of our lord William, by the grace of God, the mighty and most glorious King of Sicily, Duke of Apulia, and Prince of Capua. Amen."

Sealed with the seal of William, King of Sicily. Here follows in the original, the form of the bulla or seal, which contains around the margin the words *Dextera Domini fecit virtutem. Dextera Domini exaltavit me. Dextera Domini fecit virtutem.* "The right hand of the Lord hath created my might. The right hand of the Lord hath exalted me. The right hand of the Lord hath created my might." In the central portion is a cross surmounted by the words *Divina favente dementia Willielmus rex Siciliae et ducatus Apuliae et principatus Capuae.* "By the favour of the Divine mercy, William, King of Sicily, Duke of Apulia, Prince of Capua." The cross is supported by the following words. *Hoc signum sibi praeferri a vexillifero facit cum ad bellum aliquod procedit.* "This sign he causes to be borne before him by his standard-bearer when he goes forth to battle." [This is identical to the seal affixed to a charter issued in 1169]

From the *Ymagines Historiarum* of Ralph of Diceto

The account by Ralph of Diceto is essentially similar to those of Roger of Howden and adds only a few details, among these the route of John of Norwich, chief ambassador of the King of England, to Palermo via Auvergne, Valence, Embrun, Genoa, Gaeta and Messina. A passage recounts the terrible sea voyage of John of Norwich, his stay in Sicily and his return to England. The entry for Joanna's marriage mentions her arrival at Saint-Gilles and her wedding, performed by archbishop Walter, in February. Ralph of Diceto includes a letter from William to Henry dated 23 August 1176 at Palermo.

William's Letter to Henry

"To Henry, by the grace of God most noble King of England, your friend William, by the grace of God King of Sicily, Duke of Apulia and Prince of Capua, sends greetings.

"We have received your ambassadors in honour, and we thank you for so kindly receiving the three nobles sent to your court asking for your consent in granting us the hand of your daughter in matrimony. Likewise, your ambassadors have expressed to me your consent. As my ambassadors are authorized to act on my behalf, I did not swear a prior oath to this undertaking, but by this letter I hereby confirm their promises to you.

"As the ambassadors have explained, we shall send a fleet of galleys to Saint-Gilles to meet your embassy, from there securely transporting your daughter to our court, and I hope that the nuptials can be celebrated as soon as possible."

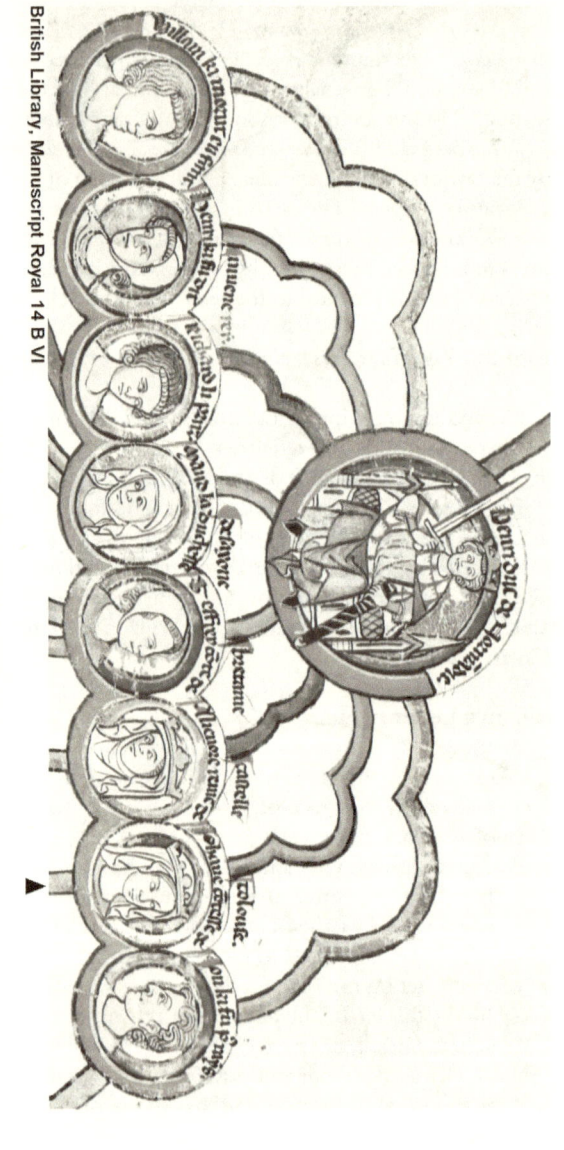

Margaret's Daughter-in-Law

Joanna of England (second from right) and her siblings as the children of King Henry II of England in a fourteenth century manuscript illumination

Appendix 4
CONSTANCE'S CROWN

The crown of Constance of Aragon, the first consort of Frederick II, was worn by her in death. It is the only crown of a Sicilian queen of this era that survives *in toto,* the others having been stolen and smelted. Three of Constance's rings (out of a total of five) are also preserved.

Fashioned of gold, leather and gemstones in the Byzantine style, the crown (shown on this book's cover) is typical of the head-dresses of the emperors and empresses of Constantinople, being a "skull cap" type of *kamelaukion* rather similar in design to a *kippah* or *taqiyah.*

It was manufactured in the workshops of Palermo, the *tiraz,* for a queen, though perhaps an earlier consort.

The silk-lined crown is decorated with numerous pearls, ten garnets, nine rubies, fourteen sapphires, three topazes and one amethyst, including one stone bearing an Arabic inscription (in reverse for sealing) and another engraved with a heraldic beast (possibly a dragon).

A pair of fillet pendants is suspended from the crown. These frame the face of the person wearing it. Its roughly hemispherical shape makes the kamelaukion appear vaguely similar in form to the Crown of Saint Stephen of Hungary, which is also of Byzantine design and has pendilia.

The crown was partially restored in 1491, the year it was first removed from Constance's tomb, which was also opened in 1781. It underwent a somewhat more extensive restoration in 1848 and is now displayed in the "treasury" museum of Palermo Cathedral.

It lacks the cross typical of royal crowns and obviously differs from the multifaceted diadems of Sicily's Norman kings (shown in mosaics in the Martorana church in Palermo and the cathedral of Monreale). This has led to much speculation.

It is possible that this kamelaukion crown was intended for less formal occasions. Perhaps it was worn when the queen walked among the common folk (not that she would have always worn a crown in such circumstances). This "informal" crown may have been designed without a cross because a Christian symbol would have been seen to alienate the Muslims and Jews of the kingdom, even though these subjects knew that their monarch was a Christian.[718]

The crown's history has been much debated, with some twentieth-century authors speculating that it was made for a king.[719] More recently, still others have made their views known.[720]

It is likely that Constance had other crowns besides this one, and those may have been more similar to the royal crown worn by Frederick II.

Regardless of its history, the crown adorned Constance of Aragon in death and in memory.

CONSTANCE'S CROWN

The crown of Constance of Aragon, consort of Frederick II, shows Byzantine influences

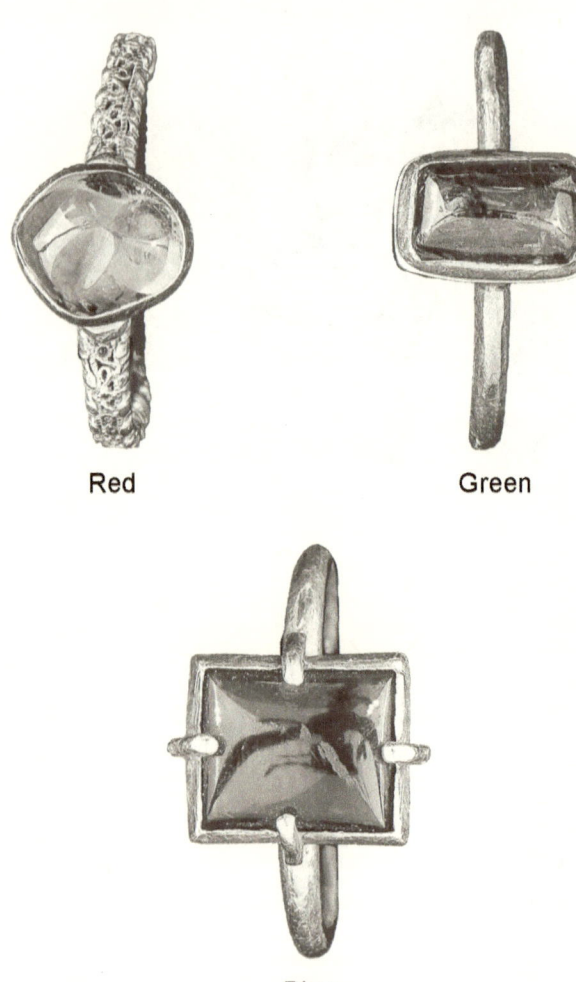

Rings of Constance of Aragon

Tesoro Museum, Palermo Cathedral

Appendix 5
THE CONTRASTO

Little is known of Cielo (Ciullo) of Alcamo, whose given name may be a form of *Michele* (Michael); in medieval Sicily *Celi* was often the shortened form of *Miceli*. Perhaps instead *Cielo* was short for *Marcello*, but what little evidence exists suggests that the poet was Sicilian and that he probably came from the town of Alcamo on the western side of the island.

The oldest surviving manuscript of his poem, the lengthiest of the Sicilian School, was copied in a "tuscanized" tongue and script late in the thirteenth century. Photos of that copy, preserved at the Vatican Library in *Codex Vaticanus Latinus 3793*, appear at the end of this appendix following the notes.

Intended to be literal and clear, this translation was effected without reference to any other. Previous English translations, such as those of Dante Gabriel Rossetti (1861) and Lorna Lancaster de'Lucchi (1922), rendered flowery, rhyming poetry which, though eloquent and appealing to the Victorian mind, was not very true to the original. That of Frede Jensen (1986) was a significant improvement.

As mentioned in this volume's introduction, Dante Alighieri and others knew of Cielo's work, which was part of an early nexus that inspired the literary, and not merely spoken, use of an Italian vernacular even though it did not influence Tuscan directly.

The *Contrasto* with which the Tuscans were familiar may have been a version more faithful to the Middle Sicilian text. It was Angelo Colocci (1474-1549), an expert in Provençal poetry and secretary to Pope Leo X, who undertook the first serious effort to identify its author, perhaps based in part on supporting documentation now lost. The first modern analysis of note was that of Bruno Panvini published in 1962, and others have since followed.

The poem was most likely composed between 1234 and 1242.[1] It might reflect an attempt to parody the Provençal themes popular in that era, but too little is known about Cielo or his intentions to draw a sound conclusion about this. Like his fellow court poet Giacomo of Lentini, Cielo may have been a royal notary or scribe. As mentioned above, his toponym suggests an association with the Sicilian town of Alcamo. Unlike Giacomo, he lacks a very substantial body of work. Indeed, the *Contrasto* is the only poem we know to be his.

As the story of a knight's successful effort to court a beguiling damsel, the *Contrasto,* or "Dialogue," is a fine example of the troubadour tradition. Was it read in the presence of Isabella of England or even Bianca Lancia? This we shall never know, but the possibility that one (or both) of these ladies heard it cannot be excluded from consideration.

The *Contrasto* was part of a trend, indeed a movement, during the age of chivalry. Cielo seems to have been familiar with *Le Roman de la Rose,* which was written a few years earlier and was widely disseminated. Here he plays on *Rosa* as the flower and the name of the damsel.

At times the author has the suitor calling the woman *madonna, mia donna* and *donna*, all terms used at court. Then in another stanza he switches to *vìtama, càrama* and *amica*, typical usage amongst commoners, as if the dialogue were actually taking place between a troubadour and a peasant girl. However, the two protagonists switch to more intimate forms of speech as the poet's intent of bedding the lady is made clear. This is evident in the use of words such as *villana*, for *peasant*, towards the lady, indicating a lower social class, and *canzoniere* (troubadour) or *zitello* (young boy) by the lady towards the suitor so as to diminish his status within the court and socially.

Whilst Cielo's *Contrasto* imitated the vernacular poetry already being composed in France and Spain, it stood at the vanguard of its form in Italy. Here in Sicily, the most obvious vestiges of the age of chivalry must be dated to the next century, when the wooden ceiling of the barons' hall in the Steri castle in Palermo was painted with colorful images depicting the persons and heraldic designs typical of courtly culture.

For all the mystery about its author, the *Contrasto,* first published in Naples in 1661, is the earliest court poetry of its length written in any of the Italian languages. It stands at the apex of the Sicilian School.

The Poem

Knight:
Rosa fresca aulentissima, chi apparj inver la state,
le donne ti disirano, pulzelle et maritate,
Trajimi de 'ste focora, si de'ste a boluntate,
per te non aviu abbento notte e dia,
penzando pur di vuy, madonna mia.

        Oh, fresh and fragrant rose that blooms during the summer,
        envied by dames and damsels alike,
        I ask you to deliver me from this raging flame,
        for I can rest neither night nor day thinking of you, my lady.

Damsel:
Si di meve trabagliti, follia lo ti fa fare:
lu mari potj arromperj avanti a semenare,
l'abere de 'sto seculo tutto quanto assembrare.
Avereme no' poteri a 'sto monnu,
avanti li cavelli m'aritonno.

> If you are suffering because you keep thinking of me,
> you are terribly foolish.
> You would have more luck plowing the sea and then
> attempting to sow it.[2] You can try to collect all the
> goods of the earth but you still will never have me in this world.
> I would sooner cut off all my hair first and become a nun.

Knight:

Si li cavelli attònniti, avanti fossi morto,
ca eu sì mi pèrdera lu sullazzo e diporto.
Quanno ci passo e veioti, rosa fresca dell'orto,
bono conforto donimi tutt'ore,
poniamo chi s'aiunga nostro amore.

> If you were to cut off your hair, I would rather be dead,
> for I would lose all my solace and delight.
> When I walk by and see you, oh, fresh rose of the garden,
> you always give me a sense of pleasure.
> Let us allow our love to unite us!

Damsel:

Chi nostro amori aiungasj?! No'boglio maltalenti!
Si ci ti trova patremo co' l'altri miei parenti,
guardanò t'aricolgono questi forti currenti.
Como ti seppi bona la venuta,
consiglio chi ti guardi la partuta.

> That our love were to unite us is something
> I do not wish to desire. If my father and my other kinsmen
> were to find you here, beware because if they return
> they'll catch you even if they have to chase you.
> As it was easy for you to get here,
> I advise you to be careful as you leave.

Knight:

Si toy parenti trovammi, chi mi pozzono farri?
Una difensa mettoci di dumilia gostari,
non mi toccara patreto per quanto ave a Bari.
Viva l'imperaduri 'n grazi'a Deu!
Intendi, bella, chi ti dico eu?

> If your father and relatives were to find me here,
> what could they do to me? They would have to pay
> a fine of two-thousand augustales.[3] Not even your father
> would try to harm me for all the riches in Bari.
> Long live the emperor, thanks be to God!
> Do you understand, my beautiful one, what I am telling you?

THE CONTRASTO

Damsel:
Tu mi no' lasci vivere né sera né mattino!
Donna mi so' di perperi, d'àuro massamotino,
si tant'avé donassemi quant'ave Saladino,
et per aiunta quanto lu Soldanu,
toccaremi no' poteri a lu manu.

> You will not let me live in peace
> neither by day nor by night.
> I am a wealthy woman with Byzantine bezants and Berber gold.
> If you were to give me as much as Saladin's gold,
> and moreover all that the sultan owns,
> you would not even be able to touch my hand.

Knight:
Multi sono le fimmini c'hanno dura la testa,
et l'omo, co' parabole, l'adimina et ammonesta,
tanto intorno percazzala, fin chi l'ave in podesta.
Femmina d'omo non si po' tenere,
guàrdati, bella, pur di ripentere.

> There are many stubborn women
> and a man is able to conquer them and persuade them;
> he hunts them down until he has them under his power.
> A woman cannot keep a man away.
> Watch out, my beautiful one, for one day you may regret it.

Damsel:
Ch'eu mi repentéssendi? Avanti fossi accesa,
ca nulla bona femmina per mi fosse ripresa.
Aersera passastici, correnno a la discesa,
acquistiti riposo, canzoneri!
Le to' paraole no' me piaczo gueri.

> I will regret it one day? I would rather die
> than learn that an honest woman could be blamed
> because of me! I saw you walking by my home last night,
> running quickly from one side to another.
> Calm down, chansonnier, I do not like your words at all.

Knight:
Quanti sono le schiantora chi m'hai mise a lu cori!
E solo purpenzànnonde, la dia quanno vo fori!
Fimmina de 'sto secolo tanto no'amai ancori,
quant'amo teve, rosa invidïata,
bene creo chi mi fosti distinata.

How much pain you have caused me to feel in my heart,
and all alone I think about it as I go out each morning!
I have never loved a woman in this world
as much as I love you, oh much envied rose.
I truly believe that you are the woman destined to be with me.

Damsel:

Si distinata fosseti, cadèra de l'altezze,
ché male messe forano in teve mie bellezze,
Si tutto addivenissemi, tagliàrami le trezze!
Eu consori m'arenno a una magione,
avanti chi m'attoccano persune.

If you were destined to be with me,
I would be lowering my expectations too much,
for my beauty would be lost in you.
If all this were to happen, I would prefer to cut off my braids
and become a nun in a convent, before you can touch my body.

Knight:

Si tu consore arenneti, donna col viso cleri,
a lu mosteru venoci et arennomi confreri,
per tanta prova vencierti, faràllo volonteri!
Con te co'stao la sera et lu mattino,
besogna chi ti tenga al meo dimino.

If you were to become a nun, oh radiant-faced woman,
I would come to the abbey and become a monk.
I would do this immediately in order to win you in this trial.
I would be with you both night and day. I must have you!

Damsel:

Oy me tapina misera, com'ào reo distinato!
Gesù Cristo l'altissimo, de 'ntutto se' airato?
Concepistimi a 'mbàttere in omo blestiemato?
Cerca la terra, ch'este granne assai,
chiù bella donna di me troverai.

Alas, poor me, what a cruel destiny is mine!
The most holy Jesus Christ must truly be angry with me
for He has allowed me to encounter a sacrilegious man.
Search the world that is very vast,
for you will find a woman more beautiful than I.

Knight:

Cercat'aio Calabria, Toscana et Lumbardia,
Pugla, Costantinopoli, Genoa, Pisa, Soria,

THE CONTRASTO

Lamagna et Babilonia, tucta Barbaria.
Donna non ci trovai tanto cortese:
per donna sovrana di mi te prese.

> I searched in Calabria, in Tuscany, in Lombardy,
> in Apulia, in Constantinople, in Genoa, in Pisa, in Syria,
> in Germany, in Babylonia, and in all of North Africa.[4]
> In none of these lands have I found such a noble woman
> as you. Therefore, I have chosen you as my sovereign lady.

Damsel:

Poy tanto trabagliastiti, faccioti meo prigheri,
chi tu vai et domannimi a mia mare et a mon peri.
Si dare mi ti degnano, menami a lu mosteri
et sposami davanti da la iente:
eu poi farò le to' comannamente!

> As you have already gone through so much distress,
> I beseech you to go see my mother and my father
> tomorrow and ask them for my hand.
> If they deign to offer me to you in marriage,
> take me to the monastery[5] and marry me before everyone.
> And then I will obey your every command.

Knight:

Di ciò chi dici, vitama, neiente non ti bale,
ca de le to' parabole fatto n'ao ponti e scale,
penne penzasti mettere, sonti cadute l'ale.
Eu dato t'aio la bolta sottana,
dunque, si poy, manteniti villana.

> What you tell me, love of my life,
> will not bring you anywhere, for I won't even mention
> what you just told me. You thought you were growing feathers
> and instead your wings fell off and I gave you the final blow.
> Therefore, if you can, defend yourself, peasant girl.

Damsel:

En paura no' mettimi di nullo manganiello!
Eu staomine 'n 'sta groria de 'sto forte castiello,
prezzo le to' parabole meno de 'no zitiello.
Si tu no' levi e vàitine di quace,
si tu ci fosse morto ben mi chiace.

> Don't even think that you are frightening me
> with a mangonel.[6] I am well-protected in my strong castle

and I consider your words less than those of a child.
If you do not leave and go away from here,
I'd be glad if you were dead.

Knight:

Dunque vorresti, vitama, ca per te fosse 'strutto!
Si morto essere debboci od intagliato tutto,
di quaci no' mi mossera, si non ayo lu frutto
lo quale staci ne lo to' jardino
disìrolo la sera et lu mattinu.

Therefore, love of my life, you wish that I be dead?
Even if I were to die or if somebody
were to cut me up into pieces, I would not leave this spot
until I eat the fruit that's in your garden.
I desire it morning and night.

Damsel:

Quello frutto non àvvero conti né cavaleri,
molto lo disirarono conti et iustizieri,
avere no' nde pottero, gìronde molto fieri.
Intendi bene chi bole dicére
me n'este di mill'unzi lo to' abere.

Neither counts nor knights have ever partaken
of that fruit. Marquesses and judges have long desired it,
but they couldn't have it. Thus they were very angry
when they left. Understand what I am trying to tell you;
your property is worth less than a thousand ounces.[7]

Knight:

Molti so' li garofani, ma non chi salma nd'hai
bella, no' dispregiaremi s'avanti no'massai.
Si vento è 'n proda, et girasi, agiunge da li prai,
arimembrare t'ao 'ste parole,
ca de 'st'ira, animella, assai mi dole.

You have many cloves[8] but not enough
to make up an entire plot of land.[9] My beautiful,
do not despise me before first granting me a chance.
If the wind is in the sails and it changes direction instead
so that I meet up with you on the shore, remember
what I told you, for in my soul I feel a terrible pain.[10]

Damsel:

Macara, si dolesseti, chi cadesse angosciato
la iente ci corresoro da traverso e da lato,

tutt'a meve dicessoro 'accorri 'sto malnato!
Non mi degnara porgere la mano,
per quant'ave lu Papa et lu Soldano.

> Even if you were to feel so much pain
> that you fell down in agony, and people would come
> to you from left and right telling me,
> "Help this poor man!" I wouldn't even hold out a hand to help you
> for all the wealth of the pope and the sultan.

Knight:
Deu lo volesse, vitama, ca fossi morto in casa
l'arma n'andèra cònsola ca di notte fantasa,
la iente ti chiamarano 'oi periura, malvasa
c'ha' morto l'omo in càsata traita,
sanz'ogni colpo levimi la vita!

> If only God would allow that I were to die in your home,
> oh love of my life! My soul that is in a delirium
> both day and night will leave comforted. People would call you:
> Oh evil liar! You killed a man in your own home,
> traitor! Alas, you kill me without even stabbing me.

Damsel:
Si tu no' levi e vàitine co' la maladizione,
li frati miei ti trovano dentro chissa magione,
bell'omi so s'eu soffero, perdici le persone,
ca meve se' venuto a sormonare.
Parente oy amico non t'ave a itare.

> If you don't get up and leave, then you shall be cursed;
> my brothers will find you in this house, and I would gladly accept
> that they kill you because you came here to bother me.
> Neither a kinsman nor a friend can come and save you.

Knight:
A meve non aì tano amichi né parenti
stranio mi sono, carama, enfra 'sta bona ienti.
Ora fa 'n'anno, vitama, ch'entrata mi se'n menti,
dicènnoti: 'Vististi lu'ntaiuto?'
Bella, da quello jorno so' feruto.

> My friends and relatives cannot help me.
> I am a foreigner, my dear, amongst these good people.
> It's been a year, oh my life's love, since you've entered my thoughts.
> Ever since you wore that dark dress of mourning.[11]
> Since that day, my beauty, have I been wounded.[12]

Damsel:
A tanto 'namorastiti, Iuda, hàilo traìto,
como si fosse porpora, iscarlatto o sciamito!
S'a le Vangelie iurimi chi mi sia marito,
avereme no' poteri a 'sto monno,
avanti in mari ièttomi a perfonno.

> Oh! So it was on that occasion that you fell in love,
> oh Judas the Traitor, as if I were wearing a scarlet dress
> or one made of another precious cloth![13] Even if you were to swear
> on the gospels that you'll become my husband,
> you cannot have me for any price in the world.
> I would rather throw myself out into the deepest sea!

Knight:
Si ne lu mari ièttiti, donna cortesi et fina,
deretro mi ti misera per tucta la marina.
Da poi ca annegàsseti, trobàrati a la rina
solo per questa cosa adimpretare,
con teco m'ayo a junjiri et peccare.

> If you were to throw yourself out into the sea,
> oh noble and fine woman, I would follow you
> all along the harbor, and after you've drowned
> I would find you on the shore to do this one thing:
> I must commit a sin by having you for my pleasure.

Damsel:
Segnomi in Patri et 'n Filio ed in santo Matteo,
si ca non se' tu retico, figlio de lu giudeo,
e cotale parabole n'odio redire anch'eu!
Mortasi la fimmina, a lo 'ntutto
perdeci lu saboru et lu desduttu.

> I make the sign of the cross in the name of the Father,
> and of the Son and of Saint Matthew.[14]
> I know that you are neither a heretic nor a Jew,
> and I've never heard such words before.
> If a woman is completely dead, you lose all the fun and pleasure.

Knight:
Bene lo faccio, carama; altro no' pozzo fare,
si quisso non accomplimi, lassone lo cantare.
Fallo, mia donna, plàzati, chi bene lo poi fare.
Ancora tu no' m'ami, molto t'amo,
sì m'hai preso come lu pesci a l'amo.

THE CONTRASTO

I know that well, my dear. There is nothing else I can do.
If you do not fulfill my desire now, I will stop singing.
Fulfill it, my woman, please me, for I know you can.
Even if you don't love me, I love you dearly.
You have caught me like a fish on a hook.

Damsel:

Sazzo chi m'ami; amoti di core paladino,
lèvati susu e vattene, tornaci a lu mattino.
Si ciò chi dico facimi, di bon cor t'amo e fino.
Quisso eu ti 'mprometto sanza faglia,
te' la mia fede, chi m'hai in toa baglia.

I know you love me, and I love you with a noble heart.
Now get up and leave. Come back tomorrow morning.
If you do as I tell you, I will love you with all my heart
and faithfully. I promise this to you truthfully.
You have my word; I put myself under your command.

Knight:

Per zò chi dici, carama, neiente non mi movo.
Innanti prenni e scannami, to 'sto cortello novo,
'sto fatto fare potesi innanti scalfi 'n'ovo.
Accompli mio talento, amica bella,
ché l'arma co' lu cori mi si 'nfella.

Because of what you're telling me, my dear,
I won't move from here at all. I would prefer
that you slaughter me. Here take this new knife to do it.
We can do this before you cook an egg.[15]
Fulfill my desire, my beautiful friend,
because my soul and my heart are overcome with sadness.

Damsel:

Ben sazzo: l'arma doleti, cumo mo ch'ave arsura.
'Sto fatto no' potèrasi per null'altra misura,
si non hai le Vangelie, chi mo ti dico: 'Jura!'
Avereme no' poi 'n toa podesta.
Innanti prenni et tagliami la testa.

I know this well. Your soul[16] hurts like a man
who is suffering from thirst. This cannot be done
in any other way. You need to have the gospels with you
so that I can ask you to swear by them.
Otherwise I will not surrender to you,
unless you take me and cut off my head.

Knight:
Le Vangelie, carama? Ch'eu le porto 'n sino,
a lu mostero presile, non c'era lu patrino.
Sovra 'sto libro juroti: mai non ti vegno mino.
Accompli mio talento in caritate,
ché l'arma me ne sta 'n suttilitate.

> The gospels, my dear? I am carrying them in my coat pocket;
> I stole them in church while the priest wasn't there.
> Upon this book I swear never to betray you.
> Fulfill my desire, I beg you, for my soul is destroying me!

Damsel:
Meu sire, poy jurastimi, eu tucta quanta incenno.
Sono a la toa presenzia, da voy non mi difenno.
S'eu minespreso àioti, merzè, a voy m'arenno.
A lo letto ne gimo, a la bon'ora,
chi chissà cosa n'è data in ventur.

> My lord, thanks to your oath my entire body
> is now burning with passion. I stand here before you
> and I give in to your requests. I ask you to forgive me
> if I've mistreated you as I now surrender.
> Let us finally go to bed together, for this is our destiny!

NOTES

1. This dating reflects two important facts. Firstly, the gold *augustale* coin mentioned in the fifth stanza was instituted in 1231. Secondly, the *Contrasto* was clearly influenced by a French poem composed around 1230, namely *Le Roman de la Rose* (by Guillaume de Lorris with later additions by Jean de Meun), which may have taken a few years to make its way to Italy. (For further commentary see the works by Panvini, Mangieri and Spampinato Beretta in Sources.)

2. This is a proverb still in use in Calabria and Sicily, *zappari a l'acqua e siminari a lu ventu,* that refers to something impossible or inconclusive.

3. The *augustale* was a gold coin issued under Frederick II beginning in 1231 and minted in Messina and in Brindisi. It was patterned after the Roman *aureus*. The obverse showed the bust of the emperor according to the classical Roman style while the reverse bore Frederick's imperial eagle. The fine refers to a statute in Frederick's Constitutions of Melfi, where article 16, *De defensis imponendis, et quis eas imponere possit,* states that somebody who was attacked could have de-

fended himself by invoking the law, and if this was not sufficient, the victim could have decided on a sum as compensation for having been attacked.

4. *Babylonia* probably refers to Cairo or Baghdad.

5. By *monastery* the poet simply means a church.

6. The mangonel was a medieval siege weapon. With the use of military terms such as mangonel, castle and the final blow, the poet is comparing the sexual conquest of a woman to a military battle. This was common use both in classical and medieval times.

7. The *ounce* was a Sicilian gold unit. One *oncia* counted as thirty *tarì,* another type of gold coin used in Sicily since Arab rule. The damsel is telling the knight that he is too poor for her.

8. Cloves refers to the spice. Many spices arrived from the east so they were quite expensive. The poet wants to say that even if the girl has much to offer, it is not enough to make her precious.

9. Here the term used is *salma,* a medieval Sicilian form of measurement for both land and weight, still in use today in the Sicilian hinterland.

10. The knight is reminding the damsel that, although she is despising him at the moment with the excuse of being wealthier than he, her fortune can change just like the wind.

11. For "dark dress of mourning," the poem states, *ti vististi di maiuto,* "you wore maiuto." Much has been debated regarding what kind of dress the author refers to, but the term is rooted in a Sicilian word of Arabic origin: *tabùt* meaning *tomb* in Arabic is still used in Sicily as *tabùto* with the same meaning. *Maiuto* is a corruption of this term, referring to a dress worn for mourning. The original text probably read, *ti vististi lo'ntavuto.*

12. That is to say, "wounded by your love," as Cupid wounds one's heart with his arrows.

13. Here the lady ridicules the suitor for having fallen in love with her while she was dressed in mourning as if what she was wearing were made of precious scarlet cloth or something similar.

14. Perhaps Saint Matthew was the woman's patron saint; for example she may have been from a town where he was venerated as the local patron (such as Salerno or Scicli).

15. "Before you can cook an egg." In the poem we find *inanti che scalfi un uovo*, which is a typical Sicilian and Southern Italian saying referring to something that happens quickly.

16. The term used here is *arma*, which means *soul* in Sicilian but *weapon* in Italian. There might be the use of a double meaning referring to the man's sexual organs. This is supported by the fact that in the same stanza the damsel is comparing the poet's sufferance to that of a man dying of thirst.

THE CONTRASTO

Manuscript of the Contrasto of Cielo of Alcamo

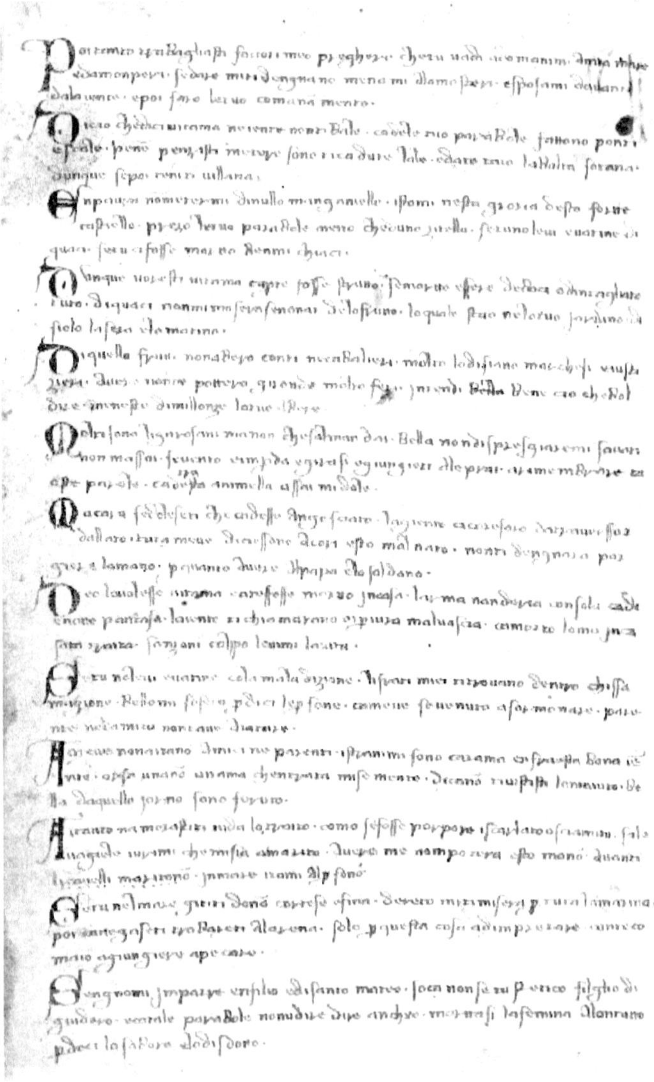

Courtesy Vatican Apostolic Library

Bene lo sdeçni cayama ab ve nompoço fare · fe quisso non ay · compli mi la sono la cun
praye · fullo mio bono plazare · be sse me lo puoi fare · Ancor a ru no ma mi molto sa
me · fomai po fe como la pesce al amo ·

Oyo ché ma m' amori di cos e pala di no · le vai su so · e vai e no lu tu i noçi di mari
no · se no ché dico fazçami di sonor o · e a mo e fi no quisso tempi metto sença fa
lgha · e la mia fede ch' e mai in mia bat gha ·

Por ch' e ssi cayama ne ve nço non mi mento · in ançi pi uni e scanta mi çello isto
cor si e la nov o · e sta fa ve fa e e pare si iomai · se al si vu uo no · Ali compli mi retorno
mia bella · Ch' e la me colo ca ve in sin fosa ·

Bensaça la ma de le pi co mo ho · e na ve u fu ça · e sto fa me non po re ssi in nulla ba mi
suo in per sona le van giu le · ho me e in co pu ra · cur ze me non puoi in tua pro ve sta ·
monti per ca i gralgha in la costa ·

L en via giu ele cayama · ch' io le po cio in fri no · il mon piaço a pro si me non e ça · lo
pai e · ma son u e so ali so i a ço i · mai non ti un gyn a o me no · di compli mi valente
in cui ç mai e · ch' el la mia men o · sin in sui chiar o ·

Mio si e po i uiu al ç mi · co çura quanto · mai uno na · sono Alama por e sem pi e in ami
Quan mi di sonno · sco mi ne spo · e se dosri meçze · amor ma sumo · Ale do ve mo i co
illa de no va · ch' e la ssa cosa ne osara pi a e no va ·

(giacomino pulgliese)

M or ne p eche mai fa vo fiça anchi guerra · chè mai selai ma donna · on de o mio
legh mi · In pover de be l' oce se mor en i vi va · in p che lo mon de le ne cru mo · n e sche
le gh mi · Vuoi ma mor te che no na pi e ses nça · di spari in amo re · via le gh bel
mi a · edai cui dolglio · lo mi a dile gi en ça · po sta in gia in sti e sença · ch' e mai colto la cia
ça di lei gi a mai · a un e e se fo lgho ·

O sto en vivo · e so la ço se gai co · vive · piu · che mi la li çe · e mai har e · c' pi e ssa os mio
gi ro · ma donna · in pa ra di so · po r tuno la ç de fre se n ça · in ma la se i a mi in pre se
ver sa e a sus · e p la mia lo vo mi de que e e co sn re · e da la do çe compagnia · ch' io mia
vea de lgha mai · e no la ver gio no le so · d a uane ri · en o ni in mi e se me pe be a · i fai fon
frante · che so lia ·

O ve o p che mai po sta in ma la pa nça · ch' io so no in ma sa so · no n si o lie mi p a r ché
mai lou ara in do che · e spo i a mi a i · pai ri mi la pui do çe · compa ri gnia · com che
fia nulla pa e no · ci o nie suisa · ma donna lo tu a uisa · ch' io lo çe no in sua bale ç a · lu
p ro in segna mente · e an co mi sa · e lo mo fran co · ce pe che in la pi e so do m
mia ·

O ue ma don na e lo suo · in segna mente la sua Bale ça · el a gi an ça na s ç en ça · le
do çe viso e lo de to · pos la ma e r g ri to di · e la do na · e la Rella sem brança · Ral sus si o
ad o pe na men to · e la sua con re si · e la sua no Bile · gen t lii sa · madon a p chui in p u n · in
vio in u lu gi m ça · o e no la ver gio ne n o he redia · e no ma de lla · si co me fa re folia · in
sua sem bran ça ·

A ef o se mio lo re an me d un ga in a con gr e ça · e la mon ça na · in fra sua in fe r me o · la po
ne oso so · di san ça fo sta · no m p i po ss a · i spa ça re figu re a de p er ce ·

Following coronations, kings and queens were acclaimed on this dais next to the cathedral.

Appendix 6
CORONATION RITE

The following *ordo* for the coronation of a Sicilian queen, conserved in the oldest surviving codex of proven provenance attesting to this ceremony, may have been used as early as the coronations of Sibylla of Burgundy and Beatrice of Rethel. Copied around 1200 in Beneventan script, the manuscript is conserved in the Biblioteca Casanatense (Casanata Library), in Rome, in Codex 614. In earlier times it was housed in the archive of Benevento's cathedral, where it seems to have been the papal copy of the *ordo* during the pontificate of Innocent III. This is the only *ordo* known with reasonable certainty to have been used in the Kingdom of Sicily during the Norman-Swabian era (see notes 117 and 119).

Based on the well-established norms set forth in certain codices contained in the "Roman-German Pontifical," the so-called *Pontificale Romano-Germanicum* (popularly the "PRG"), first published by Michel Andrieu during the last century as *Les Ordines Romani du Haute Moyen Age*, it is quite similar to the orders used for other western European queens consort during this period.[1] Indeed, several sections are nearly identical to what was used in England during the twelfth century.

The same essential elements are preserved in the only existing order of coronation still used in our times which could be said to be influenced, albeit to a limited degree, by a Norman *ordo*, that of England; however, the English ceremony now includes additional components and is the same for both kings and regnant queens, the latter most recently crowned in 1838 (Victoria) and 1953 (Elizabeth II).

Beginning with the first Sicilian coronation in 1130, the Siculo-Normans followed established Latin usage, but Elvira was not the first Norman queen to be crowned. That distinction belongs to Matilda of Flanders, wife of William the Conqueror, the first Norman king; she was crowned in 1068. It is scholarly consensus that Anglo-Saxon queens were not crowned, and the Lombards who ruled much of southern Italy immediately before the arrival of the Normans were not kings.

The Sicilian *ordo* refers to the celebrant as a "metropolitan." This was usually the Archbishop of Palermo as Primate of Sicily; in England the celebrant was the Archbishop of Canterbury or, exceptionally, the Archbishop of York (see note 191).

However, as we have seen in the preceding chapters, not all Sicilian queens of the Norman-Swabian era were crowned in Palermo's cathedral or palatine chapel. Nonetheless, either of these would normally be the first choice.

It is to be remembered that, beginning with Constance Hauteville, several queens of Sicily were also crowned Queen of the Romans (Queen of the Germans) and Holy Roman Empress, and the orders used in those ceremonies differed from this one.

Replete with abbreviations and diacritical marks, the Casanata manuscript is a condensed record. This is its first publication in a complete form with English for the rubrics; the essential format and phraseology have been retained. It was deemed appropriate to present the spoken sections, here set in *Italics*, in the original Latin (though some translations follow) because this was the liturgical language used at reginal coronations during the twelfth century; it was what our queens actually heard and spoke at the ceremony.

The notes appear at the end of this appendix.

CORONATION RITE

Incipit Ordo ad Reginam Noviter Benedicendam

Following the arrival of the neo-queen, the celebrant (archbishop) enters the church in procession.

Archbishop: *Pax huic domui.*

Queen: *Amen.*

Oath

Archbishop: *Filia, dominus noster rex, quia placuit sibi, ut cum eo unum corpus fieres, jussit nobis, ut ad regni fastigium te consecrandam sublimaremus. Vis itaque promittere, ut sis in omnibus obediens eidem domino regi et heredibus eius in regno succedentibus juxta apostolum dicentem: Omnis anima potestatibus sublimioribus subdita sit.*[2]

Queen: *Volo et promitto.*

The archbishop recites the following psalm in its entirety: *Eructavit cor meum verbum bonum dico ego opera mea regi lingua mea calamus scribae velociter scribentis. Speciosus forma prae filiis hominum diffusa est gratia in labiis tuis propterea benedixit te deus in aeternum. Accingere gladio tuo super femur tuum potentissime. Specie tua et pulchritudine tua et intende prospere procede et regna propter veritatem et mansuetudinem et iustitiam et deducet te mirabiliter dextera tua. Sagittae tuae acutae populi sub te cadent in corde inimicorum regis. Sedis tua deus in saeculum saeculi virga directionis virga regni tui. Dilexisti iustitiam et odisti iniquitatem propterea unxit te deus, deus tuus, oleo laetitiae prae consortibus tuis. Murra et gutta et cassia a vestimentis tuis a domibus eburneis ex quibus delectaverunt te. Filiae regum in honore tuo adstetit regina a dextris tuis in vestitu deaurato circumdata varietate. Audi filia et vide et inclina aurem tuam et obliviscere populum tuum et domum patris tui. Et concupiscet rex decorem tuum quoniam ipse est dominus tuus et adorabunt eum. Et filiae Tyri in muneribus vultum tuum deprecabuntur divites plebis. Omnis gloria eius filiae regis ab intus in fimbriis aureis. Circumamicta varietatibus adducentur regi virgines post eam proximae eius adferentur tibi. Adferentur in laetitia et exultatione adducentur in templum regis. Pro patribus tuis nati sunt tibi filii constitues eos principes super omnem terram. Memor ero nominis tui in omni generatione et generatione propterea populi confitebuntur tibi in aeternum et in saeculum saeculi.*[3]

Following this: *Kyrie eleison, Christe eleison, Kyrie eleison.*

The archbishop then leads the congregation in the Lord's Prayer: *Pater noster, qui es in caelis, sanctificetur nomen tuum. Adveniat regnum tuum. Fiat voluntas tua, sicut in caelo et in terra. Panem nostrum quotidianum da nobis hodie, et dimitte nobis debita nostra sicut et nos dimittimus debitoribus nostris. Et ne nos inducas in tentationem, sed libera nos a malo. Amen.*

Following this, the archbishop prays: *Domine salvam fac ancillam tuam et exaudi nos in die qua invocaverimus te. Mitte ei auxilium de sancto et de Sion tueatur te.*[4] *Domine exaudi orationem meam.*

Congregation: *Et clamor meus ad te veniat.*[5]

Archbishop: *Dominus vobiscum.*

Congregation: *Et cum spirito tuo.*

Investiture

Oration by the archbishop: *Omnipotens sempiterne deus, fons et origo tocius bonitatis, feminei sexus fragilitatem nequaquam reprobando adversaris, sed dignanter comprobando procius eligis, et qui infirma mundi eligendo forcia queque confundere decrevisti, quique eciam virtutis triumphum in manu Judith femine olim judayce plebi de hoste sevissimo resignare voluisti, respice, quesumus, preces humilitatis nostre, et super hanc famulam tuam [name], quam supplici devocione in reginam eligimus, benediccionum tuarum dona multiplica, eamque dextera tue potencie semper et ubique circumda, ut umbone muniminis tui firmiter undique protecta visibilis hostis nequicias triumphaliter expugnare valeat, et una cum Sara atque Rebecca, Lia et Rachel beatis reverendisque feminis uteris sui fecundari seu gratulari mereatur, ad decorem tocius regni statumque sancte dei ecclesie regendum necnon protegendum. Per Christum dominum nostrum, qui ex intemerate beate virginis Marie alvo nasci, visitare ac renovare hunc dignatus est mundum. Qui tecum vivit et regnat deus in unitate spiritus sancti, per omnia saecula saeculorum.*[6]

Following this oration, the archbishop vests the queen with her regalia, reciting: *Die autem tertio induta Esther regalibus vestimentis, et stetit in atrio domus regiae, quod erat interius, contra basilicam regis; at ille sedebat super solium suum in consistorio palatii contra ostium domus.*[7] *Accipe vestimenta regalia, in nomine patris et filii et spiritus sancti. Amen.*[8]

Anointing

Then the archbishop (celebrant) and other bishops process with the royal party, chanting the following antiphon: *Alma redemptoris mater, quae pervia caeli, porta manes et stella maris, succurre cadenti, surgere qui curat populo, tu quae genuisti natura mirante tuum sanctum genitorem, virgo prius ac posterius, Gabrielis ab ore sumens ilud ave, peccatorum miserere!*

Oration by the archbishop: *Deus, qui solus habes inmortalitatem lucemque habitas inacessibilem cuius providencia in sui disposicione non fallitur, qui fecisti que futura sunt et vocas ea que non sunt tamquam ea que sunt, qui superbos equo moderamine principatu deicis atque humiles dignanter in sublime provehis ineffabilem misericordiam tuam supplices exoramus, ut sicut Esther reginam Israelis causa salutis de captivitatis sue compede solutam ad regis Assueri thalamum regnique sui consorcium transire fecisti, ita hanc famulam tuam [name] humilitatis nostre benediccione plebis christiane slautis gratia ad dignam sublimemque regis nostris copulam regnique sui participium misericorditer transire concedas, et ut regalis federe coniugii semper manens pudica proximam virginitati palman continere queat, tibi deo vivo et vero in omnibus et super omnia jugiter placere desiderat, et, te inspirante, que tibi placita sunt toto corde perficiat, per omnia saecula saeculorum.*[9]

After this prayer, the following antiphon is chanted: *Tota pulchea es, Maria, et macula originalis non est in te. Tu gloria Jerusalem. Tu honorificentia populi nostri. Tu advocata peccatorum, O Maria, O Maria! Virgo prudentissima, mater clementissima. Ora pro nobis, intercede pro nobis. Ad Dominum Jesum Christum.*

Then the queen is conducted to the altar, where the archbishop asks her: *Vis sanctam fidem a catholicis viris tibi traditam tenere et operibus observare?*

Queen: *Volo.*

Then the archbishop anoints the top of the queen's head with holy oil, reciting: *Ungo te in reginam de oleo sanctificato, in nomine patris et filii et spiritus sancti.*[10]

Queen: *Amen.*

Crowning

The archbishop says the following prayer: *Sancti spiritus gratia humilitatis nostre officio in te copiosa descendat, ut sicut manibus nostris indignis oleo materiali oblita pinguescis exterius ita eius invisibili unguedine delibuta et illicita declinare tota mente et spernere discas seu valeas et utilia anime tue jugiter cogitare obtare adque operari queas, auxiliante domino nostro Jesu Christo qui cum deo patre et eodem spiritu sancto vivit et regnat deus in saecula saeculorum. Amen.*

The archbishop then places the crown upon the queen's head whilst reciting: *Officio indignitatis nostre seu congregacionis in reginam benedicta, accipe coronam regalis excellencie, que licet ab indignis episcoporum tamen manibus capiti tuo imponitur. Unde sic exterius auro sapiencie virtutumque gemmis decorari contendas, quatinus post occasum huius saeculi cum prudentibus virginibus sponso perhenni domino nostro Jesu Christo coherere valeas. Qui cum deo patre et spiritu sancto vivit et regnat per infinita saecula saeculorum. Amen.*

Enthroning

With this, the queen is conducted to a throne and seated there. The archbishop recites the following: *Gloria patri, genitaeque proli et tibi compar utriusque semper, spiritus alme, deus unus, omni tempore saecli. Amen.*

Following the celebration of the mass, the royal and archiepiscopal corteges process out of the church.

NOTES

1. The first study of this *ordo* was a concise transcription and notes published by Jacob Theodor Schwalm (1865-1931) in his "Reise nach Italien im Herbst 1894" (in Sources). See also Elze, Reinhard, "Tre Ordines per l'Incoronazione di un Re e di una Regina del Regno Normanno in Sicilia" (in Sources). See notes 6 and 9 (below) for prayers nearly identical to those used in the *ordines* of England.

2. From Romans 13:1.

3. This is Psalm 44 in the Vulgate (45 in modern texts): *My heart has uttered fine words as I write this song for the king. My tongue is the pen of a scrivener who writes swiftly. You are the most beautiful of men and you speak gracefully. God has blessed you forever. Gird your sword upon your thigh, mighty king; you are glorious and majestic. Ride on in majesty to victory for the defense of truth and justice! Your strength will win you great victories! Your arrows are sharp, they pierce the hearts of your enemies; nations fall at your feet. The kingdom that God has given you will last for ever and ever, for the sceptre of your kingdom is a sceptre of equity; you have loved what is good and detested what is evil. That is why God, your God, has chosen you and has poured upon you the oil of more joy than on any other king. Your clothes are perfumed with myrrh, aloes and cassia; musicians entertain you in palaces embellished with ivory. Among the women of your court are the daughters of kings, and to the right of your*

throne stands the queen, wearing ornaments of finest gold. Bride of the king, listen to what I say: Awake, o daughter! Forget your people and your kin. Your beauty will make the king desire you; he is your master whom you must obey. The people of Tyre will bring you gifts; the wealthy will try to win your favor. The king's daughter is in the palace; how beautiful she is! Her gown is made of gold thread. In her colorful robes she is led to the king, followed by virgin maidens, who are also brought forth. With joy and gladness they come and enter the king's palace. You, my king, will have many sons to succeed your forefathers as kings, and you will make them rulers over the whole earth. They shall remember your name throughout all generations. And the people shall sing your praises for ever and ever.

4. From Psalms 19:10 and 19:3, with the phrasing slightly altered.

5. Literally "O let my cry come to thee," liturgically "Lord, hear my prayer." From Psalm 101:2.

6. Except for minor differences in Latin spelling and style, and the addition of the name of Leah in the Sicilian version, this prayer is identical to the analogous text of the *ordo* used in England during the twelfth century; see Wickham Legg, Leopold, *English Coronation Records* (in Sources), page 37. It is translated: *Almighty and everlasting God, fount and spring of all goodness, who does not reject the frailty of woman but rather deigns to allow and choose it, and by choosing the weaker things of this earth does confound those who are stronger, who did sometimes cause your people to triumph over the cruelest foe by the hand of Judith, a woman. Hear our humble prayers and bestow your blessings upon this your servant [name] whom in all humble devotion we consecrate our queen. Defend her with your mighty hand and by your favor protect her on every side, that she may be able to overcome and triumph over all her enemies, both physical and spiritual, and that, with Sarah, Rebecca, Leah, Rachel and other blessed and honorable women, she may multiply and rejoice in the fruit of her womb, to the honor of this kingdom and your holy church. Through Our Lord Jesus Christ, who vouchsafed to be born of a purest virgin that he might visit and redeem the world, and who lives and reigns with you, O Father, in the unity of the Holy Spirit for ages and ages, world without end. Amen.*

7. From Esther 5:1.

8. Sicilian reginal regalia is not precisely described. It included a robe (actually a silk mantle in this ceremony), and probably a jeweled ring and bracelets; as an heiress, Constance Hauteville may have been invested with a sceptre (and perhaps even an orb) at her coronation in Bari. Unfortu-

nately, little is known of the details of reginal investiture in the Kingdom of Sicily during the Norman-Swabian era.

9. Except for subtle differences in style, this prayer is nearly identical to the analogous text of the *ordo* used in England during the twelfth century; see Wickham Legg, op.cit.supra, page 37. It is translated: *God, who has only immortality and dwells in light that cannot be approached by man, whose providence never fails, who has made all things that are and that shall come to be, and calls the things that are not, as the things that are, who calls down the proud from their seat and exalts the humble and meek: We humbly beseech you for your unspeakable mercy, that for the good of your people the Hebrews you delivered Queen Esther from captivity and brought her to the bed of Ahasuerus* [Xerxes] *and to the society of his kingdom. So for the good of your Christian flock, you might in your mercy and through our ministry advance your servant* [name] *to the most high and royal company of our king, that in the chastity of wedlock she may obtain the crown that is next to virginity, and that she may in all things and above all things strive always to please you, the living God, and by this holy inspiration perform those things that are acceptable to you, for ages and ages, world without end. Amen.* Interestingly, this prayer, like that in note 6, was still used in England as recently as the seventeenth century, though by then it was being recited in English (Wickham, page lix). For additional background, see Ward, Paul, "The Coronation Ceremony in Medieval England" (in Sources).

10. The celebrant probably used a gold anointing spoon similar to the one preserved in the collection of the Tower of London. (See page 162.)

Appendix 7
THE LAST QUEEN

Elisabeth Wittelsbach of Bavaria became Queen of Sicily in 1250 when her husband, Conrad, ascended the throne upon the death of his father, Frederick II. Some six centuries later, young Maria Sophia, who was born into the same Bavarian dynasty as Elisabeth, became Queen of Sicily in 1859 when her husband, Francesco II de Bourbon of the Two Sicilies, succeeded his father, Ferdinando II. (Ruled from Naples, the Kingdom of the Two Sicilies established in 1816 was coterminous to the kingdom founded by Roger II in 1130 that existed until 1282.)

Born in October 1841, Maria Sophia von Wittelsbach was the daughter of Maximilian, Duke in Bavaria. She was raised in a rather informal setting at Possenhofen Castle on the family's Alpine country estate, developing an early love for equestrian sports and country life. In this she was not unlike her siblings, and particularly her elder sister, Elisabeth ("Sissi"), who wed Emperor Franz Joseph I of Austria. The physical resemblance between Elisabeth and Maria Sophia was striking but so, it is said, was their character.

Maximilian was regarded by his contemporaries as something of an eccentric. He promoted Bavarian folk music and played the zither, and encouraged his cousin, Ludwig II, to sponsor Richard Wagner. He was a kindly man. In 1838, during a visit to Egypt, he purchased the freedom of several slave children. Though unorthodox in some ways, he seems to have been a positive influence on his daughters.

Maria Sophia's mother, Ludwiga, raised eight children (two others died in infancy) in what many would have considered a liberal environment where daughters were treated as the social equals of sons. To say that this was extremely unusual in the middle of the nineteenth century, even among royalty, would be an understatement. It seems to have left the Wittelsbach sisters with a very egalitarian view of how the world should be, and a great sense of altruism.

Like Elisabeth, Maria Sophia was rather impulsive, independent, and no slave to tradition or protocol, though she had a great sense of duty. By most contemporary accounts, both girls were intelligent as well as beautiful. Each was an exceptionally accomplished equestrienne who could wield a sabre or rifle while on horseback.

Maria Sophia and Elisabeth were especially close, while their elder sister, Helen, was a bit distant. This may be explained by an incident that occurred in 1853. Ludwiga introduced Helen to Emperor Franz Joseph I of Austria, hoping for a betrothal, and Elisabeth went along on the trip. The Emperor was smitten by Elisabeth, who became his bride, leaving Helen feeling sad and rejected. She eventually married the Prince of Thurn und Taxis.

Maximilian did not have the good fortune to provide very lavish dowries for his daughters. Maria Sophia's would be a "paltry" twenty-five thousand gold ducats, but this was of little consequence when marrying regnant royalty.

In 1859, the young Maria Sophia wed Francesco of the Two Sicilies. Then styled Duke of Calabria, he was the eldest son and heir apparent of King Ferdinando II. Maria Sophia's younger sister, Mathilde, eventually married Francesco's half-brother Luigi, a younger son of Ferdinando.

When King Ferdinando died later in the year, Francesco ascended the throne as King Francesco II. Descended from the House of Bourbon, the dynasty had reigned in Naples since 1734, and Francesco spoke Neapolitan as his mother tongue, though he was proficient in French, German and Italian.

Rarely the pragmatist, pious Francesco was not particularly well-suited to the demands of kingship in a tumultuous era. The House of Savoy had proffered the crown of a united Italy to his late father, who refused, but Ferdinando's deserved reputation as an iron-fisted warrior king willing to defend his country was sufficient to discourage any attempt at invasion. What is more, the fact that the young Francesco was greatly influenced by dogmatic Pope Pius IX did not augur well in a political pond full of anti-clericals and unificationists. The monarch's failure to extricate himself from the papal spell would write the denouement of Italy's most prosperous state.

Maria Sophia was an adamant proponent for establishment of a permanent constitution, something that was already in place in Bavaria, and she admonished her stoic husband to grant one. Alas, when he finally assented it was too late.

Ever convinced of the cause of continued sovereignty for Italy's South, Francesco II opposed the goal of Italian political unification as it was advocated by exponents in Turin. This reflected no nationalistic or dynastic bigotry. In fact, Francesco's mother, Maria Cristina (who had died giving birth to him), was a Savoy, making Francesco a cousin of King Vittorio Emanuele of Sardinia, who ruled from Turin.

Nevertheless, Piedmontese-backed troops attacked and occupied Sicily in 1860 in an undeclared war. Francesco, who commanded Italy's strongest army, failed to respond, and additional Savoyard troops eventually invaded the kingdom's mainland territories (see the map following this appendix), beginning with Calabria. Tacit support from the British navy, and treason on the part of several high officers in the Neapolitan army, made this bloody campaign that much easier for the invaders to win.

Under the command of loyal officers, the fortress of Messina held out for months, but Francesco, wishing to avoid a civilian slaughter like the one that had taken place in Palermo, abandoned Naples in favor of the coastal stronghold at Gaeta to the north.

Maria Sophia accompanied him, and during the siege in early 1861 she earned the nickname "Heroine of Gaeta."

Gaeta finally fell in February, followed by the citadel of Messina the next month, but an armed resistance continued in the hinterland, led by military officers loyal to their king. Soldiers who continued to fight were branded "brigands" and several hundred that were captured were incarcerated as the newly-united Italy's first political prisoners in Fenestrelle, an Alpine fortress.

In response to guerilla warfare, the invading troops sent from Piedmont committed the kind of atrocities that in our times earn universal opprobrium. In August, the town of Pontelandolfo suffered mass rape and murder for two long days (see note 10).

The royal Neapolitan couple were exiled following the surrender of Gaeta. A dubious referendum, showing an incredible approval of some ninety-nine percent, confirmed Vittorio Emanuele II of Savoy as "King of Italy."

Francesco and Maria Sophia then took up residence at Palazzo Farnese, a family home in Rome. (It currently houses the French Embassy.) The royal family took virtually none of their possessions or financial assets into exile, and eventually sold this palace.

Some developments during this period were nothing short of bizarre, and a particularly sobering incident said much about the credibility of the neocratic Italian state in the eyes of the world. In November 1861, a Marseille court upheld Francesco's earlier sale of two Neapolitan ships despite a vociferous protest from the hubristic Italian ambassador, who claimed that the vessels belonged to Italy. The splenetic reasoning advanced for this idea was that Francesco was no longer a reigning king when the ships were sold, and his former kingdom was by then part of the Kingdom of Italy. (History would repeat itself nine decades later when Great Britain refused to relinquish to the Italian Republic several million pounds that the "patriotic" Savoy kings had stashed in British banks.) Rarely in the decades to come would the united Italy have anything resembling a cohesive foreign policy. In the Kingdom of Italy, right up until the realm's woeful final years, subterfuge often took the place of statecraft.

It has been suggested that Maria Sophia gave birth to the daughter, or possibly twin daughters, of a military officer during her sojourn in Bavaria in 1862, but the evidence of this is scant at best, based almost entirely on hearsay emanating from questionable sources.

She was back in Rome with Francesco the next year. There, in 1869, Maria Sophia gave birth to a daughter, Maria Cristina. Her sister, Sissi, was present for the delivery. Sadly, the baby died aged only three months. The next year, papal Rome fell to the invading troops of the nascent Kingdom of Italy, and Francesco and Maria Sophia departed for Paris. Over the next decades they sometimes lived apart, travelling around Europe visiting their numerous cousins, particularly in Austria.

Admired by her contemporaries, Maria Sophia passed much of her time in Paris and Munich. The last decade of the nineteenth century was an especially trying one. Her sister Helen died in 1890. Her brother Maximilian died in 1893. Her devoted husband Francesco died in Arco, near Trent (then part of Austria), in 1894. Her younger sister, Sophia Charlotte, died in a Paris fire in 1897 at an annual charity bazar while helping the girls who worked there to escape the blaze. Maria Sophia's beloved sister Sissi was killed by an anarchist in Geneva the following year.

Plagued by riots against the government and the Savoys, the Kingdom of Italy continued to vilify the House of the Two Sicilies, which remained exiled until the Allied occupation of southern Italy during the Second World War. Much of this defamation was directed at Maria Sophia, and it said far more about the tenuous position of the Italian unitary state than it did about the woman being disparaged. Indeed, the only overtly negative commentary published about Maria Sophia was hatched in Italy, a country where she never again set foot after the age of nineteen.

The more outlandish accusations were little more than unfounded conspiracy theories associating Maria Sophia with a series of violent anarchists bent on wreaking havoc in politically fragile Italy, as if a solitary, exiled woman could bring about the country's demise. Such revisionism was part and parcel of Italian nationalist propaganda during this period, making its way into subsequent historiography; for example, the anarchist who assassinated King Umberto I in 1900 was painted as an "American" even though he was born and raised in Italy.

With the outbreak of the First World War, the last Queen of the Two Sicilies definitively abandoned Paris for Munich, where she died in January 1925, six months before her younger sister, Mathilde.

Maria Sophia was immortalised in Proust's *La Prisonnière*. She reposes with her husband and daughter in the Royal Chapel of the Basilica of Santa Chiara in Naples.

Sir Harold Acton wrote that "age spiritualised her beauty." Even as an octogenarian, Her Majesty rode the horses she so loved.

Only with the collapse of the Kingdom of Italy in 1946 following a disastrous war was there a balanced reassessment of the merits of the Neapolitan Bourbons and their role in history, and indeed a belated, pragmatic reappraisal of the Italian unification movement, the *Risorgimento*. Excoriating the fallen regime, some Italians began to question whether a federalist state along the lines of the Swiss or German models would not have been better than what was introduced in Italy. In view of the destruction and suffering wrought by the lost war, many ordinary people began to doubt the hyperbole and aphorisms that had constituted Italian political thought since 1861.

In addition to Harold Acton's books, a novel published in English translation in 1960 brought this issue to the fore. This was *The Leopard,* by Giuseppe Tomasi di Lampedusa, made into a film starring Burt Lancaster in 1963.

In a sense, the post-war establishment of Sicily as a "semi-autonomous" region confirmed Francesco's certitude that the unified Italy would always be a tenuous ensemble of culturally diverse regions, an opinion shared by a great many in our times.

In death, Francesco and Maria Sophia became greater symbols of southern identity and "regionalism" than they were in life.

The most imposing reminder of the dynasty is Caserta Palace, constructed in a large estate outside Naples on the orders of Charles III beginning in 1752. The largest royal palace in Italy, Caserta has been compared to Versailles, and it has occasionally played a part in history since the fall of Naples in 1861. Housing the Allied military command in 1945, it was the site of the signing of the formal surrender of German forces in Italy. Since then, the palace has been the location of everything from international summits to Hollywood films.

Other royal residences of note are the palaces in Naples, Capodimonte, Portici and (in Sicily) the Norman Palace and Chinese Villa in Palermo, and the Ficuzza Hunting Lodge near Corleone.

Today most would agree that it was necessary to unify the former Italian states in some way, probably as a republic rather than a monarchy. In 1861 Palermo was wealthier than Milan. The subsequent northward shift of national administration and industry left the south less industrialized and generally less affluent than the north. This provoked mass emigration.

History is based on what actually occurs, not on what might have happened otherwise. We cannot know with certainty that the Kingdom of the Two Sicilies, or perhaps a federation of united Italian states, would have avoided the succession of calamities that plagued the Kingdom of Italy established in its stead. Among these were the mass genocide perpetrated in Libya and Ethiopia, the infamous anti-Semitic laws of 1937, and Italy's suicidal alliance with Nazi Germany in its war against the Allies, during which entire historical districts of Milan and Palermo were bombed into inexistence.

Maria Sophia spent almost her entire adult life, from the age of nineteen, as an exiled queen, a footnote to history, a curiosity. For many, her very survival into the twentieth century evoked bittersweet memories of an earlier, simpler age.

Interview with Princess Urraca of the Two Sicilies

Urraca Maria Isabella Carolina de Bourbon of the Two Sicilies (1913-1999) was a granddaughter of Prince Alfonso, Count of Caserta (1841-1934), the younger half-brother and heir of King Francesco II. As a child, she knew Queen Maria Sophia.

In 1951, acting on the wishes of her father, Prince Ferdinando Pio (1869-1960), who was then head of the dynasty, Princess Urraca consigned the private papers of Francesco II to the Naples Archive of State, where the collection was catalogued two years later.

Her mother, Maria Ludwiga von Wittelsbach of Bavaria (1872-1954), was descended from the family of the Elisabeth who became Queen of Sicily in 1250. Urraca was the youngest of six children.

In December 1994, when Princess Urraca visited Palermo to observe the centennial of the death of her great uncle, King Francesco II, she was interviewed by a historian specialized in the Kingdom of Sicily who recognized her as a living link to Queen Maria Sophia.[721] The interview (translated by this book's author) is published here for the first time.

Interviewer: Your Highness, I know you used to visit Naples and Rome quite often, but had you ever been to Palermo before this trip?

Princess Urraca: Yes. The last time was some years ago, around 1977, by ship, with the Order of Malta, and our [mutual] friend Cyril Toumanoff[722] but on that occasion we went directly to visit Monreale, and spent very little time down here in the city. I had never been to the Magione church until this morning. It is beautiful.

Interviewer: My first curiosity, thinking about an era that has become the subject of historical discussion, even debate, is the exile of your father's family beginning in 1861.

Princess Urraca: Well, my mother was German, and I was raised mostly in Bavaria, so it wasn't something that touched me very noticeably, personally. My father was permitted to visit Italy at the height of Fascism, but only on the condition that he be accompanied everywhere by a police escort, not for his protection but to protect that paranoid regime. So he decided not to make such visits a habit even though my sister, Lucia, was married to a Savoy and lived for some years in Italy, until the fall of the monarchy.

Interviewer: That's when [beginning in 1946] your father could finally come here [to Italy] without those complications.

Princess Urraca: Yes. And around 1950 I began visiting Italy fairly frequently, especially Rome and Naples. I love Naples.

Interviewer: It is interesting that the Italy you've known best has been the republic, not the kingdom.

Princess Urraca: That is true, but I don't think the people had changed very much by 1950 or even 1960, and my interest has always been the people rather than the government. And especially the people of the south.

Interviewer: Yet your mother's family ruled Bavaria, which today remains one of Germany's most fiercely independent regions. Your mother's father was its last monarch. And, looking back to the thirteenth century, a woman of the Wittelsbach dynasty married a son of Frederick II. That's quite a distinguished family history.

Princess Urraca: But a little bit before my time. What I remember most are the stories my parents told me, and what I've read.

Interviewer: Anything in particular that would surprise people?

Princess Urraca: Well, when one is raised in a formerly ruling family, those stories, or their political implications, are known quite widely. I don't believe there are many secrets of substance.

Interviewer: I've heard that you knew your great aunt, who was the last Queen of the Two Sicilies, and of course a Bavarian princess by birth. What can you tell me about her?

Princess Urraca: Although she seems to have preferred Paris, she had to leave it when the war broke out in 1914. The war was terrible because it made enemies out of friends, almost overnight. That's when she came to live in Bavaria. So from my earliest years it was normal to see her around. For some time she spent the warmer months of each year in a cottage in the country outside Munich so she could be near her horses.

Interviewer: She rode often?

Princess Urraca: Almost every day, I would say, in good weather. It's something I didn't notice consciously as a little girl, but my aunt, though slender for a German lady, was not very tall. That probably added to the effect of a competent equestrienne riding a large horse. One was an Arabian, a high-spirited breed.

Interviewer: You were about twelve when she died. Do you remember any conversations with her, or perhaps between her and your mother?

Princess Urraca: Not with a great deal of detail, but what struck one most about Maria Sophia was her great dignity. It spoke for her. And even at her age, she was in good health. No problems moving or walking. Her posture was perfect, and so was her memory. My mother said that Maria Sophia looked younger than her actual age.

Interviewer: Did she ever seem melancholy, embittered about exile?

Princess Urraca: I never saw that. However, I would say that she was not very moody, so no highs and lows. She had the aura of a person to be taken seriously. She had a keen sense of humor, and even when she was scolding somebody she didn't raise her voice. She didn't have to.

Interviewer: Did she seem well-informed?

Princess Urraca: She read the newspapers in German, French and Italian. They were delivered to us in Munich a few times each week, and I recall her saving articles she felt were worth keeping. I would say she understood the politics of each country very well.

Interviewer: She held strong opinions?

Princess Urraca: That was normal between the two wars, certainly in Germany and certainly for people of her generation. But yes, the only time she ever became noticeably angry was when she read the newspapers. So, yes, I would say she was rather opinionated about some things.

Interviewer: Was she a reactionary?

Princess Urraca: I would not use that word. She was a traditionalist, but she seemed to believe in the rights of women to vote and to hold political office. I don't think she criticized women who supported social progress. After she died, I recall friends of hers, other women, saying she was very loyal to them even when she disagreed with their social or political views.

Interviewer: Was she devoutly Catholic?

Princess Urraca: Yes, but how does one measure something like devotion? She sometimes attended mass with us on Sundays.

Interviewer: I realize we're talking about a cosmopolitan woman, and that one's views can change over time, but how would you describe her sense of identity?

Princess Urraca: Very Neapolitan, by choice. She visited Italian prisoners during the war, but it transcended nostalgia. I believe she truly loved Naples, as I do.

Interviewer: A true southerner.

Princess Urraca: Yes, from southern Germany to southern Italy. The sun is always brighter in the south!

Interviewer: She had been close to her sister, Sissi. Do you recall her ever talking about the empress?

Princess Urraca: I do, but only in passing. Most of what I learned about Sissi came from my mother or my teachers, when I was sixteen or seventeen, after Maria Sophia was already gone. Bavaria has always had a close connection with Austria.

Interviewer: Was Maria Sophia reclusive?

Princess Urraca: As I knew her, she never sought attention. She was a private person, though not reclusive or shy.

Interviewer: I have researched in the family papers that your father donated to the Italian state, but there's rather little about Queen Maria Sophia, either before or after 1861.

Princess Urraca: Well, there is no single collection of Maria Sophia's correspondence, although we have some of it in Germany, so nobody has access to all of it. In the end, my aunt had very little in the way of jewels. As you may know, the king and queen took virtually nothing with them when they left Gaeta for exile, unlike the other dynasty [the Savoys] who had millions in foreign banks. They owned some property in Rome, but little else.

Interviewer: The ignorance of people in this country [Italy] regarding the unification movement, and even the Fascist regime, is appalling. Maria Sophia's life spanned both eras, yet most Italians — even southerners — have no idea that the last Queen of the Two Sicilies lived until 1925.

Princess Urraca: That is true. There has been an attempt here to bury history. Never a good thing. But our family, my cousins and I, are always very well received in Naples, so *somebody* remembers us.

Interviewer: Your grandfather [Prince Alfonso], who died in 1934, was the half-brother of King Francesco II. Did you ever discuss with him anything regarding the Kingdom of the Two Sicilies?

Princess Urraca: I saw my grandfather only rarely, as he lived in France. What little I learned of his opinions was through my father, who, of course, was his heir.

Interviewer: Was there anything in particular?

Princess Urraca: I only recall my grandfather mentioning this or that comrade from the Siege of Gaeta, things like that. Most of his attention seemed to focus on his family.

Interviewer: And of course he was the last Italian prince to lead men in cavalry charges in the manner of a medieval king commanding mounted knights.

Princess Urraca: Yes, at the Battle of the Volturno, against the Piedmontese invaders.

Interviewer: I don't want to pose too many hypothetical questions but, especially considering that, for example, Italian women were granted the right to vote only in 1945, and then only by the Allies occupying the very ground beneath us, how much worse could life have been in southern Italy if your kinsman, Francesco II, had continued to rule, without Italian unification? Or perhaps in part of a federalist state like Germany's?

Princess Urraca: Clearly, grave mistakes were made in the Kingdom of Italy. Hypothetical discussions can be very complex because one opens a box to find another inside it, and so forth. And empty because the last, smallest box, contains nothing at all. But war and death are real. I think we can all agree about that. I saw it in Germany.

Interviewer: What is life like for the Wittelsbachs in Munich?

Princess Urraca: My mother's family was never exiled, and never divested of property like the families in East Germany following the war. But it is also true that my grandfather, and his father, enjoyed a good rapport with the Bavarians, who viewed them as populists. Their family granted a constitution early in the nineteenth century, and they were never too aloof of the people they ruled.

Interviewer: Maria Sophia cited that when encouraging her husband, the king, to re-institute Sicily's constitution of 1812, which predated Piedmont's by decades.

Princess Urraca: A principle worthy of her parentage and mine.

Maria Sophia Wittelsbach (shown) was Queen Consort from 1859. Elisabeth Wittelsbach, the wife of Conrad and mother of Conradin, was Queen from 1250 to 1254. Her story is told in Chapter 17.

QUEENS OF SICILY

Royal house of Bourbon of the Two Sicilies

Lineage of Sicily's Last Dynasty

- **Louis XIV** of France
  - **Louis** The Great Dauphin
    - **Philip IV** (Philip V of Spain) 1700-1713 ⚭ **Elisabeth Farnese** of Parma
      - **Charles de Bourbon** King of Sicily 1735-1759, King of Spain 1759-1788
        - Filippo
        - Charles IV of Spain
        - **Ferdinando I of the Two Sicilies** 1759-1825
          - Carlo
          - **Francesco I** 1825-1830
            - Gennaro
            - Giuseppe
            - Leopoldo
            - Alberto
            - **Ferdinando II** 1830-1859
              - Carlo, Prince of Capua
              - Leopoldo, Count of Siracusa
              - Antonio, Count of Lecce
              - Luigi, Count of Aquila
              - Francesco, Count of Trapani
              - **Maria Sophia of Bavaria** +1925 ⚭ **Francesco II** 1859-1861 +1894
              - Luigi, Count of Trani
              - **Alfonso, Count of Caserta** +1934
                - **Maria Ludwiga of Bavaria** ⚭ **Ferdinando** +1960
                  - Urraca +1999
                - Carlo
                - Gennaro
                - Ranieri
                - Filippo
                - Gabriele
              - Gaetano, Count of Girgenti
              - Pasquale, Count of Bari
              - Gennaro, Count of Caltagirone
          - Gabriele
          - Antonio
          - Francesco Saverio
        - Filippo, Duke of Parma
        - Luigi Antonio, Count of Chinchón

+ year of death

Italian States in 1859

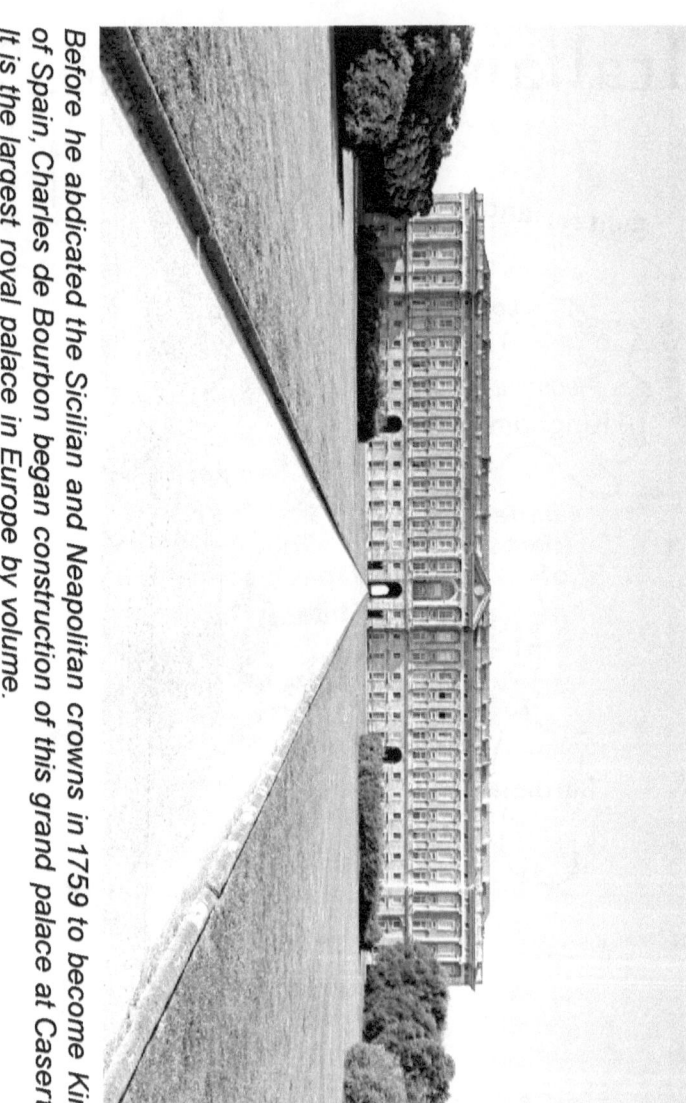

Before he abdicated the Sicilian and Neapolitan crowns in 1759 to become King of Spain, Charles de Bourbon began construction of this grand palace at Caserta. It is the largest royal palace in Europe by volume.

In 1785, Charles de Bourbon, King of Spain, formerly King of Sicily, sponsored the first Catholic parish of New York. Saint Peter's church, in Manhattan, was rebuilt in 1840.

NOTES

1. See Tuchman, Barbara. *Practicing History: Selected Essays* (in Sources), page 18.

2. For some observations about the implications of gender in the Middle Ages, see Weikert, Katherine and Woodacre, Elena, "Gender and Status in the Medieval World," *Historical Reflections,* pages 1-7.

3. See Earenfight, Theresa, "Highly Visible, Often Obscured: The Difficulty of Seeing Queens and Noble Women," *Medieval Feminist Forum* (in Sources), pages 86-90.

4. Translation by Mendola, Louis, *Sicily's Rebellion against King Charles,* pages 99, 177.

5. From *De Vulgari Eloquentia* ("On Eloquence in the Vernacular") written early in the fourteenth century, by which time Middle Sicilian was the spoken language in Sicily, much of Calabria and parts of Apulia. Tuscan did not derive from Sicilian or vice versa; each language developed on its own from Latin. The difference is that Sicilian bears the mark of many other languages, and developed somewhat earlier as a literary vernacular.

6. Trota, a woman who studied at Salerno's medical school, wrote a gynecological treatise. In an earlier era we find Hypatia of Alexandria.

7. For a contemporary account of the damage caused by the fire of 1811 to the royal tombs, see "Sopra i Reali Sepolcri del Duomo di Monreale: Memoria del Padre Don Giovan Battista Tarallo," *Giornale di Scienza, Letteratura ed Arti per la Sicilia* (Palermo), July-September 1826, page 166.

8. A growing number of books confront this, a recent entry being Angela Saini's insightful *Inferior: How Science Got Women Wrong, and the New Research That's Rewriting the Story* (2017). For a closer look at the science behind gender from an academic perspective, see *Brain Gender* (2005) by Melissa Hines.

9. The County of Barcelona was often linked to the Kingdom of Aragon and ruled by the Aragonese dynasty. The majority of Catalans voting in a widely-reported referendum held in 2017 supported secession; this led to violent police intervention in Barcelona, Spain's largest and wealthiest city, and a political crisis in Madrid. See Minder, Raphael, "Catalonia Government Declares Overwhelming Vote for Independence" in *The New York Times,* 6 October 2017; "How to Save Spain" and "Barcelona and Madrid" in *The Economist* (print edition), 5 October 2017.

10. In 2011, when Italy observed the sesquicentennial of unification, books were published decrying the atrocities of the undeclared war of 1860; ceremonies marking the commemoration in Sicily were effectively boycotted by an apathetic public, being attended by the military personnel and public officials who were paid to be there, but hardly anybody else. In some places the boycotts were more explicit. The mayor and residents of Pontelandolfo, a locality that suffered mass rape and carnage

at the hands of Piedmontese troops on 14 August 1861 during a reprisal for allegedly having supported "brigands" (partisans), blatantly refused to celebrate the sesquicentennial; newspapers reported that, on 14 August 2011, speaking for the Italian president, the national official (a former prime minister) responsible for the celebrations officially apologized to the mayors, councils and residents, declaring: *"Io vi chiedo scusa, a nome della Repubblica Italiana."* ("I apologize to you on behalf of the Italian Republic."), for which see "Pontelandolfo, scuse per un massacro: il ricordo dei civili uccisi come rappresaglia contro i briganti 150 anni fa" in the *Corriere della Sera* (Milan), 14 August 2011, page 41. Among the books published were Pino Aprile's *Terroni: All that has been done to ensure that the Italians of the South became southerners* (2011), Giordano Bruno Guerri's *Il Sangue del Sud: Antistoria del Risorgimento e del Brigantaggio* (2010), and Gianni Oliva's *Un Regno Che è Stato Grande: La Storia Negata dei Borboni di Napoli e Sicilia* (2011).

11. For some comments on "corporate monarchy" see Earenfight, Theresa, "Without the Persona of the Prince: Kings, Queens and the Idea of Monarchy in Late Medieval Europe," *Gender and History*, volume 19, number 1 (2007), pages 1-21.

12. See *A History of the House of Lords* (1988) by Frank Pakenham, Earl of Longford.

13. Green, Mary Ann Everett, *Lives of the Princesses of England from the Norman Conquest*, volume 1 (Joanna, pages 308-403), volume 2 (Isabella, pages 1-47). For a more recent scholarly study see Bowie, Colette, *The Daughters of Henry II and Eleanor of Aquitaine: A Comparative Study of Twelfth-century Women*. Not to be overlooked are fine entries in other languages, such as Ingo Runde's "Konstanze von Aragon" (see Sources).

14. See "Higher Education in Italy: A Case for Change" in *The Economist*, 15 November 2008, page 32: "...this week news emerged of a university rector who, the day before he retired on October 31st, signed a decree to make his son a lecturer. At Palermo University, as many as 230 teachers are reported to be related to other teachers." See also the article "The Ins and Outs: Italians are deeply anti-meritocratic" in the same publication, 9 June 2011, where the term *raccomandazione* (preferment) is explained. More recently: "Seven Professors Arrested in Florence University Nepotism Row" by Thomas Kington in *The Times* (London), 27 September 2017, reported from Rome; "Concorsi truccati all'università: indagati sette docenti siciliani," *Giornale di Sicilia* (Palermo), 25 September 2017. For a description of student life at Italy's public universities, see Pacitti, Domenico, "No Holiday in Rome" in *The Guardian* (London), 8 October 2002. For the high prevalence of plagiarism in Italy's universities, see Sutherland-Smith, Wendy, *Plagiarism, the Internet, and Student Learning: Improving Academic Integrity* (2008), pages 88-89. Sadly, not a single Italian university was listed in the top hundred in the *Times Higher Education World University Rankings* for 2018 (published in 2017 on the website timeshighereducation.com).

15. See *Atti del Congresso Internazionale di Studi sulla Sicilia Normanna* (Palermo 1974). The lone *professoressa* was Marina Scarlata. There was, however, a eulogy to the late Evelyn Jamison.

NOTES

16. Certain fundamental rights arrived only in very recent times; divorce, for example, was legalized in 1970. Rape became a felonious form of assault (previously it was a minor offense "against public decency") in 1996 but is rarely prosecuted because the burden of proof is ridiculously high; see Van Cleave, Rachel, "Rape and Querela Law in Italy: False Protection of Victim Agency," *Michigan Journal of Gender and Law*, volume 13, pages 273-310, January 2007 (Ann Arbor 2007). Sexual harassment is widespread in academia but only rarely taken seriously by the courts; see Hooper, John, "Sex Scandal Rocks Italian Campus: Professor acquitted of trading better grades for sex boasts of his affairs with series of young women," in *The Guardian*, 9 June 2004; also Molé, Noelle, *Labor Disorders in Neoliberal Italy: Mobbing, Well-being and the Workplace* (Indiana University Press 2012), chapter 6 ("The Sex of Mobbing"), pages 138-149, which describes reprisals against female professors who rebuke sexual advances by lecherous males to whom they report. Italy finally ratified an anti-stalking law in 2009; see De Fazio, Laura, "Criminalization of stalking in Italy: One of the last among the current European member states' anti-stalking laws," *Behavioral Sciences and the Law*, volume 29, issue 2 (March 2011), pages 317-323. In 2017, the World Economic Forum's *Global Gender Gap Report* ranked Italy 82nd out of 144 nations, immediately after Mexico and just ahead of Myanmar. While the effects of the #MeToo movement which began in the United States that year were soon echoed in Britain, they failed to arrive here in Italy; see the insightful articles by Emma Bubola, Rachel Donadio, Gaia Pianigiani, Simona Siri, Guia Soncini, Angela Giuffrida, Julian Vigo, Jason Horowitz and Nicole Winfield in the bibliography.

17. An everyday example is the belief (here in Italy) that an Italian invented the telephone. There are errors of omission as well as commission; virtually nothing is taught in Italian schools about Fascism or the atrocities perpetrated by the Italians in Africa during our nation's ill-fated colonialist escapades (see note 24).

18. Most of the tenured professors and research fellows of medieval history at Sicilian universities were born and educated here in Sicily; it is rare even to find one from the Catania orbit (from Enna eastward to the Ionian coast) teaching on the opposite side of the island in Palermo, or vice versa. This *de facto* homophily does not lend itself to the kind of diversity of thought one finds at major universities in Britain and the United States.

19. For commentary on distorted historiography in Italy, see the late Denis Mack Smith's insightful "Documentary Falsification and Italian Biography" in *History and Biography: Essays in Honour of Derek Beales* (Cambridge 1996), page 181, and the introduction of his *Italy and Its Monarchy* (1989); also *The Pursuit of Italy: A History of a Land, Its Regions, and Their Peoples* (2011) by David Gilmour; *Under the Volcano: Revolution in a Sicilian Town* (2013) by Lucy Riall. *Memorie del Sud* (1999), edited by Andrea Orlandi, presents a number of revelatory details regarding the peninsular half of the Two Sicilies and the war of 1860-1861. Another insightful work is *Darkest Italy: The Nation and Stereotypes of the Mezzogiorno 1860-1900* (1999) by John Dickie.

20. Apart from the titles mentioned in notes 10 and 19, Eric Salerno's *Genocidio in Libia* (2005) is an example of a book on a topic few Italian publishers dared to confront until very recently.

21. Not to be overlooked are specialist scholarly studies of particular aspects of certain regencies published in languages other than Italian and English. Of note is the work of Vera von Falkenhausen (see Sources).

22. Joanna of Anjou, for example, briefly visited northeastern Sicily but never actually ruled the island, over which she could be said to have reigned "by pretension." See Goldstone, Nancy, *Joanna: The Notorious Queen of Naples, Jerusalem and Sicily* (2011).

23. See *The Bourbons of Naples* (1965) and *The Last Bourbons of Naples* (1961) by Harold Acton, the definitive works for that dynasty's history from *circa* 1700 until 1861. The most detailed biography of King Francesco II is *L'Ultimo Re di Napoli* (1982) by Pier Giusto Jaeger. Arrigo Petacco's *La Regina del Sud* (1992) is the most complete biography of Queen Maria Sophia.

24. See Campbell, Ian, *The Addis Ababa Massacre: Italy's National Shame* (2017); Katz, Robert, *The Fall of the House of Savoy* (1972). See also note 20.

25. See Bucher, Michael, "Re-Discovering the Italian Kingdom of the Two Sicilies," *Time* (USA), 25 August 2016. The movements described are more regionalist than monarchist.

26. See Mendola, Louis, "English and Italian Legacy of the Norman Knight Figures of Monreale" and "Pre-Armorial Use of the Lion Passant Guardant and the Fleur-de-lis as Heraldic Badges in Norman Sicily" in Sources. Whether the repeating gold motif on the blue robe of Roger II shown in the famous mosaic in Palermo's Martorana church (see the line drawing in Chapter 5), depicts fleurs-de-lis or, conversely, crosses is a matter of scholarly debate. In 1994, Mendola wrote that the images are fleurs-de-lis; a few years later Hubert Houben stated they are crosses (presumably rendered so as to show curvature around the king's body). It should be noted that a pattern of simple Greek crosses on vestments is typical in Byzantine iconography. The Capetians did not display the fleur-de-lis heraldically (as a personally representative charge on an escutcheon), specifically as the arms blazoned *azure semé-de-lis or*, nor did the Plantagenets use the lion passant guardant heraldically, before the general inception of armorial heraldry in the second half of the twelfth century. Contrary to what some scholars have postulated, the Hautevilles' early use of these symbols may have inspired their heraldic use by the other European dynasties, and not vice versa.

27. For such descriptions we look to Mohammed ibn Hawqal in the tenth century and Abu Hussain Mohammed bin Ahmad bin Jubayr in the twelfth. Cordoba, with its magnificent mosque-cum-cathedral, is still an impressive city (and one for which the author confesses a special affinity). The Nasrid palaces in the Alhambra of Granada, and the splendid salons in Seville's Alcazar, are equally majestic. The surviving monuments to the Mudéjar style in Andalusia and Navarre differ somewhat from what one finds in Sicily, but before it fell to ruin the hammam at Cefala Diana may have been similar to the Bañuelo in Granada.

28. See Makdisi, John, op cit. in Sources.

NOTES

29. Over the years, these two accounts of the Normans' arrival in southern Italy have given rise to two schools of thought, each supporting one "theory" (tradition) or the other. It is the author's conviction that they are not mutually exclusive. In their general outlines, both descriptions mention Norman knights being in Italy for pilgrimages. Neither tradition seems slavishly faithful to fact, but neither does one contradict the substance of the other. Indeed, there may have been other bands of Norman knights errant present in Italy besides those mentioned. For more on the "Gargano" and "Salerno" traditions see Joranson, Einar, op.cit. in Sources.

30. One may very loosely describe the minor emirates that existed by 1060 as *taifas*, though they were not identical to what existed in Spain. At times the city of Bal'harm (Palermo) was, in effect, a semi-autonomous emirate. There was not much open warfare among the numerous Sicilian emirs, who all owed allegiance to the Fatimids, but neither was there much unity.

31. The best-known vestiges of this polyglot past are such monuments as Palermo's Palatine Chapel, with its Byzantine mosaic walls and Fatimid muqarnas ceiling, and of course Monreale's abbey and cloister. Biological proof of the presence of various civilizations has emerged; although genetic haplogroups do not always correlate precisely to the presence of specific peoples (and can be affected over time by such phenomena as "genetic drift"), they offer us a broad "footprint" left by the past. Research undertaken during the last two decades reveals the following Y-chromosome haplogroups (and others) in Sicily in approximately the following percentages: J (35), R (25), I (15), K (10), H (10), Others (5). These are very broadly identified with the following populations (and others) patrilineally: J1 (Arabs, Berbers, Carthaginians, Jews), J2 (Greeks, Romans, Jews), R1b (Germans, Normans, Lombards), I1 and I2b (Vikings and Normans), I and I2a (Elymians), G (Arabs and Elymians), N (Norsemen and Normans), E1b1b (Arabs and Berbers), K (Arabs, Greeks, Berbers, Carthaginians), H (Arabs), T (Phoenicians, Carthaginians). In matrilineal (mtDNA) lineage we find, among others, the "Seven Daughters of Eve," namely the haplogroups H (Helena), J (Jasmine), K (Katrine), T (Tara), U5 (Ursula), V (Velda) and X (Xenia). The reader seeking an introduction to this area of phylogeography is referred to *The Journey of Man: A Genetic Odyssey* (2004) by Spencer Wells, Explorer-in-Residence of the National Geographic Society and former student of the late Luigi Luca Cavalli-Sforza, the author of *Genes, Peoples and Languages* (2000), and *The Seven Daughters of Eve* (2001) by Bryan Sykes.

32. This was none other than William I, Duke of Normandy, known in England as "William the Conqueror." Robert of Grandmesnil (or Grantmesnil) died in 1035. See *The Ecclesiastical History of England and Normandy* by Orderic Vitalis, volume 1, page 149.

33. Ibid, page 395. The same passage also mentions how Hawisa's sister, Eremburga, bore two sons, William and Ralph of Pont-Echanfré, who ended up in Italy in the service of Robert "Guiscard" Hauteville. (In English Hawisa's name is sometimes rendered *Hawise* and Eremburga's as *Heremburge*.) Hawisa's sons by Robert of Grandmesnil were Hugh, Robert and Arnold, these being Judith's half-brothers.

34. Orderic Vitalis states very simply that Judith "became the wife of Roger, Count of Sicily." More generally, this part of the chronicle recounts the circumstances of the endowment of Saint Evroul Abbey by Hawisa's family before 1050. See also note 33.

35. See notes 33 and 34.

36. *Ecclesiastical History* (op.cit. supra), volume 1, pages 400-401.

37. Ibid, pages 401-402.

38. This description of a noblewoman's upbringing is adapted from the author's *Margaret, Queen of Sicily* (2016), pages 89-91.

39. At this early date an esquire could be knighted by an enfeoffed knight or feudal baron (thus Judith's half-brother, Robert, was an esquire of William the Bastard who dubbed him), and the ceremony was quite simple. The notion that only a king or other sovereign (being a fount of honour) could bestow knighthood emerged later. Only royal princes were knighted much before the age of twenty, usually by their own fathers.

40. By his first wife, Muriella, Tancred (980-1041) fathered William "the Iron Arm," Drogo, Geoffrey, Serlo, Humphrey and Beatrice; by his second wife, Fressenda, he sired Robert "Guiscard," Mauger, William, Alberic, Hubert, Tancred, Roger and Fressenda. Serlo, Alberic and Tancred remained in Normandy. There were other daughters besides Beatrice and Fressenda. For this our chief source is Malaterra's *De Rebus Gestis Rogerii Calabriae et Siciliae Comitis et Roberti Guiscardi Ducis Fratris Eius*, but there are others, such as Orderic Vitalis. According to *Domesday Book*, for example, a certain Alverardus of Hauteville once held manors across the Channel in Somerset; this was probably Alberic. The origin of the name of the locality called Hauteville is disputed; it may simply mean "High Town," the story of Hiallt perhaps being legendary.

41. See *Ecclesiastical History* (op.cit. supra), volume 1, page 428. See also note 34.

42. In the words of Godfrey Malaterra: *Erat enim juvenis pulcherrimus, procerae staturae, eleganti corpore, lingua facundissimus, consilio callidus, in ordinatione agendarum rerum providus, omnibus jocundus et affabilis, viribus fortis, militia ferox: quibus artibus brevi tempore omnem gratiam meruit.*

43. According to Malaterra, *diu cupitam puellam visum ire accelerat.*

44. It is possible, though unlikely, that Roger had served as an esquire or knight in the service of Judith's father (see note 39).

45. The nickname *Guiscard* comes from a Norman French word for "crafty."

46. See *Ecclesiastical History* (op.cit. supra), volume 1, page 422.

NOTES

47. Ibid, page 432.

48. Ibid, page 434.

49. Ibid, pages 439-440. This is a verbatim extract from Forester's masterful translation of Orderic's chronicle, which goes on to say that, "neither [of the two sisters] were blessed with children." That observation, as we shall see, was nonsense.

50. Mohammed ibn al-Timnah, whose domains were on the Ionian coast, had been marginalized by the other emirs. According to some accounts, he was effectively deposed in Catania and Syracuse, the "taifas" (see note 30) that constituted the greater part of his emirate.

51. This section is based chiefly on the account by Malaterra, considered the most reliable. There exists no detailed Arab account of the Battle of Messina. Interesting as some battles may be, our descriptions in this volume shall be concise.

52. The Greek city was Alontion, from which the Latin Aluntium, which minted its own coins. The vestiges of a Greek temple remain. When the Normans arrived, the inhabitants of the village were chiefly Greek Orthodox, perceived as less menacing than Muslims, and there was a Byzantine monastery dedicated to Saint Theodore. The date of the castle's construction (1061) comes to us from Malaterra, who mentions it almost as an afterthought to his report of the Normans' zealous raids around Kasr'Janni (Enna): *Cum redit, spoliis et praeda totum exercitum abundanter replevit. Per mensem itaque ibi perdurantes, totam provinciam, diversis incursionibus lacerantes, afflixerunt, sed Castro-Iohannis minime praevaluerunt. In ipso anno dux castrum Marci fecit.*

53. Malaterra refers to *Graeci* and *Sarraceni* based on the languages they spoke (see note 58), though there was an obvious religious correlation as most Byzantine Greeks were Orthodox Christian while most "Saracens" were Shia Muslim. Many Sicilians were bilingual.

54. The preceding two paragraphs are the author's translation from Malaterra's chronicle, Book II, chapter 19, titled *Comes Rogerius uxorem ducit,* and chapter 20, *Comes nuptiis celebratis in Siciliam.*

55. This detail comes to us from Malaterra.

56. See Eads, Valerie, op.cit., and Skinner, Patricia, op.cit. in Sources. In the Alexiad, Anna Comnena refers to Sichelgaita's courage.

57. This castle stood in something like its original condition until the summer of 1943, when protracted fighting between Germans (who had occupied it as a defensive position) and Americans resulted in its destruction.

58. Godfrey Malaterra states that, *Graeci vero et Sarraceni, quibus omnis patria favens pro libito patebat, plurima replebantur abundantia.* "Instead, the Greeks and Saracens received provisions from the entire region and were supplied abundantly."

59. In Malaterra's words: *Quae, quamvis juvencula, tanta strenuitate coepit esse sollicita circa castrum tuendum, ut, diatim circuens, ubi meliorandum videbat, studeret ut fierent vigiles. Reliquos omnes, quos sibi dominus suus abiens dimiserat, blande alloquens, ut sollicite, quae servanda erant, providerent, hortabatur, multa in reditu domini sui repromittens. Sed et transactum periculum, ne, segniter agendo, quid simile incurrerent, ad memoriam reducebat.*

60. See note 52 above.

61. Flandina wed Hugh of Jersey, who thereby received estates in eastern Sicily but was killed in a campaign against the Arabs in 1075, and then Henry del Vasto (brother of the woman who later wed her father); there is some debate about whether Flandina was the daughter of Judith or of Roger's second wife, Eremburga. Adelaide married Henry, Count of Mount Saint Angelo. Emma, born around 1063, though intended to marry Philip I of France (see note 68), wed William, Count of Clermont, and then Rudolf, Count of Montescaglioso. Matilda, who may have been born late in 1062, wed Raymond IV, Count of Toulouse. The identity of the mother of Roger's son, Jordan, a boy born outside marriage, is unknown. It seems that Roger's son Godfrey, Count of Ragusa, was probably born outside marriage, though he made have been a legitimate son of Judith or Eremburga by Roger.

62. Judith's half-brother, Robert, died a few years later, in 1082, and was entombed in the church he built at Saint Euphemia, near Nicastro. It is worth noting that Judith's nephew, William of Grandmesnil, son of Hugh (Abbot Robert's brother and Judith's half-brother), went to Apulia in 1084 and wed Mabel, a daughter of Robert Guiscard; see note 33. Roger I and his second wife (see the next chapter) were originally interred at the Holy Trinity Monastery at Mileto, but their Roman sarcophagi were damaged by an earthquake in 1783 and then taken to Naples during the following century. Though it is possible that Judith's tomb was transferred to Mileto after 1101, it cannot be identified. The abbey at Saint Euphemia was largely destroyed by an earthquake in 1638 and abandoned thereafter.

63. Although it has been suggested that Eremburga was the daughter of Robert, Count of Eu (and Lord of Hastings) and Beatrix of Falaise, there exists very little evidence to support such a thesis; around 1078 a betrothal of Matilda, one of Judith's daughters, was attempted with Robert of Eu. On the other hand, Malaterra, referring to Roger's subsequent marriage in 1089, states very clearly, *comes Rogerius, uxore Eremburga, filia Guillelmi, comitis Mortonensis, defuncta, aliam duxit*. (See also note 74.)

64. Present at the Battle of Hastings in 1066, Odo of Bayeux was a trusted counsellor of his half-brother King William I of England, sometimes serving as his deputy, or *de facto* regent, when the monarch was away in Normandy. Odo died in Palermo early in 1097 during a visit with Roger I *en route* to Palestine as a participant in the First Crusade. He is buried in the crypt of Palermo Cathedral.

65. This austere chapel is now the "crypt" beneath the actual Palatine Chapel.

66. Mauger (Malgerio) became Count of Troina and died at some time after 1098, probably before 1101; historians generally agree this was Eremburga's son. Matilda

married Rainulf II Drengot, Count of Alife, who died in 1139. Felicia (whose name is a subject of debate by historians) wed Coloman the Learned, King of Hungary (see note 81). Flandina (see also note 61) married Henry del Vasto. Judith wed Robert I of Bassonville, Count of Conversano, in 1110 and died in 1136. Muriella married Josbert de Lucy, whose Norman family settled in England, and died in 1119. Eremburga also gave birth to a daughter named Maximilla (sometimes Constance), who wed Conrad, King of Italy, in 1095; see the next chapter.

67. Robert of Eu had commanded some sixty ships at the Battle of Hastings in 1066.

68. This was related to the attempt of Philip I of France to marry beautiful Emma: *Hic legatos suos, apud Siciliam, ad comitem dirigens, filiam eius, nomine Emmam, quam de prima uxore Iudicta habebat, admodum speciosam puellam, sibi in matrimonium copulandam expetit.*

69. Malaterra's account: *Igitur anno Dominicae incarnationis MLXXX Raimundus, famosissimus comes Provinciarum, famem Rogerii, Siculorum comitis, audiens, propter strenuitatem, quae de ipso referabatur, legatos dignos, qui a tanto principe ad tantum mitterentur, dirigens, Matildem, filiam suam, quam de prima uxore admodum honestae faciei puellam habebat, sibi in matrimonium copulandam expostulat. Quod cum a comite concessum et ab utrisque partibus exsequendum sacramentis firmatum fuisset, die nuptiarum statuto, qui venerant, pluribus donariis a comite, ut mos erat, munificati, festiniore regressu domino suo sibi concessum renuntiant. Qua re ille non minimum gavisus — erat enim propter formositatem, quam de ipsa audierat, illam ardentissimo amore cupiens — audito termino nuptiarum, per seipsum in Siciliam accedendo, diem praevenire accelerat. Venientem comes honore condigno excipit. Pactiones renovantur; dos puellae sub testamento chirographiyatur; sponsalia, praesentibus utriusque partis praesulibus, precibus ab episcopis et sacris ordinibus catholice celebrantur. Qui iamdudum inter iuvenem et puellam paulatim adoleverat prima nocte, ut assolet, immensum excrescit. Celebratis itaque, et non sine magnarum expensarum sumptibus, nuptiis, socer generum suum aliquandiu secum retinens, tandem munificentiis benevolum, ut res ipsa expostulabat, factum, sed et iis, qui cum ipso advenerant, singulis singula, prout quemque esse sciebat, largiens, navibus apparatis, placido aequore a se cum filia dimisit. Illi autem, vela ventis accuratissime committentes, zephiro suffragante, brevi tempore unde venerant, cum sponsa reducunt.*

70. Matilda's approximate year of death is inferred from the year Raymond's third marriage was celebrated.

71. For Malaterra's observation see note 63.

72. Her tomb, which presumably indicated a date of death, was later damaged; see note 62.

73. Though preferred by Italian historians, the toponym *del Vasto* is apocryphal, first appearing in a charter issued by Frederick Barbarossa in 1162.

74. Malaterra mentions these details, describing Adelaide as very beautiful, and also notes the fact of Godfrey suffering from leprosy: *Anno igitur incarnati Salvatoris MLXXXIX comes Rogerius, uxore Eremburga, filia Guillelmi, comitis Mortonensis, defuncta,*

aliam duxit: Adelaydem nomine, neptem Bonifacii, famosissimi Italorum marchionis — filiam videlicet fratris eius — iuvenculam honestae admodum faciei; duasque sorores eiusdem puellae duobus filiis suis, Gaufredo videlicet, et Iordano, in matrimonium copulavit. Sed Gaufredus, antequam nubiles annos attigisset — quod dolor est dicere — morbo prohibente, minime eam cognovit. Iordanus autem solemnibus nuptiis duxit.

75. Malta, like Lampedusa and Pantelleria, was eventually integrated into the Kingdom of Sicily. Granted as a fief to the Knights Hospitallers in the sixteenth century, it remained part of the realm until Napoleon seized it in 1800 following a lengthy siege.

76. Later, as regent, Adelaide was to take a personal interest in several such foundations. Most of her surviving charters have been catalogued and published; for those consulted in manuscript form see A and B in Sources. Entire volumes have been written about the church in Sicily during the Norman age; for a lengthy consideration and detailed analysis of the topic, along with lists of the various abbeys founded by the Normans in Sicily, see White, Lynn Townsend, op. cit. For a study which also considers Calabria, Apulia and other peninsular regions as well as Sicily, see Loud, Graham, *The Latin Church in Norman Italy*.

77. Bohemond later sought his fortunes in the Holy Land as one of the leaders of the First Crusade. He founded a Norman monarchy in Antioch.

78. There were machinations by Robert Guiscard's widow, Sichelgaita, to make her own son (Roger Borsa) her late husband's sole heir and successor. Roger Borsa's nickname (literally "purse") is said to derive from his predilection for carefully counting his money.

79. Matilda eventually wed Rainulf of Alife, from whom her brother (Roger II) encouraged her to separate based on his alleged spousal abuse and marital infidelity. This may have been a simple pretext by which to attack Rainulf, who challenged Roger's power in the Apulia region.

80. Maximilla married Hildebrand VI Aldobrandeschi, who held extensive lands in Tuscany.

81. Malaterra describes the betrothal at some length, though without mentioning the bride's name, which is not actually known with certainty. See also note 66.

82. The very succinct entry: *Ibi se impregnavit comitissa Adelasia de comite Rogerio.*

83. This right did not survive the twelfth century. As regent for her young son (Frederick II), Roger's granddaughter, Queen Constance, renounced the apostolic legateship. However, subsequent Sicilian sovereigns occasionally invoked it.

84. What immediately comes to mind, although episcopal appointments *per se* were not its chief cause, is the jurisdictional power struggle between Henry II and Thomas Becket.

NOTES

85. Roger was entombed at Mileto; see note 62. He had fathered some eighteen children by his three wives and one or two mistresses. Our knowledge about most of Roger's children is, admittedly, sketchy.

86. Godfrey (son of Eremburga), who died after 1096, was betrothed to Adelaide's sister but the marriage was called off due to his affliction by leprosy, and Mauger (Malgerio), who held Troina, died after 1098. The other Godfrey (probably a son of Judith), who held Ragusa, died before 1120. Evidence suggests that, following the death of his bastard son Jordan in 1092, Roger may have relegated these three sons by Judith and Eremburga to a lower place in the line of succession, not that this was necessarily a formally-stated policy.

87. See Adelaide's charters under entries A, B and C in Sources. The donations in memory of Roger being cured are described in manuscripts number 7 (for 1101) and number 12 (for 1112).

88. Here our source is Orderic Vitalis in his *Ecclesiastical History*, volume 4, book 13, chapter 15 (pages 134-135 in the English edition of 1856); Thomas Forester, the translator, believes the girl was Adelaide's niece. Her name (Yolanda or Violante) is likely apocryphal, and we don't know if she was the daughter of Judith or of Eremburga, or perhaps born outside marriage. Robert was the son of Robert I of Burgundy (died 1076), himself the brother of King Henry I of France. In contrast to what was likely the *unofficial* status of Robert, Christodoulos was the official *amiratus* of the County of Sicily; see, for example, *Italia Pontificia* (in Sources), volume 10, pages 104-105.

89. A fine overview of Adelaide's monastic foundations and endowments is presented by Vera von Falkenhausen in "Zur Regentschaft der Gräfin Adelasia del Vasto in Kalabrien und Sizilien 1101-1112." See also White, Lynn Townsend, op.cit., pages 87, 95, 98, 145, 153, 155, 209, 210, 241. For the Greek monasteries specifically, see White, pages 40-46. See also the charters mentioned in note 87 above.

90. Bohemond of Taranto and Roger Borsa both died in 1111.

91. In the original, *mulier prudentissima*. See book 1, chapter 3 of Alexander's *De Rebus Gestis Rogerii Sicilia Regis*.

92. For an infamous example of Orderic's venom see note 100 below.

93. Alexander of Telese, op.cit., book 1, chapter 2, *Rogerii indotes*. This oft-quoted passage was based on hearsay, as Alexander of Telese wrote his account, essentially a biography of Roger I, around 1136. It seems unlikely that young Matilda was even present with her brothers and their friends (all males) playing the game. Nonetheless, Alexander states that the fight between brothers also involved opposing bands of boys fighting on behalf of each, which may explain little Roger's "victory."

94. Ibid, book 1, chapter 3.

95. Godfrey of Ragusa (see notes 61 and 86) was still alive. In theory, either Bohemond of Taranto or his half-brother Roger Borsa (the latter had a son) could have succeeded to Sicily. In view of Simon's untimely death, young Roger became count with (we may assume) Roger Borsa as his heir presumptive.

96. Alexander of Telese, op.cit., book 1, chapter 4: *Cum autem adolevisset, factusque miles...*

97. Historians usually determine the date by references to Roger as *miles* (knight), rather than simply *comes* (count), in certain Latin charters. Unlike the hereditary status of count, based on automatic succession upon the death of his brother, knighthood had to be conferred *ad personam*. For a charter of June 1112 see *Rogerii II Regis Diplomata Latina* (in Sources), 7-9, number 3; see also the manuscripts under entries A and B (in Sources), transcribed in Cusa's *I Diplomi Greci ed Arabi*. Another indicator may be Adelaide's release of some serfs in San Marco d'Alunzio to a nearby abbey in 1112 (an event noted earlier in the chapter), ostensibly in gratitude for her son's recovery from an illness more than a decade earlier but coincidental to him reaching majority.

98. William of Tyre, writing long after the facts mentioned, describes Adelaide's betrothal and marriage to Baldwin, and her subsequent separation from him, in book 11, chapters 21 and 29, of his chronicle, *A History of Deeds Done Beyond the Sea*. His chief source seems to have been an account by Albert of Aix (or Aachen). This will be found in the *Chronicon Hierosolymitanae Expeditionis*, book 12, chapter 13 (Quomodo conjux ducis Siciliae ad thalamum regis Baldevini cum magno apparatu properavit), and although he seems never to have visited Palestine himself, Albert may well have had access to works such as the *Chanson d'Antioche* and he probably interviewed crusaders returning from Jerusalem. He describes Adelaide's arrival and reception thus: *Rege dehinc cum omni manu sua ab insecutione hostium Ptolemaidem reverso, mense augusto inchoante, pervenit ad aures regis quomodo nobilissima conjux Roggeri ducis Siciliae, fratris Boemundi magnifici principis, post obitum et exsequias praefati mariti ad thalamum regis magnopere properaret in apparatu copioso magnarum divitiarum et plurimo militum comitatu. Fuerunt ei duae triremes, singulae cum quingentis viris bello doctissimis, cum navibus septem, auro, argento, ostro, gemmarum vestiumque pretiosarum multitudine onustis; praeter arma, loricas, gladios, galeas et clypeos auro fulgidissimos, et praeter omnem armaturam, quam ad defensionem navium solent viri potentissimi comparare. In ipsa denique nave, in qua praedicta matrona manere decreverat, malus auro purissimo tectus, procul radios ad solis claritatem exerebat, et utraque navis cornua auro et argento fabrili opere vestita, spectaculo admirationis omnibus erant ea intuentibus. In una de septem navibus viri Sarraceni et sagittarii, viri fortissimi et claritate pretiosarum vestium fulgentes inerant, dono regi adducti, et qui nullis in regione Jerusalem sagittandi arte inferiores haberentur. Hujus itaque matronae adventu et gloria audita, rex tres naves, quas vocant galeidas fetas viris egregiis et marino certamine peritissimis, misit illi in occursum; sed ventorum turbine mari intumescente, nequaquam illi occurrere aut sociari potuerunt. Ventorum enim potentia naves longe jactatae, tandem portu sinuque Ascalonis vespere sunt receptae circa horam nonam, nequaquam nautis valentibus aut frustra conantibus iter per aquas tenere, propter ventum qui eis nimium contrarius repugnabat.*

99. The same pontiff soon restored Arnulf, ordering him to "annul" a marriage (that of Adelaide to Baldwin) which was never canonically lawful in the first place.

100. In Orderic Vitalis we find blunt defamation of a kind divorced from fact and logic. From Forester's translation of the *Ecclesiastical History,* volume 4, book 13, chapter 15 (page 137 in the 1856 edition), one reads that Adelaide, "having collected money from all sources after her husband's death, amassed a great treasure. Baldwin the younger, King of Jerusalem, hearing this, coveted her wealth and sent noble proxies to demand her hand in marriage. Adelais (sic), insatiably greedy of pride, of rank, and honour, accepted the proposals of the illustrious suitors, and went to Jerusalem with a large retinue and a vast treasure. King Baldwin was pleased enough to receive her money, which he lavished on the stipendiaries who fought in the name of Christ against the pagans; but he repudiated the woman who was wrinkled with age, and had rendered herself infamous by many crimes. In consequence, the old woman returned to Sicily in confusion at her failure, and spent her declining years in general contempt." Adelaide was not yet forty.

101. The wedding between Roger and Elvira was celebrated late in 1117 but its precise date is not known.

102. Earthquakes claimed much of the medieval structure erected on Roger's orders in 1094, of which little survives except a facade and an arched portal. The "Castle of Adelaide" was likewise largely destroyed. Adelaide's tomb is not the original sarcophagus but one designed in the Renaissance style in 1557. The inscription reads: HIC JACET CORPUS NOBILIS DNE ANDILASIE REGINAE MULIERIS SERENISSIMI DNI ROGERII PRIMI REGIS SICILIE CVIVS ANIMA PER MISERICORDIAM DEI REQUIESCAT IN PACE. AMEN MCXVIII. This seems to be essentially consistent with an earlier inscription, but see also various recorded notations, such as *Necrologia Panormitana,* page 472.

103. Information about Zaida/Isabel, possibly the widow of al-Mamun, remains sketchy. However, most scholars agree about her identity and ancestry. She seems to have converted to Christianity upon her marriage to Alfonso. The given name *Zaida* comes to us from the Arabic masculine name *Zaid,* "to prosper," which is Koranic.

104. See the genealogical table at the end of this chapter.

105. The chief source for Elvira's natal family and what little we know of her betrothal is the *Chronicon Regum Legionensium,* or *Liber Chronicorum,* of Pelayo of Oviedo, which ends with the death of her father in 1109. For a good summary see Reilly, Bernard, *The Kingdom of León-Castilla under King Alfonso VI 1065-1109* (1988); see also *The Kingdom of León-Castilla under Queen Urraca 1109-1126* (1982) by the same author.

106. As his father's heir apparent, he was later Duke of Apulia. He died in 1148 or 1149 (see note 130), having fathered an illegitimate son, Tancred of Lecce.

107. Tancred, who later became Prince of Bari and Taranto, died in 1138.

108. Alfonso, sometimes Anfusus, was later Prince of Capua and Duke of Naples. He died in 1144.

109. This was the future William I.

110. Through Elvira, Margaret of Navarre, William's consort (and eventually Queen Regent of Sicily), was his third cousin once removed.

111. Adelaide (sometimes Adelisa), whose date of birth given here is somewhat conjectural, eventually wed Jocelyn, Count of Loreto, and then Robert, Count of Loritello and Conversano. She died some time after 1184. It has been suggested that she may have been the daughter of Roger's second wife; see note 136.

112. Henry died in 1145.

113. Most of our information on Roger's reign during Elvira's lifetime comes from Falco of Benevento, the *Ferraris Chronicle*, Alexander of Telese (commissioned by Roger's sister Matilda), surviving charters, and a few other sources.

114. Alexander of Telese, book 2, chapter 1.

115. Ibid, book 2, chapter 2. The chronicler refers to "princes, counts and barons."

116. Ibid, book 2, chapters 3-6.

117. Ibid, book 2, chapter 4, where the chronicler mentions anointing, *ibique unctione sacralinitus regiam sumpsisset dignitatem*. A chronicler might not always feel called upon to draw attention to a detail that was considered perfectly normal. For example, it was presumed that a *coronation* involved a crown and was performed by a high prelate, usually in a cathedral, basilica or royal chapel. By the same token, the anointing with oil would not necessarily be mentioned because it was a normal, integral part of the ceremony.

118. See Appendix 6. At least three versions of the text of a Siculo-Norman coronation rite survive, though their dating is uncertain. One of these was for queens.

119. Whatever occurred elsewhere in Europe, there did not exist parallel "classes" of queenship in the Kingdom of Sicily based on whether (or not) a queen was anointed at coronation. Assertions to the contrary seem to be rooted in analyses that exclude a serious consideration of the known references (see the two preceding notes).

120. Reproduced in this volume are folios 96r and 138r of the *Liber ad Honorem Augusti* and page 185 of the *Historia Bizantina* (manuscripts X and Y in Sources).

121. Although Matilda's actions have been attributed to various causes, including her brother's simple intent to control a defiant Rainulf and seize his feudal lands, the author of the *Ferraris Chronicle* states that she was betrayed by her husband, who had taken a concubine. See Alio, Jacqueline, *The Ferraris Chronicle*, pages 26, 102-103, 260. Falco of Benevento refers generically to the "many affronts" suffered by Matilda at the hands of her husband.

NOTES

122. The chief source here is Alexander of Telese, book 3, chapter 1. The annals of various Italian abbeys give the date as the fourth, sixth or eighth of February, if not a few days later. See also *Necrologia Panormitana,* page 474, and *Necrologium Salernitanum,* page 475.

123. This royal chapel attached to the cathedral was dismantled in 1186 or 1187 when the entire church was rebuilt. Elvira's sarcophagus was then transferred to a church of the same name nearer the royal palace, within what are now a military barracks near Porta Nuova, a city gate. Most of the royal tombs no longer exist.

124. This is a contextual use of the term *interregnum,* which more precisely denotes the interval between two reigns. Elvira was a queen consort, not a queen regnant. Here the author proposes the neologism *interreginum.*

125. For the text of this decree and others granting and confirming privileges to Adeline and her husband, Adam, manuscript entry M in Sources. See also Garufi, Carlo Alberto, *I Documenti Inediti dell'Epoca Normanna in Sicilia* (1899), part 1, pages 29-33.

126. It is possible that the new legal code was promulgated two or three years after 1140. As regards coinage, the rare *tarì* was gold, the larger *ducat* was silver, and the *follaris,* or *follis,* was copper (see the photo in this volume). The *kharruba* was a copper coin smaller than the *follaris.* The gold *dinar* sometimes seen in Sicily was slightly larger than a *tarì.* (The design of a coin, particularly its reverse, might vary from one mint to another; coins were struck at Palermo, Messina, Bari, Salerno, Capua and Amalfi.) Among the common folk, many day-to-day transactions were concluded through barter.

127. This statute was reiterated by Frederick II, King Roger's grandson, with the *Constitutions of Melfi* in 1231. By the end of the Middle Ages, it had fallen into disuse, and only rarely was anybody in Sicily charged with rape after 1500. In dilatory legislation formulated in 1930, the united Italy defined rape as a crime, but only as "an offense against public decency" akin to pornography, which rarely resulted in prison sentences. Finally, in 1996 (sic), Italy made rape a felony crime as a form of violent assault. It remains a very underreported crime, and the statute itself is not very effective; see Van Cleave, Rachel, op.cit.

128. Most of Sicily's Muslims were Shiites, but the Maliki School of jurisprudence was rooted in Sunni legal principles brought to the island in the ninth century by the conquering Aghlabids, who were Sunnis. Some principles believed to emanate from the Maliki School are the right not to testify to incriminate oneself, proscription of the use of hearsay as evidence in trials, the accused's right to trial by jury, the weight of a contract as right to possession or transfer of property (rather than actual physical possession as sole proof of title), and the importance of judges' decisions in establishing legal precedent. Among the English institutions thought to have been influenced by Islamic law are the Inns of Court and perpetual endowment. As early as 1955, Henry Cattan noted the striking similarity between the perpetual endowment of a trust and the Muslim principle of *waqf.* In contract law

we find such similarities as *force majeure* and recission. Another example is that a contract (as for the sale of goods) becomes effective immediately upon acceptance of an offer. This is expressed in Ranulf of Glanville's definition of a valid contract based on agreement and consideration. Some of the earliest efforts in this direction can be seen in the Assize of Clarendon decreed by Henry II in 1166. For more about this, see Makdisi, John, op.cit.

129. Doxopatrios was a distinguished theologian, onetime deacon of Saint Sophia in Constantinople and, in Sicily, a parishioner of the Martorana church founded by George of Antioch. Composed in Greek at King Roger's court by 1143, his treatise is titled *Orders and Ranks of the Patriarchal Thrones*.

130. Some historians give May 1148. Romuald Guarna of Salerno, who was probably present at court, states 1149, perhaps in error. King Roger may have already been planning to remarry even before his namesake's death. Tancred of Lecce is a personage we shall meet again in a later chapter.

131. Elvira and Margaret were cousins of the second degree, two generations removed. See the genealogical chart.

132. The most explicit source, or at least the nearest one, is Romuald of Salerno, but even he treats Sibylla's ephemeral queenhood perfunctorily. In his chronicle he states, quite simply, *Sibiliam sororem Ducis Burgundiae duxit uxorem, quae non multo post Salerni mortua est, et apud Caveam est sepulta*. Romuald Guarna became Salerno's bishop a few years later, in 1153, but he was from that city and had attended its medical school, keeping in regular contact from Palermo.

133. Details about the harem are elusive, sometimes expressed in a manner that lends itself to euphemism. According to some descriptions, the women in King Roger's harem were responsible for weaving silk. Yet the chronicler Hugh Falcandus refers to the palace harem specifically. Guarding the girls of the harem was one of the chief duties of the palace eunuchs, Arabs who in some cases were christianized. The description of Roger as a "baptized sultan" was coined by modern historians and much favored by Michele Amari.

134. Sibylla's year of death being 1150 was determined largely from context (Roger's movements in peninsular Italy based on the dates of his charters). Conversely, in the *Annales Casinenses* the entry for 1151, page 310, reports it as occurring in that year (1151), stating simply, *Obiit Sibilla regina*, with the additional note that during the same year *Rex Roggerius constituit Wilielmum filium suum ducem Apuliae regem*, "Roger crowned his son, William Duke of Apulia, king." Sibylla's original funerary epitaph no longer exists, but see *Necrologio del Liber Confratrum di San Matteo di Salerno*, pages 136 and 336, which supports the year 1150 as being correct, and *Necrologium Salernitanum*, page 475, which concurs with this.

135. Now Cava de' Tirreni, the Abbey of the Most Holy Trinity, famous for its cloister carved into a cave, was the most important Benedictine foundation in Italy after Cassino; unlike Cassino, it was spared the damage wrought by the Second

NOTES

World War. Its archive and library retain a wealth of manuscripts from Italy's Lombard and Norman era.

136. A daughter of Roger II named Adelaide (sometimes Adelisa) wed Jocelin, or Gozzelino, of Loreto (see Chapter 5 and note 111). Because the name of her mother is not stated in any surviving record, some historians posit that this Adelaide was either a daughter of Sibylla or perhaps born outside marriage. The author contends that Adelaide was most likely a daughter of Roger and Elvira. The hypothesis of the birth of a fraternal twin is based on the short duration of Sibylla's marriage to Roger (probably just under two years), with which three pregnancies are not easily reconciled.

137. The source for this is the *Chronica Albrici Monachi Trium Fontium* (see Sources), but some scholars suggest there may have been as many as nine children in all. It should also be noted that some historians estimate Beatrice's year of birth nearer 1135.

138. In fact, very little remains of the original town of Rethel, largely rebuilt long before the destructive "Battle of the Bulge" that began in December 1944, which was fought mostly to the northeast of the town, in Belgium and Germany.

139. The earliest known ancestor of Matilda to hold Rethel was Manasses of Omont, wed to a certain Castricia. He died before the year 1000, succeeded by his son, also Manasses.

140. The title *queen dowager* is used for lack of a better term, as *queen mother* would be imprecise.

141. For the date see *Necrologia Panormitana,* page 474.

142. For the chapel and church of Mary Magdalene see note 123 and the maps of Palermo. The royal tombs once housed in the church no longer exist, though some remains presumably rest in its crypt.

143. The day and month of Margaret's birth are unknown. The year was determined based on such factors as her father's movements and the birthdate of her sister. Additionally, two factors argue for early 1135. Firstly, near-contemporary sources concur that Blanca, Margaret's slightly older sister, was born after 1133. Secondly, sources generally agree that García Ramírez and his wife were wed around 1130. William I of Sicily, who Margaret married, was born around 1121. The birthdate of Sancho, Margaret's elder brother, is usually reported as 21 April 1132.

144. Formally, García Ramírez was King of *Pamplona*. His son was to become known, decades later, as *King of Navarre*. Navarre, like Sicily, was initially a county.

145. Consistent with standard Spanish usage, the second name of García Ramírez is a simple patronym, rather than a toponym or surname, so *García Ramírez* literally means "García, son of Ramiro." This creates obvious genealogical confusion be-

yond the identification of just one patrilineal generation. In this book's genealogical charts of this dynasty, as per general practice, the ordinals are based on given names (forenames), not patronyms. A similar convention gives us the same format for feminine names, according to which the subject of this chapter would be called *Margarita Garcés*.

146. See manuscript P in Sources.

147. See Chaytor, op.cit., page 285, for a chronological table listing the various counts of Aragon, Barcelona and Sobrarbe, including a few of the Jiménez dynasty. The author agrees with Chaytor's observation that, "The chronology and order of counts and kings earlier than 950 is extremely uncertain." One reason for this is the traditional use of patronyms rather than actual surnames (see note 145). *Jiménez* itself is a patronym, thus giving us no indication of the family's geographic origin; compare this to de Hauteville, von Hohenstaufen, de Savoie, etc.

148. Much has been written about the *Cid*. For *El Cantar de Mio Cid*, see Menéndez Pidal, op.cit. A good modern biography of the *Cid* is Fletcher, op. cit. Over time, the *Cid* became the national hero of Spain, his name standing out from the morass of Spanish kings and knights of his century; his exploits were gilded to become something like a folk legend.

149. Our information about Rotrou III "the Great" of Perche, one of several Norman adventurers seeking his fortune in Spain during the twelfth century, comes from various sources, perhaps most reliably the *Historia Ecclesiastica* of Orderic Vitalis, for which see *The Ecclesiastical History of England and Normandy*, volumes 3 and 4. See also the *Chanson d'Antioche* and Thompson, Kathleen, *Power and Border Leadership*, in Sources. A good analysis of Rotrou's movements during this period is set forth in Nelson, Lynn, op. cit. In 1166, as we shall see, Margaret herself referred to her mother's dowry (Tudela) being bequeathed by Rotrou of Perche.

150. Conserved in Gran Cartulario de la Catedral de Pamplona; *El Libro Redondo*, folio 61 recto. For a transcription see *Colección Diplomática de la Catedral de Pamplona*, page 173.

151. A document of King Alfonso I of Aragon dated July 1133 and witnessed by Rotrou still identified Tudela with Margaret's uncle. See *Colección Diplomática de Alfonso I de Aragón y Pamplona*, document number 265.

152. Conserved in Gran Cartulario de la Catedral de Pamplona; *El Libro Redondo*, folios 72-73. For a transcription see *Colección Diplomática de la Catedral de Pamplona*, pages 191-192.

153. García Ramírez did not arrange a dynastic marriage for Rodrigo as he did for Sancho, Blanca and Margaret, nor did he grant him any important position or wealthy lands in Navarre. However, though Rodrigo eventually sought his fortunes beyond the shores of his native Spain, there is no evidence of his elder half-brother, Sancho, ever actually exiling him.

NOTES

154. Hugh Falcandus, who is noted for his overtly defamatory language, is the only source to describe Margaret of l'Aigle as a harlot. No Spanish chronicle corroborates his claim that she had numerous lovers.

155. In the original, *quem ut eorum plerique qui cum ipso venerant asserebant*, "as was asserted by a number of those who arrived with him."

156. *Hunc ergo regina cum antea Rodericus dicereturm idque siculi nomen abhorrentes velut ignotum et barbarum irriderent, Henricum, appellari praecepit.* Petulant Hugh Falcandus must have known of the *Cid* even if many Sicilians did not; however, he may not have known that *Roderic* was the name of the first Visigothic King of Hispania in 710.

157. Margaret's death at around thirty-two years of age is thought to have resulted from natural causes. That would not be extremely unusual, but neither would poisoning. If she was as promiscuous as some seemed to believe, and unlikely to change her ways, her death might prove expedient.

158. Some historians have characterized Alfonso VII of Castile and León as the "overlord" of García Ramírez, as if the latter were merely a vassal. That may be an oversimplification. Clearly, however, Alfonso was the more powerful "senior partner" in the alliance. Without Alfonso's support, García Ramírez could not ensure the sovereignty of Navarre, which would be vulnerable to a military attack from the combined forces of Aragon and Catalonia (the County of Barcelona) to the east.

159. Urraca survived García Ramírez to return to her homeland, where she was regent of Asturias from 1153 until 1165, hence she is known to historians as "Urraca the Asturian."

160. In 1157, Sancho wed Urraca's half-sister Sancha, a legitimate daughter of Alfonso VII of Castile. Here the difference in age was not very great, as Sancha of Castile was only about six years younger than Sancho. Blanca was destined to marry Sancho III of Castile, a son of Alfonso VII.

161. Conserved in Gran Cartulario de la Catedral de Pamplona; *El Libro Redondo*, folio 70-71 recto. For a transcription see *Colección Diplomática de la Catedral de Pamplona*, page 222.

162. This betrothal was not finalized.

163. Rotrou III of Perche died from an arrow wound he suffered at the Siege of Rouen in 1144. His son, Stephen, was about the same age as Blanca and Margaret, if not slightly younger.

164. The other legitimate sons of King Roger II to reach the age of majority who predeceased William were Tancred in 1138, Alfonso (Anfuso) in 1144, and Roger in May 1148 (not 1149 as sometimes reported).

165. See Appendix 3.

166. See the photograph of the Pisan Tower in Chapter 7.

167. The view traces the street now called *Corso Calatafimi,* which follows the route of the path that once traversed the Genoard. Today it is difficult to imagine how this appeared without the unsightly modern buildings.

168. Even today, northern Navarre is one of Spain's greenest regions. It is worth noting that in Margaret's time much of Spain, and indeed much of Sicily, were considerably greener than they are today. In both cases, the worst deforestation began after the thirteenth century.

169. This is the so-called *Sala di Ruggero,* which can still be visited today. Although some of its mosaics already existed during Roger's reign, most are thought to have been completed after 1160.

170. The newer chapel was consecrated in 1140 and completed in 1143. Made of the timber of the Nebrodian fir of Sicily's Nebrodian and Madonian mountains, the wooden ceiling (the largest single work of Fatimid art to survive into our times) was constructed and painted independently of the chapel and then lowered into position. The author had the rare opportunity of viewing it up close on scaffolding erected during the restoration of 2005. It seems that most of the mosaics on the walls of the nave were added later, probably during the first years of William's reign, and they would inspire the mosaics of Monreale.

171. As we have stated, Roger II fathered several sons outside marriage. Prominent among them was Simon, who he made Prince of Taranto in 1144. It would develop that William did not like his illegitimate half-brother, and the antipathy was abundantly reciprocated.

172. Hugh Falcandus, ever the cynic, wrote of William that, compared to the esteem in which Roger held his other sons, "only reluctantly did the father consider him worthy of being a prince," *quem vix pater eodem dignum principatu censuerat.*

173. Strictly speaking, both Beatrice and Margaret were queen consorts. There is no juridical term for Margaret's position (upon the marriage of Roger and Beatrice) that is generally accepted by medievalists, but following Roger's death his widow was, arguably, "queen dowager." She was not, strictly speaking, "queen mother" because she was not the mother of William.

174. The loyalty of these men to King Roger was beyond cavil. As we shall see, however, they were somewhat less enthusiastic about his son.

175. For example, it seems that one of Roger's daughters was married to Robert of Loritello, a Hauteville cousin (Robert's mother was Judith, a sister of Roger), who we shall soon meet. Another, Adelaide, wed Margaret's half-brother.

176. A miscarriage would not have been recorded unless it resulted in the mother's death. Margaret gave birth to four sons between 1152 and 1158. Statistically, there

is an eighty-seven percent probability that a family of four children will be "mixed-gender," consisting of both sons and daughters.

177. Roger seems to have been ill, or at least weakened, for a month or two prior to his death. His ill-health may have been brought on by exhaustion (according to Hugh Falcandus), but it ended in a terrible fever (according to Romuald of Salerno). A stroke or heart attack cannot be ruled out.

178. The canons of Cefalù reiterated the request for sepulture there in a letter to Margaret and her son in 1169. See Alio, Jacqueline, *Margaret, Queen of Sicily,* page 410.

179. Even the late George Holmes, in *The Oxford History of Medieval Europe,* dedicated ample attention to Roger II.

180. The queen's coronation *ordo* that was probably used is presented in Appendix 6. For the relevance of reginal coronation and anointing in Norman-Swabian Sicily, see Chapter 5.

181. From the very beginning of his chronicle, Falcandus is especially critical of William's character. Romuald is less biased but for many events less detailed.

182. See Chapter 7. Henceforth, virtually nothing is recorded about Beatrice or her daughter, Constance, for the next three decades.

183. Elected on 4 December 1154 as Pope Adrian IV, Nicholas Breakspear was the only Englishman to occupy the See of Saint Peter. Ambitious Frederick I Hohenstaufen, who later historians called "Barbarossa" for his red beard, was crowned Holy Roman Emperor in Rome by Pope Adrian in June 1155; he had already been King of the Germans (King of the Romans) for three years.

184. Maio had been chancellor during the very last years of the reign of Roger II. As we have seen, the title *amiratus amiratorum,* the Arabic *amir al umara* (emir of emirs), may be the origin of the modern *admiral,* but that was not its connotation at the court of William I. During this period the chancellor answered to the *amiratus*.

185. As noted earlier, Robert's mother, Judith, was King Roger's sister. Robert of Bassonville of Loritello had held the County of Conversano until this was confiscated by Roger. Loritello, which William gave him, is now Rotello, in the Molise region.

186. For the size of Robert's army we look to Falcandus. The estimate seems accurate. The number of knights was probably surpassed by the corps of archers and foot men.

187. Falcandus claimed that King Roger had declared in a will that Robert should take William's place if the king's son proved incompetent. However, there is no ev-

idence to support this. Such a will does not survive, and Roger himself had his son crowned *rex filius*.

188. An approximate dating of William's birth (to late in 1154 or early 1155) would be based on the time during 1171 when his mother's name ceases to appear alongside his in royal charters. An earlier date (the middle of 1153) would be based on his being twelve years old at his father's death (as reported by Romuald) and thirty-six (as reported on the epitaph of his tomb) when he died late in 1189. The age of majority for a king to succeed a regency if his successor (his father) was deceased was usually the seventeenth birthday, but this varied.

189. Rather little is known of this incident, but it may be seen as an early indication of William's impetuousness, for it probably was not necessary to arrest Asclettin.

190. Neither William nor Adrian could have known that in later times the Treaty of Benevento would come to be viewed by historians as something of a turning point in papal policy because it represented an approach as politically pragmatic as it was theological. Some jurists have posited that in 1156 the papacy began to manage its affairs as a true state rather than a theocracy.

191. Today the title *Primate of Sicily* is largely symbolic. However, it should be noted that the only other primate in Italy is the Pope. Other traditional titles of this kind held by Italian archbishops are the *Patriarch of Venice* and *Archimandrite of Messina*, both of Byzantine origin. The Archbishop of Palermo is usually made a cardinal. For comparison, the Archbishop of Canterbury is the *Primate of All England*.

192. Romuald of Salerno describes this at some length. It need not concern us here except insofar as Barbarossa did not completely abandon his designs on southern Italy.

193. See Abulafia, David, *The Two Italies*.

194. Whether Idrisi was born in Ceuta (in Morocco) is unclear, though his family had mercantile ties to Sicily. It has been suggested that, following his *Book of Roger*, he composed an important geographical work for William I but, if so, it does not survive. He died in Ceuta in 1165.

195. This seems to have been rare. At least, very few written records of it survive from Sicily's Norman era, but there were feudal rolls (see note 196 below).

196. It was quite similar to other feudal rolls of its era. The name *Catalogus Baronum* was attributed to the registry in later times. The typical entry gives the name of a baron (or enfeoffed knight), the name of his manor and the number of knights he was required to provide the king.

197. In the Kingdom of Sicily, as in other medieval Norman dominions, there were two forms of property. *Royal* (or "demesnial" or "crown") lands belonged to the king, whilst *feudal* ("manorial") estates were held "in fee" by a baron, knight, bishop or abbot. Here we are using Anglice forms of the Italian terms; certain words oc-

casionally used in England to describe monarchical institutions differ from these, even though the systems in use during the twelfth century were essentially similar. As regards baronial estates, an Italian anomaly was the presence of parallel systems, namely the *Frankish* system (inheritance of an estate by a baron's eldest son) favored by the Normans, versus the *Longobard* system (inheritance by all the sons of a baron) which left estates divided into moieties. A manor such as a barony was administered by a baron or enfeoffed knight, whereas a royal town was governed by a bailiff (or governor); barons and bailiffs both answered to the king. In Sicily, feudal estates usually had at least some serfs, while certain royal lands did not. For some early Longobard codes see *The Lombard Laws* (in Sources).

198. See notes 123 and 142.

199. King Roger's occupation of Mahdia in the summer of 1148 effectively displaced the Zirid dynasty. The Almohads took the city early in 1160; their caliphate supplanted other rulers in the region, including the Almoravids in Morocco and Spain. To undertake his recent naval campaigns in Apulia and Greece, William (perhaps acting on Maio's advice) had subtracted galleys from ports like Mahdia, thus diminishing Sicilian sea power along the African coast and thereby facilitating Almohad power there. One of Roger's titles was *Rex Africae*, King of Africa.

200. Maio of Bari encouraged the latinization of Sicily's Christians. Soon after George of Antioch built the Martorana for Palermo's Greek Orthodox, Maio erected San Cataldo next to it for the Catholics (although San Cataldo may have begun its life as a personal chapel attached to Maio's residence).

201. Clementia of Catanzaro; despite holding lands in Calabria she spent much time in Palermo.

202. Falcandus quotes a speech which is partly a diatribe against Maio of Bari and partly a plea for Matthew Bonello to marry Clementia (see note 201) and join the rebels in overthrowing Maio.

203. Romuald of Salerno mentions Bohemond of Monopoli, Roger of Acerenza, Philip of Sangro and Roger of Tricarico. Falcandus mentions many more malcontents, including several who had participated in the baronial revolts in Apulia and Campania suppressed by William a few years earlier.

204. These claims come to us from the poison pen of Hugh Falcandus. Matthew of Aiello was a trusted minister who enjoyed a successful career for decades to come. He later erected the Magione church.

205. In the original: *Iamque totam fere Siciliam varii super hoc dissonique rumores impleverant, passimque vulgatum erat, admiratum diademata quedam aliaque regis insignia, quae sibi praeparaverat, multis familiaribus suis ostendisse, nec deerant qui reginam haec ei de palatio dicerent transmisisse. Nam et eius consensu totum hoc fieri eamque Maioni putabant inhonesti contractu foederis obligatam. Plerisque falso videbatur id dici.* Defamatory innuendo about Margaret is absent from the chronicle of Romuald of Salerno.

206. Margaret was not the only queen maligned in this way; some of her contemporaries in the reginal sisterhood suffered far worse, videlicet Eleanor of Aquitaine in the works of chroniclers such as Gerald of Wales. See McCracken, Peggy, op.cit. For an examination of the environment in slightly earlier times, see Stafford, Pauline, op.cit.

207. Crowns were indeed discovered among Maio's possessions following his death, and Falcandus believed this convinced the king of his guilt, but it was later revealed that, in fact, the crowns were gifts being preserved for presentation to William the following year. Maio had commissioned (with his own money) their design and manufacture.

208. Saint Martin's Day was an important feast in the Middle Ages. In Sicily, it meant that the olives had been harvested and the winter wheat planted. It no longer marks a transition of seasons; Sicily's average mean temperature was lower in the twelfth century than it is now.

209. Falcandus believed (or at least stated) that Hugh was complicit in the plot to kill Maio. This seems unlikely, though the archbishop did not greatly lament Maio's untimely passing.

210. The site of Old Saint Agatha's Gate, which was destroyed in the fifteenth century, is indicated in one of this book's maps of medieval Palermo. It was located near the church of Saint Agatha (still standing), at the intersection of what are now Via/Piazza Sant'Isidoro (an extension of Via dei Candelai) and Via Sant'Agata alla Guilla. Several segments of the old city wall, built upon the ancient Phoenician wall, are still visible along Via dei Candelai.

211. According to Falcandus: *At regina mortem Maionis multo molestius nec adeo patienter audivit, et in Mattheum Bonellum eiusque socios majori quidem impetu indignationis exarsit.*

212. See note 207.

213. According to Falcandus: *Itaque reginae ipsius freti consilio, sollicitudinis suae regi causas aperiunt asseruntque non negligendum eius capiti, nisi mature praecautum fuerit, periculum impendere.*

214. Falcandus does not elaborate on the details, but this may have been a loan against some of Bonello's landed estates: *Interim tamen, LX milia tarenorum, tam ab eo quam ab illis qui pro ipso fideiusserant, repeti iubet, quos idem olim, ut patrimonium suum reciperet, curiae spoponderat se daturum. Eorum autem solutionem admiratus, genero parcens, ignorante rege, distulerat.* The debt was grudgingly paid.

215. Adenolf, who was from northern Italy, had served at the palace since 1155.

216. Romuald Guarna, Archbishop of Salerno (the chronicler), became Archbishop of Palermo in 1166, though perhaps on a *pro tempore* basis, and remained so into the reign of William II.

NOTES

217. Taranto was much wealthier and far more important than Lecce. The reason Tancred was not deprived of Lecce is because he inherited it not from his father but through his mother, Emma. William seems to have disdained Tancred almost as much as he hated Simon.

218. It is presumed that such a meeting took place in Caccamo Castle, and that is the longstanding historical tradition. Documentation supporting its historicity is lacking.

219. The telling of the events in the following section relies almost entirely on a single account, that of Hugh Falcandus, which seems to be accurate in its essential details.

220. Falcandus and Romuald give very slightly differing (if essentially complementary) accounts of the events in this section. Falcandus' description is the more detailed but the less flattering of King William.

221. Sometimes *Henricus Aristippus,* a scholar of Greek who undertook the first Latin translation of the *Phaedo* of Plato and the *Meteorologica* of Aristotle. As an ambassador to Constantinople for two years until 1160, he brought back a copy of Ptolemy's *Almagest* for translation into Latin. William initially trusted him but changed his mind in 1162.

222. Falcandus states that William and Henry were chased down a corridor and caught. In Romuald's account William was confronted by the intruders in a room (which had a window) in the Pisan Tower.

223. From Falcandus: *Nonnulli quoque, per fenestras palatii in plebem quae foris stabat, tarenos habundantissime dispergebant.* The tarì coins were tossed out of a high window of the Pisan Tower, which overlooked a wall (much altered over successive centuries) that faced the city's Halkah and Kasr districts to the north. Compared to the copper follis and silver ducat, the gold tarì was small enough that an adult pelted with a few of these coins would not likely be injured as a result.

224. Although his intent is clear, Falcandus does not refer literally to "concubines" but to "pretty girls." He wrote: *Nec deerant qui puellarum pulchritudinem crederent lucris omnibus praeferendam. Sic homines aetate, moribus genereque diversi, variis nichilominus dissonisque rerum studiis agebantur.*

225. According to Romuald of Salerno: *Sed rex ipse captus est et in carcere positus, regina quoque cum filiis suis in quadam camera honeste est custodita.*

226. From Romuald: *Rex autem huius rei nescius et ignarus et de tam repentino casu attonitus, ad fenestram turris pisane venit, et quosque transevntes cepit ad suum auxilium convocare. Sed cum nullus esset qui succurreret, captum est palatium nemine repugnante, et ex magna parte expoliatum.*

227. The massacre was not entirely arbitrary. The eunuchs, most of whom lived in the palace, had long been viewed as partisan, given to gossip and conniving, and some among their number were known supporters of the late Maio of Bari.

228. From Falcandus: *Eunuchorum vero quotquot inveniri potuerunt nullus evasit. Plures autem eorum in initio rei ad amicorum domos confugerant, quorum plerosque repertos in via, milites occiderunt qui de castello maris exierant, aliique qui iam coeperant per civitatem discurrere.*

229. From Falcandus: *Multi quoque Sarracenorum, qui vel in apothecis suis mercibus vendendis praeerant, vel in duanis fiscales redditus colligebant, vel extra domos suas improvidi vagabantur, ab eisdem sunt militibus interfecti. Postea vero Sarraceni, perturbatione cognita, viribus se quidem ad resistendum impares arbitrati, cum eos praecedenti anno admiratus omnia arma sua curie reddere coegisset, relictis domibus quas plerique eorum in civitate media possidebant, in eam partem quae trans Papiretum est secesserunt, ubi Christianis in eos impetum facientibus, aliquam diu frustra conflictum est. Nam illi ad introitus et angustias viarum nostris tutius resistebant.*

230. This was the *Catalogus Baronum*. See note 196

231. Falcandus and Romuald are in agreement that the rebels paraded Roger down the streets of the city.

232. Walter, a Norman, was destined to be consecrated Archbishop of Palermo. For now, he was archdeacon of Cefalù, serving under Boson of Gorron, its bishop, but he spent most of his time at court, eventually becoming dean, or rector, of the Palatine Chapel as well as the royal tutor.

233. However, this was not formalized and the boy was not crowned.

234. According to Romuald, this included (besides himself) Robert of Messina, Richard Palmer of Syracuse and Justus of Mazara. It will be remembered that Romuald was Archbishop of Palermo, thus especially influential in the capital.

235. Romuald states that the arrow hit Roger in an eye, which is probably what happened. It is difficult to ascribe much credibility to the theory, advanced by Falcandus (who claims merely to be reporting rumors), that the arrow did not kill Roger but that an angry William brutally kicked the boy out of resentment for his having been proclaimed king by Walter and the people.

236. Roger was entombed with his brother in the chapel of Mary Magdalene. See notes 123 and 142.

237. See manuscript T in the Sources.

238. According to Falcandus: *Illi se coniunxerant, praeter Gillebertum Gravinae comitem, qui regis gratiam consanguineae suae reginae precibus impetraverat, et relicta societate comitum, exercitui praeerat in Apulia, Roberti comitis impetum quantum poterat moraturus.*

239. Falcandus tells us that Martin was vindictive toward Christians because his brother had been killed by them during the riots.

240. The phrase "baptized sultan" was coined by modern historians and much favored by Michele Amari.

NOTES

241. Bonello himself probably died in the prison located in the bowels of the palace.

242. Some of these Punic walls, which include an arched portal, can still be seen.

243. From Falcandus: *Illi vero spe frustrati, ad inferiorem ingressum palatii se transtulerunt, sive ut ad regem indeflexo gressu contenderent, sive ut ibidem in scholis regis filios invenirent, quos eorum preceptor Gualterius, Cephaludensis archidiaconus, in campanarium, primis rei motibus praecognitis, asportarat. Acciderat autem gayto Martino post primum januam in introitu sedenti viros quosdam assistere, quorum unus, irruentibus illis, obvium se dedit, et primos ictus excipiens, eorum impetum retardavit spemque sustulit. Interim enim gaytus Martinus, foribus obseratis, intra palatium se recepit. Ita, cum nihil eorum quae speraverant effecissent, subita virorum multitudine circumventi, quae cum Odone magistro stabuli repente confluxerant, ad unum omnes interfecti sunt. Cadavera eorum, proiecta canibus, prohibuit curia sepeliri.*

244. There were several classes of justiciar. Those described here may have been "circuit judges," called such because they travelled around the *Regnum* to hear cases.

245. Here the chief source is Falcandus: *Cum ergo regnum ab extrinsecis tumultibus aliquando quievisset, rex autem interim otio quietique vacaret, timens ne quaevis occasio voluptuosum otium impediret, familiares suos premonverat ut nihil ei quod mestitiam aut sollicitudinem posset ingerere nunciarent.*

246. A decade earlier, Idrisi counted only 130 towns, villages and other places of note in Sicily. In fact, there were hundreds of named manors, many held by barons or the church.

247. This may be the *Minenio* mentioned by Falcandus.

248. Romuald: *Eo tempore Rex Guilielmus palatium quoddam altum satis et miro artificio laboratum prope Panormum aedificari fecit, quod Zisam appellavit, et ipsum pulchris pomiferis et amoenis viridariis circumdedit, et diversis aquarum conductibus et piscariis satis delectabile reddidit.* Falcandus: *Ipse quoque palatium construeret, quod commodius ac diligentius compositum, videretur universis patris operibus praeminere.* The spacious public "garden" of concrete and majolica recently erected in front of the Zisa (immediately beyond the wall enclosing the palace) is a modern monstrosity that bears no resemblance whatsoever to the pools and gardens that graced the park in Norman times. For an idea of what such gardens looked like in the twelfth century, not only here but at the Favara (in the Brancaccio district) and the Cuba (along Corso Calatafimi), a comparison is suggested with those of the Alhambra (Granada) and the Alcazar (Seville).

249. Romuald and Falcandus both use the same phrase, *totius regni* (the entire kingdom), in defining the scope of her authority. Romuald: *Margaritam reginam uxorem suam totius regni et filiorum suorum tutricem et gubernatricem*, "entrusting Queen Margaret his wife with the governing of the entire realm and the care of his sons." Falcandus: *Reginam autem praecepit totius regni curam et administrationem, quae vulgo balium appellatur,* "to the queen was entrusted the care and administration of the whole kingdom as what is commonly known as a governor," thus explaining that this is what in common parlance was then called a *balius* (a "governor"). In the Medieval Latin of Mar-

garet's time a precise cognate for *regent* was not used, and in Italy the term *viceré* (viceroy) came into use much later.

250. Falcandus gives the date of death as 15 May. Romuald states 7 May. Historians generally seem to favour the date provided by Falcandus, which is what one reads in most books published in English and French during the last two centuries.

251. Falcandus states that the king's death was kept secret for a few days until arrangements could be made for his son's coronation, and that the late monarch's entombment in the palace was meant to be temporary. This differs slightly from Romuald's account.

252. Romuald states that young William was proclaimed king and crowned on 9 May, two days following his father's death. This seems credible as Romuald himself performed the coronation in Palermo's cathedral; it does not seem that the boy was already crowned *rex filius*. There is an additional discrepancy between Falcandus and Romuald regarding the young king's age (Falcandus states he was at least thirteen), but Romuald, as his tutor, might be presumed to be better informed on this detail.

253. Here reference is made specifically to the years of Margaret's regency (1166-1171). By contrast, Eleanor of Aquitaine, the heiress of a wealthy duchy, was Queen Consort of England (and Duchess of Normandy) as the wife of Henry II from 1154 to 1189, but she never wielded economic or military power comparable to that of the Kingdom of Sicily. Margaret's stepmother, Urraca of Castile, was Regent of Asturias (part of the Kingdom of León) until 1165, but no single Spanish kingdom of the twelfth century could compare to the Kingdom of Sicily in terms of sheer wealth and political influence. The contemporary European queen whose effective power most nearly approximated Margaret's was the Empress Maude, or Matilda, daughter of Henry I of England and consort of the (Salian) Holy Roman Emperor Henry V; by the time she died in 1167, Maude had been Imperial regent in northern Italy (for her first husband), led troops into England (for her second husband Geoffrey of Anjou), and served as regent in Normandy (for her son Henry II of England). In this regard, and though the author does not wish to engage in pedantry, it may be noted that none of the three regions (Normandy, England, northern Italy) Maude governed at one time or another was as wealthy or important as the Kingdom of Sicily during this period. Another queen sometimes included in this elite sorority is Melisende of Jerusalem, who died in 1161.

254. Following the death of his son William II, King William I was accorded the unflattering nickname "the Bad," and it was rooted largely in the harsh criticisms recorded by both Romuald and Falcandus.

255. Much of this is inferred from context and a few comments by the two chroniclers present in Palermo. Until Margaret became regent, it would have been seen as inappropriate to attribute too much political importance to her actions (except insofar as Falcandus criticized them), and at all events a certain degree of sexism was normal during this era.

256. See note 253.

NOTES

257. Romuald: *Regina vero, utpote mulier sapiens et discreta, manifeste cognoscens animos populi sui, propter molestias quas a rege Guilielmo passi fuerant, plurimum esse turbatos, illos ad amorem et fidelitatem filii sui beneficiis credidit provocandos.* Falcandus: *Itaque regina, ut plebem ac proceres sibi filioque gratos efficeret, statuit eorum gratiam copia meritorum elicere, et fidem, si fieri posset, immensis saltem beneficiis extorquere ac primum universa recludi iussit ergastula plurimamque multitudinem virorum, tam in Sicilia quam in adiacentibus insulis, liberavit. Inde redemptionis onus importabile, quod totam Apuliam Terramque Laboris ultima iam desperatione concusserat, omnino censuit amovendum, scripsitque magistris camerariis ut a nemine deinceps quicquam nomine redemptionis exigerent.*

258. In his last days, William I had abolished the redemption tax in Apulia. Margaret's policy was distinctive because it abrogated such taxes altogether, throughout the kingdom; in addition to Apulia, Falcandus (see note 257) mentions *Terra di Lavoro*, the region of Naples.

259. According to Falcandus: *Regina vero nihilominus eisdem consentiebat consiliis, nec illius ipsi persecutio displicebat, eo quod adhuc vivente marito suo, cum pro quibusdam negotiis suis aliquotiens electo preces porrigeret, ille ut in prosperis semper elatus, contemptorem induebat animum, superbe nunciis mordaciterque respondens, nunquam eius petitiones efficaciter admictebat.*

260. Richard Palmer was bishop-elect of Syracuse but because he was not yet consecrated he spent little time in that city.

261. This account comes to us from Falcandus.

262. Molise is a region north of Apulia. It reverted to the crown when the man who previously held it died without heirs some years earlier. The territories given to Richard of Mandra made his personal feudal power far greater than Gilbert's.

263. Frederick Barbarossa was indeed planning an invasion, but his chief objective was Rome, which he reached the next year. For now, a few disgruntled barons acting as his surrogates were making raids along the border the Kingdom of Sicily shared with the Papal State to the north.

264. Falcandus does not state explicitly that Margaret was privy to Matthew's manoeuvre (although she probably was), but explains that she exploited the occasion, *Hinc oportune regina, quaesitam occasionem eliciens.*

265. Cardinal John of Naples was a papal diplomat and not, as his name seems to imply, the Archbishop of Naples. He was the ambassador of Pope Alexander III to the Sicilian court and later played a role in the conflict between Thomas Becket and Henry II of England.

266. Richard Palmer was nominated (but not immediately consecrated) shortly after the death of Syracuse's last bishop and by 1166 the post had been vacant for more than a decade.

267. According to Falcandus: *Assentiente regina idque sibi gratum fore modis omnibus attestante.*

268. In good weather the travel time between Rome and Palermo was around sixteen days.

269. From Falcandus: *Regina mutato consilio respondit: Electi praesentiam curie necessariam esse, nec eum ad praesens posse quopiam proficisci, alias iturum, cum temporis oportunitas pateretur.* This is one of the few instances of anything like a precise quote being attributed to Margaret. See also note 279 (below).

270. The exiled Richard of Aquila had held Fondi, a county midway between Naples and Rome; he was now in the Papal State.

271. Divorce was a personal right in the Kingdom of Sicily, formally codified as recently as the Constitutions of Melfi in 1231. (Only in later times did the Catholic Church "outlaw" divorce altogether, supplanting it with such canonical remedies as annulment.) The dissolution of the marriage described here was more in the nature of an annulment than a divorce because it presumed that the union had never met the canonical requirements for matrimony in the first place. It should be noted that in the twelfth century there was rather little distinction between what we now call *divorce* and *annulment.* (Divorce was again legalized in Italy, quite belatedly, in 1970.)

272. According to Falcandus: *De solvendo quoque matrimonio praecepit curiae familiaribus, ut convocatis episcopis aliisque personis ecclesiasticis, et auditis utriusque partis allegationibus, quod inde dictaret aequitas expedirent.*

273. Therefore, a widower could not lawfully wed his late wife's sister (his sister-in-law) or even her first cousin (his cousin-in-law). Affinity should not be confused with consanguinity, which is kinship by blood (to siblings or cousins).

274. In fact, negotiations for the proposed betrothal continued sporadically for the next few years. According to Romuald of Salerno: Manuel Comnenus, Emperor of Constantinople, learning of the death of King William I, sent ambassadors to his young successor in Sicily to convey the message that he wished to establish, of his own volition, peace with him, William II. He proposed to William the betrothal of his only daughter, universal heiress to his [Byzantine] Empire, along with the right of succession. The Queen Regent and the King convoked a council to consider this proposal, sending and receiving many ambassadors. They renewed the traditional peace, but the negotiation of the betrothal remained open for the numerous details that had to be stipulated.

275. See note 156.

276. Not that there were extremely large casinos in Messina, but there were small gaming houses. Most of Henry's money was lost rolling dice or playing "tiles," a game somewhat similar to dominoes.

277. See manuscript D in the Sources. For Walter's status see note 282.

278. Rotrou of Rouen was Queen Margaret's first cousin, one generation removed,

being the son of Henry of Beaumont, first Earl of Warwick, and Margaret, daughter of Geoffrey of Perche (sister of Rotrou "the Great" of Perche who we met earlier). See genealogical table 5.

279. From Falcandus, who was almost certainly present, the lengthiest known quote of the words of Margaret of Navarre or any queen of Sicily during the Norman-Swabian era: *"Ecce, completum video quod plenis semper votis expetii. Nec enim aliter quam fratres proprios diligere quidem et honorare debeo filios comitis Perticensis per quem, ut verum fatear, pater meus regnum obtinuit. Nam idem comes patri meo terram amplissimam cum nepte sua, matre mea, dotem dedit, quam in Hispania multis periculis ac diuturnis laboribus expugnatam, Sarracenis abstulerat. Nec ergo mirari debetis si filium eius, matris meae consobrinum, loco mihi fratris habendum censeam, et de remotissimis partibus ad me venientem gratanter excipiam, quem quidem volo jubeoque, ut qui me filiumque meum diligere se fatentur, propensius diligant et honorent, ut eorum gratia erga nos ex hoc ipso fidei dilectionisque quantitatem emetiar."*

280. See manuscript D in the Sources.

281. According to Falcandus: *Interea regina voluntatem eius diligenter inquirens, cum intellexisset eum nolle diutius in Sicilia commorari, summa ope niti coepit ut hoc eius propositum immutaret, et gloriam ei divitiasque, quas habiturus erat si remaneret, ostentans simulque transmontanorum inopiam ei frequenter obiciens, socios quoque ipsius propositis ingentibus praemiis hortabatur, ut cum eo se promitterent remansuros, intelligens non posse mentem illius aliter ad id quod postulabat inflecti.*

282. Relying on the date indicated in a forged charter, Chalandon (op.cit.) and others report Stephen of Perche being appointed chancellor in late 1166; the earliest surviving (authentic) charters referring to him as chancellor were issued in 1167. Falcandus does not suggest his appointment before spring 1167. A charter issued in March 1167 (manuscript D in the Sources) was witnessed by a *familiare* (Matthew), the treasurer (Martin) and the royal tutor (Walter), but not by Stephen; Walter's presence is explained by his being rector of the palace chapel which is dealt with in the charter.

283. A surviving letter sent to Margaret from Thomas Becket late in 1168 thanks her for granting refuge to two of his nephews, as well as other kin, during the exile of the archbishop (and some members of his family). He makes reference to her request to assist in prompting the return of her cousin, Stephen of Perche, formerly the chancellor. The letter is borne by Thibauld, Prior of Saint-Arnoult de Crepy, who is to elucidate (verbally) more information than Thomas does in the correspondence itself. This translation is from *The Life and Letters of Thomas à Becket* (letter 24, pages 303-304), by John Allen Giles, published in 1846:

"To the most serene lady and dearest daughter in Christ, Margaret, the illustrious Queen of Sicily, Thomas, by divine appointment humble minister of the church of Canterbury, sends health, and thus to reign temporally in Sicily, that she may rejoice forever with the angels in glory!

"Although I have never seen your face, I am not ignorant of your renown, its fame supported by nobility of birth and by greatly numerous virtues. But amongst other perfections which we and others praise, we owe a debt of gratitude to your kindness, which we are now endeavouring to acknowledge, for the generosity with which you gave refuge to our fellow exiles, Christ's poor ones, our own kin who fled to your realm from him who persecutes them. You have consoled them in their distress, which is a great duty of religion. Your wealth has relieved their indigence, and the amplitude of your power protected them in their needs. By such sacrifices God is well pleased, your earthly reputation is enhanced and made known, and every blessing is poured upon you. By these means you have bound ourself also to you in gratitude, and we devote all that we possess and all we are to your service. As the first fruits of our devotion, we have used our good services to present your request to the most Christian king, as you may know by the requests which he had made to our dear friend, the King of Sicily, and by the words of the venerable prior of Crepy, whose literary attainments, single-mindedness and sense of justice make him dear to all good men. He is a man of correct life, sound doctrine, and perfect sanctity in human judgment. We beg of you to hear him with as much reverence as you would listen to the entire Western Church were it assembled at your feet. And I beseech you, not only out of respect for his person, but in high regard for the Church of Cluny, whose necessities he is charged with and which is reputed throughout all the Latin world to have possessed, within its walls, all the glory of virtue and perfection from the time of our first ancestors. In other respects also, I ask you, if it so please you, to place as much confidence in all that he shall tell you as coming from me, as if I myself had said it. Farewell."

The original:

"*Serenissime domine, et in Christo carissimae Margarete, illustri reginae Siculorum, Thomas divina dispensatione Cantuariensis ecclesiae minister humilis, salutem, et sic temporaliter regnare in Sicilia, ut cum angelis aeternaliter exultet in gloria.*

"*Licet faciem vestram non noverimus, gloriam tamen non possumus ignorare, quam et generosi sanguinis illustrat claritas, et multarum magnarumque virtutum decorat titulus, et famae celebritas numerosis praeconiis reddit insignem. Sed inter caeteras virtutes, quas cum aliis auditoribus gratanter amplectimur, liberalitati vestrae debemus, et qua nunc possumus devotione, gratias referimus ampliores, quae coexules nostros, proscriptos Christi, et consanguineos nostras, fugientes ad partes vestras a facie persecutoris, consolata est in tribulatione sua, quae profecto magna pars verae et Deo gratissimae religionis est, si pro justicia patientibus clementia ferat solatium, si pauperibus opulentia suffragetur, si sanctorum necessitatibus absoluta potestatis communicet amplitudo. Talibus enim hostiis promeretur Deus, exhilarescit et dilatatur gloria temporalis, et omnium bonorum gratiosus conciliatur affectus. His meritis inter alios specialiter tamen promeruistis et nos, qui totum id quod sumus et possumus ad vestrum devovimus obsequium. Cujus devotionis primitias, quas pro tempore potuimus excellentiae vestrae nuper optulimus, preces vestras apud regem Christianissimum promoventes, sicut perpendere potestis ex precibus ejus dilecto nostra illustri regi Siciliae porrectis, et ex verbis venerabilis prioris Crispiniacensis, quem et eruditio litterarum, et vitae sinceritas et integritas famae bonis omnibus amabilem et commendabilem reddunt. Est enim vir probatissime conversationis sanae doctrinae, et quantum ad humanum spectat examen, perfectae pro tempore sanctitatis, quem tanta reverentia a sublimitate vestra desideramus et petimus exaudiri, quanta totam occidentalem ecclesiam, si vestris pedibus assisteret, audiretis. Et hoc quidem tum pro suae personae reverentia, tum pro merito et auctoritate Cluniacensis ecclesiae, cujus procurat necessitates, quae in orbe Latino dinoscitur, a diebus patrum nostrorum in monastica religione perfectionis gloriam quasi propriam possedisse. In caeteris, quae vobis ex parte nostra dixerit, ei, si placet, credatis ut nobis. Valete.*"

NOTES

284. See note 197 for a succinct explanation of the nature of manorial property in the Kingdom of Sicily.

285. Falcandus uses the phrase *eius successores,* literally "his successors" (heirs generically), who might have been nephews; it was not unusual for a bishop to leave a substantial bequest to his kinsmen. Stephen's generosity thus enfeoffed Richard Palmer, making him a lesser manorial lord. It will be remembered that Richard had come to Italy from England, and therefore held no estates of his own in Sicily. However, the village Richard received, albeit wealthy, was not a walled town (for which the Latin word *castrum* was used) or a locality protected by a castle but what in Italy is still called a *casale,* from the Latin *casalia.* During this period many smallholdings of Sicily's Arabs and Greeks were being consolidated and absorbed into baronies (and their inhabitants forced into serfdom) while others were acquired by Catholic bishops or abbots; the *casale* granted to Richard Palmer may have been a village amidst such farms.

286. This view is shared by Falcandus and Romuald, but it should be remembered that they were writing their accounts in retrospect.

287. A decade later, Pope Alexander III ordered the prelates who had been living in Palermo for more than six years to report to their bishoprics. By then, the power-hungry clerics had already done much to harm the monarchy.

288. Falcandus implies, but does not state, that the clients were parsimonious.

289. It is interesting to note that in Italy today one must be an attorney to become a notary; this is a holdover from the Middle Ages.

290. The author cannot help commenting that in Italy notary fees are still infamously exorbitant, even subjective, and the bureaucracy is sluggish. Not without reason, Italians sometimes describe our nation's officialdom as "medieval."

291. Many charters issued in Sicily were paper rather than parchment or vellum and thus fragile; see the photo of Adelaide's letter of 1109. In 1231 Frederick II outlawed paper for the most important documents. Not all seals were wax or metal (gold or lead); some were drawn in crimson ink.

292. This is essentially a translation of the account of the incident by Hugh Falcandus. It is interesting that in Italy today there is no fixed limit on what notaries can charge their clients for witnessing documents (see note 290).

293. Here Falcandus prefers the term *stratigotus,* but in some documents the word *balius* is used. These were essentially provincial governors and urban administrators (similar to mayors).

294. According to Falcandus: *Cuius rei fama totum regnum brevi pervadens, plebisque gratiam et favorem ei concilians, tanta nomen eius celebritate diffudit, ut omnes assererent velut consolatorem angelum a Deo missum, qui curiae statu in melius immutato, aurea saecula revexisset.*

295. For some notes on the conversions of Muslims to Catholicism in Sicily during this era, see Metcalfe, Alexander, op. cit.

296. Very little evidence survives to suggest that Stephen of Perche conducted anything like a mass pogrom against the "heresy" of these relapsed converts. It appears that the allegations against them were addressed on a case-by-case basis, which is essentially the kind of approach Pope Alexander suggested for worse crimes allegedly committed by Muslims (see note 298).

297. It should be remembered that Muslims and Jews were not the only religious minorities; there were also Greek Orthodox Christians in the *Regnum*, especially in Bari, parts of Calabria and Sicily's Nebrodian region.

298. A letter from Pope Alexander III to Stephen of Perche in late 1167 refers to the matter of punishing Muslims who have raped Christian women and boys, *agendum sit de Sarracenis qui mulieres christianas et pueros rapuerint*. See *Italia Pontificia*, volume 10, page 232, document number 31.

299. From Falcandus: *Harum regina precum assiduitate permota, cancellarium primo rogat, deinde renitenti praecipit ut neminis adversus Robertum Calataboianensem accusationes admictat.*

300. From Falcandus: *Convocatis ergo curiae familiaribus et episcopis aliisque personis ecclesiasticis, Robertus sub multa frequentia plebis introducitur, omissisque furtis, rapinis, iniuriis civium homicidiis et illata constupratae virgini violentia, periurii, incestus, adulterii quaestio ventilatur.*

301. See Appendix 1, also Pennington, Kenneth, op.cit.

302. The occasional *curiae generales,* such as the meeting of barons summoned by King Roger on the eve of his coronation, was not a parliament and the baronage had no official say in royal decisions.

303. In the original: *Reginam, cum hispana sit, francum hunc consanguineum appellare, nimis ei familiariter colloqui et velut rapacibus eum oculis intueri, verendum ne sub nomine propinquitatis amor illicitus occultetur.*

304. See McCracken, Peggy, op.cit. For an examination of the environment in slightly earlier times, see Stafford, Pauline, op.cit.

305. John of Aiello was consecrated Bishop of Catania on 26 July 1168, having been elected in February. See *Italia Pontificia* (in Sources), volume 10, page 291, document 24; also page 292, document 25.

306. Bellisina may be *Beauce* or *Bellême,* both in France.

307. Aside from feudal toponyms, men were sometimes given nicknames for their towns of origin. Salerno was known for its medical school and, as Falcandus informs us, Salernus the physician was a judge in that city.

NOTES

308. It will be remembered that Romuald was the best-known physician at court.

309. Among whom were Bohemond of Manopello (who Falcandus tells us was intelligent and eloquent), William of Gesualdo and Richard of Balbano.

310. In the words of Falcandus: *Nunc reliquum quidem esse, ut aut inhonestis reginae votis deservire credatur ipsiusque cancellarii libidini seu potius incestui consentire, aut illicitam eorum familiaritatem se nescire fateatur.* At one point Henry of Montescaglioso, who was no great judge of character, suspected (or was led to believe) that Richard of Molise, rather than Stephen of Perche, was having an affair with Margaret.

311. This passage implies that Falcandus himself did not believe the rumor, which (unfortunately) has made its way into what little has ever been written about Margaret's character: *Qui, cum primum mente dubia vacillaret, dehinc ab ipsis rei principibus qui confinxerant ea cumulatius eadem audiens, plenam hiis quae sibi dicta fuerant fidem adhibuit, relictoque cancellario, consiliis eorum adhesit, quod inde suaderent se facturum pollicitus.*

312. The knights were Christians; most of the archers were Muslims.

313. Falcandus presents the conspiracy of Caïd Richard as a fact.

314. What little was left of this edifice in modern times was completely destroyed by the earthquake of 1908.

315. Neither Falcandus nor Romuald give a specific date for the supposed consecration. For papal approval, see the letters from Pope Alexander III in *Italia Pontificia*, volume 10, page 232, documents number 29 and 30. A charter Stephen witnessed at Messina in March 1168 refers to him simply as "bishop-elect" of Palermo, *datum Messane per manus Stephani Panormitane ecclesie electi et Regii Cancellarii*, for which see *I Documenti Inediti dell'Epoca Normanna in Sicilia* by Garufi, pages 101-102, document 44.

316. For a transcription see White, op.cit., pages 266-267, document 26. Note that the date (and the year of young William's reign) is very clear from the text: *Anno dominice incarnationis millesimo centesimo sexagesimo septimo, mense novembris, indictionis prime, regni vero domini Guillelmi dei gratia gloriosissimi et magnificentissimi Regis Siciliae, Ducatus Apuliae, et Principatus Capuae, anno secundo feliciter.*

317. Also known as Robert of Lauro, sometime high justiciar of northern Apulia. He came to Messina with his son, Roger of Tricarico.

318. See manuscript S in the Sources.

319. See manuscript V in the Sources. However, it is unclear whether the Messinians petitioning Margaret were referring to these same taxes.

320. This was the "mayor" of Messina. Falcandus prefers the term *stratigotus*, rather than *balius*, in referring to the local administrator of a demesnial territory.

321. Not to be confused with the "three estates" of the Middle Ages, namely the nobility, the clergy and the peasantry.

322. If only for the fact of high literacy among the Muslims and Jews, the literacy rate of Sicily's population during the twelfth century was higher than that of the population of the newly-united Italy in 1860 (when it is estimated that fewer than two in ten adults were functionally literate).

323. Most of the women known to have studied at Salerno's medical school lived after the twelfth century; an exception was Sichelgaita, the second wife of Robert "Guiscard" of Hauteville, uncle of King Roger II.

324. Here it should be remembered that in the twelfth century the death penalty was the norm in Europe.

325. Falcandus uses the phrase *Graecos et Longobardos,* literally "Greeks and Lombards" but actually the native Messinians, many of whom spoke Greek, and the (non-Norman) barons from the Italian mainland who had settled in eastern Sicily.

326. From Falcandus: *Quod ubi regina cognovit, anxia cepit distrahi sollicitudine multaeque fluctuationis aestibus agitari. Durius enim in fratrem decernere quippiam tantamque praesumptionem animadversione digna punire crudele quidem tyrampnidique proximum videbatur, sed et si fratri parceret, intelligebat cancellario non dubium capitis periculum imminere, neque posse proditores ab eo quod coeperant absterreri; simulque considerabat indignum eum esse, cui fraternus exhiberetur affectus, qui sororis posthabita reverentia, qui tot eius beneficiorum immemor id solum agere decrevisset quod ad eius dedecus et infamiam non ambigeret retorquendum, multisque rebellandi praebens materiam, regni pacem et quietem niteretur modis omnibus impedire. Huic ergo deliberationi justa succedens indignatio, fraternam ab eius animo clementiam exturbavit, placuitque, congregata curia, comitem sollemni judicio conveniri, convictumque vel confessum interim in aliqua munitionum servari, donec eius indicio ceteri possent proditores agnosci.*

327. Most of these knights were from Navarre and the other kingdoms of northeastern Spain.

328. Falcandus refers to these subjects as "Greeks," because (like the Messinians) the majority of Calabrians spoke this language and frequented churches of the Greek Orthodox rite.

329. This was Bartholomew of Lusci, whose lands near Lecce were placed in the care of Giles, the abbot of Venosa (who probably came from Navarre).

330. Roger Sorello, whose family held estates around Naples.

331. It may be remembered that Bohemond of Manopello (and Tarsia) had accompanied Henry to Palermo and befriended Stephen of Perche. He was the son of another Bohemond (who died after 1156) briefly imprisoned by King William I for allegedly usurping royal lands. See also note 309.

332. The account by Falcandus is, in itself, insufficient as an analysis of the case

against Richard of Molise. The accusations seem to reflect little more than the longstanding grievances against him.

333. Little is known of the duel, or if it even took place, but Walter of Moac (Modica) was master constable by 1171 and he was a witness to the dower charter of Joanna of England in 1177.

334. See manuscript T in the Sources.

335. See manuscript J in the Sources.

336. This church, the so-called *Badiazza* located in the San Rizzo region of the Peloritan Mountains overlooking Messina, was formerly known as *Santa Maria della Valle* (Saint Mary of the Valley), being a Greek Orthodox monastery that became Roman Catholic. In Margaret's time it was a center for the covert forgery of charters. Resembling a fortress, the structure suffered damage in the earthquake of 1908 but was restored and is still impressive.

337. See *I Documenti Inediti dell'Epoca Normanna in Sicilia* by Garufi, pages 101-102, document 44, where Stephen of Perche is identified as "bishop-elect of Palermo," not as a consecrated bishop.

338. John of Lavardin, who was enfeoffed with Caccamo and Prizzi, lands formerly held by the disgraced Bonello.

339. Specifically, these were periodic tithes (which might be paid in kind) and an annual monetary tribute. The point was that in Sicily these taxes were regulated, whereas in the baron's native France they were left more to the discretion of the local feudatory. It is implied, and indeed suggested by the available evidence, that the serfs of Norman Sicily were treated better than those in France and other regions during the same period.

340. Robert of San Giovanni and Roger of Tiron.

341. This comes to us from Falcandus.

342. Romuald does not mention the plot explicitly but does tell us that Matthew of Aiello and Caïd Richard were accused of treason.

343. These knights were already in jail by the time Matthew of Aiello was accused, shortly thereafter. According to Falcandus: *Inde capti sunt plerique milites, quos de morte ipsius jusiurandum praestitisse constabat.* The imprisoned knights probably knew the identities of the plot's three organizers; this may have been the basis for Stephen of Perche implicating Matthew of Aiello and Caïd Richard.

344. Falcandus states that Matthew of Aiello "exceeded the others in cleverness," *qui ceteris astutia praeminebat* (implying that Matthew was crafty and conniving). Romuald uses the phrase "sage and prudent," *sapiens et discretus* (thereby implying that

the *familiare* was intelligent and probably loyal). This is a good example of the chroniclers describing the same person in somewhat contrasting terms; indeed, Romuald adds that Matthew was arrested "for no reason," *sine causa capi fecit.*

345. Falcandus: *Cumque regina nullatenus consentiret ut Richardus gaytus caperetur.* The chronicler then reiterates that Caïd Richard was a chief instigator.

346. Estimates of the population of the Kingdom of Sicily before 1200 are based to a great extent on such factors as taxation, agriculture, military capacity and the number of churches and mosques, as the Normans undertook nothing like a general census and there were many peasants but (compared to most European kingdoms) few serfs to be counted. Palermo, Messina, Bari and Salerno were quite large by contemporary standards. Although there is a dearth of demographic information for this period, it seems unlikely that there were more than three million people living in the *Regnum* in Margaret's lifetime. For comparison, this may have been roughly equal to the combined population of England and Wales during the twelfth century. Italy, with its wealthy northern communes, was rather highly (and densely) populated compared to most parts of Europe.

347. There were, of course, other sympathizers, such as Roger of Gerace, an important baron, and William of Leluce.

348. This part of Sicily had once boasted a large Berber population.

349. Burgundio, of whom little is known.

350. This is the thesis advanced by Falcandus. Romuald, conversely, does not speculate in this regard. Not only is Falcandus the principal source for most of the events that transpired at Messina in 1168, for most of these he is the *only* source.

351. John Calomeno, about whom little is known.

352. Romuald states mid-April for the release of Henry of Montescaglioso, but a necrology at Chartres gives 6 April for the death of Odo which, according to Falcandus, occurred a day after Henry arrived in Messina. Andrew, the governor of Messina, probably sent a messenger to Stephen of Perche explaining the situation.

353. This important point overlooked by many historians is crucial to the analysis of subsequent events. Henry was not acting against the king or regent, but against the chancellor.

354. Like the palace, this edifice was destroyed long ago. What little of it survived into recent centuries was levelled by the earthquake of 1908.

355. Rometta's very name means "fortress," from the Greek *erymata*. It was the site of a decisive battle that prompted the arrival of thousands of troops from Constantinople in 964. This was part of a revolt of the Greeks against the ruling Kalbids; the emir Hassan al Kalbi was killed during the fighting.

356. Romuald does not mention the incident explicitly, and Falcandus refers to "promises," using the Latin cognate *promissis,* rather than monetary bribes.

357. Using the zodiac as a reference, Godfrey Malaterra states that in the summer of 1079 Roger I took control of the town following a six-month siege: *Sextus erat mensis quo fervidus eminet ensis. Piscibus obsedit servente leone recedit.*

358. This oft-quoted saying is rooted in a line from *The Tempest* (Act 2, Scene 2) by William Shakespeare: "Misery acquaints a man with strange bedfellows."

359. See note 332.

360. See Carey, Hilary, op. cit., pages 10, 27-31.

361. William's affinity for astrology was observed by bin Jubayr.

362. We cannot know precisely what it was that influenced the astrologers in casting and interpreting William's horoscope. The most noteworthy astronomical event of this period was the annual Lyrids meteor shower; the more spectacular solar eclipse of 9 April 1168 was not visible over Sicily.

363. The term *Lombard* refers in most cases to the various peninsular Italians who settled in Sicily, having arrived on the island with the Normans (see notes 197 and 325). The towns mentioned by Falcandus are Capizzi, Maniace, Nicosia, Randazzo and Vicari, but there were others having large Lombard populations and therefore willing to support the chancellor, namely Sperlinga, San Filadelfo (San Fratello), Aidone and Butera.

364. This estimate comes to us from Falcandus, and it may be based on a larger number of towns than the five he mentioned (see note 363 above).

365. Falcandus and Romuald differed in their perceptions of Matthew of Aiello. See note 344.

366. The master castellan was Ansaldo; Constantine was his assistant. Little is known of either man.

367. Roger of Avellino was a distant kinsman of the king; the ancestors of John of Lavardin held a manor on the Loire.

368. According to Falcandus, *ubi nemini liceat armis se vel militibus praemunire,* although there would have been exceptions to the rule. The author's analogy to the Rubicon, of course, refers to Julius Caesar crossing that Italian river with an armed legion in 49 BC (BCE) on his way to Rome, making him and his troops outlaws.

369. Falcandus refers to "four hundred" servants, *qui fere quadringenti erant,* a number that probably included the guards present during the day shift.

370. See note 363.

371. Scion of a Norman family, crusading Robert of Meulan was the nephew of Robert of Leicester, sometime justiciar of Henry II of England; like Stephen of Perche, he was related to Rotrou of Rouen.

372. Outside (southward) of what is now Porta Nuova, into the present Piazza Indipendenza.

373. *Tunc vero sagittarii curiae, qui nunquam in seditionibus ubi lucri spes appareat ultimi consueverunt occurrere.*

374. Falcandus mentions Carbonello and Bohemond of Manopello (see notes 309 and 331), William of San Severino, Alduin Cantuese, Hugh Lupino (now wed to Clementia of Catanzaro, with whom Matthew Bonello had flirted), and Robert of Meulan (who lived until 1203).

375. There was a church and some buildings in what is now Piazza delle Vittorie between the palace and cathedral.

376. Roger of Tiron, who held several manors in Sicily, was a competent knight and trusted advisor of Stephen of Perche. See note 340.

377. According to Falcandus, the source for this information: *Interea cum rex ad matris petitionem e palatio vellet exire ut ab obsidione populum amoveret, Mattheus notarius ceterique conspiratores qui aderant prohibuerunt egredi, dicentes non esse tutum illuc accedere, nam sagittarum ac lapidum circumquaque turbinem agitari.*

378. Stephen of Perche died in Jerusalem the following year. See *A History of Deeds Done Beyond the Sea*, by William of Tyre, book 20, chapter 3.

379. Over the next few years, the *familiares* rarely acted in unison, although we find one or another (or several at a time) witnessing royal decrees throughout the remainder of the regency. They did not all serve at the same time, and some were more influential than others. However, we find several of them witnessing the dower charter of Joanna of England in 1177.

380. The first Sicilian parliament, leading to the barons' election of Frederick of Aragon as King of Sicily, took place in 1295 and 1296. See also note 302.

381. As the "council of regency" consisting of numerous *familiares* did not survive in that form into William's majority, it did not become an enduring element in royal rule.

382. For English common law under Henry II, see Hudson, Richard, op.cit. For commentary on the Assizes of Ariano, see Pennington, Kenneth, op.cit.

383. See note 128, and Makdisi, John, op.cit.

384. This is not the place for a detailed treatise on English law during the Planta-

genet era, but (by way of comparison) it may be observed that in 1168 England did not have a "statutory" legal code quite so complex or complete as the Assizes of Ariano. However, the Charter of Liberties (issued by Henry I in 1100) is regarded by some scholars as an early precursor of the Magna Carta.

385. Like Stephen of Perche, Gilbert of Gravina ended up in the Holy Land. This is stated by Falcandus; for concordance see *Annales Casinenses,* entry for 1168, page 312.

386. Hugh of Catanzaro (Hugh Lupino) was one of the signatories of the dower charter of Joanna of England.

387. *Sed quia nullius consilii audaciae homo erat ut vel occulte paraturus insidias, vel ex praecipiti magnum ausurus aliquid timeretur, maluerunt ei parcere, sperantes eo ipso posse reginae indignationem aliquatenus mitigari.*

388. See note 305.

389. Boson was Bishop of Cefalù until his death in 1172.

390. For a translation see note 283. See also *Epistolae Sancti Thomae Cantuariensis,* volume 1, document number 192, pages 392-394.

391. Ibid, document number 193, pages 394-395.

392. Ibid, document number 150, pages 319-320.

393. Walter's supposed surname "of the Mill" is an anachronistic misnomer popularized by modern scholars in England. Reflecting a misinterpretation of such Latin words as *familiaris* and *offamilias,* it led some historians to believe that Walter was English. In fact, he was Norman French.

394. Walter may also have had a personal motive in asserting his influence in southern Sicily, as his brother, Bartholomew, became Archbishop of Agrigento in 1171.

395. *His accedebat quod Petrus Caietanus romanae curiae subdiaconus certissime promiserat electionem hanc nihil roboris habituram, septingentasque auri uncias opera studioque reginae acceperat romano pontifici deferendas.*

396. The dating is obvious from several charters referring to Walter as "archbishop-elect" regardless of whether he was already confirmed by the Pope.

397. The description suggests the earthquake's magnitude at approximately 8.0 on the Richter scale.

398. The greater part of this description comes to us from Falcandus, although a few details were reported by Romuald. See also the letters of Peter of Blois in *Petri Blesensis Opera Omnia,* number 46 on pages 138-140 and number 93 on pages 290-291.

399. Much of the apse survived, and it is the only part of the original structure standing today.

400. This is the view of bin Jubayr, who visited Sicily late in 1184. Though recorded years after the event, the quote seems to have been widely known and is probably not merely apocryphal.

401. See letter 46 in *Petri Blesensis Opera Omnia,* pages 138-140, written following the murder of Thomas Becket.

402. See note 378. Stephen's death is the last event mentioned by Hugh Falcandus.

403. For a lengthier consideration of Margaret's decrees see Alio, Jacqueline, *Margaret, Queen of Sicily,* pages 409-415.

404. Ibid.

405. This was issued at Benevento on 22 June 1169. See *Italia Pontificia,* volume 10, pages 232-233, document number 32.

406. Ibid, page 233, document number 33.

407. Manuscript E in the Sources. A photograph of the charter appears in this book.

408. See the charters of October 1170 and March 1171 in Alio (op. cit. supra); also the signature in the dower charter of Joanna of England in this volume.

409. See Giles, *The Life and Letters of Thomas à Becket,* volume 2, page 201.

410. Ibid.

411. This is the consensus of scholars based on the available evidence; no explicit statement (such as a letter) in support of Thomas Becket by Margaret survives although, as we have seen, she gave refuge to his exiled nephews.

412. See Alio, op. cit. supra.

413. This is the opinion of chroniclers such as Peter of Eboli; Peter was sometimes critical of Matthew of Aiello. Yet both *familiares* became fixtures at court throughout William's reign; Walter lived until 1190, Matthew until 1193.

414. For methods used to determine the beginning of the year during this period see Poole, op.cit., pages 41-47.

415. Romuald's description of this betrothal: At that time [1171] Manuel, Emperor of Constantinople, in the frequent messages borne by his ambassadors, had promised the betrothal of his daughter, Maria, to King William of Sicily. At the end of these negotiations, both parties were agreed that the Emperor, in the presence of

NOTES

William's representatives [as witnesses], would swear on his very soul to send his daughter to the king to a place that was mutually agreed upon. The terms of the betrothal were confirmed by an oath sworn collectively by the Imperial nobles. In the same manner, the King and those near him [the queen and court] swore to welcome the daughter of the Emperor.

416. Richard of San Germano, whose chronicle begins in 1189, uses this phrase verbatim, adding that the great men of the realm referred, in the first instance, to these two courtiers: *His duobus, quasi duabus columnis firmissimis, omnes regni magnates obsequendo adhaeserant, cum per eos quicquid a curia regia peterent, facilius impetrarent.* This may be an accurate description for the last years of the reign of King William, though it is only a retroactive (and anachronistic) characterization; being born in peninsular Italy around 1165 (if not later), Richard did not have a firsthand knowledge about the regency of Queen Margaret, but his words probably reflect prevailing perceptions. (There are various editions of Richard's chronicle, its division by year facilitates finding specific passages.)

417. See Alio, op. cit. supra.

418. The medieval city of Cairo was founded in 969 by Abu al-Hasan Jawhar al-Saqilli ("the Sicilian"). Despite his nickname, it is possible he was not born in Sicily.

419. Most of the details about Maria's planned arrival at Taranto come to us from Romuald of Salerno.

420. According to legend, Saint Michael, who was widely venerated by the Normans of Italy, appeared here during the fifth century. It was a popular pilgrimage site, visited by many pilgrims on their way to the Holy Land. The place itself (Mount Saint Angelo in Apulia) was a royal possession which came to be the personal demesne of the queen consorts of Sicily.

421. Here the source is Romuald's chronicle.

422. With the Compromise of Avranches (May 1172), Henry II of England promised to go on crusade. He also swore to guarantee papal legal jurisdiction in his kingdom in certain cases, effectively renouncing some of the rights he had obtained through the legislation that led to the conflict with Thomas Becket. The king was absolved of any guilt for Becket's death.

423. The text of William's letter to Henry II of England in 1173, translated from the *Annals of Roger de Hoveden* by Henry Riley:
"To Henry, by the grace of God the illustrious King of the English, Duke of Normandy and Aquitaine, and Count of Anjou, William, by the same grace King of Sicily, Duke of Apulia and Prince of Capua, wishes the enjoyment of health, and the desired triumph in victory over his foes.
"On the receipt of your letter, we learned a thing of which indeed we cannot without the greatest astonishment make mention, how that, forgetting the ordinary usages of humanity and violating the law of nature, the son has risen in rebellion

against the father, the begotten against the begetter. The bowels have been moved to intestine war, the entrails have had recourse to arms, and, a new miracle taking place, quite unheard of in our times, the flesh has waged war against the blood, and the blood has sought means how to shed itself.

"And, although for the purpose of checking the violence of such extreme madness, the inconvenience of the distance does not allow of our power affording any assistance, still, with all the loving kindness we possibly can, the expression of which, distance of place does not prevent, sincerely embracing your person and honour, we sympathize with your sorrow, and are indignant at your persecution, which we regard as though it were our own.

"However, we do hope and trust in the Lord, by whose judgment the judgments of kings are directed, that He will no longer allow your sons to be tempted beyond what they are able or ought to endure; and that He who became obedient to the Father even unto death, will inspire them with the light of filial obedience, whereby they shall be brought to recollect that they are your flesh and blood, and, leaving the errors of their hostility, shall acknowledge themselves to be your sons, and return to their father, and thereby heal the disruption of nature, and that the former union, being restored, will seal the bonds of natural affection."

424. Margaret founded Maniace in her own name; little explored by historians, this fact is well documented. See the charters of Nicholas, Archbishop of Messina, in March 1174 (in *Catalogo Illustrato,* page 7); Theobald, Archbishop of Monreale, in April 1177 (ibid, page 14); Nicholas, Archbishop of Messina, in May 1178 (ibid, pages 15-16).

425. In the charter of 1174 cited in note 424; also manuscripts G and U in Sources. What follows is the original text of manuscript K (in Sources), of which a photograph appears in this chapter: *Margarita, dei gratia regina domini regis. Veniet ad nos abbas sancti philippi de sancto marco quemdam de fratribus ecclesie at nos panormum transmisit cum sigillo quod ipsa ecclesia habet statum a comite rogerio qui eam condidit continens homines eiusdem ecclesie liberos esse ab omni in angaria atque servicio. Significavit autem nobis quod baiuli sancti marcii et maniachii et eorum comunitas hominibus et casalibus eius molestiis inferunt. Recipientes autem sigillum vidimus confirmatum a glorioso rege rogerio beate memorie, quapropter concessimus et confirmavimus quicquid in ipso continebatur. Precepimus igitur firmiter tibi ut baiulis maniachii et sancti marci et comuni populo precipias ut deinceps nec hominibus nec casalibus ecclesie predicte ullam inferant molestiam, et ab angaria et a lignaminibus mascali et ab muraliis et ab omni adiutorio ipsos quietos dimittant nec de forfaturis nec de decima ovium se intromittant, ut amodo super hoc nullam proclamationem audiamus, et postquam legeris cartulam des eam abbati prefate ecclesie sancti philippi pro futeris bailis. Datum panormi XXVII die mensis novembris indictionis quinte.*

426. See *Catalogo Illustrato,* pages 15-16; White, op.cit., pages 146-148.

427. Numerous charters attest to the details of the foundation of Monreale's monastery and diocese and its subsequent status. See, for example, *Italia Pontificia,* volume 10, pages 272-281; also *Catalogo Illustrato,* pages 6-32. For a list of additional original sources, see White, op.cit, pages 132-145.

428. See manuscript F in Sources.

429. The chief source for Walter's reaction is the prologue of the chronicle of Richard of San Germano. Although this was written some sixteen years after the fact, it does seem to reflect a perception held by many during the first few years of William's majority: *Quod idem archiepiscopus ad instinctum ipsius cancellarii factum intelligens (nam odio se habebant ad invicem, quamquam se in publico diligere viderentur, et per invidiam detrahentes libenter unus alteri in occulto) hanc suam injuriam et capitis diminutionem patienter portavit ad tempus. Qui tandem processu temporis cum non posset quod factum fuerat per ecclesiam revocare, hoc fieri subdole procuravit.*

430. The reconstruction of Palermo Cathedral began around 1185, long after the completion of Monreale. Although Palermo's chief basilica became the largest church in the kingdom, its beauty could not rival Monreale's. (Intending to show the cathedral as it existed in the Middle Ages, the photo in this volume is rendered with the cupola removed.)

431. For a general description, see the author's *Norman-Arab-Byzantine Palermo, Monreale and Cefalù* (2017).

432. Romuald's chronicle provides one of the most important accounts of this diplomatic event.

433. Italy's northern communes, which were under the authority of the Holy Roman Emperor, were vitally important to Frederick Barbarossa. Beyond their strategic significance, they were far wealthier than most of the cities he ruled in what are now Germany and Austria, thus providing a greater tax base. Frederick's alliance with the Kingdom of Sicily eliminated a potential threat from the south, as it was easy (and economical) for the Sicilian sovereign to send an army northward from Salerno and Naples to defend Rome if needs be.

434. William's presence at Capua in January is attested by a charter issued there; see *I Documenti Inediti dell'Epoca Normanna in Sicilia* by Garufi, pages 188-190, document 76. For his visit to Cassino in February, see *Annales Casinenses,* entry for 1183, page 313.

435. Archbishop Walter, Matthew of Aiello, and Richard Palmer (by now Archbishop of Messina) all signed the charter issued at Capua referred to at note 434. This was logical, as the royal court was, in effect, wherever the king was.

436. Margaret lived during what paleoclimatologists call the "Medieval Warm Period." The era known as the "Little Ice Age" began after the middle of the thirteenth century.

437. The only contemporary record of Margaret's date and place of death is her epitaph in Monreale Abbey (see note 438). This reports her death as the Feast of Saint Peter in Chains, which is to say the first of August. In the twelfth century the clergy usually identified a day as beginning at nightfall the previous evening.

438. Margaret's funerary epitaph (shown in a photograph in the following pages) was rendered in black on gold: *Hic regina iaces regalibus edita cunis Margarita tibi nomen,*

quod moribus unis, regia progenies per reges ducta propago, uxor regis eras et nobilitatis imago, si taceam quibus ipsa reples preconia mundum, regem Wilelmum satis est peperisse secundum, undecies centum decies octo tribus annis. Post hominem Christum migras necis eruta dampnis. Lux ea qua populis dant petri festa catene. His te de nebulis tulit ad loca lucis. Amene. This is the primary source for her date of death as it is contemporary, but it is attested in *Necrologia Panormitana,* page 473. (The sole contestation of the dating of Margaret's death is inaccurate, namely the *Necrologio del Liber Confratrum di San Matteo di Salerno,* pages 208 and 353; this gives 1182, wherein the modern editor attempts to discredit the accuracy of the Monreale epitaph by claiming it was written in mosaic "some forty years after Margaret's death," i.e. after 1222, which is nonsense, and by citing the dubious phraseology in a papal bull. For an accurate timetable of the completion of Monreale's mosaics see *The Mosaics of Norman Sicily* by Otto Demus.) Margaret's original sarcophagus was porphyry, which preserved her body remarkably well until 1811, when lightning struck the cathedral's wooden roof, setting off a fire. Fed by the resinous Nebrodian fir (a timber harvested in Sicily) of which the ceiling was constructed, the flames severely damaged her tomb and those of her sons Roger and Henry. The queen's remains were subsequently placed into a sarcophagus constructed in 1846 modelled on the original one but made of marble.

439. The chief source for the date of Joanna's birth is the *Ymagines Historiarum* of Ralph of Diceto: *Regina Alienor peperit filiam quam vocavit Johannam. Hoc eodem anno, indictione XIII, concurrentibus quatuor, anno communi, Godefridus episcopus de Sancto Asaph in basilica Sancti Albani, ad majus altare, praesente abbate Roberto et toto conventu in Coena Domini crisma confecit, et oleum sanctum, et caetera quaeque episcopalia quae ad diem ipsum pertinere videbantur, fultus virtute privilegiorum loci, sollempni peregit officio.* Roger of Wendover, in his *Flowers of History,* also mentions her birth.

440. Rosamund of Clifford, whom Joanna never met.

441. The crossing is mentioned by Ralph of Diceto under the entry for 1166: *Rex angliae transfretavit circa initium quadragesimae.* In his *Flowers of History* Roger of Wendover also notes Henry's crossing to Normandy in this year. For Henry's meeting with Louis VII of France on Easter, 24 April, see Eyton, page 112. King Henry did not return to England until the spring of 1170.

442. A number of biographies have been written of Henry II. One of the best remains that of Richard Barber, op. cit.

443. Following the death of his son, William Adelin (in 1120), Henry I willed that his heir was to be Maude (Matilda), his only surviving child. When the male line of descent from William the Conqueror died with Henry I himself in 1135, the crown was claimed by his nephew, Stephen of Blois, son of Henry's sister, Adela. Maude, contrarily, claimed that her young son, the future Henry II (who was then two years old), rather than Stephen (who was around forty), was the rightful heir to the English throne. After much chaos and bloodshed in England, hence "The Anarchy," Stephen finally renounced his own claims in 1153 and died the following year, leaving Henry II as king.

444. For more about Maude see note 253.

NOTES

445. The name *Plantagenet,* originally *Plante Genest,* is derived from Geoffrey's liking for the broom plant, *planta genista,* of which he reputedly wore a sprig from his helmet as if it were a crest.

446. Eleanor was lodged at Palermo's royal palace, where Queen Sibylla gave birth to a son a month later. During the time she spent in the city, Eleanor may have met Margaret of Navarre, whose precise date of arrival in 1149 is not known. The chief account is found in the letter of Louis VII to his trusted counsellor, Suger of Saint-Denis, for which see *Recueil des Historiens des Gaul el de la France* (in Sources), volume 15, pages 513-514, where the French monarch writes that: *In Calabriae* (sic) *partibus secundum depositionem divinam primus reditui nostro desideratae securitatus portus occurrit, applicuimusque IV kalendas augusti. Ibi siquidem ab hominibus dilectissimi nostri Rogerii, Regis Siciliae, devote reverenterque suscepti, et ab ipso quidem directis ad nos frequenter tam literis quam ninciis magnificentius honorati, fere jam per tres hebdomadas Reginae hominumque nostrorum praestolabamur adventum; quae seorsum a nobis delata navigio, post multos tandem circuitus terrae et maris, per Dei gratiam Panormam Siciliae felici cursu pervenerat, atqe inde ad nos cum omni incolumitate et gaudio properabat. sed et Lingonensis episcopi gravis quidem et incerta inter mortem et vitam infirmitas non minima causa dilationum exstiterat; et habendum cim praefato Rege colloquium redituus nostri accelerationem pariter retardabat. Eo itaque viso, caeterisque paratis quae nostro videbantur expedire itineri, viam nostram accelerare curabimus; quatinus et vos in nostris amplexibus, et nos in vestris, praestante Domino, pariter guadeamus.* (Earlier correspondence to Suger and to King Roger of Sicily appears on pages 495-496, and in the same volume see page 425 for a description from *The Deeds of Pope Eugene III* of the two kings meeting at Potenza and then going to see the pope, also the *Annales Casinenses* entry for 1149 mentioning their visit to that abbey in October.) Writing much later, William of Nangis mentions the episode with an emphasis on Louis rather than Eleanor; see *Chronique Latine de Guillaume de Nangis,* volume 1, page 46. Louis himself wrote that he landed "in Calabria," but his trek to Potenza argues for Taranto, Bari or some other port in Apulia. The *Historia Pontificalis* of John of Salisbury also records the incident, though slightly differently, stating that the galleys of Eleanor and her husband were intercepted by Byzantines but rescued by the ships of Roger II, which took the couple to Palermo; see *John of Salisbury's Memoirs of the Papal Court,* pages 60-61 (but in her footnote on page 61 Marjorie Chibnall, the editor, postulates that the copyist may have simply written Palermo instead of Potenza).

447. Marie, Countess of Champagne, and Alix, Countess of Blois, both of whom lived until 1198.

448. Under an entry for 1153 Ralph of Diceto wrote: *Alienor duci Normanniae peperit Willelmum* (young William died in 1156). For 1155, by which time Eleanor was Queen of England, an entry reads: *Natus est Lundoniae pridie kalendas Martii feria secunda filius Henrico regi Anglorum ex regina Alienor, et vocatus est Henricus, quem Ricardus Lundoniensis episcopus baptizavit.* Roger of Wendover also mentions these births.

449. Among the myriad of biographies of Eleanor of Aquitaine, two that stand out for their thoroughness are those of Jean Flori and Ralph Turner.

450. See, in particular, Yates Thompson Manuscript 12, folio 188v (shown in this

volume), and Royal Manuscript 14B.VI, membrane 6, both in the collection of the British Library, London.

451. A fair amount of study, most of it very thorough, has been undertaken into Eleanor's rapport with her children. See, in particular, Turner, Ralph, "Eleanor of Aquitaine and Her Children," and Bowie, Colette, *The Daughters of Henry II and Eleanor of Aquitaine.*

452. A fine compilation and summary based on contemporary sources such as Diceto, Howden and Gervase is Robert Eyton's *Court, Household and Itinerary of King Henry II,* cited in note 441.

453. This is not intended as a detailed biography. See the Sources for contemporary records, and the books by Duggan and Barber on the lives of (respectively) Thomas Becket and Henry II. Among those who wrote about Becket shortly after his death are John of Salisbury, Herbert of Bosham and Alan of Tewkesbury. Accounts of his death appear in the chronicles of Roger of Howden, Ralph Diceto and even Romuald of Salerno.

454. Ranulf of Glanville later wrote a detailed summary of these laws, the *Tractatus de Legibus et Consuetudinibus Regni Angliae.*

455. There may have been Maliki influences that arrived via Sicily. See note 128.

456. A small church dedicated to Saint Thomas Becket was consecrated along what is now narrow Vicolo Lombardo (in the block that extends to Via Protonotaro) in Palermo around 1180 and much altered during subsequent centuries. It was extensively damaged during the bombings of 1943. It has been suggested that this was the site of the local home of two of Becket's nephews.

457. Accounts of this encounter come to us from Herbert of Bosham and Alan of Tewkesbury.

458. See the source in note 409. This was, in effect, a criticism of Margaret as regent.

459. Henry the Young King lived from 1155 to 1183, predeceasing his father. Here he shall be referred to simply as "Prince Henry."

460. The Anglo-Castilian dynastic alliance proved more useful to Castile than to England. In 1176, Alfonso sought and received the assistance of his father-in-law, Henry II, to arbitrate a dispute with his uncle, Sancho VI of Navarre (brother of Queen Margaret of Sicily), over some territories Sancho had occupied in La Rioja during Alfonso's minority.

461. Despite much speculation by scholars, we do not know the degree to which Joanna venerated Thomas Becket, but his cult made its way to Sicily, as elsewhere, something reflected in the creation of his icon at Monreale, where he is the only saint represented who is not recognized in the Orthodox Church.

NOTES

462. See Eyton, op. cit., page 168.

463. Ibid, page 170 (citing the chronicle of Benedict of Peterborough).

464. Ibid.

465. Ibid, pages 170-171. The source quoted, which states that Humbert himself attended, seems to be in error.

466. Their fears were legitimate; the proposed marital union with the Savoy family would have extended Henry's dynastic influence into what is now southeastern France, something Louis could not have desired.

467. See the translation at note 423.

468. A notation in a Pipe Roll indicating a payment to Robert Malduit as gaoler refers to Wiltshire (where Salisbury is located), stating *Et Roberto Malduit £10 ad procurationem reginae per breve regis."* Geoffrey of Vigeois states Salisbury explicitly, *conjugem propriam, matrem filiorum, apud Angliam in terre de Salisberi per plures annos inclusit.* See Eyton, op. cit., page 180.

469. Ibid.

470. Ibid, page 197.

471. However, no existing record states explicitly that Eleanor, Joanna and John were present (see note 472 below).

472. An entry in the Pipe Rolls for September 1176 stating that the sheriff of Wiltshire charged expenses to the crown for Eleanor's household suggests that the queen was still in Salisbury until then. An entry thought to be essentially coeval with this mentions Winchester, *ad acquietandum corredium reginae apud Wintoniam per breve Regis* (see note 470). This must be reconciled with King Henry receiving the Sicilian ambassadors in April or May 1176, as he sent them to see Joanna at Winchester, not Salisbury. The most likely explanation is that Joanna was then at Winchester while her mother was still at Salisbury. There is, however, no doubt that Eleanor ended up at Winchester in time to see off Joanna.

473. For some keen observations see Bowie, Colette, *The Daughters of Henry II and Eleanor of Aquitaine,* page 42.

474. The chief source is Benedict of Peterborough (actually Roger of Howden), for which see Appendix 3, but the Pipe Rolls for Higham, Cornwall and Winchester attest to the arrival of the Sicilian ambassadors. See Eyton, op. cit., page 202.

475. For the sources of most of the betrothal details see Appendix 3.

476. While it is quite possible that Margaret corresponded with Eleanor, perhaps

sending a letter to be consigned to her by the Sicilian ambassadors, there is no firm evidence of this. The two queens shared a devotion to Saint Thomas Becket.

477. This was in March 1172. See Eyton, op. cit., page 166.

478. See note 420.

479. See the author's translation at "Peace Between the Archbishops at Winchester" in Appendix 3.

480. The text of this letter appears at the end of Appendix 3.

481. In fact, mother and daughter did meet again, in Sicily in 1191, when Joanna's brother, King Richard "Lionheart," was on the way to the Third Crusade.

482. See Appendix 3.

483. The account of Roger of Howden (see Appendix 3) mentions "a certain palace," an observation similar to Romuald's. The Cuba palace (along what is now Corso Calatafimi) was not yet built, although it may have been under construction.

484. The first coronation of William II (shortly following his father's death) was celebrated in the cathedral, which was the preferred place for such a rite. As the church of the Primate of Sicily, it would be the most appropriate venue for the wedding of a reigning monarch, and the coronation of his queen consort.

485. This palace is located along what is now Corso Calatafimi, a street that traces the route of the road to Monreale that once traversed the Genoard.

486. In the chronicler's own words: *Audivimus a quibusdam quod Johanna uxor Guillelmi regis Siciliae, filia Henrici regis Anglorum, peperit ei filium primogenitum, quem vocaverunt Boamundum. Qui cum a baptismate reverteretur, pater investivit eum ducati Apuliae per aureum sceptrum, quod in manu gerebat.* See *The Chronicle of Robert of Torigni*, page 303; also *The History of William of Newburgh and the Chronicles of Robert de Monte* in *The Church Historians of England: Pre-Reformation Period*, volume 4, part 2, page 806. Several factors argue against the accuracy of this account. Firstly, it is not corroborated elsewhere, not even by an inscription on a tomb (no tomb of a child of William and Joanna exists). Secondly, Robert was far away in Normandy, not in Sicily, so he was not a witness to events in the *Regnum*. Thirdly, a firstborn son would most likely have been named William, Roger, or even Henry (for Joanna's father or William's beloved brother), not Bohemond. Lastly, Joanna bore no other children by William, although she later gave birth to the children of her second husband, a fact that raises questions about William's ability to father children.

487. We do not have it on reliable authority that William fathered children even outside wedlock. Joanna, by contrast, was certainly fertile, giving birth to three children by her second husband, Raymond VI of Toulouse, between 1196 and her death in 1199. (See note 486 above.) Those who survived her were the future Raymond VII and Joanna (Joan).

NOTES

488. The average age of menarche in Europe in Joanna's time was around thirteen. See Amundsen and Diers, op.cit.

489. See *The Chronicle of Robert of Torigni,* page 285 (folio 229 in the manuscript).

490. For more about Majorca and the complexities of western Mediterranean politics during this period, see Abulafia's study, *A Mediterranean Emporium: The Catalan Kingdom of Majorca.*

491. This "Massacre of the Latins" was described by the chronicler Nicetas Choniates, and William of Tyre mentions it.

492. For example, in January 1179 the Archbishop of Catania gave permission to John of Messina, a pastor, to transform Catania's great mosque into a church dedicated to Saint Thomas Becket; for the charter, witnessed by thirteen monks, see Grossi, Giovanni Battista, *Catana Sacra,* pages 98-99. For the complete text of Jubayr's itinerary in English translation, see Broadhurst, Ronald, *The Travels of Ibn Jubayr.*

493. The lavish nuptials were celebrated at Milan in January 1186. On this occasion, Constance was crowned Queen of the Germans as Henry's consort. (Constance's life is the subject of a later chapter.)

494. The fact that Constance was William's designated successor (heiress) is confirmed by the chroniclers Richard of San Germano and Roger of Howden, as well as the author of the *Annales Casinenses.* This was known even to the author of the *Itinerarium Peregrinorum et Gesta Regis Ricardi* (page 203), described in the following note.

495. Since our knowledge of the activities of King Richard I in Sicily comes to us from several overlapping sources which often contradict each other in their details (and especially their chronologies), every scholar offers us a different interpretation of the events. The eyewitness account of Geoffrey of Vinsauf, published in English in *Chronicles of the Crusades* (pages 162-176), is available in the original Latin in the *Itinerarium Peregrinorum* (pages 153-177) edited by William Stubbs. The chronicle of "Benedict of Peterborough" (actually Roger of Howden) in *The Chronicle of the Reigns of Henry II and Richard I,* volume 2 (pages 124-161 passim), edited by William Stubbs based on the Cotton Manuscript, is a fine narrative. A good English translation is found in *The Annals of Roger de Hoveden,* volume 2, by Henry Riley. Other chroniclers, such as William of Newburgh and Ralph of Diceto, address these events to some degree.

496. See *Itinerarium Peregrinorum,* pages 153-157.

497. See *The Chronicle of the Reigns of Henry II and Richard I,* volume 2, page 125. Though taller than average, Richard was dressed casually, like any esquire, and thus not recognized by the local people as royalty. The fact of peasants possessing a falcon is explained by the fact that in this region hawking was not the exclusive prerogative of the aristocracy.

498. *Itinerarium Peregrinorum,* pages 158-163.

499. Ibid, pages 165-166.

500. Ibid, page 163.

501. For the details about Bagnara see *The Chronicle of the Reigns of Henry II and Richard I*, volume 2, page 127; *The Annals of Roger de Hoveden*, volume 2, page 158 mentions this and also Philip's interest in the pretty widow (see also note 504).

502. One chronicle reports that later, at Acre, Richard borrowed Joanna's dower funds with the intention of repaying her; see *La Continuation de Guillaume de Tyr*, page 104. A fine analysis is Colette Bowie's paper "To Have and Have Not."

503. *Itinerarium Peregrinorum*, pages 172-173.

504. Philip's wife, Isabella of Hainault, had died earlier in the year. William of Newburgh tells us of a marriage proposal made by Philip to Joanna in 1195; see *Chronicles of the Reigns of Stephen, Henry II and Richard I*, volume 2, page 459.

505. *Itinerarium Peregrinorum*, pages 174-176.

506. Ibid, page 176-177.

507. Part of a tower of this castle is located in Viale Principe Umberto at the Sacrario di Cristo Re, a domed church overlooking the old city.

508. *Itinerarium Peregrinorum*, page 182. An alternate account states that the ladies were shipwrecked.

509. Ibid, pages 183-194; *Chronicle of the Reigns of Henry II and Richard I*, volume 2, pages 162-167.

510. *Itinerarium Peregrinorum*, pages 195-196.

511. *Chronicle of the Reigns of Henry II and Richard I*, volume 2, pages 168-169.

512. *Itinerarium Peregrinorum*, page 182, where we read that: *Eodemque die introduxit ad se in palatium, uxorem suam reginam Angliae, et Siciliae reginam sororem suam.*

513. This incident is reported by the chronicler Baha ad-Din in *The Life of Saladin*, pages 253-254. For a more recent translation see *The Rare and Excellent History of Saladin*, page 154.

514. This is reported by Baha ad-Din in *The Life of Saladin*, pages 310-312, 326. For a modern translation see *The Rare and Excellent History of Saladin*, pages 187-188, 195-196. See also *Suite de la Troisieme Croisade*, pages 334-336.

515. Indeed, the marriage proposal may not even have been tendered. No European chronicler mentions it.

NOTES

516. The Third Crusade and its vastness of complexities are far too great to consider at length in this volume. The reader is referred to books dedicated to the subject, such as James Reston's *Warriors of God.*

517. For the journey of the queens see *Chronica Magistri Rogeri de Houedene,* volume 3, page 228; *The Annals of Roger de Hoveden* in English, volume 2, page 307.

518. Ibid.

519. Raymond VI later married the Cypriot princess (whose given name is not known but may have been Irene). By the terms of the ransom agreement that freed Richard Lionheart, she was assigned to the care of Leopold of Austria, her distant kinsman, in 1194. While living in Provence, she met Joanna again in 1199.

520. This comes to us from William of Newburgh; see Howlett's *Chronicles of the Reigns of Stephen, Henry II and Richard I,* volume 2, page 459. For Philip's marriage to the Danish princess (whereby he hoped to induce the Danes to fight against the English), see *The History of William of Newburgh and the Chronicles of Robert de Monte* in *The Church Historians of England: Pre-Reformation Period,* volume 4, part 2, page 200.

521. Ibid, page 491.

522. Ibid, page 491, footnote 2. Most contemporary annals and chronicles estimate October 1196 as the latest possible time for the wedding based on Joanna's son being born in July of the next year; it is possible that the wedding was celebrated in September. See *The Annals of Roger de Hoveden,* volume 2, page 394.

523. *The Annals of Roger de Hoveden,* volume 2, page 400.

524. Ibid, page 420.

525. Although a certain amount of hypothesis has been published about the rift between Joanna and her husband, very little of the situation is known with much certainty. However, the fact that Joanna openly separated from Raymond, to the point of seeking solace with her natal family, whilst leaving her two young children in his care (it would be normal for them to remain so), is itself remarkable.

526. See the *Chronique de Maitre Guillaume de Puylaurens sur la Guerre des Albigeois,* pages 20-21. This chronicle (more properly a history) concerned chiefly with the Cathars and the Albigensian crusades is not precisely contemporary to Joanna, as the chronicler was not born until around 1200, but we have very few other accounts of the siege of Les Cassés (see note 527). William de Puylaurens eventually became the chaplain of Joanna's son, Raymond VII, who must have been told something of these events. From Charles Lagarde's translation of 1864: *En 1196, le même Comte Raymond prit pour épouse Jeanne, illustre dame, soeur de Richard roi d'Angleterre, et devenue veuve par la mort de son premier mari, Guillaume, roi de Sicile. Il en eut un fils, Raymond, dernier du nom, l'an de grâce 1197. Cet enfant naquit à Beaucaire, dans le diocèse d'Arles. Comme sa mère était une femme énergique, prévoyante et ayant à coeur de se venger des offenses*

que bien des Grands et des Capitaines avaient faites à son mari, à peine eut-elle fait ses relevailles, qu'elle marcha contre le Sire de Saint-Félix, et assiégea le château de Casser. Mais cette attaque eut peu de succès, parce que plusieurs guerriers de son parti la trahirent pour faire passer en secret aux assiégés des armes et ce qui leur était nécessaire. Vivement émue de ces menées, elle quitta le camp, dont elle fut à peine libre de sortir; car les traîtres mirent le feu à son logis, et elle s'échappa au milieu des flammes. Poussée par le ressentiment de cette injure, elle accourut vers son frère, le roi Richard, pour en obtenir satisfaction; elle ne trouva que son cadavre. Richard avait été tué à la guerre, et ce nouveau chagrin causa la mort de Jeanne. Elle fut enterrée pres de son frère Richard, aux pieds de leur mère Éléonore de Guyenne, reine d'Angleterre, et de leur père Henri, dans l'église de Fontevrault. Tous deux décédèrent en 1199.

527. See Vaissete, Joseph, *Abregé de l'Histoire Générale de Languedoc,* volume 3, pages 246-250. Although this history published in 1749 is by its nature "secondary literature," it relies on far earlier sources such as Puylaurens (see note 526 above), some of which are believed to have been ravaged during the French Revolution. Histories recounting these events had already been published, most notably in Guillaume Catel's *Histoire des Comtes de Tolose* (1623), where in book 2, pages 223-225 he acknowledges Puylaurens and Howden. For another record see note 535.

528. Reported in the *Winchester Chronicle,* page 71, where the editor, Henry Luard, refers in marginalia to the "frightful cruelty of the Princess Joanna." Howden claims that it was the warrior Marchadés who had the man killed, q.v. *The Annals of Roger de Hoveden,* volume 2, page 454. It seems that Marchadés, who was rather capricious, had kept the crossbowman jailed even after Richard granted him clemency, and then, following the king's death, queried Joanna about a suitable punishment.

529. Eleanor's very brief stay at Fontevrault in late April 1199 is attested by her issuance of charters there, e.g. a charter of 21 April in *Layettes du Tresor des Chartes,* volume 1, number 489, page 200. She was in Poitiers by 4 May; op.cit. number 495, pages 202-204.

530. See *Calendar of Documents Preserved in France Illustrative of the History of Great Britain and Ireland 918-1206,* volume 1, documents 1102 and 1103, pages 391-392.

531. From Joanna's epitaph (or obituary) in a necrology published in 1666; see note 535. Vaissete (op.cit. page 249), whilst mentioning the presence of Luke, the Abbot of Turpenay, states that it was Hubert Walter, Archbishop of Canterbury, who was also at Rouen, who conceded Joanna her wish to become a nun at her insistence because it seemed that the abbess of Fontevrault (who had been summoned) might arrive too late to act on the request.

532. *Calendar of Documents Preserved in France Illustrative of the History of Great Britain and Ireland 918-1206,* volume 1, document 1104, page 392:
"Charter of Joanna formerly Queen of Sicily, now Duchess of the March, Countess of Toulouse, Marquise of Provence, notifying her gift to Fontevrault of a thousand shillings of rent, in Angevin coinage, from her saltpans at Agen for their kitchen and for no other purpose. This she does for the weal of her soul and that of her dearest brother King Richard, and her father, mother, brothers, and sis-

ters. Hereby witnessed: Our beloved mother the Queen Eleanor, Hubert Archbishop of Canterbury, Gautier Archbishop of Rouen, Luke Abbot of Turpenay."

533. Ibid, document 1105, pages 392-393 (catalogued at the Archives Départementales de Maine-et-Loire, 101.H.55):

"Testament of the lady the Queen Joanna of Sicily, In the name of the holy and indivisible Trinity: She leaves to Joscelin her chaplain 30 silver marks, to Geoffrey her clerk 30, to Durand her clerk 40, to Beatrice her maid of honour (domicella) 200, to Alice her maid of honour 140, to Elisabeth her maid of honour 100, to Richeold her maid 10, to Philipa her maid of honour and dear kinswoman 60, to John Pinel her servant 30, to Fulc her servant 30, to Ralf de Crolly 30, to Raolin de Gray 30, to three women of Chijnon 10 each, to Malekakxa 15, to Brito 6, to Rodric 6; to the Abbey of Fontevrault, with her body, 900 marks; to pay the debts of the abbess towards the building of the houses of the brethren of St. John the evangelist at Fontevrault, 100 marks; to the abbey of Torpenai 100, to pay its debts; to the abbey of Lauratorium 40; to all the convents of Fontevrault, except the mother house itself 300; to the Cistercian chapter 400; to the abbey of Roncevaux 100; to the nuns of Evreux 50; to the nuns of Bondeville 40; to the greater church of Rouen 50, namely 40 to the works and 10 to the convent; to the house of Pomiacrum of Graudmont 30. She gives to the above Beatrice and Alice her two coffers at Verdun and all their contents. Of her three hangings (cortinas), she gives one to St. Stephen's church at Toulouse, one to St. Mary of Orleans (?), the third to St. Saturnine. She gives a rent of 10 marks to two chaplains of Fontevrault who shall celebrate the divine service forever for her soul and those of her ancestors.

"She bequeaths to St. Katharine of Rouen 6 marks; to every religious house in Rouen two marks; to each church in the city 25 Angevin shillings; and to the church of Fontevrault, for the anniversary of (William II) the King of Sicily and herself, a rent of 20 marks. To the infirmary of Fontevrault she leaves a rent of 10 marks for the infirm sisters; to the church of St. John the Evangelist a rent of 8 marks, and one of 2 marks to its infirmary; to the abbey of Torpenai a rent of 20 marks; the convent of Ralaium a rent of 2 marks, to the convent of Logie a rent of 2 marks.

"To the lady Agatha and the lady Alice, nuns of Fontevrault, she leaves a rent of 6 marks for life, with remainder to the church of Fontevrault; to the convent of Fontevrault for buying fish, yearly, in Lent, a rent of 10 marks. The residuary 10 marks she leaves to the disposition of her lady mother the queen. To the kitchen of Fontevrault she gives a thousand shillings of rent a year from her saltpit of Agen and to the convent of Paravisum she gives half the weir fishery of Myrmande, and she transfers the right to the excise of Myrmande in wine. She directs that Peter Poitevin and the other burgesses of Agen and of Condam shall hold the saltpit of Agen and take its profits until they have been paid from it for all she has had from their stalls (trosselli), except the thousand shillings which the church of Fontevrault is to take there, yearly, forever. Provetal the Jew, also, is to have from the other revenues of the land of Agen the thousand Angevin shillings she owed him. Her horse, in the hands of Eroald Calverus, is to be given to the hospital of Roncevaux. If anything is owing to the tallager (tallendarius) of Toulouse, it shall be repaid, when proved on oath, from the revenues of the land of Agen. Her relics in the Temple at Toulouse she gives to the house of Spinatia. She directs that the land of Clairmont be restored to the knights who held it and to their kin. The remainder of those three thousand marks which the king her brother owes her she places at the disposal of the lord of Canterbury, the lord of York, her brother, and the queen her mother, and the abbot of Torpenai and the prior of Fontevrault, to be divided, according to their discretion, among religious houses and the poor, for her soul.

"Letter of Eleanor, the illustrious queen of England, duchess of Normandy and Aquitaine, countess of Anjou (addressed generally), she has gone to Gascony, taking with her the original (carta) of the testament of her dearest daughter queen Joanna, that the count of St. Gilles (Toulouse) may see it, for the testimony of the six seals attached to it, and provide its alms as far as he is concerned. She begs them, therefore, to carry out its provisions, according to the transcript of it she sends them, in the presence of William prior of Fontevrault and the brethren who have come with him to England on this matter, as they love God and her, to the honour of God and the benefit of the late queen's soul."

534. See *The Annals of Roger de Hoveden,* volume 2, page 463.

535. Joanna's funerary epitaph was defaced during the French Revolution. Fortunately, a record of her death, in the form one finds in an obituary or necrology, was published in 1666. In *La Vie du Bienheureux Robert d'Arbrissel,* under entry number 96 on page 588, Balthazar Pavillon gives an erroneous date of Joanna's death in July (as a note in the left margin) but otherwise the essential information is correct. Interestingly, the text mentions certain details of the last few months of Joanna's life, especially her becoming a nun, and is therefore a useful source record in itself: *Migrauit a saeculo domina Joanna monacha Regis Anglorum filia, Siciliae Regina Narbonae Ducissa, post mortem Patris ex assensu et consilio Patris fui Richardi Regis Anglorum Illustrissimo comiti S. Aegidii lege maritali coniuncta, eodem anno quo Rex Richardus cursum vitae finiuit. Ipsa hispanis partibus deniens, et nobis cum quibus cum nutrita fuerat paruo tempore manens apud Rothomagum pergens, super quibusdam rebus locutura cum frater suo Ioanne ibi morans decidit in aegritudinem validissimam, quae se videns ad extrema deuenire quam vis nupta viro ac praegnans, fidems de illius promissione, veritate ac misericordia qui daturus est denari operationem venienti horâ XI sicut et illi qui primâ venit, Religionis habitum fumme desiderans, nuntio et litteris festinanter Priorissam FE accersiti iubet. sed quia spatia id accelerari disserebant, sciens sibi mortem adesse praefentem Archiepiscopum Cantuar. quem hic habebat, sic alloquitur dicens. O Domine Pater miserere mei, et desiderium meum imple, armis religionis ad debellandum aduetsarium, corpus meum muni, ut anima creatori suo liberius representetur. Sio etenim credoque, Ordini Fontis Eb. sicut corde coniuncta, si coniuncta suero corpore, paenas aeternas evadere potero. Ille autem tremens dixit id non posse fieri ut domina nupta vero viventi fine eius assensu monialis sit. Sed ut eius vidit constantiam, et Dei Spiritum in câ loquentem pietate motus, precibus victus, manu proprâ facto valamine consecratam presente matre sua et Abbate de Torpeniaco, et aliis plurimis Monialibus Deo et Ordini FE obtulit. Ac ipsa gandensiam immemor doloris sui Abbate, insert se videre gloriosam Dei genitricem Mariam, et ut nobis Abbas retulic inimico suo velum suum obiiciebat dicens soror et monacha sum Fontis Eb. non timeo tali devotione roborata. Migravit ad Dom. Domina ex cuius latere infans vivus extrahitur ac Deo volente qui bonis bona accommodat à praedictis personis sacro fonte baptismatis regeneratur, et Ecclesiae B. Mariae tumulatur. Igitur Priorissa accipiens corpus v. Ioannae Reginiae ac Monachae pud FE ataulit, et ab honorificis personis in Ecclesia iuxta fratrem suum ponitur, cunius animam Dom.Iesua Christus cum SS. et electis suis requiscere faciat, etc.*

NOTES

536. In charters, Joanna's son, Raymond VII of Toulouse, was usually styled "son of Queen Joanna" immediately following his other titles. See, for example, his charter dated 2 October 1222 in *Layettes du Tresor des Chartes,* volume 1, number 1549, page 551, which reads *Raimundus, dux Narbonae, comes Tolosae, marchio Provinciae, filius Johannae reginae.*

537. For King John's donation to Fontevrault, given at Saumur on 6 October 1200, *pro salute animae suae et Johannae reginae sororis suae,* see *Layettes du Tresor des Chartes,* volume 1, number 599, page 222. It seems that Joanna was often identified as a queen even whilst married to the Count of Toulouse. See also note 536.

538. Robert of Acerra died before 1154.

539. In the chronicle of Peter of Eboli, this infamous physical description of Tancred as a "monster, crime of nature, dwarf, ape and half-man" appears in *particula* (section) 7, verses 185-187: *Ecce vetus monstrum, nature crimen, aborsum; Ecce coronatur simia, turpis homo. Huc ades Allecto, tristis proclamet Herinis; Exclament Satiri, 'semivir ecce venit.'* The sections and verses cited here and in the following notes refer to those used in the editions of Giovanni Battista Siragusa (1906) and Francesco De Rosa (2000). In her fine critical edition and translation, *Book in Honor of Augustus* (2012), Gwenyth Hood does not use this system. Several interesting papers presented about Tancred at a conference held in Lecce in 1998 were published in *Tancredi Conte di Lecce Re di Sicilia,* edited by Hubert Houben and Benedetto Vetere.

540. Peter of Eboli, rarely an unbiased source, claims that the Archbishop of Palermo initially opposed the coronation of Tancred, which was advocated chiefly by Matthew of Aiello, then vice chancellor.

541. It has been suggested that Roger of Andria had Hauteville blood, but this may have been asserted to bolster the historical legitimacy of his claim to the throne.

542. See the *Cassino Chronicle* ("Anonimo Cassinese") in *Cronisti e Scrittori Sincroni Napoletani,* volume 1, pages 471-473; also the *Annales Casinenses* entries for 1191 and 1192.

543. Ibid.

544. Ibid.

545. Peter of Eboli presents Tancred's (hypothetical) letter to Sibylla in his chronicle, section 29, verses 880-885.

546. Ibid, section 30, verses 897-938.

547. Ibid, section 33, verses 1009-1046.

548. See the *Cassino Chronicle* (cited above), page 475, which gives this information under the year 1193, which coincides with entry in the *Annales Casinenses.* Tancred's known movements in Apulia corroborate this. Writing later, Richard of San Germano

states that the nuptials took place in 1191. Roger was most likely crowned earlier, in the summer of 1192. Emma of Lecce died around 1194; see Valenziano, Maria Giovanna, "Tancredi e il Monastero di San Giovanni Evangelista in Lecce" and Frascadore, Angela, "Le Badesse del Monastero di San Giovanni Evangelista di Lecce."

549. See the *Cassino Chronicle,* page 476. Contrarily, the entry for 1194 in the *Annales Casinenses* states that young William was crowned *after* Tancred's death, implying that his coronation was overseen by Sibylla.

550. *Tancredi et Willelmi III Regum Diplomata,* page 91.

551. Although most modern historians maintain that Sibylla left her children at Caltabellotta while she defended Palermo, not every record states this explicitly. See *Cassino Chronicle,* page 476; *Patrologiae Cursus Completus,* book 214, section 18; *Annales Ceccanenses* in *Monumenta Germaniae Historica,* volume 19, pages 290-293 (and entries for 1194 and 1195 on page 292).

552. *Cassino Chronicle,* page 476; *Annales Casinenses,* entries for 1194 and 1195.

553. Contemporary chroniclers state that young William was castrated and/or blinded. Whether or not this is factual, it is consistent with what was then current practice. See, in particular, *Ottonis de Sancto Blasio Chronica,* pages 65-66 (states he was blinded); *The Annals of Roger de Hoveden,* volume 2, page 341 (states he was blinded and castrated). He probably died in 1198.

554. Though this is not stated explicitly by the Sicilian chroniclers, Roger of Howden mentions it, perhaps based on information he obtained from persons in the Kingdom of Sicily; it is consistent with the policy of Henry and Constance toward the deposed royal family. See *The Annals of Roger de Hoveden,* volume 2, page 341.

555. For both the papal request (sent with messengers) and the ladies' escape see *Patrologiae Cursus Completus,* book 214, sections 20- 22. One passage reads in part: *Sed et Sibilia, relicta regis Tancredi, cum filiabus suis, ergastulum captivitatus evasit, et in regnum Francorum confugiens, porgenitam suam Gualtero, Brenensi comiti, tradidit in uxorem.* In English translation see *The Deeds of Pope Innocent III,* pages 20-21.

556. *Patrologiae Cursus Completus,* book 214, section 25. For a translation see *The Deeds of Pope Innocent III,* pages 29-31. The text does not state that Sibylla herself traveled to Italy to meet Innocent III, but refers to her son-in-law petitioning the pope, quoting the letter.

557. See *Recueil des Historiens des Croisades, Historiens Occidentaux,* volume 2, pages 234-235 (from the "Continuation" of the history of William of Tyre written in the thirteenth century); also De Sassenay, Fernand, *Les Brienne de Lecce et d'Athènes,* pages 27-28, 30-33, 46-47, 49-52, 56; and notes 555 and 556 (above). Walter's invasion of southern Italy is described in some detail by Richard of San Germano under the chapters for the years 1201-1205; see *Cronisti e Scrittori Sincroni Napoletani,* volume 2, pages 18-20.

NOTES

558. Walter's brother, John, who we shall meet henceforth, eventually became King of Jerusalem and then Emperor of Constantinople. John's daughter, Yolanda, was destined to wed Frederick II, the son of Constance of Sicily and Henry VI.

559. This is reported in *Necrologium Liciense,* page 476, where the day of death (but not the year) of her mother, Cecilia, is also indicated.

560. The source for most of what has been recounted in this chapter thus far is the chronicler Nicetas Choniatas. See *O City of Byzantium: Annals of Nicetas Choniates* and (in the original) *Nicetae Choniatae Historia,* .

561. The precise date is not known from any contemporary Greek source; see note 548 for the Italian sources.

562. Nicetas Choniates in *Nicetae Choniatae Historia,* page 635; also *Ottonis de Sancto Blasio Chronica,* page 66.

563. In the original: *rose ane dorn, ein taube sunder gallen.* For a note on this line from the *Spruch zur Magdeburger Weihnacht* see Lachmann, Karl, *Die Gedichte Walthers von der Vogelweide, Herausgegeben,* page 144, note 13. An early copy of the ballad is found in the *Codex Manesse.* It is true enough that Walther was paid to flatter his patrons, but no known contemporary source refers to Irene in negative terms.

564. These developments are noted in several sources. See, in particular, the chronicle of Arnold of Lübeck, book 6, in *Arnoldi Chronica Slavorum,* page 219, and Nicetas Choniates in *Nicetae Choniatae Historia,* page 711. Irene herself is mentioned in passing in contemporary works such as the *Deeds of the Bishops of Halberstadt* and the chronicle of Arnold of Lübeck (see note 568), and of course by Nicetas Choniates. In the *Brunswick Chronicle,* a later source, she is referred to in such passages as *Da krönet jn und die Fravve sein, Marien die Konigin.* See *Scriptores Rerum Brunsvicensium,* volume 3, page 108, verse 114.

565. The schism worsened but Alexius was crowned, though his reign lasted only until January 1204. There exist various accounts of this. In Germany, see the chronicle of Arnold of Lübeck in *Arnoldi Chronica Slavorum,* page 249; Arnold's accounts are particularly significant not only because they are contemporary but because they consider Germany as well as the crusades. For a Byzantine Greek account by an eyewitness see *Nicetae Choniatae Historia,* page 715.

566. The fact of Irene's brother obtaining Philip's assistance lends itself to historical speculation. Had he not (with his sister's help) obtained the support of his brother-in-law, Alexius might never have returned to Constantinople with the large Frankish crusading army that caused so much death and destruction; consequently, the Latins ruled until 1261.

567. Declared an outlaw, Otto was killed in 1209 by Henry of Kalden the younger, not to be confused with Henry "Testa" (of Kalden) of Pappenheim, who served as imperial marshal for Frederick Barbarossa. (The modern consensus is that there were two Henrys, father and son.) See *Arnoldi Chronica Slavorum,* page 286.

568. Ibid, page 284.

569. Although it reflects certain findings no longer considered current, a fine study of Irene Angelina's life and times is *Irene von Byzanz*, an unpublished dissertation defended at the University of Innsbruck in 1936 by Maria Luise Mumelter (1912-2005).

570. Soon after Irene's death, Beatrix was betrothed to her father's former rival, Otto of Brunswick, who was later crowned Holy Roman Emperor. (See *Arnoldi Chronica Slavorum*, page 286.) She died in August 1212, aged just fourteen, not long after her wedding was celebrated at Nordhausen. Maria (died 1235) wed Henry II of Brabant. Kunigunde (died 1248) married Wenceslaus I of Bohemia. Elisabeth (died 1235) wed Ferdinand III of Castile. See also note 612.

571. This comes to us from Hugh Falcandus: *Nam Willelmum regem interfectum esse, Henricum fratrem eius, cum paucis militibus in castello maris clausum, obsidione vallari; alii, quibus ratione magis utentibus tam aperta falsitas huius rei fidem subtraxerat, velud moderatius astruebant, non ipsum cancellarium, sed Gaufridum quemdam eius fratrem regnaturum, et ob hoc Odonem Quarrellum cum ingenti pecunia transiturum in Gallias ut eius opera ductuque predictus Gaufridus in Siciliam transfretaret, et Constantiam, Rogerii regis filiam, uxorem duceret, inde sibi dandam occasionem existimans ut videretur regnum iustius occupare. cum ergo iam murmur invalesceret et plebis indignatio multiplicatis rumoribus augeretur, exclamavit quidam, ad eius vocem facto silentio.*

572. In the words of Richard of San Germano penned around 1216: *Erat ipsi regi amita quaedam in palatio panormitano.* This appears in the first section of his chronicle, immediately after the prologue and before the events of the year 1189. Richard seems unaware of a tradition which holds that Constance lived in a nunnery.

573. The claim that Constance went to live at the Holy Savior abbey in Palermo's Kasr district was made much later, after 1500, probably to aggrandize that convent's prestige.

574. See the *Paradiso*, canto 3, lines 113-117; like Giovanni Boccaccio (1313-1375), Dante Alighieri (1265-1321) vilified the Hohenstaufens as part of his pro-Guelph propaganda. Thomas Fazello states in his *De Rebus Siculus* (published in 1558), page 471, citing an unspecified papal document of Pope Celestine III (sic): *quin et diplomata, ac decreta Celestini Papae, quibus Constantia votiva virginitate absoluta ad legitimas cum Henrico nuptias admisit, quae hucusque et in Archivio Romano et in decretis publicis leguntur, in id consentiunt.* For commentary on this see White, *Latin Monasticism in Norman Sicily*, page 125, note 2 (Agostino Gallo's assessment of a manuscript in a publication of 1823 is questionable), and Scaduto, *Il Monachesimo Basiliano nella Sicilia Medievale*, pages 161-162. It is quite possible that the papal document Fazello saw was a forgery written three centuries earlier.

575. See, among others, Fröhlich, Walter, "The Marriage of Henry VI and Constance of Sicily: Prelude and Consequences."

576. Though he was parroting Dante, his recent predecessor, Giovanni Boccaccio's concise, superficial commentary may be considered the first "biography"

of Constance. As a manuscript composed around 1361, *De Claris Mulieribus* ("On Distinguished Women") was widely copied, to be published as an incunable in 1473. The narrative reflects the jaundiced Guelphic (and anti-Ghibelline) view of the Hohenstaufen dynasty that colored Italian historiography for centuries. What is more, Boccaccio errs in identifying Constance's father as William I (rather than Roger II), and overstating the queen's age at the time of her pregnancy. For a fine English translation see Virginia Brown's *Giovanni Boccaccio: Famous Women*, pages 221-223.

577. Sources refer to as much as 40,000 gold livres, which were actually Sicilian tarì.

578. This is mentioned in numerous chronicles and annals. A good reference is *Ottonis de Sancto Blasio Chronica*, pages 39-40. The *Notae Sancti Georgii Mediolanenses*, among other sources, states that Frederick Barbarossa was present at the wedding. For a slightly more detailed description see the *Annales Marbacenses*, page 163.

579. For a contemporary report on the dispute between Baldwin "the Brave" of Hainaut and his uncle, Henry "the Blind" of Luxembourg, and Constance's intervention in the case, see *Gisleberti Chronicon Hanoniense*, page 186. Admittedly, the *Chronicle of Hainaut* is biased in favor of Baldwin as the patron of Gislebert of Mons. The essential facts are that Henry, a widower lacking children, had willed his nephew, Baldwin, some important lands. After Henry, as a septuagenarian, remarried and subsequently fathered a daughter, he rewrote his will to exclude Baldwin, effectively disinheriting him. This provoked Baldwin to attack some of Henry's lands. Constance's influence with the Holy Roman Emperor tipped the scales of imperial justice in Baldwin's favor by granting him Nemur and other territories, although contested Luxembourg fell to neither litigant, instead becoming an imperial county. (The kinship of Baldwin and Henry to Constance is shown in the genealogical table in Chapter 7 of this volume; Baldwin was Constance's first cousin once removed, while Henry was her great uncle.)

580. Albert was murdered in November 1192, when Constance and Henry were both in Germany following their unsuccessful military expedition to the Kingdom of Sicily. There are two contemporary sources for the incident. The *Vita Alberti Episcopi Leodiensis* is sympathetic to Albert of Louvain, whereas the account in the *Chronicle of Hainaut* favors Baldwin and his cousin. For a keen analysis see Schmandt, Raymond, "The Election and Assassination of Albert of Louvain, Bishop of Liège 1191-1192." (See also the following note.)

581. The perception that Henry VI was involved in the assassination of Albert of Louvain was quite widespread. Even Roger of Howden mentioned it; see *The Annals of Roger de Hoveden*, volume 2, page 295. The modern scholarly consensus is that if there was indeed any imperial complicity in the murder, it was most likely initiated by an overzealous courtier and not by Henry himself.

582. This was Henry of Kalden the elder; see note 567.

583. See *The Historical Works of Ralph de Diceto*, volume 2, page 81.

584. There are various contemporary references to this detail. See, for example, *The Annals of Roger de Hoveden,* volume 2, page 197.

585. What is presented in the remainder of this chapter comes to us chiefly from Peter of Eboli, Richard of San Germano, Godfrey of Viterbo and the *Annales Casinenses,* sources nearer the events than Roger of Howden and others. See also the *Patrologiae Cursus Completus,* series 2, book 214. Some of these facts are the subject of notes (above) supporting the previous three chapters. Other sources are cited as appropriate.

586. The author's translation, from the chronicle of Peter of Eboli, section 25, verses 724-741. Except for the address of Queen Margaret upon the arrival in Palermo of Stephen of Perche, quoted by Hugh Falcandus (who may have been present to hear it), this is the lengthiest verbatim passage attributed to one of the queens whose story appears in these pages.

587. See, amongst other sources, *Ottonis de Sancto Blasio Chronica,* page 56, and *The Annals of Roger de Hoveden,* volume 2, page 254.

588. For an account from the English perspective, see *The Historical Works of Ralph de Diceto,* volume 2, pages 104, 127-128.

589. Richard's misadventure at the hands of Leopold and Henry has been chronicled by Geoffrey of Vinsauf, Richard of Devize, Roger Howden, Ralph of Diceto and others.

590. A minor Milanese annal mentions that in 1194 (on her way southward for the imperial coronation) a pregnant Constance stayed at the Meda convent near Milan: *Et eodem anno dicta Constantia venit in Mediolano, et hospitata fuit in monasterio de Meda et tunc erat graveda de Fedricho.* See *Memoriae Mediolanenses,* page 400. Despite some historians' claims, we cannot know if this was, in fact, Constance's first pregnancy, just that it was the only one she carried to term.

591. This coronation was important news across Europe; see *The Annals of Roger de Hoveden,* volume 2, pages 340-341.

592. The earliest charter currently known to us was issued at Palermo on 25 June 1195 reiterating ecclesiastical jurisdiction of the Benedictine abbey of Monreale as established by William II. See *Constantiae Imperatricis Diplomata,* document 1, page 40; other decrees of Constance appear in the same compilation, the most complete record of her charters published to date.

593. An idea, parroted by some, that Constance instigated a revolt against her own husband does not seem to have much substance, though it is very old; see *The Annals of Roger de Hoveden,* volume 2, page 406. The *Ferraris Chronicle* (pages 148-149), brings us this dubious, if colorful, account: "In 1197, the emperor subjected the entire kingdom to increased taxes. Many of the barons he mistreated and oppressed went into exile. Henry ordered the burning of the head cantor of the church of Palermo. He commanded that a deacon be drowned in the sea with some nobles. It is said

that, when the queen reproved him for this, the emperor angrily threatened her at sword-point and would have killed her were it not for the intervention of Markward of Anweiler. Hearing of these incidents, the Sicilians, Latins and Greeks as well as Arabs, rebelled against the emperor. But when leaders of the army they gathered learned the queen was safe, the people were placated and submitted to the emperor."

594. See *Constantiae Imperatricis Diplomata,* documents 41-71, pages 127-281.

595. See *Patrologiae Cursus Completus,* series 2, book 214, sections XXXVIII, XLIII, LII.

596. *Constantiae Imperatricis Diplomata,* pages 279-281.

597. Ibid, pages 277-278. This was either Sancha, born in 1186, or Dulcia, born in 1192.

598. Ibid.

599. See *Chronicon Budense,* pages 53, 190; *Gesta Hungarorum* (Simon of Keza), page 95; *Chronicon Pictum Vindobonense,* page 221, *Indices Rerum ab Aragoniae Gestarum,* page 59.

600. *Chronicon Pictum Vindobonense,* page 221. Ladislas was probably born late in 1199.

601. See *Historia Salonitanorum atque Spalatinorum Pontificum,* pages 140-144; also *Chronicon Budense,* page 191.

602. *Indices Rerum ab Aragoniae Gestarum,* page 64.

603. *Continuatio Admuntensis,* pages 590-591; *Chronicon Budense,* page 191. This basilica is now in ruins and the tombs have been destroyed.

604. *Chronicon Budense,* pages 191-194.

605. For a discussion with reference to correspondence between Innocent III and Peter II, see Smith, Damian, *Innocent III and the Crown of Aragon,* pages 30, 56, 68, 272.

606. Peter's initial motivation was the papal annulment of his marriage to Marie of Montpelier, who in the event died in Rome in April 1213 as she was about to return to Aragon, having convinced Pope Innocent III to preserve her conjugal union.

607. *Historia Diplomatica Friderici Secundi,* volume 1, part 1, pages 131-133, 139-140.

608. Ibid, pages 169-170.

609. For Richard of San Germano see *Cronisti e Scrittori Sincroni Napoletani,* volume 2, page 21 (as noted above it is simplest to refer to Richard's chronicle by year be-

cause there exist many editions of it); also *Codex Diplomaticus Hungariae Ecclesiasticus ac Civilis,* pages 57-58.

610. For a reliable account from a source near the events, see the *Annales Casinenses* entries for 1209-1211. Other descriptions come to us from the *Ferraris Chronicle,* page 156, and from Richard of San Germano.

611. Alfonso died in Palermo; see *Historia Diplomatica Friderici Secundi,* volume 2, part 2, page 893. His remaining knights were soon needed in Spain. Peter II of Aragon participated in the Battle of Las Navas de Tolosa in 1212. He was killed at the Battle of Muret the following year whilst defending his brother-in-law, Raymond VI of Toulouse, and the Cathars against an invasion led by Simon IV of Montfort; to Peter, this was more a question of familial loyalty and territory than a fight against the papacy's Albigensian Crusade. See Marvin, Laurence, *The Occitan War.*

612. The betrothal of Beatrix Hohenstaufen probably took place in the autumn of 1208, after the death of her widowed mother (Irene) but before Otto of Brunswick was crowned emperor. It was arranged by Walter of Palear, who was briefly chancellor of Frederick II following a few years as the young king's *de facto* regent, and it may be one of the unspoken reasons why this prelate was subsequently dismissed. See also note 570.

613. She was still in Messina in May 1212; see *Historia Diplomatica Friderici Secundi,* volume 2, part 2, page 685.

614. See *Historia Diplomatica Friderici Secundi,* volume 1, part 1, pages 232-234, 241-242.

615. Ibid, pages 253-255, 265-266, 282-283.

616. Michael Scot probably arrived at the Sicilian court after Constance's death; he is mentioned here merely as an example.

617. Although Sicilian was likely spoken (and certainly written) before Tuscan or Umbrian, those languages do not derive from it. These Italian languages and others, like Calabrian, all evolved independently from Latin. One is not a "dialect" of the other.

618. Frederick likely fathered several children whose names are lost to time. Among those known to us are Enzio of Sardinia, born around 1218 to Adelaide, who was probably of the Swabian Urslingen family, Constance (later Anna), born around 1230 to Bianca Lancia, and Manfred, later born to the same mistress.

619. The author does not wish to digress upon a biography of Frederick II. For a fine narrative and analysis the reader is referred to Abulafia, David, *Frederick II: A Medieval Emperor.*

620. *Historia Diplomatica Friderici Secundi,* volume 2, part 2, page 468. Years earlier, Nicholas, the son of the vice chancellor Matthew, had supported Sibylla against Constance (see Chapter 10).

NOTES

621. Ibid, pages 484, 895.

622. This is the first passage in the chronicle of Richard of San Germano for the year 1121 and it mentions Constance explicitly. These movements are attested in *Historia Diplomatica Friderici Secundi,* volume 2, part 1, pages 106 (Frederick at Sessa in January), 137-156.

623. *Historia Diplomatica Friderici Secundi,* volume 2, part 1, pages 178-182.

624. Ibid, pages 196-197.

625. Ibid, pages 204-224 passim.

626. Ibid, pages 254-257.

627. Ibid, page 258. Also *Necrologium Liciense,* page 476; *Necrologia Panormitana,* page 472; Richard of San Germano, entry for 1222.

628. *Yolande* initially seems to have been preferred by French historians, while *Isabelle,* which some used, derives directly from *Elizabeth.* Some give both forms; see the note in *Recueil des Historiens des Croisades, Historiens Occidentaux,* volume 2, page 311.

629. Ibid, page 320.

630. Ibid, pages 343-344.

631. See the chronicle of Richard of San Germano for that year; also *Historia Diplomatica Friderici Secundi,* volume 2, part 1, page 327.

632. Ibid, pages 394-395, referring to August 1223. In 1215 the Fourth Lateran Council relaxed diriment impediment to the fourth degree of consanguinity (using the old canonical measurement). The most recent common ancestor of Frederick and Yolanda was Agnes Waiblingen of Germany, who died in 1143. She was a great great grandmother to each spouse.

633. The lengthiest contemporary account of the marriage of Yolanda of Jerusalem is found in the "Chronicle of the Holy Land" in *Gestes des Chiprois,* pages 19-25. (See also note 634.)

634. For the wedding, see *Recueil des Historiens des Croisades, Historiens Occidentaux,* volume 2, pages 356-361; also *Chronique d'Ernoul,* pages 449-450.

635. See Richard of San Germano and the other sources cited above; also *Historia Diplomatica Friderici Secundi,* volume 2, part 1, page 525.

636. See the *Chronique d'Ernoul,* page 451. Even if this distasteful incident never occurred, the flirtatious cousin in question is a historical personage. The chronicle refers simply to "a niece of King John," without mentioning the woman's name.

If anybody, it was probably Margaret of Reynel (daughter of John's sister Ida), who wed Balian Grenier of Sidon, later a supporter of Frederick over John, around 1218 and died in 1253; see *Recueil des Historiens des Croisades, Historiens Occidentaux,* volume 2, pages 332 (also footnote h) and 441 (also footnote n). Balian and Margaret were present at Yolanda's coronation at Acre in 1225; ibid, pages 357-358.

637. This was at Foggia in December 1225; see *Historia Diplomatica Friderici Secundi,* volume 2, part 1, page 526-527.

638. Ibid, pages 536-538.

639. Ibid, page 541.

640. Richard of San Germano states that this is when John, who resented his son-in-law's blatant claim to be King of Jerusalem, parted company with Frederick. In fact, Frederick enjoyed the support of the Hierosolymitan baronage. The overt antipathy between Frederick and John was generally known to contemporaries in Italy; see the *Ferraris Chronicle,* pages 168-169.

641. He was at Messina in January and Catania in February; *Historia Diplomatica Friderici Secundi,* volume 2, part 2, pages 706, 712.

642. Although Frederick did not take Yolanda on most of his travels, there is no evidence to support the modern speculation that she was kept in "seclusion" or otherwise mistreated.

643. Reported by Richard of San Germano, attested by other sources.

644. Reports of Yolanda's date of death vary by several days; see, for example, *Breve Chronicon de Rebus Siculis,* page 80. See also *Recueil des Historiens des Croisades, Historiens Occidentaux,* volume 2, page 420.

645. *Recueil des Historiens des Croisades, Historiens Occidentaux,* volume 2, pages 369-373. Also *Breve Chronicon de Rebus Siculis,* pages 80-92, which offers what is probably an eyewitness account of Frederick's crusade.

646. For more about John see Perry, Guy, *John of Brienne.*

647. See Powell, James, *The Liber Augustalis or Constitutions of Melfi.*

648. See *Matthaei Parisiensis, Chronica Majora,* volume 4, page 175.

649. *Chronicon de Lanercost,* page 13; the note on page 372 cites the *Close Roll* for her confinement at Gloucester Castle from 3 December 1214. Roger of Wendover also alludes to the incident. The chronicler Matthew Paris famously observed that Isabella of Angoulême "ought to be called a wicked Jezebel rather than Isabel." When she died in 1246, he wrote that she was "much in need of the spiritual benefit to be derived from the alms of the pious." See *Matthew Paris's English History,* volume 2, page 166. (See also note 651.)

650. The author begs the reader's indulgence for this perfunctory treatment of a fascinating era of English history, as a detailed exposition would be a lengthy digression from the subject of this chapter. For an introduction, three fine works are highly recommended (see the bibliography): *King John* by Ralph Turner; *Magna Carta* by Dan Jones; *William Marshal* by David Crouch.

651. Before she was a teenager, pretty Isabella of Angoulême was betrothed to the father of Hugh X of Lusignan, namely Hugh IX "le Brun," and went to live in his castle until she was old enough to marry. When John of England expressed a prurient interest in the beautiful girl, her father, thinking an important king a better match than a lowly count, snatched her away from Hugh and affianced her to John, who she wed in 1200. For this, historians sometimes refer to Isabella of Angoulême as "the Helen of Troy of the thirteenth century." Later, in 1214, John betrothed his daughter, Joan, to Hugh X as if in compensation for taking Isabella from his father, Hugh IX, fourteen years earlier. Little Joan was even sent to be raised at the Lusignan court. It is said that in 1220 when Hugh X (who was 37) met the widowed Isabella (then about 32) he was struck by her beauty and chose her over her daughter. Economic considerations may also have come into play. Joan was eventually sent back to England, to be betrothed to Alexander II of Scotland. (For Isabella's personality see note 649.)

652. Unlike most of the other queens considered in this volume, Isabella and her aunt, Joanna, are the subject of fine biographies published long ago. For the former, see Mary Anne Everett Green's *Lives of the Princesses of England,* volume 2, pages 1-47; for the latter see volume 1 of that work. Mrs Green's scholarship, though typically Victorian and in certain respects superseded by more recent research, has generally withstood the test of time quite well.

653. The royal children also lived at Marlborough, Westminster and elsewhere, based on the movements of Henry as king. This was for administrative reasons as well as safety. See *Historia Anglicana,* page 110.

654. Margaret of Biset, who was related to a landed family of Kidderminster (see note 661), was already receiving a salary noted in the *Close Roll* of Henry III for 1218; see Green, op. cit. supra, page 2; also *Close Rolls,* volume 1, page 65. She is later mentioned, with Isabella's usher ("sergeant") and cook, as receiving a pension; see *Patent Rolls,* volume 3, pages 103-105. For Margaret's sons see *Close Rolls,* volume 1, pages 159, 249.

655. *Patent Rolls,* volume 1, page 235; *Foedera,* volume 1, part 1, page 81.

656. Correspondence mentioning this appears in *Lettres de Rois,* volume 1, pages 44-49 (document 35). Citing (and quoting) reference to it in a response made by the council of Henry III in 1225, Green (op.cit. supra, pages 443-445) estimates its dating to that year even if the compiler of *Lettres de Rois* makes an unconvincing case for 1236. To support her rebuttal, Green also quotes from the *Annales Godefridi.* Contextually, it is reasonable to believe that an effort would be made to betroth Isabella rather soon considering that her sisters, one her junior, were already married.

657. *Close Rolls,* volume 1: pages 233 (Henry's letter to his kinsman Otto I of Brunswick-Lüneburg regarding aborted marriage proposal in 1229), 453 (Isabella at Marlborough in 1230), 482 (Easter 1231 at Marlborough), 502 (Katherine the damsel betrothed at royal expense), 533 (two red deer sent to Isabella at Marlborough for venison). *Close Rolls,* volume 2: Marlborough, pages 35 (fish sent to Isabella), 235-236, 249 (deer sent to Isabella for venison), 430 (wine and deer sent to Isabella); Gloucester, pages 65, 79 (a red deer sent to Isabella), 107; London, pages 517, 540 (sweet wine sent to Isabella at the Tower of London in October 1234); clothes purchased at the fair, pages 4-5; gift of silverware, pages 9-10, 43; personal chaplain assigned to Isabella, page 229; the *hostiario* (house manager) William Pilet receives a horse, page 370.

658. *Close Rolls,* volume 3: pages 73 (chaplain), 58 (gift of almonds). For Isabella's attendant, or friend, Isolda of Kidderminster, see note 661.

659. According to Matthew Paris, Frederick actually offered to begin such a campaign immediately after Henry approved the betrothal of Isabella. See *Matthew Paris's English History,* volume 1, page 11.

660. *Foedera,* page 121. For Henry's letter to his sister, Joan, informing her of the marriage see *Royal and Other Historical Letters,* volume 1, pages 459-460, citing the Close Roll, q.v. *Close Rolls,* volume 3, page 167. For the transportation preparations, ibid, page 84.

661. *Foedera,* pages 120-121, 123-124, 126, 130. Some of these patents are misdated in this compilation; for example the dowry money was withdrawn from the exchequer (page 130) in June 1235, not 1236. For the tax levied in Ireland, see *Close Rolls,* volume 3, pages 510, 571, 573; for debts forgiven, ibid, pages 81 (royal debt to several English Jews) and 241 (debt of Thomas Daniel who wed Isabella's attendant Isolda of Kidderminster).

662. *Patent Rolls,* volume 3, pages 103-105. For Roger Pilet's kinsman William, the manager of Isabella's household, see *Close Rolls,* volume 2, page 370.

663. See *Matthaei Parisiensis, Chronica Majora,* volume 3, pages 318-319; also *Roger of Wendover's Flowers of History,* volume 2, pages 607-609 (excerpted).

664. See manuscript DD in Sources. For the horses sent to Henry by Frederick from Germany, *Close Rolls,* volume 3, page 309.

665. The following passages are quoted from the eloquent Victorian translation by John Giles, published in 1848 as *Roger of Wendover's Flowers of History,* volume 2, pages 607-610 passim.

666. Henry's trial took place in early July; he was condemned and placed under arrest. Frederick's younger son, Conrad, was present for both the trial and the wedding.

NOTES

667. *Roger of Wendover's Flowers of History,* volume 2, page 610. For Frederick's offer of military support see also note 659.

668. See, for example, *Monumenta Wormatiensia,* pages 150, 174-175, 210, 216.

669. Ibid, page 175. *Act Imperii Inedita,* pages 298, 786.

670. See, for example, *Foedera,* pages 133-135; *Royal and Other Historical Letters,* volume 2, pages 8-9, 25-29.

671. This is mentioned by Richard of San Germano. Some historians identify the girl as Agnes, others as Margaret; see note 678. It is possible that a boy (apocryphally identified as Jordan) was born to Isabella in the spring of 1236 but died in infancy. There is, however, much doubt about this.

672. For the visit of Walter, the clerk, *Patent Rolls,* volume 3, page 145. For Henry's letter, *Foedera,* page 128: *Rex imperatrici, et cetera, et jocunda prosperitate diu gaudere. Affectionem sinceram, quam de status nostri prosperitate certiorari desideratis, plenius attendentes ex intimo desiderio, quo vestram scire cupimus laeitiam et jocunditatem, serenitati vestrae significamus nos et reginam, uxorem nostram, benedictus Deus, esse sanos et incolumes. Placeat igitur dilectioni vestrae statum vestrum, utinam prosperum, nobis renuntiare, et inde nos reddere velitis laetiores. Significantes insuper nobis si quid penes nos vestrae placuerit excellentiae, ad quod nos semper pronos inveniet dilectio vestra.*

673. *Foedera,* page 130; also *Petri de Vineis Friderici II Imperatoris Epistolarum,* volume 1, book 3, chapter 21, pages 419-420.

674. Among her other titles, Isabella was Queen of Jerusalem. Henceforth, however, Frederick's status as King of Jerusalem began to fall into that of pretender. The Franks, and therefore the Christians, lost the city in 1244.

675. *Chronica Majora,* volume 4, pages 145-147, where Matthew Paris reports that Richard saw Isabella at Palermo and that Frederick was present. That is inaccurate, but historians have often conflated Matthew's account with what little is known of the meeting in Faenza. See also Richard of San Germano. For Frederick's movements see *Historia Diplomatica Friderici Secundi,* volume 5, part 2, pages 1130-1167.

676. Peter della Vigna, who generally restricts his mention of Isabella and her children to births and deaths, would be an ideal source because, unlike Richard of San Germano and Matthew Paris, he was at court (when he wasn't traveling on diplomatic missions for Frederick) and actually knew Isabella. See *Petri de Vineis Friderici II Imperatoris Epistolarum,* volume 1, book 3, chapter 21, pages 419-420; volume 1, book 3, chapter 70, pages 502-504; volume 1, book 3, chapter 71, pages 504-506; volume 2, book 4, chapter 2, pages 6-7.

677. *Chronica Majora,* volume 4, page 83.

678. Some historians believe this child to be Margaret, who did survive. This suggests that she was born in 1241 rather than 1236/1237. See note 671.

679. *Foedera,* page 140; *Chronica Majora,* volume 4, page 175. For Frederick's letter to Henry see also *Historia Diplomatica Friderici Secundi,* volume 6, part 1, page 26.

680. *Chronica Majora,* volume 5, pages 571-573. Matthew Paris wrote this around 1256 to explain the paternity, royal status and legitimacy of Bianca's son, Manfred Hohenstaufen. Scholars often cite the wording of the marriage contract of Bianca's son, Manfred (to Beatrice of Savoy), as evidence that the wedding between Bianca and Frederick was not celebrated until 1247 or 1248, as Frederick's charter of April/May 1247 refers to "Manfred *Lancia,* son of the emperor." For this see *Historia Diplomatica Friderici Secundi,* volume 6, part 1, pages 526-528. By December 1248, Frederick was referring to his wife's kinsman, Marquis Manfred Lancia, as *dilectus affinis noster,* implying canonical affinity through marriage; see *Historia Diplomatica Friderici Secundi,* volume 6, part 2, page 672.

681. For the chronicle, see *Frederick, Conrad and Manfred of Hohenstaufen, Kings of Sicily 1210-1258: The Chronicle of Nicholas of Jamsilla.*

682. See *Bianca Lancia d'Agliano: Fra il Piemonte e il Regno di Sicilia* (1992), edited by Renata Bordone. This is a compilation of papers presented at a conference held at Agliano in April 1990 dedicated exclusively to Bianca Lancia.

683. *Chronica Majora,* volume 5, page 196. For [what may be] the declaration of Frederick's sons, see *Historia Diplomatica Friderici Secundi,* volume 6, part 2, page 810-812. For [what may be] Frederick's testament, ibid pages 805-810.

684. Through the Hohenstaufen line, Elisabeth and Conrad were third cousins, their most recent common ancestor being their great-great grandfather, Frederick "the One-Eyed," Duke of Swabia, who died in 1147. See the genealogical table at the end of this chapter.

685. For the text of the betrothal agreement, see *Historia Diplomatica Friderici Secundi,* volume 6, part 2, page 875-876.

686. We find Elisabeth mentioned in passing in the "Jamsilla Chronicle." Unlike the chronicles of Bartholomew of Nicastro and Saba Malaspina, which were penned later (and from a Guelphic point of view), this was written contemporaneously by somebody (of Ghibelline sympathy) at Manfred's court. As published originally, Jamsilla lacks division into chapters; for convenience see the translation by Louis Mendola, *Frederick, Conrad and Manfred of Hohenstaufen, Kings of Sicily 1210-1258: The Chronicle of Nicholas of Jamsilla,* pages 104, 211-212.

687. Ibid, page 104.

688. Ibid, pages 105-109.

689. Ibid, page 144. Jamsilla's statement that young Henry was governor of Sicily is

attested by a letter written by Frederick II to Henry III of England, the boy's uncle, in February 1247; see *Historia Diplomatica Friderici Secundi*, volume 6, part 1, page 502.

690. After English baronial support for the costly "Sicilian business" evaporated, other candidates were sought. Pope Urban IV, a Frenchman, eventually chose Charles of Anjou as the most suitable among them. In England, the Italian ambitions of Henry III were one of the causes of the Second Barons' War (1264-1267).

691. The Battle of Tagliacozzo followed the earlier Battle of Benevento (1266). These events are considered at greater length in Chapter 19. The chief source for Conradin's campaign is the chronicler Andrew of Hungary, although Saba Malaspina (book 4, chapters 1-16) also recounts it in detail, as does Bartholomew of Nicastro (chapters 8-10).

692. Saba Malaspina, book 4, chapter 16. This is the author's translation; Malaspina's chronicle has not been published in its entirety in English.

693. This is Santa Maria del Carmine (Our Lady of Mount Carmel) at the end of Piazza Mercato. This square, or one near it, was the site of Conradin's execution on 29 October 1268. Most contemporary sovereigns did not condone the murder of Conradin by Charles of Anjou; see, for example, the "Invective" of Peter of Pretio.

694. The precise year of birth of Manfred III del Vasto is not known, but while quite young he succeeded his grandfather (his father having died) in 1212. Much has been written about the Savoys, particularly after they united Italy under their aegis in the nineteenth century. Unfortunately, a great deal of this scholarship was authored by Italian nationalist apologists seeking to glorify the dynasty, thus exaggerating its antiquity or importance. Beatrice herself is mentioned in contemporary sources, such as the chronicles indicated here (see note 698) and the charters confirming her betrothals; for her time in Saluzzo, see *Chronaca di Saluzzo*, columns 895, 897, and *Regesto dei Marchesi di Saluzzo*.

695. For the betrothal finalized in April 1247, see *Historia Diplomatica Friderici Secundi*, volume 6, part 1, pages 526-528; the compensation of a thousand silver marks is mentioned. For an affirmation of Frederick's alliance with the Savoys and the Marquesses of Saluzzo expressed in a charter of January 1246, ibid, volume 6, part 2, page 916. Although the exact date of the wedding is unknown, the fact that it took place before March 1249 is clear from a charter issued by Frederick II in that month, ibid, pages 703-704.

696. For the manors granted to the Savoys as a dower for Beatrice, ibid, pages 664-665.

697. See notes 680 and 695.

698. None of these passing references says much about Beatrice other than identifying her. For example, in the chronicle of Saba Malaspina: book 1, chapter 1, we read of Manfred's wife described as, "a noble lady, Beatrice, daughter of Amedeo, Count of Savoy."

699. To support this hypothesis, historians cite the testaments of Amedeo IV, Beatrice's father (issued in 1252 and 1253), which refer to her as "my daughter Beatrice, wife of the late Manfred, Marquis of Saluzzo" and "Beatrice, Marchioness of Saluzzo," rather than identifying her as the wife of Manfred Hohenstaufen. In connection with the rather tenuous thesis of a "divorce" or "formal separation" (anachronistic to the thirteenth century), it should be remembered that Manfred was not yet King of Sicily but simply regent (vicar) of the realm acting on behalf of his half-brother, King Conrad, and therefore had no official, hereditary title. Whatever the state of her marriage, there is no record of Beatrice actually leaving Manfred to return to live at Saluzzo, even if it is reasonable to believe that she made a trip to visit her children there.

700. *Frederick, Conrad and Manfred of Hohenstaufen,* page 153.

701. In the chronicle of Saba Malaspina, book 3, chapter 4, we read that, "With the death of Queen Beatrice, the king, negotiating a union with Michael Comnenus Ducas, a great and illustrious Greek, took as his wife this man's daughter, who was of young but marriageable age, sage and prudent beyond her years, who bore him several children, of whom only a daughter survived into adulthood." Jamsilla does not mention Beatrice being present at Manfred's coronation, but too much should not be made of that oversight. Beatrice's place and date of death are unknown, but a longstanding theory holds that she was interred in Sicily

702. See Saba Malaspina, book 2, chapter 6. Based on her Hohenstaufen blood, Constance became Queen of Sicily two decades later as a result of the War of the Sicilian Vespers, which saw her husband crowned king. This led to the Aragonese rule of the island, with the mainland under the Angevins.

703. See Domenico Forges Davanzati's detailed *Dissertazione sulla Seconda Moglie del Re Manfredi e sù Loro Figliuoli,* published in 1791, which cites an obscure Apulian chronicle as the source of this information regarding Helena's arrival (pages 11-13), for which there is concordance in other sources. Davanzati's book, arguably the first modern biography published of any of the women profiled herein, is especially useful because it includes the first printed transcriptions of various charters (some then archived but not yet catalogued) issued in Helena's time or shortly thereafter, preceding by a half-century the collections compiled by historians such as Bartolommeo Capasso. Apart from chronicles such as those of Jamsilla, Nicastro, Malaspina and Villani, Davanzati consulted unedited charters kept at Cassino, Cava, Naples (the royal archive), Salerno, Bari, Trani, Rome and elsewhere. In consulting Davanzati's work, and his citations, it should be borne in mind that cataloguing systems have changed since 1791. The major shortcoming in the work is that Davanzati, like certain other modern historians, occasionally cites the chronicle of "Matthew Spinelli," which was actually a forgery. In his compendium *Historia Diplomatica Regni Siciliae,* pages 176-177 (document 315), Capasso cites Malaspina and also the chronicler of Trani mentioned by Davanzati.

704. For an analysis of the culture of Manfred's court see *Translating at Court,* by Pieter De Leemans. There are several modern biographies of Manfred Hohen-

NOTES

staufen, most notably Giuseppe Di Cesare's *Storia di Manfredi,* published in 1837. Another work worthy of mention is Giuseppe Del Giudice's *La Famiglia di Re Manfredi.* The author also consulted the typescript of the forthcoming monograph, *Manfred King of Sicily,* by Louis Mendola, due for publication soon.

705. The dowry lands were mentioned explicitly in a charter of Charles II issued in 1273; see Davanzati (op.cit. supra), page LIII, document LX. The marriage is also mentioned in *Historia Diplomatica Regni Siciliae,* pages 188-191 (document 327).

706. Helena may have given birth to twins; see Davanzati (op.cit. supra), page 10.

707. The dating is disputed, but see *Historia Diplomatica Regni Siciliae,* pages 217-221 (documents 368, 369). By July 1262, Manfred and his family seem to have been in Palermo, where a charter was issued to the preceptor of the Teutonic Knights witnessed by John of Procida; see manuscript EE. The account of Helena's meeting with the Aragonese written by "Matthew Spinelli" may be dismissed as fantasy; see note 703.

708. A highly-recommended introduction to this era and its complexities is Sir Steven Runciman's history, *The Sicilian Vespers.*

709. Ibid. For chroniclers' contemporary accounts see note 691; also Mendola, Louis, *The Battle of Benevento according to Andrew of Hungary and Saba Malaspina.* As stated in the Introduction, the fall of the Hohenstaufens in 1266 (and definitively two years later) signalled several obvious developments over the next century and thereafter: (1) The cultural nexus of "Italy" and its literary vernacular shifted northward, with Tuscan and Umbrian popularized over Sicilian and Neapolitan. (2) The Guelphic views expressed in the Italian (Tuscan) works of Dante and Boccaccio demonized Frederick II, Manfred, and the Ghibellines generally. (3) Successive cultural and artistic movements, most notably the Renaissance, flourished chiefly in the Italian north whilst the Angevin and Aragonese dynasties ruling the south failed to patronize the arts to the same degree (and in the same manner) as the rulers or patriciates of cities like Florence, Milan, Pisa, Venice and even Rome. (4) The remaining Muslim population of Italy (in Apulia, Basilicata, Calabria) was forcibly converted to Catholicism whilst the Jews in most cities were increasingly restricted and confined to ghettos. (5) In the kingdoms of Naples and Sicily, the Hohenstaufen legal code, the Constitutions of Melfi, was soon supplanted by a complex, confusing, disunified, inconsistent farrago of statutes which by 1400 was inefficient and indeed unworkable, with certain fundamental rights all but abandoned. (6) A Latin ("Italian") monoculture permeated most of what is now Italy.

710. Charles and his successor (Charles II "the Lame") did indeed occupy some of these Albanian lands during the next few years. The Neapolitan Angevins eventually controlled Corfu and much of mainland Greece.

711. Henry of Castile (1230-1303), a cousin of Charles, supported the Angevins at Benevento but changed allegiance and supported Conradin (also his cousin) at Tagliacozzo two years later.

712. Davanzati (op.cit. supra), pages XXX-XXXI (document 32 issued at Lucera in July 1269) and XXXIV (document 27, same place and date).

713. Ibid, page XXXVII (document 33 issued at Capua in March 1270), mentioning the forty ounces to be sent to the castellan of Nocera.

714. Ibid, pages XLIII-XLIV (document 44).

715. For Beatrice Hohenstaufen's renunciation, betrothal and dowry, see *Codice Diplomatico dei Re Aragonesi,* volume 1, pages 330-341. King Peter's son, James, had succeeded him as King of Sicily by this time (October 1286).

716. Ibid, page 336.

717. Among various charters, see Davanzati, page LXXXIII (document 91 issued in Naples in April 1297), which attests to the three brothers' presence at Castel del Monte.

718. See Lipinsky, Angelo, "Sicaniae Regni Corona" and "Le Insegne Regali" in Sources.

719. See Lipinsky (the preceding note); also Maria Accascina's commentary in *Oreficeria di Sicilia,* pages 78-79, and Josef Deér's passing remarks in *The Dynastic Porphyry Tombs,* page 171. In his 32-page monograph *La Corona di Costanza,* Gregorio La Grua, by stated intent (on page 7) does not respond directly to all of the affirmations of Lipinsky, Accascina or Deér.

720. In "From Her Head to Her Toes," Christopher Mielke examines Deér's tenuous thesis while citing several papers published after 1990 but does not mention the earlier work of Lipinsky (see note 718), Accascina or La Grua (note 719).

721. Louis Mendola, author of *The Kingdom of Sicily 1130-1860.*

722. Born the same year as Princess Urraca, Prince Cyril Toumanoff was a native of Saint Petersburg where, as a boy, he witnessed the Russian Revolution. Following retirement from a longtime professorship of history at Georgetown University, where one of his many students was a young Bill Clinton, he resided in the Palazzo di Malta in Rome, serving as High Historical Consultant of the Sovereign Military Order of Malta. He died in 1997.

SOURCES AND BIBLIOGRAPHY

Manuscript Sources

For concordance, a number of charters and other documents were consulted at archives in Italy and Spain. For the benefit of scholars wishing to consult these manuscripts, it should be noted that cataloguing systems change over time, so since 2007 the collection at the Palermo Archive of State formerly known as *Pergamene Varie* (sundry manuscripts) has been known as *Pergamene di Diversa Provenienza,* literally "manuscripts from various sources," and it is presently housed in the more modernized, more secure Catena division rather than the Gancia off Via Alloro at the opposite end of Piazza Marina. The *Fondo Messina* (Messina Collection) of the Fundación Casa Ducal de Medinaceli, formerly housed in Seville, is now conserved at the archive of the Hospital de Tavera (de San Juan Bautista) in Toledo. Other idiosyncrasies confront the researcher; for example, most Spanish charters and chronicles of the twelfth century are dated with reference to the "Spanish era" dating system that begins with the year 38 BC (BCE), probably based on the infelicitous date that a certain Roman tax was imposed in Iberia. A few charters, letters and chronicles may be consulted online, where some published transcriptions and extracts are also made available. For convenience in identification, the letters A-FF correspond to references to each manuscript in this volume's endnotes.

A) Archivio di Stato di Palermo, Tabulario dei Monasteri di San Filippo di Fragalà e di Santa Maria di Maniace: Manuscript 6 (decree issued on parchment before 1113, probably *circa* 1110, by Adelaide in the name of her son Roger II renewing to the monastery privileges granted by her late husband replacing the previous decree written on paper).

B) Archivio di Stato di Palermo, Tabulario dei Monasteri di San Filippo di

Fragalà e di Santa Maria di Maniaci: Manuscripts 7, 11, 12 (decrees made into 1112 endowing the monastery on Adelaide's initiative); Manuscript 10 (reissue in 1109 of former decree of Roger I delimiting territory of abbey of Saint Barbarus).

C) Archivio di Stato di Palermo, Tabulario dei Monasteri di San Filippo di Fragalà e di Santa Maria di Maniace: Manuscript 9 (paper letter of March 1109 in Greek on upper half and Arabic on lower half from Adelaide commanding jurats of Kasr'Janni, now Enna, to protect the monastery of Saint Philip of Demenna, in the San Marco Valley, under her personal patronage).

D) Tabulario Cappella Palatina: Manuscript number 13 (royal concession of ecclesiastical property in Palermo by Margaret and young William, in March 1167, bearing signatures of Matthew of Aiello, Qaid Martin and Walter the rector and future archbishop).

E) Tabulario della Cattedrale di Palermo: Manuscript number 21 (royal concession of the feudal rights of the mills on the manor of Brucato, the Arabic *Bur-Ruqqad,* to Walter, the newly-consecrated Archbishop of Palermo, in September 1169).

F) Tabulario della Cattedrale di Palermo: Manuscript number 22 (William grants Archbishop Walter of Palermo rights to judge adulterers except for claims falling under civil jurisdiction, 15 April 1172).

G) Tabulario di Santa Maria Nova, Monreale (in the Biblioteca Centrale della Regione Siciliana, Palermo): Manuscript number 8, 1 March 1174, (Nicholas, Archbishop of Messina, exempts Abbey of Maniace founded by Margaret from taxation).

H) Tabulario di Santa Maria Nova, Monreale (in the Biblioteca Centrale della Regione Siciliana): Manuscript number 20, March 1177, (Theobald, Bishop of Monreale, establishes rights of Abbey of Maniace).

I) Archivio di Stato di Palermo, Pergamene Varie: Manuscript number 3, November 1146 (recorded in Greek, confirms the sale of familial property near the Martorana by the children of Eugenius for a thousand gold tarì, includes epitaph to George of Antioch, founder of the Martorana, dated 1151).

SOURCES AND BIBLIOGRAPHY

J) Archivio di Stato di Palermo, Tabulario di Santa Maria Maddalena of Messina: Manuscript number 50 (Margaret and William order nobles to exempt a monastery from taxation based on established policy, in 1168).

K) Archivio di Stato di Palermo, Tabulario dei Monasteri di San Filippo di Fragalà e di Santa Maria di Maniace: Manuscript 17 (TSFF17), 27 November 1171 (unsealed, probably a copy of an original, sealed charter; recorded in Greek and Latin, confirms privileges of Roger II protecting said monasteries, exempting them from the obligation to provide timber and livestock, lodge men-at-arms, and so forth, effectively exempting them from local civic authority).

L) Tabulario della Cattedrale di Palermo: Manuscript number 29 (Queen Constance's assignment of some serfs, formerly under the feudal jurisdiction of the late Archbishop Walter, to the authority of the notary Rainaldo, dated April 1196).

M) Tabulario di Santa Maria Nova, Monreale (in the Biblioteca Centrale della Regione Siciliana): Manuscript number Balsamo 31, 30 December 1174, (Pope Alexander III grants status and privileges of "major abbey" to Monreale's Benedictine monastery).

N) Archivio di Stato di Palermo, Tabulario della Magione: Manuscripts 3 (April 1136) and 4 (January 1145) both copied in February 1291 (King Roger II grants serfs and lands to Adeline, the wet nurse of his late son Henry, near Vicari).

O) Vatican Apostolic Library: Codice Vaticano Latino 3880, "Liber Privilegiorum Sanctae Montis Regalis Ecclesiae" chartulary (transcriptions of royal and papal charters relative to Monreale Abbey, several during the reign of William II).

P) Archivo de la Catedral de Tudela: Cajón 1, D. Manuscript number 20 (marriage charter between García Ramírez and Margaret l'Aigle).

Q) British Library, London: Harley Manuscript 5786, folio 79r (trilingual psalter composed in Sicily in Latin, Greek and Arabic during the reign of Roger II).

R) Archivio di Stato di Palermo: Direzione Centrale Statistiche (maps drawn between 1820 and 1850 showing medieval manors in Sicily).

S) Fundación Casa Ducal de Medinaceli (Toledo), Fondo Messina: Manuscript number 1118, November 1167 (Caïd Martin, acting on orders of Margaret and William II, issues this directive in Greek and Arabic restoring authority to Nicholas, Archbishop of Messina; only the Greek text mentions Margaret).

T) Fundación Casa Ducal de Medinaceli (Toledo), Fondo Messina: Manuscript number 109, March 1168, 1st indiction (William II and Margaret cede the Agrò Woods to the Holy Savior monastery of Messina).

U) Fundación Casa Ducal de Medinaceli (Toledo), Fondo Messina: Manuscript number 528, November 1176, 10th indiction (Margaret renews a donation effected five years earlier of some flat land near Milazzo to the Cistercian monastery of Santa Maria at Novara).

V) Fundación Casa Ducal de Medinaceli (Toledo), Fondo Messina: Manuscript number 522, May 1161, 9th indiction (William I confirms to the eldest sons of feudal vassals their hereditary rights to succeed their fathers killed in the service of the king, while conceding the citizens of Messina certain tax exemptions).

W) Vatican Apostolic Library: Codex Pal. Lat 1071. King Manfred's copy of Frederick's treatise *De Arte Venandi cum Avibus*.

X) Biblioteca Nacional de España (Madrid): Codex number VITR/26/2 (bdh0000022766), the *Historia Bizantina* ("Synopsis of Histories") of Ioannes Skylitzes, copied in Greek in Palermo circa 1130 from an older manuscript, chronicling years 811-1057.

Y) Burgerbibliothek, Berne: Codex number 120.2, *Liber ad Honorem Augusti sive de Rebus Siculis* by Peter of Eboli, written in Latin verse in Palermo after 1197.

Z) Vatican Apostolic Library: Codex Vaticanus Latinus 3793 (electronic ID 214430), pages 60, 61, 62. *Contrasto* of Cielo d'Alcamo.

AA) British Library, London: Yates Thompson Manuscript 12, folio 188v (French translation executed and illuminated after 1232 of the *Historie d'Outremer* originally written in Latin by William of Tyre).

BB) British Library, London: Royal Manuscript 14B.VI ("Royal Chronicle" showing genealogy of kings of England, composed around 1300, featuring illumination of a young, blonde Joanna).

CC) British Library, London: Royal Manuscript 20A.II, folios 152v and 154r (copy of a letter attributed to Queen Joanna written to Hugh IV, King of Cyprus).

DD) British National Archives, Kew: Document C47/3/3 (account of fabric issued at Easter 1135 for trousseau of Isabella of England).

EE) Archivio di Stato di Palermo, Tabulario della Magione: Manuscripts 94, 96, charters of July 1262 (Manfred confirms rights of Magione commandery of Teutonic Order in Palermo).

FF) Biblioteca Casanatense, Rome: Codex 614, folios 33-36 (rite of reginal coronation).

Primary Sources in Print

This list includes a few works in translation.

Acti Imperii Inedita seculi XIII, Urkunden un Briefe. Collection. Edited by Winkelmann, Eduard (1880).

Alexiad of Anna Comnena. Translated by Sewter, Edgar Robert Ashton (1969).

Annales Beneventani, in *Monumenta Germaniae Historica,* volume 3. Edited by Pertz, Georg (1839).

Annales Casinenses, in *Monumenta Germaniae Historica,* volume 19. Edited by Pertz, Georg Heinrich (1866), pages 303-320.

Annales Cavenses, in *Monumenta Germaniae Historica,* volume 3. Edited by Pertz, Georg (1839).

Annales Ceccanenses, in *Monumenta Germaniae Historica,* volume 19. Edited by Pertz, Georg Heinrich (1866), pages 275-302.

Annales Marbacenses, in *Monumenta Germaniae Historica,* volume 17. Edited by Pertz, Georg (1861), pages 142-180.

Annales Siculi, in *Rerum Italicarum Scriptores,* volume 5. Edited by Muratori, Lodovico (1774, reprint Bologna 1928).

Arnoldi Chronica Slavorum, in the *Scriptores Rerum Germanicarum* series. Edited by Pertz, Georg (1868).

The Battle of Benevento according to Andrew of Hungary and Saba Malaspina. Translation and notes. Mendola, Louis (2019).

Book in Honor of Augustus by Pietro da Eboli. Translation and notes. Hood, Gwenyth. (2012).

Book of King Roger by Abdullah al Idrisi: *Il Libro di Ruggero* (2008), Italian translation by Umberto Rizzitano; *La Sicilia di al-Idrisi ne Il Libro di Ruggero* (2010) by Luigi Santagati; *Carte Comparèe de la Sicile* (1859) by Michele Amari.

Breve Chronicon de Rebus Siculis, in *Monumenta Germaniae Historica,* volume 72. Edited by Stürner, Wolfgang (2004).

Calendar of Documents Preserved in France Illustrative of the History of Great Britain and Ireland 918-1206, volume 1. Round, Horace, editor (1899).

Catálogo de los Cartularios Reales del Archivo General de Navarra 1007-1384. Idoate, Florencio (1974).

Catalogo Illustrato del Tabulario di Santa Maria Nuova in Monreale. Garufi, Carlo Alberto (1902).

Catalogus Baronum. Jamison, Evelyn (1972). See also Del Re's *Cronisti,* volume 1, below.

La Chanson d'Antioche. Edited by Graindor de Douai (1862).

Chronica Adefonsi Imperatoris. Edited by Sánchez Belda, Luis (1950).

Chronica Albrici Monachi Trium Fontium of Alberic of Trois-Fontaines, in *Monumenta Germaniae Historica,* volume 23. Edited by Pertz, Georg Heinrich (1874), pages 631-950.

SOURCES AND BIBLIOGRAPHY

The Chronicle of Ibn al-Athir for the Crusading Period from al-Kamil fi'l-Ta'rikh by Ali ibn al-Athir. Part 2, 541-589/1146-1193. Richards, Donald (2007).

Chronica Magistri Rogeri de Houedene (4 volumes). Edited by Stubbs, William (1870).

Chronica Monasterii Casinensis, in *Monumenta Germaniae Historica,* volume 34. Edited by Hoffmann, Hartmut (1980).

Chronicle of Alfonso the Emperor. Translation of the *Chronica Adefonsi Imperatoris* by Lipskey, Glenn Edward (1972).

Chronicles of the Reigns of Stephen, Henry II and Richard I, volume 2. Edited by Howlett, Richard (1885).

The Chronicle of Robert of Torigni. Edited by Howlett, Richard (1889).

Chronicon Budense post Elapsos ab Editione. Edited by Podhradczky, Josef (1838).

Chronicon Hierosolymitanae (1584); first print edition of the chronicle of Albert of Aix (or Aachen).

Chronicon de Lanercost. Edited by Stevenson, Joseph (1839).

Chronicon Pictum Vindobonense, in *Historiae Hungaricae Fontes Domestici,* part 1 (Scriptores), volume 2, pages 100-315. Edited by Florian, Matyas (1883).

Chronicon Vulturnense de Monaco Giovanni, 3 volumes. Edited by Federici, Vincenzo (1925-1938).

Chronique d'Ernoul et de Bernard le Trésorier. Edited by de Mas Latrie, Louis (1871).

Chronique Latine de Guillaume de Nangis, volume 1. Géraud, Hercule, editor. (1843).

Chronique de Maitre Guillaume de Puylaurens sur la Guerre des Albigeois. Translation, Lagarde, Charles (1864).

Chronaca di Saluzzo, in *Monumenta Historiae Patriae, Scriptores,* volume 3. Edited by Della Chiesa, Goffredo (1848).

O City of Byzantium: Annals of Nicetas Choniates. Translation. Magoulias, Harry (1984).

Close Rolls of the Reign of Henry III Preserved in the Public Record Office (London 1902-1916), volumes: 1 (1227-1231), 2 (1231-1234), 3 (1234-1237), 4 (1237-1242), 5 (1242-1247).

Codex Diplomaticus Cavensis. Compilation. Morcaldi, Michele, chief editor (1893).

Codex Diplomaticus Hungariae Ecclesiasticus ac Civilis, series 3, volume 1. Compilation. Fejér, Georg (1829).

Codex Diplomaticus Regni Siciliae, volumes 1-5. Compilation. Various editors (1982).

Codice Diplomatico dei Re Aragonesi di Sicilia 1282-1355. Compilation. La Mantia, Giuseppe (1918).

Codice Diplomatico del Regno di Carlo I e Carlo II d'Angio 1265-1309. Compilation. Del Giudice, Giuseppe (1863).

Codice Diplomatico di Sicilia sotto il Governo degli Arabi. Compilation. Airoldi, Alfonso (1790).

Codice Diplomatico Verginiano. Compilation. Tropeano, Placido Maria (1977).

Colección Diplomática de Alfonso I de Aragón y Pamplona 1104-1134. Edited by Lema Pueyo, José (1990).

Colección Diplomática de la Catedral de Pamplona, volume 1 (829-1243). Compilation. Edited by Gaztambide, José Goñi (1997).

Colección Diplomática Medieval de la Rioja 923-1225 (2 volumes). Rodríguez de Lama, Ildefonso (1976).

Constantiae Imperatricis Diplomata, in *Monumenta Germaniae Historica, Diplomata Regum et Imperatorum Germaniae,* volume 11, part 3. Compilation. Koelzer, Theo (1990).

SOURCES AND BIBLIOGRAPHY

Constantiae Imperatricis et Reginae Siciliae Diplomata, in *Codex Diplomaticus Regni Siciliae,* series 2, part 1. Compilation. Koelzer, Theo (1983).

Continuatio Admuntensis, in *Monumenta Germaniae Historica,* volume 9, pages 579-593. Edited by Pertz, Georg (1851).

La Continuation de Guillaume de Tyr. Translation. Morgan, Margaret (1982).

Corónicas Navarras. Edited by Ubieto Arteta, Antonio (1989).

Constitutionum Regni Siciliarum, volume 3, Constitutions of Melfi (1773).

Cronica Fratis Salimbene de Adam Ordinis Minorum, in *Monumenta Germaniae Historica,* volume 32. Edited by Pertz, Georg (1913).

Crónica Nájerense. Edited by Ubieto Arteta, Antonio (1985).

Crónica Nájerense. Translated by Estévez Sola, Juan (2003).

Crónica Navarro-Aragonesa, in *Crónica de los Estados Peninsulares.* Edited by Ubieto Arteta, Antonio (1955).

Cronisti e Scrittori Sincroni Napoletani, volume 1 ("Normanni"), edited by Del Re, Giuseppe (Naples 1845); pages 5-71 and 559-563 (Romuald of Salerno); pages 88-156 (Alexander of Telese); pages 160-276 (Falco of Benevento); pages 277-391 (Hugh Falcandus); pages 405-439 (Peter of Eboli); pages 461-480 (Cassino Chronicle); pages 571-616 (Catalogus Baronum).

Cronisti e Scrittori Sincroni Napoletani, volume 2 ("Svevi"), edited by Del Re, Giuseppe (Naples 1868); pages 5-100 (Richard of San Germano); pages 101-200 ("Nicholas Jamsilla"); pages 201-408 (Saba Malaspina); pages 409-627 (Bartholomew of Nicastro).

The Deeds of Frederick Barbarossa. Translation of the *Gesti Friderici Imperatoris* of Otto of Freising. Mierow, Charles (1953).

The Deeds of Pope Innocent III: By an Anonymous Author. Translation of the *Gesti Innocenti* from the *Patrologiae Cursus Completus,* q.v. Powell, Joseph (2004).

De Vita sua Opusculum. Memoir of Michael VIII of Constantinople (1885).

I Diplomi della Cattedrale di Messina. Compilation of the Antonino Amico index. Starrabba, Raffaele (1876-1890).

I Diplomi Greci ed Arabi di Sicilia Pubblicati nel Testo Originale, Tradotti ed Illustrati (2 volumes). Cusa, Salvatore (1868).

I Documenti Inediti dell'Epoca Normanna in Sicilia. Compilation. Garufi, Carlo Alberto (1899).

Documentos de Sigena, volume 1. Compilation. Ubieto Arteta, Antonio (1972).

The Ecclesiastical History of England and Normandy, 4 volumes. Translaton and notes of the *Historia Ecclesiastica* of Orderic Vitalis. Forester, Thomas (1853-1856).

Epistolae Sancti Thomae Cantuariensis, volume 1. Compilation. Giles, John (1845).

Das Falkenbuch Friedrichs II. Photography and notes of Vatican codex *Pal. Lat 1071.* Walz, Dorothea, and Willemsen, Carl (2000).

The Ferraris Chronicle: Popes, Emperors, and Deeds in Apulia 1096-1228. Translation and notes. Alio, Jacqueline (2017).

Foedera, Conventiones, Literae et Cujuscunque Generis Acta Publica inter Reges Angliae, third edition, volume 1, parts 1 and 2. Edited by Rymer, Thomas (1869).

Friderici II Diplomata, in *Monumenta Germaniae Historica,* volume 14, parts 1 and 2. Compilation. Koch, Walter (2002, 2007).

Frederick, Conrad and Manfred of Hohenstaufen, Kings of Sicily 1210-1258: The Chronicle of Nicholas of Jamsilla. Translation by Mendola, Louis (2016).

Gesta Francorum et aliorum Hierosolimitanorum. Parallel Latin/English text. Hill, Rosalind (1967).

Gesta Henrici VI of Godfrey of Viterbo, in *Monumenta Germaniae Historica,* volume 22, pages 334-338. Compilation. Pertz, Georg (1872).

SOURCES AND BIBLIOGRAPHY

Gesta Hungarorum of Simon of Keza, in *Historiae Hungaricae Fontes Domestici*, part 1 (Scriptores), volume 2, pages 52-99. Edited by Florian, Matyas (1883).

Gesta Hungarorum - The Deeds of the Hungarians. Translated by Vezprémy, Laszlo (1999).

Gesta Regis Henrici Secundi Benedicti Abbatis (formerly attributed to Benedict of Peterborough) in *Rerum Britannicarum Medii Aevi Scriptores* (2 volumes). Stubbs, William (1867).

Gesta Roberti Wiscardi of William of Apulia. Mathieu, Marguerite (1961).

The Gesta Tancredi of Ralph of Caen: A History of the Normans on the First Crusade. Translation. Bachrach, Bernard (2016).

Gestes des Chiprois of Philip of Navarre and Gerard of Monreal. Raynaud, Gaston (1887).

Gisleberti Chronicon Hanoniense, in the *Scriptores Rerum Germanicarum* series. Edited by Arndt, Wilhelm (1869).

Historia Bizantina ("Synopsis of Histories") of John Skylitzes (PDF file of codex). See Manuscript source X.

Historia Diplomatica Friderici Secundi. Compilation. Huillard-Bréholles, Jean (1852-1857).

Historia Diplomatica Regni Siciliae inde ab anno 1250 ad annum 1266. Compilation. Capasso Bartolommeo (1874).

Historia Rerum Angicarum Willelmi Parvi de Newburgh. Edited by Hamilton, John (1856).

Historia Roderici, o Gesta Roderici Campi Docti. Edited by Risco, Manuel (1792).

Historia Salonitanorum atque Spalatinorum Pontificum by Thomas of Split. Edited and translated by Sweeney, James, and Karbic, Damir (2006).

The Historical Works of Ralph de Diceto, Dean of London (2 volumes). Stubbs, William (1876).

A History of Deeds Done Beyond the Sea, by William, Archbishop of Tyre. Translation of *Historia Rerum in Partibus Transmarinis Gestarum* with notes. Babcock, Emily, and Krey, August (1943).

History of the Lombards by Paul the Deacon. Translated by Foulke, William (1907), edited by Peters, Edward (1975).

Indices Rerum ab Aragoniae Gestarum, book 3, in *Hispaniae Illustrata,* volume 3, pages 1-231. Compilation. Schott, Andreas (1606).

Die Innsbrucker Briefsammlung: Eine neue Quelle zur Geschichte Kaiser Friedrichs II und König Konrads IV, in *Monumenta Germaniae Historica, Briefe des späteren Mittelalters,* volume 3. Compilation and notes. Riedmann, Josef (2017).

Italia Pontificia, volumes 1 (Rome), 2 (Lazio), 3 (Tuscany), 8 (Campania), 9 (Molise, Apulia, Basilicata), 10 (Calabria and islands). Compilation. Kehr, Paul (1906-1975).

Itinerarium Peregrinorum et Gesta Regis Ricardi in *Chronicles and Memorials of the Reign of Richard I,* volume 1. Edited by Stubbs, William (1864).

The Itinerary of Benjamin of Tudela (1907). Translation and commentary by Adler, Marcus Nathan; *The Itinerary of Rabbi Benjamin of Tudela* (1840) by Asher, Adolf (with Hebrew text).

John of Salisbury's Memoirs of the Papal Court. Transcription and translation of the *Historia Pontificalis of John of Salisbury* by Chibnall, Marjorie (1956).

Kitab al-masalik w'al-mamalik. Mohammed ibn Hawqal, in *Bibliotheca Geographorum Arabicorum* (Leiden 1873).

Das Kitab surat al-ard des Abu Gafar Muhammad ibn Musa al-Huwarizmi. Translation by von Mzik, Hans (1926).

Layettes du Tresor des Chartes in *Inventaires ed Documents,* volume 1. Edited by Teulet, Alexandre (1863).

Lettera a un Tesoriere di Palermo sulla Conquista Sveva di Sicilia. Tramontana, Salvatore (1988).

SOURCES AND BIBLIOGRAPHY

Lettres de Rois, Reines et Autres Personnages des Cours de France et d'Angleterre, volume 1. Edited by Champollion-Figeac, Jacques-Joseph (1839).

Liber ad Honorem Augusti di Pietro da Eboli. De Rosa, Francesco (2000).

Liber ad Honorem Augusti di Pietro da Eboli. Siragusa, Giovanni Battista (1906).

The Liber Augustalis or Constitutions of Melfi. Translation and notes. Powell, James (1971).

The Life of Saladin by Baha ad-Din Yusuf ibn Rafi ibn Shaddad, volume 12. Translation. Palestine Pilgrims' Text Society (1897).

The Lombard Laws. Translation and notes. Drew, Katherine (1973).

Mann aus Apulien: Die privaten Papiere del italienischen Staufers. Compilation by Stern, Horst (2015).

Materials for the History of Thomas Becket, Archbishop of Canterbury (7 volumes). Compilation. Robertson, James (1877).

Matthaei Parisiensis, Chronica Majora (5 volumes). Edited by Luard, Henry (1877).

Matthew Paris's English History (2 volumes). Translated by Giles, John (1853).

Memoriae Mediolanenses, in *Monumenta Germaniae Historica,* volume 8, pages 399-402. Edited by Pertz, Georg (1863).

Miscellany of Hebrew Literature. Includes writings of Obadja da Bertinoro. Edited by Neubauer, Adolf (1872).

Monumenta Wormatiensia, Annalen und Chroniken. Edited by Boos, Heinrich (1893).

Monumenti Storici, series 1 ("Cronache"), *Ignoti Monachi Cisterciensis: Sancta Mariae de Ferraria Chronica et Ryccardi de Sancto Germano Chronica Priora.* Edited by Gaudenzi, Augustus (1888).

Necrologia Panormitana, in *Forschungen zur Deutschen Geschichte,* pages 471-475. Edited by Winkelmann, Eduard (1878).

Necrologio del Liber Confratrum di San Matteo di Salerno. Edited by Garufi, Carlo Alberto (1922).

Necrologium Liciense, in *Forschungen zur Deutschen Geschichte,* pages 476-477. Edited by Winkelmann, Eduard (1878).

Necrologium Salernitanum, in *Forschungen zur Deutschen Geschichte,* page 475. Edited by Winkelmann, Eduard (1878).

Nicetae Choniatae Historia. Edited by Bekker, Immanuel (1835).

Ottonis de Sancto Blasio Chronica, in the *Scriptores Rerum Germanicarum* series. Edited by Hofmeister, Adolf (1912).

Patent Rolls of the Reign of Henry III, volume 1 (1216-1225), volume 3 (1232-1247). Edited by Lyte, Henry Maxwell (1901, 1906).

Patrologiae Cursus Completus, series 2, book 214. Edited by Migne, Jacques Paul (1855).

Petri Blesensis Opera Omnia (volume 1), Letters of Peter of Blois. Giles, John (1847).

Petri de Vineis Friderici II Imperatoris Epistolarum (2 volumes), Letters of Peter della Vigna. Edited by Iselin, Johann Rudolf (1740).

The Rare and Excellent History of Saladin. Translation. Richards, Donald (2002).

De Rebus Gestis Rogerii Calabriae et Siciliae Comitis et Roberti Guiscardi Ducis Fratris Eius of Godfrey Malaterra, *Rerum Italicarum Scriptores,* volume 5, part 1. Pontieri, Ernesto (1928).

Recueil des Historiens des Croisades - Historiens Occidentaux, 5 volumes (1844-1895).

Recueil des Historiens des Gaul el de la France, 19 volumes. Edited by Brial, Michel Jean (1878).

Regesto dei Marchesi di Saluzzo 1091-1340. Edited by Tallone, Armando (1906).

SOURCES AND BIBLIOGRAPHY

Registro della Cancelleria 1239-1240. Carcani, Gaetano (1786).

Le Rime della Scuola Siciliana, volume 1. Compilation and translations by Panvini, Bruno (1962).

Robert the Monk's History of the First Crusade: Iherosolimitana. Translation. Sweetenham, Carol (2006).

The Annals of Roger de Hoveden (2 volumes). Translation. Riley, Henry (1853).

Roger of Wendover's Flowers of History (2 volumes). Translation. Giles, John (1849).

Rogerii II Regis Diplomata Latina (Codex Diplomaticus Regni Siciliae), Diplomata Regum et Principum e Gente Normannorum (series 1). Brühl, Carlrichard (1987).

Rollus Rubeus: Privilegia Ecclesie Cephaleditane, a Diversis Regis et Imperatoribus Concessa, Recollecta et in hoc Volumine Scripta. Mirto, Corrado (1972).

Royal and Other Historical Letters Illustrative of the Reign of Henry III (2 volumes). Compilation by Shirley, Walter (1862).

Scriptores Rerum Brunsvicensium, volume 3. Leibnitz, Gottfried (1711).

Select Charters and Other Illustrations of English Constitutional History (eighth edition). Compilation. Stubbs, William (1905).

Sicily's Rebellion against King Charles: The Story of the Sicilian Vespers. Translation and notes of the *Rebellamentu* of John of Procida. Mendola, Louis (2015).

Suite de la Troisieme Croisade, in *Bibliotheque des Croisades (Chroniques Arabes),* volume 4. Edited by Michaud, Joseph (1829).

Tabulario di San Filippo di Fragalà e Santa Maria di Maniace. Silvestri, Giuseppe (1887).

Tabularium Regiae et Imperialis Cappellae Collegiatae Divi Petri in Regio Palermitano Palatio. Garofalo, Luigi (1835).

Tancredi et Willelmi III Regum Diplomata, in *Codex Diplomaticus Regni Siciliae,* series 1, volume 5. Zielinski, Herbett (1982).

The Life and Letters of Thomas à Becket (2 volumes). Documents in translation. Giles, John (1846).

St Thomas of Canterbury: An Account of His Life and Fame from the Contemporary Biographers and other Chroniclers. Hutton, William (1899).

The Travels of Ibn Jubayr. Broadhurst, Ronald (1952, 2008).

Urkunden und Kanzlei der Kaiserin Konstanze, Königin von Sizilien 1195-1198, in *Monumenta Germaniae Historica,* volume 6, part 3. Compiled by Kölzer, Theo (1983).

Vita Sancti Thomae by William Fitzstephen and Herbert of Bosham, in *Materials for the History of Thomas Becket,* volume 3 (see above).

The History of William of Newburgh and the Chronicles of Robert de Monte in *The Church Historians of England: Pre-Reformation Period.* Edited by Stevenson, Joseph (1856).

The Winchester Chronicle, in *Annales Monastici,* volume 2. Edited by Luard, Henry (1865), pages 3-128.

The World of El Cid: Chronicles of the Spanish Reconquest (2000); includes the *Chronicon Regum Legionensium,* or *Liber Chronicorum,* of Pelayo of Oviedo. Translation by Barton, Simon and Fletcher, Richard.

L'Ystoire de li Normant of Amatus of Montecassino. *Storia dei Normanni.* Parallel French/Italian text. Tamburrini, Alberto (1999).

Secondary Literature

Abulafia, David. "The Crown and the Economy under Roger II and his Successors," *Dumbarton Oaks Papers,* number 37 (Washington DC, 1983), pages 1-14.

Abulafia, David. *Frederick II: A Medieval Emperor* (1988).

Abulafia, David. *A Mediterranean Emporium: The Catalan Kingdom of Majorca* (1994).

Abulafia, David. *The Two Italies: Economic Relations Between the Norman Kingdom of Sicily and the Northern Communes* (1977).

Abun-Nasr, Jamil. *A History of the Maghrib in the Islamic Period* (1987).

Accascina, Maria. *Oreficeria di Sicilia dal XII al XIX Secolo* (1974).

Acton, Harold. *The Bourbons of Naples* (1965); *The Last Bourbons of Naples* (1961).

SOURCES AND BIBLIOGRAPHY

Agius, Dionisius. *Siculo Arabic* (1996).
Agnello, Giuseppe. *L'Architettura Sveva in Sicilia* (1935).
Ahmad, Aziz. *A History of Islamic Sicily* (1975).
Alio, Jacqueline. *Margaret, Queen of Sicily* (2016).
Amari, Michele. *Biblioteca Arabo-Sicula* (1880).
Amari, Michele. *La Guerra del Vespro Siciliano* (1876).
Amari, Michele. *Un Periodo delle Istorie Siciliane del Secolo XIII* (1842).
Amari, Michele. *Storia dei Musulmani di Sicilia* (1854).
Amico, Vito. *Dizionario Topografico della Sicilia* (1859).
Amundsen, Darrel, and Diers, Carol Jean. "The Age of Menarche in Medieval Europe," *Human Biology*, number 45, volume 3 (Detroit 1973), pages 363-369.
Angeli Murzaku, Ines, and Crostini, Barbara. *Greek Monasticism in Southern Italy: The Life of Neilos in Context* (2017).
Arbel, Benjamin, et al. *Latins and Greeks in the Eastern Mediterranean after 1204* (1989).
Arblaster, Paul. *A History of the Low Countries*, second edition (2012).
Ardizzone, Maria Luisa, et al. *Dante as Political Theorist: Reading Monarchia* (2018).
Backman, Clifford. *The Decline and Fall of Medieval Sicily: Politics, Religion and Economy in the Reign of Frederick III, 1296-1337* (1995).
Bagehot, Walter. *The English Constitution* (second edition, 1872).
Barber, Malcolm. *The Crusader States* (2012).
Barber, Richard. *Henry Plantagenet* (1964).
Barlow, Frank. "Roger of Howden," *The English Historical Review*, volume 65, number 256 (July 1950), pages 352-360.
Bates, David, et al. *People, Texts and Artefacts: Cultural Transmission in the Medieval Norman Worlds* (2017).
Bates, David. "The Representation of Queens and Queenship in Anglo-Norman Royal Charters," *Frankland: The Franks and the World of the Early Middle Ages* (2008).
Bates, David, and Crick, Julia (editors). *Writing Medieval Biography 750-1250: Essays in Honour of Professor Frank Barlow* (2006).
Beckwith, John. *Early Christian and Byzantine Art* (1979).
Beihammer, Alexander. "Defection across the Border of Islam and Christianity: Apostasy and Cross-Cultural Interaction in Byzantine-Seljuk Relations," *Speculum*, volume 86, number 3 (July 2011), pages 597-651.
Bellafiore, Giuseppe. *La Zisa di Palermo* (1994).
Bennett, Judith, and Karras, Ruth (editors). *The Oxford Handbook of Women and Gender in Medieval Europe* (2013).
Berg, Beverly. "Manfred of Sicily and Urban IV: Negotiations of 1262"

Mediaeval Studies (the journal of the Pontifical Institute of Mediaeval Studies, Toronto), volume 55 (1993), pages 111-136.

Blud, Victoria. *The Unspeakable, Gender and Sexuality in Medieval Literature 1000-1400* (2017).

Bordone, Renata. "Il 'Famosissimo Marchese Bonifacio,' Spunti per una storia degli Aleramici detti del Vasto," *Bollettino Storico-bibliografico Subalpino,* volume 81 (1983), pages 586-602.

Bowie, Colette. *The Daughters of Henry II and Eleanor of Aquitaine: A Comparative Study of Twelfth-century Women* (2014).

Bowie, Colette. "To Have and Have Not: The Dower of Joanna Plantagenet, Queen of Sicily," *Queenship in the Mediterranean: Negotiating the Role of the Queen in the Medieval and Early Modern Eras* (2013), pages 27-50.

Bradbury, Jim. *The Routledge Companion to Medieval Warfare* (2004).

Brand, Charles. "The Byzantines and Saladin 1185-1192: Opponents of the Third Crusade," *Speculum,* volume 37, number 2 (April 1962), pages 167-181.

Brandileone, Francesco. *Il Diritto Romano nelle Leggi Normanne e Sveve del Regno di Sicilia* (1884).

Brantl, Markus. "Itinerar und Regesten Manfreds 1250-1266," in *Studien zum Urkunden und Kanzleiwesen König Manfreds von Sizilien*, pages 226-448 (2005).

Bresc, Henri. *Palermo al Tempo dei Normanni* (2012).

Brown, Virginia. *Giovanni Boccaccio: Famous Women* (2003).

Brühl, Carlrichard. *Urkunden und Kanzlei König Rogers II von Sizilien* (1978).

Bubola, Emma. "Locker-room talks: Italian politics and normalized sexism," *Al Jazeera,* 11 March 2018.

Bucaria, Nicolò. *Sicilia Judaica: Guida alle Antichità Giudaiche della Sicilia* (1996).

Bucaria, Nicolò, and Cassuto, David. "La Sinagoga e i Miqweh di Palermo alla Luce dei Documenti e delle Scoperte Archeologiche," *Archivio Storico Siciliano,* Series 4, Volume 31 (Palermo 2005), pages 171-209.

Bucher, Michael. "Re-Discovering the Italian Kingdom of the Two Sicilies," *Time* (USA), 25 August 2016.

Buchthal, Hugo. "The Beginnings of Manuscript Illumination in Norman Sicily," *Papers of the British School at Rome,* volume 24 (London, November 1956), pages 78-85.

Bucossi, Alessandra, et al. *John Komnenos, Emperor of Byzantium: In the Shadow of Father and Son* (2016).

Burkhardt, Stefan, et al. *Norman Tradition and Transcultural Heritage: Exchange of Cultures in the "Norman" Peripheries of Medieval Europe* (2013).

Buscemi, Niccolò. *La Vita di Giovanni di Procida, Privata e Pubblica* (1836).

Cahen, Claude. *Le Régime Féodal de l'Italie Normande* (1940).

Catel, Guillaume. *Histoire des Comtes de Tolose* (1623).

Catlos, Brian. *Muslims of Medieval Latin Christendom c. 1050-1614* (2014).
Campbell, Ian. *The Addis Ababa Massacre: Italy's National Shame* (2017).
Canning, Joseph. *A History of Medieval Political Thought 300-1450* (1996).
Caperna, Umberto. *Cronaca Santa Maria della Ferraria* (2008).
Caravale, Mario. "La Feudalità nella Sicilia Normanna," *Atti del Congresso Internazionale di Studi sulla Sicilia Normanna* (Palermo 1974), pages 21-50.
Carey, Hilary. *Courting Disaster: Astrology at the English Court and University in the Later Middle Ages* (1992).
Caruso, Stefano. "Echi della Polemica Bizantina Antilatina dell' XI-XII Secoli nel *De Oeconomia Dei* di Nilo Doxapatres," *Atti del Congresso Internazionale di Studi sulla Sicilia Normanna* (Palermo 1974), pages 403-432.
Caspar, Erich. *Roger II und die Gründung der Normannische-sicilischen Monarchie* (1904).
Chalandon, Ferdinand. *Histoire de la Domination Normande en Italie et en Sicile* (Paris 1907).
Chappuys, Gabriel. *L'Historie du Royaume de Navarre* (1616).
Chaytor, Henry. *A History of Aragon and Catalonia* (1933).
Chiarelli, Leonard. *A History of Muslim Sicily, Second Edition* (2018).
Chiarelli, Leonard. "The Ibadi Communities in Muslim Sicily," *Ibadi Jurisprudence: Origins, Development and Cases*, in the series *Studies on Ibadism and Oman*, volume 6 (2015), pages 159-166.
Chibnall, Marjorie. *The Empress Matilda: Queen Consort, Queen Mother, and Lady of the English* (1991).
Chibnall, Marjorie. *Piety, Power and History in Medieval England and Normandy* (2000).
Cilento, Adele and Routt, David. "Foundation of a Monastery in Byzantine Calabria 1053/54" *Medieval Italy: Texts in Translation* (2009), pages 506-507.
Clarke, Peter, and Duggan, Anne (editors). *Pope Alexander III 1159-1181: The Art of Survival* (2012).
Cobb, Paul. *The Race for Paradise: An Islamic History of the Crusades* (2014).
Collins, Roger. *The Basques* (1990).
Collura, Paolo. *Le Più Antiche Carte dell'Archivio Capitolare di Agrigento 1092-1282* (1961).
Columba, Gaetano. "Note di Topografia Medievale Palermitana," *Archivio Storico Siciliano* (Palermo 1910), pages 325-350.
Conti, Emanuele. "L'Abbazia della Matina," *Archivio Storico per la Calabria*, volume 35 (Rome 1967), pages 11-30.
Coulton, George. *From St Francis to Dante: Translations from the Chronicle of the Franciscan Salimbene 1221-1288* (1907).
Crook, David, et al. *The Growth of Royal Government Under Henry III* (2015).

Crouch, David. *The Birth of Nobility: Constructing the Aristocracy in England and France 900-1300* (2005).
Crouch, David. *William Marshal: Knighthood, War and Chivalry 1147-1219* (2002).
Cuozzo, Errico. *Catalogus Baronum: Commentario* (1984).
D'Angelo, Edoardo. *Pseudo Ugo Falcando: De Rebus circa Regni Siciliae Curiam Gestis* (2014).
Davanzati, Domenico Forges. *Dissertazione sulla Seconda Moglie del Re Manfredi e sù Loro Figliuoli (*1791).
Davies, Norman. *Vanished Kingdoms* (2012).
De Fazio, Laura, "Criminalization of stalking in Italy: One of the last among the current European member states' anti-stalking laws," *Behavioral Sciences and the Law,* volume 29, issue 2 (March 2011), pages 317-323.
De Leemans, Pieter, et al. *Translating at Court: Bartholomew of Messina and Cultural Life at the Court of Manfred, King of Sicily* (2014).
De Sassenay, Fernand. *Les Brienne de Lecce et d'Athènes* (1869).
Deér, Josef. *The Dynastic Porphyry Tombs of the Norman Period in Sicily* (1959).
Del Giudice, Giuseppe. *La Famiglia di Re Manfredi* (1896).
Delogu, Paolo. *I Normanni in Italia: Cronache della Conquista e del Regno* (1984).
Demus, Otto. *The Mosaics of Norman Sicily* (1950).
Di Cesare, Giuseppe. *Storia di Manfredi Re di Sicilia e di Puglia* (1837).
Geanakoplos, Deno John. *Emperor Michael Palaeologus and the West 1258-1282: A Study in Byzantine-Latin Relations* (1959).
Di Giovanni, Vincenzo. "Appendice alla Topografia Antica di Palermo," *Archivio Storico Siciliano* (Palermo 1899), pages 379-396.
Di Giovanni, Vincenzo. "Il Quartiere degli Schiavoni nel Secolo X," *Archivio Storico Siciliano* (Palermo 1887), pages 40-64.
Di Giovanni, Vincenzo. *La Topografia Antica di Palermo dal Secolo X al XV* (1890).
Domínguez Fernandez, Enrique, and Larrambebere Zabal, Miguel. *García Ramírez el Restaurador 1134-1150* (1986).
Donadio, Rachel. "The Missing Piece in Italian Politics: Women," *The Atlantic* (Washington DC, 10 March 2018).
Donovan, Joseph. *Pelagius and the Fifth Crusade* (1950).
Drell, Joanna. *Kinship and Conquest: Family Strategies in the Principality of Salerno during the Norman Period 1077-1194* (2002).
Duggan, Anne. *Queens and Queenship in Medieval Europe: Proceedings of a Conference Held at King's College, London, April 1995* (1997).
Duggan, Anne. *Thomas Becket* (2004).
Dujcev, Ivan. "I Normanni e l'Oriente Bizantino," *Atti del Congresso Internazionale di Studi sulla Sicilia Normanna* (Palermo 1974), pages 105-131.

Dunbabin, Jean. *Charles I of Anjou: Power, Kingship and State-Making in Thirteenth-Century Europe* (1998).
Dunbabin, Jean. *The French in the Kingdom of Sicily 1266-1305* (2011).
Eads, Valerie. "Sichelgaita of Salerno: Amazon or Trophy Wife?" *Journal of Medieval Military History*, volume 3 (2005), pages 72-87.
Earenfight, Theresa, "Highly Visible, Often Obscured: The Difficulty of Seeing Queens and Noble Women," *Medieval Feminist Forum*, volume 44, issue 1 (2008), pages 86-90.
Earenfight, Theresa. *Queenship in Medieval Europe* (2013).
Earenfight, Theresa, "Without the Persona of the Prince: Kings, Queens and the Idea of Monarchy in Late Medieval Europe," *Gender and History*, volume 19, number 1 (2007), pages 1-21.
Edbury, Peter. *The Conquest of Jerusalem and the Third Crusade: Sources in Translation* (1998).
Egidi, Pietro. *La Colonia Saracena di Lucera e la Sua Distruzione* (1912).
Elze, Reinhard. "Tre Ordines per l'Incoronazione di un Re e di una Regina del Regno Normanno in Sicilia," *Atti del Congresso Internazionale di Studi sulla Sicilia Normanna* (Palermo 1974), pages 438-459.
Elze, Reinhard. "The Ordo for the Coronation of King Roger II of Sicily: An Example of Dating from Internal Evidence," *Coronations: Medieval and Early Modern Monarchic Ritual* (1990), pages 165-178.
Enzensberger, Horst. "Il Documento Regio come Strumento del Potere," *Potere, Società e Popolo nell'Età dei Due Guglielmi* (Bari 1981), pages 104-138.
Enzensberger, Horst. "Chanceries, Charters and Administration in Norman Sicily," *The Society of Norman Italy* (Leiden 2002), pages 117-150.
Epifanio, Vincenzo. "Ruggero II e Filippo di Al Mahdiah," *Archivio Storico Siciliano* (Palermo 1905), pages 471-501.
Epstein, Stephan. *An Island for Itself: Economic Development and Social Change in Late Medieval Sicily* (2003).
Evans, Michael. *Inventing Eleanor: The Medieval and Post-Medieval Image of Eleanor of Aquitaine* (2014).
Eyton, Robert William. *Court, Household and Itinerary of King Henry II, Instancing also the Chief Agents and Adversaries of the King in his Government, Diplomacy and Strategy* (1878).
von Falkenhausen, Vera. "Zur Regentschaft der Gräfin Adelasia del Vasto in Kalabrien und Sizilien 1101-1112," *AETOS: Studies in Honor of Cyril Mango Presented to Him on April 14, 1998* (Stuttgart 1998), pages 87-115.
Fazello, Thomas. *De Rebus Siculus* (1558-1560).
Fernandez Perez, Gregorio. *Historia de la Iglesia y Obispos de Pamplona* (1820).

Fletcher, Richard. *The Quest for El Cid* (1991).
Flori, Jean. *Eleanor of Aquitaine: Queen and Rebel* (English edition, 2007).
Fodale, Salvatore. *Comes et Legatus Siciliae: Sul privilegio di Urbano II e la pretesa Apostolica Legazia dei Normanni in Sicilia* (1970).
Frascadore, Angela. "Le Badesse del Monastero di San Giovanni Evangelista di Lecce," *Tancredi Conte di Lecce Re di Sicilia* (2004), pages 233-286.
Freed, John. *Frederick Barbarossa: The Prince and the Myth* (2016).
Fried, Johannes. *Charlemagne* (2016).
Fröhlich, Walter. "The Marriage of Henry VI and Constance of Sicily: Prelude and Consequences," *Anglo Norman Studies 15* (1993), pages 99-125.
Fuhrmann, Horst. *Germany in the High Middle Ages c. 1050-1200* (1986).
Fuiano, Michele. "La Fondazione del *Regnum Siciliae* nella Versione di Alessandro di Telese," *Papers of the British School at Rome*, volume 24 (London, November 1956), pages 65-77.
Gabrieli, Francesco. "Ibn Hawqal e gli Arabi in Sicilia," *L'Islam nella Storia: Saggi di storia e storiografia musulmana* (1966), pages 57-67.
Garufi, Carlo Alberto. "Monete e Conii nella Storia del Diritto Siculo dagli Arabi ai Martini," *Archivio Storico Siciliano* (Palermo 1898), pages 11-171.
Gelin, Marie-Pierre, et al. *The Cult of Saint Thomas Becket in the Plantagenet World c. 1170-c.1220* (2016).
Giordano, Nicola. "Nuovo Contributo alla Determinazione dei Rapporti tra Stato e Chiesa in Sicilia al Tempo dei Normanni," *Archivio Storico Siciliano* (Palermo 1916), pages 25-48.
Giuffrida, Angela. "Italy's highest court accused of victim blaming over rape case," *The Guardian* (London, 17 July 2018).
Giunta, Francesco. *Bizanti e Bizantinismo nella Sicilia Normanna* (1950).
Giunta, Francesco. "Federico II e Ferdinando III di Castiglia," *Papers of the British School at Rome*, volume 24 (London, November 1956), pages 137-141.
Goldstone, Nancy, *Joanna: The Notorious Queen of Naples, Jerusalem and Sicily* (2011).
Goodman, Jennifer. *Medieval England and Iberia: A Chivalric Relationship* (2007).
Goskar, Tehmina. "Material Worlds: The Shared Cultures of Southern Italy and Its Mediterranean Neighbours in the Tenth to Twelfth Centuries," *Al-Masaq: Journal of the Medieval Mediterranean*, volume 23, issue 3 (London 2011), pages 189-204.
Granara, William. "Ibn Hawqal in Sicily," *Alif: Journal of Comparative Poetics*, number 3, (Cairo, 1983), pages 94-99.
Grant, Lindy. *Blanche of Castile, Queen of France* (2016).
Grassotti, Hilda. "Homenaje de García Ramírez a Alfonso VII dos Documentos Ineditos," *Principe de Viana*, volume 25 (number 94-95), 1964, pages 57-66.

Green, Mary Ann Everett. *Lives of the Princesses of England from the Norman Conquest,* volumes 1 and 2 (1850).
Green, Monica. "Medicine in Southern Italy, Twelfth-Fourteenth Centuries: Six Texts," *Medieval Italy: Texts in Translation* (2009), pages 311-327.
Grillo, Paolo. *L'Aquila e il Giglio: La Battaglia di Benevento* (2015).
Gross, Thomas. *Lothar III und die Mathildischen Güter* (1990).
Grossi, Giovanni Battista. *Catana Sacra* (1654).
Hamilton, Bernard. "Women in the Crusader States: The Queens of Jerusalem 1100-1190," *Studies in Church History: Medieval Women* (Oxford 1978), pages 143-174.
Hanley, Catherine. *Louis: The French Prince Who Invaded England* (2016).
Harris, Carolyn. *1000 Years of Royal Parenting* (2017).
Haskins, Charles Homer. "England and Sicily in the Twelfth Century," *English Historical Review,* volume 26 (July 1911), pages 432-447, 641-665.
Haskins, Charles Homer. "Michael Scot and Frederick II," *Isis,* volume 4, number 2 (1921), pages 250-275.
Haskins, Charles Homer. "Science at the Court of Frederick II," *American Historical Review,* volume 27, number 4 (July 1922), pages 669-694.
Haskins, Charles Homer. "The Sicilian Translators of the Twelfth Century and the First Latin Version of Ptolemy's Almagest," *Harvard Studies in Classical Philology,* volume 21 (1910), pages 75-102.
Haverkamp, Alfred. *Medieval Germany 1056-1273.* Translation (1992).
Herrin, Judith. *Byzantium: The Surprising Life of a Medieval Empire* (2009).
Herrin, Judith. *Unrivalled Influence: Women and Empire in Byzantium* (2013).
Hildt, John. "The Ministry of Stephen of Perche During the Minority of William II of Sicily," *Smith College Studies in History,* number 3 (April 1918).
Hill, Barbara. *Imperial Women in Byzantium 1025-1204: Power, Patronage and Ideology* (1999).
Hilton, Lisa. *England's Medieval Queens* (2010).
Hines, Melissa. *Brain Gender* (2005).
Hodgson, Natasha. "Nobility, Women and Historical Narratives of the Crusades and the Latin East," *Al-Masaq: Journal of the Medieval Mediterranean,* volume 17, issue 1 (London 2005), pages 61-85.
Hoffmann, Hartmut. "Die Anfänge der Normannen in Süditalien" *Quellen und Forschungen aus Italienischen Arxhiven un Bibliotheken,* number 49 (Tübingen 1969), pages 95-144.
Holmes, George. *The Oxford History of Medieval Europe* (1988).
Hood, Gwenyth. "Falcandus and Fulcaudus Epistola ad Petrum liber de Regno Sicilie: Literary Form and Author's Identity," *Studi Medievali* (June 1999), 3rd Series, XL, pages 1-41.

Horowitz, Jason. "In Italy, #MeToo is More Like 'Meh'" in *The New York Times* (New York, 16 December 2017).
Houben, Hubert. "Adelaide 'del Vasto' nella Storia del Regno di Sicilia," *Itinerari di Ricerca Storica,* number 4 (Lecce 1990), pages 9-40.
Houben, Hubert. *Roger II von Sizilien* (1997).
Houben, Hubert, and Vetere, Benedetto. *Tancredi Conte di Lecce Re di Sicilia* (2004).
Hoving, Thomas. "A Newly Discovered Reliquary of St Thomas Becket," *Gesta,* volume 4, spring 1965 (New York 1965), pages 28-30.
Howard-Johnston, James. "The Chronicle and Other Forms of Historical Writing in Byzantium," *The Medieval Chronicle,* number 10 (Leiden 2015), pages 1-22.
Howell, Margaret. *Eleanor of Provence: Queenship in Thirteenth-Century England* (1998).
Hudson, Richard. "The Judicial Reforms of the Reign of Henry II," *Michigan Law Review,* volume 9, number 5 (Ann Arbor 1911), pages 385-395.
de Huesca, Ramon. *Teatro Historico de las Iglesias del Reyno de Aragón* (1785).
Hurlburt, Holly. "Women, Gender and Rulership in Medieval Italy," *History Compass,* volume 4, number 3 (2006), pages 528-535.
Hurlock, Kathryn, and Oldfield, Paul, et al. *Crusading and Pilgrimage in the Norman World* (2015).
Ingraiti, Gaetano. "Sulla Legittimità della Legazia Apostolica in Sicilia," *Atti del Congresso Internazionale di Studi sulla Sicilia Normanna* (Palermo 1974), pages 460-466.
Jaeger, Pier Giusto. *L'Ultimo Re di Napoli* (1982).
Jamison, Evelyn. A*dmiral Eugenius of Sicily: His Life and Work and Authorship of the Epistola ad Petrum and the Historia Hugonis Falcandi Siculi* (London 1957).
Jamison, Evelyn. "Alliance of England and Sicily in the Second Half of the Twelfth Century," *Journal of the Warburg and Courtauld Institutes,* volume 6 (London 1943), pages 20-32.
Jamison, Evelyn. "Judex Tarentinus: The Career of Judex Tarentinus *Magne Curie Justiciarius* and the Emergence of the Sicilian *Regalis Magna Curia* under William I and the Regency of Margaret of Navarre, 1156-72," *Proceedings of the British Academy,* volume I, iii (London 1968), pages 289-344.
Jensen, Frede. *The Poetry of the Sicilian School* (1986).
Jimeno Jurío, José María. *¿Dönde fue la batalla de Roncesvalles?* (1974).
Jimeno Jurío, José María. *Historia de Pamplona: Síntesis de una Evolución* (1974).
Johns, Jeremy. *Arabic Administration in Norman Sicily: The Royal Diwan* (2002).
Johns, Jeremy. "The Norman Kings of Sicily and the Fatimid Caliphate," *Anglo-Norman Studies XV* (1995), pages 133-159.

Johns, Jeremy. "Parchment versus Paper: Countess Adelaide's Bilingual Mandate of 1109," *Documenting Multiculturalism* (Oxford, November 2018).

Johns, Susan. *Noblewomen, Aristocracy and Power in the Twelfth-Century Anglo-Norman Realm* (2003).

Jones, Dan. *Magna Carta: The Birth of Liberty* (2016).

Joranson, Einar. "The Inception of the Career of the Normans in Italy: Legend and History," *Speculum*, volume 23, number 3 (July 1948), pages 353-396.

Jordan, Edouard. "La Politique Ecclésiastique de Roger I et les Origines de la Légation Sicilienne," *Le Moyen Age* (1922), volume 2, pages 237-273.

Jordan, Erin. *Women, Power and Religious Patronage in the Middle Ages* (2006).

Jordan, William, et al. *The Capetian Century 1214-1314* (2017).

Kantorowicz, Ernst. *Friedrich der Zweite* (1927).

Kapitaikin, Lev. "The Daughter of Al-Andalus: Interrelations between Norman Sicily and the Muslim West," *Al-Masaq: Journal of the Medieval Mediterranean*, volume 25, issue 1 (London 2013), pages 113-134.

Karras, Ruth. *Sexuality in Medieval Europe: Doing Unto Others* (2005).

Karst, August. *Geschichte Manfreds vom Tode Friedrichs II bis ze seiner Krönung 1250-1258* (1897).

Katz, Robert, *The Fall of the House of Savoy* (1972).

Kehr, Karl Andreas. "Ergänzungen zu Falco von Benevent," *Neues Archiv der Gesellschaft für ältere deutsche Geschichtskunde*, number 27 (Hannover and Leipzig, 1902), pages 445-472.

Kelly, Amy. "Eleanor of Aquitaine and Her Courts of Love," *Speculum*, volume 12, number 1 (January 1937), pages 3-17.

King, Edmund, et al. *The Anarchy of King Stephen's Reign* (1994).

Kitzinger, Ernst. "The Mosaics of the Cappella Palatina in Palermo," *Art Bulletin*, number 31 (New York 1949), pages 290-319.

Kitzinger, Ernst and Curcic, Slobodan. *The Mosaics of St Mary's of the Admiral in Palermo* (1990).

Kreutz, Barbara. *Before the Normans: Southern Italy in the Ninth and Tenth Centuries* (1996).

Krönig, Wolfgang. "Sul Significato Storico dell'Arte sotto i Due Guglielmi," *Potere, Società e Popolo nell'Età dei Due Guglielmi* (Bari 1981), pages 292-310.

Lachmann, Karl. *Die Gedichte Walthers von der Vogelweide, Herausgegeben* (1827).

La Corte, Giorgio. "Appunti di Toponomastica sul Territorio della Chiesa di Monreale nel Secolo XII," *Archivio Storico Siciliano* (Palermo 1902), pages 336-345.

La Grua, Gregorio. *La Corona di Costanza di Aragona Regina di Sicilia* (1988).

Madden, Thomas. "The Venetian Version of the Fourth Crusade: Memory and the Conquest of Constantinople in Medieval Venice," *Speculum,* volume 87, number 2 (April 2012), pages 311-344.

La Mantia, Giuseppe. "Su l'Uso della Registrazione nella Cancelleria del Regno di Sicilia dai Normanni a Federico III d'Aragona 1130-1377," *Archivio Storico Siciliano* (Palermo 1908), pages 197-209.

La Mantia, Giuseppe. "Su gli Studi di Topografia Palermitana del Medio Evo e su la Fonte detta dagli Arabi Ayb-Rum," *Archivio Storico Siciliano* (Palermo 1917), pages 317-357.

Landon, Lionel. *The Itinerary of King Richard I, with Studies on Certain Matters of Interest Connected with his Reign* (1935).

Langley, Ernest. *The Poetry of Giacomo da Lentino, Sicilian Poet of the Thirteenth Century* (1915).

Larner, John. *Italy in the Age of Dante and Petrarch 1216-1380* (1983).

La Via, Mariano. "Le Così Dette 'Colonie Lombarde' in Sicilia," *Archivio Storico Siciliano* (Palermo 1899), pages 1-35.

Lello, Giovanni Luigi. *Descrizione del Real Tempio di Santa Maria Nuova di Monreale* (1702).

Levtzion, Nehemia. "Ibn-Hawqal, the Cheque, and Awdaghost," *Journal of African History,* volume 9, number 2 (Cambridge 1968), pages 223-233.

Lewis, Matthew. *Henry III: The Son of Magna Carta* (2016).

Licinio, Raffaele. *Castelli Medievali: Puglia e Basilicata dai Normanni a Federico II e Carlo d'Angio* (1994).

Lieberman, Max. "A New Approach to the Knighting Ritual," *Speculum,* volume 90, number 2 (April 2015), pages 391-423.

Lipinsky, Angelo. "Le Insegne Regali dei Sovrani di Sicilia e la Scuola Orafa Palermitana," *Atti del Congresso Internazionale di Studi sulla Sicilia Normanna* (Palermo 1974), pages 162-194.

Lipinsky, Angelo. "Sicaniae Regni Corona: Il Kamelaukion detta Cuffia di Costanza nel Tesoro del Duomo di Palermo," *Bizantino-Sicula II: Miscellanea di Scritti in Memoria di Giuseppe Rossi Taibbi* (Palermo 1975), pages 347-370.

Loewenthal, Leonard Joseph Alphonse. "For the Biography of Walter Ophamil Archbishop of Palermo," *English Historical Review,* volume 87 (January 1972), pages 75-82.

Loud, Graham. "The Chancery and Charters of the Kings of Sicily 1130-1212, *English Historical Review,* volume 124, number 509 (August 2009), pages 779-810.

Loud, Graham. "The Image of the Tyrant in the Work of 'Hugo Falcandus,'" *Nottingham Medieval Studies,* Number 57 (January 2013), pages 1-20.

Loud, Graham. "The Genesis and Context of the Chronicle of Falco of Benevento," *Anglo-Norman Studies IV: Proceedings of the Battle Conference 1992* (1993).
Loud, Graham. "History Writing in the Twelfth-Century Kingdom of Sicily," *Chronicling History: Chroniclers and Historians in Medieval and Renaissance Italy* (2007).
Loud, Graham. *The Latin Church in Norman Italy* (2007).
Loud, Graham. *Roger II and the Creation of the Kingdom of Sicily* (2012).
Louda, Jiri and Maclagan, Michael. *Heraldry of the Royal Families of Europe* (1988). Also published as *Lines of Succession*.
Lourie, Elena. "The Will of Alfonso I 'El Batallador,' King of Aragon and Navarre: A Reassessment," *Speculum,* volume 50, number 4 (October 1975), pages 635-651.
Lucas-Avenel, Marie-Agnés. "Le récit de Geoffroi Malaterra ou la légitimation de Roger, grand comte de Sicile," *Anglo-Norman Studies 34: Proceedings of the Battle Conference* (2012), pages 169-192.
Lupo, Carmelina. "I Normanni di Sicilia di Fronte al Papato," *Archivio Storico Siciliano per la Sicilia Orientale,* volume 20 (Catania 1924), pages 1-74.
Magdalino, Paul. *The Empire of Manuel I Komnenos 1143-1180* (1993).
Makdisi, John. "The Islamic Origins of the Common Law," *North Carolina Law Review,* volume 77, number 5, June 1999, pages 1635-1737.
Mallette, Karla. *The Kingdom of Sicily 1100-1250: A Literary History* (2005).
Mangieri, Cono Antonio. *Il Contrasto di Cielo d'Alcamo: Introduzione, testo manoscritto e diplomatico, testo critico-congetturale, traduzione e note* (2005).
Marongiù, Antonio. "La Legislazione Normanna," *Atti del Congresso Internazionale di Studi sulla Sicilia Normanna* (Palermo 1974), pages 195-212.
Marongiù, Antonio. "Concezione della Sovranità di Ruggero II," *Atti del Convegno Internazionale di Studi Ruggeriani* (Palermo 1955), pages 195-212.
Martorana, Pierluigi. *La Monetazione Aurea in Sicilia* (2007).
Marvin, Laurence. *The Occitan War: A Military and Political History of the Albigensian Crusade 1209-1218* (2008).
Massetti, Marco. *Zoologia della Sicilia Araba e Normanna 827-1194* (2016).
Matthew, Donald. "The Chronicle of Romuald of Salerno" in *The Writing of History in the Middle Ages: Essays Presented to Richard William Southern* (Oxford 1981), pages 239-274.
Matthew, Donald. "Modern Study of the Norman Kingdom of Sicily," *Reading Medieval Studies,* volume 18 (1992), pages 34-56.
Matthew, Donald. *The Norman Kingdom of Sicily* (1992).
Maurici, Ferdinando. *Palermo Araba: Una sintesi dell'evoluzione urbanistica 831-1072* (2015).

Maurolico, Francesco. *Sicanicarum Rerum Compendium* (1562).
Mazzarese Fardella, Enrico. "La Condizione Giuridica della Donna nel Liber Augustalis" in *Archivio Storico Siciliano,* Series 4, Volume 21-22 (Palermo 1997).
Mazzarese Fardella, Enrico. "La Struttura Amministrativa del Regno Normanno," *Atti del Congresso Internazionale di Studi sulla Sicilia Normanna* (Palermo 1974), pages 213-224.
McCracken, Peggy. *The Romance of Adultery: Queenship and Sexual Transgression in Old French Literature* (1998).
Mendola, Louis. "English and Italian Legacy of the Norman Knight Figures of Monreale," *The Coat of Arms,* journal of The Heraldry Society, London, edited by John P. Brooke-Little, Norroy and Ulster King of Arms; NS Volume X, Number 166 (London 1994), pages 245-254 (a correction to a typesetting error appears in the next issue).
Mendola, Louis. *The Kingdom of Sicily 1130-1860* (2015).
Mendola, Louis. "Pre-Armorial Use of the Lion Passant Guardant and the Fleur-de-lis as Heraldic Badges in Norman Sicily," *The Coat of Arms,* journal of The Heraldry Society, London, edited by John P. Brooke-Little, Norroy and Ulster King of Arms; NS Volume X, Number 165 (London 1994), pages 210-212.
Menéndez Pidal, Ramón. *Cantar de Mio Cid: Texto, Gramática y Vocabulario* (1908).
Metcalfe, Alexander. *Muslims and Christians in Norman Sicily: Arabic Speakers and the End of Islam* (2011).
Metcalfe, Alexander. *The Muslims of Medieval Italy* (2009).
Meyendorff, John. *Orthodoxy and Catholicity* (1966).
Mielke, Christopher. "From Her Head to Her Toes: Gender-Bending Regalia in the Tomb of Constance of Aragon, Queen of Hungary and Sicily," *Royal Studies Journal,* volume 5, number 2 (2018), pages 49-62.
Millunzi, Gaetano. "Il Mosaicista Mastro Pietro Oddo ossia Restauri e Restauratori del Duomo di Monreale nel Secolo XVI," *Archivio Storico Siciliano* (Palermo 1890), pages 195-251.
Millunzi, Gaetano. *Il Tesoro, la Biblioteca ed il Tabulario della Chiesa di Santa Maria Nuova in Monreale: Studi e Documenti* (1904).
Molé, Noelle. *Labor Disorders in Neoliberal Italy: Mobbing, Well-being and the Workplace* (Indiana University Press 2012), chapter 6 (The Sex of Mobbing), pages 138-149.
Morris, Marc. *King John: Treachery and Tyranny in Medieval England, The Road to Magna Carta* (2015).
Morrison, James Cotter. *The Life and Times of Saint Bernard, Abbot of Clairvaux* (1877).

Morrison, Susan Signe. *A Medieval Woman's Companion: Women's Lives in the European Middle Ages* (2016).
Morso, Salvadore. *Descrizione di Palermo Antico* (1827).
Morton, James. "A Byzantine Canon Law Scholar in Norman Sicily: Revisting Neilos Doxapatre's 'Order of the Patriarchal Thrones,'" *Speculum*, volume 92, number 3 (July 2017), pages 724-754.
Moshe, Gil. "The Jews in Sicily under Muslim Rule in the Light of Geniza Documents," *Italia Judaica 1* (1983), pages 87-134.
Mumelter, Maria Luise. *Irene von Byzanz*, University of Innsbruck (1936); Universitäts und Landesbibliothek Tirol, C87782809.
Naro, Massimo. *Gloria di Cristo: I Mosaici del Duomo di Monreale* (2006).
Nef, Annliese. *Conquérir et Gouverner: La Sicile Islamique aux XIe et XIIe Siècles* (2011).
Nelson, Lynn. "Rotrou of Perche and the Aragonese Reconquest," *Traditio*, number 26 (New York 1970), pages 113-133.
Neville, Leonora. *Anna Komnene: The Life and Work of a Medieval Historian* (2016).
Niccolini, Giovanni Battista. *Storia della Casa di Svevia in Italia* (1873).
Norwich, John Julius. *The Kingdom in the Sun 1130-1194* (London 1970).
Oeillet des Murs, Marc-Athanase. *Historie des Comtes du Perche de la Famille des Rotrou de 943 a 1234* (1856).
Oldfield, Paul. *City and Community in Norman Italy* (2009).
Omodei, Filoteo. "La Versione Italiana della Historia di Ugo Falcando," *Archivio Storico Siciliano* (Palermo 1898), pages 465-477.
Orlando, Diego. *Il Feudalismo in Sicilia* (1847).
Palmarocchi, Roberto. "Sul Feudo Normanno," *Studi Storici* (Pavia 1912), pages 349-376.
Paoli, Sebastiano. *Codice Diplomatico del Sacro Militare Ordine Gerosolimitano, oggi di Malta* (1733).
Paratore, Ettore. "Esame delle Varianti dei Codici Vaticano e Cassinense delle Leggi," *Atti del Congresso Internazionale di Studi sulla Sicilia Normanna* (Palermo 1974), pages 477-479.
Parker, John. "The Attempted Byzantine Alliance with the Sicilian Norman Kingdom 1166-1167," *Papers of the British School at Rome*, volume 24 (London, November 1956), pages 86-93.
Parsons, John Carmi, et al. *Medieval Queenship* (1993).
Pavillon, Balthazar. *La Vie du Bienheureux Robert d'Arbrissel, Patriarche des Solitaires de la France et Instituteur de l'Ordre de Font-Evraud* (1666).
Pennington, Kenneth. "The Birth of the Ius Commune: King Roger II's Legislation," *Rivista Internazionale del Diritto Comune*, number 17 (Enna 2006).
Perla, Raffaele. *Le Assise de'Re di Sicilia* (1881).

Perry, Charles. *A Baghdad Cookery Book*. Translation of the *Kitab al-Tabikh* of Muhammad al Baghdadi (2009).
Perry, Guy. *John of Brienne: King of Jerusalem, Emperor of Constantinople* (2013).
Petacco Arrigo. *La Regina del Sud* (1992).
Pianigiani, Gaia. "Women Could Decide Italy's Election, but They Feel Invisible," *The New York Times* (New York, 3 March 2018).
Pick, Lucy. *Her Father's Daughter: Gender, Power and Religion in the Early Spanish Kingdoms* (2017).
Pieri, Piero. "I Saraceni di Lucera nella Storia Militare Medievale" *Atti del Terzo Congresso Storico Pugliese*, number 6 (1953), pages 94-101.
Pirri, Rocco. *Chronologia Regum Penes Quos Siciliae* (1643).
Pirri, Rocco, et al. *Sicilia Sacra Disquisitionibus et Notitiis Illustrata*, 4 volumes (1647).
Pispisa, Enrico. *Il Regno di Manfredi: Proposte di Interpretazioni* (1991).
Pontieri, Ernesto. "La madre di re Ruggero: Adelasia del Vasto, contessa di Sicilia, regina di Gerusalemme," *Atti del Covegno Internazionale di Studi Ruggeriani*, volume 1 (Palermo 1955), pages 327-432.
Poole, Reginald. *Medieval Reckonings of Time* (1918).
Powell, James. *Innocent III: Vicar of Christ or Lord of the World?* (1963).
Powell, James. *The Papacy, Frederick II, and Communal Devotion in Medieval Italy* (2014).
Quintana Prieto, Augusto. *La Documentation Pontificia de Innocencio IV 1243-1254* (1987).
Radici, Benedetto. "Il Casale e l'Abbazia di Santa Maria di Maniace," *Archivio Storico Siciliano* (Palermo 1909), pages 1-104.
Re, Edward. "The Roman Contribution to the Common Law," *Fordham Law Review*, number 447 (New York 1961), pages 447-494.
Reilly, Bernard. *The Kingdom of León-Castilla under Queen Urraca 1109-1126* (1982).
Reilly, Bernard. *The Kingdom of León-Castilla under King Alfonso VI 1065-1109* (1988).
Reilly, Bernard. *The Kingdom of León-Castilla under King Alfonso VII 1126-1157* (1998).
Resta, Gianvito. "La Cultura Siciliana dell'Età Normanna." *Atti del Congresso Internazionale di Studi sulla Sicilia Normanna* (Palermo 1974), pages 263-278.
Reston, James. *Warriors of God: Richard the Lionheart and Saladin in the Third Crusade* (2002).
Richardson, Henry Gerald. "The Letters and Charters of Eleanor of Aquitaine," *The English Historical Review*, volume 74, number 291 (April 1959), pages 193-213.
Riley-Smith, Jonathan. *The First Crusade and the Idea of Crusading* (1986).

Rizzitano, Umberto. "La Cultura Araba nella Sicilia Normanna," *Atti del Congresso Internazionale di Studi sulla Sicilia Normanna* (Palermo 1974), pages 279-297.
Rohlfs, Gerhard. *La Sicilia nei Secoli: Profilo Storico Etnico Linguistico* (1984).
Rohr, Zita Eva, and Benz, Lisa (editors). *Queenship, Gender and Reputation in the Medieval and Early Modern West 1060-1600* (2016).
Runciman, Steven. *Byzantine Civilisation* (1933, 1969).
Runciman, Steven. *The Eastern Schism: A Study of the Papacy and the Eastern Churches during the XIth and XIIth Centuries* (1955).
Runciman, Steven. *The Sicilian Vespers: A History of the Mediterranean World in the Later Thirteenth Century* (1958).
Runde, Ingo. "Konstanze von Aragon," *Die Kaiserinnen des Mittelalters* (2011), pages 232-248.
Ruffino, Giovanni, et al. *Lingue e Culture in Sicilia* (2013).
Russo, Rocco. *La Magione di Palermo negli Otto Secoli della Sua Storia* (1975).
Saini, Angela. *Inferior: How Science Got Women Wrong, and the New Research That's Rewriting the Story* (2017).
San Martino de Spucches, Francesco. *Storia dei Feudi e dei Titoli Nobiliari di Sicilia,* 10 volumes (1927).
Santoro, Rodolfo. "Architettura Castellana della Feudalità Siciliana," *Archivio Storico Siciliano,* Series 4, Volume 7 (Palermo 1981), pages 59-113.
Sapio Vitrano, Francesco. *Il Nummarium Islamico e Normanno della Biblioteca Comunale di Palermo* (1975).
Sauer, Michelle. *Gender in Medieval Culture* (2015).
Savagnone, Guglielmo. "Il Diploma di Fondazione della Cappella Palatina di Palermo 1140," *Archivio Storico Siciliano* (Palermo 1901), pages 66-83.
Sayers, Jane. *Innocent III: Leader of Europe 1198-1216* (1994).
Scaduto, Mario. *Il Monachesimo Basiliano nella Sicilia Medievale* (1947).
Scarlata, Marina. "Sul Declino del Regno Normanno e l'Assunzione al Trono di Tancredi," *Atti del Congresso Internazionale di Studi sulla Sicilia Normanna* (Palermo 1974), pages 480-499.
Schlunz, Thomas Paul. *Archbishop Rotrou of Rouen 1164-1183: A Career Churchman in the Twelfth Century* (1984).
Schmandt, Raymond. "The Election and Assassination of Albert of Louvain, Bishop of Liège 1191-1192," *Speculum,* volume 42, number 4 (October 1967), pages 639-660.
Schwalm, Jacob. "Reise nach Italien im Herbst 1894," *Neues Archiv der Gesellschaft für ältere Deutsche Geschichtskunde,* number 23 (1898), pages 21-22.

Sentis, Franz Jacob. *Die Monarchia Sicula* (1869).
Setton, Kenneth. *The Papacy and the Levant 1204-1571* (1976).
Seward, Desmond. *The Monks of War: The Military Religious Orders* (1972).
Shadis, Miriam. *Berenguela of Castile and Political Women in the High Middle Ages* (2009).
Shepard, Mary, et al. *The Cloisters: Studies in Honor of the Fiftieth Anniversary* (1992), page 226.
Simonsohn, Shlomo. *Between Scylla and Charybdis: The Jews in Sicily* (2011).
Simpson, Alicia. *Niketas Choniates: A Historiographical Study* (2013).
Siragusa, Giovanni Battista. *Il Regno di Guglielmo I in Sicilia* (1885, 1929).
Siri, Simona. "Having a misogynist leader has consequences. And no, I don't mean Trump." *The Washington Post* (Washington DC, 14 December 2017).
Skinner, Patricia. "Halt, Be Men!: Sikelgaita of Salerno, Gender and the Norman Conquest of Southern Italy," *Gender and History*, volume 12, issue 3 (2000), pages 622-641.
Skinner, Patricia. *Women in Medieval Italian Society 500-1200* (2001).
Skinner, Patricia. *Family Power in Southern Italy: The Duchy of Gaeta and Its Neighbors 850-1139* (1995).
Smith, Damian. *Innocent III and the Crown of Aragon: The Limits of Papal Authority* (2004).
Smith, Denis Mack. "Documentary Falsification and Italian Biography" *History and Biography: Essays in Honour of Derek Beales* (Cambridge 1996), page 181.
Smith, Jennifer. "Women, Land and Law in Occitania 1130-1250," *Medieval Women and the Law* (2000), pages 19-40.
Soncini, Guia. "The Failure of Italian Feminism," *The New York Times* (New York, 26 October 2017).
Spahr, Rodolfo, *Le Monete Siciliane dai Bizantini a Carlo I d'Angio 582-1282* and *Le Monete Siciliane dagli Aragonesi ai Borboni 1282-1836* (1959).
Spampinato Beretta, Margherita. *Poeti della Corte di Federico II*, volume 2 in the series *I Poeti della Scuola Siciliana* (2008).
Spata, Giuseppe. *Le Pergamene Greche Esistenti nel Grande Archivio di Palermo Tradotte ed Illustrate* (1862).
Spiegel, Gabrielle. *The Past as Text: The Theory and Practice of Medieval Historiography* (1999).
Stafford, Pauline. *Queens, Concubines and Dowagers: The King's Wife in the Early Middle Ages* (1983).
Stafford, Pauline. "Writing the Biography of 11th-century Queens," *Writing Medieval Biography 750-1250: Essays in Honour of Professor Frank Barlow* (2006), pages 99-109.

Stalls, Clay. *Possessing the Land: Aragon's Expansion into Islam's Ebro Frontier under Alfonso the Battler 1104-1134* (1995).
Stanton, Charles. *Norman Naval Operations in the Mediterranean* (2011).
Starrabba, Raffaele. "Del Dotario delle Regine di Sicilia," *Archivio Storico Siciliano* (Palermo 1874), pages 7-25.
Staub, Martial, et al. *The Making of Medieval History* (2017).
Stenton, Doris Mary. "Roger of Howden and Benedict," *The English Historical Review*, volume 68 (October 1953), pages 574-582.
Stephenson, Carl. *Mediaeval Feudalism* (1942).
Stern, Horst. *Mann aus Apulien: Die privaten Papiere del italienischen Staufers* (2015).
Stevenson, Joseph. *The Chronicles of Robert de Monte* (1991).
Strauss, Raphael. *Die Juden im Königreich Sizilien unter Normannen und Staufen* (1910).
Symes, Carol, et al. *Sicily, al-Andalus and the Maghreb: Writing in Times of Turmoil,* special issue of *The Medieval Globe*, volume 5, number 1 (2019).
Szabados, György. "Aragóniai Konstancia Magyar Királyné," *Királylányok Messzi Földrol: Magyarország és Katalónia a Középkorban* (2009), pages 163-175.
Takayama, Hiroshi. *The Administration of the Norman Kingdom of Sicily* (1993).
Takayama, Hiroshi. "Familiares Regis and the Royal Inner Council in Twelfth-Century Sicily," *English Historical Review*, volume 104, number 411 (April 1989), pages 357-372.
Tarallo, Giovanni. "Sopra i Reali Sepolcri del Duomo di Monreale: Memoria del Padre Don Giovan Battista Tarallo," *Giornale di Scienza, Letteratura ed Arti per la Sicilia* (Palermo), July-September 1826, page 166.
Taylor, Julie Anne. *Muslims in Medieval Italy: The Colony at Lucera* (2003).
Testa, Francesco. *De Vita, et Rebus Gesti Guilelmi II, Siciliae Regis, Monregalensis Ecclesii Fundatoris,* 4 volumes (1705-1773).
Thompson, Kathleen. "The Lords of Laigle: Ambition and Insecurity on the Borders of Normandy," *Anglo-Norman Studies XVIII* (1996), pages 177-180.
Thompson, Kathleen. *Power and Border Leadership in Medieval France: The County of the Perche 1000-1226* (2002).
Thornton, Hermann. "The Poems Ascribed to Frederick II and Rex Fredericus," *Speculum*, volume 1, number 1 (January 1926), pages 87-100.
Thumser, Matthias. "Der König un sein Chronist: Manfred von Sizilien in der Cronik des sogenannten Nikolaus von Jamsilla" *Die Reichskleinodien: Herrschaftszeichen des Heiligen Römischen Reiches,* pages 222-242 (1997).
Toomaspoeg, Kristjan. *Les Teutoniques en Sicile 1197-1492* (2003).

Tramontana, Salvatore. "Gestione del Potere, Rivolte e Ceti al Tempo di Stefano di Perche," *Potere, Società e Popolo nell'Età dei Due Guglielmi* (Bari 1981), pages 79-101.

Tramontana, Salvatore. *L'Isola di Allah* (2014).

Tramontana, Salvatore. *La Monarchia Normanna e Sveva* (1986).

Travaini, Lucia. "La Monetazione del Regno di Sicilia al Tempo di Tancredi" *Tancredi, Conte di Lecce Re di Sicilia* (2004), pages 193-206.

Travaini, Lucia. *La Monetazione nell'Italia Normanna,* second edition (2016).

Treviño, Gloria. *Santa María la Real de Nájera* (2012).

Trindade, Ann. *Berengaria: In Search of Richard the Lionheart's Queen* (1999).

Tronzo, William. *The Cultures of His Kingdom: Roger II and the Cappella Palatina of Palermo* (1997).

Tronzo, William. *Intellectual Life at the Court of Frederick II* (1994).

Tuchman, Barbara Wertheim. *Practicing History: Selected Essays* (1982).

Turner, Ralph. *Eleanor of Aquitaine: Queen of France, Queen of England* (2009).

Turner, Ralph. "Eleanor of Aquitaine and Her Children: An inquiry into medieval family attachment," *Journal of Medieval History,* volume 14, issue 4 (1988), pages 321-335.

Turner, Ralph. *King John* (1992, 2009).

Vaissete, Joseph. *Abregé de l'Histoire Générale de Languedoc,* volume 3 (1749).

Valenziano, Maria Giovanna. "Tancredi e il Monastero di San Giovanni Evangelista in Lecce," *Tancredi Conte di Lecce Re di Sicilia* (2004), pages 217-232.

Van Cleave, Rachel. "Rape and Querela Law in Italy: False Protection of Victim Agency," *Michigan Journal of Gender and Law,* volume 13, pages 273-310, January 2007 (Ann Arbor 2007).

Van Cleve, Thomas Curtis. *The Emperor Frederick II of Hohenstaufen, Immutator Mundi* (1972).

Van Cleve, Thomas Curtis. *Markward of Anweiler and the Sicilian Regency* (1937).

Varvaro, Alberto. *Lingua e Storia in Sicilia* (2000).

Varvaro, Alberto, et al. *Vocabolario Storico-Etimologico del Siciliano* (2014).

Venuti, Antonino. *De Agricultura Opusculum* (1516).

Vetere, Benedetto. "Tancredi di Lecce nella Storiografia Medievale," *Tancredi, Conte di Lecce Re di Sicilia* (2004), pages 1-32.

Vigo, Julian. "Tight Jeans, Rape and Technology," *Forbes* (New York, 22 July 2018).

Vitrano, Francesco Sapio. "La Zecca di Palermo dai Primi Insediamenti Fenici al 1836," *Archivio Storico Siciliano,* Series 3, Volume 20 (Palermo 1970), pages 107-202.

Waley, Daniel. "'Combined Operations' in Sicily AD 1060-1078," *Papers of the British School at Rome*, volume 22 (London, November 1954), pages 118-125.
Ward, Paul. "The Coronation Ceremony in Medieval England," *Speculum*, volume 14, number 2 (April 1939), pages 160-178.
Wayno, Jeffrey. "Rethinking the Fourth Lateran Council of 1215," *Speculum*, volume 93, number 3 (July 2018), pages 611-637.
Weber, Hans. *Der Kampf Zwischen Papst Innocenz IV und Kaiser Friedrich II, bis zur Flucht des Papstes nach Lyon* (1900).
Weikert, Katherine and Woodacre, Elena, "Gender and Status in the Medieval World," *Historical Reflections*, volume 2, issue 1, spring 2016 (Oxford 2016), pages 1-7.
Weiler, Björn. *Henry III of England and the Staufen Empire 1216-1272* (2006).
Weir, Alison. *Eleanor of Aquitaine: By the Wrath of God, Queen of England* (1999).
Weir, Alison. *Queens of the Conquest: England's Medieval Queens* (2017).
Wellas, Michael. *Griechisches aus dem Umkreis Kaiser Friedrichs II* (1983).
White, Lynn Townsend. "The Byzantinization of Sicily," *American Historical Review*, volume 41, number 1 (October 1936), pages 1-21.
White, Lynn Townsend. *Latin Monasticism in Norman Sicily* (1938).
Wickham Legg, Leopold. *English Coronation Records* (1901).
Wieruszowski, Helene. "Roger II of Sicily, *Rex-Tyrannus*, in Twelfth-century Political Thought," *Speculum*, volume 38, number 1 (January 1963), pages 46-78.
Wilson, Henry Austin. *The Pontifical of Magdalen College with an Appendix of Extracts from Other English Manuscripts of the Twelfth Century* (1910).
Winfield, Nicole. "Italian Court Ruling That a Woman Was Too Ugly to Be Raped Sparks Outrage," *Time* (USA), 14 March 2019.
Winkelmann, Eduard. *Kaiser Friedrich II* (1889-1898).
Wolf, Kenneth. *Making History: The Normans and their Historians in Eleventh-century Italy* (1995).
Woodacre, Elena (editor). *Queenship in the Mediterranean: Negotiating the Role of the Queen in the Medieval and Early Modern Eras* (2013).
Woodacre, Elena, and Fleiner, Carey (editors). *Royal Mothers and Their Ruling Children: Wielding Political Authority from Antiquity to the Early Modern Era* (2015).
Zecchino, Ortensio. *Le Assise di Ariano: Testo Critico, Traduzione e Note* (1984).

HISTORIA HV-
GONIS FALCANDI SICVLI DE
rebus geſtis in Siciliæ regno, iam primùm typis
excuſa, ſtudio & beneficio Reuerendi D. Domini
Matthæi Longogęi Sueſsionũ pontificis & regni
Galliæ ab interiore ac penitiore conſilio.

Huc accefsit in librum præfatio, & hiſtoricæ lectionis Encomi
um per Geruaſium Tornacæum Suefsionenſem.

PARISIIS

Apud Mathurinum Dupuys via Iacobea,
ſub inſigni Hominis ſylueſtris, & Frobenij.
M. D. L.

CVM PRIVILEGIO REGIS.

Editio princeps of the chronicle of Hugh Falcandus, 1550

INDEX

The focus of these entries is the period from 1000 to 1300. Names of persons are listed according to common usage, e.g. *Michael Scot* and *Dante Alighieri* but *Boccaccio, Giovanni*. Most individuals are listed by given name rather than surname or toponym. Some names, particularly those in Arabic, are shortened based on popular usage as mononyms, e.g. *Saladin,* and also note spellings such as *Koran* rather than *Quran* and *Comnena* instead of *Komnena*. Places named for saints vary as well, so the town of Saint-Gilles is listed under the letter G and the abbey of Saint Euphemia under E but the castle of San Marco d'Alunzio under S.

Aachen, 417
Abbasids, 303
abbeys, 10, 17, 21, 43, 53, 76, 109, 115, 359, 398. *See also* Cassino, Cava, Monreale, *etc.*
Abruzzi, 53, 54, 68, 237
Abu'l Kasim, 231
Acerra, 52, 54, 357-359
Achard of Lecce, 358, 359
Acre, 119, 121, 339
Adelaide Hauteville (daughter of Roger I), 94, 96
Adelaide Hauteville (daughter of Roger II), 129, 141, 608n111
Adelaide del Vasto, 30, 50, 52, 107-126, 129
Adelard of Bath, 264
Adeline, nurse, 137
Adenolf, chamberlain, 189
Adrian IV, Pope, 176-179
adultery, 139, 213, 228, 240, 296, 456, 518
affinity *defined,* 213
Africa, 29, 56, 63, 72, 75, 78, 129, 140, 149, 180. *See also* Cairo, Mahdia, Tunisia, *etc.*

705

St Agatha's Gate, 59, 186
Aghlabids, 78, 80
agriculture, 80, 85, 171, 182, 219. *See also* olives, *etc.*
Agrigento (Girgenti), 55, 65, 72, 204, 254-256, 280, 419
Agrò forest, 249
Ahmed es-Sikeli. *See* Caïd Peter
Aix-la-Chapelle. *See* Aachen
Albania, 475-477, 483
Alberic Hauteville, 600n40
Albert of Louvain, 386-387, 393
Albert of Rethel, 159, 386
Albigensian crusades, 417
Alcazar (Seville), 33, 146
Alcherio, bishop, 109
Aleramid dynasty, 107, 453
Alexander II of Scotland, 437
Alexander III, Pope, 158, 179, 185, 229, 242, 280, 285, 295, 298, 319, 331
Alexander of Telese, 116, 118, 130
Alexiad, 16
Alexius IV Angelus, Emperor, 371, 375
Alfonso II of Aragon, 342, 409
Alfonso VIII of Castile, 18, 282-283, 287, 298, 320
Alfonso of Aragon (brother of Constance), 410-413 passim
Alfonso of Portugal, 147, 148
algebra, 79
Alhambra (Granada), 19

Almohads, 63, 184, 284, 331
Almoravids, 147
Aloet, Alfred, 438, 440
Amalfi, 111, 129
Amari, Michele, 14, 610n133
Amatus of Montecassino, 684
Amedeo IV of Savoy, 469
amiratus, 44, 114, 129, 131, 137, 176
Anacletus II, Pope, 129, 130, 135, 138
Anagni, 285, 419
Anarchy (in England), 314
Anastasius IV, Pope, 157
Ancona, 53, 54, 67, 396, 413
Andalusia, 19, 52, 71, 172
Andrew II of Hungary, 411-412, 418
Andrew, governor of Messina, 257-259
Andria, 361, 431, 447, 449
Angers, 313, 316
Angevin dynasty (in Italy), 465, 478-481 passim, 486
Anglo-French War, 417, 436
Anjou region, 313, 357, 436
Anna Comnena, historian, 16, 601n56
anointings, royal, 130-131, 175, 329, 372, 455, 570-571. *See also* coronations
Ansaldo, castellan, 268, 269
Antioch, 112, 116, 119
apostolic (papal) legateship, 26,

INDEX

112, 114, 132, 179, 210, 276, 401, 414
Apulia (Puglia). *See* Bari, Brindisi, Taranto, *etc.*
Arabic language, 10, 11, 44, 79, 117, 200, 330, 400, 416, 545
Arabic numerals. *See* Hindu-Arabic
Arabs *defined*, 79
Arabs, 24, 34, 45, 77-80, 81, 82, 89, 91, 102-120 passim, 129, 158, 194, 209, 226, 255, 264. *See also* Aghlabids, Berbers, Fatimids, Kalbids, Muslims, *et al.*
Aragon: 13, 35, 128, 163-164, 401, 409, 412, 485; Crown of, 23, 410, 485
archers, x, 93, 111, 178, 195, 271, 345, 478-479
architecture, 19, 29, 83, 146, 153-154, 161, 202, 297, 301-304, 310, 330, 353, 368, 378-379, 421-423, 438, 501. *See also* Norman-Arab
archon. *See* familiare
Arda of Edessa, 119
Ardennes, 155
Ariano, Assizes of, 17, 21, 132, 138, 182, 202, 228, 241, 267, 418, 509-531
aristocracy. *See* baronage
Armenia, 73
Armenia, Lesser, 426-427
Arnolf of Capaccio, bishop, 324, 327, 537, 538
Arnulf of Chocques, 120, 121
Arta, 52, 475, 483
Arthur of Brittany, 338, 362
artichokes, 69, 219
Ascalon, 341, 606n98
Asclettin, general, 177, 178
astrology, 264, 265, 445
astronomy, 264, 496
augustale coin, 45, 552, 560
Aversa, 390
Ayyubids, 289, 297, 340, 341, 427, 432, 448
Baghdad, 80, 172, 289, 333, 372
Bagnara, 338
Baha ad-Din, 340
Baldwin I of Jerusalem, 119-121
Baldwin II of Jerusalem, 155
Baldwin of Hainaut, 386-387, 655n579
Bal'harm. *See* Palermo
Ballarò souk, 20
Barcelona, 58, 169, 170, 305, 410, 423, 477, 486
Bari, 53, 54, 76, 81, 135-136, 178, 236, 396, 504
Barletta, 53, 54, 292, 431
baronage, 35, 44, 116, 120, 130, 138, 175, 181-184, 189, 193, 206, 364
Barons' Crusade, 448
Bartholomew, familiare, 284
Bartholomew of Lusci, 247
Bartholomew of Parisio, 212,

243, 249
Basilicata. *See* Lucania
Basque region, 58, 164. *See also* Navarre
bastardy. *See* illegitimacy
baths. *See* hammams, mikvehs
Batu Khan, 447, 506
Bavaria, 52, 341, 375, 461, 462
Beatrice Hohenstaufen, daughter of Frederick I Barbarossa, 294
Beatrice of Rethel, 50, 52, 155-161, 174, 294, 295, 329, 334
Beatrice of Savoy, 50, 52, 469-473
Beatrice of Sicily, daughter of Manfred, 477, 480-482
Becket home (Palermo), 59, 221
Belisarius, 75
Benedictines, 9, 53, 76, 149, 295, 296, 357, 390, 393
Benevento: 53, 54, 176, 177, 285; Battle of, x, 2, 8, 465, 478, 486; Treaty of, 179, 184, 214
Benjamin of Tudela, 291
Berbers, 78, 255
Berengaria of Navarre, 338-345 passim
Berthold of Hohenburg, 463, 472
betrothals, 103, 148, 170, 376, 410, 412, 470, 537-543
Bianca Lancia, 50, 52, 131, 432, 453-460
Blanca of Navarre, 163-169 passim, 173, 179, 180, 300, 303

Boccaccio, Giovanni, 9, 384
Bohemond of Manopello (Tarsia), 234, 235, 248
Bohemond of Taranto (and Antioch), 112, 116, 119
Boioannes, Basil, 81
Bologna, 418
Boson of Gorron, bishop, 250, 266, 278
Bourbon-Sicilies, House of, 40, 575-593
Breakspear, Nicholas. *See* Adrian IV
Brindisi, 53-54, 178, 363, 372, 429, 431
Bulot, Baldwin, 538, 540
Burgundy, 52, 57, 62, 114
Byzantine Christians. *See* Orthodox Church
Byzantine (Eastern Roman) Empire, 16, 57, 63, 77, 81, 102, 140, 176, 180, 292, 371, 398, 475
Byzantine Greeks (in Sicily), 10, 43, 44, 75-77, 80, 416
Byzantium. *See* Constantinople
Caccamo, 55, 185, 187, 190, 195
Cairo, 80, 289
Calabria, 68, 76, 77, 80, 82, 87, 89, 94, 102, 114, 185, 259, 265, 332, 338, 388, 415. *See also* Cosenza, Mileto, *etc.*
Calomeno, John, 259
Caltabellotta, 364; Peace of, 486
Campania, 135, 137, 178, 209,

237. *See also* Salerno, Capua, *etc.*
canals. *See* kanats
Cantuese, Alduin, 271
Capetians, 37, 78, 114, 147-149, 313, 336, 439, 465
Capua, 53-54, 111, 140, 212, 293, 390, 418, 419
Carthaginians, 70-73, 78, 599n31
Cassino abbey, 53-54, 76, 357, 361, 390, 391, 419
Castel dell'Ovo (Naples), 447, 480, 481
castles, 44, 55, 84-85, 91, 94, 97, 112, 115, 135, 163, 185, 187, 190, 193, 195, 259, 262, 281, 315, 337, 340, 342, 343, 364, 373, 385, 422, 429, 436, 447, 461, 479
Castrogiovanni (Enna). *See* Kasr' Janni
San Cataldo chruch, 154, 199, 290
Catalogus Baronum, 43, 182, 196
Catalonia, 19, 23, 58, 164, 170, 410, 413
Catania, 71, 191, 198, 231, 265, 281, 285, 338, 419
Catanzaro, 277
Cathars, 344, 417
Catholicism. *See* abbeys, Benedictines, crusades (by number), Lateran councils, popes (by name), *etc.*
Cava abbey, 53-54, 76, 149, 480

Cefalù, 53, 55, 66, 69, 172, 175, 250, 266, 268, 278, 332
Celestine III, Pope, 341, 342, 362, 363, 386, 389, 393
Ceprano, 393
Charles I (Anjou) of Naples, 465, 478-481 passim
Charles II (Anjou) of Naples, 480, 481, 486
Charles the Simple, 86
charters (royal writs, diplomas, decrees), 6, 15, 16, 17, 32, 113, 117, 123-125, 132, 137, 158, 165, 166, 216, 219, 223-225, 239, 281, 284, 286, 288, 296, 306-308, 346, 389, 398, 400, 415, 454, 480
chess, 34, 85, 172
Chibnall, Marjorie, 7, 38
China, 29
chivalry. *See* knighthood, minstrels, poetry, tournaments, troubadours
Christodoulos, amiratus, 114, 129
Cielo of Alcamo, 10, 11-13, 416, 549-565
Cistercians, 368, 397, 465
city-states. *See* communes
Ciullo. *See* Cielo of Alcamo
Clement III, Pope, 334
Clement IV, Pope, 478
Clementia of Catanzaro, 185, 277
Cluniacs, 87
coats of arms. *See* heraldry

coinage, 24, 45, 133, 139, 192, 361, 369, 385, 560
Coloman of Hungary, 111
communes (in northern Italy), 179, 398, 440, 446, 447. *See also* Milan, *etc.*
Comnenus dynasty, 16, 136, 176, 214, 291, 334, 339, 341, 371-372, 375, 377, 475, 482
Conrad I of Sicily (Conrad IV of Germany), 17, 431, 457, 461-468 passim
Conrad II of Sicily (Conradin), 463-466 passim, 467, 479, 488
Conrad II of Germany and Italy (son of Emperor Henry IV), 102, 111-112
Conrad of Montferrat, King of Jerusalem, 394-395, 426
Constance of Aragon, 11, 21, 134, 401, 409-423, 471, 545-547
Constance (Hauteville) of Sicily, daughter of Roger II, 24, 28, 30, 48, 132, 142, 157, 158, 238, 258, 294, 295, 330, 334, 343, 360-386 passim, 381-407, 488
Constance (Hohenstaufen) of Sicily, daughter of Manfred, 12, 471, 472, 473, 477, 480, 485-486, 488
Constance (city). *See* Konstanz
Constans II, Emperor, 77
Constantine the Great, 73
Constantinople (Byzantium), 74-77 passim, 81, 119, 136, 176, 196, 214, 274, 282, 291, 315, 331, 334, 371-372
consuocera *defined,* 329
Contrasto (Dialogue), 10, 11-13, 416, 549-565
Cordoba, 19, 80, 100, 333, 598n27
Corfu, 292, 341, 476
Corno Grande (mountain), 68
coronations, 119, 120, 130-131, 150, 157, 158, 167, 173, 175, 201, 329, 334, 339, 360, 362, 363, 372, 374, 385, 396, 399, 400, 455-456, 472, 476, 567-574
Cosenza, 332
cotton, 80
counsellors. *See* familiares
crowns, 133-135, 142-145, 545-547
crusades. *See* First, Second, Barons, *etc.*
Cuba palace, 19, 59, 60, 330
cuisine, 29, 47, 80
Cyprus, 339-342 passim, 426, 429
Damietta, 419, 427
Dante Alighieri, 9, 13, 382, 549
dar al-hikma, 264
Davanzati, Domenico, 36
Decameron. *See* Boccaccio
decrees. *See* charters
deer, 69, 486

Dialogue (poem). *See* Contrasto
Diceto, Ralph of, 543
Dietpold of Schweinspünt, 402
ad-Din, Baha, 340
dinar coin, 609n126
diplomas. *See* charters
diversity. *See* multiculturalism
divorce, 34, 212-214, 597n16
diwan (treasury), 114, 182, 193, 204, 285
DNA. *See* genetics
dowers and dowries, 18, 43, 149, 169-170, 325, 335, 336-338 passim, 343, 346, 410-411, 412, 418, 436, 440, 454-455, 470-471, 539-543
Drengot family, 103, 111, 491
ducat coin, 45, 138, 369
Dürnstein, 342, 394
dysentery, 200
earthquakes, 115, 281, 332
Eastern Christians. *See* Orthodox church
Edmund of England, 464, 478
Edrisi. *See* Idrisi
education. *See* literacy
El Cid. *See* Rodrigo Diaz
Eleanor of Aquitaine, 16, 31, 149, 283, 313-323 passim, 389, 395
Eleanor of England (daughter of Henry II). *See* Leonor
Eleanor of Provence, 439
Elias of Gesualdo, 391
Elias of Troia, bishop, 324, 327, 537-542 passim
Elisabeth of Bavaria, 20, 50, 52, 461-467
Elvira of Castile, 46, 48, 50, 52, 127-137, 141, 494
Elvira Hauteville, 365, 367
Emeric (Imre) of Hungary, 410-412
emirates (Sicily), 24, 78, 82, 89, 90, 599n30
Emma of Lecce, 140, 358, 359, 363
England, 31, 35, 101, 158, 180, 202, 267, 287, 313-326, 435-446. *See also* Henry II, London, Westminster, *etc.*
Enna. *See* Kasr'Janni
Enzio of Sardinia, 447, 464
Epirus, 475-476, 483
Eremburga of Mortain, 50, 52, 101-105
Erice (Eryx), 71
Erveo of Tropea, bishop, 188
esquire rank, 84-85, 113
Etna, Mt, 55, 67, 281
Eugene III, Pope, 157, 315
Eugene of Palermo, 396
eunuchs, 9, 189, 193, 196, 197, 204, 206, 226-231 passim, 254, 283
St Euphemia abbey (Calabria), 90, 91, 95
Euphemius, 78
St Evroul abbey, 84, 86, 88

Falco of Benevento, 17, 138, 510
falconry, 336, 416, 458
familiare *defined,* 28, 44, 130
familiares, 130, 135, 190, 200-211 passim, 216, 220-224 passim, 232, 241, 250, 275, 277, 278, 288, 384
Fascism, 37, 39, 41, 597n17, 598n24
Fatimids, 79-81, 289
Favara palace, 200
Fazello, Thomas, xi
Felicia Hauteville, 102, 111
feminism, 5, 22, 26, 28-31
Ferentino, 428
Ferraris Chronicle, 17, 45, 608n113
feudalism. *See* manorialism
Fifth Crusade, 427
First Crusade, 103, 112, 119, 425
fleur-de-lis (heraldry), 598n26
Florio of Camerota, 324, 327, 537-539 passim
follaris (follis) coin, 45, 369, 609n126
Fontevrault, 320, 346-347, 355
forgeries, 15, 139
Fourth Crusade, 375, 475
Francesco II, 575-582 passim, 587
Frankish feudal law, 616n197
Franks (Catholic Europeans), 80, 114, 117, 257, 334, 341, 375, 427, 448, 475

Frederick I Barbarossa, Emperor, 157, 158, 176-179 passim, 208, 247, 294, 298, 334, 362
Frederick II: 7, 8, 11, 488, 490; childhood (minority), 396, 398-409; crusade, 431-432; laws, 432, 458; marriages, 423-474 passim
Frederick of Antioch, 464
freedom of expression, 38
Fressenda, 489, 600n40
al-Furat, Asad, 78
Gagliano, 78-79
Gaiseric, 75
gaming (gambling), 216
García Ramírez, 163-169 passim
Gargano tradition, 599n29
Mt Gargano, 292
gender, 5, 11, 25-26, 29-30, 33, 34
genetics (DNA), 4, 70, 599n31
Genghis Khan, 398
Genoans, 179, 390
Genoard park, 59, 60, 171, 199, 200
genocide, 582
Genseric, 75
Gentile Tuscus, bishop, 204-206 passim, 251, 254-256, 266, 275, 288
Geoffrey of Ely, 327-328, 538-540
Geoffrey Malaterra. *See* Godfrey Malaterra
Geoffrey of Perche, 382

INDEX

geography (topography), 7, 19, 20, 67-69, 90, 171

George of Antioch, 129, 131, 135, 140, 199, 290

George Maniakes, 81

Gerace (Calabria), 92, 266, 496

Germany. *See* Bavaria, Swabia, Worms, *etc.*

Ghibellines, 9, 417, 471, 478

Giacomo of Lentini, 10, 12, 416, 550

Gilbert Foliot, 538

Gilbert (Perche) of Gravina, 181, 185, 190, 196, 205-209 passim, 212, 217, 236, 237, 243-251 passim, 277-278

Giles of Anagni, 393

Giles of Evreux, bishop, 328, 539-540

St Gilles (town), 327-328, 538-539, 543

Gloucester, 52, 435, 437

Godfrey Hauteville, 102, 108

Godfrey Malaterra, 91-93 passim, 103, 111, 600n40

Goths. *See* Ostrogoths, Visigoths

Granada, 19, 598n27. *See also* Alhambra

Gran Sasso Mountains, 68

Greeks, ancient, 67, 70-73

Greeks, medieval. *See* Byzantine Greeks

Gregory IX, Pope, 439

Gromoald Alferanites, 135

Guaimar III, 81

Guelphs, 9, 37, 417, 478

Halkah district (Palermo), 59, 171

Halycos river, 72

Hamelin of Warenne, 327, 539

hammams, 598n27

Harald Hardrada Sigurdsson, 81

harems, 9, 148, 189, 192, 196, 197, 254, 417, 610n133

Hasan as-Samsam, 82

Haskins, Charles, 32

Hauteville dynasty, x, 82, 86, 87, 90-94 passim, 103, 104, 108, 110. *See also* Roger I, Roger II, William I, William II, *et al.*

Hawisa of Echauffour, 83-84

ibn Hawqal, Abdullah (emir), 510

ibn Hawqal, Mohammed (traveler), 347, 598n27

Helena Angelina of Epirus, 21, 50, 52, 475-483

Henry II of England, 158, 180, 202, 220, 264, 282, 285, 298, 313-323 passim, 348

Henry III of England, 18, 35, 436-437, 441, 445. 448, 464

Henry VI, Emperor, 31, 343, 362, 364, 372, 384-385, 387, 391, 393, 395-400, 490

Henry Aristippo, deacon, 191, 192, 196

Henry of England, the Young King, 290, 295, 319, 637n423

Henry of Kalden, 389

713

Henry the Lion (of Saxony and Bavaria), 323, 341, 387-389 passim, 394
Henry of Luxembourg, 386, 655n579
Henry of Malta, 429
Henry of Montescaglioso. *See* Rodrigo of Navarre
Henry of Sicily (son of Constance of Aragon), 414, 415, 418-419, 439, 445, 447, 462
Henry del Vasto (brother of Adelaide), 130, 602n61
Henry the Younger of Sicily (son of Isabella of England), 447, 450, 463-464
heraldry (coats of arms), 47, 598n26
Hervé the Florid, 270
Hindu-Arabic numerals, 29, 175
historiography, 2-6, 9, 31, 35, 37, 580, 597n19
Hohenems Castle, 364
Hohenstaufen dynasty, 8, 62, 158, 294, 334, 366, 373, 374, 375. *See also* Frederick, I, Frederick, II, Henry VI, Manfred, *et al.*
Holy Land. *See* Jerusalem, Palestine
Holy Roman Empire, 44, 52, 57, 62, 111, 158, 294, 298, 365, 374, 386, 388, 391, 418, 443, 447. *See also* Frederick II, Henry VI, *et al.*
Honorius II, Pope, 129

Honorius III, Pope, 402, 418, 427
Hospitallers (knights), 334, 426
Howden (Hoveden), Roger of, 537, 539, 543
Hrolf (Rollo), 83, 86
Hugh II of Burgundy, 147-148, 151
Hugh III of Burgundy, 336
Hugh of Catanzaro, 277
Hugh Falcandus, 15, 17, 167, 174, 185, 204, 215, 218, 271
Hugh of Palermo, bishop, 179, 199
Hymera, Battle of, 71
Iato. *See* Jato
Ibadi Islam, 80
icons, 9, 99, 131, 145, 153, 172, 311, 349
identity, Sicilian, 23, 42-43
Idrisi (geographer), 158, 174, 180
Iesi, 396
illegitimacy, 42, 101, 457
India, 29
Innocent II, Pope, 135, 136, 137
Innocent III, Pope, 365, 374, 401, 412, 414
Ireland, 289
Irene Angelina of Constantinople, 50, 52, 363, 364, 371-377
Irene Palaeologue, 371
irrigation. *See* kanats
Iruña. *See* Pamplona
Isaac II Angelus Comnenus, Emperor, 334, 363, 371, 375, 377

INDEX

Isaac Comnenus of Cyprus, 339
Isabella of Angoulême, 435, 436, 661n651
Isabella of Brienne. *See* Yolanda of Jerusalem
Isabella of England, 4, 50, 52, 435-451
Isabella of Jerusalem. *See* Yolanda of Jerusalem
Islam. *See* Muslims
Istanbul. *See* Constantinople
Italian language. *See* Tuscan
Italy (modern nation state), xi, 8, 14, 21, 36-41, 574-588
Ja'far al-Kalbi (emir), 495
Jamison, Evelyn, 7, 38
Jato (Iato), 419
Jerusalem, 29, 119-121 passim, 155, 274, 282, 289, 333-334, 341, 394, 426, 431-432
Jesi, 396
Jesus Christ, 73, 172, 297, 311, 573
Jews, 64-65, 115, 139, 288, 291
Jiménez dynasty, 58, 121, 128, 140, 494. *See also* Elvira, Margaret
Joanna of England, x, 50, 52, 285, 295, 299, 313-355, 361-362
John II Comnenus, 136, 493
John of Aiello, bishop, 231, 281, 284
John of Brienne, 425-429 passim, 432, 433
John of England, 435, 436, 451
St John of the Hermits, 161, 237
St John, Knights of. *See* Hospitallers
John of Lavardin, 251, 268
John of Malta, bishop, 274, 275
John of Naples, cardinal, 209-214 passim
John of Procida, 12, 477
John Skylitzes, 16, 134, 144
Jordan Hauteville (son of Roger I), 101, 102, 109, 110, 489
bin Jubayr, 332-333
Judaism. *See* Jews
Judith of Evreux, 50, 52, 83-100, 102, 108
jure uxoris *defined*, 132, 294
justiciars, 198, 203, 223, 233, 238, 241, 244, 248, 255, 324
Justinian, Code of, 132, 138, 139, 509
Justus (apothecary), 233
Justus of Mazara, bishop, 542
Kala district (Palermo), 59, 61, 198
Kalbids, 80, 82
kanats, 59, 60, 187
Kantorowicz, Ernst, 24
Kasr district (Palermo), 59, 102, 117, 268
Kasr'Janni (Enna), 55, 80, 90, 117
Kemonia river, 59, 60, 330
al-Kenani. *See* bin Jubayr
Khalesa district (Palermo), 60,

kharruba coin, 609n126
knighthood, 10-11, 23, 43, 182, 206, 416, 549-550, 600n39, 616n196
knightly orders. *See* Hospitallers, Templars, Teutonic Order
Koloman. *See* Coloman
Komnenus. *See* Comnenus
Konstanz, Treaty of, 157
Koran, 79, 298, 607n103
Kuba. *See* Cuba palace
Ladislas III of Hungary, 411-412, 420
La Guardia (Navarre), 58, 163
Lancia family, 453-456 passim
Lateran Councils: First, 500; Second, 500; Third, 331; Fourth, 659n632
Latin Empire, 375, 477, 480
Latins. *See* Franks
Latins, massacre of, 334
law: 17, 138; canon, 214; codes, 132, 458, 509-531; feudal, 112; Frankish, 616n197; Lombard, 616n197; Maliki, 276, 609n128; rape, 23, 34, 139, 432, 597n16; Salic, 16
Lecce, 67-68, 358-359
legateship. *See* apostolic legateship
Leonor (Eleanor) of England, 283, 287, 320
Leopold V of Austria, 341
Leopold VI of Austria, 411, 430
Leo Tornikios Kontoleon, 81
leprosy, 108, 603n74, 605n86
Les Cassés, 344-345
Liguria, 107, 108
lion passant (heraldry), 598n26
literacy, 29, 34, 117
Lombard feudal law, 616n197
Lombard League. *See* communes
Lombards (and Longobards), 76-81 passim, 89, 92, 111, 138, 446
Lombardy. *See* Milan, *etc.*
London: 80, 319, 325, 537; Tower of, 438, 441
Longobards. *See* Lombards
Lothar of Hochstaden, 386
Lothair II, Emperor, 136
Louis (Ludwig) III of Thuringia, 389
Louis VII of France, 149, 313, 315, 321-323 passim, 640n441
Louis IX of France, 439, 446, 465, 478, 507
Lucania (Basilicata), 53-54, 82, 149, 391, 395
Lucera, 13, 53-54, 476, 479
Lucius III, Pope, 214, 331
Mabel Hauteville, 602n62
Madonian Mountains, 55, 67, 69
Magdalen chapels, 59, 61, 136, 158, 183, 199, 609n123
Magione (Holy Trinity) church, 61, 290, 364, 368, 397
Magna Carta, 35, 276, 436
Magna Graecia, 67

Mahdia, 184
Mainz, 374, 400
Maio of Bari, 174, 176, 179, 184-193 passim, 290
Majorca, 331
Malaga, 70
malaria, 463
Malaterra, Godfrey (Geoffrey), 91, 92, 93, 103, 111, 600n40
Maliki law, 276, 609n128
Mallorca. *See* Majorca.
Malta, xi, 68-70, 109
Manfred III of Saluzzo, 469
Manfred of Sicily, 131, 432, 453-460, 463, 464, 470, 472, 476-481 passim
Maniace, 295-296, 633n363, 638n424
manorialism (feudalism), 83, 181, 182-183, 298. *See also* baronage
Manuel I Comnenus, Emperor, 176, 214-215, 291-293 passim
markets. *See* souks
Margaret of l'Aigle, 163-167 passim
Margaret of Biset, 436, 438, 440
Margaret of Navarre, 28, 50, 52, 150, 156, 163-312, 494
Margaritus of Brindisi, 334, 337, 361, 363, 364, 390
Maria of Montferrat, Queen of Jerusalem, 425
Maria Porphyrogenita, 214, 288, 291

St Maria delle Scale, 250
Maria Sophia of Bavaria, 575-590
mark (coin), 346, 395, 412, 470
Markward of Anweiler, 401, 402
Marlborough, 437, 438, 661n652
marriages. *See* betrothals
Caïd Martin, 196, 201, 216, 284
Martorana church, 59, 131, 145, 147, 154, 199, 290, 333
St Mary of the Latins, 59, 290
Mary Magdalene church. *See* Magdalen chapels
Mategriffon castle, 337-339
Matilda (Maud), Empress, 202, 314, 348, 622n253
Matilda of England (daughter of Henry II), 316, 323, 348, 394
Matilda Hauteville (daughter of Adelaide), 110, 116, 122, 129, 135, 604n79
Matthew of Aiello, 179, 185-187 passim, 196, 200, 204, 208, 216-217, 231, 233, 241, 247, 255-258 passim, 266, 268, 272-277 passim, 284, 287, 293
Matthew Bonello, 185-197 passim, 219, 265, 277
Matthew Paris, 18, 445, 448, 454, 457, 660n649, 662n659
Mauger Hauteville (son of Roger I), 102, 105
Mazara, 55, 78
Mecca, 77
Meda (San Vittore) convent,

656n590
medicine, 25, 34, 293, 390
Meinhard of Gorizia, 464
Melfi: 82; Constitutions of, 34, 45, 432
Melisende of Jerusalem, 622n253
Melus, 81
Messina, Battle of (1061), x, 88-90
Michael II, Emperor, 78
Michael II Comenus Doukas, 475, 476
Michael VIII of Nicaea, 476, 477
microhistory, 14
Middle Sicilian. *See* Sicilian language
mikvehs, 64
Milan, 74, 158, 385, 389
Milazzo, 250
Mileto, 82, 91, 92, 108
minstrels, 11, 91
Minturno, 78
misogyny. *See* sexism
Mistretta, 194
Mohammed, Prophet, 77
monasteries. *See* abbeys
Monreale, 21, 296-299 passim, 330
Montecassino. *See* Cassino
Monte San Giuliano. *See* Erice
Montferrat, dynasty of, 107, 394, 426, 469
Morso, Salvadore, 14
mosaics, 131, 133, 145, 153, 167, 171, 172, 297, 311, 349, 598n26
mosques, 79, 100, 109, 172, 379, 598n27
Motya (Mozia), 70
Mount Saint Angelo, 43, 325, 412, 440, 454, 540-541
Mudéjar architecture, 100, 146, 160, 379, 422, 598n27
Muhammed. *See* Mohammed
multiculturalism (diversity), xi, 10, 19, 28-31, 82, 104, 128, 160, 171, 486, 599n31
muqarnas, 172, 353
Muriella (wife of Tancred Hauteville), 489, 600n40
Muslims, 29, 77, 78, 79, 80, 103, 112, 127, 133, 139, 194, 197, 226, 231, 298, 331, 332-333. *See also* Ibadi, Maliki, Shia, Sunni
Naples, 40, 111, 170, 178, 203, 328, 364, 389, 390, 395, 419, 447, 465, 575, 577, 580
Nasrid architecture, 19, 598n27
Navarre, 19, 52, 57, 58, 128, 163-173 passim. *See also* La Guardia, Pamplona, *etc.*
Neapolitan language, 577, 667n709
Nebrodian Mountains, 55, 67, 69, 90, 91, 109. *See also* Maniace, Troina, *etc.*
neolithic sites, 68-69
Nicaea: 475-477 passim, 483; Council of, 74

Nicastro, 90, 602n62; Bartholomew of, 454, 471
Nicea. *See* Nicaea
Nicetas Choniates, 315, 645n491
Nicholas II, Pope, 82, 88
Nicholas of Aiello, 390-391, 396, 417
Nicodemus, bishop, 109
Nicosia (Sicily), 92
Nilos Doxopatrios, 139
nobility. *See* baronage
Nocera, 135, 479
Norman-Arab architecture, 19, 153-154, 161, 199-200, 290, 296, 310-311, 353, 368, 378
Normandy, 52, 63, 81, 83, 86, 87, 101, 202, 287
Norman French language, 10, 11, 115, 165, 218, 325, 332, 416
Norman Palace (Palermo), 7, 59-60, 102, 117, 126, 130, 161, 167, 171-172, 581
Norsemen, 81, 83, 86
Norwich (Viscount), John Julius Cooper, 32
Noto, 55, 104, 109, 215
Occitan language, 332, 343
Ockham, William of, 14
Odo II of Burgundy, 148
Odo of Bayeux, 101, 498
Odo Quarrel, 220, 221, 249, 256-261 passim
Odoacer, 75
olives, 70

Orderic Vitalis, 84, 88, 116, 121
Orthodox church, 44, 82, 109, 114, 139, 154, 199, 249, 290, 333
Ostrogoths, 75-76
Otranto, 431
Otto I, Emperor, 107
Ouche, 88
Paestum, 67
Palatine Chapel (Palermo), 102, 118, 153, 171, 172, 191, 201, 329
Palermo: 19, 20, 29, 78, 82, 102, 108, 109, 120, 128, 130, 137, 149, 170; Battle of (1071), 94-95
Palestine, 103, 112, 119, 134, 140, 338, 340. *See also* Jerusalem
Pamplona, 58, 128, 163, 166, 168-169
Pantocrator, 153, 172, 297, 311
papacy (as institution), 76, 79, 109, 112, 114, 179
paper making, 29, 117
Papyrus (Papireto) River, 59-60, 187, 193
Paris of Rochester, 538, 539
parliaments, 35, 275
Paschal II, Pope, 120
Patti, 121
Paul of Tarsus, 73
Pelayo of Oviedo, 607n105
Caïd Peter (Ahmed), 204-209 passim, 227, 247-248

Peter II of Aragon, 401, 410

Peter III of Aragon, 12, 472, 473, 480, 485, 488

Peter of Blois, 218, 219, 264, 278, 282

Peter of Eboli, 16, 48, 134, 156, 358, 392, 636n413

Peter of Gaeta, 280

Peter delle Vigna, 440, 448, 449, 663n676

Peter, notary, 223-225

Petronella of Aragon, 409, 420, 494

Philip II of France, 15, 335-338, 342, 343, 365, 417

Philip of Swabia, 373-375 passim, 399-402 passim, 413

Phoenicians, 70-71

phylogeography, 4, 599n31

Piedmont, 107, 108, 111, 426, 469. *See also* Montferrat, *etc.*

Pilet, Roger, 438, 440, 662n662

Pisa (and Pisans), 111, 331, 342, 375

Pisan Tower, 161, 191, 192, 254, 271

Pizzo Carbonara (mountain), 67

Plantagenet dynasty. *See* Henry II, Joanna, *et al.*

Platani river, 72

poetry, 10, 12, 13, 416, 549-562. *See also* Sicilian School

Poitiers, 320, 327, 342, 346, 352, 538

popes. *See* Nicholas II, *et al.*

Portugal, 52, 147, 148, 409

Potenza, 315, 479

Provençal culture, 10, 550

Provence, 104, 342, 647n519

Puglia (Apulia). *See* Bari, Brindisi, Taranto, *etc.*

Punics. *See* Carthaginians, Phoenicians

queenship, study of, 5, 6, 14, 22-25, 40, 42, 46, 130-133

Quran. *See* Koran

Rainulf of Alife, 129, 135-137 passim, 604n79

Ranulf of Glanville, 318

rape legislation, modern, 432, 597n16. *See also* law

Raymond IV of Toulouse, 103-104

Raymond V of Toulouse, 342

Raymond VI of Toulouse, 342, 343

redemption tax, 203

regalia, 131, 133-135, 185, 192, 207, 545-547

Reginald of Bath, bishop, 329, 533

Regnum Siciliae *defined,* 10

religions. *See* Catholicism, Islam, Judaism, Orthodox church, papacy

revisionism, historical, 580

Rhodes, 339

rice, 80, 107

INDEX

Richard I Lionheart, 316, 335, 362, 389, 391, 394, 409
Richard I of Normandy, 83
Caïd Richard, 216, 235-236, 238, 251-252, 258, 272, 284
Richard of Acerra, 358, 361, 364, 371, 396
Richard of Aigle, 220
Richard of Aversa, 239-240, 243, 257
Richard of Balbano, 629n309
Richard of Camville, 538, 540
Richard of Cornwall, 448, 464
Richard of Mandra and Molise, 207-211 passim, 216, 233-234, 241, 247-249, 262-263, 277, 284
Richard Palmer, bishop, 197, 200, 204-286 passim, 328
Richard of Sai (Say), 212-214, 243
Rieti, 385
Risorgimento (Italian unification movement), 37, 38, 577, 581, 595n10
Robert of Bellisina, 231-232
Robert of Burgundy, 114
Robert of Calatabiano, 198, 199, 225-229
Robert of Caserta, 238, 239, 328
Robert of Eu, 602n63, 603n67
Robert of Grandmesnil (abbot), 84, 87, 90
Robert (Guiscard) Hauteville, 82, 87, 90, 110, 114
Robert of Loritello (Bassonville), 176-184 passim, 196, 249, 278-279, 282, 285, 614n175, 615n185
Robert of Meulan, 269, 271
Robert of Neubourg, 217
Robert of Normandy (brother of William I of England), 96, 101, 105
Robert of Sablé, 336
Robert of Selby, 157, 174
Robert of Torigni, 330-331
Rodrigo Diaz of Vivar (El Cid), 165, 300
Rodrigo (Henry) of Navarre of Montescaglioso, 166-167, 215-216, 233-235
Roffred of Liri, abbot, 393
Roger I: x, 43; ancestry, 86, 489; marriages, 83-126 passim; Sicilian conquest, 87-90, 94, 109
Roger II: x, 35, 36, 113, 488; birth, 110; coronation, 130; legislation of, 131-132, 138-139, 509-511; marriages,127-161 passim; posterity, 24, 140
Roger III, 363, 367, 475, 482
Roger of Acerenza, 185, 617n203
Roger of Acerra, 358, 367
Roger of Andria, 361
Roger of Avellino, 268, 270, 271
Roger Borsa, 110, 111, 112, 116, 118, 604n78
Roger of Gerace, 266, 275
Roger of Martorano, 185

Roger of Tiron, 251, 272
Roger of Wendover, 441-445
Rollo. *See* Hrolf
Roman Empire, 72-74
Rome, 72, 76, 88, 157, 178, 229, 285, 341, 342, 362, 386, 389, 414, 418, 478
Rometta, 79, 262
Romuald of Salerno, 166, 179, 201, 221, 232, 275, 384
Rosa fresca aulentissima. *See* Contrasto
Rotrou of Perche, 165, 169, 181
Rotrou of Rouen, bishop, 217, 279, 217, 279
Rouen, 83, 217, 322, 343, 346, 347
Saladin (An-Nasir Salah ad-Din Yusuf ibn Ayyub), 289, 297, 334, 340, 341, 426
Salerno, 76, 81, 149, 178, 203, 221, 293, 328, 362, 390, 395, 396, 430
Salerno tradition, 80-81, 599n29
Salernus, physician, 232-233
Salic Law, 16
Sancho III of Castile, 282
Sancho VI of Navarre, 163, 168, 180, 249, 283, 287
San Marco d'Alunzio, 55, 90, 94, 102, 111-113, 117, 129, 158, 238
San Martino (Calabria), 91
Saphadin (Al-Adil), 340
Saqaliba district (Palermo), 59

Saragossa. *See* Zaragoza
Sari al Kadi district (Palermo), 59, 193
Sarum (Salisbury), 323
Savona, 107, 108
Savoy, 322, 469
Scibene palace, 60, 200
Schism of 1054, 77
Scot, Michael, 415
seals, 117, 132, 134, 223-224, 355, 398, 407, 441, 541, 543
Second Crusade, 140, 149, 315
Segesta (Egesta), 67, 71, 72
serfs (and serfdom), 44, 112-113, 117, 137, 139, 181, 242, 251, 298, 404, 606n97, 616n197
Sessa Arunca, 419
Seville, 33, 127, 379
sexism, 4, 34, 36, 38, 139, 290
sexuality, 5, 10, 22, 167, 213, 227. *See also* harems
Shia Islam, 80, 609n128
Sibylla of Acerra, 50, 52, 335, 357-370, 381
Sibylla of Burgundy, 50, 52, 147-154
Sicanians, 68-71 passim
Sichelgaita, 34, 92, 114, 601n56, 604n78, 630n323
Sicilian identity, 23, 42-43
Sicilian language, 10-11, 23, 200, 416
Sicilian School, 10, 11-13, 416, 549-565

INDEX

Sicily. *See* Palermo, *etc.*
Sicily, Kingdom of, *defined,* x, 40, 45, 53, 67-68, 480, 575
Caïd Siddiq, 231
sieges, 78, 95, 135, 176, 178-179, 258, 272, 334, 339, 344, 390-391, 427
Sigena, 412
Sila Mountains, 54, 68, 247
silk making, 80, 115
Simon, King of Sicily, 110, 112, 114-116, 122, 489
Simon of Taranto, 140, 189, 191, 358, 489
Siponto, 325, 540
al-Siqilli, Jawhar, 80, 637n418
Sixth Crusade, 431-432
slavery, 73, 197, 199, 576
sonnet, 10
souks, 20, 59, 137
sovereignty, concepts of, 42, 313, 317, 375, 510, 577
Speyer, 394, 415
Spoleto, 413
Staufen (town), 373, 375. *For the dynasty see* Hohenstaufen
Stephen of England, 640n443
Stephen of Perche, 216-275 passim, 278, 282
Stephen of Rethel, 158
Stephen of Turnham, 341
Strickland, Agnes, 33
sugar cane, 80
Suger of Saint-Denis, 641n446

suks. *See* souks
Sunni Islam, 78, 80, 289, 333
Swabia, 57, 62, 63. *See also* Staufen
synagogues, 64, 65, 75, 168
Syracuse (Siracusa), 53, 55, 71-79 passim, 209, 210, 281
Tagliacozzo, Battle of, 8, 465, 479, 486
taifas, 82, 599n30
Tancred of Hauteville (dynastic progenitor), 82, 489
Tancred of Lecce, King of Sicily, 140, 191, 194, 297, 334-338 passim, 343, 358-366 passim, 371, 372, 387
Taormina, 55, 71, 72, 249, 250, 262-264, 281, 412
Taranto, 53, 54, 110, 137, 178, 183, 236, 245, 291-292, 364, 365
tarì coin, 45, 192, 609n126
Templars (knights), 24, 282, 426, 441
Termini Imerese, 71, 234, 332
Teutonic Order, 397-398, 429, 430, 667n707
Theobald of Monreale (abbot), 542, 638n424, 670
Theodora Petraliphaina, 475
Theodora of Sai (Say), 212-214
Theodoric, 75
Theodosius I, 74
Third Crusade, 334, 335, 339-341, 389, 394, 426

Thomas Becket, 220-221, 278, 285-287 passim, 295, 297, 311, 317-320, 349, 533-536
Thomas Brown. *See* Thomas le Brun
Thomas le Brun, 174, 180
al-Timnah, Mohammed ibn, 89
torture, x, 184, 197, 198, 229, 345, 364, 435, 506
Toulouse, 52, 58, 103, 341, 343-346
tournaments, 11, 416
Trani, 54, 476, 479
treason, 139, 203, 185, 229, 252, 258, 266
Tremestieri, 89
Trifels Castle, 385, 393, 395, 446, 462
Tripoli (Lebanon), 103, 425
Troia, 81, 248, 338
Troina (Traina), 91-94 passim
Trota, 34, 595n6
troubadours, 11, 332, 343, 416, 550
Tudela, 58, 163, 165, 166, 181, 218, 291, 304
Tunisia, 56, 57, 71, 75, 78, 140, 184, 289, 331
Turgisio of Troia, 248
Tuscan language, 12, 549-550, 595n5
Tuscany, 373, 374. *See also* Pisa, *etc.*
Two Sicilies, Kingdom of, 40, 41, 480, 575-579, 582, 591

Tyre, 426, 573, 606n98
Urban II, Pope, 111, 112
Urraca "the Reckless" of Castile (daughter of Alfonso VI), 127, 128
Urraca of Castile (daughter of Alfonso VII), 167-168
Vandals, 74-75
Varangian Guard, 81
Venetians, 475
Venice: 366, 476; Treaty of, 298, 330, 384
Vercelli, 470
Vespers war, 12, 13, 40, 480, 485
Vesuvius, Mt, 68
Vicari, 137, 633n363
Vikings. *See* Norsemen
Visigoths, 74-75, 409
Walter III of Brienne, 365
Walter, archbishop, 44, 198, 216-221 passim, 275, 278, 279-281, 284-290 passim, 293, 296-297, 329
Walter of Moac, 249
Walter of Palear, 400, 402, 414, 658n612
Walther von der Vogelweide, 373-374
Welf dynasty, 374, 387, 389, 399, 400, 413, 417, 436, 461
Westminster, 323, 438, 440, 441
William I of England (Duke of Normandy), 83, 84, 87, 88, 101, 119

William I of Sicily, 30, 128, 132, 140, 148-150, 157, 169-180 passim, 184-201 passim, 203-204, 488, 489, 610n134
William II of Apulia, 129
William II of Sicily, 134, 177, 201, 202, 214, 239, 245, 299, 319, 321, 322, 334, 360, 488, 489
William III of Sicily, 359, 363, 364
William of Capparone, 402
William of Gesualdo, 629n309
William of Leluce, 632n347
William Marshal, 436, 437
William of Mortain, 101
William of Pavia, 220
William of San Severino, 238-239
William of Tyre, 606n98
Winchester, 323, 324, 436, 538, 643n472
wine, 93, 163, 437
Wittelsbach dynasty, 375, 461-462, 464, 466, 467, 575, 589
women's movements. *See* feminism
Women's Studies. *See* feminism
Worms: 374, 443, 444, 445; Concordat of, 499
Xerxes, 71, 574
Ximenez. *See* Jiménez
Yolanda (Isabella) of Jerusalem, 50, 52, 425-431, 433, 449, 453, 457
Zaida of Seville, 127, 141, 146
Zaragoza, 58, 128, 169, 410, 422
Ziani, Peter, 366
Zirids, 617n199
Zisa palace, 19, 59, 60, 200, 202, 329, 330, 335, 353
Ziyadat Allah I, 78

This book was first printed simultaneously in Italy and in the United States of America in April 2019. The text is set in Garamond, a typeface developed in Paris by the engraver Claude Garamont during the sixteenth century.

www.ingramcontent.com/pod-product-compliance
Lightning Source LLC
Chambersburg PA
CBHW021136080526